A UNIFIED INTRODUCTION TO MATHEMATICAL ECONOMICS

A UNIFIED INTRODUCTION TO MATHEMATICAL ECONOMICS

BARRY BRESSLER
Richmond College of the City University of New York

Harper & Row, Publishers
New York   Evanston   San Francisco   London

To my parents
for all their efforts

Sponsoring Editor: John Greenman
Project Editor: Eleanor Castellano
Designer: T. R. Funderburk
Production Supervisor: Will C. Jomarrón

A UNIFIED INTRODUCTION TO MATHEMATICAL ECONOMICS

Library of Congress Cataloging in Publication Data
Bressler, Barry.
  A unified introduction to mathematical economics.

  Includes index.
  1. Economics, Mathematical. I. Title.
HB135.B74   330'.01'51   75-5689
ISBN 0-06-040952-5

CONTENTS

The following list is a directory of all discussions in the text labeled CAUTION which serve as critiques of the theory presented:

1. Within Section 4.6: Limitations of *Ceteris Paribus* Theory
2. Within Section 4.7: Limitations of Equilibrium Theory
3. Section 4.9: Pure Competition and Reality
4. Within Section 12.3: Consumer Sovereignty Versus Contrived Demand
5. Section 12.7: Shortcomings of Ordinal Utility Theory
6. Within Section 12.8: Shortcomings of Revealed Preference Theory
7. Within Section 12.9: Shortcomings of the Neumann-Morgenstern Approach
8. Section 13.8: The Profit Maximization Hypothesis
9. Within Section 13.9: Production Functions and Reality
10. Section 13.10: Nonphysical Production
11. Within Section 13.11: Limitations of Static Analysis
12. Section 14.12: The Giant Corporation
13. Within Section 15.2: Consumption of Durables Versus Nondurables
14. Within Section 15.3: Investment in Plant and Equipment versus Residential Construction
15. Within Section 15.4: Interactions Between Governmental and Nongovernmental Expenditures
16. Within Section 15.5: Limitation of Multiplier Analysis
17. Within Section 15.6: Limitations of Liquidity Preference Analysis
18. Within Section 15.7: Some Shortcomings of the Complete Macro Model

PREFACE

Like most works, this book has gone through a long developmental process. It was initially conceived when I taught my first mathematical economics course at the City College of New York. I became quickly convinced that none of the existing books accomplished what I thought was necessary for such a course, that is, to provide a self-contained introduction to the body of mathematical economic results without the need of a separate book or supplement to provide the requisite mathematical background.

Other books in this field fall into two categories. One type presents topics in mathematical economics and assumes that the student has already mastered the necessary mathematical techniques. Such books, at most, provide a short and much-too-concise supplement on mathematical techniques. Another type of book provides an introduction to the use of mathematical methods without presenting in any organized, systematic, or comprehensive manner the results of mathematical economic theory. These books use relatively few results of mathematical economics to illustrate mathematical techniques but do not develop any body of mathematical economics. The present book, on the other hand, presents a limited but significant body of mathematical economic results, and provides an introduction to the use and understanding of mathematical techniques. This explains the term "unified" that appears in the title of the book.

It is also my view that an introductory mathematical economics text should integrate the mathematics and economics portions. Material is therefore presented in a logical economic sequence with the requisite mathematics brought in wherever necessary. As a consequence, the student is in a better position to see the immediate application of the mathematics he or she is learning.

A key feature of this book is its exposition. Explanations are more detailed and comprehensive than is generally customary in mathematically oriented books. Illustrations and exercises are given for virtually every mathematical and economic theorem, method, and approach. Answers to selected exercises are provided at the end of the book. Moreover, mathematical concepts are motivated from an economic point of view before they are introduced in technical language.

Another major objective of this book is to demonstrate that the mathematical method can be used to point out the limitations and lack of realism underlying certain portions of existing economic theory. Every major theoretical result is followed by a discussion labeled *caution* indicating its possible shortcomings. The reader who takes all of these discussions together will have a critique of modern economic theory. In this respect, the book has benefited from the passage of time and contemporary concerns which have convinced me that it is now necessary to show that mathematical economics is a neutral and useful tool regardless of one's viewpoint on political, economic, or social issues.

This book does not assume any mathematical background beyond high school mathematics. No prior knowledge of calculus, set theory, or matrices is necessary. It would be useful for the reader to have had an introductory economics course at the college level. But interested students from other disciplines can also profit from the book even if they have taken no previous economics courses. The book is, then, as self-contained as possible. Upon completion, the student will have a working knowledge and good comprehension of calculus, set theory, matrix algebra, and elements of difference and differential equations. A rigorous treatment of microeconomic and macroeconomic theory is also offered to the student.

Although an attempt was made to provide broad coverage of topics and methods, several subjects could not be included in the book. This explains the omission of chapters on programming, input-output analysis, and trigonometric functions. In the case of programming, it was felt that adequate coverage would require a sizeable portion of the book and would therefore be best left for a separate volume. In regard to the other omissions, it was apparent that if the book was to be held to a manageable size, some topics would just have to be left for supplementary books. A decision was made at the early stages—and adhered to throughout—that the first priority of the book would be to cover the included topics in the most intelligible manner possible even if it meant elaborate explanations and thus necessitating the deletion of certain topics. A good text is one which makes a difficult subject easy to follow. I therefore attempted, as far as possible, not to skip steps and to reinforce certain concepts and results by expressing them in alternate ways. Proofs of mathematical theorems are included wherever they are instructive for future work. Some particularly intricate or difficult proofs or formulations are relegated to appendices which appear at the end of several chapters so as not to detour the average student. In any event, the *introductory* nature of this book is to be stressed. Needless to say, much more in the realm of mathematical economics exists. Hopefully, the interested reader will eventually move on to more advanced books.

The material in this book is ideally suited for courses in "mathematical economics" and "mathematics for economists" on either an undergraduate or graduate level. Exact coverage of chapters will, of course, vary from instructor to instructor and depend on student background and on whether the course is a full or one-half year course. Thus students with good backgrounds in calculus, set theory, or matrix algebra while benefiting from a reformulation of these topics in economic terms, will be able to proceed more quickly to the chapters which are primarily concerned with deriving mathematical economic theorems and results. On the other hand, students with less mathematical background will spend more time on those chapters devoted to mathematical techniques and methods. Intermediate courses in Price Theory (microeconomics) and Income and Employment Theory (macroeconomics) designed so as to present a mathematical formulation of those subjects will find the book extremely useful either as a primary or supplementary text. For courses taught on a graduate level, it is expected that more topics would be covered and, in general, treatment would be more intensive than on an undergraduate level.

As all authors well know, a great deal goes into writing a book. Even when the name of a single author appears on the title page, books are, in reality, cooperative ventures. I express my gratitude to my wife, Rebecca, for all the time she so cheerfully relinquished to allow me to work unhampered on my manuscript and to my young daughter, Shoshana, who also yielded—not always so cheerfully—time that was rightfully hers. I bequeath my hope that some day she will agree it was all worth it.

I am indebted to Professors Eric Lee of Fairleigh Dickinson University and Nilan Norris of Herbert Lehman College of the City University of New York, who carefully read the manuscript and made helpful suggestions and comments, and to a true friend, Marie Cooper, who provided invaluable aid, particularly with manuscript prepartion.

I also commend my students in the numerous mathematical economics courses I have taught at the City College of New York, Richmond College (Staten Island, New York), and the Graduate Center of the City University of New York. Their enthusiastic responses to such materials and their insistence that a text such as this was necessary gave me renewed encouragement and desire to complete the task.

Finally, to all my colleagues past and present who have made contributions to mathematical economics and economic theory, I express my appreciation. They were the "giants" upon whose shoulders I stood.

BARRY BRESSLER

A UNIFIED INTRODUCTION TO MATHEMATICAL ECONOMICS

1

THE EVOLUTION, USE, AND MISUSE OF MATH-EMATICAL ECONOMICS

> The description of the enormous complexity of the sociosphere even at a single moment in time must involve abstraction to an extreme degree. It is the principal business of the social sciences, indeed, to develop those abstractions which are most useful and which give us the most significant information. It is a very fundamental principle, indeed, that knowledge is always gained by the orderly loss of information, that is, by condensing and abstracting and indexing the great buzzing confusion of information that comes from the world around us into a form which we can appreciate and comprehend.
>
> —Kenneth Boulding

Mathematical economics can be defined as the use of mathematical methods and techniques in an effort to construct rigorous and logical economic theories. The actual tools employed in this pursuit include algebra, calculus, matrix methods, set theory, and other branches of mathematics. A related field of study is *econometrics*, which is the attempt to measure economic phenomena empirically and to test whether economic theories accord with the empirical data. For this purpose, the key tools are modern methods of statistical inference.

In the real world, where the numbers of events, facts, and actions approach infinity, theoretical frameworks are essential. Massive piles of data and information, by themselves, show precious little. They certainly do not enable us to understand why things happened, how they operate, what was responsible for change, and what is likely or unlikely to cause future change. Alas, the human mind is severely restricted in its ability to comprehend and sort out a multitude of facts. Only with the aid of theory can we make any sense of the complexity around us. By making simplifying assumptions and building deductively upon these, theory enables us, hopefully, to recognize and identify patterns, relations, and principles that govern the course of events in general and economic events in particular. The derived results, to be sure, will be no more than approximations to reality. Just how good will be such approximations depends upon the purpose for which they are to be used and, in any event, should stand the test of empirical verification.

Mathematical economics is valuable because it frequently enables us to develop theories of economic behavior in a more precise, efficient, and effective manner than literary economics (which is nonquantitative and depends solely upon words). It should, at the same time, be conceded that the very power of mathematical formulation can, upon occasion, lead us into intellectual traps if we do not proceed with proper caution.

If mathematical economics makes its contribution to the development of economic theory, econometrics provides us with the wherewithal to test whether the theories accord sufficiently well with reality. In this way, mathematical economics and econometrics complement each other.

This book is about mathematical economics; the province of econometrics is left to other authors. In the present chapter we provide a brief sketch of the origin and development of mathematical economics and then consider in detail the advantages and disadvantages of using the mathematical method.

SECTION 1·1 THE EVOLUTION OF MATHEMATICAL ECONOMICS

Before plunging into the actual study of mathematical economics, the reader may be interested in the historical development of the subject. A concise summary of the evolution and growth of mathematical economics will now be given. Emphasis is placed on the general tenor of mathematical activity during different periods of time rather than on the analysis of the works of particular authors. A full, in-depth history of mathematical economic thought would enrich the literature but is beyond the scope of this volume.[1]

---

[1] There are several scattered works that provide material for the reader interested in the history of mathematical economics. See Joseph A. Schumpeter, *History of Economic Analysis* (New York: Oxford University Press, 1954), pp. 954–963; James C. Charlesworth (ed.), *Mathematics and the Social Sciences* (Philadelphia: American Academy of Political and Social Science, 1963), pp. 1–29; James A. Gherity, *Economic Thought* (New York:

As we survey the role that mathematics has played in economics, we delineate several different periods based on their distinguishing characteristics. It is not always easy to determine precisely the end of one period and the beginning of another, but for convenience, we divide the total history into the following stages:

1) Pre–1838: Nonexistence
2) 1838–1870: Neglected Infant
3) 1870–1930: Rediscovery
4) 1930–1950: Active Growth—Flexing Muscles
5) 1950–Late 1960s: Supremacy
6) Late 1960s–Early 1970s: Firmly in Control but Under Attack

We shall now consider each of these in turn.

Pre–1838: Nonexistence

There were several scattered attempts to introduce the use of mathematics in dealing with economic problems as early as the eighteenth century. The Italian, Ceva, in 1711 and the Englishman, H. Lloyd, in 1771 employed algebraic formulations in their discussions of monetary matters, while the famous Swiss mathematician, Daniel Bernoulli, in 1738 introduced calculus concepts in his analysis of utility. In the early nineteenth century we find mathematical methods used by that advanced German writer, Von Thunen, whose first work was published in 1826.

Notwithstanding these efforts, the science of mathematical economics was not yet born, because there was no systematic mathematical treatment of a substantial body of economic theory until Cournot's 1838 work.

1838–1870: Neglected Infant

Antoine Augustin Cournot, the French writer, is generally acknowledged to be the "father of mathematical economics." His pioneering 1838 work made extensive use of the calculus in the analysis of demand,

---

Random House, 1965), pp. 264–281 and 326–429; Ben B. Seligman, *Main Currents in Modern Economics* (New York: Free Press, 1962), pp. 367–441 and 771–784; John F. Bell, *A History of Economic Thought* (New York: Ronald Press, 1967), pp. 680–708; Kenneth J. Arrow and F. H. Hahn, *General Competitive Analysis* (San Francisco: Holden-Day, 1971), pp. 1–15.

supply, price, monopoly, competition, oligopoly, and taxation. The publication of this work, however, hardly made a ripple and was almost universally ignored for more than 30 years. Mathematical economics, although born, did not begin growing until the early 1870s.

1870–1930: Rediscovery

In the 1870s Walras and Jevons rediscovered and loudly praised Cournot's work. As a result, it finally began to be carefully studied and applauded by such leading economists as Marshall, Edgeworth, and Seligman. The rediscovery of Cournot's work, together with the mathematical writings of Walras and Jevons, combined to increase interest in the mathematical approach to economic analysis. The number of economics works in mathematical form gradually increased. Some of the prominent writers who adopted this approach during this period were Edgeworth, Wicksell, Pareto, Irving Fisher, Slutsky, and Cassel.

In spite of the progress made by the mathematical writers during this period, the mathematical approach continued to be used only by a minority of writers and did not stand in the forefront of economic methodology.

1930–1950: Active Growth—Flexing Muscles

In the decades of the 1930s and 1940s mathematical economics took enormous strides both in the spreading use of its methodology and in the theoretical results it was able to derive. It is this period that produced the advances in value theory made by Hicks and Allen, the analysis of stability of equilibrium and revealed preference theory of Samuelson, the first rigorous treatment of general equilibrium theory by Wald, the study of economic dynamics by Tinbergen, Frisch, Kalecki, and Samuelson, the input–output analysis of Leontieff, and the path-breaking work on the theory of games by Von Neumann and Morgenstern. Mathematical economists had, at last, succeeded in showing that their method was capable and, indeed, amenable to pushing forward the frontiers of economic theory. One could not, however, say that mathematical economics, by itself, dominated the field of economic theory during most of this period.

1950–Late 1960s: Supremacy

By the dawn of the decade of the 1950s, it became increasingly evident that the mathematical method had moved to a position of supremacy, at least as far as economic theory was concerned. Such sentiment is expressed in the statement made by Samuelson in 1952 that "it has been correctly said that mathematical economics is flying high these days."[2] Virtually all of the work in economic theory during the decades of the 1950s and 1960s was mathematically oriented, whether in micro, macro or any of the specialized areas of economics. A sampling of some of the more prominent names of this period includes Arrow, Debreu, McKenzie, Gale, and Uzawa for their work in general equilibrium analysis; Koopmans for his activity analysis of production; Dantzig, Kuhn, and Tucker for their pioneer work in linear and nonlinear programming; and Solow, Morishima, Tobin, and Klein for their contributions to macroeconomics and other areas. There was little doubt, indeed, that anyone aspiring to labor in the vineyards of economic theory would be at an almost fatal disadvantage without a thorough knowledge of mathematics. Moreover, even students of economics who wished to center their activities in applied areas constantly encountered mathematical formulations in the relevant economics journals.

Late 1960s—Early 1970s: Firmly in Control but Under Attack

A definitive analysis of the significance of contemporaneous events must, of course, await the test of time. Nonetheless, certain developments during recent years are of interest as we near the end of our survey on the evolution of mathematical economic thought. On the one hand, mathematical economics seems solidly entrenched and firmly in control of ongoing research and education in economic theory. The economics journals show no abatement whatever in their proclivity toward sophisticated mathematical model building. Indicative of this continuing trend is the following statement by Samuelson, who is probably the leading present-day spokesman for the mathematical economists:

> In the middle third of the twentieth century, mathematics has everywhere swept through economics like an epidemic of measles sweeping through a new continent. He who would occupy a chair at a great university, advise the Prince or the Chairman of the Board, must serve his apprenticeship in this difficult art. Deplore it or applaud it, the fact is there—like the Dead Sea or Pike's Peak.[3]

On the other hand, for the first time in decades, we are experiencing a vociferous and sustained dissent to the use of mathematics in economics

[2] Paul A. Samuelson, "Economic Theory and Mathematics, An Appraisal," *American Economic Review*, XLII (May 1952), p. 56.

[3] Paul A. Samuelson, "Foreward" to *Analytical Economics* by Nicholas Georgescu-Roegen (Cambridge, Mass.: Harvard University Press, 1966), p. vii.

by those who describe themselves as radical economists. Bronfenbrenner, in his review of radical economics, best summarizes their thought in this matter:

> The final methodological revolt of radical economics is against the gnostic esotericism of the technical specialist and the use of higher mathematics and statistics as expository devices. Here the argument is against discouraging the general public from serious consideration of economic problems by making the problems appear somehow beyond the layman's understanding.[4]

How have mainstream economists responded to this argument? For the most part, attacks on the use of mathematics have been ignored and theorists have remained unshaken in their adherence to the mathematical method. Samuelson, for instance, in his Nobel speech quipped: "Just recently I was reading an article by a writer of the New Left. It was written in blank verse, which turns out to be an extremely inefficient medium for communication but which a dedicated scholar must be prepared to struggle through in the interest of science."[5]

One indication of the great esteem in which mathematical economists are held—radical critics notwithstanding—is the number of such economists who have been awarded Nobel Prizes. The Nobel award for economics was established by Riksbank, the Swedish bank, in celebration of its 300th anniversary. The winner of the annual award is selected by the Swedish Academy of Science. The list of winners to date follows:

1969　Ragnar Frisch (Norway) and Jan Tinbergen (Netherlands)
1970　Paul A. Samuelson (United States)
1971　Simon Kuznets (United States)
1972　Kenneth J. Arrow (United States) and John R. Hicks (United Kingdom)
1973　Wassily Leontief (United States)

The reader will perhaps have noticed that six of the seven men honored happen to be mathematical economists who were mentioned in our survey of the history of mathematical economics. As a matter of fact, even the seventh, Kuznetz, while not a mathematical economist per se, has dealt almost exclusively with quantitative or statistical data, so that he too can be labeled a quantitative economist.[6]

---

[4] Martin Bronfenbrenner, "Radical Economics in America 1970," *Journal of Economic Literature*, VIII (September 1970), p. 753.
[5] Paul A. Samuelson, "Maximum Principles in Analytical Economics," *American Economic Review*, LXII (June 1972), p. 261.
[6] After this book had gone into production, word was received that the 1974 winners were Myrdal and Hayek, neither of whom is a mathematical economist. It is much too early to say whether this represents the onset of a new trend.

Our survey of mathematical economics through the years has shown that there has often been a communications gap between mathematical and other economists. This certainly goes a long way in explaining the difficulty encountered in launching the field and then in attracting followers to it. It is possible that a lack of adequate communication still exists today. Unfortunately, mathematical economists have not found it rewarding enough to translate their results and to show the true nature of their field in a clear and intelligible manner to the nonmathematical economist. As fairly typical of the attitude taken by most mathematical economists, consider the following passage from a classic in the field:

> In the beginning it was hoped that the discussion could be made nontechnical. Very quickly it became apparent that such a procedure, while possible, would involve a manuscript many times the present size. . . . The laborious literary working over of essentially simple mathematical concepts . . . is not only unrewarding from the standpoint of advancing the science, but involves as well mental gymnastics of a peculiarly depraved type.[7]

Thus, even though it is granted that a nontechnical translation is possible, it is rejected, first because of the projected size of such a manuscript and second because it is unrewarding. Neither of these contentions can be accepted if we are truly interested in spreading economic knowledge.

In this book we hope partially to bridge the gap that has arisen between mathematical and nonmathematical economists by showing that the mathematical method can be used by all—whether to defend or to criticize the "conventional wisdom" of accepted economic theory. To this end, we use the mathematical approach not only to present the basic body of micro and macro theory, but also to show the limitations and shortcomings of such theories. It should be recognized that there are those who do not accept the existing political and economic system of our country and who desire structural change in such institutions. Mathematical economics can even be helpful to such persons, because its methods can be used not only to attack the existing system but also to build a theoretical edifice for alternative political-economic structures.

At the same time, we readily concede that the mathematical method can be overplayed and overemphasized. It can be used to build elegant but empty theoretical boxes and to ignore the real world. Mathematical economists have unfortunately sometimes been guilty of such vices. The essential point, however, is that when this occurs, it is not the mathematical method that is at fault, but rather the practitioner.

In the next section we delineate more specifically the benefits and limitations associated with use of the mathematical method.

[7] Paul A. Samuelson, *Foundations of Economic Analysis* (New York: Atheneum, 1965), p. 6.

SECTION 1·2   THE USES AND MISUSES
OF MATHEMATICAL ECONOMICS

It is worthwhile to consider explicitly the various advantages and disadvantages that may accrue from utilization of the mathematical approach. We outline these in succeeding paragraphs.

Advantages Gained Through Use of the Mathematical Method

1. Mathematical language is very clear and usually free of ambiguity. Assumptions are generally made explicit. This is not the case, in the main, for literary writing. Words are not usually defined very precisely. Invariably, there are different shades of meaning for any word or phrase.
2. Conclusions of a mathematical argument follow rigorously. There is, almost invariably, agreement among all mathematicians as to whether a particular mathematical argument is valid. Loose thinking is thus eliminated. When literary arguments are presented, it is not unusual for there to be disputes as to inferences drawn. This is because it is possible for literary economics to talk without a careful delineation of a logical structure.
3. The mathematical method is more efficient. It is easier and quicker to prove many propositions by use of mathematics than by ordinary logic in verbal form.
4. The mathematical approach has the advantage of generality. Through the use of symbols, it is usually possible to deal simultaneously with a whole family of conceivable situations and to generalize results to a large number of variables.
5. Through the use of mathematics, we may derive results that may never be achieved otherwise. The mathematical method is the only way to solve certain problems. As an elementary illustration, think of solving a set of simultaneous equations through methods of literary logic.
6. The application of mathematics to economics enables us to understand concepts that are otherwise not clearly comprehensible. As an example, consider the marginal cost of producing a product. Do we mean the cost of the last unit produced or of the next one that would be produced? On occasion, a significant difference may appear, and the concept is ambiguous unless we introduce the derivative as shown in later chapters.

Disadvantages Inherent in the
Use of the Mathematical Method

1. Mathematical economists often state only mathematical assumptions
    such as the nature of functions used (linear, homogeneous, etc.), while
    obscuring the economic assumptions (rationality, perfect knowledge,
    etc.).
2. It frequently happens that the assumptions made are mathematically
    convenient but unrealistic from an economic point of view, thus
    giving unrealistic and nonuseful results. The construction of math-
    ematically elegant—even if unrealistic—models may become an end
    in itself. As Boulding has so aptly stated, "Mathematics in any of its
    applied fields is a wonderful servant but a very bad master; it is so
    good a servant that there is a tendency for it to become an unjust
    steward and usurp the master's place.[8]
3. Mathematical models often totally ignore qualitative variables such
    as attitudes, beliefs, and expectations.
4. The process of making simplifying assumptions contains within it a
    greater danger when the mathematical method is used as opposed to
    the literary approach, because after some time these assumptions are
    forgotten and lost sight of in a maze of formulas and symbols.
5. There is the danger that mathematical economics gives one the feel-
    ing of possessing absolute knowledge and being beyond the possi-
    bility of being challenged.
6. Mathematics is often used when it is unnecessary, merely to give the
    impression of being esoteric.

We thus see that while mathematical tools may be very potent, there
are, at the same time, dangers lurking in our path as we use them. This
should not deter us from utilizing such methods and reaping as much as
we can from them. But it does mean that we must be wary of the possible
dangers and examine closely every step of our procedures.

---

[8] Kenneth E. Boulding, *Economics as a Science* (New York: McGraw-Hill, 1970), p. 115.

2

SET THEORY AND DEDUCTIVE LOGIC

> The mathematical method is character-
> ized not so much (if at all) by what it deals
> with as by the way in which it formulates
> and handles a problem. There have, of
> course, been changes over the years in
> what the mathematicians themselves
> regard as acceptable. But three aspects
> seem to stand out: the use of symbolism,
> axiomatic structure, a treasury of accu-
> mulated techniques and results.
> —Leonid Hurwicz

This chapter seeks to introduce the student to logic in general and mathematical reasoning in particular. Elementary set theory is an ideal topic
with which to begin, because it can be understood by students regardless
of their mathematical background and can be mastered relatively quickly.
It also shows that no one need be intimidated by symbolic notation. In
recent years set theory and axiomatic structures have assumed increasing
importance in mathematical economic reasoning. The trend promises to
continue unabated.

SECTION 2·1 SETS

There are a multitude of objects and beings in the world. We often group
some of these together. Such collections of clearly defined objects or
beings are known as *sets*. Thus we can speak of

the set of all college students
the set of all people weighing more than 200 lb
the set of all books

Economic analysis frequently utilizes the concept of sets. It deals
with

the set of all consumers
the set of all business firms
the set of all monopolists
the set of all capital
the set consisting of General Motors, Chrysler, and Ford Motors

Every member of a set is said to be an *element* of that set. For example, U.S. Steel is an element of the set of all business firms.

The concept of sets is also applicable when considering a collection of actions, ideas, or possibilities. We can therefore speak of the set of possible reactions by one oligopolist to a 10 percent price reduction by a competitor. The elements within this set could consist of a 50 percent price reduction, a 20 percent price reduction, a zero price reduction, and so on.

Any set must be described in an unambiguous manner so that it is clear what is and what is not included in that set. One way to describe a set is to specify a common characteristic. All objects or beings having this characteristic are then elements of the set. The set of all persons who bought new automobiles in 1970 is an example of such a set. Such descriptions must be precise. A collection of the most powerful business firms in the nation is not a set, because we cannot determine objectively how many powerful firms are to be included, or for that matter, what criteria are used to measure power. Similarly, the collection of all the large investors in the economy does not constitute a set, because there is no way to determine whether any particular person is a large enough investor. But the collection of all persons who invested more than $1 million in 1970 is a well-defined set.[1]

A second way of describing a set is to enumerate all the elements of the set. The set consisting of General Motors, Chrysler, and Ford Motors falls into this category, because all its elements are specified.

In describing a set, it is customary to use a pair of braces to indicate the elements contained in that set. Thus, one way to write the set of all persons who bought new automobiles in 1970 is the following:

$\{X \mid X$ is a person who bought a new automobile in 1970$\}$

The symbol within the braces (in this case X) indicates a typical element in the set. This is followed by a vertical line, which in turn is followed by

---

[1] In popular terminology, the term "jet set" is often used to refer to the class of people who unhesitatingly employ jets to hop around the world. This, however, does not truly constitute a set, because there is no way of deciding unambiguously whether one must travel once a month, twice a month, and so on.

the criterion for membership in this set. The statement can thus be read as the set of all X such that X is a person who bought an automobile in 1970.

If a set is defined by enumerating all its elements, such as the set consisting of General Motors, Chrysler, and Ford Motors, it could be written as

{General Motors, Chrysler, Ford Motors}

Here, all the elements of the set are specified within the braces.

To simplify discussions, any set may be denoted by a letter. Thus, for the set given above, we would have

A = {General Motors, Chrysler, Ford Motors}

which indicates that A is the set consisting of General Motors, Chrysler, and Ford Motors. We can then refer to elements of A without repeating the full description of the set. To denote a particular element of this set, we could simply write GM $\in A$, which means that GM is an element of the set A. We can also denote elements that are not within the set. Thus we could write American Motors $\notin A$.

SECTION 2·2 SUBSETS

If A is any set, it may be that all its elements are contained within another set B. In this case we say that A is a *subset* of B. We denote this by writing $A \subset B$ or A is contained within B. An equivalent way of expressing this is to say B includes A, which is denoted by $B \supset A$.

Illustration.
1) The set of all males is a subset of the set of all humans.
2) The set of consumers of 1970 automobiles is a subset of the set of consumers of all 1970 products.
3) The set of nonskilled labor is a subset of the set of all labor.

Note that any set has many subsets. Thus the set of semiskilled labor, the set of skilled labor, the set of all labor other than skilled labor are all subsets of the set of all labor. Note, too, that any subset is a set in itself and has, in turn, its own subsets. Thus the set of skilled labor is one subset of the set of all labor. The set of professional workers is, in turn, a subset of the set of skilled labor.

When considering subsets of some particular set, the original, all-inclusive set is referred to as the *universal set* and denoted by the symbol I. A set that contains no elements is referred to as the *empty set* or the *null set* and denoted by the symbol $\emptyset$. Thus we may refer to the set of all workers as the universal set, the set of nonskilled workers as a subset, the set of skilled workers as another subset, the set of all workers 100 ft tall as the null set. However, the set of all professional workers and their wives is not a subset of the set of all workers, even though the two sets may have common elements, namely, professional workers.

SECTION 2·3   OPERATIONS ON SETS

Two sets A and B are said to be equal if each element in A is an element in B and if each element in B is an element in A. Thus $A = B$ if and only if $A \subset B$ and $B \supset A$. This implies that A and B have identical elements.

Illustration. If $A = \{X \mid X$ is a U.S. automobile manufacturer$\}$ and $B = \{$General Motors, Ford, Chrysler, American Motors$\}$, then $A = B$ because A and B contain precisely the same elements.

Illustration. If $A = \{$skilled workers, nonskilled workers, semiskilled workers$\}$ and $B = \{$nonskilled workers, semiskilled workers, skilled workers$\}$, then $A = B$. Thus a set is unchanged even if elements in the set are rearranged.

If we have two sets denoted by A and B, we can form a new set by taking together all the elements in both sets. The resulting set is known as the *union* of these two sets and is denoted by $A \cup B$. Any element in either of the two sets will then be in the union set.

Illustration.   Given two sets A and B, where

$A = \{$Cadillacs, Oldsmobiles, Buicks, Pontiacs, Chevrolets$\}$

$B = \{$Chevrolets, Plymouths, Fords$\}$

The union of the two sets is

$A \cup B = \{$Cadillacs, Oldsmobiles, Buicks, Pontiacs, Chevrolets, Plymouths, Fords$\}$

If we are given two sets A and B, we may form another new set by taking together all the elements that are common to both sets. The resulting set is known as the *intersection* of these two sets and is denoted by

$A \cap B$. Only those elements that appear in both sets are in the intersection set.

Illustration. Given the two sets A and B defined as in the above illustration. Then

$A \cap B = \{\text{Chevrolets}\}$

The intersection set contains only one element, that is, Chevrolets, because this is the only element included in both A and B.

Two sets that contain no common elements are said to be *disjoint*.

Illustration. Given two sets A and B, where

$A = \{\text{Cadillacs, Oldsmobiles, Buicks, Pontiacs, Chevrolets}\}$

$B = \{\text{Plymouths, Dodges, Chryslers}\}$

Then $A \cap B = \varnothing$, or the intersection set is the *null set* because it contains no elements. Thus A and B are disjoint.

These operations can be better visualized by drawing *Venn diagrams*. The universal set is represented by a rectangle and any subsets by circlelike figures. We would then have

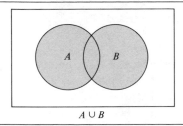
$A \cup B$
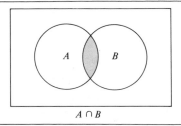
$A \cap B$

Circle A represents set A, while circle B represents set B. The union $A \cup B$ is the total area within both circles. The intersection $A \cap B$ is the area common to both A and B, that is, the shaded portion of the second diagram.

Two disjoint sets C and D would be represented by circles C and D in the following diagram.

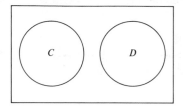

The set of all elements of the universal set not included in set *A* is known as the *complement* of *A* and is denoted by *A'*.

Illustration. If *A* is the set of all people weighing 200 lb or more, then *A'* is the set of all people weighing less than 200 lb.

Illustration. If $A = \{$skilled labor, semiskilled labor$\}$, then *A'* is the set of unskilled labor.

Sets and their complements can be visualized by the following Venn diagram:

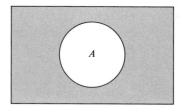

The shaded area in the box is the complement of *A*. Note in particular that the complement of the universal set is the null set and that the complement of the null set is the universal set.

If we consider two sets *A* and *B*, we can then form a new set $B - A$, which is composed of all the elements in *B* but not in *A*.

Illustration. If $A = \{$skilled labor, semiskilled labor$\}$ and $B = \{$all workers$\}$, then

$$B - A = \{\text{unskilled workers}\}$$

This notation enables us to express the complement of *A* as $I - A$.

We are now in a position to prove various theorems concerning sets and operations on sets. Note that some of these propositions may seem self-evident from an intuitive point of view. They, however, require formal proof to establish their truth beyond question.

Theorem.   If A and B are any two sets, then

$$A \cup B = B \cup A$$

Proof.   To prove the equality of sets, we must show that every element in the first set is also an element in the second set and that every element in the second set is an element in the first set.

Therefore let X represent any element in $A \cup B$. This implies that X is either in A or in B. But if this is so, then X is also in $B \cup A$.

Similarly, let Y represent any element in $B \cup A$. This implies that Y is either in B or in A. But if this is so, then Y is also in $A \cup B$.

We could also use Venn diagrams to establish the validity of this theorem.

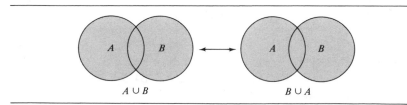

$$A \cup B \qquad\qquad\qquad B \cup A$$

Illustration.   The above theorem would assert that the set composed of workers who are either professionals or over 40 years of age is the same as the set composed of workers who are either over 40 or professionals.

Theorem.   If A, B, and C are any three sets, then

$$(A \cup B) \cup C = A \cup (B \cup C)$$

Proof.   Let X be any element in $(A \cup B) \cup C$. Then X is either an element in $A \cup B$ or an element in C. But being an element in $A \cup B$ implies being an element in either A or B. Thus X is an element in either A or B or C. But then X is either an element in A or in $B \cup C$. This is the same as saying that X is an element in $A \cup (B \cup C)$. Therefore every element in $(A \cup B) \cup C$ is an element in $A \cup (B \cup C)$.

Let Y be any element in $A \cup (B \cup C)$. Then Y is either an element of A or of $B \cup C$. But being an element of $B \cup C$ is the same as being an element of B or C. Thus Y is an element of either A or B or C. But then Y is either an element of $(A \cup B)$ or of C, which is the same as saying that Y is an element of $(A \cup B) \cup C$. Therefore every element in $A \cup (B \cup C)$ is an element of $(A \cup B) \cup C$.

We can also use Venn diagrams to demonstrate the validity of this theorem.

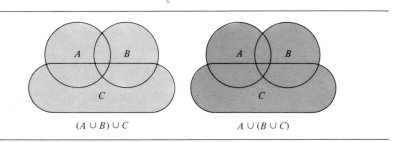

$(A \cup B) \cup C$ $A \cup (B \cup C)$

Illustration. Let A be the set of professional workers, B the set of teen-age workers, and C the set of workers earning more than \$7000 a year. Then $(A \cup B) \cup C$ is the set of all workers who are either professionals or teen-agers or those workers earning more than \$7000 a year. $A \cup (B \cup C)$ is the set of all workers who are professionals or who are either teen-agers or earning more than \$7000 a year. Thus $(A \cup B) \cup C$ and $A \cup (B \cup C)$ refer to the same set of workers.

Theorem. If A, B, and C are any sets, then

$$A \cap (B \cup C) = (A \cap B) \cup (A \cap C)$$

Proof. Let X be any element in $A \cap (B \cup C)$. Then X is an element of A and of $B \cup C$, which is equivalent to saying that X is an element of A and of either B or C. Thus X is an element of either $A \cap B$ or of $A \cap C$. This implies that X is an element of $(A \cap B) \cup (A \cap C)$. Therefore every element in $A \cap (B \cup C)$ is an element of $(A \cap B) \cup (A \cap C)$.

Let Y be any element in $(A \cap B) \cup (A \cap C)$. Then Y is an element of either $A \cap B$ or $A \cap C$, which means that Y is an element of either A and B or of A and C. Thus Y is an element of A and of either B or C. This is the same as saying that Y is an element of $A \cap (B \cup C)$. Therefore every element in $(A \cap B) \cup (A \cap C)$ is an element of $A \cap (B \cup C)$.

We can again use Venn diagrams to demonstrate the validity of the theorem.

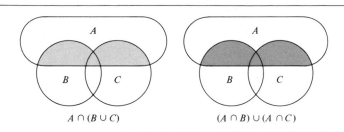

$A \cap (B \cup C)$ $(A \cap B) \cup (A \cap C)$

Illustration.   Let A be the set of workers earning more than \$10,000 a year, B the set of professional workers, and C the set of workers over 40. Then $A \cap (B \cup C)$ is the set of workers who earn more than \$10,000 a year and who are either professionals or over 40.

    $(A \cap B) \cup (A \cap C)$ is the set of workers who either earn more than \$10,000 a year and are professionals or who earn more than \$10,000 a year and are over 40.

Exercises

1. If A is the set of all males, B the set of all professional workers, and C the set of all employed workers over 50, find
    a) $A \cup B$
    b) $B \cap C$
    c) $(A \cap B) \cap C$
    d) $A \cup (B \cap C)$
    e) $(A \cap B) \cup (B \cap C)$
    f) $A' \cap B$
2. Decide whether each of the following is a set:
    a) all the best workers
    b) all unemployed workers
    c) all young workers
3. Specify all of the subsets of {General Motors, Ford, Chrysler Motors}.
4. Prove and give an economic example:
    a) $A \cap B = B \cap A$
    b) $(A \cap B) \cap C = A \cap (B \cap C)$
    c) $A \cup (B \cap C) = (A \cup B) \cap (A \cup C)$
    d) $I \cap A = A$
    e) $\varnothing \cup A = A$
    f) $I \cup A = I$
    g) $\varnothing \cap A = \varnothing$

  h) $A \cup A = A$
  i) $A \cap A = A$
  j) $A \cup (B \cup C) = (A \cup B) \cup (A \cup C)$
  k) $A \cap (B \cap C) = (A \cap B) \cap (A \cap C)$
5. Prove and give economic examples:
  a) $A \cup (A \cap B) = A$
  b) $A \cap (A \cup B) = A$
  c) $(A \cup B)' = A' \cap B'$
  d) $(A \cap B)' = A' \cup B'$

SECTION 2·4   DEDUCTIVE LOGIC

Deductive logic is the process of arriving at conclusions that follow inescapably from given statements. These given statements are known as *hypotheses. Conclusions* that are logical consequences of the hypotheses are said to be *valid.*

  It is important to realize that the validity of a statement does not imply its truth. A conclusion is valid if it follows logically from the given hypothesis. But the hypothesis may be false, in which case the conclusion might also be false. The validity of a conclusion implies only that *if* the hypothesis is true, then the conclusion is true.

  The validity of arguments can be tested by using Venn diagrams.

Illustration.
Hypotheses. a) All steel producers are business firms.
     b) All business firms are pure competitors.
Conclusion. All steel producers are pure competitors.
  The following diagram depicts these hypotheses.

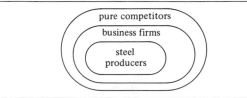

  The first hypothesis tells us that the set of steel producers is a subset of the set of business firms. We therefore place all steel producers within the larger boundary of all business firms. The second hypothesis tells us that the set of all business firms is itself a subset of the set of pure competitors. Thus all business firms are placed within the boundary of pure competitors.

We now notice that an unavoidable consequence of these hypotheses is that the set of all steel producers is found within the set of pure competitors. Hence we have an inescapable conclusion that all steel producers are pure competitors, and the argument is valid even though the conclusion is not a true one. A valid conclusion implies only that if the hypothesis is true, the conclusion is true. In this case, if all business firms were, indeed, pure competitors, then all steel producers would be pure competitors. But, in truth, all steel producers are not pure competitors.

We have just seen an illustration of a conclusion that was valid but nevertheless untrue because the hypothesis was untrue. But this does not mean that when the hypotheses are untrue, valid conclusions will always be untrue. Consider the following example:

Hypotheses.   a)   All engineers are farmers.
                  b)   All farmers are skilled workers.
Conclusion.   All engineers are skilled workers.
We represent this argument by the following diagram.

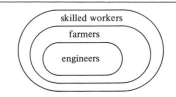

The conclusion is indeed inescapable, and the reasoning is valid. But note that the hypotheses are patently false. Yet the conclusion is true.

We have thus shown that if valid reasoning is used, then the conclusion must be true if the hypotheses are true. If the hypotheses are untrue, then the conclusions might or might not be true.

The fact that a conclusion is a true statement does not by itself ensure that the argument is a valid one, as the following example will show.

Hypothesis.   a)   All professional workers are in favor of higher wages.
                 b)   All skilled workers are in favor of higher wages.
Conclusion.   All professional workers are skilled workers.
This argument is represented by the following diagram.

those who favor higher wages

professional
workers

skilled
workers

All of these statements are true. Yet the reasoning is invalid, because the conclusion does not follow inescapably from the hypotheses. There is nothing in the hypotheses that compels us to place the set of professional workers within the set of skilled workers. The hypotheses do compel us to place both the set of professional workers and the set of skilled workers within the set of those who favor higher wages. But these two subsets could just as well be disjoint.

This example also illustrates the point that in order for an argument to be valid, the conclusion must follow inescapably from the hypotheses. If a conclusion is possible but not inescapable, we say that it is invalid because there is insufficient reason to deduce it from the hypotheses.

The illustrative statements given above apply to complete classes such as all steel producers, all firms, all nonskilled workers, and so on. Many statements concern only some members of a class. Still other statements are phrased in negative terminology. We illustrate these below.

Illustration.
Hypotheses.   a)   Some business firms make less than 10 percent profit.
     b)   All pure competitors are business firms.
Conclusion.   Some pure competitors make less than 10 percent profit.
  This argument can be analyzed by means of the following diagram:

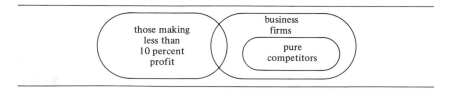

those making
less than
10 percent
profit

business
firms

pure
competitors

By hypothesis, we know that some firms make less than 10 percent profit. This means that at least one firm makes less than 10 percent profit. It may be that more than one firm or, indeed, all firms make less than 10 percent profit. But we are certain only that this applies to at least one firm. We therefore cannot draw the set of business firms as a subset of those making less than 10 percent profit. Consequently, we have drawn the set of business firms so that it intersects the set of those making less than 10 percent profit.

We also know, by hypothesis, that the set of pure competitors is entirely included within the set of business firms. It may be that some of the pure competitors are business firms that make less than 10 percent profit, in which case a portion of the set of pure competitors would fall into the intersection of business firms and those making less than 10 percent returns. But we were not given any information establishing that this is so. Therefore we place the set of pure competitors within the region of business firms that does not intersect the set of those making less than 10 percent.

The proposed conclusion is therefore seen to be invalid, because it may be that no pure competitors make less than 10 percent. The conclusion is not inescapable from the hypotheses, so it is invalid.

This serves to illustrate the point that a statement concerning some objects in a set refers to at least one object, but tells us nothing concerning the other members of the set. This is contrary to popular usage, where the term "some" indicates not all.

Statements asserting that no elements of a set are members of another set are represented by two nonintersecting disjoint circles as in the following.

Illustration.
Hypotheses.   a)   No skilled workers are under 25 years of age.
                 b)   Some skilled workers earn more than $20,000 a year.
Conclusion.   Some workers who earn more than $20,000 a year are not under 25 years of age.

We represent this argument by the following diagram:

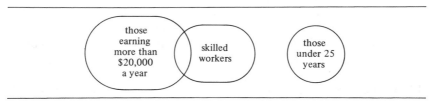

The set of skilled workers is disjoint or completely separated from the set of those under 25 years of age. We know that they have no common elements. But the set of skilled workers intersects the set of those earning more than $20,000, because there is at least one skilled worker who earns more than $20,000. We therefore can validly conclude that some workers who earn more than $20,000 a year are not under 25 years, because at least one skilled worker earns more than $20,000 a year and he is excluded from the set of those under 25 years.

We often encounter arguments that are invalid as they stand but that can be made valid by the insertion of additional hypotheses.

Illustration.
Hypotheses. a) All firms producing at levels other than where marginal revenue = marginal cost do not maximize profits.
  b) Jones does not know the meaning of either marginal revenue or marginal cost.
Conclusion. Jones does not maximize profits.

This argument is invalid as stated unless we assume that because Jones does not know the meaning of marginal revenue and marginal cost, he cannot be producing at a level where marginal revenue equals marginal cost. But this assumption is not one of the hypotheses. In fact, it could well be that Jones produces at a level where marginal revenue equals marginal cost even though he does not know the meaning of the terms.

The argument could be made valid by the insertion of an additional hypothesis, namely, that all those who do not know the meaning of marginal revenue and marginal cost cannot be producing at a level where marginal revenue equals marginal cost.

SECTION 2·5 CONVERSES

Consider an argument of the form, A implies B; that is, if A is true, then B is true. The *converse* of this argument is the argument, B implies A; that is, if B is true, then A is true. Thus the converse of an argument is formed by interchanging hypothesis and conclusion. The converse of a valid argument may or may not be valid.

Illustration.
Hypothesis. All firms seek to maximize profits.
Conclusion. Firm A seeks to maximize profits.

This argument is valid. The converse argument would appear as

Hypothesis. Firm A seeks to maximize profits.
Conclusion. All firms seek to maximize profits.

This, however, is not a valid argument.

An argument of the form:
1)   If A is true, then B is true.
can be written as A is a *sufficient condition* for B.

The converse of this argument is the following:
2)   If B is true, then A is true.
This can be written as A is a *necessary condition* for B. Thus the statement that A is a necessary and sufficient condition for B is equivalent to statement (1) and its converse (2).

Statement (1) is also sometimes written as A is true only if B is true. Thus the statement A is true if and only if B is true is equivalent to (1) and its converse.

If statement (1) implies its converse (2) and statement (2) implies its converse (1), we say that (1) and (2) are *equivalent*.

Illustration.   Consider the following argument and its converse:
a)   If a firm is to maximize profits, it must set $MR = MC$.
b)   A firm that sets $MR = MC$ will maximize profits.

Statement (a) could also be written as " Profit maximization is a sufficient condition for setting $MR = MC$," or in the following manner: "A firm maximizes profits only if it sets $MR = MC$."

Statement (b) could be written as " Profit maximization is a necessary condition for setting $MR = MC$," or in the following manner: "A firm maximizes profits if it sets $MR = MC$."

Statements (a) and (b) together could be written as " Profit maximization is a necessary and sufficient condition for setting $MR = MC$", or as "A firm maximizes profits if and only if it sets $MR = MC$."

Exercises

Test the validity of each of the following arguments.
1.   Hypotheses: a)   All monopolists equate MR and MC.
                   b)   Company X equates MR and MC.
     Conclusion: Company X is a monopolist.
2.   Hypotheses: a)   All consumers are rational.
                   b)   All workers are rational.
     Conclusions: a)   All workers are consumers.
                   b)   No workers are consumers.
                   c)   Some workers are consumers.
                   d)   Some workers are not consumers.
                   e)   Some consumers are workers.
                   f)   Some consumers are not workers.

3. Hypotheses: a) All spending on consumer durables is included in investment spending.
   b) All investment spending is included in GNP.
   Conclusion: All spending on consumer durables is included in GNP.

4. Hypotheses: a) No U.S. producer experiences increasing returns to scale.
   b) Some monopolists do not experience increasing returns to scale.
   Conclusion: Some monopolists are U.S. producers.

5. Hypotheses: a) All workers are factors of production.
   b) No children are factors of production.
   Conclusion: No children are workers.

6. Hypotheses: a) All oligopolists seek to maximize profits.
   b) Some oligopolists are steel producers.
   c) Some auto producers are oligopolists.
   Conclusions: a) Some profit maximizers are steel producers.
   b) Some profit maximizers are auto producers.
   c) Some steel producers are auto producers.
   d) Some steel producers are not auto producers.
   e) Some steel producers are not oligopolists.
   f) Some steel producers are not profit maximizers.

7. Hypotheses: a) All X's are Y's.
   b) Some Z's are Y's.
   c) Some W's are not Y's.
   Conclusions: a) Some W's are Z's.
   b) No W's are X's.
   c) Some W's are Y's.
   d) Some W's are not X's.
   e) Some Y's are not X's.

8. a) What is the converse of the following argument? If a consumer is to maximize his satisfaction, he must equate marginal utility per last dollar spent for all products.
   b) According to the argument of part (a), is the equating of marginal utility per last dollar for all products a necessary or a sufficient condition for the maximization of satisfaction?

9. What additional hypothesis would make the following a valid argument?
   Hypotheses: a) Any worker, knowing all the alternative wages he could command, would choose the highest-paying one available.
   b) Mr. Robinson says that he knows all the alternative wages he can command.

Conclusion: Mr. Robinson will choose the highest-paying job
available to him.

10. a)   What is the converse of the following argument? If an equilibrium level of national income is to be attained, then desired
savings must equal desired investment.

  b)   According to the argument of part (a), is the attainment of an
equilibrium level of national income a necessary or a sufficient
condition for the equality of desired savings and desired
investment?

SECTION 2·6   PROPOSITIONS AND STATEMENTS

In previous sections we have dealt with logical statements concerning sets
of elements. We showed how to determine whether some such statements
implied other statements known as conclusions. In this section, we consider statements in general and the conditions that determine their truth
or falsity.

A *proposition* is a *statement*, or an assertion that is either true or
false but not both.

Illustrations.   The following are statements or propositions:
1)   The average income of lawyers is higher than the average income of
teachers.
2)   More General Motors automobiles were sold in 1970 than Chrysler
automobiles.
3)   Consumers, at any time, will buy more color TVs at low prices than
at high prices.
4)   Consumers, at any time, will buy more color TVs at high prices than
at low prices.
5)   Wheat farmers will offer more bushels for sale at higher prices than at
lower prices.
6)   A person, at any time, will derive greater utility from the first unit of a
product than from the second unit.
7)   Any firm wishing to maximize profits will produce until the point
where marginal revenue equals marginal cost.

Note that propositions may be either true or false. It is quite
obvious that propositions (3) and (4) above cannot both be true. If one is
true, then the other is false. Nevertheless, they are both propositions. One
is a true proposition and the other is a false proposition. The truth or
falsity of a statement is called its *truth value* and is denoted by either T
(for true) or F (for false).

Not all sentences or phrases are propositions or statements. This is illustrated by the following:

Illustrations.
1)   Why did the consumer buy the automobile?
2)   Don't grant any wage increases.
3)   When prices increase.
4)   Recession and unemployment.

In each of these cases no assertions are made. The phrases are neither true nor false.

Propositions can be denoted by letters such as $p, q, r, \ldots$.

Some statements are composites of two or more substatements. Such statements are known as *compound statements or propositions.*

Illustration.   Let p denote the proposition that consumers will purchase less wheat at high prices than at low prices and let q be the proposition that farmers will supply more wheat at high prices than at low prices. We can assert that both of these propositions are true by stating the compound proposition: Consumers will purchase less wheat at high prices than at low prices, and farmers will supply more wheat at high prices than at low prices. We denote this compound statement by $p \wedge q$.

Thus the compound statement $p \wedge q$ asserts that both p and q are true. The symbol $\wedge$ is read as "and."

Alternatively, we could make the assertion that either p or q is true. This would be denoted by $p \vee q$. The symbol $\vee$ is read as "or."

We could also make the assertion that one of the statements is not true. An example of this would be "Farmers will not supply more wheat at high prices than at low prices." This would be written as $\sim q$. The symbol $\sim$ is read as "not."

There are many varieties of compound statements. Thus we could say $p \wedge \sim q$, which would assert that consumers will purchase less wheat at high prices than at low prices *and* farmers will *not* supply more wheat at high prices than at low prices.

The truth value of a compound statement depends upon the truth values of its components. This dependence is clearly shown by the construction of a *truth table*, which shows all the possible truth values of the component statements together with the corresponding truth values of the compound statement.

The truth table for the compound statement $p \wedge q$ is given by the following.

p	q	$p \wedge q$
T	T	T
T	F	F
F	T	F
F	F	F

The table indicates that if statements p and q are both true, then $p \wedge q$ is true. If p is true while q is false, or if p is false while q is true, or if both p and q are false, then $p \wedge q$ is false. The table thus considers all the possible truth values of the component statements and the truth value of the compound statement for each of these possibilities.

For the compound statement $p \vee q$, we would have the following truth table:

p	q	$p \vee q$
T	T	T
T	F	T
F	T	T
F	F	F

This indicates that the compound statement $p \vee q$ is true if either of its components are true and certainly if both components are true. The only possible way for $p \vee q$ to be false is if both p and q are false. Notice that the symbol $p \vee q$, which indicates p or q, does not exclude the possibility of both p and q being true. This is to be contrasted to popular usage of the term "or," which often is taken to mean "one or the other" but not "both."

Compound statements can, of course, be much more intricate than those already mentioned. Consider the statement $\sim (p \wedge \sim q)$. Its truth table is given below.

p	q	$\sim q$	$p \wedge \sim q$	$\sim (p \wedge \sim q)$
T	T	F	F	T
T	F	T	T	F
F	T	F	F	T
F	F	T	F	T

The first two columns of the table are for the component propositions p and q, while the last column is for the compound proposition itself. The intermediate columns are for the steps used in arriving at the compound proposition. Thus in the above table the third column is for $\sim q$ and the fourth column for $p \wedge \sim q$.

Illustration. The following is the truth table for the statement $(p \wedge q) \vee (\sim p \wedge \sim q)$.

p	q	$(p \wedge q)$	$\sim p$	$\sim q$	$(\sim p \wedge \sim q)$	$(p \wedge q) \vee (\sim p \wedge \sim q)$
T	T	T	F	F	F	T
T	F	F	F	T	F	F
F	T	F	T	F	F	F
F	F	F	T	T	T	T

Consider a proposition whose truth table contains only T in the last column on the far right. This indicates that the proposition is true for all possible truth values of the component statements; that is, the proposition is true regardless of whether its components are true or false. Such propositions are called *tautologies*.

Illustration. The proposition $p \vee \sim p$ is a tautology, as demonstrated by the following truth table:

p	$\sim p$	$p \vee \sim p$
T	F	T
F	T	T

Thus the proposition, "Either the consumer will purchase the cheaper product or he will not," is a tautology.

On the other hand, a proposition whose truth table contains only F in the column on the far right is known as a self-contradiction. Such propositions are false regardless of whether their components are true or false.

Illustration. The proposition $p \wedge p$ is a self-contradiction, as demonstrated by its truth table:

p	$\sim p$	$p \wedge \sim p$
T	F	F
F	T	F

Thus the proposition, "A consumer will both purchase and not purchase the cheaper product," is a self-contradiction.

Illustration. "A consumer will purchase the cheaper product or he will not purchase both the cheaper and the more expensive product." We can best analyze this statement by putting it into symbolic language. We would then have p is "A consumer will purchase the cheaper product" and q is "A consumer will purchase the more expensive product." The compound statement is then $p \vee \sim (p \wedge q)$.

p	q	$(p \wedge q)$	$\sim (p \wedge q)$	$p \vee \sim (p \wedge q)$
T	T	T	F	T
T	F	F	T	T
F	T	F	T	T
F	F	F	T	T

The statement is thus shown to be a tautology.

Two propositions are equivalent if they have identical truth values. (Equivalence is denoted by $\equiv$.)

Illustration. We can demonstrate that the proposition $\sim (p \wedge q) \equiv \sim p \vee \sim q$.

p	q	$p \wedge q$	$\sim (p \wedge q)$	p	q	$\sim p$	$\sim q$	$\sim p \vee \sim q$
T	T	T	F	T	T	F	F	F
T	F	F	T	T	F	F	T	T
F	T	F	T	F	T	T	F	T
F	F	F	T	F	F	T	T	T

Because the truth values are the same, the two propositions are equivalent. Thus the statement, "A consumer will not buy both the cheaper and the more expensive product," is equivalent to the statement, "A consumer will either not buy the cheaper or not buy the more expensive product."

Many statements are not outright assertions but rather are conditional. They are in the form "If p then q" and can be denoted by $p \rightarrow q$, which is read "p implies q." An example of such a statement is the following: "If consumer income increases, consumers will purchase more of all commodities." Another example is "If demand for any product increases, the market price will increase."

A conditional statement $p \rightarrow q$ is said to be true in all cases except if p is true and q is not true. Thus the truth table of $p \rightarrow q$ appears as

p	q	$p \rightarrow q$
T	T	T
T	F	F
F	T	T
F	F	T

The table indicates that if q is true when p is true, it is true that $p \rightarrow q$. On the other hand, if q is false when p is true, then it is not true that $p \rightarrow q$. The remaining two rows of the table refer to the case when p is false. In this case, it is immaterial whether q is true or false. The implication $p \rightarrow q$ is said to hold even if q is false, because the statement implies only that q is true when p is true.

Thus the conditional statement, "If consumer income increases, consumers will purchase more of all commodities," is true unless we know that when consumer income increases, consumers will not purchase more.

Conditional statements are sometimes the equivalents of noncondi- tional statements; that is, they assert the same thing.

Illustration. Consider the proposition $\sim p \vee q$, whose truth table is given by

p	q	$\sim p$	$\sim p \vee q$
T	T	F	T
T	F	F	F
F	T	T	T
F	F	T	T

It is evident that the truth values of $\sim p \vee q$ are identical to those of $p \rightarrow q$ given above, or

$$p \rightarrow q \equiv \sim p \vee q$$

Thus the conditional proposition, "If consumer income increases, con- sumers will purchase more of all commodities," is equivalent to the prop- osition, "Either consumer income will not increase or consumers will purchase more of all commodities."

A special type of conditional statement occurs in the form "p if and only if q" or $p \leftrightarrow q$; that is, p implies q and q implies p. Such statements are called *biconditional*. They imply that if p is true then q is true, and if q is true then p is true. p cannot be true without q being true, and q cannot be true without p being true. Thus either p and q are both true or they are both false. The truth table of $p \leftrightarrow q$ is given by the following:

p	q	$p \leftrightarrow q$
T	T	T
T	F	F
F	T	F
F	F	T

To illustrate, consider the statement $MU_x > (P_x)(MU$ of dollar$) \leftrightarrow$ consumer will purchase more of X. The statement says that if the marginal utility of any product is greater than the marginal utility of the money that must be paid to purchase the product, the consumer will purchase more of the product. Also, if the consumer purchases more of a product, it implies that the MU of the product is greater than the MU of the money that must be paid for the product. This is equivalent to saying that a consumer will purchase more of a product if and only if the MU of the product is greater than the MU of the money that must be paid to purchase the product.

Consider a conditional proposition $p \rightarrow q$. Then we say that the statement $q \rightarrow p$ is the converse of the first proposition. Note then that if $p \leftrightarrow q$, this means that the statement $p \rightarrow q$ and its converse are true. The statement $\sim p \rightarrow \sim q$ is known as the inverse of the first proposition, while the statement $\sim q \rightarrow \sim p$ is the contrapositive of the first statement. The truth tables for these conditional propositions are now given:

p	q	$\sim p$	$\sim q$	Conditional $p \rightarrow q$	Converse $q \rightarrow p$	Inverse $\sim p \rightarrow \sim q$	Contrapositive $\sim q \rightarrow \sim p$
T	T	F	F	T	T	T	T
T	F	F	T	F	T	T	F
F	T	T	F	T	F	F	T
F	F	T	T	T	T	T	T

This demonstrates that a conditional statement is not equivalent to its converse or inverse. However, a conditional statement is equivalent to its contrapositive.

Illustration.   Consider the statement, "If demand for any product increases, the market price will increase." This is not equivalent to the
converse statement, "If market price of any product increases, demand
for the product will increase." It is also not equivalent to the inverse
statement, "If demand for any product does not increase, market price
will not increase." However, it is equivalent to the contrapositive statement, "If market price for any product does not increase, demand for the
product has not increased."

We sometimes encounter statements with undefined terms, as for
example:

"If the price of X increases, the demand for beef will increase."

Such statements are not assertions unless a meaning has been assigned to
the variable X. When a meaning is given to the undefined term, the result
may be a true statement, a false statement, or a nonsensical statement.
Thus if X stands for chicken, then the statement becomes a true proposition. If X stands for soda, then the statement is a false proposition. If X
stands for reading, then the statement is nonsensical and is not a proposition at all.

Statements containing undefined terms are termed *propositional
functions*. When the undefined terms are given meanings that make the
statement true or false, they become propositions.

Exercises

1. Let p be "Consumers given a choice between two products will
    purchase the cheaper one," and let q be "Consumers given a choice
    between two products will purchase the one giving greater utility."
    What would the following compound statements indicate?
    a) $p \vee q$
    b) $p \wedge \sim q$
    c) $\sim p \vee \sim q$
    d) $p \vee \sim q$
    e) $\sim (p \wedge q)$
    f) $\sim (p \vee q)$
    g) $\sim (\sim p \vee \sim q)$
2. "Monopolists restrict output and raise prices."
    "Monopolists do not restrict output but do raise prices."
    "Monopolists do not restrict output nor raise prices."
    "Monopolists either restrict output or raise prices."

"Monopolists either restrict output or do not raise prices."
"Monopolists either do not restrict output or do not raise prices."
a)   Write the above statements in symbolic form.
b)   Construct truth tables for the above statements.
3.   Construct truth tables for the following:
   a) $\sim (p \wedge q)$
   b) $p \wedge \sim q$
   c) $p \vee q \vee \sim p$
   d) $\sim [(p \vee q) \wedge (\sim p \vee \sim q)]$
   e) $\sim (p \vee q) \wedge p$
   f) $(p \vee q) \vee \sim (q \vee p)$
4.   Decide whether each of the following is a tautology or a self-contradiction and give an illustrative economic example of the statement.
   a) $(p \wedge q) \vee (\sim p) \vee (\sim q)$
   b) $(p \wedge q) \vee (p \wedge [\sim q])$
   c) $(p \wedge q) \wedge \sim (p \vee q)$
5.   Prove: $(p \wedge q) \wedge r \equiv p \wedge (q \wedge r)$
6.   Prove: $p \vee (q \wedge r) \equiv (p \vee q) \wedge (p \vee r)$
7.   Prove De Morgan's laws:
   a) $\sim (p \wedge q) \equiv \sim p \vee \sim q$
   b) $\sim (p \vee q) \equiv \sim p \wedge \sim q$
8.   Prove that the following are equivalent:
   a) $\sim (p \rightarrow q) \equiv p \wedge \sim q$
   b) $\sim (p \leftrightarrow q) \equiv p \leftrightarrow \sim q \equiv \sim p \leftrightarrow q$
9.   Is the following a tautology?

   $(p \wedge q) \rightarrow (p \vee q)$

10.   Determine the converse, inverse, and contrapositive of the statements:
   a)   If consumer income increases, consumers will purchase more of all commodities.
   b)   If a producer wishes to maximize profits, he will equate MR to MC.

SECTION 2·7   INDUCTIVE LOGIC

Suppose that by observing many production processes in the short run, we notice that diminishing returns is always present. We might then generalize our findings and conclude that diminishing returns is ever present in the short run. Such reasoning is an example of *inductive logic*, which is the process of reaching conclusions on the basis of observations.

Illustration.   On the basis of statements made by many consumers of various amounts of several products, we may conclude: "As more of a product is consumed, the marginal utility derived therefrom decreases." This is an example of inductive logic.

It should be noted that conclusions derived by the use of inductive logic are always only *probable conclusions*. There may be an overwhelming probability that they are correct, but one can never be 100 percent certain. Thus if, on the basis of observing the production of 1 million firms, we notice that diminishing returns is present in each case, we may feel very confident in expecting it to occur in other firms. But we cannot be absolutely certain, because it is possible that diminishing returns could occur in the 1 million firms we happened to observe and not in the firms we failed to observe. However, because the probability of this happening is so low, we conclude that diminishing returns is ever present. Similar considerations apply to the conclusion regarding diminishing marginal utility. Regardless of how many consumers and products were observed before reaching the conclusion, it is just possible that it will not hold for other consumers or products.

Inductive logic is to be contrasted to deductive logic, discussed earlier, which reaches conclusions from assumptions rather than from observations. Conclusions drawn through the use of deductive logic are inescapable if the hypotheses apply.

In spite of the fact that inductive logic reaches conclusions that are only probable, it is, nevertheless, a very potent method of reasoning. It is, for example, indispensable for any experimental science. Moreover, inductive logic is very often used to provide suggestions as to what we should attempt to prove deductively or to provide realistic hypotheses.

Illustration.   By inductive logic, we reach the conclusion of diminishing marginal utility. Using diminishing marginal utility as a hypothesis, we can, as shown in price theory, deductively arrive at conditions for consumer equilibrium such as

$$\frac{\text{marginal utility}_X}{\text{price}_X} = \frac{\text{marginal utility}_Y}{\text{price}_Y}$$

Exercises

1.   Show how both inductive and deductive logic are used to reach the following conclusions:

   a)   A monopolist reaches equilibrium at a level where $MR = MC$.
   b)   Supply curves are generally upward sloping.
   c)   Demand curves are generally downward sloping.
2.   Can you think of any other illustrations?

CHAPTER

3

THE NUMBER SYSTEM

One has to be able to count if only so that
at fifty one doesn't marry a girl of twenty.
—Maxim Gorky

We all make use of numbers every day of our lives. Invariably, we deal
with numbers mechanically or by rote. In this chapter we seek to understand the concept of a number, the different types of numbers and how
operations with numbers are defined.

SECTION 3·1   NATURAL NUMBERS

Consider, in turn, a monopolist, a monopsonist, a single market price, a
single factor of production. All of these are distinct entities. They,
however, have a feature in common, which is their singleness or unique-
ness. We represent this characteristic with the number *one*. The number
one is thus an abstract concept that refers to the set of all collections
with only a single member.

Suppose that we now consider all collections consisting of an element and another element. We represent their common characteristic by
the number *two*. We could then refer to a two-seller market, that is,
duopoly; a two-price commodity, that is, price discrimination is
practiced; two plants producing the same commodity; two factors of
production; two machines; two workers; and so on.

In a similar manner, the numbers three, four, . . . , and so on, are
defined to refer to sets that have as their common characteristic the same
number of elements.

The endless succession of numbers 1, 2, 3, . . . are known as *natural
numbers*. Note that they include all the positive integers but no other
numbers. Negative numbers, the number zero, and fractions are not natural numbers.

If we have any two natural numbers, we can define a process known as *addition*, which consists of taking together the elements of both sets and forming a new set. The symbol $+$ is used to denote addition. Thus adding $2 + 3$ implies taking all the elements of a set of two members and all the elements of another set of three members and putting them together to form a new set that has five members in it and can therefore be represented by the number five. We then say that the sum of 2 and 3 is 5. Addition of any two natural numbers is defined in the same manner. Of course, to find sums, we generally do not think of the process in such detail. But this is because tables of addition enable us to arrive quickly at the equivalent answer.

We also define the operation of *multiplication*, by which we mean the process of repeated additions of the same natural number. Thus to multiply four by three, we take four different sets of three members each and array them together. This yields a new set containing 12 members. We then say that the product of 4 and 3 or $4 \cdot 3$ is 12. Tables of multiplication give us quick but equivalent answers.

The operation of subtraction of any two natural numbers is denoted by $a - b$ and means a natural number x such that $b + x = a$ provided that such a number exists. Thus $6 - 2 = 4$ because $2 + 4 = 6$.

The operation of division of any two natural numbers is denoted by $a \div b$ and means a natural number x such that $bx = a$ provided that such a number exists. Thus $6 \div 2 = 3$ because $2 \cdot 3 = 6$.

If we add any two natural numbers, the sum will also be a natural number. We indicate this by saying that the set of natural numbers is closed under addition. The set of natural numbers is also closed under multiplication, because the product of any two natural numbers is itself a natural number.

The system of natural numbers is, however, not closed under subtraction, because the difference $a - b$ is not always a natural number. Thus we earlier showed that $6 - 2 = 4$, which is a natural number. But $2 - 6$ does not exist within the system of natural numbers, because there is no natural number x such that $6 + x = 2$.

Similarly, the system of natural numbers is not closed under division, because the quotient $a \div b$ is not always a natural number. Thus $6 \div 2 = 3$, which is a natural number. But $2 \div 6$ does not exist within the system of natural numbers, because there is no natural number x such that $6 \cdot x = 2$.

Illustration.   If the supply for automobiles is represented by $q_s = 100p$, then at any price p, where p is any natural number, we could find the quantity supplied. The result would also be a natural number. Thus if $p = 3000$, q_s would be 300,000 automobiles.

SECTION 3·2   FRACTIONS

Natural numbers are sufficient for some purposes. This is the case in the above illustration, because the number of automobiles supplied is a positive whole number. However, we often deal with quantities that are not integers or whole numbers. Thus if we consider the supply of yarn, it is possible, indeed likely, that at certain prices the amount of yarn supplied will not be a whole number but will involve some portion of a whole number. This makes it necessary to introduce a new set of numbers, which we call fractions.

A *fraction* consists of two natural numbers a and b and is written $\frac{a}{b}$ or a/b, where a is the numerator and b the denominator of the fraction. A fraction a/b represents a parts out of b. Thus 3/4 of an item indicates that the item is to be divided into four equal parts and three of the four are to be selected. We assume the usual rules encountered in grade-school mathematics for the addition, subtraction, multiplication, and division of fractions.

Any natural number a can be expressed as a fraction by putting it into the form $a/1$. We also link the process of division with that of forming fractions by the following definition: $a \div b = a/b$.

Illustration.   Given the following supply function for a yarn: $q_s = 110p$. If $p = \frac{3}{4}$, then $q_s = \frac{330}{4}$.

We have earlier seen that the system of natural numbers is not closed under division. The system of fractions is, however, closed under division. If any fraction is divided by another fraction, the quotient will be a fraction. But the system of fractions is not closed under subtraction; we can easily see that $\frac{1}{2} - \frac{3}{4}$ is undefined, because we have defined only positive integers and positive fractions.

SECTION 3·3   SIGNED NUMBERS

The fact that the system of fractions is not closed under subtraction is one reason for seeking to extend the number system. Another reason is that there are many practical applications where we would like to indicate not only magnitude or quantity but also direction. Consider a firm that receives for each unit it sells $1 more than its variable costs of production but that also has $1000 of fixed costs regardless of how much is produced.

If this firm sells 10,000 units, its profit will be $9000. If it sells 1900 units, its profits will be $900. If it sells only 100 units, it will suffer a loss of $900. Now we would like to have numbers that will distinguish between a profit of $900 and a loss of $900.

We therefore introduce a system of *signed* or *directed numbers.* Thus for each natural number and fraction, such as the number *a*, we define two new symbols, $+a$ and $-a$. Those with + sign are called *positive numbers*; those with − sign are called *negative numbers.* Thus we would indicate a profit of $900 as $+900$ and a loss of $900 as -900. But we still have no number to indicate the possibility of earning neither a profit nor a loss, which in the preceding example would occur if 1000 units are sold.

We are therefore led to define another number, 0, read *zero*, which is neither positive nor negative. In the above illustration, we would say that if 1000 units are sold, there is 0 profit.

The numbers $0, +1, +2, +3, \ldots$ and $-1, -2, -3, \ldots$ are termed *integers*, either positive or negative. We also have positive and negative fractions. All these numbers can be referred to as signed or directed numbers. They can be visualized by selecting a point as the origin and drawing a horizontal line of infinite length to the right and to the left. If we choose a certain length as a unit length, the remaining numbers can be represented by proportional distances from the origin, to the right for positive numbers and to the left for negative numbers.

We would then have

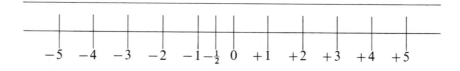

The number $+5$ could be depicted as moving 5 units to the right, while the number -5 would mean moving 5 units to the left. Fractions would be interpreted in like manner. Thus the number $-\frac{1}{2}$ would indicate a movement of $\frac{1}{2}$ unit to the left.

We assume the usual rules encountered in grade-school mathematics for the addition, subtraction, multiplication, and division of fractions.

The reader will have noticed that the symbol + has been used in two ways, namely, to indicate the process of addition and also to indicate a positive number. Similarly, the symbol − has been used to indicate the process of subtraction and also to indicate a negative number. This, however, poses no difficulty. We also adopt the convention of writing the number $+a$ simply as the number *a*. Thus 5 and $+5$ are interchangeable.

SECTION 3·4 RATIONAL NUMBERS

We have, so far, introduced the following numbers: zero; the positive and negative integers; the positive and negative fractions. The totality of all of these numbers are known as the *rational numbers*. The term "rational" is derived from the word ratio, and not from the words reason or reasonable. Every rational number can be expressed as the ratio of two integers a/b, where $b \neq 0$. Conversely, any number that can be expressed as the ratio of two integers a/b, with $b \neq 0$, is rational. It should be noted that all integers can be expressed as ratios by simply inserting a denominator of 1.

We have been careful to exclude the fraction $a/0$ from the system of rational numbers, because $a/0$ is equivalent to $a \div 0$, which is seen to be undefined when we seek a number x such that $0 \cdot x = a$. Consider first the case where $a \neq 0$. Then no number will satisfy the condition $0 \cdot x = a$. On the other hand, if $a = 0$, then the condition is equivalent to $0 \cdot x = 0$, which is satisfied by any number whatsoever. The condition is thus meaningless because it does not identify any particular number. Therefore division by zero is an undefined operation.

Earlier, we saw that the system of natural numbers is closed under the operations addition and multiplication. But it is not closed under subtraction or division. The system of positive fractions was found to be closed under addition, multiplication, and division but not under subtraction. We can now say that the system of rational numbers is closed under addition, multiplication, subtraction, and division, with the single exception that division by zero must be excluded.

SECTION 3·5 POWERS AND ROOTS

Suppose that the government has made a new investment of $1000 and the marginal propensity to consume in the economy is $\frac{9}{10}$. Then in the next income period, consumers will spend 0.9 of the initial new investment. In the second income period, consumers will respend $(0.9)(0.9)$ of the new investment. In the fifth income period, respending will be $(0.9)(0.9)(0.9)(0.9)(0.9)$ of the new investment. In the nth period, respending will be

$$\underbrace{(0.9)(0.9)(0.9) \cdots}_{n \text{ times}}$$

It is convenient to invent a shorthand symbol to denote repeated multiplication of the same number. We therefore define the symbol x^n as referring to the repeated multiplication of x by itself, where n indicates the number of repeated factors. Thus in the illustration given above, responding in the fifth income period would be $(0.9)^5(1000)$ and in the nth period, $(0.9)^n(1000)$.

The expression x^n is referred to as the nth power of x, and n is said to be the exponent of x. In particular, x^2 is called x square and x^3 is called x cube.

The definition of power thus far given is limited to positive integer exponents, because it refers to a number of repeated self-multiplications. Thus, for example, it is not possible to multiply something by itself -3 times or $\frac{1}{2}$ times. This means that we have, thus far, defined x^n only where n is a positive integer.

If we have a number x such that $x^n = a$, then x is known as the nth root of a. In particular, if $x^2 = a$, then x is known as the square root of a, and if $x^3 = a$, then x is the cube root of a. We write the nth root of a by putting the a under a radical sign ($\sqrt{}$) and indicating the index of the root as such $\sqrt[n]{a}$. Thus the fifth root of a is written as $\sqrt[5]{a}$. In the case of square roots of a, we write $\sqrt{a}$, where it is understood that the lack of a specific index indicates that the second root of a is to be taken.

Our definition of powers and roots applies only where the exponent n is a positive integer, so the symbol X^{-n} (where n is positive) has no meaning as yet. We find it convenient to denote the expression $1/X^n$ (where $X \neq 0$) as X^{-n}. Note that X^{-n} does not imply that X is to be multiplied by itself $-n$ times. Obviously, this is nonsensical. X^{-n} simply indicates the reciprocal of X^n or $1/X^n$, which has a well-defined meaning, namely, the number 1 divided by X multiplied by itself n times.

We have defined X^n for all positive or negative integer values of n. The one remaining integer is zero. We now define X^0 as being equal to 1.

We next turn to the case where n is a fraction and make the following definition: $X^{p/q} = (\sqrt[q]{x})^p$, that is, the qth root of X^p. Thus $8^{2/3} = 4$, because the cube root of 8 is 2, which when squared equals 4.

SECTION 3·6   IRRATIONAL NUMBERS

Suppose that the production possibilities of a firm are given by the following: $q = \sqrt{L + C}$; that is, total production will be the square root of the number of units of labor employed plus the number of units of capital employed. In particular, suppose that 1 unit of labor and 1 unit of capital are employed. Total production will then be $\sqrt{2}$. We shall now prove that no rational number can be a square root of 2. We must, however, first make some definitions and then prove some preliminary theorems called lemmas.

Definition. An integer is called even if and only if it can be expressed as $2X$, where X is some integer.

Definition. An integer that is not even is called odd. Every odd integer can be expressed as $2X + 1$, where X is an integer.

Lemma 1. If p is even, then p^2 is even.
Proof.
Given that p is even.
$\therefore p = 2X$, where X is an integer.[1]
$\therefore p^2 = (2X)^2 = 4X^2$.
$\therefore p^2 = 2(2X^2)$.
X is an integer. Therefore so is X^2 and $2X^2$, because the product of two integers is also an integer.
$\therefore p^2$ is 2 times some integer.
$\therefore p^2$ is even.

Lemma 2. If p is odd, then p^2 is odd.
Proof.
Given that p is odd.
$\therefore p = 2X + 1$, where X is an integer.
$\therefore p^2 = (2X + 1)^2 = 4X^2 + 4X + 1$.
$\therefore p^2 = 2(2X^2 + 2X) + 1$.
X is an integer. Therefore so is X^2, $2X^2$, and $2X^2 + 2X$, because the products and sums of two integers are integers.
$\therefore p^2$ is 2 times an integer plus 1.
$\therefore p^2$ is odd.

Lemma 3. If p is an integer and P^2 is even, then p is even.
Proof.
Given that p is an integer.
$\therefore p$ is either even or odd.
If p were odd, then p^2 would be odd by Lemma 2.
But we are given that p^2 is even.
$\therefore p$ must be even
because this is the only remaining possibility.

---

[1] The symbol $\therefore$ is shorthand for the word "therefore."

Theorem.   No rational number can be a square root of 2.
Proof.
1)   Either $\sqrt{2}$ is a rational number or it is not.
2)   Assume that $\sqrt{2}$ is rational. It could then be expressed as a fraction and be reduced to lowest terms so that we would have $\sqrt{2} = p/q$, where p and q are integers with no common factors except ± 1.
3)   Then $p^2/q^2 = 2$.
4) $p^2 = 2q^2$.
5)   Because q is an integer, so is q^2. Thus p^2 is an even integer because it is two times an integer.
6)   By Lemma 3, p must be even.
7) $\therefore$ q must be odd, because p and q have no common factor and if q were even, p and q would have a common factor of 2.
8) $p = 2X$, where X is an integer because p is even.
9) $\therefore$ substituting into step (4), we have
10) $(2X)^2 = 2q^2$.
11) $4X^2 = 2q^2$.
12) $q^2 = 2X^2$.
13)   Thus q^2 is even.
14) $\therefore$ q is even by Lemma 3.
15)   We have thus been led to a self-contradiction, because in step (7) we showed that q must be odd and now we have shown that q is even.
16) $\therefore$ the assumption that $\sqrt{2} = p/q$ must be rejected, because it leads to a contradiction.
17)   The only remaining possibility is that $\sqrt{2}$ cannot be expressed as a rational number.

The preceding theorem was proved indirectly by a method known as *reductio ad absurdum.* It consists of showing that if the supposition that a statement is true leads to a self-contradiction, then the statement must be false.

It has already been shown that the system of rational numbers is closed under the operations of addition, subtraction, multiplication, and division with the exception of division by zero. Our present theorem, however, demonstrates that the system of rational numbers is not closed under the operation of taking square roots. The square root of a rational number is not necessarily a rational number. We have seen that there are economic quantities that cannot necessarily be given precisely by rational numbers. The case of total production amounting to $\sqrt{2}$ serves as one such illustration.

Because the system of rational numbers is insufficient for our purposes, we invent *irrational numbers.* These are numbers that cannot be expressed as fractions but can nevertheless be represented as points on a straight line that are definite distances from a chosen origin.

We have shown that $\sqrt{2}$ is one such irrational number. There are many others, such as $\sqrt{3}$, $\sqrt{5}$, $\sqrt{6}$, $\sqrt[3]{2}$, $\sqrt[3]{3}$, and so on. The number $\pi = 3.14159\ldots$ is also irrational.

The word irrational should not be taken to mean unreasonable. It simply means not expressible as a ratio of two integers.

SECTION 3·7   REAL NUMBERS

The system of *real numbers* consists of all the rational numbers and the irrational numbers. Thus the set of rational numbers is a subset of the set of real numbers.

Every real number can be represented by a point on a straight line. This is illustrated below. A point is chosen as the origin and represents the number 0. If a certain length is chosen as a unit length, the remaining numbers can be represented by points either to the right or to the left of the origin.

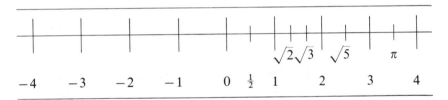

Not only can every real number be represented by a point on the straight line, but it can be shown that every point on the straight line represents a real number. Thus the system of real numbers leaves no gaps on the straight line.

Numbers are often expressed in decimal notation. This is merely a shorthand way of writing numbers in terms of powers of ten. Thus the number 45,162.176 is a concise way of writing

$$4 \cdot 10^4 + 5 \cdot 10^3 + 1 \cdot 10^2 + 6 \cdot 10 + 2 + \frac{1}{10} + \frac{7}{10^2} + \frac{6}{10^3}$$

It is quite evident that if a decimal terminates, it represents a rational number because it can be expressed as a fraction whose denominator is some power of ten. Thus the number 2.723 is a rational number that can be expressed as 2723/1000.

Decimals that do not terminate, that is, that continue on without end, are of two kinds. Either they are periodic, which means they repeat themselves in blocks, or they are nonperiodic. The number $\frac{2}{3}$, for example, can be represented by the nonterminating periodic decimal 0.66666.... Similarly, the number $\frac{1}{7}$ can be represented by 0.142857142857142857.... It can be shown that every periodic decimal also represents a rational number.

A nonterminating decimal that is also nonperiodic represents an irrational number. Thus all rational numbers can be expressed either as a terminating decimal or as a periodic nonterminating decimal. When expressed in decimal notation, irrational numbers are neither terminating nor periodic. This implies that every real number can be expressed as a decimal either terminating or nonterminating and, conversely, that every decimal expression represents a real number.

SECTION 3·8   COMPLEX NUMBERS

One of the reasons for introducing irrational numbers was the discovery that the square roots of many rational numbers were not rational. We therefore extended the number system to include all real numbers. But we now notice that even the system of real numbers is not closed under the operation of taking square roots. This is because of the following theorem.

Theorem.   No negative number N has a square root among the real numbers.
Proof.
Let X be any real number.
Either X is positive, negative, or zero.
If X is positive, then X^2 is positive and cannot be equal to N.
If X is negative, then X^2 is also positive and cannot be equal to N.
If X is zero, then X^2 is zero and cannot be equal to N.
Thus no real number can be the square root of a negative number.

We therefore introduce a new set of numbers, which we call *pure imaginary numbers*, that consists of all the square roots of negative numbers. Now the square root of any negative number can always be put into the form $\sqrt{a}\sqrt{-1}$. For example, $\sqrt{-9} = \sqrt{9}\sqrt{-1} = 3\sqrt{-1}$. Thus every pure imaginary number can be written as the product of a real number and $\sqrt{-1}$. We denote $\sqrt{-1}$ by the letter i, which implies that $i^2 = -1$. Therefore $\sqrt{-9} = 3i$ and $\sqrt{-7} = \sqrt{7}\,i$.

We now have in our number system both real numbers and pure imaginary numbers. If we add some real number with some pure imaginary number, we get a number that has a real component and an imaginary component.

We therefore define the system of *complex numbers* to consist of all numbers of the form $a + bi$, where a and b are real and $i = \sqrt{-1}$. a is said to be the real part and bi the imaginary part of the complex number $a + bi$. We also make the following definitions:

Definition. $a + bi = c + di$ if and only if $a = c$ and $b = d$.

Definition. $(a + bi) + (c + di) = (a + c) + (b + d)i$.

Thus, to add two complex numbers, we add separately the real part and the imaginary part.

Illustration. $(5 + 2i) + (3 + 4i) = 8 + 6i$.

Definition. To multiply complex numbers, we follow the usual multiplication rules while at the same time noting that $i^2 = -1$.

Illustration. To multiply $(5 + 2i)$ by $(3 + 4i)$ we do the following:

$$5 + \quad 2i$$
$$3 + \quad 4i$$
$$15 + \quad 6i$$
$$\quad + 20i + 8i^2$$
$$15 + 26i - 8 = 7 + 26i$$

Subtraction of one complex number from another is accomplished by subtracting the real part of the first from the real part of the second and the imaginary part of the first from the imaginary part of the second.

Illustration. $(5 + 2i) - (3 + 4i) = 2 - 2i$.

Note that $(3 + 4i) + (2 - 2i) = 5 + 2i$, which accords well with our earlier definition of subtraction, that is, $a - b = X$ such that $b + X = a$.

Definition. The *conjugate* of any complex number $a + bi$ is defined as $a - bi$.

Division of one complex number by another is accomplished by multiplying numerator and denominator by the conjugate of the denominator.

Illustration.

$$\frac{5+2i}{3+4i} = \frac{5+2i}{3+4i}\frac{3-4i}{3-4i} = \frac{15+6i-20i-8}{9-12i+12i+16} = \frac{7-14i}{25}$$

The system of complex numbers $a + bi$ includes all numbers previously introduced. Thus real numbers are complex numbers with $b = 0$, such as $7 + 0i$. Imaginary numbers are complex numbers where $b \neq 0$, such as $7 + 2i$. Pure imaginary numbers are complex numbers where $a = 0$, such as $0 + 2i$.

The set of pure imaginary numbers is a subset of the set of imaginary numbers. The set of imaginary numbers, in turn, is a subset of the set of complex numbers. The set of real numbers is also a subset of the set of complex numbers. The totality of all real and imaginary numbers make up the set of complex numbers.

It can be shown that even though imaginary numbers have no physical representation, that is, that they cannot be related to any familiar objects or concepts, they have important economic applications in dynamic analysis. If we are considering economic activity over time, it is possible to describe movements of economic variables by equations with various types of solutions. The form of the solution indicates the pattern of growth or fluctuations exhibited by the system. In particular, if the equations have solutions that are imaginary numbers, this indicates a definite type of cyclical fluctuation in economic activity over time.

Exercises

1. a) Prove that if a is even, then a^3 is even.
    b) Prove that if a is odd, then a^3 is odd.
    c) Prove that if n is an integer and n^3 is even, then n is even.
    d) Prove that no rational number is equal to $\sqrt[3]{2}$.
2. Prove that no rational number is equal to $\sqrt[4]{2}$.
3. Prove that the sum of two even numbers is even.
4. Prove that the product of two odd numbers is odd.
5. Prove that the product of any natural number and an even number is even.
6. Show that each of the following numbers is irrational:

    a) $1 + \sqrt{2}$

    b) $3\sqrt{2}$

    c) $\dfrac{3 - \sqrt{2}}{5}$

7. Perform the indicated operations:

a) $(5 + \sqrt{-4}) + (2 + \sqrt{-9})$

b) $5 + 7i - (2 - 3i)$

c) $(2 + 3i) - (5 + i)$

d) $2i(5 + 3i)$

e) $(3 + 2i)(5 - 3i)$

f) $(2 + 3i) + (7 + i)$

g) $(2 - 3i)(4 + 2i)$

h) $(3 + i\sqrt{2})(3 - i\sqrt{2})$

i) $\dfrac{2 - 3i}{3 + 2i}$

j) $\dfrac{6i - 2}{3 - 2i}$

k) $\dfrac{1}{i}$

l) $\dfrac{2 + i}{3i}$

m) $\dfrac{3 + 2i}{1 - 2i}$

SECTION 3·9   INEQUALITIES

If a and b are any real numbers, then we say that a is *greater than* b (denoted by $a > b$) if and only if $a - b$ is positive. This is equivalent to saying that $a > b$ if and only if there exists a positive number X such that $a = b + X$. If a is not greater than b, then a must either be less than b (denoted by $a < b$) or a is equal to b (denoted by $a = b$). If we wish to indicate that a is either greater than or equal to b, we write $a \geqslant b$. If a is either smaller than or equal to b, we write $a \leqslant b$.

Statements of the form $a > b$ or $a < b$ are termed *inequalities*. Inequalities have certain properties, which are given by the following theorems.

Theorem.   If $a > b$ and $b > c$, then $a > c$.
Proof.
By hypothesis, $a - b = X$ and $b - c = Y$, where X and Y are positive.
$\therefore (a - b) + (b - c) = X + Y$, because equals added to equals are equal.
$\therefore a - c = X + Y$.
$\therefore a > c$, because X and Y are positive.

Illustration.   If the marginal cost of producing the tenth unit of a product (MC_{10}) is greater than the marginal cost of the ninth unit (MC_9), and the marginal cost of the ninth unit is greater than the marginal cost of the eighth unit (MC_8), then $MC_{10} > MC_8$ by the above theorem.

Theorem. If $a > b$, then $a + c > b + c$, where c is any real number.
Proof.
By hypothesis, $a = b + X$, where X is positive.
Adding c to both sides of the equation gives

$$a + c = b + c + X$$

$$\therefore a + c > b + c.$$

Illustration. If the $MC_{10} > MC_9$ and a tax of \$5 per unit is imposed on each unit produced, then we would have

$$MC_{10} + 5 > MC_9 + 5$$

which implies that even with the tax cost included, the marginal cost of the tenth unit is greater than that of the ninth unit.

Theorem. If $a > b$ and c is positive, then

$$ac > bc$$

This implies that the sense of an inequality, that is, the direction of the inequality, is unchanged if both sides are multiplied by the same positive number.
Proof.
By hypothesis, $a = b + X$, where X is positive.
Multiplying both sides of the equation by c, we have

$$ac = bc + Xc$$

Now Xc is positive, because both X and c are positive.
$\therefore ac > bc.$

Illustration. If profits of firm A are given by X and those of firm B by Y, and $X > Y$, then if profits for all firms double, we have

$$2X > 2Y$$

so that A's profits remain greater than B's profits.

Theorem. If $a > b$ and c is a negative number, then

$$ac < bc$$

that is, the sense of an inequality is reversed if both sides are multiplied by the same negative number.

Proof.

By hypothesis, $a = b + X$, where X is positive.
Multiplying both sides of the equation by c, we have

$$ac = bc + Xc$$

which is equivalent to $bc = ac - Xc$.
Now Xc is negative, because X is positive and c is negative.
$\therefore$ $-Xc$ is positive.
$\therefore$ $bc = ac + $ some positive number.
$\therefore$ $bc > ac$.
or $ac < bc$.

Illustration.   If firm A's profit is greater than firm B's profit in 1970, we
have $X_{1970} > Y_{1970}$, where X is A's profit and Y is B's profit. In 1971
both firms had losses twice as great as their 1970 profits. By the above
theorem we would have

$$-2X_{1971} < -2Y_{1971}$$

implying that in 1971, A's profit is less than B's profit, that is, A's loss is
greater than B's loss.

Exercises

Prove the following:

1.   If $2X - 10 < 0$, then $X < 5$ and conversely.
2.   If $3X - 4 < X + 8$, then $X < 6$.
3.   If $a > b$ and $c > d$, then $a + c > b + d$.
4.   If a, b, c, d are positive and if $a > b$ and $c > d$, then $ac > bd$.
5.   If a and b are positive and $a > b$, then $a^2 > b^2$.
6.   If $2X + 4Y < 12$, then $X < 6 - 2Y$.
7.   If $4X + 2Y < 8$, then $X < 2 - \frac{1}{2}Y$.
8.   If $6X - 2Y < 9$, then $Y > 3X - \frac{9}{2}$.

SECTION 3·10   ABSOLUTE VALUE

Suppose that we wish to compare the movements in aggregate consumption to those in aggregate investment. We might then show that investment is much more volatile than consumption by presenting the changes
that occur in the former in contrast to the changes in the latter. Assume,

for example, that we have the following data for successive income periods.

PERIOD	CHANGE IN CONSUMPTION (IN BILLIONS OF DOLLARS)	CHANGE IN INVESTMENT (IN BILLIONS OF DOLLARS)
1	+5	+20
2	+10	+100
3	-2	-30
4	+1	-15
5	-3	-40

In considering the totality of changes in each variable, it would be misleading simply to add the changes arithmetically, because the negative changes will partially cancel out the positive changes. This will give the impression that the total changes are less than they really are. In fact, both negative changes and positive changes indicate volatility. We should therefore add all changes regardless of sign. In such cases, we are interested in the *absolute values* of the changes in consumption and investment.

The absolute value of a real number X is denoted by $|X|$ and defined by

$$|X| = \begin{cases} X & \text{if} \quad X \geqslant 0 \\ -X & \text{if} \quad X < 0 \end{cases}$$

that is, if X is positive or zero, $|X|$ is simply X, but if X is negative, then $|X|$ is $-X$.

The absolute changes in consumption and investment would then be given by

PERIOD I	ABSOLUTE CHANGE IN C	ABSOLUTE CHANGE IN I
1	5	20
2	10	100
3	2	30
4	1	15
5	3	40
sum	21	205

As a result of the definition of absolute value, it follows that the statement $|X| < a$, where a is some positive number, is equivalent to

$-a < X < a$. To illustrate, if ΔC is the change in consumption and $|\Delta C| < 25$, then $-25 < \Delta C < 25$. This means that ΔC is more than -25 but less than 25.

SECTION 3·11   NUMBER SCALES

Consider the number 423. This number consists of three digits, 4, 2, and 3, where the position of each digit is significant. Indeed, every one of our real numbers is some combination of the ten digits, 0, 1, 2, 3, 4, 5, 6, 7, 8, 9. We can get by with so few digits because all numbers are expressed in powers of ten. Thus the number 423 is a shorthand way of writing

$4 \cdot 10^2 + 2 \cdot 10 + 3$

As we proceed from right to left, each digit is multiplied by a successively higher power of ten. The individual terms are then summed.

The number 6,357 would stand for

$6 \cdot 10^3 + 3 \cdot 10^2 + 5 \cdot 10 + 7$

It is likely that the central role played by the number ten evolved from the fact that humans first learned to count on their ten fingers. But the number system could just as well be expressed in terms of other powers, such as five.

Thus the number 63, by which we mean

$6 \cdot 10 + 3$

could also be written in terms of powers of five as

$2 \cdot 5^2 + 2 \cdot 5 + 3$

We would then write this number as $223_{(5)}$. The subscript 5 indicates that the individual digits are expressed in terms of powers of five or that the scale 5 is being used.

If no subscript is attached to a number, it is understood that the scale 10 is being employed. Notice that when the 5 scale is employed, the only possible digits are 0, 1, 2, 3, 4, because any higher number would be some power of 5.

Numbers can similarly be written in any other scale. Thus the number 17, which means

$1 \cdot 10 + 7$

can be written as

$1 \cdot 2^4 + 0 \cdot 2^3 + 0 \cdot 2^2 + 0 \cdot 2 + 1$

which is abbreviated by $10001_{(2)}$. Note that the only possible digits in the 2 scale are 0 and 1.

From a logical point of view, there is no reason to prefer one number scale over another. However, for certain purposes, it is more convenient to use a scale other than 10. The 2 scale, for instance, has been very important in the development of electronic computers. Moreover, by comprehending the equivalencies of different notations, we better understand the meaning conveyed by numbers.

Exercises

1. Write each of the following numbers in (a) the 4 scale, (b) the 3 scale, (c) the 9 scale, (d) the 2 scale:
   a)   twenty-three
   b)   thirty-four
   c)   nine
2. The following numbers are written in the 2 scale. Rewrite them in the 10 scale.
   a) $1111_{(2)}$
   b) $1011_{(2)}$
   c) $11010_{(2)}$
3. Rewrite the number $231_{(4)}$ in the 8 scale.

4

ALGEBRAIC FUNCTIONS AND MARKET EQUILIBRIUM UNDER PURE COMPETITION

> Mathematics possesses not only truth, but supreme beauty—a beauty cold and austere, like that of sculpture, without appeal to any part of our weaker nature, sublimely pure, and capable of a stern perfection such as only the greatest art can show.
>
> —Bertrand Russell

In this chapter we deal with the simplest types of associations between variables in general and economic factors in particular. We show that even simple algebraic techniques can be helpful in understanding market mechanisms.

SECTION 4·1 FUNCTIONS

Consider the demand for a product. We generally say that the quantity demanded depends upon the price of the product. In other words, there is a relationship or association between price and quantity demanded. For each possible price, there is some unique quantity that will be demanded. As the former changes, the latter changes. Implied, of course, is the assumption that all other factors are fixed. This is the same as saying that quantity demanded is a *function* of price, which is written as

$$q_d = f(p)$$

Any letter can be used to denote a functional relationship. In particular, if we wish to distinguish the above demand function from a different demand function, we could write the latter in the form

$$q_d = g(p)$$

We can better understand the meaning of a function by making use of the concept of a set. Let the set of all possible prices be denoted by P and the set of all possible quantities demanded by Q. Then if to each element in P we can assign a unique element of Q, we say that quantity demanded is a function of price.

In general then, if to each element in a set A there is assigned a unique element of set B, we refer to such correspondences as functions. If a is any element in A (i.e., $a \in A$), then the corresponding element in B that is assigned to a is called the *image* of a and is denoted by $f(a)$. The set of all values of A is referred to as the *domain* of the function, while the set of all elements that appear as images of these values is referred to as the *range* of the function.

Consider a function where each different element in A has a different image; that is, no two different elements in A have the same image. We then say that this function is *one to one*.

Illustration.   The demand for a particular product is given by

$$q_d = \begin{cases} 100 - 2p & \text{if} \quad 0 \leqslant p \leqslant 50 \\ 0 & \text{if} \quad\quad p > 50 \end{cases}$$

This is a demand function because for each possible price, that is, $p \geqslant 0$, there corresponds a unique quantity demanded. We say that p is the *independent variable* and q_d is the *dependent variable*, which means that for a given value of p, there results a specific value of q_d. Thus, q_d depends upon P.

In particular, at a price of \$3.00, we could find the corresponding quantity demanded, or the image of $p = 3$, by substituting in the formula that expressed the functional relation. We would have

$$f(3) = 100 - 2(3) = 94$$

The domain of the function is the set of all possible values of p, which is $p \geqslant 0$. The range of the function is $0 \geqslant q_d \geqslant 100$, because quantity demanded varies between 0 and 100. The function is not one to one, because at any $p \geqslant 50$, we have $q_d = 0$, which means that many prices have the same image.

Illustration. The demand for a product is given by

$$q_d = \begin{cases} 100 - \sqrt{p} & \text{if} \quad 0 \leqslant p \leqslant 10{,}000 \\ 0 & \text{if} \quad \quad p > 10{,}000 \end{cases}$$

This is not a function, because a unique quantity demanded is not associated with each price. For example, if $p = 25$, we get

$$q_d = 100 - \sqrt{25}$$
$$= 100 \pm 5$$
$$= 105 \text{ or } 95$$

Quantity demanded may be either 105 or 95 when price is 25. This is known as a *relation*, because there is a definite association between price and quantity—albeit not unique.

The above relation could be made into a function if we make the assumption that whenever square roots are to be taken, only the positive root is to be considered. For every p, there would then be a unique q_d.

Illustration. The demand for a product is given by

$$q_d = \frac{1000}{2p} \qquad \text{when} \quad p > 0$$

This is a function, because for each possible price, that is, $p > 0$, there corresponds a unique quantity demanded. Furthermore, no two values of p yield identical values for q_d. Thus the function is one to one.

In the above illustrations, the functional relationship was given by a formula. This is the most common form of expressing a function. But functions can be given in other forms as well. Thus a function could be given by simply listing the totality of corresponding values for both variables. Such a function is considered in the following example.

Illustration. The table below presents the average unemployment rate for each of the years in the 1950s. As such it provides a functional representation between years in the 1950s and the unemployment rate. The X variable is the year, while the Y variable is the average annual unemployment rate.

X	1950	1951	1952	1953	1954	1955	1956	1957	1958	1959
Y	5.3	3.3	3.1	2.9	5.6	4.4	4.2	4.3	6.8	5.5

There is no need for a formula representation, because the unemployment
rate is given for each possible year of the 1950s.

It is easily seen that functions listing the totality of all values can
only be given where there exists only a finite number of possibilities.

Exercises

1. $q_d = \begin{cases} 40 - \frac{1}{2}p & \text{if} \quad 0 \leqslant p \leqslant 20 \\ 0 & \text{if} \quad\quad p > 20 \end{cases}$

    a) Is this a function?
    b) Is it one to one?
    c) Find $f(10), f(1), f(a), f(a-5)$.

2. $q_s = \begin{cases} 4p - 10 & \text{if} \quad p \geqslant 2.5 \\ 0 & \text{if} \quad p < 2.5 \end{cases}$

    a) Is this a function?
    b) Is it one to one?
    c) Find $f(5), f(2), f(100), f(a^2)$.

3. $q_d = \begin{cases} 50 - 2\sqrt{p} & \text{if} \quad 0 \leqslant p \leqslant 625 \\ 0 & \text{if} \quad\quad p > 625 \end{cases}$

    a) Is this a function?
    b) Is it one to one?
    c) Find $f(25), f(144)$.

4. $q_s = 5p$ for $p \geqslant 0$

    a) Is this a function?
    b) Is it one to one?
    c) Find $f(15), f(150), f(11a)$.

5. $Y = X^2 - 4$

    a) Is this a function?
    b) Is it one to one?
    c) Find $f(1), f(2), f(0), f(4), f(-3)$.

6. $Y = 3X - 10$

    a) Is this a function?
    b) Is it one to one?
    c) Find $f(0), f(3), f(-1)$.

SECTION 4·2   ORDERED PAIRS[1]

Consider the set of all possible prices and the set of all possible quantities demanded for a product. Suppose that we select an element *a* from the first set and an element *b* from the second set. We can represent this by the *ordered pair* (*a*, *b*).

Two ordered pairs (*a*, *b*) and (*c*, *d*) are equal if and only if $a = c$ and $b = d$. The order of the elements is definitely significant. Thus the ordered pairs (20, 60) and (60, 20) are not the same.

Let *P* and Q_d represent the sets of all possible prices and quantities demanded, respectively. Consider now all conceivable ordered pairs (*a*, *b*) where $a \in P$ (i.e., *a* is a possible price) and $b \in Q_d$ (i.e., *b* is a possible quantity demanded). These taken together are known as the *product set* of *P* and Q_d, denoted by $P \times Q_d$ and read *P cross* Q_d.

This is equivalent to the following:

$$P \times Q_d = \{(a, b) \mid a \in P, b \in Q_d\}$$

that is, the product set of *P* and Q_d is the set of all ordered pairs where the first element is a member of the set of prices and the second is a member of the set of quantities demanded.

Illustration.   Assume that the price of a certain product is given in whole dollars and that price controls exist so that the maximum price that can be charged is $2. Also, assume that the maximum conceivable amount that would be demanded is 4 units. Then

$$P = \{1, 2\} \quad \text{and} \quad Q_d = \{1, 2, 3, 4\}$$

The product set would thus be

$$P \times Q_d = \{(1, 1), (1, 2), (1, 3), (1, 4), (2, 1), (2, 2), (2, 3), (2, 4)\}$$

The product set $P \times Q_d$ is also known as the *Cartesian product* of *P* and Q_d.

If we allow *X* and *Y* to assume any and all real values, then the Cartesian product of *X* and *Y* consists of all ordered pairs with real elements and can be represented by a coordinate diagram such as:

---

[1] This section can be omitted without disturbing the continuity of accompanying sections.

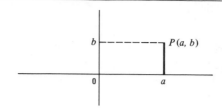

Every ordered pair such as P, which is the ordered pair (a, b), is represented by a point that has a horizontal distance of a from the origin and a vertical distance of b from the origin.

Any set of ordered pairs makes up a *relation*. Thus, referring back to the preceding illustration, the set

$$\{(1, 3), (1, 4), (2, 1), (2, 2)\}$$

represents a relation between P and Q_d and indicates that with a price of $1, quantity demanded could be either 3 or 4, and with a price of $2, quantity demanded could be either 1 or 2. We write this simply as $P \, R \, Q_d$, or P is related to Q_d.

Any relation, R, is thus some subset of a Cartesian product of two sets. We can see that the set defined by the relation just given is a subset of the Cartesian product $P \times Q_d$ given in the preceding illustration.

We are now able to define functions in terms of sets of ordered pairs. Consider the Cartesian product $P \times Q_d$. If we take a subset of $P \times Q_d$ in which each element of P appears as the first element in one and only one ordered pair, we have a function.

Illustration. Consider the product set given previously, consisting of possible prices and quantities demanded, namely,

$$P \times Q_d = \{(1, 1), (1, 2), (1, 3), (1, 4), (2, 1), (2, 2), (2, 3), (2, 4)\}$$

If we now take the subset

$$\{(1, 4), (2, 1)\}$$

we have a correspondence between the possible prices of the product and unique quantities that will be demanded at each possible price.

Note that the relation given earlier also associated possible prices with quantities demanded, but it did not define unique quantities for each price. In older terminology, relations were referred to as multivalued functions. But in modern terminology the practice is to distinguish between functions and relations.

Note, too, that it is possible for different prices to be associated with the same quantity and still represent a function. All that is required is that for each price there is associated one and only one quantity. If, in addition, every price is associated with a different quantity, then the function is said to be one to one.

Illustration.   The previous illustration considered a very simple function, where the only possible prices were $1 and $2. Let us now return to an earlier illustration, where demand was given by

$$q_d = \begin{cases} 100 - 2p & \text{if} \quad 0 \leqslant p \leqslant 50 \\ 0 & \text{if} \qquad p > 50 \end{cases}$$

The set of possible prices is given by $P = \{0, 0.01, 0.02, \ldots, 1.00, \ldots\}$, while the set of possible quantities demanded is $Q_d = \{0, 0.01, 0.02, \ldots, 1.00, \ldots\}$. The product set consisting of possible prices and quantities demanded is

$P \times Q_d = \{(0, 0), (0, 0.1), (0, 0.2), \ldots, (0, 1.00), \ldots,$

$\quad (0.01, 0), (0.01, 0.01), (0.01, 0.02), \ldots,$

$\quad (0.01, 1.00), \ldots, (0.02, 0), (0.02, 0.01),$

$\quad (0.02, 0.02), \ldots, (0.02, 1.00), \ldots, (1.00, 0),$

$\quad (1.00, 0.01), (1.00, 0.02), \ldots, (1.00, 1.00), \ldots\}$

The given formula assigns for each p a unique value. These assigned values form a subset of the product set, and appear as

$\{(0, 100.00), (0.01, 99.98), \ldots, (1.00, 98.00), \ldots,$

$(2.00, 96.00), \ldots, (50.00, 0)\}$

Thus we have a set of ordered pairs where the first element represents a possible price and the second element a unique quantity associated with that price. That is, with a price of 0.00, the quantity demanded is 100 units; with a price of 0.01, q_d is 99.98; with a price of $1.00, q_d is 98; and so on.

We therefore say that q_d is a function of p, with the functional relationship being expressed by the above formula.

The definition of functions in terms of ordered pairs is equivalent to the definition given earlier. For some purposes it is useful to think of functions as ordered pairs, while for other purposes it suffices to think of functions as associations or relationships between variables.

SECTION 4·3   GRAPHICAL REPRESENTATION
OF TWO VARIABLES

It is often desirable to express a functional relationship in graphical form. This is done, for example, when we portray a demand function by a downward-sloping demand curve or a supply function by an upward-sloping curve.

To do this, we select a point as our origin and draw two perpendicular lines that intersect at the origin. These lines are known as *coordinate axes*. If our two variables are denoted by X and Y, we can take the horizontal line as the X axis and the vertical line as the Y axis. Movements rightward from the origin along the X axis indicate positive units of X, while movements to the left of the origin indicate negative units of X. Movements in an upward direction from the origin along the Y axis indicate positive units of Y, while movements downward indicate negative units of Y.

The axes would then appear as

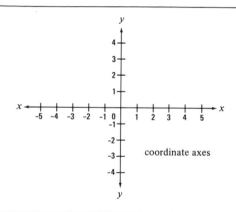

coordinate axes

Any function could then be visualized graphically by plotting various pairs of X and Y values. Every pair of values is represented by a point located by moving the indicated number of units along the X axis and then moving vertically according to the indicated Y value.

Illustration.   Graph the function $Y = X^2 + 2$.

We select a number of X values, such as $-4, -3, -2, -1, 0, 1, 2, 3, 4$, and find the corresponding Y values. These are given by the following table.

X	−4	−3	−2	−1	0	1	2	3	4
Y	18	11	6	3	2	3	6	11	18

Every pair of X, Y values is represented by a point on the graph. Thus, to represent the pair $(-4, 18)$, we begin at the origin and move along the X axis, 4 units to the left and then 18 units upward. This point is said to have coordinates $(-4, 18)$, where -4 is the X coordinate and 18 is the Y coordinate. We locate several points on the graph so that, by connecting them, the general shape of the resulting curve is evident. Following this procedure for the above table of values, we arrive at the following graph.

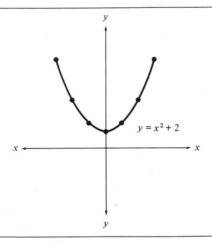

The graph indicates quite clearly that as X increases in magnitude, whether positively or negatively, Y increases positively. Also, Y increases at a much faster rate than X. Moreover, Y is never negative and, indeed, never falls below a value of 2. Thus $Y = 2$ is a minimum point of the function.

A graph with this particular shape is called a *parabola*.

Illustration.   Consider the demand function introduced earlier, namely,

$$q_d = \begin{cases} 100 - 2p & \text{if} \quad 0 \leqslant p \leqslant 50 \\ 0 & \text{if} \quad p > 50 \end{cases}$$

We select the following sets of coordinates:

p	5	10	15	20	25	30	35	40	45	50	60
q_d	90	80	70	60	50	40	30	20	10	0	0

To graph this relationship, we draw a p axis and a q axis. We have already seen that the independent variable is generally represented by the horizontal axis and the dependent variable by the vertical axis. In the case of price and quantity, the tradition has arisen to plot p on the vertical axis and q on the horizontal axis. Mathematically, it makes no difference which variable is plotted on which axis. The relation portrayed is the same in any case.

We then plot the points given above. The result appears as a straight line:

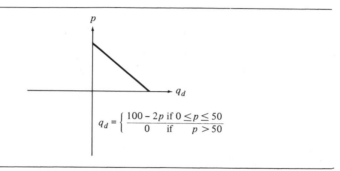

$$q_d = \begin{cases} 100 - 2p & \text{if } 0 \le p \le 50 \\ 0 & \text{if } \quad p > 50 \end{cases}$$

It is evident from the graph that as price increases, quantity demanded decreases.

A function that is represented graphically by a straight line is called a *linear function*. A function $Y = f(X)$ will be linear if X appears raised to the first power and no other power in the functional representation. Conversely, any function that can be represented by a straight line must have its X term raised to the first power and to no other power.

Illustration.   The function $Y = X^2 + 2$, which was considered earlier, could not be a linear equation because X appears to the second power. On the other hand, $Y = X + 2$ is a linear function, because X appears only to the first power.

Exercises

1–6.   Graph functions 1–6 of Section 4.1.
  7.   Graph $q_s = 2p^2 - p + 4$.
  8.   Graph $q_s = p^3 - 3p$.

9. Graph $q_d = (p + 2)/p$.
10. Graph $y = x^2$.
11. Graph $y = 2/X^2$.

SECTION 4·4 EQUATIONS

An *equation* is a statement that asserts that one expression is equivalent to another. Thus $X + 2 = 10$ is an equation that is a true statement only if $X = 8$. Some equations are true statements for all values of X, for instance, $2(X + 1) = 2X + 2$. Such equations are called *identities*. In general, however, an equation is a true statement only for certain values of X. A value of X that makes the equation a true statement is called a *root*. Thus $X = 8$ is a root of $X + 2 = 10$. When we talk of solving an equation, we mean finding all its roots.

An equation that can be written in the form $ax + b = 0$, where $a \neq 0$ and where a and b are constants, is termed a *linear equation* or an equation of *first degree*.

Illustration. $X + 2 = 10$ is a linear equation, because it can be written as $X - 8 = 0$.

We may also have linear equations in two or more variables, if all variables appear raised only to the first power.

Illustration. $X + 2Y = 4$ is a linear equation in two variables. Both X and Y are raised to the first power.

SECTION 4·5 LINEAR FUNCTIONS AND THEIR PROPERTIES

We have already shown that a function $Y = f(X)$, where both variables appear to the first power, can be represented by a straight line. In other words, a function of the form $Y = aX + b$ is a linear function and represented graphically by a straight line. Conversely, any straight line can be expressed in the form $Y = aX + b$.

A straight line is completely determined by two points. Once we know any two points, we can immediately specify the equation of the line.

If the two points are (X_1, Y_1), (X_2, Y_2), then the equation of the straight line is

$$Y - Y_1 = \frac{Y_2 - Y_1}{X_2 - X_1}(X - X_1)$$

Let

$$\frac{Y_2 - Y_1}{X_2 - X_1} = m$$

We then have

$$Y - Y_1 = m(X - X_1)$$

or

$$Y = mX - mX_1 + Y_1$$

If we set

$$-mX_1 + Y_1 = b$$

we have $Y = mX + b$, which is the same form as the general straight line we considered above, that is, $Y = aX + b$.

The expression

$$\frac{Y_2 - Y_1}{X_2 - X_1} = m$$

is called the *slope* of the line. It is the ratio of change in Y (i.e., $Y_2 - Y_1$) to change in X (i.e., $X_2 - X_1$).

A straight line has the property of a constant slope; that is, m remains the same regardless of which points on the line are chosen.

Illustration.   Find the equation of the line passing through the two points (10, 80) and (15, 70).

We first find the slope of the line, which is given by

$$m = \frac{Y_2 - Y_1}{X_2 - X_1} = \frac{70 - 80}{15 - 10} = \frac{-10}{5} = -2$$

This means that for every unit increase in X, there is a 2 unit decrease in Y. Note that in computing the slope we took the Y coordinate of one point minus the Y coordinate of the other point and divided by the difference of the X coordinates.

The straight line is therefore given by

$$Y - Y_1 = m(X - X_1)$$

or

$$Y - 80 = -2(X - 10)$$
$$Y = -2X + 20 + 80$$
$$= -2X + 100$$

Now that we have the equation of the line, we can find all the points on that line. Thus if $X = 25$, we would have

$$Y = -2(25) + 100$$
$$= 50$$

indicating that $(25, 50)$ is another point on the line. Similarly, $(45, 10)$ is a point on the line.

If we now compute the slope of the line from these two points we have just found, we have

$$m = \frac{10 - 50}{45 - 25} = \frac{-40}{20} = -2$$

which is exactly the same as the slope computed from the original two points given. This illustrates that the slope of a straight line is constant throughout.

Note that if we substitute q_d for Y and p for X, we have the demand curve that we considered earlier in Section 4.3. In that section, we began with a given equation and from it derived points on the curve. In this section, we began with two points and from that derived the equation of the straight line passing through them.

When Y is given as a direct function of X such as $Y = aX + b$, we say that Y is an *explicit function* of X. Sometimes Y may be given as an indirect function of X, such as $AX + BY + C = 0$. Notice that once a particular value for X is specified, then Y is determined. We say that Y is in this case an *implicit function* of X.

Illustration.   Given the implicit function $6X + 3Y - 300 = 0$. If $X = 5$, then Y must be 90. Similarly, we can find the corresponding Y value for other values of X.

We can also convert this implicit equation into an explicit equation by solving for Y:

$$3Y = -6X + 300$$

$$Y = -2X + 100$$

which is seen to be an equation of a straight line. However, it should be noted that in some cases an implicit equation cannot be put into explicit form.

Earlier we represented a straight line as $Y = aX + b$. We can now see that another way to express a straight line is by

$$AX + BY + C = 0$$

because the latter can always be converted into the former:

$$BY = -AX - C$$

$$Y = -\frac{A}{B}X - \frac{C}{B}$$

which is in the form of $Y = aX + b$, where $a = -A/B$ and $b = -C/B$.

Exercises

1. Find the equation of the line passing through $(5, 8)$ and $(8, 17)$.
   a) What is the slope of this line?
   b) If $X = 6$, what is the corresponding Y value?
   c) Graph the straight line.
2. Find the equation of the line passing through $(-1, 2)$ and $(-3, -2)$.
   a) What is the slope of this line?
   b) If $X = 4$, what is the corresponding Y value?
   c) Graph the straight line.
3. Find the equation of the line passing through $(-3, 4)$ that has a slope of (a) 3; (b) -2; (c) 0. Graph the straight line.
4. Find the equation of the line passing through $(2, 3)$ that has a slope of (a) $\frac{1}{2}$; (b) -5.
5. What is the slope of the straight line represented by $9X + 3Y - 120 = 0$?
6. What is the slope of the straight line represented by $5X - 15Y + 100 = 0$?

SECTION 4·6 DEMAND AND SUPPLY

We have already seen how demand curves are represented algebraically. As an illustration, the following demand curve was considered:

$$q_d = 100 - 2p \quad \text{where} \quad p \text{ and } q_d \geq 0$$

A number of comments should be made regarding this representation.

1. It is assumed in the above formulation that the quantity demanded of a product depends upon its price alone and not on such other factors as income or prices of related products. In reality, of course, these other factors do influence quantity demanded. They are, however, assumed to be held constant and unchanging in the market situation under consideration. This is known as *ceteris paribus*, that is, other things the same. It is justified either because the other variables change rather slowly and over a long period of time, as in the case of income, or because the other variables do not have a very direct or potent effect, as in the case of prices of related products. Demand functions can therefore be constructed for the purpose of relating quantity demanded to product price with the other factors at fixed levels. If the other factors do undergo significant change, the demand functions must be altered to take account of such changes.

Limitations of Ceteris Paribus Theory

A word of *caution* is, however, in order. In the final analysis, the usefulness of such simple demand functions depends on how realistic it is to assume constancy of these other factors. In some cases, as where a product has a close substitute, this is totally unrealistic. Thus the demand for butter clearly depends not only upon the price of butter but also upon the price of margarine. It would be of dubious validity to assume a fixed price for margarine and then specify the demand for butter, because the price of margarine depends on the price of butter. For each possible price of butter, there would probably be a different price of margarine. In such a situation, it is essential to express demand as a function of more than one variable. We consider such formulations in the following chapter.

2. The demand function given above is linear; that is, it can be represented graphically by a straight line. We do not really have any basis to assume that this is generally true. We choose, at the outset, to work with this function only because of its simplicity. Subsequently, we

shall have to examine other types of functions and see whether they
lead to different conclusions.

3.   The demand function given above has a negative slope. It can be
     written as $q_d = mp + 100$, where $m = -2$. In general, for linear
     demand functions we have

$$q_d = b - ap$$

where $a > 0, b \geqslant 0, p \geqslant 0, q_d \geqslant 0$. This implies that as p increases, q_d
decreases and that as p decreases, q_d increases. It seems reasonable to
expect that as the price of a product increases, consumers wish to
purchase fewer units and vice versa. However, the underlying
justification for this assertion is presented in Chapter 12.

Supply functions can also be represented algebraically by expressing quantity supplied as a function of price.

Illustration.   Consider the supply function $q_s = 3p - 50$, where $q_s \geqslant 0$
and $p \geqslant 0$. For each possible price, we can find the corresponding quantity supplied. Thus, at a price of $20, ten units will be supplied. At a price
of $50/3, nothing will be supplied. Obviously, at any lower price there will
also be nothing forthcoming from suppliers.

A number of comments should now be made in connection with
supply functions.

1.   The above formulation assumes that the quantity supplied of a prod-
     uct depends upon its price alone and not on such other factors as the
     wage rate to be paid workers or the necessary payments to other
     factors of production. These variables are assumed to be held
     constant. Supply functions therefore relate quantity supplied to prod-
     uct price with other factors at fixed levels. If these other factors
     undergo change, the supply functions must be altered to take account
     of such changes.
2.   The supply function given above is linear. As in the case of demand
     functions, this is assumed, at the outset, only because of its simplicity.
     In later sections we shall encounter other types of supply functions.
3.   The supply function given above has a positive slope. It can be writ-
     ten as $q_s = mp - 50$, where $m = 3$. In general, for linear supply func-
     tions we have

$$q_s = cp - d$$

where $c > 0$, $d \geqslant 0$, $p \geqslant 0$, $q_s \geqslant 0$. This implies that as p increases, q_s increases and that as p decreases, q_s decreases. It seems reasonable to expect that as the price of a product increases, suppliers wish to offer more for sale and vice versa. However, the underlying justification for this assertion will be found in Chapter 13.

Exercises

1. Given the market demand function $q_d = 200 - 5p$, where p and $q_d \geqslant 0$.
   a) Find the price if quantity demanded is 100.
   b) Find the quantity demanded if the price is $21.50.
   c) If the price of the product increases by $2.00, what would happen to quantity demanded?

2. Given the market demand function $q_d = 40 - \frac{1}{2}p$, where p and $q_d \geqslant 0$.
   a) Find the quantity demanded if the price is $9.20.
   b) Find the price if quantity demanded is 20.
   c) What would demand be if the product were a free good?
   d) What is the highest price anyone would pay for this product?
   e) If the price of the product increases by $0.50, what would happen to quantity demanded?

3. Given the market demand function $3q_d + 4p = 240$, where p and $q_d \geqslant 0$.
   a) Find the quantity demanded if the price is $12.
   b) What would demand be if the product were a free good?
   c) If the price of the product decreases by $3.00, what would happen to quantity demanded?

4. Given the market demand function $q_d = 120 - ap$, where a, p and $q_d \geqslant 0$.
   a) Find quantity demanded if price is $20.
   b) What would demand be if the product were a free good?
   c) If the price of the product decreases by $1.00, what would happen to quantity demanded?

5. Given the market demand function $q_d = b - 3p$, where b, p, and $q_d \geqslant 0$.
   a) Find quantity demanded if price is $4.00.
   b) What would demand be if the product were a free good?
   c) If the price of the product increases by $4.00, what would happen to quantity demanded?

6. Given the market supply function $q_s = 4p - 60$, where p and $q_s \geqslant 0$.
   a) Find the quantity supplied if the price is $101.
   b) Find the price if the quantity supplied is 20.
   c) What is the lowest price at which the product will be offered on the market?
   d) If the price of the product decreases by $2.00, what would happen to quantity supplied?

7. Given the market supply function $q_s = 7.5p - 10$, where p and $q_s \geqslant 0$.
   a) Find the quantity supplied if the price is $16.
   b) If the price of the product increases by $6.00, what would happen to quantity supplied?

8. Given the market supply function $q_s = cp - 20$, where c, p, and $q_s \geqslant 0$.
   a) Find the quantity supplied if the price is $5.00.
   b) If the price of the product decreases by $3.00, what would happen to quantity supplied?

9. Given the market supply function $q_s = 4p - d$, where d, p, and $q_s \geqslant 0$.
   a) Find the quantity supplied if the price is $12.25.
   b) If the price of the product increases by $1.00, what would happen to quantity supplied?

SECTION 4·7 MARKET PRICE DETERMINATION UNDER PURE COMPETITION

Pure competition is a market structure under which no seller or buyer can control or even affect market price. The number of buyers and sellers is so great that any one buyer or seller is only an infinitesimal portion of the total. Furthermore, all firms sell homogeneous or identical products. Thus the wheat produced by one farmer is essentially identical to that produced by any other farmer. Pure competition is also characterized by free entry and exit from the market. Any firm attracted by the profit potentials existing in such an industry can enter the industry. Conversely, any firm disenchanted with an industry can make its exit.

Price in a purely competitive context is given by the market and cannot be determined by any individual buyer or seller. How then will the market price be determined? The price to which the market, after some initial haggling, will finally settle down is known as the *equilibrium* price. For equilibrium to occur, it must be that participants in the market achieve what they desire. Otherwise they would not be in a state of rest.

They would continue to act to achieve their desires. This implies that for equilibrium to be established at some price, p_0, it must be that at that price, consumers are able to buy as much as they wish. Suppliers must also be able to sell as much as they wish at the equilibrium price. A necessary condition for equilibrium is therefore that market price must be at a level where

q_d in the market $= q_s$ in the market

because if $q_d > q_s$, consumers wish to buy more than is available for sale and if $q_d < q_s$, suppliers wish to sell more than will be bought.

To find the equilibrium market price, we need only set quantity demanded in the market equal to quantity supplied in the market and then solve for p.

Illustration. Given the following demand and supply functions for a purely competitive market:

$$q_d = 100 - 2p \qquad q_s = 3p - 50 \qquad p, q_d, \text{ and } q_s \geqslant 0$$

Find the equilibrium market price.

We set $q_d = q_s$, which gives

$$100 - 2p = 3p - 50$$

$$150 = 5p$$

$$p = 30$$

At a price of \$30, $q_d = 40$ and $q_s = 40$. Thus the equilibrium price is \$30, and at that price 40 units will be demanded and 40 units offered for sale.

It is easy to see what would happen if some other price ensued. Assume that the market price was \$40. At that price, consumers would wish to buy only 20 units, while suppliers would offer 70 units for sale. Such a state could not long continue. Price would be bid down, as some anxious sellers would offer to sell for a lower price in order not to be stuck with a surplus. Similarly, if the price was \$20, consumers would demand 60 units but suppliers would be willing to offer only 10 units for sale. Price would then be bid up, as some anxious buyers would offer a higher price to be sure of getting the product.

Illustration. Given the following linear demand and supply functions in general terms:

$$q_d = b - ap \qquad q_s = cp - d \qquad \text{where} \quad p, q_d, q_s, b, d \geqslant 0 \quad \text{and} \quad a, c$$
$$> 0$$

Find the equilibrium market price assuming a purely competitive market.
We set $q_d = q_s$, which gives

$$b - ap = cp - d$$

$$b + d = cp + ap$$

$$b + d = (c + a)p$$

$$p = \frac{b + d}{c + a}$$

Note that the numerator depends solely on the constant terms in the
supply and demand equations, while the denominator depends solely on
the coefficients of the p term in the two equations.

The equilibrium quantity is

$$q = b - a\left(\frac{b + d}{c + a}\right)$$

$$= b - \frac{ab + ad}{c + a}$$

$$= \frac{bc - ad}{c + a}$$

Assume that government imposes price controls. What effect will
this have in the market? Consider the illustration given above, where

$$q_d = 100 - 2p \quad \text{and} \quad q_s = 3p - 50$$

We have seen that equilibrium occurs at a price of $30 and a quan-
tity of 40 units. If this price is deemed excessively high, the government
might set a price ceiling of $25. But at this price, the demand function
shows that consumers would wish to buy 50 units, while the supply
function shows that only 25 units will be supplied. This will necessitate
some form of rationing.

On the other hand, if the equilibrium price is deemed too low to
provide adequate incomes for the suppliers, government might set a minimum price of $35. But at this price, quantity demanded would be only 30
units, while quantity supplied would be 55 units. The result would therefore be the accumulation of surplus product.

Limitations of Equilibrium Theory

Caution: Economic theory generally assumes that market equilibria are attainable. It is true that, if market price is something other than equilibrium price, forces will be brought into operation that will tend to move the market price toward the equilibrium price. Thus, if the market price is above the equilibrium price, excess quantities of the product will appear and remain unsold. Some suppliers, fearing that they will be stuck with unsold goods, will probably offer to sell at lower prices. Buyers will also, in all probability, be cognizant of the impending excess supply and will realize that they can procure the product at lower prices. The purchase prices they offer will then decrease. These tendencies will continue until market price falls to equilibrium price, at which there will be no pressures to alter the price. An analogous process will ensue if market price is below equilibrium price. The forces would merely work in the opposite direction.

This analysis, however, does have definite limitations arising from the lack of any complete theory of how buyers and sellers act when not in a state of equilibrium. The chain of reasoning relies on what buyers and sellers would *probably* do but conceivably might not do. Thus, with a market price above equilibrium, some sellers, sensing a price that is too high, could cut their prices somewhat and quickly sell all they have before the price falls even further. Such sales could be made at a whole range of prices, depending upon how quickly the participants sense the supply and demand conditions. No one uniform price would then apply to what is exchanged in the market. Moreover, with some sellers having sold all their output and some buyers having made their purchases before any equilibrium ensued, the demand and supply functions would be altered. Thus the equilibrium solution predicted by the original demand and supply functions might never be achieved even if some equilibrium were eventually attained.

Illustration. In an earlier illustration, we considered the following demand and supply functions:

$$q_d = 100 - 2p \qquad q_s = 3p - 50$$

We concluded that the equilibrium market price would be $30. Assume, for example, a market price of $40. We saw that consumers would desire to purchase only 20 units and producers would supply only 70 units. This, we reasoned, would cause prices to be bid downward. Such forces would be in operation as long as the market price was above $30. This might be generally true. However, it is possible that the price might, for some reason (possibly even chance factors), be set at $40. Some sellers with good insight into the general supply and demand conditions might then offer to sell their output at, say, $38, quickly disposing of their total output before the price falls. As other buyers and sellers get a clearer picture of conditions, some sellers might next offer to sell at $35, quickly disposing of all their output. The demand and supply functions would, as a consequence, be altered, and might then appear as

$$q_d = 80 - 2p \qquad q_s = 3p - 65$$

The resulting equilibrium price would not be $30, which would be predicted by the original demand and supply functions. Based on the subsequent functions, the equilibrium price would be $31. Thus some of the product would have been sold at $38, some at $35, and some at $29, with the possibility that none would be sold at $30. Moreover, we have no way of knowing how many of such quick sales would occur.

This is not to say that equilibrium analysis should not be used, only that it should be interpreted and applied with care.

Exercises

In each of the following cases, assume a purely competitive market.

1.   Given the following market demand and supply functions:

$$q_d = 200 - 5p \qquad q_s = 4p - 79 \qquad \text{where} \quad p, q_d, q_s \geq 0$$

a)   Find the equilibrium price and quantity.
b)   What would happen if government set a maximum price of $20?
c)   What would happen if government set a minimum price of $35?

2.   Given the following market demand and supply functions:

$$q_d = 40 - \tfrac{1}{2}p \qquad q_s = 7.5p - 10 \qquad \text{where} \quad p, q_d, q_s \geq 0$$

a)   Find the equilibrium price and quantity.
b)   What would happen if government set a maximum price of $5?
c)   What would happen if government set a minimum price of $10?

3.   Given the following market demand and supply functions:

$$q_d = 120 - ap \qquad q_s = cp - 20 \qquad \text{where} \quad a, c, p, q_d, q_s \geq 0$$

a)   Find the equilibrium price and quantity.
b)   What values would have to be assigned to c and a in order for the equilibrium price to be $20?

4.   Given the following market demand and supply functions:

$$q_d = b - 3p \qquad q_s = 4p - d \qquad \text{where} \quad b, d, p, q_d, q_s \geqslant 0$$

a)   Find the equilibrium price and quantity.
b)   What values would have to be assigned to b and d in order for the equilibrium price to be $6?
c)   If the values of b and d doubled, what effect would this have upon equilibrium price?

SECTION 4·8   SHIFTS IN DEMAND AND SUPPLY

We have seen that a demand function identifies a certain quantity demanded for every price. If price changes from p_1 to p_2, then quantity demanded will change from q_1 to q_2. This is not, however, a change in demand, because the original demand function has not been altered. It is just that a different point on the curve becomes pertinent.

On the other hand, assume that there is a change in the original demand function so that $q_d = f_1(p)$ does not pertain any longer, and in its place we have $q_d = f_2(p)$. We then say that there has been a change or *shift* in demand.

Shifts in demand occur because of changes in the factors assumed fixed. Thus, if $q_d = f_1(p)$ is a demand function constructed on the assumption that income is at a level Y_1, then an increase in income brings about a new demand function $q_d = f_2(p)$, where more will be demanded at each price.

Similar remarks apply to supply functions. If $q_s = h(p)$ and costs of production increase, a new supply function pertains reflecting the fact that less will be offered for sale at each price.

Illustration.   Assume a shift in demand such that the demand function changes from $q_d = 100 - 2p$ to $q_d = 200 - 2p$. This increase in demand could be caused by an increase in income, an increase in the price of substitutes, a decrease in the price of complements, or an increase in consumer tastes.

Similarly, suppose that supply shifts from $q_s = 3p - 50$ to $q_s = 3p - 100$. This decreased supply could be caused by increasing costs.

Illustration.   Consider the general case of linear demand and supply functions. What are the effects of changes in these functions upon market equilibrium?

Linear demand and supply functions are given in general form as

$$q_d = b - ap \qquad q_s = cp - d \qquad \text{where} \quad b, d \geqslant 0 \quad \text{and} \quad a, c > 0$$

We saw earlier that equilibrium will occur when

$$p = \frac{b + d}{c + a} \quad \text{and} \quad q = \frac{bc - ad}{c + a}$$

Now an increase in demand implies that b increases, which therefore leads to a higher equilibrium price and quantity.

An increase in supply implies that d is reduced, which therefore leads to a lower equilibrium price and higher equilibrium quantity.

Exercises

1. a) Assume that the demand of Exercise 1, Section 4.7, changes to $q_d = 407 - 5p$. What is the new equilibrium?
    b) Assume that the demand of Exercise 1, Section 4.7, remains unchanged, but that supply changes to $q_s = 4p - 106$. What is the new equilibrium?
    c) Assume now that demand changes to $q_d = 407 - 5p$ and supply to $q_s = 4p - 106$. What is the new equilibrium?
2. a) Assume that the demand of Exercise 2, Section 4.7, changes to $q_d = 30 - \frac{1}{2}p$. What is the new equilibrium?
    b) Assume that the demand of Exercise 2, Section 4.7, remains unchanged, but that supply changes to $q_s = 7.5p - 16$. What is the new equilibrium?
    c) Assume now that demand changes to $q_d = 30 - \frac{1}{2}p$ and supply to $q_s = 7.5p - 16$. What is the new equilibrium?
3. Assume that the demand of Exercise 4, Section 4.7, changes to $q_d = 3b - 3p$ and supply to $q_s = 4p - 2d$. What is the new equilibrium?
4. How would the supply function of Exercise 3, Section 4.7, have to change in order for the equilibrium price to double? Assume an unchanged demand function.

SECTION 4·9   PURE COMPETITION AND REALITY

Caution: The purely competitive market structure cannot be said to typify the majority of markets in the United States. It is true that there are markets that satisfy at least approximately the assumptions of pure competition, such as many of the agricultural industries and some security markets. However, most products are bought and sold under market structures that do not satisfy the assumptions of the purely competitive model. We must therefore not expect purely competitive solutions necessarily to apply to other market conditions. The primary value of the purely competitive model is its simplicity, which makes it useful as a first step. But we must be able eventually to relax and alter its restrictive assumptions in order to arrive at better insights into other, more realistic and prevalent market structures. It is generally found that this approach is more productive than attempting to go directly to the more prevalent but also more complex market structures. Other market structures are therefore considered after a complete treatment of the purely competitive market model. In the final analysis, the usefulness of the model depends upon how much light it sheds upon the understanding of the real economic world.

SECTION 4·10   THE EFFECT OF A SPECIFIC TAX ON PURELY COMPETITIVE EQUILIBRIUM

A specific tax is a tax that collects a fixed amount per unit of a product sold regardless of the actual selling price. Suppose that the market demand and supply functions are initially

$$q_d = 100 - 2p \qquad q_s = 3p - 50$$

and a specific tax of $5 per unit is imposed upon suppliers. This means that a price of p_0 will not bring forth the same quantity supplied as without the tax. Instead, a price of p_0 will only have the effect that a price of $p_0 - 5$ would have had before the imposition of the tax, because a price of p_0 implies that the supplier receives only $p_0 - 5$. A new supply function is therefore appropriate. This is derived by replacing p in the initial supply function by $p - 5$. We then have[2]

$$q'_s = 3(p - 5) - 50$$
$$= 3p - 15 - 50$$
$$= 3p - 65$$

---

[2] Those who are familiar with calculus notation may recall that the prime notation (i.e., ′) is sometimes used to denote a derivative. However, it can also be used to indicate a changed function. This is the sense in which it is used in this chapter.

The equilibrium market price in a purely competitive market is found by equating demand and supply functions, which yields

$$100 - 2p = 3p - 65$$
$$165 = 5p$$
$$p = \$33$$

This compares with an equilibrium price of \$30, which we earlier computed for the initial demand and supply functions.

Thus equilibrium price increases by \$3 as a result of the tax. This is somewhat less than the tax per unit, which was \$5. The consumer ends up paying \$3 of the tax on each unit in the form of the higher price. The supplier receives \$33 on each unit but must pay the government \$5, thus remaining with \$28 as opposed to the \$30 he could keep without the imposition of the tax. The supplier therefore pays the remaining \$2 per unit of the tax.

Equilibrium quantity is also affected by the tax. Without the tax, the equilibrium quantity would be 40 units, but this is reduced to 34 units as a result of the tax. The government, when imposing a \$5 per unit tax on an industry selling 40 units, should not expect to receive ($5)(40) = \$200 tax revenue. As the illustration demonstrates, tax revenue would be only ($5)(34) = \$170.

Illustration. Consider the following general linear demand and supply functions:

$$q_d = b - ap \qquad q_s = cp - d \qquad \text{where} \quad b, d \geqslant 0 \quad \text{and} \quad a, c > 0$$

Assume that a tax of $\$t$ per unit is imposed on the supplier. We then have

$$q_d = b - ap \qquad q'_s = c(p - t) - d$$
$$= cp - ct - d$$

Equilibrium is then determined by setting $q_d = q'_s$, which gives

$$b - ap = cp - ct - d$$
$$b + d + ct = cp + ap$$
$$b + d + ct = (c + a)p$$
$$p = \frac{b + d + ct}{c + a}$$

We had earlier found that equilibrium price with the initial demand and supply functions would be

$$p = \frac{b + d}{c + a}$$

Thus equilibrium price increases by

$$\frac{ct}{c + a} = \frac{t}{1 + (a/c)}$$

This shows that the price increase is less than the full tax, which is t.

The exact proportion of the tax burden borne by the consumer will vary depending upon the ratio of the slopes of the demand and supply functions, that is, a/c. The smaller the absolute slope of the demand function (a) in relation to the slope of the supply function (c), the greater the proportion of the tax that will be borne by the consumer.

Assume now that instead of a specific tax levied on the supplier, a similar per-unit tax is levied on the consumer. Let us begin with the same initial demand and supply functions as above:

$$q_d = 100 - 2p \qquad q_s = 3p - 50$$

If a tax of $5 per unit is imposed upon the consumer, the demand function is altered. At a price of p_0 the product would really cost the consumer $p_0 + 5$. The new demand function is therefore derived by replacing p with $p + 5$. This gives us

$$q'_d = 100 - 2(p + 5)$$
$$= 100 - 2p - 10$$
$$= 90 - 2p$$

The equilibrium market price is then found by equating demand and supply functions:

$$90 - 2p = 3p - 50$$
$$140 = 5p$$
$$p = \$28$$

The equilibrium market price is thus $2 below the equilibrium market price with the initial demand and supply functions. The consumer pays $28 plus $5 tax for each unit. The total cost to the consumer is thus $33. He therefore ends up paying $3 of the tax, while the supplier pays $2

in the form of receiving a lower price. Equilibrium quantity is again
reduced to 34 units as a result of the tax.

The result of a per-unit tax on the consumer is thus identical in all
respects to a similar tax on the supplier.

Illustration. Consider the general linear demand and supply functions

$$q_d = b - ap \qquad q_s = cp - d \qquad \text{where} \quad b, d \geqslant 0 \quad \text{and} \quad a, c > 0$$

Assume that a tax of $\$t$ per unit is imposed on the consumer. We have

$$q_d' = b - a(p + t) \qquad q_s = cp - d$$
$$ = b - ap - at$$

Equilibrium is then determined by setting $q_d' = q_s$, which gives

$$b - ap - at = cp - d$$
$$b + d - at = cp + ap$$
$$b + d - at = (c + a)p$$
$$p = \frac{b + d - at}{c + a}$$

Equilibrium price with the initial demand and supply functions is

$$p = \frac{b + d}{c + a}$$

Therefore equilibrium price decreases by

$$\frac{at}{c + a}$$

But this increase is more than balanced by the tax the consumers must
pay, which is t. Adding the tax onto the price, we get the total cost to the
consumer:

$$\frac{b + d - at}{c + a} + t = \frac{b + d - at + t(c + a)}{c + a}$$
$$= \frac{b + d + ct}{c + a}$$

This is exactly what the consumer pays when the tax is levied on the
supplier. Thus it makes no real difference whether the tax is imposed on
consumer or supplier.

Exercises

1. a) Given the demand and supply functions of Exercise 1, Section 4.7, what is the effect on equilibrium price and quantity of a specific tax of $9 imposed on the supplier? What proportion of the tax is borne by the consumer?
   b) How much revenue will the government collect as a result of the tax?
2. a) Given the demand and supply functions of Exercise 2, Section 4.7, what is the effect on equilibrium price and quantity of a specific tax of $4 imposed on the consumer? What proportion of the tax is borne by the consumer?
   b) How much revenue will the government collect as a result of the tax?
3. Given the demand and supply functions of Exercise 3, Section 4.7, what is the effect on equilibrium price of a specific tax of $1 on the supplier?
4. Given the demand and supply functions of Exercise 4, Section 4.7, what is the effect on equilibrium price of a specific tax of $4 imposed on the consumer?
5. Given the demand and supply functions of Exercise 1, Section 4.7. A specific tax of t is imposed upon the supplier, and equilibrium price rises by $4.00. What is the value of t?

SECTION 4·11   THE EFFECT OF A SALES TAX ON PURELY COMPETITIVE EQUILIBRIUM

A sales tax differs from a specific tax in that the former collects a fixed percentage of the product price instead of a fixed amount per unit of product. Assume the same initial demand and supply functions as in the previous section,

$$q_d = 100 - 2p \qquad q_s = 3p - 50$$

but now a sales tax of 5 percent is imposed on the supplier. This means that when the seller receives a price of p_0, he is able to keep only $p_0 - 0.05p_0$. The new supply function is therefore derived by replacing p with $p - 0.05p$. We then have

$$q'_s = 3(p - 0.05p) - 50$$

$$= 3p - 0.15p - 50$$

$$= 2.85p - 50$$

The equilibrium market price is found by equating demand and supply functions, which yields

$$100 - 2p = 2.85p - 50$$

$$150 = 4.85p$$

$$p = \$30.93$$

The 5 percent sales tax thus raises equilibrium price from $30 to $30.93. The supplier, however, must pay the tax on this amount, which is $(0.05)(30.93) = \$1.55$. He thus remains with $30.93 - 1.55 = \$29.38$, as opposed to the $30 he would keep without the imposition of the sales tax. The supplier therefore pays $0.62 of the tax, while the consumer pays $0.93 of the tax in the form of a higher price.

The effects of a sales tax are thus similar to those for a specific tax. In either case, quantity sold is reduced as a result of the tax. Both taxes are shifted in part to the consumer.

Illustration.   Consider the general linear demand and supply function

$$q_d = b - ap \qquad q_s = cp - d \qquad \text{where} \quad b, d \geqslant 0 \quad \text{and} \quad a, c > 0$$

A sales tax of amount h is imposed on the supplier. We then have

$$q_d = b - ap \qquad q'_s = c(p - hp) - d$$

$$= cp - chp - d$$

$$= (c - ch)p - d$$

Equilibrium is then determined by setting $q_d = q'_s$, which yields

$$b - ap = (c - ch)p - d$$

$$b + d = (c + a - ch)p$$

$$p = \frac{b + d}{c + a - ch}$$

Comparing this to the equilibrium price without any taxes of

$$p = \frac{b + d}{c + a}$$

we see that equilibrium price increases due to the sales tax.

Assume now that a 5 percent sales tax is imposed on the consumer instead of the supplier. The initial demand and supply functions are as above:

$$q_d = 100 - 2p \qquad q_s = 3p - 50$$

As a result of the sales tax, there is a change in the demand function, because at a price of p_0 the product would really cost the consumer $p_0 + 0.05p_0$. The new demand function is therefore derived by replacing p with $p + 0.05p$. This yields

$$q'_d = 100 - 2(p + 0.05p)$$
$$= 100 - 2p - 0.10p$$

The equilibrium market price is then found by equating demand and supply functions:

$$100 - 2p - 0.10p = 3p - 50$$
$$5p + 0.10p = 150$$
$$5.10p = 150$$
$$p = \frac{150}{5.1}$$
$$p = \$29.41$$

In addition to the market price of $29.41, the consumer must pay a tax of $(0.05)(29.41) = \$1.47$. The total cost of the product to the consumer is therefore $29.41 + $1.47 = $30.88. Without the imposition of any tax, the equilibrium market price would be $30. Therefore the consumer pays $0.88 of the tax, while the supplier pays the other $0.59 in the form of receiving a lower price.

The government thus collects $0.08 less in taxes per unit in this case than when the tax is imposed on the supplier ($1.47 compared to $1.55). The consumer pays $0.05 less ($30.88 compared to $30.93), while the supplier pays $0.03 less ($0.59 compared to $0.62) when the tax is imposed upon the consumer.

The reason for this result is that when levied on the seller, the tax is a percentage of the full selling price, including the additional amount that the consumer is paying because of the tax. On the other hand, when levied on the consumer, the tax is a percentage of the price before taxes. Thus, in the illustration above, the tax when levied on the seller was 5 percent of $30.93, but when levied on the consumer it was 5 percent of $29.41.

Generally, sales taxes are imposed on the consumer with the provision that the seller collect the tax.

Illustration. Consider the general linear demand and supply functions

$$q_d = b - ap \qquad q_s = cp - d \qquad \text{where} \quad b, d \geq 0 \quad \text{and} \quad a, c > 0$$

A sales tax of amount h is imposed on the consumer. We have

$$q_d' = b - a(p + hp) \qquad q_s = cp - d$$

$$= b - ap - ahp$$

$$= b - (a + ah)p$$

Equilibrium is then determined by setting $q_d' = q_s$, which yields

$$b - (a + ah)p = cp - d$$

$$cp + (a + ah)p = b + d$$

$$p = \frac{b + d}{c + a + ah}$$

The consumer must pay this price plus a tax of

$$h\left(\frac{b + d}{c + a + ah}\right)$$

Exercises

1. a) Given the demand and supply functions of Exercise 1, Section 4.7, what is the effect on equilibrium price and quantity of a sales tax of 6 percent imposed on the supplier?
    b) How much revenue will the government collect as a result of the tax?

2. a) Given the demand and supply functions of Exercise 2, Section 4.7, what is the effect on equilibrium price and quantity of a sales tax of 4 percent imposed on the consumer?
    b) How much revenue will the government collect as a result of the tax?

3. Given the demand and supply functions of Exercise 3, Section 4.7, what is the effect on equilibrium price of a sales tax of 5 percent imposed on the consumer?

4. Given the demand and supply functions of Exercise 4, Section 4.7, what is the effect on equilibrium price of a sales tax of 1 percent imposed on the consumer?

5. Given the demand and supply functions of Exercise 1, Section 4.7. A sales tax of amount h is imposed upon the consumer, and equilibrium price falls by $5.00. What is the value of h?

6. Given the demand and supply function of Exercise 2, Section 4.7. A specific tax of $$t$ and a sales tax of 2 percent is imposed on the consumer, and equilibrium price falls by $0.25. What is the value of t?

7. Given the following demand and supply functions

$$q_d = 250 - 3p \qquad q_s = 8p - 14$$

where p, q_d, q_s are positive.

a) What is the effect on equilibrium price and quantity of a specific tax of $3.00 imposed on the supplier combined with a sales tax of 1 percent imposed on the consumer?

b) Compare this to the effect of imposing only a specific tax of $3.00 on the supplier and to the effect of imposing only a sales tax of 1 percent on the consumer.

SECTION 4·12   QUADRATIC FUNCTIONS AND EQUATIONS

Until this point, we have dealt extensively with linear functions. But other functions are also important. If we have a function $y = f(x)$, where x appears to a power other than the first, the function is nonlinear. In particular, if the function is of the form

$$y = ax^2 + bx + c$$

where $a \neq 0$ and a, b, c are constants, then it is said to be a *quadratic function* or a function of *second degree*.

Illustration. $y = x^2 + 2$ is a quadratic function or equation. Its graph was drawn in Section 4.3. It is quite evident that it does not have the slope of a straight line. Its graphical shape is known as a parabola.

Illustration. $q_d = 50 - 4p - 2p^2$ for $0 \leqslant p < 4$ is a quadratic demand function.

We may also encounter functions of higher degree.

Illustration. $q_d = 100 - 2p^4$ is a fourth-degree function.

Demand and supply curves or functions are often assumed to be linear or first degree. This is not because we expect such curves to be typically linear. Rather, we do so because of the simplicity of working with linear functions. In this way, we derive certain conclusions which can then often be shown to apply even in the case of nonlinear functions.

We shall now carry forth the work we have done with linear demand and supply functions to the case of quadratic functions.

Suppose that we have the following quadratic market demand and supply functions:

$$q_d = \begin{cases} 50 - 4p - 2p^2 & \text{for} \quad 0 \leqslant p < 4 \\ 0 & \text{for} \quad p > 4 \end{cases}$$

$$q_s = \begin{cases} 3p^2 + 6p - 25 & \text{for} \quad p \geqslant 2.10 \\ 0 & \text{for} \quad p < 2.10 \end{cases}$$

We know that competitive market equilibrium is achieved by setting

$$q_d = q_s$$

Therefore we have

$$50 - 4p - 2p^2 = 3p^2 + 6p - 25$$

which by solving should yield any possible equilibrium price.

This is equivalent to

$$0 = 5p^2 + 10p - 75$$

or dividing each side by 5, we have

$$p^2 + 2p - 15 = 0$$

We now need to be able to solve a quadratic equation in the variable p. Let us therefore consider the general method of solving such equations.

Solving Quadratic Equations

Assume that we wish to solve any quadratic equation that can be written as

$$ax^2 + bx + c = 0$$

If the expression can be written as a product of two factors each of the first degree, we can easily solve by setting each factor equal to zero and solving two linear equations. This can be done because when a product of two factors equals zero, it must be that at least one of the factors equals zero. If we find a value of x that makes either factor equal zero, then the product of factors will also equal zero. Such a value will therefore satisfy the original quadratic equation.

Illustration.   Solve $2x^2 - 9x - 5 = 0$.
　　　Factoring, we have

$$(2x + 1)(x - 5) = 0$$

A product of two factors will equal zero if either factor equals zero. Therefore we set each factor equal to zero.

$$2x + 1 = 0 \quad \text{and} \quad x - 5 = 0$$
$$x = -\tfrac{1}{2} \qquad\qquad x = 5$$

Thus $x = -\tfrac{1}{2}$ and $x = 5$ are roots of the original equation. This can easily be verified by substitution into the original quadratic equation.

For the case where the quadratic expression cannot be factored, we must derive a general formula that will give us the roots of the equation. Suppose that we have

$$ax^2 + bx + c = 0 \quad\quad \text{where} \quad a \neq 0$$

Divide both sides of this equation by a. We then have

$$x^2 + \frac{b}{a}x + \frac{c}{a} = 0$$

which is equivalent to

$$x^2 + \frac{b}{a}x = -\frac{c}{a}$$

Now add $(b/2a)^2$ to both sides of the equation. We have

$$x^2 + \frac{b}{a}x + \left(\frac{b}{2a}\right)^2 = -\frac{c}{a} + \left(\frac{b}{2a}\right)^2$$

This is equivalent to

$$\left(x + \frac{b}{2a}\right)^2 = -\frac{c}{a} + \left(\frac{b}{2a}\right)^2$$

or

$$\left(x + \frac{b}{2a}\right)^2 = \frac{b^2 - 4ac}{4a^2}$$

Therefore,

$$x + \frac{b}{2a} = \frac{\pm\sqrt{b^2 - 4ac}}{2a}$$

$$x = -\frac{b}{2a} \pm \frac{\sqrt{b^2 - 4ac}}{2a}$$

$$= \frac{-b \pm \sqrt{b^2 - 4ac}}{2a}$$

We have thus solved the quadratic equation for x in terms of a, b, and c, which are the coefficients of the original equation. Therefore, given any quadratic equation, to solve for x, we merely substitute the particular values for a, b, and c.

Illustration. Solve $x^2 - 8x + 13$.
In this case $a = 1$, $b = -8$, and $c = 13$. Therefore, using the formula, we have

$$x = \frac{-(-8) \pm \sqrt{(-8)^2 - 4(1)(13)}}{2}$$

$$= \frac{8 \pm \sqrt{12}}{2} = \frac{8 \pm 2\sqrt{3}}{2} = 4 \pm \sqrt{3}$$

The two roots are therefore $4 + \sqrt{3}$ and $4 - \sqrt{3}$.

Illustration. Solve $x^2 - 6x + 13$.
In this case $a = 1$, $b = -6$, and $c = 13$.

$$x = \frac{-(-6) \pm \sqrt{(-6)^2 - 4(1)(13)}}{2} = \frac{6 \pm \sqrt{-16}}{2} = \frac{6 \pm 4\sqrt{-1}}{2}$$

$$= 3 \pm 2i$$

The two roots are therefore $3 + 2i$ and $3 - 2i$, where $i = \sqrt{-1}$ as we recall from Chapter 3.

Let us now return to the problem we earlier considered where, after setting $q_d = q_s$, we arrived at

$$p^2 + 2p - 15 = 0$$

We now see that this can be factored into

$$(p + 5)(p - 3) = 0$$

or

$$p + 5 = 0 \quad \text{and} \quad p - 3 = 0$$
$$p = -5 \qquad\qquad p = 3$$

Price cannot be negative, so we are left with one equilibrium price, $p = 3$. At this price equilibrium quantity can be found by referring back to either the demand or the supply function. It is found to be $q = 20$.

Illustration.   Given the following demand and supply functions for a competitive market. Find the equilibrium market price.

$$q_d = 20 - 5p - p^2 \qquad \text{where} \quad q_d \geqslant 0$$
$$q_s = 6p^2 + 5p - 5 \qquad \text{where} \quad q_s \geqslant 0$$

Market equilibrium is achieved at the point where

$$q_d = q_s$$

Therefore we have

$$20 - 5p - p^2 = 6p^2 + 5p - 5$$

or

$$7p^2 + 10p - 25 = 0$$

In this case, $a = 7$, $b = 10$, and $c = -25$. Therefore, using the formula, we have

$$p = \frac{-10 \pm \sqrt{(10)^2 - 4(7)(-25)}}{2(7)} = \frac{-10 \pm \sqrt{800}}{14}$$

$$= \frac{-10 \pm 20\sqrt{2}}{14} = \frac{-5 \pm 10\sqrt{2}}{7}$$

The two possible equilibrium prices are

$$p = \frac{-5 + 10\sqrt{2}}{7} \quad \text{and} \quad p = \frac{-5 - 10\sqrt{2}}{7}.$$

Now $\sqrt{2}$ is approximately equal to 1.4. Thus the second possibility yields a negative price, which is clearly impossible by the nature of the problem. Therefore we are left with one equilibrium price,

$$p = \frac{-5 + 10\sqrt{2}}{7}$$

which is approximately equal to $\frac{9}{7}$ or \$1.29.

Of course, demand and supply functions may take many forms. Upon occasion, we may be able to reduce the resulting equilibrium condition to a linear or quadratic form that facilitates finding solutions.

Illustration.   Given the following demand and supply functions in a competitive market. Find equilibrium market price.

$$q_d = \frac{400}{p - 2} \qquad q_s = 2p \qquad \text{where} \quad q_d \text{ and } q_s \geq 0$$

For equilibrium, we must have $q_d = q_s$, or

$$\frac{400}{p - 2} = 2p$$

Multiplying both sides of the equation by $p - 2$ gives

$$400 = 2p(p - 2)$$
$$400 = 2p^2 - 4p$$

or

$$2p^2 - 4p - 400 = 0$$

which is the same as $p^2 - 2p - 200 = 0$.

We can now use the quadratic equation formula, for which we have $a = 1$, $b = -2$, $c = -200$. Therefore

$$p = \frac{2 \pm \sqrt{4 - 4(1)(-200)}}{2} = \frac{2 \pm \sqrt{804}}{2}$$

$$= \frac{2 \pm 2\sqrt{201}}{2} = 1 \pm \sqrt{201}$$

The only possible equilibrium price is thus $p = 1 + \sqrt{201}$, which is approximately \$15. To verify that this is in fact a root, we can substitute back into the original equation and find that it does check.

Illustration.   Given the following demand and supply functions in a competitive market. Find equilibrium market price.

$$q_d = 5 - p \qquad q_s = \sqrt{2p - 1} \qquad \text{where} \quad q_d \text{ and } q_s \geqslant 0$$

For equilibrium, we must have $q_d = q_s$ or

$$5 - p = \sqrt{2p - 1}$$

Squaring both sides of the equation gives

$$25 - 10p + p^2 = 2p - 1$$

or

$$p^2 - 12p + 26 = 0$$

We can now use the quadratic formula, for which we have $a = 1$, $b = -12$, $c = 26$. Therefore

$$p = \frac{12 \pm \sqrt{144 - 4(1)(26)}}{2} = \frac{12 \pm \sqrt{40}}{2} = \frac{12 \pm 2\sqrt{10}}{2}$$

$$= 6 \pm \sqrt{10}$$

Now there are two possible solutions, $p = 6 + \sqrt{10}$ and $p = 6 - \sqrt{10}$. But if $p = 6 + \sqrt{10}$, then q_d would be negative, which is not possible. Therefore the only possible equilibrium point is at $p = 6 - \sqrt{10}$. To make sure that this is, indeed, a root, we can substitute back into the original equation and see that $p = 6 - \sqrt{10}$ does check.

Exercises

1.   Solve $x^2 + 7x + 6 = 0$.

2.   Solve $2x^2 + 7x + 3 = 0$.

3.   Solve $x^2 - 4x + 1 = 0$.

4.   Solve $3x^2 - 11x - 20 = 0$.

Given the following demand and supply functions, where q_d and $q_s > 0$.
Find equilibrium market price.

5. $q_d = 600 - 3p - 3p^2$, $q_s = 3p^2 + 9p - 84$

6. $q_d = 640 - 4p - 4p^2$, $q_s = 4p^2 - 20p$

7. $q_d = 100 - 5p - p^2$, $q_s = 4p^2 + 5p$

8. $q_d = 40 - 2p - 3p^2$, $q_s = p^2 + 3p - 10$

9. $q_d = \dfrac{100}{p - 5}$, $q_s = 4p - 4$

10. $q_d = \sqrt{16 - 4p}$, $q_s = 3p - 2$

11. Given the demand and supply functions of Exercise 5, what will be
     the equilibrium price if a specific tax of $2 is imposed on the
     producer?

12. Given the demand and supply functions of Exercise 6, what will be
     the equilibrium price if a specific tax of $5 is imposed on the
     consumer?

SECTION 4·13   LOGARITHMS

Consider the following relationship between price and quantity supplied:

$$p = b^{q_s}$$

where p is price, q_s is quantity supplied, and b is some positive constant
not equal to 1.

Another way of expressing the above relationship is to write

$$q_s = \log_b p$$

where log denotes the *logarithm* of a number to the base b.

Thus the logarithm of a number is merely the exponent to which a
given base must be raised to yield the original number.

Illustration. $\log_{10} 100 = 2$ is a shorthand way of stating that the base 10
must be raised to the second power to yield 100.

Logarithms can be taken to any base. However, some are especially
convenient for various purposes. The base 10 is usually most convenient
from a computational point of view. Logarithms to the base 10 are called
common logarithms. Whenever the log of a number is written without
reference to a specific base, it is understood that the base 10 is meant.

Logarithmic expressions have certain properties that greatly facilitate many computations. These are given by the following theorems.

Theorem 1. $\log_b b = 1.$
Proof.
Let $\log_b b = x$, where x is some unknown quantity.
Then $b^x = b$ by the definition of a logarithm stated earlier.
Therefore $x = 1$.
$\therefore \log_b b = 1.$

Theorem 2. $\log_b(uv) = \log_b u + \log_b v$; that is, the logarithm of a product is the sum of the logarithms of the factors.
Proof.
Let $\log_b u = x$ and $\log_b v = y$.
Then $b^x = u$ and $b^y = v$ by definition of logarithm.
Therefore $uv = b^x b^y$ and $uv = b^{x+y}$.
This is equivalent to $\log_b uv = x + y$ by definition of logarithm.
But $\log_b u + \log_b v = x + y$.
$\therefore \log_b(uv) = \log_b u + \log_b v.$

Theorem 3. $\log_b(u/v) = \log_b u - \log_b v$; that is, the logarithm of a quotient is the logarithm of the numerator minus the logarithm of the denominator.
Proof.
Let $\log_b u = x$ and $\log_b v = y$.
Then $b^x = u$ and $b^y = v$ by definition of logarithm.
Therefore

$$\frac{u}{v} = \frac{b^x}{b^y} = b^{x-y}$$

This is equivalent to $\log_b(u/v) = x - y$ by definition of logarithm.
But $\log_b u - \log_b v = x - y$.
$\therefore \log_b(u/v) = \log_b u - \log_b v.$

Theorem 4. $\log_b u^n = n \log_b u$; that is, the logarithm of any number raised to a power is equivalent to the exponent multiplied by the logarithm of that number.
Proof.
Let $\log_b u = x$.
Then $u = b^x$ by definition of logarithm and $u^n = (b^x)^n = b^{xn}$.

This is equivalent to $\log_b u^n = xn$ by definition of logarithm.
But $n \log_b u = nx$.
$\therefore \log_b u^n = n \log_b u$.

Illustration.   Consider the following supply function:

$$q_s = \log\left(\frac{10p^2}{p + 1}\right)$$

By the above theorems, this is equivalent to

$$q_s = \log(10p^2) - \log(p + 1)$$

$$= \log 10 + \log p^2 - \log(p + 1)$$

$$= 1 + 2 \log p - \log(p + 1)$$

We have already pointed out that logarithms are often taken to the base 10. The evaluation of such logarithms is greatly facilitated by the use of a table of logarithms. If we wish to find the logarithm of a number, we express that number as a product of a number between 1 and 10 and an integral power of 10. Thus, if we wish to find $\log 624$ we write

$$624 = 6.24(10^2)$$

and therefore

$$\log 624 = \log 6.24 + 2 \log 10$$

$$= \log 6.24 + 2$$

The log of 6.24 is then found from the table of logarithms at the end of the book. The first two digits are located in the first column and the third digit in the top row. The entry corresponding to the three digits 624 turns out to be 7952. A decimal must be placed before the first digit because the logarithm of a number between 1 and 10 must be somewhere between 0 and 1. Therefore

$$\log 624 = .7952 + 2$$

$$= 2.7952$$

An analogous procedure would be followed for any other number.

Illustration.   Find $\log 62.4$.

We express 62.4 as a product of a number between 1 and 10 and an integral power of 10. Thus

$$62.4 = 6.24(10^1)$$

and

$\log 62.4 = \log 6.24 + \log 10$

$\quad\quad\quad = .7952 + 1$

$\quad\quad\quad = 1.7952$

Illustration.   Find $\log 0.00624$.
   We proceed as above.

$0.00624 = 6.24(10^{-3})$

and

$\log 0.00624 = \log 6.24 + \log(10^{-3})$

$\quad\quad\quad\quad\quad = \log 6.24 - 3 \log 10$

$\quad\quad\quad\quad\quad = \log 6.24 - 3$

$\quad\quad\quad\quad\quad = .7952 - 3$

which is generally written as $7.7952 - 10$, where we note that $7 - 10$ is the same as -3.

   When a logarithm is expressed with a positive decimal portion, then the integral portion is called its *characteristic* and the decimal portion its *mantissa*.

   We can easily see that the table of logarithms is really a table of mantissas, because the characteristic is readily determined from the integral power of 10. Moreover, all numbers with the same sequence of digits beginning with the first nonzero digit have the same mantissas. Thus we have seen that the mantissas of $\log 624$, $\log 62.4$, and $\log 0.00624$ are all identical. But the characteristics are 2, 1, and -3, respectively.

   We can now appreciate why $.7952 - 3$ is written as $7.7952 - 10$ rather than as -2.2048. The former expression makes clear that the characteristic is $7 - 10$ or -3 and the mantissa is $.7952$, while the latter does not indicate either the characteristic or mantissa.

   Upon occasion, we may wish to find a number whose logarithm is known to us. To do this, we look for the mantissa or the closest thing to it in the table of logarithms. The table will indicate which digits correspond to the mantissa. The decimal point is then inserted in accordance with the characteristic.

Illustration.   If $\log x = 2.9400$, find x.
Solution.   In the table of logarithms, we find that the digits corresponding to 9400 are 871. The characteristic is 2, so x must be a number

between 10^2 and 10^3. Therefore we place the decimal after the 1 and $x = 871$.

Illustration. If $\log x = 8.9400 - 10$, find x.

Solution. The digits in the table of logarithms corresponding to 9400 are 871. The characteristic is $8 - 10 = -2$, so the number must be between $10^{-2} = 0.01$ and $10^{-1} = 0.1$. Therefore the number is 0.0871.

The table of logarithms at the end of the book provides the mantissa for three-digit numbers. If we wish to find the mantissa of a four-digit number, we may take the closest entry in the table as an approximation. Alternatively, we may use more detailed tables or we may interpolate between the two closest three-digit numbers.

Logarithmic Demand and Supply Functions

Suppose now that we have logarithmic demand and supply functions. We arrive at equilibrium price in a manner analogous to that used for linear or quadratic functions.

Illustration. Given the following demand and supply functions for a competitive market, find the equilibrium market price.

$$q_d = 10 - \log p \qquad \text{where} \quad q_d \geq 0$$

$$q_s = 4 \log p \qquad \text{where} \quad q_s \geq 0$$

Equilibrium is determined by setting $q_d = q_s$, which yields

$$10 - \log p = 4 \log p$$
$$5 \log p = 10$$
$$\log p = 2$$
$$p = 10^2 = 100$$

At $p = 100$, we have

$$q = 4 \log 100$$
$$= (4)(2) = 8$$

Thus equilibrium occurs at $p = 100$ and $q = 8$.

Illustration. Given the following demand and supply functions.

$q_d = 100 - 2 \log p$ where $q_d > 0$

$q_s = 50 \log p - 80$ where $q_s > 0$

a) Find quantity demanded and supplied at a price of $87.
b) Find equilibrium price and quantity.
Solution.
a) At $p = 87$

$q_d = 100 - 2 \log 87 = 100 - 2(1.9395) = 96.12$

$q_s = 50 \log 87 - 80 = 50(1.9395) - 80 = 16.98$

b) Equilibrium is determined by setting $q_d = q_s$, which yields

$100 - 2 \log p = 50 \log p - 80$

$52 \log p = 180$

$\log p = 3.46$

$p = 2220$

At $p = 2220$, we have

$q = 100 - 2 \log(2220)$

$= 100 - 2(3.46)$

$= 93$

Exercises

1. Find the log of the following numbers.

a) 314   b) 23.4   c) 5.21   d) 0.0621   e) 0.00542

2. Find x if $\log x$ is equal to

a) 2.7348   b) 0.7348   c) 8.7348 − 10

3. Find

$\log \dfrac{(314)^2}{23.4}$

4.   Find

$$\log \frac{3(5.21)^4}{0.0621}$$

5.   Given the following demand and supply functions:

$q_d = 50 - 5 \log p$ where $q_d \geqslant 0$

$q_s = 20 \log p - 25$ where $q_s \geqslant 0$

a)   Find quantity demanded and supplied at a price of $30.
b)   Find equilibrium price and quantity.

6.   Given the following demand and supply functions:

$q_d = 80 - 10 \log p$ where $q_d \geqslant 0$

$q_s = 30 \log p - 40$ where $q_s > 0$

a)   Find quantity demanded and supplied at a price of $111.
b)   Find equilibrium price and quantity.

7.   Given the following demand and supply functions:

$q_d = 120 - 8 \log p$ where $q_d > 0$

$q_s = 50 \log p - 60$ where $q_s > 0$

a)   Find quantity demanded and supplied at a price of $19.
b)   Find equilibrium price and quantity.

5

MATRIX ALGEBRA AND THE SOLUTION OF SYSTEMS OF EQUATIONS

The effort of the economist is to see, to picture the interplay of economic elements. The more clearly cut these elements appear in his vision, the better, the more elements he can grasp and hold in mind at once, the better. The economic world is a misty region. The first explorers used unaided vision. Mathematics is a lantern by which what before was dimly visible now looms up in firm, bold outlines. The old phantasmagoria disappear. We see better. We also see further.

—Irving Fisher

In this chapter we show how to deal with several equations simultaneously. The method of elimination of variables is used, at first, to find solutions for such systems. We then introduce the concept of a matrix, show how operations with matrices are performed, and then use matrix methods to solve systems of equations.

SECTION 5·1   DEMAND AND SUPPLY AS FUNCTIONS OF MORE THAN ONE VARIABLE

The demand functions we previously considered were all functions of one variable, that is, product price. They were constructed on the assumption that the quantity demanded of a particular product can be expressed as a function of the price of that product, and that all other factors that might affect the quantity demanded remain constant.

If we wish instead to consider the effect of simultaneous variations in the prices of several products upon the demand for a particular product, we express demand as a function of more than one variable. We then have

$$q_{d_A} = f(P_A, P_B, P_C, \ldots)$$

where q_{d_A} denotes the quantity demanded of product A; P_A is the price of product A, P_B is the price of product B, and so on. Products $B, C, \ldots$ may be either substitutes or complements of product A.[1]

Similarly, the demand function for product B would be expressed as a function of the prices of products A, B, and so on.

Market equilibrium in a purely competitive market is determined by equating demand and supply for each product. Thus, if there are n products, we have n equations in n unknowns, which would then be solved simultaneously.

Illustration. Given the following demand and supply functions in a purely competitive market. Find the equilibrium prices and quantities:

$$q_{d_A} = 100 - 2p_A - 2p_B + p_C$$

$$q_{d_B} = 135 - 4p_A - 3p_B + 2p_C$$

$$q_{d_C} = 140 + p_A + p_B - 2p_C$$

$$q_{s_A} = 3p_A - 65$$

$$q_{s_B} = 5p_B - 95$$

$$q_{s_C} = 6p_C - 10$$

We note that as the price of product B increases, the quantity demanded of product A decreases. A and B are said to be *complementary* products. They are used in conjunction with each other. Therefore as the price of B increases, less of both B and A are used.

We also note that as the price of product C increases, the quantity demanded for products A and B increases. Product C is thus a *substitute*, to some degree, for both A and B. Therefore as the price of C increases, less of C is used and more of A and B is substituted for C.

It is evident that the quantity demanded of A is not a simple function of the price of A alone but also depends upon the prices of other

---

[1] It has already been shown that we can view functions involving two variables as sets of ordered pairs. Similarly, functions involving three variables can be viewed as sets of ordered triplets. In general, for n variables, functions are sets of ordered n-tuples.

products. In fact, quantity demanded may depend upon still other variables such as consumer income. Similarly, supply could depend upon other factors.

Let us then equate demand and supply for each product. This yields three equations in three unknowns:

$$100 - 2p_A - 2p_B + p_C = 3p_A - 65$$
$$135 - 4p_A - 3p_B + 2p_C = 5p_B - 95$$
$$140 + p_A + p_B - 2p_C = 6p_C - 10$$

which are equivalent to

$$5p_A + 2p_B - p_C = 165 \tag{1}$$
$$4p_A + 8p_B - 2p_C = 230 \tag{2}$$
$$-p_A - p_B + 8p_C = 150 \tag{3}$$

We can solve this system by the process of elimination, that is, multiplying the equations by suitable constants so that successive variables can be eliminated. In this case, we see that if we multiply equation (1) by -2 and add the result to equation (2), we shall have an equation containing only the two variables, p_A and p_B:

$$-10p_A - 4p_B + 2p_C = -330$$
$$\underline{4p_A + 8p_B - 2p_C = 230}$$
$$-6p_A + 4p_B = -100 \tag{4}$$

Similarly, we can multiply equation (2) by 4 and add the result to equation (3). This will give us another equation containing only the two variables, p_A and p_B:

$$16p_A + 32p_B - 8p_C = 920$$
$$\underline{-p_A - p_B + 8p_C = 150}$$
$$15p_A + 31p_B = 1070 \tag{5}$$

If we take equations (4) and (5) together, we have two equations in two unknowns, which we can solve by eliminating one of the remaining variables.

$$-6p_A + 4p_B = -100 \tag{4}$$
$$15p_A + 31p_B = 1070 \tag{5}$$

We now multiply equation (4) by 15 and equation (5) by 6 and add
the results. We have

$$-90p_A + 60p_B = -1500$$

$$90p_A + 186p_B = 6420$$

$$\overline{ 246p_B = 4920}$$

$$p_B = \$20$$

p_A can then be determined from equation (4) or (5), which yields

$$p_A = \$30$$

p_C can then be determined from equation (1), (2), or (3):

$$p_C = \$25$$

Referring back to the demand or supply functions of A, B, and C, we
now find that at these equilibrium prices, quantities purchased will be

$$q_A = 25$$

$$q_B = 5$$

$$q_C = 140$$

This solution should be verified by substituting the values of p_A, p_B,
and p_C into the three equations (1), (2), and (3). When this is done it will
be seen that they check.

A similar procedure would be used to solve a system of four linear
equations in four unknowns. We would first reduce the system to one
involving three equations in three unknowns by eliminating the same
unknown from three different pairs of the four equations. The resulting
system of three equations in three unknowns would then be solved as
above, that is, by eliminating the same unknown from two pairs of the
three equations and by solving the resulting system of two equations in
two unknowns.

Exercises

Given the following demand and supply functions. Find the equilibrium prices and quantities and determine which of the products are
complements and which are substitutes.

1. $q_{d_A} = 285 - 5p_A - 10p_B$

$q_{d_B} = 373 - 3p_A - 15p_B$

$$q_{s_A} = 4p_A - 14$$
$$q_{s_B} = 3p_B - 20$$

2. $q_{d_A} = 320 - 4p_A - 2p_B + 2p_C$

$q_{d_B} = 200 - 2p_A - 3p_B + 6p_C$

$q_{d_C} = 190 + 6p_A + 4p_B - 10p_C$

$q_{s_A} = 6p_A - 80$

$q_{s_B} = 2p_B - 90$

$q_{s_C} = 23p_C - 10$

3. $q_{d_A} = 33 - 3p_A + 9p_B - p_C$

$q_{d_B} = 10 + 2p_A - 5p_B + 4p_C$

$q_{d_C} = 217 - 6p_A + p_B - 3p_C$

$q_{s_A} = 3p_A - 60$

$q_{s_B} = 80$

$q_{s_C} = 2p_C$

4. $q_{d_A} = 150 - 2p_A - p_B + p_C$

$q_{d_B} = 280 - 3p_A - 5p_B + 4p_C$

$q_{d_C} = 140 + p_A + 2p_B - 7p_C$

$q_{s_A} = 12p_A - 43$

$q_{s_B} = 7p_B - 144$

$q_{s_C} = 15p_C - 18$

5. $q_{d_A} = 68 - 2p_A - 2p_B - p_C + p_D$

$q_{d_B} = 39 - p_A - p_B - 2p_C + p_D$

$q_{d_C} = 95 - 2p_A - p_B - p_C + 2p_D$

$q_{d_D} = 44 + 2p_A + 2p_B + 2p_C - 2p_D$

$q_{s_A} = 2p_A - 20$

$q_{s_B} = p_B$

$q_{s_C} = 50$

$q_{s_D} = 100$

SECTION 5·2   MATRICES

Consider the three equations (1), (2), and (3) given in the previous section, which represent the equilibrium conditions in a purely competitive market.

$$5p_A + 2p_B - p_C = 165$$

$$4p_A + 8p_B - 2p_C = 230$$

$$-p_A - p_B + 8p_C = 150$$

One way to write this system of equations compactly is to array in order the coefficients of the variables and the constant terms:

$$\begin{pmatrix} 5 & 2 & -1 & 165 \\ 4 & 8 & -2 & 230 \\ -1 & -1 & 8 & 150 \end{pmatrix}$$

The numbers in the first column are the coefficients of the first variable; those in the second column are the coefficients of the second variable; those in the third column are the coefficients of the third variable; and those in the final column are the constant terms.

Such an ordered array of numbers, enclosed by parentheses, is known as a *matrix*.[2] In this particular case there are three rows and four columns, and the matrix is then said to be a 3 by 4 or 3×4 matrix. In general, a matrix can have any number of rows (say, m) and columns (say, n) and is referred to as an $m \times n$ matrix. Each entry in a matrix is known as an *element* of that matrix.

Some matrices have an equal number of rows and columns (n rows and columns). These are said to be *square matrices* of order n. If, in the previous illustration, we arrayed only the coefficients of the variables without the constant terms, we would have a square matrix of order 3. This would be referred to as the coefficient matrix and would appear as

$$\begin{pmatrix} 5 & 2 & -1 \\ 4 & 8 & -2 \\ -1 & -1 & 8 \end{pmatrix}$$

Matrices arise in many different contexts. Input–output analysis, which is concerned with how the outputs of certain sectors of the economy become the inputs for other sectors, makes extensive use of the matrix representation. Thus a transactions matrix can be derived to show the purchases made by each sector from every other sector during a

---

[2] Sometimes brackets [ ] or double bars ‖ ‖ are used instead of parentheses.

specified period, say 1 year. In simplified form, assuming only a very few broad sectors, this could be illustrated by the following 3 × 5 matrix:

	Agriculture	Industry	Services	Consumers	Total
Agriculture	3	8	1	5	17
Industry	7	20	2	60	89
Services	1	9	4	25	39

The first row is the agriculture row, which reflects in, say, billions of dollars, how the total agricultural output was utilized. Thus $3 billion was used in the production of other agricultural products, $8 billion served as input for industrial products, $1 billion was used by the service industry, and $5 billion of agricultural output was purchased directly by consumers. This accounts for the $17 of agricultural output that was produced. A similar interpretation is given to the industry output row. Of $89 billion of total industrial output, $7 billion was utilized as input for the agricultural sector, $20 billion for the production of other industrial products, $2 billion for the service sector, and $60 billion was purchased directly by consumers. The final row, which represents output from the services industry, is interpreted in the same way.

As another illustration of the possible use of matrices, consider the following matrix, which provides information concerning price, quantity, and total revenue of a certain product.

$$\begin{pmatrix} 1 & 20 & 20 \\ 2 & 16 & 32 \\ 3 & 10 & 30 \\ 4 & 3 & 12 \end{pmatrix}$$

The first or price column represents four possible prices for a particular product. The second or quantity column provides the quantities that would be bought at each price, while the third or total revenue column shows how much revenue would accrue at each price and quantity level.

Vectors

A matrix with only one row is known as a *row vector*. To illustrate, consider the following row vector, which shows the price of a product, the quantity purchased at that price, and the resulting total revenue:

(6   12   72)

Similarly, a matrix with only one column is known as a *column vector*.

The following column vector, for example, shows several different prices of a product at different times:

$$\begin{pmatrix} 8 \\ 5 \\ 2 \\ 4 \\ 6 \\ 10 \end{pmatrix}$$

Transpose of a Matrix

If the rows and columns of a matrix are interchanged, the resulting matrix is the transpose of the original. The original matrix may be denoted by A and the transposed matrix by A'. To illustrate, suppose that

$$A = \begin{pmatrix} 5 & 2 & -1 & 165 \\ 4 & 8 & -2 & 230 \\ -1 & -1 & 8 & 150 \end{pmatrix}$$

then the transpose of A would be given by

$$A' = \begin{pmatrix} 5 & 4 & -1 \\ 2 & 8 & -1 \\ -1 & -2 & 8 \\ 165 & 230 & 150 \end{pmatrix}$$

In the event that $A = A'$, A is said to be a *symmetric matrix*. The following matrix is an example of a symmetric matrix:

$$B = \begin{pmatrix} 5 & 2 & -1 \\ 2 & 8 & -1 \\ -1 & -1 & 8 \end{pmatrix}$$

It is easily seen that all symmetric matrices are square matrices.

If all nondiagonal elements of a square matrix are zero, the matrix is said to be a *diagonal matrix*. An example óf such a matrix is given by the following:

$$C = \begin{pmatrix} 5 & 0 & 0 \\ 0 & 8 & 0 \\ 0 & 0 & 8 \end{pmatrix}$$

A special type of diagonal matrix occurs when all diagonal elements are one. The resulting matrix is then a *unit or identity matrix*. The following matrices are examples of identity matrices.

$$I_2 = \begin{pmatrix} 1 & 0 \\ 0 & 1 \end{pmatrix}$$

$$I_3 = \begin{pmatrix} 1 & 0 & 0 \\ 0 & 1 & 0 \\ 0 & 0 & 1 \end{pmatrix}$$

$$I_4 = \begin{pmatrix} 1 & 0 & 0 & 0 \\ 0 & 1 & 0 & 0 \\ 0 & 0 & 1 & 0 \\ 0 & 0 & 0 & 1 \end{pmatrix}$$

If all elements of a matrix are zero, it is termed a *null or zero matrix*. A null matrix need not be a square matrix.

Equality of Matrices

Two matrices are said to be equal if and only if they are of the same order and their corresponding elements are identical.

Matrix Addition

The operation of addition is defined only for two matrices of like dimension, that is, both are $m \times n$ matrices. If A and B are both $m \times n$ matrices, then $A + B = C$, where each element in C is the sum of the corresponding elements in A and B. Two matrices of like dimension are said to be *conformable* for addition. It will be seen that this definition of matrices guarantees that $A + B = B + A$, where A and B are any two conformable matrices.

Illustration.   Find $A + B$, where

$$A = \begin{pmatrix} 20 & 18 \\ 16 & 13 \\ 10 & 12 \\ 3 & 7 \end{pmatrix} \qquad B = \begin{pmatrix} 14 & 17 \\ 19 & 18 \\ 11 & 14 \\ 4 & 6 \end{pmatrix}$$

Solution.   Both A and B are 4×2 matrices, so they are conformable for addition; we get the sum $A + B$ by merely adding corresponding terms.

$$A + B = \begin{pmatrix} 34 & 35 \\ 35 & 31 \\ 21 & 26 \\ 7 & 13 \end{pmatrix}$$

Suppose that the rows in A represent four different products, the columns two different markets, and the elements in A represent the quantities purchased of each product in each market during 1971. The matrix B is given the same interpretation except that it refers to quantities purchased in 1972. The sum $A + B$ will then give the total combined quantities purchased for each product in each market for the 2-year period 1971–1972.

Matrix Subtraction

The operation of subtraction is defined in a completely analogous manner as the addition of matrices. Subtraction is defined only for two matrices of like dimension. If A and B are both $m \times n$ matrices, then they are said to be conformable for subtraction, and $A - B = C$, where each element of C is the difference of the corresponding elements in A and B.

Illustration. Find $A - B$, where

$$A = \begin{pmatrix} 34 & 35 & 15 \\ 35 & 31 & 20 \\ 21 & 26 & 18 \\ 7 & 13 & 4 \end{pmatrix} \qquad B = \begin{pmatrix} 14 & 17 & 5 \\ 19 & 18 & 8 \\ 11 & 14 & 12 \\ 4 & 6 & 3 \end{pmatrix}$$

Solution. Both A and B are 4×3 matrices, so they are conformable for subtraction; we get the difference $A - B$ by merely subtracting corresponding terms.

$$A - B = \begin{pmatrix} 20 & 18 & 10 \\ 16 & 13 & 12 \\ 10 & 12 & 6 \\ 3 & 7 & 1 \end{pmatrix}$$

Suppose that the rows in A represent four different products, the columns three different markets, and the elements in A represent the quantities purchased of each product in each market during the 2-year period 1971–1972. The matrix B has the same interpretation except that it refers to quantities purchased in 1972. The difference $A - B$ then gives the quantities purchased for each product in each market for the year 1971.

Scalar Multiplication (ROCK)

A scalar is any single number; it is not a matrix. To multiply a matrix by any scalar, we merely multiply each element of the matrix by the scalar.

Illustration. Find $3A$, where

$$A = \begin{pmatrix} 6 & 2 & 7 & 5 \\ 8 & 1 & 3 & 2 \\ 3 & 4 & 3 & 10 \end{pmatrix}$$

Solution. We simply multiply each element of the matrix by 3, which gives

$$3A = \begin{pmatrix} 18 & 6 & 21 & 15 \\ 24 & 3 & 9 & 6 \\ 9 & 12 & 9 & 30 \end{pmatrix}$$

Suppose that the rows in A represent three different products, the columns four different markets, and the elements in A represent the prices of each product in each market. The matrix $3A$ then represents a tripling of the prices of each product in each market.

Matrix Multiplication

The multiplication of two matrices AB is defined only where A is an $m \times n$ matrix and B an $n \times p$ matrix. This is equivalent to saying that only if the number of columns of A is equal to the number of rows of B is A conformable to B for multiplication. If this is the case, then to find the product AB it is necessary to multiply each row of A by each column of B. The multiplication of a row of one matrix by a column of another matrix is, in turn, effected by multiplying each element of the row by the corresponding element of the column and then adding the results. This means that AB is a matrix such that the element in the ith row and jth column is found by multiplying each element of the ith row of A by the corresponding element of the jth column of B and adding the results. If A is an $m \times n$ matrix and B an $n \times p$ matrix, then AB will be an $m \times p$ matrix, that is, the product AB will have the number of rows of A and the number of columns of B.

As an illustration, let

$$A = \begin{pmatrix} a & d \\ b & e \\ c & f \end{pmatrix} \qquad B = \begin{pmatrix} g & i \\ h & j \end{pmatrix}$$

A is a 3×2 matrix, while B is a 2×2 matrix. The number of columns of A is the same as the number of rows of B, so A is conformable to B for multiplication. To find AB, we take the first row of A and multiply by the first column of B, which gives $ag + dh$. We then multiply the first row of A by the second column of B, which gives $ai + dj$. Next, we take the second row of A and multiply by each column of B, and similarly for the final row of A. This gives

$$AB = \begin{pmatrix} ag + dh & ai + dj \\ bg + eh & bi + ej \\ cg + fh & ci + fj \end{pmatrix}$$

We have multiplied a 3×2 matrix by a 2×2 matrix, and the result is a 3×2 matrix (i.e., the number of rows of the first matrix and the number of columns of the second).

Illustration. Find AB, where

$$A = \begin{pmatrix} 14 & 16 & 5 & 9 \\ 19 & 18 & 8 & 15 \\ 11 & 14 & 12 & 10 \end{pmatrix} \qquad B = \begin{pmatrix} 2 & 1 \\ 1.5 & 2 \\ 3 & 2 \\ 4 & 3 \end{pmatrix}$$

Suppose that the rows in A represent three different products, the columns four different markets, and the elements in A the quantities purchased of each product in each market during the year 1975. The rows of B give the multiple by which it is expected that the quantities in the four markets will change over the ensuing decade. The two columns in B represent two different estimates of such multiples. Show that the elements of AB represent expected total sales for each product in 1985 according to each of the two estimates.

Solution. We note that A is a 3×4 matrix and B a 4×2 matrix. The number of columns of A is the same as the number of rows of B, so A is conformable to B for multiplication. We find the product AB by multiplying the first row of A by each column of B, and then similarly for the second and third rows of A. This gives us

$$AB = \begin{pmatrix} (14)(2) + 16(1.5) + 5(3) + 9(4) & (14)(1) + 16(2) + 5(2) + 9(3) \\ 19(2) + 18(1.5) + 8(3) + 15(4) & 19(1) + 18(2) + 8(2) + 15(3) \\ 11(2) + 14(1.5) + 12(3) + 10(4) & 11(1) + 14(2) + 12(2) + 10(3) \end{pmatrix}$$

and

$$AB = \begin{pmatrix} 103 & 83 \\ 149 & 116 \\ 119 & 93 \end{pmatrix}$$

AB is thus a 3×2 matrix (i.e., the number of rows of the first matrix and the number of columns of the second matrix).

The elements in A, we are told, represent the quantities purchased of three different products in four different markets. The elements of B represent the multiples of change in the quantities according to two different estimates. Therefore, when we take the first row of A and multiply it by the first column of B, we get total sales in all markets of the first product in 1985 according to the first estimate, that is, $14(2) + 16(1.5) + 5(3) + 9(4) = 103$. This is what the element in the first row and column of AB indicates. Similarly, when we multiply the first row of A by the second column of B, we get total sales of the first product in 1985 according to the second estimate, that is, $14(1) + 16(2) + 5(2) + 9(3) = 83$. This appears as the element in the first row and second column of AB. In an analogous manner the two elements in the second row of AB represent total sales of the second product according to the two estimates, and likewise for the third row in AB.

The matrix AB is thus a matrix of projected 1985 sales for three products (the three rows) according to two estimates (the two columns).

It may at first seem odd that the multiplication of matrices is defined in such an unusual manner, that is, multiplying the rows of one matrix by the columns of another. However, the motive for the definition lies in the fact that it enables us to express a system of equations in compact form. Suppose that we are dealing with the three equations given in Section 5.1, namely,

$$5p_A + 2p_B - p_C = 165$$

$$4p_A + 8p_B - 2p_C = 230$$

$$-p_A - p_B + 8p_C = 150$$

The algebra of matrices enables us to write this system as

$$AP = B$$

where

$$A = \begin{pmatrix} 5 & 2 & -1 \\ 4 & 8 & -2 \\ -1 & -1 & 8 \end{pmatrix} \qquad P = \begin{pmatrix} p_A \\ p_B \\ p_C \end{pmatrix} \qquad B = \begin{pmatrix} 165 \\ 230 \\ 150 \end{pmatrix}$$

If we apply the definition of multiplication of matrices to AP, we get

$$AP = \begin{pmatrix} 5p_A + 2p_B - p_C \\ 4p_A + 8p_B - 2p_C \\ -p_A - p_B + 8p_C \end{pmatrix}$$

The statement $AP = B$ implies equality between elements of the matrix AP and the matrix B. This, in turn, amounts to the same expression as is contained in the three equations written above. Thus we have shown that the single expression $AP = B$ is identical to the three equations written above. The real importance of this compact notation, as we shall see later, appears when various operations such as, finding solutions, are to be performed with the equations.

It is essential to recognize that matrix multiplication does not possess the same properties as ordinary multiplication of numbers. Thus, as an illustration will presently show, the product AB is not necessarily the same as BA, where A and B are matrices. In fact, A may be conformable to B for multiplication while B is not conformable to A for multiplication, thus allowing AB to be defined while keeping BA undefined. Furthermore, even if both AB and BA are defined, they may not be the same.

Illustration. Find AB and BA, where

$$A = \begin{pmatrix} a & d \\ b & e \\ c & f \end{pmatrix} \qquad B = \begin{pmatrix} g & i \\ h & j \end{pmatrix}$$

Solution. A is a 3×2 matrix and B is a 2×2 matrix, so A is conformable to B for multiplication. We earlier found that, by the definition of matrix multiplication, we have

$$AB = \begin{pmatrix} ag + dh & ai + dj \\ bg + eh & bi + ej \\ cg + fh & ci + fj \end{pmatrix}$$

When we next proceed to find BA, we see that B is a 2×2 matrix and A is a 3×2 matrix. The number of columns of the first matrix (i.e., B) is not the same as the number of rows of the second matrix (i.e., A), so we conclude that B is not conformable to A for multiplication. Thus BA is undefined.

Illustration. Find AB and BA, where

$$A = \begin{pmatrix} 2 & -1 \\ 1 & -1 \end{pmatrix} \qquad B = \begin{pmatrix} 3 & 2 \\ 0 & 1 \end{pmatrix}$$

Solution. A is a 2×2 matrix and B is a 2×2 matrix. The number of columns of A is equal to the number of rows of B, so A is conformable to B for multiplication. We find

$$AB = \begin{pmatrix} 6 & 3 \\ 3 & 1 \end{pmatrix}$$

We next wish to find BA. The number of columns of B is equal to the number of rows of A, so B is conformable to A for multiplication. We find

$$BA = \begin{pmatrix} 8 & -5 \\ 1 & -1 \end{pmatrix}$$

Thus even though AB and BA are both defined, they are not the same. $AB \neq BA$.

We have seen illustrations where $AB \neq BA$. This, however, does not imply that AB is never equal to BA for matrices. Under special circumstances it may, indeed, be true that $AB = BA$. However, that is certainly not the general case.

Other familiar properties from the algebra of numbers also do not necessarily carry over to the algebra of matrices. Thus if $AB = 0$, where A and B are two matrices and 0 is the null matrix, it does not hold that either $A = 0$ or $B = 0$. This is shown by the following example. Consider the matrices A and B, defined as follows:

$$A = \begin{pmatrix} 2 & -1 \\ -4 & 2 \end{pmatrix} \qquad B = \begin{pmatrix} 3 & 0 \\ 6 & 0 \end{pmatrix}$$

When we compute the product AB, we see that

$$AB = \begin{pmatrix} 0 & 0 \\ 0 & 0 \end{pmatrix}$$

Yet neither A nor B is a zero or null matrix.

These examples serve to illustrate the point that the algebra of matrices is distinct from the algebra of numbers. In performing operations with matrices, we must therefore go back to the definition of the operations. We cannot carry over rules from other algebraic systems unless we prove that they hold for matrices. Some, but not all properties of numbers are applicable for matrices. As an example of a rule that pertains for both numbers and matrices, think of addition, where we have already found that $A + B = B + A$, where A and B are conformable matrices.

It can easily be seen that if any matrix is multiplied by an appropriate identity matrix, the result will be the original matrix. Thus if A is an $m \times n$ matrix,

$$I_m A = A$$

Illustration. Show that $IA = A$, where

$$A = \begin{pmatrix} 5 & 2 \\ 2 & 8 \\ -1 & -1 \end{pmatrix}$$

Solution. A is a 3×2 matrix, so we select the 3×3 identity matrix. We then have

$$IA = \begin{pmatrix} 1 & 0 & 0 \\ 0 & 1 & 0 \\ 0 & 0 & 1 \end{pmatrix} \begin{pmatrix} 5 & 2 \\ 2 & 8 \\ -1 & -1 \end{pmatrix} = \begin{pmatrix} 5 & 2 \\ 2 & 8 \\ -1 & -1 \end{pmatrix}$$

Thus $IA = A$.

We have defined the operations of addition, subtraction, and multiplication for matrices. The operation of division is not defined. Thus we cannot speak of A/B, where A and B are matrices. However, in Section 5.4 we shall show how to find an inverse for certain matrices. Inverses exhibit some of the properties usually found in division, but division as such will remain undefined.

Exercises

1–5. For each exercise at the end of Section 5.1, write the equilibrium equations in matrix form.

6. Find the transpose A' of the following matrices:

a)

$$A = \begin{pmatrix} 6 & 4 & 7 \\ -1 & 0 & -2 \\ 2 & 3 & 5 \end{pmatrix}$$

b)

$$A = \begin{pmatrix} 6 & 4 \\ -1 & 0 \\ 2 & 3 \end{pmatrix}$$

c)

$$A = (2 \quad 4 \quad -1 \quad 0)$$

d)

$$A = \begin{pmatrix} 2 & 4 & -1 & 0 \\ 3 & 1 & 5 & -2 \end{pmatrix}$$

e)

$$A = \begin{pmatrix} 3 & 5 & 1 \\ 1 & 2 & -3 \\ 0 & -1 & 7 \\ -4 & -1 & 2 \end{pmatrix}$$

7. Fill in the missing elements in order to make the matrix
    a)   a symmetric matrix
    b)   a diagonal matrix

$$\begin{pmatrix} 7 & - & - \\ - & -2 & - \\ - & - & 1 \end{pmatrix}$$

8. Fill in the missing elements in order to make the matrix
    a)   a diagonal matrix
    b)   an identity matrix

$$\begin{pmatrix} 1 & 0 & - & - \\ - & - & - & - \\ - & - & - & - \\ - & - & - & - \end{pmatrix}$$

9. Fill in the missing elements in order to make the matrix
    a)   an identity matrix
    b)   a null matrix

$$\begin{pmatrix} - & 0 \\ 0 & - \end{pmatrix}$$

10. Find $A + B$ and give an economic interpretation, where

$$A = \begin{pmatrix} 6 & 4 & 7 \\ 1 & 0 & 2 \\ 2 & 3 & 5 \end{pmatrix} \qquad B = \begin{pmatrix} 2 & 3 & 4 \\ 1 & 0 & 1 \\ 9 & 8 & 5 \end{pmatrix}$$

11. Find $A + B$ and give an economic interpretation:

$$A = \begin{pmatrix} 6 & 4 \\ 1 & 0 \\ 2 & 3 \\ 1 & -3 \end{pmatrix} \qquad B = \begin{pmatrix} -2 & 3 \\ 1 & 0 \\ 9 & -8 \\ 7 & 2 \end{pmatrix}$$

12.   Find $A + B$ and give an economic interpretation:

$$A = \begin{pmatrix} 1 \\ 2 \\ 5 \\ 3 \\ 4 \end{pmatrix} \qquad B = \begin{pmatrix} 2 \\ 7 \\ 3 \\ 1 \\ 4 \end{pmatrix}$$

13.   Find $A + B$ and give an economic interpretation:

$$A = \begin{pmatrix} 6 & 4 & 7 \\ 1 & 0 & 2 \\ 2 & 3 & 5 \end{pmatrix} \qquad B = \begin{pmatrix} 2 & 3 \\ 1 & 0 \\ 9 & 8 \end{pmatrix}$$

14.   Find $A - B$ and give an economic interpretation:

$$A = \begin{pmatrix} 6 & 4 & 7 \\ 1 & 0 & 2 \\ 2 & 3 & 5 \end{pmatrix} \qquad B = \begin{pmatrix} 2 & 3 & 4 \\ 1 & 0 & 1 \\ 0 & 2 & 3 \end{pmatrix}$$

15.   Find $A - B$ and give an economic interpretation:

$$A = \begin{pmatrix} 6 & 4 \\ 1 & 0 \\ 2 & 3 \\ 1 & -3 \end{pmatrix} \qquad B = \begin{pmatrix} -2 & 3 \\ 1 & 0 \\ 9 & -8 \\ 7 & 2 \end{pmatrix}$$

16.   Find $B + A$, where A and B are defined as in Exercise 10.
17.   Find $B - A$, where A and B are defined as in Exercise 15.
18.   Find $8A$ and give an economic interpretation, where A is defined as in Exercise 11.
19.   Find $4A + 2B$, where A and B are defined as in Exercise 10.
20.   Find $4A - 2B$, where A and B are defined as in Exercise 10.
21.   Find AB and BA and give economic interpretations, where A and B are defined as in Exercise 10.
22.   Find AB and BA and give economic interpretations, where A and B are defined as in Exercise 13.
23.   Find AB and BA and give economic interpretations, where A and B are defined as in Exercise 11.
24.   Find AB and BA and give an economic interpretation, where

$$A = \begin{pmatrix} 1 \\ 2 \\ 5 \\ 3 \\ 4 \end{pmatrix} \qquad B = (3 \quad 7 \quad 2 \quad 1 \quad 1)$$

25. Find AB and BA, where

$$A = \begin{pmatrix} 7 & 4 \\ 1 & 0 \\ 6 & 3 \\ 3 & 1 \end{pmatrix} \qquad B = \begin{pmatrix} 1 & 0 & 1 & 5 \\ 2 & 3 & 4 & 8 \end{pmatrix}$$

26. Find AB and BA, where

$$A = \begin{pmatrix} -1 & 0 & 4 \\ 3 & 2 & -3 \end{pmatrix} \qquad B = \begin{pmatrix} 5 & -2 \\ -1 & -4 \end{pmatrix}$$

27. Find IA and AI, where A is defined as in Exercise 10.
28. Find IA and AI, where A is defined as in Exercise 11.
29. Show by the construction of an example that $AB = 0$ does not imply either $A = 0$ or $B = 0$, where A and B are matrices.
30. Prove that $A + B = B + A$, where A and B are any 4×4 matrices. This is known as the commutative law for addition.
31. Prove that $A + (B + C) = (A + B) + C$, where A, B, and C are any 3×3 matrices. This is known as the associative law for addition.
32. Show that $AB = AC$ but that $B \neq C$, where

$$A = \begin{pmatrix} 2 & -1 \\ -4 & 2 \end{pmatrix} \qquad B = \begin{pmatrix} 1 & 2 \\ 3 & 2 \end{pmatrix} \qquad C = \begin{pmatrix} 0 & 1 \\ 1 & 0 \end{pmatrix}$$

33. Prove that $(AB)C = A(BC)$, where A is any 3×2 matrix, B is any 2×4 matrix, and C is any 4×2 matrix. This is known as the associative law for multiplication.
34. Prove that $A(B + C) = AB + AC$, where A is any 3×2 matrix, B is any 2×4 matrix, and C is any 2×4 matrix.
35. Find $(A')'$, where A is defined as in Exercise 6(a).
36. Find $(A + B)'$ and $A' + B'$, where A and B are defined as in Exercise 10.
37. Find $(2A)'$ and $2A'$, where A is defined as in Exercise 6(a).
38. Find $(AB)'$ and $B'A'$, where A and B are defined as in Exercise 13.
39. Prove that $(A')' = A$, where A is any 3×2 matrix.
40. Prove that $(A + B)' = A' + B'$, where A and B are any 3×2 matrices.
41. Prove that $(aA)' = aA'$, where a is any scalar and A is any 3×2 matrix.

SECTION 5·3   DETERMINANTS, LINEAR EQUATIONS, AND CRAMER'S RULE

Every square matrix has a number associated with it that is known as its *determinant*. For 2×2 matrices such as

$$\begin{pmatrix} a_1 & b_1 \\ a_2 & b_2 \end{pmatrix}$$

the determinant is defined as

$$D = \begin{vmatrix} a_1 & b_1 \\ a_2 & b_2 \end{vmatrix} = a_1 b_2 - a_2 b_1$$

Thus a determinant is not the array of numbers, but a single number (or scalar) associated with the array. To distinguish the determinant from the array itself, it is enclosed by single vertical bars instead of parentheses. Determinants are defined only for square matrices.

Illustration.   Consider the following equilibrium conditions.

$$3p_A - 2p_B = 18$$
$$-5p_A + 20p_B = 70$$

The coefficients form a 2×2 matrix, which is

$$\begin{pmatrix} 3 & -2 \\ -5 & 20 \end{pmatrix}$$

The determinant associated with this matrix is

$$D = \begin{vmatrix} 3 & -2 \\ -5 & 20 \end{vmatrix} = 3(20) - (-2)(-5) = 60 - 10 = 50$$

Thus the determinant is a single number, namely 50, while the matrix is the full array of coefficients.

Suppose that we wish to solve a system of two equations in two unknowns. In general form we have the following two equations:

$$a_1 x + b_1 y = k_1$$
$$a_2 x + b_2 y = k_2$$

Multiply the first equation by b_2 and the second by $-b_1$ and add together. We then get

$$a_1 b_2 x + b_1 b_2 y = b_2 k_1$$

$$-a_2 b_1 x - b_1 b_2 y = -b_1 k_2$$

$$\overline{(a_1 b_2 - a_2 b_1)x = b_2 k_1 - b_1 k_2}$$

$$x = \frac{b_2 k_1 - b_1 k_2}{a_1 b_2 - a_2 b_1} \quad \text{provided that} \quad a_1 b_2 - a_2 b_1 \neq 0$$

Next, multiply the first equation by $-a_2$ and the second by a_1 and add. We then have

$$-a_1 a_2 x - a_2 b_1 y = -a_2 k_1$$

$$a_1 a_2 x + a_1 b_2 y = a_1 k_2$$

$$\overline{(a_1 b_2 - a_2 b_1)y = a_1 k_2 - a_2 k_1}$$

$$y = \frac{a_1 k_2 - a_2 k_1}{a_1 b_2 - a_2 b_1} \quad \text{provided that} \quad a_1 b_2 - a_2 b_1 \neq 0$$

If we substitute the values of x and y back into the original equations, we can demonstrate that they check as solutions.

We now note that the solutions can be written in determinant form as

$$x = \frac{\begin{vmatrix} k_1 & b_1 \\ k_2 & b_2 \end{vmatrix}}{\begin{vmatrix} a_1 & b_1 \\ a_2 & b_2 \end{vmatrix}} \quad \text{and} \quad y = \frac{\begin{vmatrix} a_1 & k_1 \\ a_2 & k_2 \end{vmatrix}}{\begin{vmatrix} a_1 & b_1 \\ a_2 & b_2 \end{vmatrix}}$$

provided that

$$\begin{vmatrix} a_1 & b_1 \\ a_2 & b_2 \end{vmatrix} \neq 0$$

This follows from the fact that

$$\begin{vmatrix} a_1 & b_1 \\ a_2 & b_2 \end{vmatrix} = a_1 b_2 - a_2 b_1$$

$$\begin{vmatrix} k_1 & b_1 \\ k_2 & b_2 \end{vmatrix} = b_2 k_1 - b_1 k_2$$

$$\begin{vmatrix} a_1 & k_1 \\ a_2 & k_2 \end{vmatrix} = a_1 k_2 - a_2 k_1$$

We have therefore derived a method for solving two equations in two unknowns by the use of determinants. This is known as *Cramer's rule* for the case of two equations in two unknowns. It is possible to solve for any unknown by taking the ratio of two determinants, where the denominator is the determinant associated with the matrix of coefficients and the numerator is the same determinant except that the column of coefficients of the unknown being sought is replaced by the column of constant terms.

Illustration.   Given the following demand and supply functions for products A and B.

$$q_{d_A} = 10 - p_A + 2p_B \qquad q_{s_A} = 2p_A - 8$$
$$q_{d_B} = 60 + 5p_A - 15p_B \qquad q_{s_B} = 5p_B - 10$$

Find the equilibrium prices for A and B in a competitive market.

Solution.   To achieve equilibrium, quantity demanded must equal quantity supplied for each product. Therefore

$$10 - p_A + 2p_B = 2p_A - 8$$

and

$$60 + 5p_A - 15p_B = 5p_B - 10$$

This is equivalent to

$$3p_A - 2p_B = 18$$
$$-5p_A + 20p_B = 70$$

We now have two equations in two unknowns, that is, p_A and p_B. Cramer's rule tells us that the solutions are given by

$$p_A = \frac{\begin{vmatrix} 18 & -2 \\ 70 & 20 \end{vmatrix}}{\begin{vmatrix} 3 & -2 \\ -5 & 20 \end{vmatrix}} = \frac{360 + 140}{60 - 10} = \frac{500}{50} = \$10$$

and

$$p_B = \frac{\begin{vmatrix} 3 & 18 \\ -5 & 70 \end{vmatrix}}{\begin{vmatrix} 3 & -2 \\ -5 & 20 \end{vmatrix}} = \frac{210 + 90}{60 - 10} = \frac{300}{50} = \$6$$

When these values are inserted into the original equations, it is easily seen that they check.

Notice that in each case the denominator is the determinant associated with the matrix of coefficients, while the numerator is the same determinant except that the column of coefficients of the unknown being sought is replaced by the column of constant terms.

We now turn to 3×3 matrices such as

$$\begin{pmatrix} a_1 & b_1 & c_1 \\ a_2 & b_2 & c_2 \\ a_3 & b_3 & c_3 \end{pmatrix}$$

The determinant associated with this third-order matrix is defined as

$$\begin{vmatrix} a_1 & b_1 & c_1 \\ a_2 & b_2 & c_2 \\ a_3 & b_3 & c_3 \end{vmatrix} = a_1 \begin{vmatrix} b_2 & c_2 \\ b_3 & c_3 \end{vmatrix} - a_2 \begin{vmatrix} b_1 & c_1 \\ b_3 & c_3 \end{vmatrix} + a_3 \begin{vmatrix} b_1 & c_1 \\ b_2 & c_2 \end{vmatrix}$$

Definition. The *minor* of an element of a determinant is the determinant formed by deleting the row and column of the element and retaining the remaining elements of the original array.

Thus, the minor of a_1 is derived by deleting the row and column containing a_1. This yields

$$\begin{vmatrix} b_2 & c_2 \\ b_3 & c_3 \end{vmatrix}$$

as the minor of a_1.

It is now evident that a third-order determinant can be evaluated by multiplying each element of the first column by its minor, provided that the middle term is multiplied by -1. It can also be shown that the same result can be achieved by multiplying each element of *any* column or row by its minor, provided that each term in the ith row and jth column is multiplied by -1 if $i + j$ is odd.

Illustration. Evaluate

$$\begin{vmatrix} 5 & 2 & -1 \\ 4 & 8 & -2 \\ -1 & -1 & 8 \end{vmatrix}$$

Solution.

$$\begin{vmatrix} 5 & 2 & -1 \\ 4 & 8 & -2 \\ -1 & -1 & 8 \end{vmatrix} = 5 \begin{vmatrix} 8 & -2 \\ -1 & 8 \end{vmatrix} - 4 \begin{vmatrix} 2 & -1 \\ -1 & 8 \end{vmatrix} - 1 \begin{vmatrix} 2 & -1 \\ 8 & -2 \end{vmatrix}$$

$$= 5(64 - 2) - 4(16 - 1) - 1(-4 + 8)$$

$$= 5(62) - 4(15) - (4)$$

$$= 310 - 60 - 4 = 246$$

Alternatively, this determinant could be evaluated by taking the minors of any other column or row. Suppose that we take the second row. We then have

$$\begin{vmatrix} 5 & 2 & -1 \\ 4 & 8 & -2 \\ -1 & -1 & 8 \end{vmatrix} = -4 \begin{vmatrix} 2 & -1 \\ -1 & 8 \end{vmatrix} + 8 \begin{vmatrix} 5 & -1 \\ -1 & 8 \end{vmatrix} + 2 \begin{vmatrix} 5 & 2 \\ -1 & -1 \end{vmatrix}$$

$$= -4(16 - 1) + 8(40 - 1) + 2(-5 + 2)$$

$$= -60 + 312 - 6 = 246$$

Notice that the element in the first column of the second row, that is, 4, was multiplied by -1 because the sum of its row and column position, $2 + 1$, is odd; while the element in the second column of the second row, that is, 8, was multiplied by $+1$ because its row and column position, $2 + 2$, is even; and the element in the third column of the second row, that is, -2, was multiplied by -1 because its row and column, $2 + 3$, is odd.

In general, the sign associated with the minor of any element of a determinant can easily be determined by the following checkerboard approach

$$\begin{vmatrix} + & - & + & - & \cdots \\ - & + & - & + & \cdots \\ + & - & + & - & \cdots \end{vmatrix}$$

In other words, the sign alternates, whether vertically or horizontally, beginning with a plus in the upper left-hand corner.

We can express the expansion of a determinant in a slightly different form if we introduce a new term. The *cofactor of any element a_{ij}* is the signed minor associated with that element. The appropriate sign is as previously indicated $(-1)^{i+j}$, where i and j indicate the row and column position, respectively, of the element a_{ij}. Thus a third-order determinant can be evaluated by multiplying each element of any row or each element of any column by its cofactor. This is, in effect, what was done in the previous illustration.

Suppose now that we wish to solve a system of three equations in three unknowns, given by

$$a_1 x + b_1 y + c_1 z = k_1$$
$$a_2 x + b_2 y + c_2 z = k_2$$
$$a_3 x + b_3 y + c_3 z = k_3$$

We can now use Cramer's rule applied to three equations in three unknowns. We can solve for any unknown by taking the ratio of two determinants, where the denominator is the determinant associated with the matrix of coefficients and the numerator is the same determinant except that the column of coefficients of the unknown being sought is replaced by the column of constant terms.

Thus we have

$$x = \frac{\begin{vmatrix} k_1 & b_1 & c_1 \\ k_2 & b_2 & c_2 \\ k_3 & b_3 & c_3 \end{vmatrix}}{\begin{vmatrix} a_1 & b_1 & c_1 \\ a_2 & b_2 & c_2 \\ a_3 & b_3 & c_3 \end{vmatrix}} \qquad y = \frac{\begin{vmatrix} a_1 & k_1 & c_1 \\ a_2 & k_2 & c_2 \\ a_3 & k_3 & c_3 \end{vmatrix}}{\begin{vmatrix} a_1 & b_1 & c_1 \\ a_2 & b_2 & c_2 \\ a_3 & b_3 & c_3 \end{vmatrix}} \qquad z = \frac{\begin{vmatrix} a_1 & b_1 & k_1 \\ a_2 & b_2 & k_2 \\ a_3 & b_3 & k_3 \end{vmatrix}}{\begin{vmatrix} a_1 & b_1 & c_1 \\ a_2 & b_2 & c_2 \\ a_3 & b_3 & c_3 \end{vmatrix}}$$

provided that

$$\begin{vmatrix} a_1 & b_1 & c_1 \\ a_2 & b_2 & c_2 \\ a_3 & b_3 & c_3 \end{vmatrix} \neq 0$$

Illustration.   Given the following demand and supply functions for products A, B, and C.

$$q_{d_A} = 100 - 2p_A - 2p_B + p_C \qquad q_{s_A} = 3p_A - 65$$
$$q_{d_B} = 135 - 4p_A - 3p_B + 2p_C \qquad q_{s_B} = 5p_B - 95$$
$$q_{d_C} = 140 + p_A + p_B - 2p_C \qquad q_{s_C} = 6p_C - 10$$

Find equilibrium prices for A, B, and C.

Solution. To achieve equilibrium, quantity demanded must equal quantity supplied for each product. Therefore

$$100 - 2p_A - 2p_B + p_C = 3p_A - 65$$

$$135 - 4p_A - 3p_B + 2p_C = 5p_B - 95$$

$$140 + p_A + p_B - 2p_C = 6p_C - 10$$

This is equivalent to

$$5p_A + 2p_B - p_C = 165$$

$$4p_A + 8p_B - 2p_C = 230$$

$$-p_A - p_B + 8p_C = 150$$

We have already solved this system of equations in Section 5.1 by the process of elimination. Let us now solve by using Cramer's rule. The solutions are given by

$$p_A = \frac{\begin{vmatrix} 165 & 2 & -1 \\ 230 & 8 & -2 \\ 150 & -1 & 8 \end{vmatrix}}{\begin{vmatrix} 5 & 2 & -1 \\ 4 & 8 & -2 \\ -1 & -1 & 8 \end{vmatrix}} \qquad p_B = \frac{\begin{vmatrix} 5 & 165 & -1 \\ 4 & 230 & -2 \\ -1 & 150 & 8 \end{vmatrix}}{\begin{vmatrix} 5 & 2 & -1 \\ 4 & 8 & -2 \\ -1 & -1 & 8 \end{vmatrix}}$$

$$p_C = \frac{\begin{vmatrix} 5 & 2 & 165 \\ 4 & 8 & 230 \\ -1 & -1 & 150 \end{vmatrix}}{\begin{vmatrix} 5 & 2 & -1 \\ 4 & 8 & -2 \\ -1 & -1 & 8 \end{vmatrix}}$$

Now

$$\begin{vmatrix} 165 & 2 & -1 \\ 230 & 8 & -2 \\ 150 & -1 & 8 \end{vmatrix} = 165 \begin{vmatrix} 8 & -2 \\ -1 & 8 \end{vmatrix} - 230 \begin{vmatrix} 2 & -1 \\ -1 & 8 \end{vmatrix} + 150 \begin{vmatrix} 2 & -1 \\ 8 & -2 \end{vmatrix}$$

$$= 165(64 - 2) - 230(16 - 1) + 150(-4 + 8)$$

$$= 165(62) - 230(15) + 150(4)$$

$$= 10,230 - 3450 + 600$$

$$= 7380$$

$$\begin{vmatrix} 5 & 165 & -1 \\ 4 & 230 & -2 \\ -1 & 150 & 8 \end{vmatrix} = 5\begin{vmatrix} 230 & -2 \\ 150 & 8 \end{vmatrix} - 4\begin{vmatrix} 165 & -1 \\ 150 & 8 \end{vmatrix} - 1\begin{vmatrix} 165 & -1 \\ 230 & -2 \end{vmatrix}$$

$$= 5(1840 + 300) - 4(1320 + 150) - (-330 + 230)$$

$$= 5(2140) - 4(1470) - (-100)$$

$$= 10,700 - 5880 + 100$$

$$= 4920$$

$$\begin{vmatrix} 5 & 2 & 165 \\ 4 & 8 & 230 \\ -1 & -1 & 150 \end{vmatrix} = 5\begin{vmatrix} 8 & 230 \\ -1 & 150 \end{vmatrix} - 4\begin{vmatrix} 2 & 165 \\ -1 & 150 \end{vmatrix} - 1\begin{vmatrix} 2 & 165 \\ 8 & 230 \end{vmatrix}$$

$$= 5(1200 + 230) - 4(300 + 165) - (460 - 1320)$$

$$= 5(1430) - 4(465) - (-860)$$

$$= 7150 - 1860 + 860$$

$$= 6150$$

and we have in an earlier illustration found that

$$\begin{vmatrix} 5 & 2 & -1 \\ 4 & 8 & -2 \\ -1 & -1 & 8 \end{vmatrix} = 246$$

It then follows that

$$p_A = \frac{7380}{246} = \$30$$

$$p_B = \frac{4920}{246} = \$20$$

$$p_C = \frac{6150}{246} = \$25$$

To check these values, we insert them back into the original equations and see that the equations are satisfied.

We can now generalize to matrices of any order such as

$$\begin{pmatrix} a_{11} & a_{12} & a_{13} & \cdots & a_{1n} \\ a_{21} & a_{22} & a_{23} & \cdots & a_{2n} \\ a_{31} & a_{32} & a_{33} & \cdots & a_{3n} \\ \vdots & \vdots & \vdots & & \vdots \\ a_{n1} & a_{n2} & a_{n3} & \cdots & a_{nn} \end{pmatrix}$$

The determinant associated with this $n \times n$ matrix is

$$
\begin{vmatrix}
a_{11} & a_{12} & a_{13} & \cdots & a_{1n} \\
a_{21} & a_{22} & a_{23} & \cdots & a_{2n} \\
a_{31} & a_{32} & a_{33} & \cdots & a_{3n} \\
\vdots & \vdots & \vdots & & \vdots \\
a_{n1} & a_{n2} & a_{n3} & \cdots & a_{nn}
\end{vmatrix}
$$

$$
= a_{11}
\begin{vmatrix}
a_{22} & a_{23} & \cdots & a_{2n} \\
a_{32} & a_{33} & \cdots & a_{3n} \\
\vdots & \vdots & & \vdots \\
a_{n2} & a_{n3} & \cdots & a_{nn}
\end{vmatrix}
- a_{21}
\begin{vmatrix}
a_{12} & a_{13} & \cdots & a_{1n} \\
a_{32} & a_{33} & \cdots & a_{3n} \\
\vdots & \vdots & & \vdots \\
a_{n2} & a_{n3} & \cdots & a_{nn}
\end{vmatrix}
$$

$$
+ a_{31}
\begin{vmatrix}
a_{12} & a_{13} & \cdots & a_{1n} \\
a_{22} & a_{23} & \cdots & a_{2n} \\
\vdots & \vdots & & \vdots \\
a_{n2} & a_{n3} & \cdots & a_{nn}
\end{vmatrix}
\cdots
$$

$$
+ (-1)^{n+1} a_{n1}
\begin{vmatrix}
a_{12} & a_{13} & \cdots & a_{1n} \\
a_{22} & a_{23} & \cdots & a_{2n} \\
a_{32} & a_{33} & \cdots & a_{3n} \\
\vdots & \vdots & & \vdots \\
a_{n-1,2} & a_{n-1,3} & \cdots & a_{n-1,n}
\end{vmatrix}
$$

Thus a determinant of any order can be evaluated by multiplying each element of the first column by its minor, providing that every alternate term is multiplied by -1. An equivalent way of expressing the same idea is that a determinant of any order can be evaluated by multiplying every element of the first column by its cofactor. An identical result will ensue if any other column or row is used instead of the first column.

Illustration. Evaluate

$$
\begin{vmatrix}
2 & -1 & 0 & 2 \\
1 & -2 & 1 & -1 \\
-1 & 0 & -1 & -1 \\
0 & 1 & 0 & 1
\end{vmatrix}
$$

Solution. By the method of minors or cofactors, the above determinant is equal to

$$
2
\begin{vmatrix}
-2 & 1 & -1 \\
0 & -1 & -1 \\
1 & 0 & 1
\end{vmatrix}
- 1
\begin{vmatrix}
-1 & 0 & 2 \\
0 & -1 & -1 \\
1 & 0 & 1
\end{vmatrix}
$$

$$
- 1
\begin{vmatrix}
-1 & 0 & 2 \\
-2 & 1 & -1 \\
1 & 0 & 1
\end{vmatrix}
- 0
\begin{vmatrix}
-1 & 0 & 2 \\
-2 & 1 & -1 \\
0 & -1 & -1
\end{vmatrix}
$$

Notice that we multiply each term of the first column by its minor and also multiply each alternate term by -1. We then evaluate each of the above determinants:

$$\begin{vmatrix} -2 & 1 & -1 \\ 0 & -1 & -1 \\ 1 & 0 & 1 \end{vmatrix} = -2 \begin{vmatrix} -1 & -1 \\ 0 & 1 \end{vmatrix} - 0 \begin{vmatrix} 1 & -1 \\ 0 & 1 \end{vmatrix} + 1 \begin{vmatrix} 1 & -1 \\ -1 & -1 \end{vmatrix}$$

$$= -2(-1) - 0 + 1(-1-1) = 2 - 2 = 0$$

$$\begin{vmatrix} -1 & 0 & 2 \\ 0 & -1 & -1 \\ 1 & 0 & 1 \end{vmatrix} = -1 \begin{vmatrix} -1 & -1 \\ 0 & 1 \end{vmatrix} - 0 \begin{vmatrix} 0 & 2 \\ 0 & 1 \end{vmatrix} + 1 \begin{vmatrix} 0 & 2 \\ -1 & -1 \end{vmatrix}$$

$$= -1(-1) - 0 + 1(0+2) = 1 + 2 = 3$$

$$\begin{vmatrix} -1 & 0 & 2 \\ -2 & 1 & -1 \\ 1 & 0 & 1 \end{vmatrix} = -1 \begin{vmatrix} 1 & -1 \\ 0 & 1 \end{vmatrix} - 2 \begin{vmatrix} 0 & 2 \\ 0 & 1 \end{vmatrix} + 1 \begin{vmatrix} 0 & 2 \\ 1 & -1 \end{vmatrix}$$

$$= -1(1) - 2(0) + 1(0-2) = -1 - 2 = -3$$

Therefore the original determinant is equal to

$$2(0) - 1(3) - 1(-3) - 0 = -3 + 3 = 0$$

Cramer's rule can be generalized to find the solutions of n linear equations in n unknowns. Solutions can be written as

$$X_j = \frac{|A_j|}{|A|} \quad \text{provided that} \quad |A| \neq 0$$

where X_j is the jth unknown, $|A|$ is the determinant arising from the coefficient matrix, and $|A_j|$ is the determinant of the coefficient matrix, where the coefficients of X_j are replaced by the constant terms.

Thus any unknown can be solved for by taking the ratio of two determinants. The denominator is the determinant associated with the matrix of coefficients, and the numerator is the same determinant except that the column of coefficients of the unknown being sought is replaced by the column of constant terms.

This process will guarantee a unique solution for all variables as long as the determinant associated with the coefficient matrix, that is, $|A|$, is not equal to zero. In the event that $|A| = 0$, however, Cramer's rule has no meaning, but this does not necessarily mean that no solutions exist. We shall, in fact, consider this case in Section 5.5.

We now state a number of theorems concerning determinants that are frequently very useful.

Theorem 1.   The value of a determinant is unchanged if corresponding rows and columns are interchanged.

Illustration.   It can easily be verified that

$$
\begin{vmatrix} 5 & 2 & -1 \\ 4 & 8 & -2 \\ -1 & -1 & 8 \end{vmatrix} \text{ and } \begin{vmatrix} 5 & 4 & -1 \\ 2 & 8 & -1 \\ -1 & -2 & 8 \end{vmatrix}
$$

have the same value.

Theorem 2.   If all the elements of any column or row of a determinant are zero, the value of the determinant is zero.
Proof.   Such a determinant could be evaluated by multiplying each element of the zero column or row by its respective minor. But because each term in the expansion would then include a factor of zero, the value of the determinant will be zero.

Theorem 3.   If two columns or rows of a determinant are interchanged, the sign of the determinant is reversed.

Illustration.   It can easily be verified that the determinants

$$
\begin{vmatrix} 5 & 2 & -1 \\ 4 & 8 & -2 \\ -1 & -1 & 8 \end{vmatrix} \text{ and } \begin{vmatrix} 5 & -1 & 2 \\ 4 & -2 & 8 \\ -1 & 8 & -1 \end{vmatrix}
$$

are the negatives of each other.

Theorem 4.   If two columns or rows of a determinant are identical or proportional, the value of the determinant is zero.

Illustration.   It can easily be verified that

$$
\begin{vmatrix} 5 & 5 & -1 \\ 4 & 4 & -2 \\ -1 & -1 & 8 \end{vmatrix} = 0 \text{ and } \begin{vmatrix} 15 & 5 & -1 \\ 12 & 4 & -2 \\ -3 & -1 & 8 \end{vmatrix} = 0
$$

Theorem 5.   If each of the elements of a column or row of a determinant is multiplied by some number K, the value of the determinant is multiplied by K.

Proof. Select the column or row whose terms have been multiplied by K. Multiply each such element by its respective minor, taking into account the proper sign to be attached in each case. The result is the value of the determinant where each element in a column or row has been multiplied by K. The value of the original determinant can be found by multiplying each element of the same column or row by its respective minor, taking into account the proper signs. The expansion of the original determinant will therefore involve the same terms as the expansion of the determinant where each term in a column or row has been multiplied by K, except that in the latter case each term in the expansion will have an additional factor of K. Thus the entire determinant will be multiplied by K.

Illustration.   It can easily be verified that

$$\begin{vmatrix} 15 & 5 & -1 \\ 12 & 4 & -2 \\ -3 & -1 & 8 \end{vmatrix} = 3 \begin{vmatrix} 5 & 5 & -1 \\ 4 & 4 & -2 \\ -1 & -1 & 8 \end{vmatrix}$$

Theorem 6.   If each element of any column (or row) of a determinant is multiplied by some number K and then added to the corresponding element of any other column (or row), the value of the determinant is unchanged.

Illustration.   Consider the following determinant:

$$\begin{vmatrix} 5 & 2 & -1 \\ 4 & 8 & -2 \\ -1 & -1 & 8 \end{vmatrix}$$

If we multiply each term of the third column by -2 and then add to the corresponding terms of the first column, we have

$$\begin{vmatrix} 7 & 2 & -1 \\ 8 & 8 & -2 \\ -17 & -1 & 8 \end{vmatrix}$$

It can easily be verified that this determinant has the same value as the original determinant.

It is possible, through judicious use of Theorem 6, to reduce substantially the computations involved in evaluating determinants. The basic aim is to convert any determinant to a determinant of equivalent value, but with zeros as elements in some column or row. This diminishes the number of minors that have to be evaluated.

Illustration.   Evaluate

$$\begin{vmatrix} 5 & 2 & -1 \\ 4 & 8 & -2 \\ -1 & -1 & 8 \end{vmatrix}$$

If we select any column or row of the determinant as given, we would have to evaluate three minor determinants. Instead, let us attempt to convert this determinant to one that has two zeros in the first column. To do this, multiply each element of the third row by 5 and add to the corresponding elements of the first row. We get

$$\begin{vmatrix} 0 & -3 & 39 \\ 4 & 8 & -2 \\ -1 & -1 & 8 \end{vmatrix}$$

Now multiply each element of the third row by 4 and add to the second row. We get

$$\begin{vmatrix} 0 & -3 & 39 \\ 0 & 4 & 30 \\ -1 & -1 & 8 \end{vmatrix}$$

We shall now expand this determinant by selecting the first column and its minors. But because we have zeros in the first two elements of the column, the determinant is simply

$$-1\begin{vmatrix} -3 & 39 \\ 4 & 30 \end{vmatrix} = -1(-90 - 156) = 246$$

The method just outlined is especially useful in higher-order determinants.

Illustration.   We have earlier evaluated

$$\begin{vmatrix} 2 & -1 & 0 & 2 \\ 1 & -2 & 1 & -1 \\ -1 & 0 & -1 & -1 \\ 0 & 1 & 0 & 1 \end{vmatrix}$$

But we had to consider a number of third-order minor determinants. We can more easily find its value by first multiplying each element of the third row by 2 and adding to the corresponding elements of the first row, which yields

$$\begin{vmatrix} 0 & -1 & -2 & 0 \\ 1 & -2 & 1 & -1 \\ -1 & 0 & -1 & -1 \\ 0 & 1 & 0 & 1 \end{vmatrix}$$

Next add each term of the second row to those of the third row, which yields

$$\begin{vmatrix} 0 & -1 & -2 & 0 \\ 1 & -2 & 1 & -1 \\ 0 & -2 & 0 & -2 \\ 0 & 1 & 0 & 1 \end{vmatrix}$$

Expanding the determinant by taking the signed minors of the first column, we see that the determinant is equal to

$$-1 \begin{vmatrix} -1 & -2 & 0 \\ -2 & 0 & -2 \\ 1 & 0 & 1 \end{vmatrix}$$

This, in turn, can be expanded by finding the signed minors of the second column. We then have

$$\begin{vmatrix} -1 & -2 & 0 \\ -2 & 0 & -2 \\ 1 & 0 & 1 \end{vmatrix} = 2 \begin{vmatrix} -2 & -2 \\ 1 & 1 \end{vmatrix} = 2(-2 + 2) = 0$$

Therefore the original determinant $= -1(0) = 0$, which is the result we obtained earlier.

Exercises

1–5. Given the demand and supply functions of Exercises 1–5, Section 5.1, find the equilibrium price in each case by using Cramer's rule to solve a system of equations.

6. The following two determinants are equal. Fill in the missing element.

$$\begin{vmatrix} 2 & -3 & 4 & 1 \\ 0 & 1 & 5 & -7 \\ 3 & -4 & 2 & 4 \\ 7 & 2 & 1 & 0 \end{vmatrix} \qquad \begin{vmatrix} 2 & 0 & 3 & 7 \\ -3 & 1 & -4 & 2 \\ 4 & — & 2 & 1 \\ 1 & -7 & 4 & 0 \end{vmatrix}$$

7. The following two determinants are equal. Fill in the missing elements.

$$\begin{vmatrix} 4 & 1 & 3 & 2 \\ -1 & 3 & 0 & 6 \\ 2 & -1 & 1 & -3 \\ -2 & 0 & 1 & 2 \end{vmatrix} \qquad \begin{vmatrix} 1 & 4 & 2 & 3 \\ 3 & -1 & 6 & — \\ -1 & — & -3 & 1 \\ 0 & -2 & 2 & 1 \end{vmatrix}$$

8. Find the value of the following determinant without expanding:

$$\begin{vmatrix} 3 & 3 & 6 & -12 \\ 1 & 5 & 3 & -20 \\ -1 & 0 & 1 & 0 \\ 0 & -7 & 5 & 28 \end{vmatrix}$$

9. Find the value of the following determinant without expanding:

$$\begin{vmatrix} 2 & 1 & 3 \\ 3 & 2 & -1 \\ 8 & 4 & 12 \end{vmatrix}$$

10. Evaluate by use of Theorem 6:

$$\begin{vmatrix} 2 & 4 & 1 \\ 3 & -2 & 3 \\ -1 & 2 & -2 \end{vmatrix}$$

11. Evaluate by use of Theorem 6:

$$\begin{vmatrix} 2 & 1 & 3 \\ 4 & 4 & 2 \\ -3 & 4 & -2 \end{vmatrix}$$

12. Evaluate by use of Theorem 6:

$$\begin{vmatrix} 3 & 1 & -1 & 2 \\ -1 & 2 & 2 & 1 \\ 1 & 0 & 1 & -1 \\ 2 & -1 & 2 & 1 \end{vmatrix}$$

SECTION 5·4   THE SOLUTION OF A SYSTEM OF LINEAR EQUATIONS BY THE INVERSE MATRIX METHOD

Singular and Nonsingular Matrices

A square matrix A is said to be *singular* if its determinant is equal to zero, that is, $|A| = 0$. A square matrix A is *nonsingular* if its determinant is not equal to zero, that is, $|A| \neq 0$.

Illustration.   A 3×3 matrix A is given by

$$A = \begin{pmatrix} 4 & 2 & 0 \\ 1 & 2 & 1 \\ 0 & 3 & 2 \end{pmatrix}$$

Is it a singular matrix?

Solution.   We evaluate the determinant of A using minors:

$$|A| = \begin{vmatrix} 4 & 2 & 0 \\ 1 & 2 & 1 \\ 0 & 3 & 2 \end{vmatrix} = 4\begin{vmatrix} 2 & 1 \\ 3 & 2 \end{vmatrix} - 1\begin{vmatrix} 2 & 0 \\ 3 & 2 \end{vmatrix}$$

$$= 4(1) - 1(4) = 0$$

Thus A is a singular matrix

Rank of a Matrix

The rank of a matrix is the order of the largest nonsingular square submatrix contained within it. A submatrix is derived from a matrix by striking out any number of rows or columns.

Illustration.   Find the rank of the following matrix:

$$A = \begin{pmatrix} 1 & 7 \\ 2 & 0 \\ -1 & -3 \end{pmatrix}$$

Solution.   The largest square submatrix contained within A is a 2×2 matrix, which is derived by striking out any of the three rows. Suppose that we consider the following submatrix:

$$\begin{pmatrix} 1 & 7 \\ 2 & 0 \end{pmatrix}$$

Its determinant is

$$\begin{vmatrix} 1 & 7 \\ 2 & 0 \end{vmatrix} = 1 - 14 = -13 \neq 0$$

Therefore the matrix A is said to be of rank 2.

Illustration.   Find the rank of the following matrix:

$$A = \begin{pmatrix} 1 & 2 & 0 & 1 \\ 7 & -2 & 2 & -2 \\ 1 & -6 & 0 & -3 \end{pmatrix}$$

Solution.   The largest square submatrix contained within A is a 3×3 matrix, which is derived by striking out any of the four columns. Suppose that we strike out the first column. We get the following matrix:

$$\begin{pmatrix} 2 & 0 & 1 \\ -2 & 2 & -2 \\ -6 & 0 & -3 \end{pmatrix}$$

The determinant of this matrix, it can easily be verified, is equal to zero:

$$\begin{vmatrix} 2 & 0 & 1 \\ -2 & 2 & -2 \\ -6 & 0 & -3 \end{vmatrix} = 0$$

We can, however, strike out the second column instead, in which case we get the following matrix:

$$\begin{pmatrix} 1 & 0 & 1 \\ 7 & 2 & -2 \\ 1 & 0 & -3 \end{pmatrix}$$

The determinant of this matrix, it can be verified, is not equal to zero:

$$\begin{vmatrix} 1 & 0 & 1 \\ 7 & 2 & -2 \\ 1 & 0 & -3 \end{vmatrix} = -8 \neq 0$$

There is some 3×3 nonsingular matrix within A, so the rank of A is 3.

Illustration. Find the rank of the following matrix:

$$A = \begin{pmatrix} 4 & 2 & 0 \\ 1 & 2 & 1 \\ 0 & 3 & 2 \end{pmatrix}$$

Solution. The largest square submatrix contained within A is A itself, which is a 3×3 matrix. We have evaluated its determinant in an earlier illustration and found

$$\begin{vmatrix} 4 & 2 & 0 \\ 1 & 2 & 1 \\ 0 & 3 & 2 \end{vmatrix} = 0$$

Let us therefore consider any 2×2 submatrix contained within A. Strike out the first row and first column and get

$$\begin{pmatrix} 2 & 1 \\ 3 & 2 \end{pmatrix}$$

Its determinant is easily evaluated to be nonzero:

$$\begin{vmatrix} 2 & 1 \\ 3 & 2 \end{vmatrix} = 1 \neq 0$$

Therefore A is of rank two.

Inverse of a Matrix

The *inverse* of a square matrix A is another square matrix denoted by A^{-1} such that $AA^{-1} = I = A^{-1}A$; that is, postmultiplication or premultiplication of A by its inverse yields the identity matrix.

For some purposes the inverse of a matrix may be viewed as analogous to the reciprocal of a number. Any number multiplied by its reciprocal yields the number 1; that is,

$$a \cdot \frac{1}{a} = 1$$

Similarly, a square matrix multiplied by its inverse is equal to the identity matrix; that is,

$$AA^{-1} = I$$

Furthermore, division of any number a by another number b can be viewed as multiplication of a by the reciprocal of b; that is,

$$a \div b = a \cdot \frac{1}{b}$$

For matrices, too, we can talk about the multiplication of a matrix A by the inverse of B, that is, AB^{-1}, and consider it as analogous to division. The analogy is, however, imperfect. For one thing, inverses are defined only for square matrices. Second, we shall soon see that, under certain conditions, the inverse matrix is undefined even for a square matrix. Therefore, as noted in Section 5.2, we do not talk about the division of matrices as such, although we do consider inverses of matrices.

To find the inverse of a square matrix A, we follow a three-step procedure.
1) Begin with the matrix A and replace each element by its cofactor.
2) Transpose the resulting matrix. This result is known as the *adjoint* of A.
3) Divide each element of the adjoint by the value of the determinant $|A|$. The result is the inverse.

In the event that the determinant $|A| = 0$, that is, A is a singular matrix, then an inverse cannot be found. Singular matrices thus do not have inverses.

Illustration.   Find the inverse of

$$A = \begin{pmatrix} 5 & 2 & -1 \\ 4 & 8 & -2 \\ -1 & -1 & 8 \end{pmatrix}$$

Solution. We first find the matrix of cofactors, remembering that the cofactor of any element is its signed minor. The cofactor matrix is therefore

$$\begin{pmatrix} 62 & -30 & 4 \\ -15 & 39 & 3 \\ 4 & 6 & 32 \end{pmatrix}$$

The next step is to transpose the cofactor matrix, which will give the adjoint. This yields

$$\text{adjoint} = \begin{pmatrix} 62 & -15 & 4 \\ -30 & 39 & 6 \\ 4 & 3 & 32 \end{pmatrix}$$

We have already computed the determinant of A in the previous section. We found that

$$|A| = 246$$

Therefore

$$A^{-1} = \begin{pmatrix} \dfrac{62}{246} & \dfrac{-15}{246} & \dfrac{4}{246} \\ \dfrac{-30}{246} & \dfrac{39}{246} & \dfrac{6}{246} \\ \dfrac{4}{246} & \dfrac{3}{246} & \dfrac{32}{246} \end{pmatrix}$$

This result can be checked by computing the product AA^{-1} or $A^{-1}A$ and verifying that it is equal to I.

We now consider a system of n linear equations in n unknowns.

$$a_{11}x_1 + a_{12}x_2 + \cdots + a_{1n}x_n = k_1$$

$$a_{21}x_1 + a_{22}x_2 + \cdots + a_{2n}x_n = k_2$$

$$\vdots \qquad \vdots \qquad \qquad \vdots \qquad \vdots$$

$$a_{n1}x_1 + a_{n2}x_2 + \cdots + a_{nn}x_n = k_n$$

This system can be written as

$$AX = K$$

where A is the $n \times n$ coefficient matrix

$$\begin{pmatrix} a_{11} & a_{12} & \cdots & a_{1n} \\ a_{21} & a_{22} & \cdots & a_{2n} \\ \vdots & \vdots & & \vdots \\ a_{n1} & a_{n2} & \cdots & a_{nn} \end{pmatrix}$$

X is the $n \times 1$ vector of unknowns

$$X = \begin{pmatrix} X_1 \\ X_2 \\ \vdots \\ X_n \end{pmatrix}$$

and K is the $n \times 1$ vector of constant terms

$$K = \begin{pmatrix} K_1 \\ K_2 \\ \vdots \\ K_n \end{pmatrix}$$

The reader should verify that when the matrix multiplication AX is performed and the product set equal to the matrix K, the result will be identical to the system of equations given above.

If we next multiply each side of the equation

$$AX = K$$

by A^{-1} (assuming that the inverse of A exists), we get

$$A^{-1}AX = A^{-1}K$$

or

$$IX = A^{-1}K$$

and

$$X = A^{-1}K$$

This means that we need only derive A^{-1} in order to arrive at the solutions of the system of equations. Once having found A^{-1}, we would take the product $A^{-1}K$ and set it equal to X. Because X is an $n \times 1$ vector containing only $X_1, X_2, \ldots, X_n$ terms, we would get the value of any X_i by merely equating it to the corresponding element in the $n \times 1$ vector $A^{-1}K$. (The reader can verify that $A^{-1}K$ is an $n \times 1$ vector by noting that A^{-1} is an $n \times n$ matrix and K is an $n \times 1$ matrix.)

The calculation of inverse matrices therefore provides us with an alternative to Cramer's rule for finding unique solutions to a system of equations. It can be seen that this method, like Cramer's rule, applies only if A is a nonsingular matrix, because if $|A| = 0$, the inverse matrix A^{-1} does not exist. We shall, however, consider this special case where $|A| = 0$ in the next section.

Illustration.   Given the following demand and supply functions for products A, B. and C.

$$q_{d_A} = 100 - 2p_A - 2p_B + p_C \qquad q_{s_A} = 3p_A - 65$$

$$q_{d_B} = 135 - 4p_A - 3p_B + 2p_C \qquad q_{s_B} = 5p_B - 95$$

$$q_{d_C} = 140 + p_A + p_B - 2p_C \qquad q_{s_C} = 6p_C - 10$$

Find equilibrium prices for A, B, and C.

Solution.   To achieve equilibrium, quantity demanded must equal quantity supplied for each product. Therefore

$$100 - 2p_A - 2p_B + \quad p_C = 3p_A - 65$$

$$135 - 4p_A - 3p_B + 2p_C = 5p_B - 95$$

$$140 + \quad p_A + \quad p_B - 2p_C = 6p_C - 10$$

This is equivalent to

$$5p_A + 2p_B - p_C = 165$$

$$4p_A + 8p_B - 2p_C = 230$$

$$-p_A - p_B + 8p_C = 150$$

We have already solved this system of equations in previous sections both by the method of elimination and by Cramer's rule. We now show how to arrive at solutions through use of the inverse method.

The three equations in three unknowns, p_A, p_B, and p_C, can be written in the form

$$AP = K$$

where

$$A = \begin{pmatrix} 5 & 2 & -1 \\ 4 & 8 & -2 \\ -1 & -1 & 8 \end{pmatrix}$$

$$P = \begin{pmatrix} p_A \\ p_B \\ p_C \end{pmatrix}$$

$$K = \begin{pmatrix} 165 \\ 230 \\ 150 \end{pmatrix}$$

This is equivalent to

$$P = A^{-1}K$$

It is therefore necessary to find the inverse matrix A^{-1}. We have already done this in the previous illustration, when we showed that if

$$A = \begin{pmatrix} 5 & 2 & -1 \\ 4 & 8 & -2 \\ -1 & -1 & 8 \end{pmatrix}$$

then

$$A^{-1} = \begin{pmatrix} \dfrac{62}{246} & \dfrac{-15}{246} & \dfrac{4}{246} \\[2mm] \dfrac{30}{246} & \dfrac{39}{246} & \dfrac{6}{246} \\[2mm] \dfrac{4}{246} & \dfrac{3}{246} & \dfrac{32}{246} \end{pmatrix}$$

We can therefore write

$$\begin{pmatrix} p_A \\ p_B \\ p_C \end{pmatrix} = \begin{pmatrix} \dfrac{62}{246} & \dfrac{-15}{246} & \dfrac{4}{246} \\[2mm] \dfrac{-30}{246} & \dfrac{39}{246} & \dfrac{6}{246} \\[2mm] \dfrac{4}{246} & \dfrac{3}{246} & \dfrac{32}{246} \end{pmatrix} \begin{pmatrix} 165 \\ 230 \\ 150 \end{pmatrix}$$

The next step is to perform the indicated multiplication of the matrices on the right-hand side of the equation, that is, $A^{-1}K$. A^{-1} is a 3×3 matrix, while K is a 3×1 matrix, so the matrices are conformable for multiplication. The result will be a 3×1 matrix as follows:

$$\begin{pmatrix} \dfrac{62}{246} & \dfrac{-15}{246} & \dfrac{4}{246} \\[2mm] \dfrac{-30}{246} & \dfrac{39}{246} & \dfrac{6}{246} \\[2mm] \dfrac{4}{246} & \dfrac{3}{246} & \dfrac{32}{246} \end{pmatrix} \begin{pmatrix} 165 \\ 230 \\ 150 \end{pmatrix} = \begin{pmatrix} 30 \\ 20 \\ 25 \end{pmatrix}$$

This leads us to

$$\begin{pmatrix} p_A \\ p_B \\ p_C \end{pmatrix} = \begin{pmatrix} 30 \\ 20 \\ 25 \end{pmatrix}$$

By the definition of equality of matrices, we conclude that

$$p_A = 30$$

$$p_B = 20$$

$$p_C = 25$$

which is, of course, the same set of solutions arrived at by use of the process of elimination and Cramer's rule.

The advantage of using matrix methods may not be readily apparent to the reader at the outset. However, continued use of mathematical theory and methods will show the matrix approach to be most efficient. One indication of this is the compact notation made possible through matrix terminology, that is, $AX = K$. More important are the operations that can be performed with systems of equations expressed in such simple form and the ease of dealing with systems involving large numbers of variables.

We should, however, note that matrix algebra is applicable only to linear equations. While many other types of equations invariably arise, it is often possible to approximate such relationships and equalities by linear equations. This makes it possible to use matrix algebra in a wide range of applications.

Exercises

1. Determine whether each of the following matrices is singular:

a)

$$\begin{pmatrix} 2 & 5 & 1 \\ -1 & -10 & 7 \\ 3 & 7 & 2 \end{pmatrix}$$

b)

$$\begin{pmatrix} 1 & -1 & 4 & 0 \\ -1 & 2 & 2 & -1 \\ 2 & 0 & 1 & 0 \\ 4 & 3 & 0 & -1 \end{pmatrix}$$

c)

$$\begin{pmatrix} 4 & 2 & 8 & -2 \\ 2 & 3 & 0 & 1 \\ 0 & 1 & -1 & 0 \\ -1 & 2 & -3 & -1 \end{pmatrix}$$

d)

$$\begin{pmatrix} 3 & -15 \\ -2 & 10 \end{pmatrix}$$

e)

$$\begin{pmatrix} 2 & -1 \\ 1 & 1 \end{pmatrix}$$

f)

$$\begin{pmatrix} 3 & -1 & 2 \\ 1 & 2 & 1 \\ 0 & 4 & 0 \end{pmatrix}$$

g)

$$\begin{pmatrix} 2 & 1 & 7 & 0 & 2 \\ 1 & 2 & 1 & 0 & -1 \\ -1 & -2 & 2 & 0 & 1 \\ 3 & 4 & -3 & 0 & 3 \\ 2 & 1 & 1 & 0 & -2 \end{pmatrix}$$

2. Find the rank of each of the matrices in Exercise 1.
3. Find the rank of each of the following matrices:

a)

$$\begin{pmatrix} 2 & 3 & 1 \\ -1 & 4 & -2 \end{pmatrix}$$

b)

$$\begin{pmatrix} 2 & 7 & 1 \\ -1 & 1 & 3 \\ 0 & -1 & 2 \\ 1 & 2 & -1 \\ 3 & 0 & 1 \end{pmatrix}$$

c)

$$\begin{pmatrix} -1 & 2 & 0 & 3 \\ 2 & 1 & 3 & 0 \\ 1 & -1 & -3 & 0 \end{pmatrix}$$

d)

$$\begin{pmatrix} 7 \\ -4 \\ 3 \end{pmatrix}$$

e)

$$\begin{pmatrix} 3 & 5 \\ -6 & -10 \\ 1 & -1 \end{pmatrix}$$

f)

$$\begin{pmatrix} 2 & -6 & 10 & 4 \\ 1 & -3 & 5 & 2 \\ -1 & 3 & -5 & -2 \end{pmatrix}$$

4. Find the inverse of the following matrices:

a)

$$\begin{pmatrix} 1 & -1 & 4 & 0 \\ -1 & 2 & 2 & -1 \\ 2 & 0 & 1 & 0 \\ 4 & 3 & 0 & -1 \end{pmatrix}$$

b)

$$\begin{pmatrix} 2 & -1 \\ 1 & 1 \end{pmatrix}$$

c)

$$\begin{pmatrix} 3 & -1 & 2 \\ 1 & 2 & 1 \\ 0 & 4 & 0 \end{pmatrix}$$

d)

$$\begin{pmatrix} 2 & 5 & 1 \\ -1 & -10 & 7 \\ 3 & 7 & 2 \end{pmatrix}$$

e)

$$\begin{pmatrix} 3 & -2 \\ -5 & 20 \end{pmatrix}$$

f)

$$\begin{pmatrix} -1 & 2 & 0 & 3 \\ 1 & -1 & -3 & 0 \\ 2 & 1 & 3 & 0 \end{pmatrix}$$

g)

$$\begin{pmatrix} -1 & -2 & 3 \\ 2 & 0 & 1 \\ 1 & -1 & -2 \end{pmatrix}$$

5. Find the adjoint of the following matrices:

a)

$$\begin{pmatrix} 1 & -1 & 4 & 0 \\ -1 & 2 & 2 & -1 \\ 2 & 0 & 1 & 0 \\ 4 & 3 & 0 & -1 \end{pmatrix}$$

b)

$$\begin{pmatrix} 2 & -1 \\ 1 & 1 \end{pmatrix}$$

c)

$$\begin{pmatrix} 3 & -1 & 2 \\ 1 & 2 & 1 \\ 0 & 4 & 0 \end{pmatrix}$$

d)

$$\begin{pmatrix} 3 & -2 \\ -5 & 20 \end{pmatrix}$$

e)

$$\begin{pmatrix} -1 & -2 & 3 \\ 2 & 0 & 1 \\ 1 & -1 & -2 \end{pmatrix}$$

6. Prove that the adjoint of a 3×3 diagonal matrix is also a diagonal matrix.

7. Given the following demand and supply functions for products A and B.

$$q_{d_A} = 10 - p_A + 2p_B \qquad q_{s_A} = 2p_A - 8$$
$$q_{d_B} = 60 + 5p_A - 15p_B \qquad q_{s_B} = 5p_B - 10$$

Find the equilibrium prices by using the inverse matrix method of solving a system of equations.

8–12. Given the demand and supply functions of Exercises 1–5, Section 5.1. Find the equilibrium price in each case by using the inverse matrix method of solving a system of equations.

SECTION 5·5   GENERAL CONDITIONS FOR THE SOLUTION OF m LINEAR EQUATIONS IN n UNKNOWNS

In previous sections we considered systems of equations involving n equations in n unknowns (i.e., the number of equations and unknowns were the same). We saw that we could arrive at solutions either through Cramer's rule or the inverse matrix method, provided that the determinant of the coefficient matrix is not equal to zero. We now wish to consider the general case of m equations in n unknowns and determine under what conditions a solution can or cannot be found. Furthermore, even in the case of n equations in n unknowns, we must determine whether solutions are possible when the determinant of the coefficient matrix is equal to zero.

In this connection, it is interesting to note that we frequently encounter statements to the effect that solutions to linear equations exist as long as the number of equations is equal to the number of unknowns. This is not strictly the case, because we have already encountered difficulty in finding solutions when the coefficient matrix has a zero determinant. Moreover, even when the number of unknowns is greater than the number of equations, it may be possible to arrive at some form of solution, even if not a unique solution.

Let us consider any system of m linear equations in n unknowns $X_1, X_2, \ldots, X_n$.

$$a_{11}X_1 + a_{12}X_2 + \cdots + a_{1n}X_n = K_1$$

$$a_{21}X_2 + a_{22}X_2 + \cdots + a_{2n}X_n = K_2$$

$$\vdots \qquad \vdots \qquad \vdots \qquad \vdots \qquad \vdots$$

$$a_{m1}X_1 + a_{m2}X_2 + \cdots + a_{mn}X_n = K_m$$

When such a system has a solution (i.e., a set of values for the unknowns that satisfies all the equations), it is said to be *consistent*. If there is no set of values that simultaneously satisfies all the equations, the system is said to be *inconsistent*.

The system of equations given above can be written in matrix terminology as

$$AX = K$$

where A is the $m \times n$ matrix

$$A = \begin{pmatrix} a_{11} & a_{12} & \cdots & a_{1n} \\ a_{21} & a_{22} & \cdots & a_{2n} \\ \vdots & \vdots & \vdots & \vdots \\ a_{m1} & a_{m2} & \cdots & a_{mn} \end{pmatrix}$$

X is the $n \times 1$ matrix

$$X = \begin{pmatrix} X_1 \\ X_2 \\ \vdots \\ X_n \end{pmatrix}$$

and K is the $m \times 1$ matrix

$$K = \begin{pmatrix} K_1 \\ K_2 \\ \vdots \\ K_m \end{pmatrix}$$

The matrix A is known as the *coefficient matrix*. If we now consider a matrix containing all the terms of the coefficient matrix and also the constant terms, we have the following:

$$\begin{pmatrix} a_{11} & a_{12} & \cdots & a_{1n} & K_1 \\ a_{21} & a_{22} & \cdots & a_{2n} & K_2 \\ \vdots & \vdots & & \vdots & \vdots \\ a_{m1} & a_{m2} & \cdots & a_{mn} & K_m \end{pmatrix}$$

This $m \times n + 1$ matrix is known as the *augmented matrix*.

We now state the fundamental theorem concerning systems of linear equations.

Theorem. A system of m linear equations in n unknowns, $AX = K$, is consistent if and only if the coefficient matrix and the augmented matrix have the same rank.

This theorem enables us to distinguish among several possibilities.

1. If the number of variables is equal to the number of unknowns, then the coefficient matrix will be an $n \times n$ matrix and the augmented matrix an $n \times n + 1$ matrix. In the event that the determinant of the coefficient matrix is nonzero, that is, $|A| \neq 0$, the rank of the coefficient matrix is n. The augmented matrix is the coefficient matrix with one additional column and no additional rows, so the highest-order nonzero determinant contained within it will be an $n \times n$ determinant. The augmented matrix will consequently also be of rank n. This case is illustrated by the systems of equations given in previous sections. We saw that the solution can be found by using Cramer's rule or the inverse matrix method. The solution arrived at will be unique; that is, there will be only one set of values for $X_1, X_2, \ldots, X_n$ that will satisfy the system of equations.

2. Assume again that the number of variables and unknowns are equal
    (*n*), but that the determinant of the coefficient matrix is zero, that is,
    $|A| = 0$. The rank of the coefficient matrix is therefore *r*, which is
    some number smaller than *n*. There are now two possibilities: (a) If
    the augmented matrix is also of rank *r*, then by the theorem above,
    the system is consistent. In this event, it is possible to solve for *r*
    variables in terms of the remaining $n - r$ variables. This means that if
    the $n - r$ variables are assigned any values whatever, the remaining *r*
    variables would be determined. In fact, there would then ensue an
    infinite number of solutions—one for each set of assigned values.
    (b) If the augmented matrix is not of rank *r*, then the system is incon-
    sistent; that is, there is no solution. We have thus seen that if
    $|A| = 0$, there may be infinitely many solutions or no solution at all.
3. If the number of variables (*n*) is greater than the number of equations
    (*m*), then the rank of the coefficient matrix will be *r*, which is some
    number smaller than *n*. There are then two possibilities: (a) If the
    augmented matrix is also of rank *r*, the system is consistent and it is
    possible to solve for *r* variables in terms of the remaining $n - r$
    variables. (b) If the augmented matrix is not of rank *r*, the system is
    inconsistent.
4. If the number of variables (*n*) is smaller than the number of equations
    (*m*) and the rank of the coefficient matrix is *n*, then there are two
    possibilities: (a) If the augmented matrix is also of rank *n*, the system
    is consistent and a unique solution exists. (b) If the augmented matrix
    is not of rank *n*, the system is inconsistent.
5. Assume again that the number of variables (*n*) is smaller than the
    number of equations (*m*), but that the rank of the coefficient matrix is
    r, which is some number smaller than *n*. There are again two possibili-
    ties: (a) If the augmented matrix is also of rank *r*, the system is
    consistent and it is possible to solve for *r* variables in terms of the
    remaining $n - r$ variables. (b) If the augmented matrix is not of rank
    r, the system is inconsistent.

The following examples illustrate these general principles or rules.

Illustration 1.   Does the following system of equations have a solution?

$$5p_A + 2p_B - p_C = 165$$
$$4p_A + 8p_B - 2p_C = 230$$
$$-p_A - p_B + 8p_C = 150$$

Solution.   We have a system of three equations in three unknowns. The determinant of the coefficient matrix is

$$\begin{vmatrix} 5 & 2 & -1 \\ 4 & 8 & -2 \\ -1 & -1 & 8 \end{vmatrix} \neq 0$$

Therefore, by Rule 1 above, the system has a unique solution, which can be found by use of Cramer's rule or by the inverse matrix method. In fact, we have already found the solution to this system in Sections 5.3 and 5.4.

Illustration 2.   Does the following system of equations have a solution?

$$3X_1 + 4X_2 - X_3 = 100$$

$$5X_1 + 2X_2 - 3X_3 = 150$$

$$X_1 + 6X_2 + X_3 = 50$$

Solution.   This is a system of three equations in three unknowns. The determinant of the coefficient matrix is

$$\begin{vmatrix} 3 & 4 & -1 \\ 5 & 2 & -3 \\ 1 & 6 & 1 \end{vmatrix} = 0$$

Rule 2 therefore applies. The rank of the coefficient matrix is 2. The augmented matrix is

$$\begin{pmatrix} 3 & 4 & -1 & 100 \\ 5 & 2 & -3 & 150 \\ 1 & 6 & 1 & 50 \end{pmatrix}$$

All possible 3×3 determinants turn out to be equal to zero. The rank of the augmented matrix is therefore 2, which is the same rank as the coefficient matrix. The system is therefore consistent. In this case, $n = 3$ and $r = 2$ ($r = $ rank). Thus two variables can be solved for in terms of the third. This is done as follows. Let us solve for X_2 and X_3 in terms of X_1. We have

$$4X_2 - X_3 = -3X_1 + 100 \tag{1}$$

$$2X_2 - 3X_3 = -5X_1 + 150 \tag{2}$$

First, eliminate X_3 by multiplying the first equation by 3 and then subtracting the second equation from the first. This gives

$$10X_2 = -4X_1 + 150$$

$$X_2 = -\tfrac{2}{5}X_1 + 15$$

We have thus expressed X_2 in terms of X_1. Second, eliminate X_2 by multiplying equation (2) by 2 and then subtracting it from equation (1). We have

$$5X_3 = 7X_1 - 200$$

$$X_3 = \tfrac{7}{5}X_1 - 40$$

This gives us X_3 in terms of X_1. If we take together both expressions

$$X_2 = -\tfrac{2}{5}X_1 + 15$$

$$X_3 = \tfrac{7}{5}X_1 - 40$$

we have a *complete solution* of the system. For any particular value of X_1, X_2 and X_3 will assume fixed values. For example, if $X_1 = 5$, we would find $X_2 = 13$, $X_3 = -33$. This would be a *particular solution* of the system. There would, in fact, be infinitely many particular solutions.

Both the complete solution and the particular solutions can be verified by substituting back into the original equations.

Illustration 3.   Does the following system of equations have a solution?

$$3X_1 + 4X_2 - X_3 = 100$$

$$5X_1 + 2X_2 - 3X_3 = 150$$

$$X_1 + 6X_2 + X_3 = 75$$

Solution.   This is again a system of three equations in three unknowns. The determinant of the coefficient matrix is, as in the previous illustration, equal to zero. The rank of the coefficient matrix is 2. The augmented matrix is

$$\begin{pmatrix} 3 & 4 & -1 & 100 \\ 5 & 2 & -3 & 150 \\ 1 & 6 & 1 & 75 \end{pmatrix}$$

If we take the determinant formed by the elements of the last three columns, we have

$$\begin{vmatrix} 4 & -1 & 100 \\ 2 & -3 & 150 \\ 6 & 1 & 75 \end{vmatrix} \neq 0$$

Therefore the rank of the augmented matrix is 3. The coefficient and augmented matrices have different ranks, so the system is inconsistent. No solution is possible.

Illustration 4.   Does the following system of equations have a solution?

$$2X_1 - X_2 + 3X_3 = 200$$
$$X_1 + 3X_2 - 2X_3 = 120$$

Solution.   This is a system of two equations in three unknowns. Rule 3 therefore applies. The rank of the coefficient matrix is easily seen to be 2. The augmented matrix is also of rank 2. The system is consistent, and it is possible to solve for two variables in terms of the remaining unknowns. Let us solve for X_1 and X_2 in terms of X_3. We have

$$2X_1 - X_2 = -3X_3 + 200$$
$$X_1 + 3X_2 = 2X_3 + 120$$

Multiply the second equation by 2 and subtract it from the first to get

$$-7X_2 = -7X_3 - 40$$
$$X_2 = X_3 + \tfrac{40}{7}$$

We have thus expressed X_2 in terms of X_3. To find X_1 in terms of X_3, we eliminate X_2 by multiplying the first equation by 3 and adding to the second, which gives

$$7X_1 = -7X_3 + 720$$
$$X_1 = -X_3 + \tfrac{720}{7}$$

If we take together

$$X_2 = X_3 + \tfrac{40}{7}$$
$$X_1 = -X_3 + \tfrac{720}{7}$$

we have a complete solution of the system, which can be verified by substituting back into the original equations.

Illustration 5.   Does the following system of equations have a solution?

$$2X_1 - X_2 = 50$$
$$3X_1 + 4X_2 = -200$$
$$X_1 + 2X_2 = -100$$

Solution.   This is a system of three equations in three unknowns. The ranks of the coefficient and augmented matrices are each 2. Rule 4 applies, and the system is consistent. The rank is the same as the number of unknowns, so a unique solution exists and can be found by elimination, Cramer's rule, or the inverse matrix method.

Let us use Cramer's rule to find the actual solution. If we work with the first two equations, we get

$$X_1 = \frac{\begin{vmatrix} 50 & -1 \\ -200 & 4 \end{vmatrix}}{\begin{vmatrix} 2 & -1 \\ 3 & 4 \end{vmatrix}} = \frac{0}{11} = 0$$

$$X_2 = \frac{\begin{vmatrix} 2 & 50 \\ 3 & -200 \end{vmatrix}}{\begin{vmatrix} 2 & -1 \\ 3 & 4 \end{vmatrix}} = \frac{-550}{11} = -50$$

These solutions, that is, $X_1 = 0$, $X_2 = -50$, can be verified by substituting back into the three given equations.

Exercises

Determine whether each of the following systems of equations have any solutions, and find them wherever possible.

1. $3X_1 + 4X_2 = 44$
    $2X_1 + 2X_2 = 24$
2. $3X_1 + 15X_2 = 50$
    $2X_1 + 10X_2 = 40$
3. $3X_1 + 15X_2 = 60$
    $2X_1 + 10X_2 = 40$
4. $2X_1 + X_2 + 3X_3 = 16$
    $3X_1 + 2X_2 - X_3 = 24$
    $8X_1 + 4X_2 + 12X_3 = 64$
5. $5X_1 + 2X_2 - X_3 = 20$
    $3X_1 - 2X_2 + 2X_3 = 15$
    $X_1 + 5X_2 - 3X_3 = 10$
6. $2X_1 + X_2 + 3X_3 = 16$
    $3X_1 + 2X_2 - X_3 = 24$
    $8X_1 + 4X_2 + 12X_3 = 48$
7. $3X_1 + 3X_2 + 6X_3 - 12X_4 = 60$
    $X_1 + 5X_2 + 3X_3 - 20X_4 = 30$
    $-X_1 + X_3 = 10$
    $-7X_2 + 5X_3 + 28X_4 = 50$

8. $3X_1 + 3X_2 + 6X_3 - 12X_4 = 50$
$X_1 + 5X_2 + 3X_3 - 20X_4 = 40$
$-X_1 + X_3 = 8$
$-7X_2 + 5X_3 + 28X_4 = 20$

9. $X_1 + 2X_2 - X_3 + X_4 = 15$
$2X_1 + 3X_2 + X_3 - 2X_4 = 0$
$-X_1 - X_2 + 3X_3 + 2X_4 = 25$
$3X_1 - 2X_2 + 5X_3 - X_4 = 21$

10. $5X_1 + 2X_2 - X_3 = 20$
$3X_1 - 2X_2 + 2X_3 = 15$

11. $2X_1 + 8X_2 - 6X_3 = 10$
$3X_1 + 12X_2 - 9X_3 = 15$

12. $2X_1 + 8X_2 - 6X_3 = 10$
$3X_1 + 12X_2 - 9X_3 = 15$

13. $2X_1 + X_2 + 3X_3 = 16$
$3X_1 + 2X_2 - X_3 = 24$

14. $3X_1 + 3X_2 + 6X_3 - 12X_4 = 50$
$X_1 + 5X_2 + 3X_3 - 20X_4 = 40$
$-X_1 + X_3 = 8$

15. $3X_1 + 3X_2 + 6X_3 - 12X_4 = 50$
$X_1 + 5X_2 + 2X_3 - 20X_4 = 40$
$-X_1 - 2X_3 = 8$

16. $3X_1 + 3X_2 + 6X_3 - 12X_4 = 36$
$X_1 + 5X_2 + 2X_3 - 20X_4 = 12$
$-X_1 - 2X_3 = -12$

17. $5X_1 + 2X_2 = 20$
$3X_1 - 2X_2 = 15$
$X_1 + 5X_2 = 10$

18. $5X_1 + 2X_2 = 35$
$3X_1 - 2X_2 = 21$
$X_1 + 5X_2 = 7$

19. $-X_1 + 2X_2 + 3X_4 - 2X_5 = 25$
$2X_1 + X_2 + 3X_3 + X_5 = 18$
$X_1 - X_2 - 3X_3 - X_5 = 4$

20. $5X_1 + 2X_2 - X_3 + X_4 = 22$
$3X_1 - 2X_2 + 2X_3 + 2X_4 = 19$

21. $6X_1 + 15X_2 = 20$
$2X_1 + 5X_2 = 15$
$8X_1 + 20X_2 = 10$

22. $6X_1 + 15X_2 = 30$
$2X_1 + 5X_2 = 10$
$8X_1 + 20X_2 = 40$

23. $5X_1 + 2X_2 = 20$

$$3X_1 - 2X_2 = 15$$
$$X_1 + 5X_2 = 10$$
$$2X_1 + 3X_2 = 12$$

24. $5X_1 + 2X_2 = 35$
$$3X_1 - 2X_2 = 21$$
$$X_1 + 5X_2 = 7$$
$$2X_1 + 3X_2 = 14$$

25. $6X_1 + 15X_2 = 30$
$$2X_1 + 5X_2 = 10$$
$$8X_1 + 20X_2 = 40$$
$$4X_1 + 10X_2 = 20$$

26. $2X_1 + 7X_2 + X_3 = 70$
$$-X_1 + X_2 + 3X_3 = 10$$
$$X_1 + 2X_2 - X_3 = 20$$
$$3X_1 + X_3 = 0$$

27. $2X_1 + 7X_2 + X_3 = 70$
$$-X_1 + X_2 + 3X_3 = 10$$
$$X_1 + 2X_2 - X_3 = 20$$
$$3X_1 + X_3 = 5$$

28. $2X_1 + 7X_2 - 4X_3 = 70$
$$-X_1 + X_2 + 2X_3 = 10$$
$$X_1 + 2X_2 - 2X_3 = 20$$
$$3X_1 - 6X_3 = 0$$

29. $2X_1 + 7X_2 - 4X_3 = 70$
$$-X_1 + X_2 + 2X_3 = 10$$
$$X_1 + 2X_2 - 2X_3 = 20$$
$$3X_1 - 6X_3 = 0$$
$$4X_1 + X_2 - 8X_3 = 10$$

30. $2X_1 + 7X_2 - 4X_3 = 70$
$$-X_1 + X_2 + 2X_3 = 10$$
$$X_1 + 2X_2 - 2X_3 = 20$$
$$3X_1 - 6X_3 = 0$$
$$4X_1 + X_2 - 8X_3 = 15$$

31. $5X_1 + 2X_2 - X_3 = 0$
$$3X_1 - 2X_2 + 2X_3 = 0$$
$$X_1 + 5X_2 - 3X_3 = 0$$

32. $5X_1 + 15X_2 - X_3 = 0$
$$3X_1 + 9X_2 + 2X_3 = 0$$
$$X_1 + 3X_2 - 3X_3 = 0$$

33. $3X_1 + 3X_2 + 6X_3 - 12X_4 = 0$
$$X_1 + 5X_2 + 3X_3 - 20X_4 = 0$$
$$-X_1 + X_3 = 0$$
$$-7X_2 + 5X_3 + 28X_4 = 0$$

34.
$$X_1 + 2X_2 - X_3 + X_4 = 0$$
$$2X_1 + 3X_2 + X_3 - 2X_4 = 0$$
$$-X_1 - X_2 + 3X_3 + 2X_4 = 0$$
$$3X_1 - 2X_2 + 5X_3 - X_4 = 0$$

35.
$$2X_1 + X_2 + 3X_3 = 0$$
$$3X_1 + 2X_2 - X_3 = 0$$
$$8X_1 + 4X_2 + 12X_3 = 0$$

36.
$$3X_1 + 4X_2 = 0$$
$$2X_1 + 2X_2 = 0$$

37.
$$3X_1 + 15X_2 = 0$$
$$2X_1 + 10X_2 = 0$$

38.
$$5X_1 + 2X_2 = 0$$
$$3X_1 - 2X_2 = 0$$
$$X_1 + 5X_2 = 0$$
$$2X_1 + 3X_2 = 0$$

CHAPTER

6

LIMITS AND CONTINUITY

The study of mathematics, like the Nile, begins in minuteness, but ends in magnificence.

—C. C. Colton

In the preceding chapter we considered functions and their values at specific points. We now consider the behavior of functions in the neighborhood of selected points. This leads to the concept of limits and continuity. In this chapter we shall develop and apply these concepts to economic problems.

SECTION 6·1 LIMITS

Consider the following supply function: $q_s = p^2 - 1$. From this functional relation we derive the following table of values, showing the quantity that will be supplied at each price:

p	$1.00	$1.10	$1.20	$1.30	$1.40	$1.50	$1.60	$1.70
q_s	0	0.21	0.44	0.69	0.96	1.25	1.56	1.89

p	$1.80	$1.90	$1.95	$1.96	$1.97	$1.98	$1.99	$2.00
q_s	2.24	2.61	2.80	2.84	2.88	2.92	2.96	3.00

Suppose that p can never reach $2.00 because of price controls. We then ask what will happen to quantity supplied as the price is raised higher and higher, say, from $1.00 to 1.10 to 1.20 to ... 1.90, and so on. In other words, price is increased in the neighborhood of $2.00, but not quite up to $2.00. From the table of values we see that as price increases so does quantity supplied, until it eventually comes closer and closer to 3 units. But it will never actually reach 3 units.

We note that we can get the supply as close as we desire to 3.00 units merely by raising the price closer and closer to $2.00. Thus if we want to be within 0.20 of $q_s = 3.00$, we raise p to $1.95; if we want to be still closer, say, within 0.10 of $q_s = 3.00$, we can raise p to $1.98; and so on. (A similar process would occur if we were to lower price from somewhat above \$2.00 closer and closer to \$2.00 but never reaching \$2.00. This situation might occur if we had a minimum price enforced by the government.)

We then say that the *limit* of $q_s = f(p)$ as p approaches \$2.00 is equal to 3.00 units. This can be written as $f(p) \to 3.00$, as $p \to \$2.00$, or as

$$\lim_{p \to \$2.00} f(p) = 3.00$$

Note that we are not concerned with the value of $f(p)$ when $p = \$2.00$. Indeed, we have specifically excluded this value. We are concerned only with the values of $f(p)$ when p is close to but not equal to \$2.00.

Analogously, we define the limit of any function $f(x)$ as x approaches a in the following manner:

$$\lim_{x \to a} f(x) = L$$

if for $x \neq a, f(x)$ is as close as we desire to L when x is sufficiently close to a.

Note: See the appendix to this chapter for a more formal and rigorous expression of limits.

Illustration.   Consider the demand function given by

$$q_d = 50 - 4p - 2p^2$$

Find $\lim_{p \to 3} q_d$

Solution.   As p moves closer and closer to 3, $4p$ approaches 12 and $2p^2$ approaches 18. Therefore $f(p) = 50 - 4p - 2p^2$ will be as close as we desire to $50 - 12 - 18 = 20$ as long as p is sufficiently close to 3. Therefore,

$$\lim_{p \to 3} f(p) = 20.$$

Note that

$$\lim_{p \to 3} f(p) = f(3).$$

But this need not always be true.

Illustration.

$$q_s = \frac{p^2 + 2p - 3}{p - 1}$$

Find $\lim\limits_{p \to 1} q_s$

We notice that as $p \to 1$, the numerator $\to 0$ and the denominator also $\to 0$. But we cannot determine what the whole fraction approaches, because $\frac{0}{0}$ does not yield a value. But we do notice that the numerator $p^2 + 2p - 3$ can be factored into $(p - 1)(p + 3)$. Thus we have

$$q_s = \frac{p^2 + 2p - 3}{p - 1} = \frac{(p - 1)(p + 3)}{p - 1}$$

Now $(p - 1)$ can be canceled from both the numerator and denominator provided that $p \neq 1$ (if $p = 1$ this would mean dividing by zero, which is not permissible). Therefore we can say that if $p \neq 1$, then

$$q_s = \frac{(p - 1)(p + 3)}{p - 1} = p + 3 \quad \text{and} \quad \lim_{p \to 1} q_s = 4$$

Notice that when $p = 1$ the function q_s is undefined. Yet we can speak of $\lim\limits_{p \to 1} q_s$ because we are not concerned with the value of q_s at $p = 1$, but only with its value as p comes close to 1 without being equal to 1.

SECTION 6·2 INFINITE LIMITS

In the preceding examples we have seen that the functions we considered approached definite limits as $x \to a$. But it may happen that as $x \to a$ the function $f(x)$ may not approach a definite limit, but instead continue to increase without end. We denote this by saying that

$$\lim_{x \to a} f(x) = \infty$$

The symbol ∞ is read "infinity." It is not a number, but simply a term that indicates the behavior of the variable.

Illustration. Consider the long-run supply function of a constant-cost industry.

$$q_s = p^2 + \frac{1}{(p - 10)^2}$$

Let us find $\lim\limits_{p \to 10} q_s$. We are interested in the behavior of the supply function as the price moves closer and closer to $p = 10$ without actually reaching $p = 10$. We note that as p moves closer and closer to $p = 10$, the quantity supplied increases without end. We can make supply as great as we desire simply by increasing the price to make it sufficiently close to $p = 10$. Therefore,

$$\lim_{p \to 10} \left(p^2 + \frac{1}{(p - 10)^2} \right) = \infty$$

Illustration.   Consider the demand function

$$q_d = \frac{100}{(p - 1)^2}$$

Find

$$\lim_{p \to 1} q_d.$$

We are interested in knowing the behavior of the demand function as the price of the product comes closer and closer to $p = 1$ without actually reaching $p = 1$. We notice that as p moves closer and closer to $p = 1$, the quantity demanded increases without end. We can achieve a demand as great as we desire simply by reducing the price sufficiently close to $p = 1$. Therefore

$$\lim_{p \to 1} \frac{100}{(p - 1)^2} = \infty$$

To be precise, we say that

$$\lim_{x \to a} f(x) = \infty$$

if $f(x)$ is greater than an arbitrarily large positive number when x is sufficiently close to a.

In a similar manner, it may happen that as $x \to a, f(x)$ may become larger and larger negatively without end. We therefore say that

$$\lim_{x \to a} f(x) = -\infty$$

if $f(x)$ becomes larger and larger negatively as $x \to a$.

Illustration.

$$\lim_{x \to 4} \frac{-5}{(x - 4)^2} = -\infty$$

SECTION 6·3   LIMITS FOR AN INFINITE VARIABLE

Until this point we have considered how a function behaves as x approaches some definite number. We may also inquire as to what occurs to a function as x gets larger and larger without end.

Consider the supply function

$$q_s = 100 - \frac{100}{p}$$

which applies in the very short run. As p becomes larger and larger, q_s moves closer and closer to 100 because $(100/p) \to 0$. We can get q_s as close as we please to 100 simply by making p large enough. Thus, if we want q_s to be within 1 unit of 100, we set $p = \$100$. If we want q_s still closer to 100, say, to within $\frac{1}{10}$ of a unit, then we set $p = \$1000$. We therefore conclude that

$$\lim_{p \to \infty} \left(100 - \frac{100}{p}\right) = 100$$

In more general terms, we say that the

$$\lim_{x \to \infty} f(x) = L$$

if $f(x)$ is as close as we desire to L whenever x is sufficiently large.

Illustration.   Consider the demand function

$$q_d = \frac{100}{(p - 1)^2}$$

$\lim_{p \to \infty} q_d = 0$, because as p gets larger and larger,

$$\frac{100}{(p - 1)^2} \to 0$$

Exercises

1. $q_s = (p^2 - 3)$ Find $\lim_{p \to 3} q_s$

2. $q_d = 4 - p^2$ Find $\lim_{p \to 2} q_d$

3. $q_d = \dfrac{p + 2}{p}$ Find $\lim_{p \to 4} q_d$

4. $q_s = \left(\dfrac{9-1}{p^2}\right)$ Find $\lim\limits_{p \to 3} q_s$

5. $q_d = \dfrac{2}{p^2 + 4}$ Find $\lim\limits_{p \to \infty} q_d$

6. $q_d = 2 + \dfrac{3}{p^2}$ Find $\lim\limits_{p \to \infty} q_d$

7. $q_s = \dfrac{p^2 - 4}{p - 2}$ Find $\lim\limits_{p \to 2} q_s$

8. $q_d = \dfrac{p - 1}{p^2 - 1}$ Find $\lim\limits_{p \to 1} q_d$

9. $q_s = \dfrac{p^2 - p}{p^2 - 1}$ Find $\lim\limits_{p \to 1} q_s$

10. $q_s = \dfrac{3p^2 + p - 1}{2p^2 - 2p + 1}$ Find $\lim\limits_{p \to \infty} q_s$

(*Hint:* Divide numerator and denominator by p^2.)

11. $q_s = 5p + \dfrac{1}{(4 - p)^2}$ Find $\lim\limits_{p \to 4} q_s$

12. $q_d = \dfrac{4000}{p^4}$ Find $\lim\limits_{p \to 0} q_d$

SECTION 6·4 OPERATIONS WITH LIMITS

We state the following theorems without proof. In all cases we assume that

$$\lim_{x \to a} f(x) \quad \text{and} \quad \lim_{x \to a} g(x)$$

exist.

Theorem 1.

$$\lim_{x \to a}[f(x) + g(x)] = \lim_{x \to a} f(x) + \lim_{x \to a} g(x)$$

In other words, the limit of a sum of functions is the sum of the limits of the individual functions.

Theorem 2.

$$\lim_{x \to a}[f(x)g(x)] = \lim_{x \to a} f(x) \lim_{x \to a} g(x)$$

that is, the limit of the product of functions is the product of the limits of the individual functions.

Theorem 3.

$$\lim_{x \to a} \frac{f(x)}{g(x)} = \frac{\lim_{x \to a} f(x)}{\lim_{x \to a} g(x)} \quad \text{where} \quad \lim_{x \to a} g(x) \neq 0$$

that is, the limit of the quotient of functions is the quotient of the limits of the individual functions.

Theorem 4.

$$\lim_{x \to a}[f(x)]^n = \left[\lim_{x \to a} f(x)\right]^n$$

that is, the limit of a power of a function is the power of the limit of the function.

Illustration.

$$\lim_{p \to 2} \frac{3p^3 - p + 2}{p^2 + 4} = \frac{\lim_{p \to 2}(3p^3 - p + 2)}{\lim_{p \to 2}(p^2 + 4)}$$

$$= \frac{\lim_{x \to 2}(3p^3) + \lim_{x \to 2}(-p) + \lim_{x \to 2}(2)}{\lim_{x \to 2}(p^2) + \lim_{x \to 2}(4)}$$

$$= \frac{24 - 2 + 2}{4 + 4} = \frac{24}{8} = 3$$

Exercises

1. $q_s = 2p^2 - p + 4$ Find $\lim_{p \to 4} q_s$

2. $q_s = p + \dfrac{1}{p}$ Find $\lim_{p \to 2} q_s$

3. $q_s = \dfrac{p - 1}{p + 1}$ Find $\lim\limits_{p \to 0} q_s$

4. $q_d = \dfrac{p^2 + 1}{p^2 + p + 1}$ Find $\lim\limits_{p \to 3} q_d$

5. $q_s = p^2 + 1 - \dfrac{1}{p - 2}$ Find $\lim\limits_{p \to 5} q_s$

6. $q_d = 100 - \dfrac{p - 1}{p^2}$ Find $\lim\limits_{p \to 10} q_d$

7. $q_s = p - 4 + \sqrt{p + 1}$ Find $\lim\limits_{p \to 8} q_s$

8. $q_s = 5p - \sqrt{p^2 - 4}$ Find $\lim\limits_{p \to 2} q_s$

9. $q_d = \dfrac{3}{p^2 + 1}$ Find $\lim\limits_{p \to \infty} q_d$

SECTION 6·5   CONTINUITY

Definition. A function $f(x)$ is *continuous* at $x = a$ if $f(a)$ exists, $f(x)$ approaches some limit as x approaches a, and

$$\lim_{x \to a} f(x) = f(a)$$

A function that is not continuous at $x = a$ is said to be *discontinuous* at $x = a$.

Note that a function can be continuous at certain points and discontinuous at other points. If within a certain interval $f(x)$ is continuous at all values of x, then we say that $f(x)$ is continuous in the interval. If it is stated that $f(x)$ is continuous without any further specification, then this is taken to mean that it is continuous for all values of x.

Illustration 1. We have already considered the supply function $q_s = p^2 - 1$. We showed that

$$\lim_{p \to 2}(p^2 - 1) = 3.$$

We also know that $f(2) = 3$. Thus

$$\lim_{p \to 2} f(p) = f(2)$$

Therefore $f(p)$ is continuous at $p = 2$. We could also take

$$\lim_{p \to a} f(p)$$

for any a, and we would see that

$$\lim_{p \to a} f(p) = f(a)$$

Therefore this supply function is continuous for all values of p.

Illustration 2.   We have previously considered the supply function

$$q_s = \frac{p^2 + 2p - 3}{p - 1}$$

We have shown that

$$\lim_{p \to 1} q_s = 4.$$

But $f(1)$ itself is undefined. Therefore, $f(p)$ is discontinuous at $p = 1$.

The graph of a continuous function is a continuous curve, that is, an unbroken curve. Graphs of discontinuous functions have at least one break.

Illustration 3.   We have shown that the supply function

$$q_s = p^2 - 1$$

is continuous for all values of p. Its graph for all relevant values, that is, for positive p and q, is shown below. It is an unbroken curve.

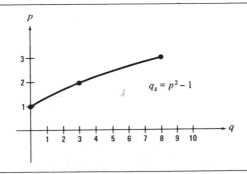

On the other hand, we showed that the supply function

$$q_s = \frac{p^2 + 2p - 3}{p - 1}$$

is discontinuous at $p = 1$. We know that for $p \neq 1$,

$$f(p) = \frac{p^2 + 2p - 3}{p - 1} = \frac{(p - 1)(p + 3)}{p - 1} = p + 3$$

Thus $f(p)$ is the straight line $q = p + 3$ for $p \neq 1$. However, $f(p)$ is undefined for $p = 1$. Therefore the curve that depicts the function is a straight line with a hole in it at $p = 1$. It is a broken curve:

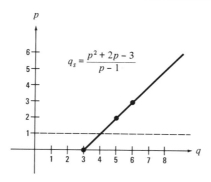

Illustration 4. Consider the following demand function for some precious stone that is desired primarily because of the status or prestige it bestows.

$$q_d = \begin{cases} 1000 - 2p & \text{for} \quad 0 \leqslant p < 500 \\ 3000 - \dfrac{p}{2} & \text{for} \qquad p > 500 \end{cases}$$

For prices greater than 500 there is a certain relationship between p and q_d. But when the price of the stone falls to below 500, a great deal of its social luster is lost, and a different relationship between p and q_d

ensues. The price of 500 is the boundary between these two different relationships. It is not known exactly how consumers will react to the boundary price, that is, whether or not the stone is still a prestige item at $p = 500$.

Thus $f(500)$ is undefined. Therefore $f(p)$ is discontinuous at $p = 500$. Its graph is shown below. It has a break at $p = 500$.

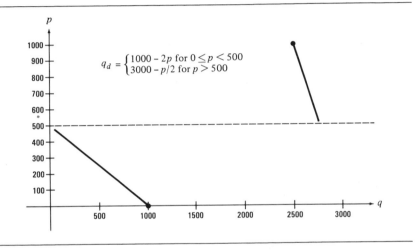

$$q_d = \begin{cases} 1000 - 2p \text{ for } 0 \le p < 500 \\ 3000 - p/2 \text{ for } p > 500 \end{cases}$$

Now consider a slight variation of this example, where we have the same demand function except that it is defined for $p = 500$:

$$q_d = \begin{cases} 1000 - 2p & \text{for} \quad 0 \le p < 500 \\ 3000 - \dfrac{p}{2} & \text{for} \qquad p \ge 500 \end{cases}$$

Thus for all prices $p \ge 500$, the stone carries prestige; while if $p < 500$, its prestige is lost.

Let us find

$$\lim_{p \to 500} f(p)$$

We notice that as we approach $p = 500$ from the left side, that is, from prices lower than 500, the function q_d approaches a value of 0. However, if we approach $p = 500$ from the right side, that is, from prices higher than 500, q_d approaches a value of 2750. Such limits are referred to as one-sided limits. Because the one-sided limits do not coincide, we cannot say that

$$\lim_{p \to 500} f(p)$$

exists regardless of the direction from which $p \to 500$. Therefore $f(p)$ is discontinuous at $p = 500$. Its graph is shown below.

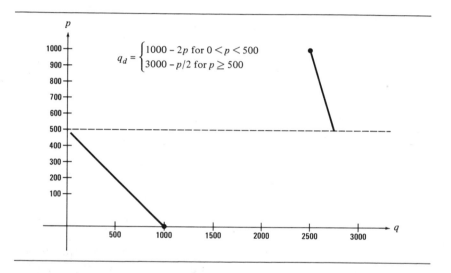

Illustration 5. Consider the following supply function of shoe company xyz.

$$q_s = \begin{cases} 10p - 100 & \text{for} \quad 10 \leqslant p < 50 \\ 20p & \text{for} \qquad p > 50 \end{cases}$$

For prices below 50, there is a certain relationship between p and the quantity of shoes put on the market. But this relationship changes when the price is greater than 50. The price of 50 is the boundary between these two different relationships. It is unknown exactly how much will be supplied at $p = 50$, because that price may be a signal of a forthcoming change in the relationship between p and q_s.

Thus $f(50)$ is undefined, and therefore $f(p)$ is discontinuous at $p = 50$. Its graph is shown below. It has a break at $p = 50$.

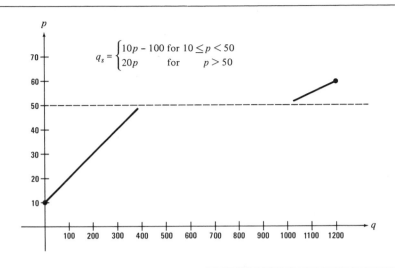

$$q_s = \begin{cases} 10p - 100 & \text{for } 10 \le p < 50 \\ 20p & \text{for } \quad\; p > 50 \end{cases}$$

Moreover, even if $f(50)$ is defined, as in the following,

$$q_s = \begin{cases} 10p - 100 & \text{for} \quad 10 \leqslant p < 50 \\ 20p & \text{for} \quad\quad p \geqslant 50 \end{cases}$$

$f(p)$ is still discontinuous at $p = 50$, because the one-sided limits do not coincide. As $p \to 50$ from the left, that is, from below, the function $q_s \to 400$, while as $p \to 50$ from the right, that is, from above, $q_s \to 1000$.

We have seen illustrations of functions $f(x)$ that were discontinuous at $x = a$ either because $f(a)$ did not exist or because $\lim\limits_{x \to a} f(x)$ did not exist, or because both $f(a)$ and $\lim\limits_{x \to a} f(x)$ did not exist. Thus the function given in Illustration 2 was discontinuous at $p = 1$ because $f(1)$ did not exist. The functions given at the end of Illustrations 4 and 5 were discontinuous at $p = 500$ and $p = 50$, respectively, because $\lim\limits_{p \to 500} f(p)$ and $\lim\limits_{p \to 50} f(p)$ did not exist even though $f(500)$ and $f(50)$ did exist. The remaining possibility of $f(x)$ being discontinuous at $x = a$ arises when both $f(a)$ and $\lim\limits_{x \to a} f(x)$ exist but $\lim\limits_{x \to a} f(x) \neq f(a)$. This is illustrated below.

Illustration 6.   Consider the supply function of Illustration 2 with the amendment that $f(1)$ is now defined and given as

$$q_s = \begin{cases} \dfrac{p^2 + 2p - 3}{p - 1} & \text{for } p \neq 1 \\[2mm] 5 & \text{for } p = 1 \end{cases}$$

When $p \neq 1$, we have

$$f(p) = \frac{p^2 + 2p - 3}{p - 1} = \frac{(p - 1)(p + 3)}{p - 1} = p + 3$$

$$\lim_{p \to 1} f(p) = 4$$

But $f(1) = 5$.

Thus, although $\lim_{p \to 1} f(p)$ and $f(1)$ both exist, the function is discontinuous at $p = 1$ because

$$\lim_{p \to 1} f(p) \neq f(1)$$

The graph of the function appears below and has a break at $p = 1$.

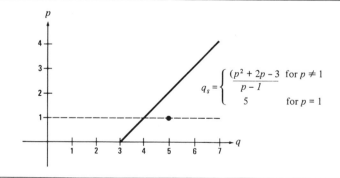

In deciding whether a particular function is continuous, we have in each case referred directly to the definition of continuity. This is not always necessary. Very often, we can make use of the following theorem, which states that a function that is constructed by adding, subtracting, multiplying, or dividing continuous functions, is itself continuous.

Theorem 5. If $f(x)$ and $g(x)$ are both continuous at $x = a$, then

1) $f(x) + g(x)$ is continuous at $x = a$.
2) $f(x) - g(x)$ is continuous at $x = a$.
3) $f(x)g(x)$ is continuous at $x = a$.
4) $f(x)/g(x)$ is continuous at $x = a$, provided that $g(a) \neq 0$.

Proof of (1). Let $h(x) = f(x) + g(x)$.

Now $h(a)$ exists because, by hypothesis, $f(a)$ and $g(a)$ exist. Also,

$$\lim_{x \to a} h(x) = \lim_{x \to a} f(x) + \lim_{x \to a} g(x)$$

by Theorem 1 of Section 6.4.
But

$$\lim_{x \to a} f(x) = f(a) \quad \text{and} \quad \lim_{x \to a} g(x) = g(a)$$

by the hypothesis of continuity.
Therefore

$$\lim_{x \to a} h(x) = f(a) + g(a)$$
$$= h(a)$$

Thus $h(x)$ is continuous.

Conclusions 2–4 follow similarly from the remaining limit theorems of Section 6.4. They are left as exercises for the student.

Theorem 5 enables us to establish the continuity of a great number of functions. Thus we can show that $f(p) = p^n$ is continuous where n is a positive integer by first showing that $f(p) = p$ is continuous because of the definition of continuity and by then applying Conclusion 3 repeatedly.

Similarly, $f(p) = cp^n$ can be shown to be continuous by showing that $f(p) = c$ is continuous because of the definition of continuity and by then applying Conclusion 3.

In the same manner, if $f(p)$ is any polynomial, it can be shown to be continuous because it is the sum of a number of continuous functions, and Conclusion 1 guarantees that the result is continuous.

It can also be shown that if $f(p)$ is a rational function, that is, a quotient of two polynomials, it is continuous at all points where it is defined. This follows from Conclusion 4, because a rational function is a quotient of polynomials that themselves are continuous.

Exercises

Find the points of discontinuities, if any, of the following functions and graph the functions.

1. $q_s = \dfrac{p^2 - 4}{p - 2}$

2. $q_d = \dfrac{p - 1}{p^2 - 1}$

3. $q_d = 4 - p^2$

4. $q_d = \begin{cases} 500 - 4p & \text{for} \quad 0 \leqslant p < 100 \\ 500 - p & \text{for} \qquad\quad p > 100 \end{cases}$

5. $q_d = \begin{cases} 500 - 4p & \text{for} \quad 0 \leqslant p < 100 \\ 500 - p & \text{for} \qquad\quad p \geqslant 100 \end{cases}$

6. $q_s = \begin{cases} 5p - 4 & \text{for} \quad p < 20 \\ 10p & \text{for} \quad p > 20 \end{cases}$

7. $q_s = p^2 - 3$

8. $q_s = \begin{cases} \dfrac{p^2 - 4}{p - 2} \end{cases}$ for $p \neq 2$; 5 for $p = 2$

9. $q_s = \begin{cases} \dfrac{p^2 - 4}{p - 2} \end{cases}$ for $p \neq 2$; 4 for $p = 2$

10. Prove Conclusion 2 of Theorem 5.

11. Prove Conclusion 3 of Theorem 5.

12. Prove Conclusion 4 of Theorem 5.

APPENDIX : LIMITS

In the text of the chapter, we discussed the concept of a limit and showed how to calculate limits. We now wish to give a more formal and rigorous definition of a limit.

Definition. A function $f(x)$ is said to approach a limit L as x approaches a if for any positive number ε, there is a positive number δ such that

$$|f(x) - L| < \varepsilon \quad \text{when} \quad 0 < |x - a| < \delta$$

This is equivalent to saying that $f(x)$ approaches the limit L as x approaches a if we can bring the value of $f(x)$ within any ε distance from L (no matter how small ε may be) by bringing x to within some distance, δ, from a.

Illustration.

$$q_s = 3p - 50$$

Show that

$$\lim_{p \to 20} q_s = 10$$

We must show that the value of q_s can be made as close as we please to 10 by simply taking p sufficiently close to 20.

Now, we can readily see that if we were challenged to bring the value of q_s to within 0.1 of 10, we could do this by taking a p of 19.97, because

$$f(19.97) = 3(19.97) - 50 = 9.91$$

Thus $q_s = 9.91$, which is within 0.1 of 10.

Suppose that we were challenged further to bring the value of q_s to within 0.001 of 10. We could achieve this by taking a p of 19.9997. We would then have

$$f(19.9997) = 3(19.9997) - 50 = 9.99991$$

Thus $q_s = 9.9991$, which is within 0.001 of 10.

We might now expect that we could, indeed, make q_s as close as desired to 10. It is, however, necessary to prove that this holds for all possibilities.

Consider, therefore, the general case where we are challenged to bring q_s to within ε of 10. We must show that

$$10 - \varepsilon < 3p - 50 < 10 + \varepsilon$$

that is, $3p - 50$ is within $\pm\varepsilon$ of 10, provided that $20 - \delta < p < 20 + \delta$, that is, p is within $\pm\delta$ of 20.

Now,

$$10 - \varepsilon < 3p - 50 < 10 + \varepsilon$$

is equivalent to

$$60 - \varepsilon < 3p < 60 + \varepsilon$$

or to

$$20 - \frac{\varepsilon}{3} < p < 20 + \frac{\varepsilon}{3}$$

Therefore, if we choose our δ as $\varepsilon/3$, we shall be guaranteed that

if $20 - \delta < p < 20 + \delta$

then $10 - \varepsilon < 3p - 50 < 10 + \varepsilon$

Infinite Limits

In the text of this chapter we discussed the case of a function increasing without end or becoming infinite as $x \to a$. The question that arises is how much the function has to increase in order to be considered as becoming infinite. We therefore state the following definition.

Definition.   A function $f(x)$ is said to approach an infinite limit as $x \to a$ if for any positive number M, there is a positive number δ such that

$$|f(x)| > M \quad \text{when} \quad 0 < |x - a| < \delta$$

Illustration.

$$q_d = \frac{100}{(p - 1)^2}$$

Show that

$$\lim_{p \to 1} q_d = \infty$$

We must show that the value of q_d can be made as large as desired by taking p sufficiently close to 1.

If we were challenged to make the value of $q_d > 1,000,000$, we could do this by taking p to be some number slightly smaller than 1.01. For example, if $p = 1.009$, then $q_d > 1,000,000$.

For the general case, where we may be challenged to make $q_d > M$ for any M, we wish to show that

$$\frac{100}{(p - 1)^2} > M$$

provided that

$$1 - \delta < p < 1 + \delta$$

Now

$$\frac{100}{(p-1)^2} > M$$

is equivalent to

$$\frac{100}{M} > (p-1)^2$$

or to

$$\pm(p-1) < \frac{10}{\sqrt{M}}$$

or to

$$1 - \frac{10}{\sqrt{M}} < p < 1 + \frac{10}{\sqrt{M}}$$

Therefore, if we choose our δ as $10/\sqrt{M}$, we shall be guaranteed that

$$\text{if} \quad 1 - \delta < p < 1 + \delta$$

$$\text{then} \quad \frac{100}{(p-1)^2} > M$$

Limits for an Infinite Variable

In the text of this chapter we also discussed the case of a function $f(x)$ approaching a definite limit as x increases without end or becomes infinite. The following definition makes this more clear.

Definition. A function $f(x)$ is said to approach a limit L as x becomes infinite if for any positive number ε, there is a positive number M such that

$$|f(x) - L| < \varepsilon \quad \text{when} \quad x > M$$

Illustration.

$$q_s = 100 - \frac{100}{p}$$

Show that

$$\lim_{p \to \infty} q_s = 100.$$

We must show that the value of q_s can be made as close as we please to 100 by taking p sufficiently large.

If we were challenged to bring the value of q_s to within 0.01 of 100, we could do this by taking $p > 10,000$.

For the general case, where we may be challenged to bring q_s to within ε of 100, we wish to show that

$$100 - \varepsilon < 100 - \frac{100}{p} < 100 + \varepsilon$$

provided that $p > M$. Now,

$$100 - \varepsilon < 100 - \frac{100}{p} < 100 + \varepsilon$$

is equivalent to

$$-\varepsilon < \frac{100}{p} < \varepsilon$$

or

$$p > \frac{100}{\varepsilon}$$

Therefore, if we choose our $M = 100/\varepsilon$, we shall be guaranteed that if $p > M$, then

$$100 - \varepsilon < 100 - \frac{100}{p} < 100 + \varepsilon$$

Exercises

1. $q_s = 2p - 15$ Show that $\lim_{p \to 10} q_s = 5$

2. $q_d = 100 - 2p$ Show that $\lim_{p \to 10} q_d = 80$

3. $q_s = 4p - 10$ Show that $\lim_{p \to 5} q_s = 10$

4. $q_d = \dfrac{10}{p^2}$ Show that $\lim\limits_{p \to 0} q_d = \infty$

5. $q_d = \dfrac{4}{(p-2)^2}$ Show that $\lim\limits_{p \to 2} q_d = \infty$

6. $q_s = 40 - \dfrac{1}{p}$ Show that $\lim\limits_{p \to \infty} q_s = 40$

7. $q_s = 1000 - \dfrac{10}{p}$ Show that $\lim\limits_{p \to \infty} q_s = 1000$

8. $q_d = \dfrac{10}{(p-1)^2}$ Show that $\lim\limits_{p \to \infty} q_d = 0$

DERIVATIVES, ELASTICITY, AND MARGINAL REVENUE

Under the guidance of Cournot and in a less degree of Von Thunen, I was led to attach great importance to the fact that our observations of nature, in the moral as in the physical world, relate not so much to aggregate quantities as to increments of quantities.

—Alfred Marshall

The concepts of limits and continuity that were considered in the last chapter lead us directly to rates of change of functions and derivatives.

SECTION 7·1 DERIVATIVES OF DEMAND FUNCTIONS

Consider any demand function $q_d = f(p)$. We know that as p changes, so does q_d, the quantity demanded. The question we now pose is how great will these changes in q_d be? For some demand functions the resulting change in q_d will be great, while in other instances it will be minute. Moreover, even with one particular demand function, the reaction of quantity demanded to changes in price will vary depending upon the range of consideration.

To illustrate, consider the demand function $q_d = 50 - 4p - 2p^2$. At what rate is q_d changing? Because the answer depends upon the range of consideration, we must stipulate a specific range. We can then restate the question and ask at what rate is q_d changing when $\$1 \leqslant p \leqslant \$2$? But we now note that in any interval that we choose, the rate of change may and usually does vary throughout the interval. All we can then do is find the average rate of change for the interval. This we accomplish by computing

$$\frac{\text{change in } q_d \text{ (denoted by } \Delta q_d)}{\text{change in } p \text{ (denoted by } \Delta p)}$$

For our illustration we have $f(2) = 34$, $f(1) = 44$, and

$$\frac{\Delta q_d}{\Delta p} = \frac{34 - 44}{2 - 1} = \frac{-10}{1} = -10$$

This indicates that for this interval, a \$1 increase in p will, on the average, cause a 10-unit reduction in quantity demanded.

Notice, however, that if we consider only the first half of the interval, $\$1 < p < 1.50$, then

$$\frac{\Delta q_d}{\Delta p} = \frac{39.50 - 44}{1.50 - 1.00} = -9$$

Thus we see that in the first half of the original interval the rate of change was not -10. In the same manner, we could take different segments of the original interval and show that the rates of change vary. The essence of the situation is that for any interval these computations only give average rates of change.

In speaking of rates of change, we would like to consider the rate of change of q_d at a particular point $p = p_0$. This is known as the *instantaneous rate of change*. It eliminates any misleading or ambiguous conclusions, because there is then no averaging.

We notice that as we take smaller and smaller intervals, our average rate of change shows less and less fluctuation. Computations from small intervals will therefore give us better approximations to the rate of change at a particular point.

This suggests the following procedure for finding the rate of change of the variable at any point. Form an interval that includes the particular point in question. Then compute the average rate of change for this interval. Repeat the procedure with intervals whose lengths approach zero. If these average rates of change approach a limit, then this limit is the rate of change at the desired point.

Return to our illustration of the demand function $q_d = 50 - 4p - 2p^2$. At the price of \$1.00, how fast is q_d changing? Consider the interval from $p = 1.00$ to $p = 1.00 + \Delta p$, where Δp is some small change in price. The average rate of change for this interval is given by

$$\frac{\Delta q_d}{\Delta p} = \frac{f(1.00 + \Delta p) - f(1)}{(1.00 + \Delta p) - 1.00}$$

that is, Δq_d is computed by evaluating the demand function at the price $1.00 + \Delta p$ and subtracting from this the quantity demanded at $p = \$1.00$.

Δp is evaluated by subtracting one price, which is \$1.00, from the other price, which is \$1.00 + Δp.

Now,

$$f(1.00 + \Delta p) = 50 - 4(1.00 + \Delta p) - 2(1.00 + \Delta p)^2$$
$$= 50 - 4 - 4\,\Delta p - 2 - 4\,\Delta p - 2(\Delta p)^2$$

and

$$f(1.00) = 50 - 4 - 2$$

Thus

$$f(1.00 + \Delta p) - f(1.00) = -8\,\Delta p - 2(\Delta p)^2$$

and

$$\frac{\Delta q_d}{\Delta p} = \frac{-8\,\Delta p - 2(\Delta p)^2}{\Delta p} = -8 - 2\,\Delta p$$

Next, allow Δp to become smaller and smaller and consider what effect this will have on the ratio $\Delta q_d / \Delta p$. We then have

$$\lim_{\Delta p \to 0} \frac{\Delta q_d}{\Delta p} = -8$$

because as $\Delta p \to 0$, $-2\,\Delta p \to 0$.

This means that at a price of \$1.00, quantity demanded is decreasing at a rate of 8 times as much as p is increasing.

We have thus shown how to find the rate of change in the quantity demanded at a price of $p = \$1.00$. We now wish to consider the rate of change in q_d at any price, whatever it may be.

We have $q_d = 50 - 4p - 2p^2$. Consider the interval from p to $p + \Delta p$, where p may be any price. Then

$$\frac{\Delta q_d}{\Delta p} = \frac{f(p + \Delta p) - f(p)}{\Delta p}$$

and

$$f(p + \Delta p) = 50 - 4(p + \Delta p) - 2(p + \Delta p)^2$$
$$= 50 - 4p - 4\,\Delta p - 2p^2 - 4p\,\Delta p - 2(\Delta p)^2$$
$$f(p) = 50 - 4p - 2p^2$$
$$f(p + \Delta p) - f(p) = -4\,\Delta p - 4p\,\Delta p - 2(\Delta p)^2$$

Thus

$$\frac{\Delta q_d}{\Delta p} = \frac{-4\,\Delta p - 4p\,\Delta p - 2(\Delta p)^2}{\Delta p} = -4 - 4p - 2\,\Delta p$$

$$\lim_{\Delta p \to 0} \frac{\Delta q_d}{\Delta p} = -4 - 4p$$

This gives us the rate of change in quantity demanded for any p. In particular, at $p = \$2.00$, the rate of change is -12.

This leads us to the following definition. If $q_d = f(p)$, then the rate of change of q_d at price p is

$$\lim_{\Delta p \to 0} \frac{\Delta q_d}{\Delta p} = \lim_{\Delta p \to 0} \frac{f(p + \Delta p) - f(p)}{\Delta p}$$

The rate of change of q_d at price p expresses the responsiveness or sensitivity of q_d to changes in p. We call this rate of change the *marginal demand*.

The rate of change of q_d at price p, that is,

$$\lim_{\Delta p \to 0} \frac{\Delta q_d}{\Delta p}$$

is also written in shorthand as

$$f'(p) \quad \text{or} \quad \frac{dq_d}{dp} \quad \text{or} \quad q'.$$

All these expressions are interchangeable. Note that

$$\frac{dq_d}{dp}$$

is definitely not the same as

$$\frac{\Delta q_d}{\Delta p}.$$

Instead,

$$\frac{dq_d}{dp} = \lim_{\Delta p \to 0} \frac{\Delta q_d}{\Delta p}$$

This rate of change is known as the *derivative* of q_d with respect to p. Notice that the derivative of a function of p is also a function of p. The process of finding a derivative is known as *differentiation*.

SECTION 7·2 ELASTICITY OF DEMAND

The marginal demand concept, which we have introduced to measure the responsiveness of quantity to price, turns out to be inadequate for many purposes. One shortcoming arises when a variable can be expressed in different units such as cents or dollars. If p is then converted from dollar terms to cents terms, there will be a very great difference in the resulting rate of change even though there is no actual change. Furthermore, if one product is to be compared to another product, our measure is again insufficient, because a Δq_d of 5 automobiles is quite different from a Δq_d of 5 bushels of wheat.

To rectify these inadequacies, we customarily employ percentage changes in price and quantity instead of absolute changes. Thus, in place of Δq_d and Δp, which are absolute quantities, we shall use

$$\frac{\Delta q_d}{q_d} \quad \text{and} \quad \frac{\Delta p}{p}$$

which are the percentage changes in quantity and price, respectively.

We then define *elasticity of demand* (E_d) at a certain point by the following, which is a simple modification of marginal demand.

$$E_d = \lim_{\Delta p \to 0} \frac{\Delta q_d / q_d}{\Delta p / p} = \lim_{\Delta p \to 0} \frac{\Delta q_d}{\Delta p} \frac{p}{q_d} = \frac{p}{q_d} \lim_{\Delta p \to 0} \frac{\Delta q_d}{\Delta p}$$

Thus

$$E_d = \frac{p}{q_d} \frac{dq_d}{dp} = \frac{p}{q_d} f'(p)$$

Elasticity of demand is merely the derivative of q_d with respect to p multiplied by p/q_d.

Illustration.   We have shown that for the demand function $q_d = 50 - 4p - 2p^2$, marginal demand is given by

$$\frac{dq_d}{dp} = -4 - 4p.$$

To compute elasticity, we have

$$E_d = \frac{p}{q_d} \frac{dq_d}{dp} = \frac{p}{q_d}(-4 - 4p) = \frac{-4p}{q_d} - \frac{4p^2}{q_d}.$$

For a specific point, say, $p = \$2.00$, we have marginal demand $= -4 - 4(2) = -12$. This indicates that at a price of \$2.00, quantity demanded is decreasing at a rate of 12 times as much as price is increasing. It follows that

$$E_d = \text{elasticity} = \frac{p}{q_d}(-12).$$

Now, when $p = \$2.00$, our demand function shows us that $q_d = 34$. Therefore,

$$E = \tfrac{2}{34}(-12) = -\tfrac{12}{17}.$$

This indicates that at a price of $\$2.00$, there is $\tfrac{12}{17}$ of a percent decrease in quantity demanded for every percent increase in price.

SECTION 7·3   ELASTICITY OF SUPPLY

We have, until this point, been concerned with the elasticity of the demand function. In a completely analogous manner, we can define elasticity of supply. Thus, if we have a supply function $q_s = f(p)$, then *marginal supply* is given by

$$\frac{dq_s}{dp}$$

and *elasticity of supply* by

$$\frac{p}{q_s}\frac{dq_s}{dp}.$$

Just as elasticity of demand expressed the percentage rate of change of quantity demanded in response to a price change, so does elasticity of supply express the percentage rate of change of quantity supplied in response to a price change.

Illustration.   Consider the supply function $q_s = 3p^2 + 6p - 25$.

$$\frac{\Delta q_s}{\Delta p} = \frac{f(p + \Delta p) - f(p)}{\Delta p}$$

and

$$f(p + \Delta p) = 3(p + \Delta p)^2 + 6(p + \Delta p) - 25$$
$$= 3p^2 + 6p\,\Delta p + 3(\Delta p)^2 + 6p + 6\,\Delta p - 25$$
$$f(p) = 3p^2 + 6p - 25$$
$$f(p + \Delta p) - f(p) = 6p\,\Delta p + 3(\Delta p)^2 + 6\,\Delta p$$

and

$$\frac{\Delta q_s}{\Delta p} = \frac{6p \, \Delta p + 3(\Delta p)^2 + 6 \, \Delta p}{\Delta p} = 6p + 3 \, \Delta p + 6$$

$$\text{marginal supply} = \lim_{\Delta p \to 0} \frac{\Delta q_s}{\Delta p} = f'(p) = 6p + 6$$

and

$$\text{elasticity of supply} = \frac{p}{q_s}(6p + 6) = \frac{6p^2}{q_s} + \frac{6p}{q_s}.$$

At a price of $3.00, marginal supply $= 6(3) + 6 = 24$. This indicates that at a price of $3.00, quantity supplied is increasing at a rate 24 times as much as price is increasing. It follows that

$$\text{elasticity of supply} = \frac{p}{q_s}(24).$$

Now, when $p = \$3.00$, the supply function shows that $q_s = 20$. Therefore,

$$\text{elasticity of supply} = \tfrac{3}{20}(24) = \tfrac{18}{5}.$$

This indicates that at a price of $3.00, there is a $3\tfrac{3}{5}$ percent increase in quantity supplied for each percent increase in price.

Exercises

1. $q_s = 2p^2 - p + 4$. Find marginal supply and elasticity of supply.

2. $q_d = 50 - 4p - p^2$. Find marginal demand and elasticity of demand.

3. $q_s = p^2 - 4p$. Find marginal supply and elasticity of supply at $p = 5$.

4. $q_d = 60 + p - 5p^2$. Find marginal demand and elasticity of demand at $p = 3$.

5. $q_s = p^3 - 3p$. Find marginal supply and elasticity of supply at $p = 5$.

6. $q_d = \dfrac{p + 2}{p}$. Find marginal demand and elasticity of demand.

7. $q_d = \dfrac{2}{p^2 + 4}$. Find marginal supply and elasticity of supply.

SECTION 7·4   DERIVATIVES IN GENERAL

We have spoken of rates of change of quantity demanded and quantity supplied in response to changes in price. But the concept of rates of change is a general one, and can be applied to any function $y = f(x)$.

We define the *instantaneous rate of change* of $y = f(x)$ with respect to x as

$$\lim_{\Delta x \to 0} \frac{\Delta y}{\Delta x} = \lim_{\Delta x \to 0} \frac{f(x + \Delta x) - f(x)}{\Delta x}$$

provided that this limit exists. This rate of change is called the *derivative of y with respect to x*, and is denoted by

$$f'(x) \quad \text{or} \quad y' \quad \text{or} \quad \frac{dy}{dx}.$$

This rate of change is also called the *slope of the function*, because it gives the slope of the tangent line to the curve of the function. The process of finding a derivative is known as *differentiation.*

We note that $f'(x)$, in turn, is also a function of x. To find the rate of change at any particular point, we merely evaluate $f'(x)$ at that point.

In the appendix to this chapter it is proved that if a function $f(x)$ has a derivative at $x = x_0$, then $f(x)$ is continuous at $x = x_0$. Thus, continuity is a necessary condition for differentiability; that is, a function can have a derivative only if it is continuous.

The rate of change of $q_d = f(p)$ with respect to p, which we considered above, is merely a special case, or one example, of the general definition of rates of change for any function.

It is important to note that

$\dfrac{dy}{dx}$ is not defined as a fraction.

$\dfrac{dy}{dx}$ is merely the value of the limit approached by

$\dfrac{\Delta y}{\Delta x} \quad$ as $\quad \Delta x \to 0$

Exercises

Find the derivative of each of the following functions.

1. $y = x^2$

2. $y = x^3$

3. $y = 2x^2 + 3$

4. $y = \dfrac{2}{x^2}$

5. $y = \dfrac{x}{x + 1}$

Find the slope of the following curves at the points indicated.

6. $y = 3x - x^2$ at $x = 1$

7. $y = x^2 - 3x + 2$ at $x = 2$

SECTION 7·5   RELATION BETWEEN DEMAND AND TOTAL REVENUE

Consider the demand function facing a firm given by $q_d = f(p)$. An equivalent way to write this is to solve for p in terms of q, so that the same demand relation can be written as $p = h(q_d)$.

Illustration.   Given the following demand function facing a certain firm: $q_d = 100 - 2p$. This is equivalent to $2p = 100 - q_d$ or $p = 50 - \frac{1}{2}q_d$, so that the demand function is put into the form $p = h(q_d)$.

Total revenue received by a firm is the quantity it sells multiplied by the price. Thus, total revenue (denoted by TR) $= qp = qh(q)$.

Illustration.   Consider the demand function above, which was written as $p = 50 - \frac{1}{2}q_d$. We have $TR = qp = q(50 - \frac{1}{2}q) = 50q - \frac{1}{2}q^2$.

Thus total revenue is itself a function depending upon the quantity sold.

SECTION 7·6   MARGINAL REVENUE

We are very often interested in determining the change that will occur in total revenue due to a small increase in sales. But how small an increase in sales shall we consider—1 unit, $\frac{1}{2}$ unit, $\frac{1}{10}$ unit? Our aim is to consider an increase as small as possible. We are therefore led to the instantaneous rate of change of the revenue function. Anything short of this will give us only the average rate of change of revenue over some small interval instead of at some definite point.

We therefore define

$$marginal\ revenue\ (MR) = \lim_{\Delta q \to 0} \frac{\Delta TR}{\Delta q}.$$

Marginal revenue is thus another example of the general definition of a derivative. It expresses the instantaneous rate of change of the revenue function in response to a change in sales (i.e., q).

Illustration. In the previous illustration we showed that a certain demand function implied a revenue function of

$$TR = 50q - \tfrac{1}{2}q^2.$$

Therefore,

$$\frac{\Delta TR}{\Delta q} = \frac{f(q + \Delta q) - f(q)}{\Delta q}$$

and

$$f(q + \Delta q) = 50(q + \Delta q) - \tfrac{1}{2}(q + \Delta q)^2$$
$$= 50q + 50\,\Delta q - \tfrac{1}{2}q^2 - q\,\Delta q - \tfrac{1}{2}(\Delta q)^2$$
$$f(q) = 50q - \tfrac{1}{2}q^2$$
$$f(q + \Delta q) - f(q) = 50\,\Delta q - q\,\Delta q - \tfrac{1}{2}(\Delta q)^2$$

and

$$\frac{\Delta TR}{\Delta q} = \frac{50\,\Delta q - q\,\Delta q - \tfrac{1}{2}(\Delta q)^2}{\Delta q} = 50 - q - \tfrac{1}{2}\,\Delta q$$

$$MR = \lim_{\Delta q \to 0} \frac{\Delta TR}{\Delta q} = 50 - q$$

At a level of sales $q = 10$, we would have $MR = 50 - 10 = 40$. This indicates that at $q = 10$, total revenue is increasing by 40 times as much as sales are increasing.

In general, we shall find that in all cases where the term marginal is employed, reference is being made to a derivative. This applies to such well-known economic concepts as marginal cost, marginal utility, marginal physical product, marginal propensity to consume. We shall consider each of these in more detail at a later point, in the proper economic context.

Exercises

125 1. If $q_d = 40 - \frac{1}{2}p$, find (a) total revenue; (b) marginal revenue.
126 2. If $q_d = 60 - 3p$, find TR and MR at $q = 6$.
127 3. If $TR = 2q^2 + 5q - 3$, find MR.
128 4. If $TR = q^2 - 3q + 2$, find MR at $q = 4$.

SECTION 7·7 SIGNIFICANCE OF THE SIGN OF A DERIVATIVE

Consider a function $y = f(x)$. Assume that the derivative $y' = f'(x)$ is positive at the point $x = x_1$. This means that y is changing in the same direction as x; that is, as x increases, y increases and as x decreases, y decreases. Either case would make $\Delta y/\Delta x$ positive and therefore $\lim \Delta y/\Delta x$ positive.

On the other hand, if $f'(x)$ is negative at $x = x_1$, then y is changing in the opposite direction of x; that is, as x increases, y decreases and as x decreases, y increases. Either case would make $\Delta y/\Delta x$ negative and therefore $\lim \Delta y/\Delta x$ negative.

Illustration. We have already considered the demand function $q_d = 50 - 4p - 2p^2$ and have shown that $dq_d/dp = -8$ at $p = \$1.00$. This implies that as price is increased, quantity demanded falls, and as price is decreased, quantity demanded increases. On the other hand, for the supply function $q_s = 3p^2 + 6p - 25$, we showed that $dq_s/dp = 24$ at a price of $\$3.00$. This implies that as price is increased, quantity supplied increases, and as price decreases, quantity supplied decreases.

Demand: One of the basic economic theorems is that, except for rare cases, there is an inverse relation between price and quantity demanded; that is, as price increases, quantity demanded decreases, and as price decreases, quantity demanded increases.

In more precise terminology, it states that with a demand function $q_d = f(p)$, it follows that $dq_d/dp = f'(p) < 0$ for all values of p. In other words, the derivative of the demand function, that is, marginal demand, will be negative at all points. This is equivalent to saying that demand is a negatively sloped or downward-sloping function.

We know that elasticity of demand is given by

$$\frac{p}{q_d} \frac{dq_d}{dp}.$$

Now dq_d/dp is always negative. p and q_d are always positive or zero by the

nature of the problem; that is, price and quantity cannot be negative.
Therefore elasticity of demand, E_d, is always negative.

Supply: Supply functions usually exhibit a direct relation between
price and quantity supplied; that is, price and quantity move in the same
direction.

In precise terminology, this means that for a supply function
$q_s = f(p)$, it follows that

$$\frac{dq_s}{dp} = f'(p) > 0 \qquad \text{for all values of } p.$$

This implies that as price increases, quantity supplied increases, and as
price decreases, quantity supplied decreases. This is equivalent to saying
that supply is a positively sloped or upward-sloping function.

Similarly, elasticity of supply, which is given by

$$\frac{p}{q_s} \frac{dq_s}{dp}$$

will be positive, because each term is positive.

Total revenue: We have considered the total revenue function
$TR = 50q - \frac{1}{2}q^2$ and shown that $MR = 50 - q$ (recall that MR is the
derivative of TR). At a quantity of 10 we have shown that $MR = 40$,
indicating that at that level as quantity increases, TR will increase, and as
quantity decreases, TR will decrease.

However, at a quantity of 60 we would have $MR = 50 -
60 = -10$. This would indicate that at that level of sales, as quantity
increases, TR will decrease, and as quantity decreases, TR will increase.

More generally, we can determine at which points MR is positive
and at which points negative by solving the following:

$$MR = 50 - q > 0 \qquad MR = 50 - q < 0$$
$$50 > q \qquad\qquad 50 < q$$
$$q < 50 \qquad\qquad q > 50$$

This shows that for $q < 50$, MR will be positive and for $q > 50$, MR
will be negative. This implies that for any $q < 50$, as q increases, TR will
increase and for any $q > 50$, as q increases, TR will decrease.

Exercises

1. For each of the exercises after Section 7.6, determine at which points
    MR is positive and at which points negative.

APPENDIX

We now wish to establish the theorem that states that differentiability implies continuity.

Theorem.
Hypothesis.   The derivative of $f(x)$ at $x = a$ exists.
Conclusion. $f(x)$ is continuous at $x = a$.
Proof. $f'(a)$ exists by hypothesis.

$$\lim_{\Delta x \to 0} \frac{f(a + \Delta x) - f(a)}{\Delta x}$$

exists. This implies that $f(a + \Delta x)$ and $f(a)$ exist. Now

$$f(a + \Delta x) - f(a) = \Delta x \frac{f(a + \Delta x) - f(a)}{\Delta x} \qquad \text{if } \Delta x \neq 0$$

and

$$\lim_{\Delta x \to 0} [f(a + \Delta x) - f(a)] = \lim_{\Delta x \to 0} \Delta x \left[\lim_{\Delta x \to 0} \frac{f(a + \Delta x) - f(a)}{\Delta x} \right]$$

because of a previous theorem stating that the limit of a product is the product of the limits.

$$= 0f'(a) = 0$$

$$\therefore \ \lim_{\Delta x \to 0} [f(a + \Delta x) - f(a)] = 0$$

$$\therefore \ \lim_{\Delta x \to 0} f(a + \Delta x) = f(a)$$

But

$$\lim_{\Delta x \to 0} f(a + \Delta x) = \lim_{x \to a} f(x)$$

$$\therefore \ \lim_{x \to a} f(x) = f(a)$$

Therefore $f(x)$ is continuous at $x = a$.

We have shown that differentiability implies continuity. The converse, is, however, not true. All continuous functions are not necessarily differentiable. This is illustrated by the following.

Illustration.   Consider the following demand function for some precious stone.

$$q_d = \begin{cases} 1000 - 2p & \text{for} \quad 0 < p < 100 \\ 8p & \text{for} \quad p \geqslant 100 \end{cases}$$

There is an inverse relation between price and quantity as long as $p < 100$; that is, as the price increases, quantity demanded decreases. However, for prices greater than or equal to 100, there is a direct relationship between price and quantity, that is, as price increases, quantity demanded increases. This is a prestige item, where a higher price attached to the good produces greater prestige value.

The graph of the function is shown below.

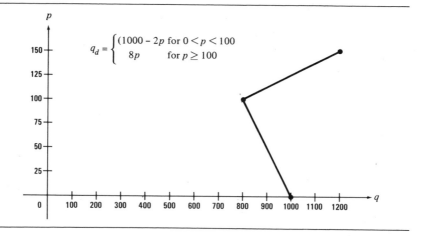

Let us now show that this function is continuous at $p = 100$ but not differentiable, that is, has no derivative, at $p = 100$.

$$\lim_{p \to 100} f(p) = 800$$

because as $p \to 100$ from either the right or left side,

$$f(p) \to 800$$

Also

$$f(100) = 800$$

Therefore

$$\lim_{p \to 100} f(p) = f(100)$$

Therefore, $f(p)$ is continuous at $p = 100$. This is further supported by the graph of the function, which is seen to be an unbroken curve.

To find the derivative of $f(p)$ at $p = 100$, we must evaluate

$$\lim_{\Delta p \to 0} \frac{f(100 + \Delta p) - f(100)}{\Delta p}$$

Now, when $\Delta p > 0$, we have

$$\lim_{\Delta p \to 0} \frac{f(100 + \Delta p) - f(100)}{\Delta p} = \lim_{\Delta p \to 0} \frac{8(100 + \Delta p) - 8(100)}{\Delta p}$$

$$= \lim_{\Delta p \to 0} \frac{8 \, \Delta p}{\Delta p} = \lim_{\Delta p \to 0} (8) = 8$$

But when $\Delta p < 0$, we have

$$\lim_{\Delta p \to 0} \frac{f(100 + \Delta p) - f(100)}{\Delta p} = \lim_{\Delta p \to 0} \frac{1000 - 2(100 + \Delta p) - 800}{\Delta p}$$

$$= \lim_{\Delta p \to 0} \frac{-2 \, \Delta p}{\Delta p} = \lim_{\Delta p \to 0} (-2) = -2$$

Thus the right-hand and left-hand limits do not coincide, and therefore

$$\lim_{\Delta p \to 0} \frac{f(100 + \Delta p) - f(100)}{\Delta p}$$

does not exist. This means that the derivative of $f(p)$ at $p = 100$ does not exist.

This fact is portrayed by the graph, which has a kink at $p = 100$.

Exercises

Investigate the following functions for continuity and differentiability and graph the functions.

1. $q_s = \begin{cases} 10p - 50 & \text{for} \quad 5 < p < 20 \\ 250 - 5p & \text{for} \qquad\quad p \geqslant 20 \end{cases}$

2. $q_d = \begin{cases} 1000 - 2p & \text{for} \quad 0 < p < 100 \\ 10p & \text{for} \qquad\quad p \geqslant 100 \end{cases}$

3. $q_d = \begin{cases} 100 - p & \text{for} \quad 0 < p \leqslant 50 \\ 2p - 50 & \text{for} \qquad\quad p > 50 \end{cases}$

8

DIFFERENTIATION TECHNIQUES APPLIED TO ECONOMIC FUNCTIONS

Method is good in all things.
—Jonathan Swift

In the previous chapter we found derivatives of a number of different functions. In each case, we had to go through the complete $\Delta y/\Delta x$ process. We now present certain rules that will enable us to find derivatives much more easily than if we had to go through the whole $\Delta y/\Delta x$ process each time.

SECTION 8·1 DIFFERENTIATION RULES

These rules are derived by applying the $\Delta y/\Delta x$ process to general functional forms and then employing the result for all functions of the same category. Included in the text are derivations that are enlightening or instructive and that improve the understanding of basic concepts. Derivations that were judged to be more indirect or of a one-shot variety will be found in the appendix to this chapter.

SECTION 8·2 DERIVATIVE OF A CONSTANT

Theorem 1. If $y = c$, where c is a constant, then

$$\frac{dy}{dx} = 0$$

that is, the derivative of a constant is zero.

Proof. $f(x) = c$ and $f(x + \Delta x) = c$ by hypothesis

$$\therefore \ \frac{f(x + \Delta x) - f(x)}{\Delta x} = \frac{c - c}{\Delta x} = 0$$

and

$$\lim_{\Delta x \to 0} \frac{f(x + \Delta x) - f(x)}{\Delta x} = 0$$

Illustration. Consider the following fixed supply function:

$$q_s = 1000$$

Marginal supply is given by

$$\frac{dq_s}{dp} = 0$$

This indicates that there is a zero rate of change in quantity supplied as price changes. Indeed, this is what a fixed supply implies.

SECTION 8·3 DERIVATIVE OF A POWER OF THE INDEPENDENT VARIABLE

Theorem 2. If $y = x^n$, where n is any rational number, then

$$\frac{dy}{dx} = nx^{n-1}$$

that is, the derivative of a power of the independent variable is equal to the exponent multiplied by the variable raised to a power one less than the original power.

Proof. We shall prove the theorem for the case where n is a positive integer and leave the cases where n is a negative integer or a rational number for the appendix to this chapter.

$$f(x) = x^n$$

where n is a positive integer by hypothesis. Therefore

$$f(x + \Delta x) = (x + \Delta x)^n$$

The binomial theorem tells us that

$$(x + \Delta x)^n = x^n + nx^{n-1}(\Delta x) + \frac{n(n-1)}{2} x^{n-2}(\Delta x)^2$$

$$+ \text{ (terms involving higher powers of } \Delta x)$$

Therefore

$$f(x + \Delta x) - f(x) = nx^{n-1}(\Delta x) + \frac{n(n-1)}{2} x^{n-2}(\Delta x)^2$$

$$+ \text{(terms involving higher powers of } \Delta x)$$

and

$$\frac{f(x + \Delta x) - f(x)}{\Delta x} = nx^{n-1} + \frac{n(n-1)}{2} x^{n-2}(\Delta x)$$

$$+ \text{(terms involving higher powers of } \Delta x).$$

Now all terms after the first contain Δx as a factor. Therefore,

$$\lim_{\Delta x \to 0} \frac{f(x + \Delta x) - f(x)}{\Delta x} = nx^{n-1}$$

and

$$\frac{dy}{dx} = \lim_{\Delta x \to 0} \frac{f(x + \Delta x) - f(x)}{\Delta x} = nx^{n-1}$$

Note that this derivation applies only for the case where the exponent, n, is a positive integer. It was this assumption that enabled us to apply the binomial theorem. In fact, the same differentiation formula holds true when n is a negative integer or a rational number, that is, a fraction. This is proved in the appendix to this chapter.

Illustration.

(a) $y = x^3$

$$\frac{dy}{dx} = 3x^2$$

(b) $q_s = p^6$

$$\frac{dq_s}{dp} = 6p^5$$

(c) $q_s = p$

$$\frac{dq_s}{dp} = 1 \cdot p^0$$

$$= 1$$

(d) $q_s = p^{2/3}$

$$\frac{dq_s}{dp} = \tfrac{2}{3}p^{(2/3)-1}$$

$$= \tfrac{2}{3}p^{-1/3}$$

(e) $q_d = \dfrac{100}{p^4} = 100p^{-4}$

$$\frac{dq_d}{dp} = 100(-4)p^{-5}$$

$$= -400p^{-5}$$

$$= -\frac{400}{p^5}$$

SECTION 8·4 DERIVATIVE OF A CONSTANT TIMES A FUNCTION

Theorem 3. If $y = cu$, where c is a constant and u is a differentiable function of x, then

$$\frac{dy}{dx} = c\frac{du}{dx}$$

that is, the derivative of a constant times a function is the constant times the derivative of the function.

Proof. $y = cu$, where u is a function of x by hypothesis. Now, when x changes by Δx, u changes by some amount Δu and, consequently, y changes by some amount Δy. We shall then have

$$y + \Delta y = c(u + \Delta u)$$
$$= cu + c(\Delta u)$$

Subtracting y from $y + \Delta y$, we have

$$\Delta y = c(\Delta u)$$

and

$$\frac{\Delta y}{\Delta x} = c \frac{\Delta u}{\Delta x}$$

$$\lim_{\Delta x \to 0} \frac{\Delta y}{\Delta x} = \lim_{\Delta x \to 0} c \frac{\Delta u}{\Delta x}$$

$$= c \lim_{\Delta x \to 0} \frac{\Delta u}{\Delta x} \text{ by Theorem 2 of Section 6.4.}$$

Now

$$\lim_{\Delta x \to 0} \frac{\Delta y}{\Delta x} = \frac{dy}{dx} \quad \text{and} \quad \lim_{\Delta x \to 0} \frac{\Delta u}{\Delta x} = \frac{du}{dx}$$

$$\therefore \quad \frac{dy}{dx} = c \frac{du}{dx}$$

Illustration.   (a) $y = 7x^5$.

This is in the form $y =$ a constant multiplied by a function u, where $u = x^5$. Therefore,

$$\frac{dy}{dx} = 7(5x^4) = 35x^4$$

(b) $q_s = 25p^2$.

$$\frac{dq_s}{dp} = 25(2p) = 50p$$

SECTION 8·5   DERIVATIVE OF A SUM OF FUNCTIONS

Theorem 4.   If $y = u + v$, where u and v are differentiable functions of x, then

$$\frac{dy}{dx} = \frac{du}{dx} + \frac{dv}{dx}$$

that is, the derivative of a sum of functions is the sum of the derivatives of each function.

Proof. $y = u + v$, where u and v are differentiable functions of x, by hypothesis.

When x changes by Δx, u changes by some amount Δu, v by some amount Δv, and, consequently, y changes by some amount Δy. We then have

$$y + \Delta y = (u + \Delta u) + (v + \Delta v)$$

Subtracting y from $y + \Delta y$, we have

$$y = \Delta u + \Delta v$$

$$\frac{\Delta y}{\Delta x} = \frac{\Delta u}{\Delta x} + \frac{\Delta v}{\Delta x}$$

$$\lim_{\Delta x \to 0} \frac{\Delta y}{\Delta x} = \lim_{\Delta x \to 0} \left(\frac{\Delta u}{\Delta x} + \frac{\Delta v}{\Delta x}\right)$$

$$= \lim_{\Delta x \to 0} \frac{\Delta u}{\Delta x} + \lim_{\Delta x \to 0} \frac{\Delta v}{\Delta x}$$

because the limit of a sum is the sum of the limits by a previous theorem.

$$\therefore \quad \frac{dy}{dx} = \frac{du}{dx} + \frac{dv}{dx}$$

If y is a sum of three or more functions, a similar formula would hold (see Exercises for this section).

Illustration. (a) $y = 2x^3 - 3x^2$.

This is in the form of $y = $ a sum of two functions, where the first function is $2x^3$ and the second function is $-3x^2$. Therefore

$$\frac{dy}{dx} = \frac{d(2x^3)}{dx} + \frac{d(-3x^2)}{dx}$$

$$= 2 \cdot 3x^2 - 3 \cdot 2x$$

$$= 6x^2 - 6x$$

(b) $q_d = 500 + \frac{1}{2}p^2 - 2p^3 - \frac{1}{10}p^4$.

$$\frac{dq_d}{dp} = 0 + \frac{1}{2} \cdot 2p - 2 \cdot 3p^2 - \left(\frac{1}{10}\right)4p^3$$

$$= p - 6p^2 - \frac{2}{5}p^3$$

Exercises

Find the derivative of each of the functions in Exercises 1–9.

1. $y = 3x^9$
2. $y = x^{4/3}$
3. $y = x^{-2}$
4. $q_s = 2p^2 - 4p + 3$
5. $q_s = 3p^{-1} - \frac{1}{2}p^{-2}$
6. $q_d = 40 + 3p - 2p^2$
7. $q_d = 100 - p^{2/3}$
8. $q_s = \frac{1}{2}p^3 - \frac{1}{4}p^2 - 2p + 10$
9. $q_d = 100 - 3p^3 + 4p$
10. Prove that the derivative of a sum of three functions is the sum of the derivatives of each of the three functions.
11. If $q_d = 30 - 2p$, find TR and MR.
12. If $p = 100 - 3q_d^3 + 4q_d$, find TR and MR at $q = 2$.

SECTION 8·6   DERIVATIVE OF A PRODUCT OF FUNCTIONS

Theorem 5.   If $y = uv$, where u and v are differentiable functions of x, then

$$\frac{dy}{dx} = u\frac{dv}{dx} + v\frac{du}{dx}$$

that is, the derivative of a product of two functions is the first function multiplied by the derivative of the second function plus the second function multiplied by the derivative of the first function.

Proof. $y = uv$, where u and v are differentiable functions of x, by hypothesis.

When x changes by Δx, u changes by some amount Δu, v by some amount Δv, and, consequently, y changes by some amount Δy. We then have

$$y + \Delta y = (u + \Delta u)(v + \Delta v)$$

$$= uv + u(\Delta v) + v(\Delta u) + (\Delta u)(\Delta v)$$

Subtracting y from $y + \Delta y$, we have

$$\Delta y = u(\Delta v) + v(\Delta u) + (\Delta u)(\Delta v)$$

$$\frac{\Delta y}{\Delta x} = u\frac{\Delta v}{\Delta x} + v\frac{\Delta u}{\Delta x} + \Delta u\frac{\Delta v}{\Delta x}$$

Now,

$$\lim_{\Delta x \to 0} \Delta u = \lim_{\Delta x \to 0} \left(\frac{\Delta u}{\Delta x} \Delta x \right) = \lim_{\Delta x \to 0} \left(\frac{\Delta u}{\Delta x} \right) \lim_{\Delta x \to 0} (\Delta x) = \frac{du}{dx} \cdot 0 = 0$$

Thus, as $\Delta x \to 0$, so does Δu, and

$$\lim_{\Delta x \to 0} \frac{\Delta y}{\Delta x} = \lim_{\Delta x \to 0} u \frac{\Delta v}{\Delta x} + \lim_{\Delta x \to 0} v \frac{\Delta u}{\Delta x} + \lim_{\Delta x \to 0} \Delta u \frac{\Delta v}{\Delta x}$$

$$= \lim_{\Delta x \to 0} u \lim_{\Delta x \to 0} \frac{\Delta v}{\Delta x} + \lim_{\Delta x \to 0} v \lim_{\Delta x \to 0} \frac{\Delta u}{\Delta x} + \lim_{\Delta x \to 0} \Delta u \lim_{\Delta x \to 0} \frac{\Delta v}{\Delta x}$$

$$= u \frac{dv}{dx} + v \frac{du}{dx} + 0$$

Note that we have made use of our earlier theorems on the sum and product of limits.

$$\therefore \frac{dy}{dx} = u \frac{dv}{dx} + v \frac{du}{dx}$$

Illustration.   (a) $y = (3x - 1)(2x^2 + 3)$.

This is in the form of $y =$ a product of two functions uv, where $u = 3x - 1$ and $v = 2x^2 + 3$. Therefore,

$$\frac{dy}{dx} = (3x - 1) \frac{d}{dx} (2x^2 + 3) + (2x^2 + 3) \frac{d}{dx} (3x - 1)$$

$$= (3x - 1)(4x) + (2x^2 + 3)(3)$$

$$= 12x^2 - 4x + 6x^2 + 9$$

$$= 18x^2 - 4x + 9$$

(b) $q_s = (p + 4)(p^3 - 1)$.

$$\frac{dq_s}{dp} = (p + 4)(3p^2) + (p^3 - 1)(1)$$

$$= 3p^3 + 12p^2 + p^3 - 1$$

$$= 4p^3 + 12p^2 - 1$$

(c) $y = x^2(x - 1)(x - 2)$.

In this case y is a product of three factors. But we differentiate by successive use of the product rule. If we let $u = x^2(x - 1)$ and $v = x - 2$, we have

$$\frac{dy}{dx} = x^2(x - 1)\frac{d}{dx}(x - 2) + (x - 2)\frac{d}{dx}[(x^2)(x - 1)]$$

The product rule must now be applied to the term in brackets:

$$\frac{dy}{dx} = x^2(x - 1)(1) + (x - 2)[x^2(1) + (x - 1)(2x)]$$

$$= x^3 - x^2 + (x - 2)[x^2 + 2x^2 - 2x]$$

$$= x^3 - x^2 + (x - 2)[3x^2 - 2x]$$

$$= x^3 - x^2 + 3x^3 - 2x^2 - 6x^2 + 4x$$

$$= 4x^3 - 9x^2 + 4x$$

SECTION 8·7 DERIVATIVE OF A QUOTIENT OF FUNCTIONS

Theorem 6. If $y = u/v$, where u and v are differentiable functions of x, then

$$\frac{dy}{dx} = \frac{v\left(\dfrac{du}{dx}\right) - u\left(\dfrac{dv}{dx}\right)}{v^2}$$

that is, the derivative of a quotient of two functions is the denominator multiplied by the derivative of the numerator minus the numerator multiplied by the derivative of the denominator, all divided by the denominator squared.

Proof. $y = u/v$, where u and v are differentiable functions of x, by hypothesis.

When x changes by Δx, u changes by some amount Δu, v by some amount Δv, and, consequently, y changes by some amount Δy. We then have

$$y + \Delta y = \frac{u + \Delta u}{v + \Delta v}$$

Subtracting y from $y + \Delta y$, we have

$$\Delta y = \frac{u + \Delta u}{v + \Delta v} - \frac{u}{v}$$

$$= \frac{uv + v(\Delta u) - uv - u(\Delta v)}{v(v + \Delta v)} = \frac{v(\Delta u) - u(\Delta v)}{v(v + \Delta v)}$$

$$\frac{\Delta y}{\Delta x} = \frac{v(\Delta u/\Delta x) - u(\Delta v/\Delta x)}{v(v + \Delta v)}$$

Now,

$$\lim_{\Delta x \to 0} (\Delta v) = \lim_{\Delta x \to 0} \left(\frac{\Delta v}{\Delta x} \Delta x\right) = \lim_{\Delta x \to 0} \left(\frac{\Delta v}{\Delta x}\right) \lim_{\Delta x \to 0} (\Delta x) = \frac{dv}{dx} \cdot 0 = 0$$

Thus, when $\Delta x \to 0$, we also have $\Delta v \to 0$, and

$$\lim_{\Delta x \to 0} \frac{\Delta y}{\Delta x} = \frac{\lim_{\Delta x \to 0} v(\Delta u/\Delta x) - \lim_{\Delta x \to 0} u(\Delta v/\Delta x)}{\lim_{\Delta x \to 0} v(v + \Delta v)}$$

$$= \frac{\lim_{\Delta x \to 0} v \lim_{\Delta x \to 0} (\Delta u/\Delta x) - \lim_{\Delta x \to 0} u \lim_{\Delta x \to 0} (\Delta v/\Delta x)}{\lim_{\Delta x \to 0} v \lim_{\Delta x \to 0} (v + \Delta v)}$$

$$= \frac{v\dfrac{du}{dx} - u\dfrac{dv}{dx}}{v^2}$$

Note that we have made use of our earlier theorems on the sum, product and quotients of limits.

$$\therefore \frac{dy}{dx} = \frac{v\dfrac{du}{dx} - u\dfrac{dv}{dx}}{v^2}$$

Illustration.

$$\text{(a)} \quad y = \frac{2x^2 + 3}{3x - 1}$$

This is in the form of $y =$ a quotient of two functions, u/v, where $u = 2x^2 + 3$ and $v = 3x - 1$. Therefore,

$$\frac{dy}{dx} = \frac{(3x-1)\frac{d}{dx}(2x^2+3) - (2x^2+3)\frac{d}{dx}(3x-1)}{(3x-1)^2}$$

$$= \frac{(3x-1)(4x) - (2x^2+3)(3)}{(3x-1)^2}$$

$$= \frac{12x^2 - 4x - 6x^2 - 9}{(3x-1)^2}$$

$$= \frac{6x^2 - 4x - 9}{(3x-1)^2}$$

(b) $q_d = \dfrac{20}{p}$

$$\frac{dq_d}{dp} = \frac{p\frac{d}{dp}(20) - 20\frac{d}{dp}(p)}{p^2}$$

$$= \frac{(p)(0) - (20)(1)}{p^2}$$

$$= \frac{-20}{p^2}$$

(c) $q_d = \dfrac{60+p}{p^3+1}$

$$\frac{dq_d}{dp} = \frac{(p^3+1)\frac{d}{dp}(60+p) - (60+p)\frac{d}{dp}(p^3+1)}{(p^3+1)^2}$$

$$= \frac{(p^3+1)(1) - (60+p)(3p^2)}{(p^3+1)^2}$$

$$= \frac{p^3 + 1 - 180p^2 - 3p^3}{(p^3+1)^2}$$

$$= \frac{1 - 180p^2 - 2p^3}{(p^3+1)^2}$$

Exercises

Find the derivative of each of the following functions.

1. $y = (x + 2)(x^2 - 3)$

2. $y = (x^3 - 1)(x^2 - 1)$

3. $q_s = p^2(p^4 - 2)$

4. $q_s = (p - 4)(p^2 + 1)$

5. $q_s = (p + 1)(p - 3)(p + 2)$

6. $y = \dfrac{4x^2}{x + 2}$

7. $q_d = \dfrac{p - 1}{p^2 + 9}$

8. $q_d = \dfrac{p}{p + 10}$

9. $q_d = 100 - 2p + \dfrac{p}{p + 1}$

10. $q_d = 500 - \dfrac{p^3 - 4}{p^2}$

SECTION 8·8   DERIVATIVE OF A FUNCTION OF A FUNCTION: THE CHAIN RULE

Let $y = g(u)$ and $u = h(x)$. In this case, y is a function of u and u is a function of x, which means that y is really a function of x. We therefore say that y is a *function of a function* or a *composite function*.

Theorem 7.   If $y = g(u)$ is differentiable with respect to u and $u = h(x)$ is differentiable with respect to x, then

$$\frac{dy}{dx} = \frac{dy}{du}\frac{du}{dx}$$

that is, if y is a function of u and u is a function of x, then the derivative of y with respect to x is the derivative of y with respect to u multiplied by the derivative of u with respect to x.

This is known as the *chain rule* of differentiation.

Proof. $y = g(u)$ is differentiable with respect to u and $u = h(x)$ is differentiable with respect to x by hypothesis.

When x changes by Δx, u changes by some amount Δu, and, consequently, y changes by some amount Δy. We then have

$$\frac{\Delta y}{\Delta x} = \frac{\Delta y}{\Delta u}\frac{\Delta u}{\Delta x} \qquad \text{provided that } \Delta u \neq 0$$

In the rare case where $\Delta u = 0$, a somewhat different proof is required. This is beyond the scope of this text.

Now,

$$\lim_{\Delta x \to 0} \Delta u = \lim_{\Delta x \to 0} \left(\frac{\Delta u}{\Delta x}\Delta x\right) = \lim_{\Delta x \to 0}\frac{\Delta u}{\Delta x} \lim_{\Delta x \to 0} \Delta x = \frac{du}{dx}\cdot 0 = 0$$

Thus, as $\Delta x \to 0$, it is also true that $\Delta u \to 0$.

$$\therefore \lim_{\Delta x \to 0}\frac{\Delta y}{\Delta x} = \lim_{\Delta x \to 0}\left(\frac{\Delta y}{\Delta u}\frac{\Delta u}{\Delta x}\right)$$

$$= \left(\lim_{\Delta x \to 0}\frac{\Delta y}{\Delta u}\right)\left(\lim_{\Delta x \to 0}\frac{\Delta u}{\Delta x}\right)$$

$$= \left(\lim_{\Delta u \to 0}\frac{\Delta y}{\Delta u}\right)\left(\lim_{\Delta x \to 0}\frac{\Delta u}{\Delta x}\right)$$

and

$$\frac{dy}{dx} = \frac{dy}{du}\frac{du}{dx}$$

Illustration.

(a) $y = 2u^2 + 3$ and $u = x^2 - 2x$

In this case, y is a function of u and u, in turn, is a function of x.
Now

$$\frac{dy}{du} = 4u \quad \text{and} \quad \frac{du}{dx} = 2x - 2$$

Therefore

$$\frac{dy}{dx} = \frac{dy}{du}\frac{du}{dx}$$

$$= (4u)(2x - 2)$$

We know that $u = x^2 - 2x$.

$\therefore 4u = 4x^2 - 8x$

and

$$\frac{dy}{du} = (4x^2 - 8x)(2x - 2)$$

(b) $q_d = u^2 + 100$ and $u = \dfrac{10}{p}$

$$\frac{dq_d}{du} = 2u \quad \text{and} \quad \frac{du}{dp} = -\frac{10}{p^2}$$

$$\therefore \frac{dq_d}{dp} = \frac{dq_d}{du}\frac{du}{dp}$$

$$= 2u\left(-\frac{10}{p^2}\right)$$

We know that

$$u = \frac{10}{p} \quad \text{and} \quad 2u = \frac{20}{p}$$

$$\therefore \frac{dq_d}{dp} = \frac{20}{p}\left(-\frac{10}{p^2}\right)$$

$$= \frac{-200}{p^3}$$

Exercises

1. $y = 2u^2 - 5u + 3$ and $u = 3x + 2$ Find $\dfrac{dy}{dx}$

2. $q_s = 2u^{2/3}$ and $u = p^2 + 1$ Find $\dfrac{dq_s}{dp}$

3. $q_d = 40 + u^{-1} - u^2$ and $u = 3p$ Find $\dfrac{dq_d}{dp}$

4. $y = \dfrac{1 - 4u}{u}$ and $u = \dfrac{4 - x}{4 + x}$ Find $\dfrac{dy}{dx}$

5. $q_s = u^3 - 2u^2 + 3u - 5$ and $u = 3p^2 - p$ Find $\dfrac{dq_s}{dp}$

6. $q_d = u^3 + 10$ and $u = \dfrac{6}{p^2}$ Find $\dfrac{dq_d}{dp}$

SECTION 8·9 DERIVATIVE OF A POWER OF A FUNCTION

In Section 8.3 we considered the case where the independent variable, x, was raised to a power. We showed that

$$\frac{d}{dx}(x^n) = nx^{n-1}.$$

But suppose that we have functions such as $y = (x + 1)^n$ or $y = (x^2 - 4)^5$? How do we find dy/dx? In general, we are interested in the case $y = u^n$, where u itself is a function of x.

Theorem 8. If $y = u^n$, where u is a differentiable function of x and n is any rational number, then

$$\frac{dy}{dx} = nu^{n-1}\frac{du}{dx}$$

that is, the derivative of a power of a function is equal to the exponent multiplied by the function raised to a power one less than the original power, all multiplied by the derivative of the function.

Note that a special case of the above rule occurs when $u = x$, in which case the general power rule reduces itself to the simple formula for a power of the independent variable given earlier.

Proof. $y = u^n$, where u is a differentiable function of x, by hypothesis.

Consider first the case where n is a positive integer. Then

$$\frac{dy}{du} = nu^{n-1} \qquad \text{by Theorem 2 of Section 8.3}$$

and

$$\frac{dy}{dx} = \frac{dy}{du}\frac{du}{dx} \qquad \text{by Theorem 7 of Section 8.8}$$

Thus,

$$\frac{dy}{dx} = nu^{n-1}\frac{du}{dx}$$

The proof of the theorem for the case where n is any rational number is given in the appendix to this chapter.

Illustration.

(a) $y = (x^2 + 4)^3$

This is in the form of $y = u^3$, where $u = x^2 + 4$. Therefore,

$$\frac{dy}{dx} = 3(x^2 + 4)^2 \frac{d}{dx}(x^2 + 4)$$

$$= 3(x^2 + 4)^2(2x)$$

$$= 6x(x^2 + 4)^2$$

(b) $q_d = \sqrt{200 - p^2} = (200 - p^2)^{1/2}$

This is in the form $q_d = u^{1/2}$, where $u = 200 - p^2$. Therefore,

$$\frac{dq_d}{dp} = \frac{1}{2}(200 - p^2)^{-1/2}\frac{d}{dp}(200 - p^2)$$

$$= \frac{1}{2}(200 - p^2)^{-1/2}(-2p)$$

$$= \frac{-p}{\sqrt{200 - p^2}}$$

(c) $q_d = \frac{400p^2}{(1 + p^2)^3}$

To differentiate this function, we must first use the quotient rule and then the power rule. Thus,

$$\frac{dq_d}{dp} = \frac{(1 + p^2)^3 \frac{d}{dp}(400p^2) - 400p^2 \frac{d}{dp}(1 + p^2)^3}{(1 + p^2)^6}$$

$$= \frac{(1 + p^2)^3(800p) - 400p^2[3(1 + p^2)^2(2p)]}{(1 + p^2)^6}$$

$$= \frac{(1 + p^2)^3(800p) - 2400p^3(1 + p^2)^2}{(1 + p^2)^6}$$

$$= \frac{(1 + p^2)(800p) - 2400p^3}{(1 + p^2)^4}$$

$$= \frac{800p + 800p^3 - 2400p^3}{(1 + p^2)^4}$$

$$= \frac{800p - 1600p^3}{(1 + p^2)^4}$$

Exercises

Differentiate each of the following functions.

1. $y = (5x + 2)^4$

2. $q_d = \dfrac{100}{p} \pm \dfrac{200}{p^2}$

3. $q_s = p\sqrt{p} - \dfrac{2}{p^2}$

4. $y = \dfrac{\sqrt{x}}{1 + x^2}$

5. $q_s = 10p - \dfrac{2}{p^3}$

6. $q_s = (p + 10)\sqrt{p}$

7. $q_d = \dfrac{4000}{(p^2 + 1)^3}$

8. $q_s = \sqrt{p^2 + 25}$

9. $q_s = p^2\sqrt{p^3 + 1}$

10. $q_d = 1000 - (p + 4)\sqrt{p + 1}$

11. $q_d = 500 - \dfrac{p^2}{\sqrt{1 + p^2}}$

SECTION 8·10 DERIVATIVE OF AN INVERSE FUNCTION

In the process of considering functional relationships between variables, it is often desirable to consider one variable as independent for some purposes and the other as independent for other purposes. Thus the quantity demanded for a certain product may be expressed as a function of price, $q_d = f(p)$. This would indicate how many units consumers would wish to purchase at each possible price. However, we may upon occasion be interested in determining the prices that could be charged for various quantities offered in the market. It would then be convenient to express the function as $p = h(q_d)$, which would indicate the price that could be charged for every possible quantity offered. The two functions, f and h, are said to be *inverse functions*.

The reader will recall from Chapter 4 that q_d is said to be a function of p if and only if, for every p under consideration, there corresponds a unique q_d. This does not preclude the possibility of the same q_d corresponding to more than one value of p. However, in order for the inverse function to exist, it is necessary that for every q_d, there corresponds a unique p. Thus, for a function and its inverse to exist, it must be that for every p there corresponds a unique q_d and for every q_d, a unique p. In this case there is a one-to-one relationship between p and q_d.

The following theorem will help us in deciding whether a function has an inverse.

Theorem 9. If a function $q_d = f(p)$ is continuous and steadily increasing (or steadily decreasing)[1] in an interval from $p = a$ to $p = b$, then p is a continuous and steadily increasing (or steadily decreasing) function of q_d within the corresponding q_d interval and can be written as $p = h(q_d)$.

In such cases $p = h(q_d)$ is said to be the inverse function of $q_d = f(p)$ within the pertinent interval.[2]

Illustration. Given the following demand function facing a certain firm:

$$q_d = 100 - 2p \qquad 0 \leqslant p \leqslant 50$$

We have shown in Section 6.5 that any polynomial function is continuous. Thus $q_d = 100 - 2p$ is continuous. It is also a steadily decreasing

---

[1] This is the same as saying that the function is monotonically increasing (or monotonically decreasing).

[2] See the appendix to this chapter for an illustration of a function that does not possess an inverse.

function. Therefore Theorem 9 enables us to say that the inverse of q_d exists.

We can then find the inverse function by solving the equation $q_d = 100 - 2p$ for p in terms of q_d:

$$q_d = 100 - 2p$$

$$2p = 100 - q_d$$

$$p = 50 - \tfrac{1}{2}q_d$$

The demand function is thus put in the form $p = h(q_d)$.

The following theorem enables us to find derivatives of inverse functions merely by knowing the derivative of the original function.

Theorem 10.   If the inverse of $y = f(x)$ is given by $x = h(y)$, then

$$\frac{dx}{dy} = \frac{1}{dy/dx} \qquad \text{provided that } \frac{dy}{dx} \neq 0$$

Illustration.

(a) $q_d = 100 - 2p$ for $0 \leqslant p \leqslant 50$

$$\frac{dq_d}{dp} = -2$$

$$\therefore \frac{dp}{dq_d} = \frac{1}{-2} = -\frac{1}{2}$$

(b) $y = x^2 - 2x$ for $x > 1$

$$\frac{dy}{dx} = 2x - 2$$

$$\therefore \frac{dx}{dy} = \frac{1}{2x - 2}$$

Exercises

1. $q_s = 20p - 100$ Find $\dfrac{dp}{dq_s}$

2. $q_d = 150 - \tfrac{1}{2}p^2$ Find $\dfrac{dp}{dq_d}$

3. $q_s = p^3 - 2p + 30$ Find $\dfrac{dp}{dq_s}$

4. $y = \dfrac{x^2 + 2}{x - 1}$ Find $\dfrac{dx}{dy}$

SECTION 8·11   DERIVATIVES OF IMPLICIT FUNCTIONS

We have been dealing with functions where one variable was expressed directly as a function of a second variable, such as $y = f(x)$. These are known as *explicit functions*. Sometimes, however, we are given a relation between x and y that is not solved for x in terms of y but is instead expressed as $F(x, y) = 0$. Such a relation is known as an *implicit function*, because the value of y is not made explicit. An example of such an implicit function is $2x^2 - xy + y^2 + 6 = 0$. The equation is not solved for y.

In general, for any implicit function $F(x, y) = 0$, the derivative of y with respect to x is found by differentiating $F(x, y) = 0$ term by term while considering y as a function of x. The result is then solved for dy/dx.

Illustration. $2x^2 - xy + y^2 + 6 = 0$. We differentiate each term with respect to x. Thus x is the independent variable; y is a function of x and is treated like any other function of x. Therefore we get

$$4x - \left(x\frac{dy}{dx} + y\right) + 2y\frac{dy}{dx} = 0$$

Note that the derivative of xy is the derivative of a product and the product rule must be used.

$$\therefore\ 4x - x\frac{dy}{dx} - y + 2y\frac{dy}{dx} = 0.$$

We now bring to one side of the equation those terms involving dy/dx:

$$4x - y = x\frac{dy}{dx} - 2y\frac{dy}{dx}$$

$$4x - y = (x - 2y)\frac{dy}{dx}$$

$$\frac{dy}{dx} = \frac{4x - y}{x - 2y}$$

Illustration.   Consider the following demand function, where quantity demanded is given as an implicit function of price.

$$p + pq_d + q_d - 2 = 0$$

Let us find elasticity of demand at a price of $0.50.
We differentiate each term with respect to p. We then have

$$1 + p\frac{dq_d}{dp} + q_d + \frac{dq_d}{dp} = 0$$

$$p\frac{dq_d}{dp} + \frac{dq_d}{dp} = -1 - q_d$$

$$(p + 1)\frac{dq_d}{dp} = -1 - q_d$$

$$\frac{dq_d}{dp} = \frac{-1 - q_d}{p + 1}$$

Now,

$$\text{elasticity of demand} = \frac{p}{q_d}\frac{dq_d}{dp} = \frac{p}{q_d}\left(\frac{-1 - q_d}{p + 1}\right)$$

From the original demand function, we find that when $p = 0.50$, $q_d = 1.00$. Therefore, elasticity of demand at a price of 0.50

$$= \frac{0.50}{1.00}\left(\frac{-2}{1.50}\right) = -0.667$$

Exercises

1. $5p - 3q_s = 2$. Find $\dfrac{dq_s}{dp}$ by implicit differentiation.

2. $pq_d = 1000$. Find $\dfrac{dq_d}{dp}$ by implicit differentiation.

3. $p^2 - q_s^2 = 100$. Find $\dfrac{dq_s}{dp}$ by implicit differentiation.

4. $q_d^2 + 4p^2 = 160$. Find $\dfrac{dq_d}{dp}$ by implicit differentiation.

5. $10p^2q_d = 7$. Find $\dfrac{dq_d}{dp}$ by implicit differentiation.

6. $x^2 + y^2 - 4y = 0$. Find $\dfrac{dy}{dx}$ by implicit differentiation.

7. $y^2 - 3xy = 5$. Find $\dfrac{dy}{dx}$ by implicit differentiation.

8. $x^2 + 2xy - 5y^2 = 4$. Find $\dfrac{dy}{dx}$ by implicit differentiation.

SECTION 8·12 DERIVATIVES OF PARAMETRIC FUNCTIONS

We sometimes encounter a functional relationship between x and y expressed in terms of an auxiliary variable such as

$$x = f(t) \qquad y = g(t)$$

In this case, for every value of t, there corresponds unique values of x and y. Thus there is a unique value of y associated with each value of x and therefore y is a function of x. The auxiliary variable t is said to be a *parameter*.

In some instances, the parameter t may be eliminated by solving both equations for t, thus yielding an equation connecting x and y directly. In most cases, however, such a procedure is cumbersome, inconvenient, or unnecessary.

Illustration.

$$x = 2t - 10 \qquad y = 100 - \tfrac{1}{2}t$$

For each value of t, we have unique x and y values. For example, if $t = 20$, $x = 30$, and $y = 90$. Similarly, every other t value would associate a particular x value with a particular y value.

We can, if we so choose, eliminate the parameter by solving each equation for t:

$$2t = x + 10 \qquad \tfrac{1}{2}t = 100 - y$$

$$t = \frac{x + 10}{2} \qquad t = 200 - 2y$$

$$\frac{x + 10}{2} = 200 - 2y$$

$$x + 10 = 2(200 - 2y)$$
$$x + 10 = 400 - 4y$$
$$4y = 400 - 10 - x$$
$$4y = 390 - x$$
$$y = \frac{390 - x}{4}$$

y is then expressed directly as a function of x. Note that if $x = 30$, $y = 90$, which is what we found from the parametric equations.

Illustration.

$$x = t^3 + 2t + 20 \qquad y = 60 + 5t - t^2$$

For each value of t, we have unique x and y values. For example, when $t = 2$, $x = 32$ and $y = 66$. Similarly, for every t value there will be a correspondence between a particular x value and a particular y value. This establishes y as a function of x. We do not attempt to eliminate the parameter.

The following theorem enables us to find derivatives of parametric functions.

Theorem 11. If y is a function of x given by the parametric equations $x = f(t)$, $y = g(t)$, where $f(t)$ and $g(t)$ are differentiable and where $f'(t) \neq 0$, then

$$\frac{dy}{dx} = \frac{\dfrac{dy}{dt}}{\dfrac{dx}{dt}}$$

Proof.

$$x = f(t) \qquad y = g(t)$$

where $f(t)$ and $g(t)$ are differentiable, and where $f'(t) \neq 0$ by hypothesis. It follows by Theorem 10 that the function $x = f(t)$ has an inverse $t = h(x)$.
Consider now the functions

$$y = g(t) \qquad t = h(x)$$

y is thus a function of t, and t is a function of x. We can therefore use the chain rule of Section 8.8.

We therefore have

$$\frac{dy}{dx} = \frac{dy}{dt}\frac{dt}{dx} \qquad \text{by the chain rule}$$

But by Theorem 10 of Section 8.10,

$$\frac{dt}{dx} = \frac{1}{\dfrac{dx}{dt}}$$

$$\therefore \frac{dy}{dx} = \frac{\dfrac{dy}{dt}}{\dfrac{dx}{dt}}$$

Illustration.

$$x = 2t - 10 \qquad y = 100 - \tfrac{1}{2}t$$

Find dy/dx.

We proceed as follows:

$$\frac{dx}{dt} = 2 \qquad \frac{dy}{dt} = -\frac{1}{2}$$

$$\therefore \frac{dy}{dx} = \frac{\dfrac{dy}{dt}}{\dfrac{dx}{dt}} = \frac{-\tfrac{1}{2}}{2} = -\frac{1}{4}$$

Illustration.

$$x = t^3 + 2t + 20 \qquad y = 60 + 5t - t^2$$

$$\frac{dx}{dt} = 3t^2 + 2 \qquad \frac{dy}{dt} = 5 - 2t$$

$$\frac{dy}{dx} = \frac{\dfrac{dy}{dt}}{\dfrac{dx}{dt}} = \frac{5 - 2t}{3t^2 + 2}$$

Illustration. Given the following demand function facing a certain firm.

$$q_d = 100 - p^2$$

Find marginal revenue at $q = 36$.

In the previous chapter we saw that

$$MR = \frac{d(TR)}{dq},$$

that is, marginal revenue is the derivative of the total revenue function with respect to quantity. To find MR, we solved demand functions for p in terms of q_d and then multiplied p by q_d to give TR. But this procedure can sometimes be difficult, inconvenient, or impossible. We are now in a position to employ an alternative method making use of derivatives of parametric equations.

Because $TR = pq_d$, we shall multiply q_d by p. We then have

$$TR = 100p - p^3$$

where TR is the revenue received by selling any number of units. Thus the total revenue received from selling $q = 36$ units would be found by computing the price that corresponds to $q_d = 36$, which is $p = 8$. Thus when $p = 8$,

$$TR = 100(8) - (8)^3 = 800 - 512 = 288$$

Now, marginal revenue is defined as

$$MR = \frac{d(TR)}{dq_d}$$

But TR and q_d are each functions of p. Therefore we can consider them as parametric equations and use the formula for derivatives of parametric functions. We then have

$$MR = \frac{d(TR)}{dq_d} = \frac{\dfrac{d(TR)}{dp}}{\dfrac{dq_d}{dp}} = \frac{100 - 3p^2}{-2p}$$

At $q = 36$, $p = 8$, and

$$MR = \frac{100 - 3(64)}{-2(8)} = \frac{-92}{16} = 5.75$$

Exercises

For Exercises 1–3, find dy/dx without eliminating the parameter.

1. $x = 3t^2 + 5$ $y = \frac{1}{3}t^3$

2. $x = 2t^{1/3} + t \qquad y = 3t^{2/3} - 7$

3. $x = \dfrac{100}{2 + t} \qquad y = \dfrac{t}{t^2 + 1}$

For Exercises 4–7, find MR at the indicated quantity without changing the form of the demand function.

4. $q_d = 100 - 2p \qquad$ Find MR at $q = 20$

5. $q_d = 100 - p^{1/2} \qquad$ Find MR at $q = 90$

6. $q_d = 100 - 2p - p^2 \qquad$ Find MR at $q_d = 1$

7. $q_d = 54 - p^3 \qquad$ Find MR at $q_d = 27$

SECTION 8·13   DERIVATIVES OF LOGARITHMIC FUNCTIONS

In Chapter 4, the concept of logarithms was explained. We now wish to find derivatives of functions containing logarithms.

Theorem 12.   If $y = \log_a u$, where u is a differentiable function of x and a is any base greater than 1, then

$$\frac{dy}{dx} = \log_a e \, \frac{1}{u}\frac{du}{dx}$$

where e is an irrational number whose approximate value is

$e = 2.71828$

Proof. $y = \log_a u$, where u is a differentiable function of x and a is any base greater than 1.

When x changes by Δx, u changes by some amount Δu and, consequently, y changes by some amount Δy. We then have

$y + \Delta y = \log_a(u + \Delta u)$

Subtracting y from $y + \Delta y$, we have

$$\Delta y = \log_a(u + \Delta u) - \log_a u$$

$$= \log_a \left(\frac{u + \Delta u}{u} \right)$$

by the theorem on the logarithm of a quotient

$$= \log_a \left(1 + \frac{\Delta u}{u} \right)$$

$$\frac{\Delta y}{\Delta u} = \frac{1}{\Delta u} \log_a\left(1 + \frac{\Delta u}{u}\right)$$

$$= \frac{1}{u}\frac{u}{\Delta u} \log_a\left(1 + \frac{\Delta u}{u}\right) \qquad \text{where we multiplied by } \frac{u}{u}$$

$$= \frac{1}{u} \log_a\left(1 + \frac{\Delta u}{u}\right)^{u/\Delta u}$$

by the theorem on a logarithm to a power

$$\therefore \lim_{\Delta u \to 0} \frac{\Delta y}{\Delta u} = \lim_{\Delta u \to 0} \left[\frac{1}{u}\log_a\left(1 + \frac{\Delta u}{u}\right)^{u/\Delta u}\right]$$

$$= \frac{1}{u}\log_a\left[\lim_{\Delta u \to 0}\left(1 + \frac{\Delta u}{u}\right)^{u/\Delta u}\right] \qquad .$$

Now, in advanced works it is shown that

$$\lim_{h \to 0}(1 + h)^{1/h} = e$$

where e is an irrational number whose approximate value is 2.71828. If we then let $\Delta u/u = h$, we have

$$\lim_{\Delta u \to 0}\left(1 + \frac{u}{u}\right)^{u/\Delta u} = \lim_{h \to 0}(1 + h)^{1/h} = e$$

$$\therefore \lim_{\Delta u \to 0} \frac{\Delta y}{\Delta u} = \frac{1}{u}\log_a e$$

and

$$\frac{dy}{du} = \frac{1}{u}\log_a e$$

But because u is a function of x, the chain rule tells us

$$\frac{dy}{dx} = \frac{dy}{du}\frac{du}{dx}$$

and

$$\frac{dy}{dx} = \frac{1}{u}\log_a e \frac{du}{dx}$$

In Chapter 4 we pointed out that logarithms can be taken to any base. Logarithms taken to the base e are known as *natural logarithms* and denoted by ln x. The table of natural logarithms at the end of the book enables us easily to evaluate such logarithms.

If, in Theorem 12, we deal with logarithmic functions to the base e, then $a = e$ and we have the following corollary.

Corollary 1.

$$\frac{d}{dx}(\ln u) = \frac{1}{u}\frac{du}{dx}$$

where u is a differentiable function of x.

This follows from the fact that $\log_e e = 1$. Thus the derivative of the natural logarithm of a function is the derivative of that function divided by the function.

In fact, e is the base most frequently used in connection with the calculus.

Illustration.

$$q_s = \ln\sqrt{p^2 - 1} = \ln(p^2 - 1)^{1/2}$$

Find dq_s/dp.

The given function is in the form of $q_s = \ln u$, where $u = (p^2 - 1)^{1/2}$

$$\therefore \frac{dq_s}{dp} = \frac{1}{(p^2 - 1)^{1/2}}\frac{d}{dp}(p^2 - 1)^{1/2} = \left[\frac{1}{(p^2 - 1)^{1/2}}\right][\tfrac{1}{2}(p^2 - 1)^{-1/2}(2p)]$$

$$= \frac{p}{p^2 - 1}$$

Illustration.

$$q_s = \ln(3p^4)$$

Find dq_s/dp.

This is in the form of $q_s = \ln u$, where $u = 3p^4$.

$$\therefore \frac{dq_s}{dp} = \frac{1}{3p^4}\frac{d}{dp}(3p^4) = \frac{1}{3p^4}(12p^3) = \frac{4}{p}$$

Exercises

1. $q_s = \ln(10p^3)$ Find $\dfrac{dq_s}{dp}$

2. $q_d = \ln\left(\dfrac{400}{p}\right)$ Find $\dfrac{dq_d}{dp}$

3. $q_d = 500 - p^2 \ln p$ Find $\dfrac{dq_d}{dp}$

4. $q_s = 10 + \ln(p^2 + 1)^2$ Find $\dfrac{dq_s}{dp}$

5. $q_d = 50 - \ln(\ln p)$ Find $\dfrac{dq_d}{dp}$

6. $q_s = \sqrt{\ln p} - 6$ Find $\dfrac{dq_s}{dp}$

7. $q_d = 100 - \ln \sqrt{2p^2 - 4}$ Find $\dfrac{dq_d}{dp}$

8. $q_d = \ln\left(\dfrac{p}{p^2 - 1}\right)$ Find $\dfrac{dq_d}{dp}$

9. $q_s = p \ln(4 - p) - 5$ Find $\dfrac{dq_s}{dp}$

SECTION 8·14   LOGARITHMIC DIFFERENTIATION

When presented with the problem of differentiating a complicated expression involving products, quotients, or powers, it is often useful to take logarithms of both sides of the equation and then differentiate. This procedure is known as *logarithmic differentiation*.

Illustration.

$$q_s = \frac{2p^3 - 3}{p(p^2 - 2)^{1/2}}$$

This expression could be differentiated directly. But it would be quite involved, requiring application of the quotient rule, the product rule, and the power rule to complicated expressions. Instead, we take logarithms of both sides of the equation, which gives us

$$\ln q_s = \ln\left[\frac{2p^3 - 3}{p(p^2 - 2)^{1/2}}\right]$$
$$= \ln(2p^3 - 3) - \ln[p(p^2 - 2)^{1/2}]$$
$$= \ln(2p^3 - 3) - \ln p - \tfrac{1}{2}\ln(p^2 - 2)$$

We now differentiate both sides of the equation, remembering that p is the independent variable and q_s is a function of p.

$$\therefore \frac{1}{q_s}\frac{dq_s}{dp} = \left(\frac{1}{2p^3 - 3}\right)\frac{d}{dp}(2p^3 - 3) - \frac{1}{p} - \frac{1}{2}\left(\frac{1}{p^2 - 2}\right)\frac{d}{dp}(p^2 - 2)$$

$$\frac{1}{q_s}\frac{dq_s}{dp} = \left(\frac{1}{2p^3 - 3}\right)(6p^2) - \frac{1}{p} - \frac{1}{2}\left(\frac{1}{p^2 - 2}\right)(2p)$$

$$= \left(\frac{6p^2}{2p^3 - 3}\right) - \frac{1}{p} - \left(\frac{p}{p^2 - 2}\right)$$

We wish to solve for dq_s/dp. We therefore multiply both sides of the equation by q_s and get

$$\frac{dq_s}{dp} = q_s\left[\left(\frac{6p^2}{2p^3 - 3}\right) - \frac{1}{p} - \left(\frac{1}{p^2 - 2}\right)\right]$$

At the outset, we were given

$$q_s = \frac{2p^3 - 3}{p(p^2 - 2)^{1/2}}$$

$$\therefore \frac{dq_s}{dp} = \left(\frac{2p^3 - 3}{p(p^2 - 2)^{1/2}}\right)\left[\left(\frac{6p^2}{2p^3 - 3}\right) - \frac{1}{p} - \left(\frac{p}{p^2 - 2}\right)\right]$$

Exercises

Use logarithmic differentiation to find the derivative of each of the following:

1. $q_d = \dfrac{(10p + 1)^2}{(p^2 - 4)^3}$

2. $q_s = \dfrac{\sqrt{4p^2 - 1}}{(p + 1)^{1/3}}$

3. $q_s = \dfrac{4p^4 - 2}{p\sqrt{p^2 - 2}}$

4. $q_s = \dfrac{p^2\sqrt{p^2 - 4}}{\sqrt{3p^2 - 2}}$

5. $q_d = \dfrac{(p^2 + 3)\sqrt{2p - 1}}{\sqrt[3]{p + 2}}$

SECTION 8·15 DERIVATIVES OF EXPONENTIAL FUNCTIONS

Suppose that we are given the function $y = a^u$, where a is any constant > 1 and u is a function of x. We wish to find dy/dx. However, we cannot use the power rule, because it applies only where the variable is raised to a constant power. In our case we have a constant raised to a variable power. We call this an *exponential function* and derive the following theorem.

Theorem 13. If $y = a^u$, where u is a differentiable function of x and a is greater than 1, then

$$\frac{dy}{dx} = \ln a \, a^u \frac{du}{dx}$$

Proof. $y = a^u$, where u is a differentiable function of x and a is any base greater than 1.

Using logarithmic differentiation, we have

$$\ln y = \ln a^u = u \ln a$$

$$\frac{1}{y}\frac{dy}{dx} = \ln a \frac{du}{dx}$$

$$\frac{dy}{dx} = y \ln a \frac{du}{dx}$$

$$\frac{dy}{dx} = a^u \ln a \frac{du}{dx}$$

If in Theorem 13 we use a base of e, then $a = e$ and we have the following corollary.

Corollary 2.

$$\frac{d}{dx}(e^u) = e^u \frac{du}{dx}$$

because $\ln_e e = 1$; that is, the derivative of an exponential function with base e is the same exponential function multiplied by the derivative of the exponent.

Illustration.

$$q_d = e^{-p^2}$$

Find dq_d/dp.

The given function is in the form $y = e^u$, where $u = -p^2$. Therefore,

$$\frac{dq_d}{dp} = e^{-p^2}\frac{d}{dp}(-p^2) = e^{-p^2}(-2p) = -2pe^{-p^2}$$

Illustration.

$$q_s = \frac{e^p}{p}$$

Find dq_s/dp.

This is a quotient of two functions, one of which happens to be an exponential function. Therefore,

$$\frac{dq_s}{dp} = \frac{p\dfrac{d}{dp}(e^p) - e^p\dfrac{d}{dp}(p)}{p^2}$$

$$= \frac{pe^p - e^p}{p^2}$$

Exercises

1. $q_d = 5^{-p}$ Find $\dfrac{dq_d}{dp}$

2. $q_s = 3e^{p/2}$ Find $\dfrac{dq_s}{dp}$

3. $q_d = e^{-2p}$ Find $\dfrac{dq_d}{dp}$

4. $q_s = 2e^{\sqrt[3]{p}}$ Find $\dfrac{dq_s}{dp}$

5. $q_s = 10e^p + \frac{1}{2}e^{-p}$ Find $\dfrac{dq_s}{dp}$

6. $q_s = p^2e^{2p}$ Find $\dfrac{dq_s}{dp}$

7. $q_d = 500 - pe^{p/10}$ Find $\dfrac{dq_d}{dp}$

8. $q_d = 1000 - e^{-p} \ln 4p$ Find $\dfrac{dq_d}{dp}$

9. $q_s = \dfrac{e^{2p}}{p}$ Find $\dfrac{dq_s}{dp}$

SECTION 8·16   RELATION BETWEEN ELASTICITY AND MARGINAL REVENUE

Consider a demand function $q_d = f(p)$ facing a firm. We have seen in Section 7.5 that this can be converted into p as a function of q or $p = h(q_d)$. We have also seen that $TR = qp = qh(q)$. This is the general expression for total revenue. Now, MR is the derivative with respect to q of the TR function. Therefore, let us compute this derivative from the general expression $TR = qp$. Notice that it is necessary to use the product rule. We then have

$$MR = \frac{d(TR)}{dq} = \frac{d(qp)}{dq} = \frac{q\,dp}{dq} + p = p\left(\frac{q\,dp}{p\,dq} + 1\right)$$

Now, elasticity of demand,

$$E_d = \frac{p\,dq_d}{q_d\,dp}$$

$$\therefore \frac{1}{E_d} = \frac{1}{\dfrac{p\,dq_d}{q_d\,dp}} = \frac{q_d}{p}\frac{1}{dq_d}\;$$

But by the derivative of an inverse function, we know that

$$\frac{1}{\dfrac{dq_d}{dp}} = \frac{dp}{dq_d}$$

$$\therefore \frac{1}{E_d} = \frac{q_d}{p}\frac{dp}{dq_d}$$

and

$$\therefore MR = p\left(1 + \frac{1}{E_d}\right).$$

We have thus derived a relation connecting elasticity of demand and marginal revenue.

Illustration.   Consider the demand function $q_d = 100 - 2p$.

$$\frac{dq_d}{dp} = -2 \quad \text{and} \quad E_d = \frac{p}{q_d}(-2).$$

At $p = 45$,

$$q_d = 10 \quad \text{and} \quad E = \tfrac{45}{10}(-2) = -9$$

Using our formula, we then have

$$MR = 45\left(1 + \frac{1}{-9}\right)$$

$$\therefore MR = 40 \qquad \text{at } q = 10$$

Illustration.   Consider the demand function

$$q_d = 200 - \tfrac{1}{2}\sqrt{1 + 2p}$$

We wish to find the marginal revenue of the 199th unit.
        We first find

$$\frac{dq_d}{dp} = -\frac{1}{2} \cdot \frac{1}{2}(1 + 2p)^{-1/2}(2)$$

$$= -\frac{1}{2(1 + 2p)^{1/2}}$$

Therefore

$$E_d = \left(\frac{p}{q_d}\right)\left(-\frac{1}{2(1 + 2p)^{1/2}}\right)$$

We are given $q_d = 200 - \tfrac{1}{2}\sqrt{1 + 2p}$. Therefore, when $q_d = 199$, we
have

$$199 = 200 - \tfrac{1}{2}\sqrt{1 + 2p}$$

$$\tfrac{1}{2}\sqrt{1 + 2p} = 1$$

$$\sqrt{1 + 2p} = 2$$

$$1 + 2p = 4$$

$$2p = 3$$

$$p = 1.50$$

Therefore, at $q_d = 199$, $p = 1.50$.

$$E_d = \left(\frac{1.50}{199}\right)\left(-\frac{1}{2(1 + 3)^{1/2}}\right) = -\frac{1.5}{792} = -\frac{3}{1584} = -\frac{1}{528}$$

and

$$MR = p\left(1 + \frac{1}{E_d}\right)$$

$$= 1.5(1 - 528)$$

$$= 1.5(-527) = -790.50$$

Thus, at $q = 199$, marginal revenue is negative. This implies that the sale of an additional unit, which invariably is associated with a price reduction, results in a reduction in total revenue.

Exercises

Using the relationship developed in Section 8.16, find marginal revenue for each of the following functions at the specified points.

1. $q_d = 40 - \frac{1}{2}p$ at $q = 30$

2. $q_d = 60 - 3p$ at $q = 6$

3. $q_d = 100 - p^{2/3}$ at $q = 96$

4. $q_d = \dfrac{p}{p + 10}$ at $q = 5$

5. $q_d = 150 - \frac{1}{2}p^2$ at $q = 100$

6. $pq_d = 1000$ at $q = 50$

7. $q_d = 100 - p^{1/2}$ at $q = 90$

SECTION 8·17 ELASTICITY PROPERTIES

If elasticity of demand is greater in absolute value than 1, that is, $|E_d| > 1$, we say that demand is *elastic*. If elasticity of demand is smaller in absolute value than 1, that is, $|E_d| < 1$, we say that demand is *inelastic*. Finally, if elasticity of demand is equal in absolute value to 1, that is, $|E_d| = 1$, we say that demand is *unitary*.

Consider the case of elastic demand, that is, $E_d > 1$. We have already seen in Section 7.7 that except for rare cases elasticity of demand is negative. Therefore E_d must be a negative number larger than 1. It follows that $1/E_d$ must be a negative number smaller than 1 in absolute magnitude. This means that $(1 + 1/E_d)$ will be a positive number, which in turn implies that MR will be positive. The fact that MR (i.e., the derivative of TR) is positive implies that as q increases, so will TR, and as q decreases, so will TR. Assume now that price increases. This will cause a decrease in quantity sold, resulting in a decline in TR. On the other hand, if price falls, quantity sold will increase, resulting in an increase in TR.

We have therefore proved that for elastic demand, if p increases, TR decreases and if p decreases, TR increases. Thus price and total revenue move inversely for elastic demand.

Consider next the case of inelastic demand, that is, $E_d < 1$. E_d must be a negative number smaller than 1 in absolute magnitude. It follows that $1/E_d$ will be a negative number larger than 1 in absolute magnitude. This means that $(1 + 1/E_d)$ will be a negative number, which in turn implies that MR will be negative. The fact that MR is negative implies that as q increases, TR decreases, and as q decreases, TR increases. Assume now that price increases. This will cause a decrease in quantity sold, resulting in an increase in TR. On the other hand, if price falls, quantity sold will increase, resulting in a decrease in TR.

We have therefore proved that for inelastic demand, if p increases, TR increases, and if p decreases, TR increases. Thus price and total revenue move in the same direction for inelastic demand.

Consider, finally, the case where demand is unitary, that is, $|E_d| = 1$. E must be equal to -1. It follows that $1/E_d = -1$. This implies that $(1 + 1/E_d) = 0$, which in turn means that $MR = 0$. The fact that MR is zero implies that as q changes in either direction, TR remains unchanged. Of course, if price increases, there will be a decrease in quantity sold, and if price decreases, there will be an increase in quantity sold. But in either case, TR will remain unchanged.

We have therefore proved that for unitary demand, whether p increases or decreases, TR will remain unchanged.

SECTION 8·18   RELATION BETWEEN ELASTICITY OF MARKET DEMAND AND ELASTICITY OF INDIVIDUAL BUYER'S DEMAND

A market demand function is derived by summing the numerous demand functions of all individual buyers. We wish to derive a relation between the elasticity of the market demand function and the elasticity of the individual buyer's demand function.

Assume that we have n individual buyers whose demand functions are given by $q_1 = f_1(p); q_2 = f_2(p); \ldots; q_n = f_n(p)$. Then market demand is merely the summation $Q_d = q_1 + q_2 + \cdots + q_n$. Elasticity of market demand is then

$$\frac{p}{Q_d} \frac{dQ_d}{dp} = \frac{p}{Q_d} \left(\frac{dq_1}{dp} + \frac{dq_2}{dp} + \cdots + \frac{dq_n}{dp} \right)$$

where to compute dQ_d/dp we took the derivative of each term in the sum. This is justified by the rule on differentiation of a sum of functions (Theorem 4). Removing parentheses, we have

$$\frac{p}{Q_d} \frac{dQ_d}{dp} = \frac{p}{Q_d} \frac{dq_1}{dp} + \frac{p}{Q_d} \frac{dq_2}{dp} + \cdots + \frac{p}{Q_d} \frac{dq_n}{dp}$$

$$= \frac{q_1}{Q_d} \frac{p}{q_1} \frac{dq_1}{dp} + \frac{q_2}{Q_d} \frac{p}{q_2} \frac{dq_2}{dp} + \cdots + \frac{q_n}{Q_d} \frac{p}{q_n} \frac{dq_n}{dp}$$

Now let E_{q1} denote elasticity of the first demand function and E_{q2} elasticity of the second demand function, E_{qn} elasticity of the nth demand function, and E_Q elasticity of the market demand. Then

$$E_Q = \frac{q_1}{Q_d} E_{q1} + \frac{q_2}{Q_d} E_{q2} + \cdots + \frac{q_n}{Q_d} E_{qn}$$

Thus we have proved that elasticity of market demand is the weighted average of the elasticities of the individual demand functions, the weights being the relative quantities purchased by each buyer.

SECTION 8·19   HIGHER DERIVATIVES

Consider a utility function $u = f(q)$, which expresses the utility derived from consuming various quantities of a certain product. q denotes the quantity of the product and u the utility associated with the acquisition of that quantity.

In the usual case, u will be an increasing function of x; that is, as x increases, so will the utility derived therefrom. This implies that

$$\frac{du}{dq} > 0.$$

The precise magnitude of $\dfrac{du}{dq}$ will indicate the amount of increase in utility for each unit increase in x. $\dfrac{du}{dq}$ is known as the *marginal utility* of the product.[3]

We are also interested in the rate of change of the first derivative, that is: Does $\dfrac{du}{dq}$ become smaller or larger as q increases? If $\dfrac{du}{dq}$ becomes smaller as q increases, this means that u is increasing by smaller and smaller amounts. But if $\dfrac{du}{dq}$ becomes larger as q increases, then u is increasing by larger and larger amounts.

We have earlier seen that the derivative of a function $y = f(x)$ is itself a function of x. As such, this resulting function can also be differentiated with respect to x. The result is then known as the second derivative of $y = f(x)$, and is denoted by

$$\frac{d^2y}{dx^2} \quad \text{or} \quad f''(x) \text{ or } y''$$

Therefore, with a utility function $u = f(q)$, the first derivative would be given by

$$\frac{du}{dq}$$

and the second derivative would be derived by differentiating $\dfrac{du}{dq}$. The result would be denoted by

$$\frac{d^2u}{dq^2}$$

and would indicate the rate of change in the first derivative. Thus if

$$\frac{d^2u}{dq^2} > 0$$

then $\dfrac{du}{dq}$ becomes larger as x increases, which, in turn, implies that u is increasing by larger and larger amounts. On the other hand, if

$$\frac{d^2u}{dq^2} < 0$$

[3] The concept of utility has been introduced at this point only to illustrate second derivatives. A full discussion of the various aspects of utility, including the question of its measurability, will be found in Chapter 12.

then $\dfrac{du}{dq}$ becomes smaller as x increases, which implies that u is increasing by smaller and smaller amounts.

Economists usually postulate what is called the law of diminishing marginal utility. This means simply that

$$\frac{d^2u}{dq^2} < 0$$

which indicates that $\dfrac{du}{dq}$ becomes smaller as x increases. This, in turn, implies that u is increasing but by smaller and smaller amounts.

Illustration.   Consider the utility function $u = q^{1/2}$, where only positive square roots are to be taken. Then

$$\frac{du}{dq} = \tfrac{1}{2}q^{-1/2},$$

which is > 0 because $q > 0$. The fact that the first derivative of the utility function, or marginal utility, is positive indicates that utility is an increasing function of x. In other words, additional units of the product add somewhat to utility. But

$$\frac{d^2u}{dq^2} = \frac{-1}{4}x^{-3/2}$$

which is < 0 because $q > 0$. The fact that the second derivative is negative indicates that the first derivative or marginal utility is decreasing. This indicates diminishing marginal utility. As more of the product is acquired, utility increases but by diminishing amounts.

Upon occasion, we may be interested in the rate of change of second derivatives. If we differentiate a second derivative, we have a third derivative. The third derivative of $y = f(x)$ is denoted by

$$\frac{d^3y}{dx^3} \quad \text{or} \quad f'''(x) \quad \text{or} \quad y'''$$

Analogously, the nth derivative of $y = f(x)$ is denoted by

$$\frac{d^ny}{dx^n} \quad \text{or} \quad f^n(x) \quad \text{or} \quad y^n$$

Illustration.

$$y = x^3 - 4x^2 + 2$$

$$\frac{dy}{dx} = 3x^2 - 8x$$

$$\frac{d^2y}{dx^2} = 6x - 8$$

$$\frac{d^3y}{dx^3} = 6$$

$$\frac{d^4y}{dx^4} = 0$$

$$\frac{d^5y}{dx^5} = 0$$

$$\frac{d^ny}{dx^n} = 0 \qquad n \geqslant 4$$

Exercises

Find the second derivative of each of the following functions.

1. $y = 3x^9$
2. $y = x^{4/3}$
3. $q_s = 2p^2 - 4p + 3$
4. $q_d = 100 - 3p^3 + 4p$
5. $q_s = p^2(p^4 - 2)$
6. $u = 3x^{2/3}$
7. $u = \ln x$
8. $u = 20 \ln \frac{1}{2}x$

Appendix

Proof of the Power Rule for Any Rational Exponent

In the text of this chapter we proved the power rule for positive integral exponents. We shall now extend the proof for all rational exponents.

Let $y = u^n$, where u is a differentiable function of x and n is a positive fraction.

Because n is a positive fraction, it can be written as $n = p/q$, where p and q are positive integers with no common factors. Thus,

$$y = u^n = u^{p/q}$$

$$\therefore y^q = u^p$$

Using the power rule for positive integral exponents, we can differentiate both sides of the equation with respect to x. We then have

$$qy^{q-1} \frac{dy}{dx} = pu^{p-1} \frac{du}{dx}$$

and

$$\frac{dy}{dx} = \frac{pu^{p-1}}{qy^{q-1}} \frac{du}{dx}$$

$$= \frac{p}{q} \frac{u^{p-1}}{(u^{p/q})^{q-1}} \frac{du}{dx} \qquad \text{remembering that } y = u^{p/q}$$

$$= \frac{p}{q} \frac{u^{p-1}}{u^{p-p/q}} \frac{du}{dx}$$

$$= \frac{p}{q} u^{(p/q)-1} \frac{du}{dx}$$

Thus,

$$\frac{d}{dx}(u^{p/q}) = \frac{p}{q} u^{(p/q)-1} \frac{du}{dx}$$

and we have proved the power rule for positive fractional exponents.

Consider now the case $y = u^n$, where u is a differentiable function of x and n is a negative rational number.

We can then write

$$y = u^{-m} = \frac{1}{u^m}$$

where m is some positive rational number.

$$\therefore \frac{dy}{dx} = \frac{d}{dx}\left(\frac{1}{u^m}\right) = \frac{-\dfrac{d}{dx}(u^m)}{u^{2m}} \qquad \text{by the quotient rule}$$

$$\frac{d}{dx}(u^m) = mu^{m-1}\frac{du}{dx} \qquad \text{because } m \text{ is a positive rational number}$$

$$\therefore \frac{dy}{dx} = \frac{-mu^{m-1}\dfrac{du}{dx}}{u^{2m}}$$

$$= -mu^{-m-1}\frac{du}{dx}$$

$$= nu^{n-1}\frac{du}{dx}$$

We have thus shown that

$$\frac{d}{dx}(u^n) = nu^{n-1}\frac{du}{dx}$$

for any rational exponent.

Inverse Functions

It was pointed out in the text that a function may or may not have an inverse. The functions discussed in the text were those that had inverses. We shall here present an illustration of a function that does not possess an inverse.

Illustration.   Consider the function $y = x^2$.

For every x there corresponds a unique y, and thus y is a function of x. However, if we solve for x, we have $x = \sqrt{y}$. Now, for any value of y there correspond two values of x, the positive square root of y and the negative square root of y. For example, if $y = 4$, then x could be either $+2$ or -2. Because there is no unique x associated with every value of y, we say that the original function does not have an inverse.

However, if it is made clear that only positive square roots are to be taken, then there would be only one value of x associated with every value of y. In this case, the inverse function would exist.

9

MAXIMIZING AND MINIMIZING FUNCTIONS OF ONE VARIABLE WITH ECONOMIC ILLUSTRATIONS

Here, where we reach the sphere of mathematics, we are among processes which seem to some the most inhuman of all human activities and the most remote from poetry. Yet it is here that the artist has the fullest scope of his imagination.

—Havelock Ellis

In previous chapters we were concerned with functions, the values they could attain, and their rates of change. In this chapter we shall show how to find maximum and minimum values of functions.

SECTION 9·1 MAXIMUM AND MINIMUM POINTS

Consider the following total revenue function,

$$TR = -2q^3 + 35q^2 - 100q$$

defined for $4 \leqslant q \leqslant 14$. What quantity level will maximize and what quantity level will minimize the value of total revenue? We must first define what we mean by a maximum or a minimum value. In so doing, we distinguish between an absolute maximum or minimum and a relative maximum or minimum.

An *absolute maximum point* for any function

$$y = f(x) \qquad \text{where} \quad a \leqslant x \leqslant b$$

is a point $x = x_1$ such that $f(x_1)$ is greater than $f(x)$ for any other x within the interval $a \leqslant x \leqslant b$. Similarly, an *absolute minimum point* for any such function is a point $x = x_2$ such that $f(x_2)$ is smaller than $f(x)$ for any other x within the stated interval.

A point $x = x_3$ is said to be a *relative maximum point* for the above function if $f(x_3)$ is greater than $f(x)$ for any other x within some neighborhood of x_3. This neighborhood must stretch both to the right and to the left of x_3 if x_3 is an interior point of the interval $[a, b]$. If x_3 is an end point of the interval $[a, b]$, then the neighborhood need stretch in only one direction, that is, to include points within the interval where the function is defined. In either case, the neighborhood may be very large or very small.

Analogously, a point $x = x_4$ is said to be a *relative minimum point* for the above function if $f(x_4)$ is smaller than $f(x)$ for any other x within some neighborhood of x_4.

Relative maximum and minimum points are sometimes referred to as *extreme points*.

The following diagram illustrates these definitions graphically:

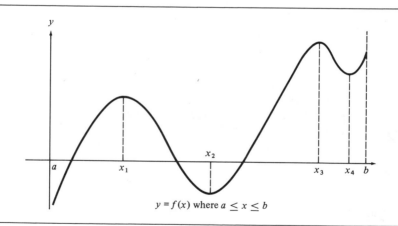

$y = f(x)$ where $a \leq x \leq b$

This function attains its absolute minimum at $x = a$ and its absolute maximum at $x = x_3$. $x = x_1$ is a relative maximum point, because we may choose a neighborhood extending to the right and left of x_1 for which $f(x_1) > f(x)$. For similar reasons, $x = x_3$ is also a relative maximum point. In considering $x = b$, we need only choose a neighborhood that extends to the left, because $x = b$ is an end point. The point $x = b$ is then seen to be a relative maximum because we can, indeed, find a neighborhood stretching to the left for which $f(b) > f(x)$. $x = x_2$ and $x = x_4$

are relative minimum points because, in both cases, we may choose neighborhoods stretching to the right and left where $f(x_2) < f(x)$ and $f(x_4) < f(x)$. For $x = a$, we need only choose a neighborhood that extends to the right, because $x = a$ is an end point. $x = a$ is then seen to be a relative minimum point, because we can find a neighborhood stretching to the right of $x = a$ for which $f(a) < f(x)$.

Now that we have defined maxima and minima, we are interested in being able to locate such points from the functional representation. The succeeding theorems will help us in this task.

Theorem 1.   Suppose that $f(x)$ is defined for $a \leqslant x \leqslant b$ and has a relative maximum or minimum at $x = c$, where c is an interior point (i.e., $a < c < b$). Suppose also that the derivative $f'(x)$ exists at $x = c$. Then we can conclude that

$$f'(c) = 0$$

In other words, this theorem states that if a function has a relative maximum or minimum at an interior point of an interval and if its derivative is defined at that point, then that derivative is equal to zero.

Proof.   We shall provide the proof for the case of a relative maximum. The proof for the case of a relative minimum is quite similar.

Because $x = c$ is a relative maximum and an interior point, we know that for some neighborhood stretching to the right and left of $x = c$, $f(c) > f(x)$. This is the same as saying that for some small Δx, $f(c) > f(c + \Delta x)$. Now, Δx may be either a positive or a negative number. Consider the case where Δx is positive. Then

$$\frac{f(c + \Delta x) - f(c)}{\Delta x} < 0$$

because the numerator is negative while the denominator is positive. This expression takes on only negative values, so its limit, if such a limit exists, can only be either a negative value or zero. Consider next the case where Δx is negative. Then

$$\frac{f(c + \Delta x) - f(c)}{\Delta x} > 0$$

because both the numerator and denominator are negative. This expression takes on only positive values, so its limit, if such a limit exists, can only be either a positive value or zero. But we were given that $f'(c)$ exists, which implies that

$$\lim_{\Delta x \to 0} \frac{f(c + \Delta x) - f(c)}{\Delta x}$$

exists and has the same value regardless of whether $\Delta x \to 0$ through positive or through negative values.

We have, however, already determined that

$$\lim_{\Delta x \to 0} \frac{f(c + \Delta x) - f(c)}{\Delta x} \begin{array}{l} \leq 0 \quad \text{if} \quad \Delta x \text{ is positive} \\ \geq 0 \quad \text{if} \quad \Delta x \text{ is negative} \end{array}$$

The existence of the derivative implies that this limit has the same value regardless of whether Δx is positive or negative, so it must follow that

$$\lim_{\Delta x \to 0} \frac{f(c + \Delta x) - f(c)}{\Delta x} = 0$$

This implies that $f'(c) = 0$.

It should be noted that the theorem says nothing about the conditions for a maximum or minimum at points where $f'(x)$ is undefined. If such points exist, they may be either maxima, minima, or neither. The theorem also does not apply to the end points of the interval of definition. Such points may be maxima, minima, or neither even if $f'(x) \neq 0$.

If the theorem does apply and $f'(c) = 0$, we are nevertheless not assured that $x = c$ is a relative maximum or minimum. The theorem merely asserts that if a function is differentiable at $x = c$, then $f'(c) = 0$ is a *necessary* condition for the existence of a relative maximum or minimum point. It is not, however, a *sufficient* condition. Given the circumstances of the theorem, it is not possible for a point to be a maximum or minimum without $f'(c) = 0$, but the converse does not hold. It is possible for $f'(c) = 0$ without $x = c$ being either a maximum or minimum.

In cases where $f'(c) = 0$, we need some way of verifying whether $x = c$ is a maximum point, minimum point, or neither. The following theorem supplies us with such a method.

Theorem 2.   Suppose that $f(x)$ is defined for $a \leq x \leq b$ and that the derivative $f'(x)$ exists over an interval that includes $x = c$ as an interior point. Suppose also that $f'(c) = 0$. We can then conclude that

1) $f(x)$ has a relative maximum at $x = c$, provided that $f'(x)$ is positive for values of x immediately to the left of $x = c$ and negative for values of x immediately to the right of $x = c$.

2) $f(x)$ has a relative minimum at $x = c$, provided that $f'(x)$ is negative for values of x immediately to the left of $x = c$ and positive for values of x immediately to the right of $x = c$.

3) $f(x)$ has neither a relative maximum or minimum at $x = c$ if $f'(x)$ is positive for values of x on both sides of $x = c$ or if $f'(x)$ is negative for values of x on both sides of $x = c$.

Proof. Consider Case 1. $f(x)$ is an increasing function for points to the left of $x = c$ because $f'(x)$ is positive. $f(x)$ is a decreasing function for points to the right of $x = c$ because $f'(x)$ is negative. This implies that $x = c$ is a relative maximum point.

The proofs for the other cases follow analogously.

This theorem establishes what may be called the *first-derivative test* for verifying maxima or minima. Values of x for which $f'(x) = 0$ are termed *critical values* for the function $f(x)$. Our procedure will generally consist of finding critical values and then testing to see whether they are actually maximum points, minimum points, or neither.

Illustration. Find any maximum and minimum points for the function

$$y = x^3 - 6x^2 + 9x + 1$$

Solution. We first proceed to find the critical values of the function by setting $f'(x) = 0$, which yields

$$f'(x) = 3x^2 - 12x + 9$$
$$= 3(x^2 - 4x + 3)$$
$$= 3(x - 3)(x - 1)$$

and

$$3(x - 3)(x - 1) = 0$$

$x = 3$, $x = 1$ are critical points and are possible maximum or minimum points.

Can there be any other maxima or minima? According to Theorem 1, the only other possibilities are at points where the derivative $f'(x)$ does not exist or at the end points of the function. But in our case $f'(x) = 3(x - 3)(x - 1)$ is defined for every value of x. Moreover, there are no end points of the function, because the function is defined for all possible values of x. Therefore, if there are any relative maxima or minima, they can occur only at $x = 3$ or $x = 1$.

We must now use the first-derivative test to establish whether these critical points are maximum points, minimum points, or neither.

Consider values of x for which $x < 1$. We then have

$$f'(x) = 3(x - 3)(x - 1) > 0$$

that is, $f'(x)$ is positive because both factors involving x are negative and their product, consequently, is positive. If x has a value slightly greater than 1, one factor $(x - 1)$ is then positive but the other $(x - 3)$ is negative, causing the product to be negative. Therefore $f'(x)$ is positive for values of x to the left of $x = 1$ and negative for values of x to the right of $x = 1$. By Theorem 2, $x = 1$ is a maximum point.

Consider values of x immediately to the left of $x = 3$, that is, x is somewhat smaller than 3. The result is that $(x - 3)$ is negative and $(x - 1)$ positive, causing the product and the derivative to be negative. If x has a value greater than 3, both factors are positive so that the derivative is positive. Therefore $f'(x)$ is negative for values of x to the left of $x = 3$ and positive for values of x to the right of $x = 3$. By Theorem 2, $x = 3$ is a minimum point.

We therefore conclude that the only relative maximum is at $x = 1$, for which $y = 5$, and that the only relative minimum is at $x = 3$, for which $y = 1$.

While $x = 1$ is a relative maximum point, it is certainly not an absolute maximum point because when x is very large, y is certainly more than 5. The function, in fact, has no absolute maximum, because there is no end point. As x is taken larger and larger beyond $x = 3$, the function can be made as large as one pleases. Similarly, the function has no absolute minimum, because it can be made as small as one wishes by taking x to be a large negative number.

In the illustration above, we employed the first derivative test to verify maxima and minima. We can also use an alternative test, which often is more convenient and simpler. This is known as the *second-derivative test* and is formulated by the following theorem.

Theorem 3. Suppose that $f(x)$ is defined for $a \leqslant x \leqslant b$ and that the derivative $f'(x)$ exists over an interval that includes $x = c$ as an interior point. Suppose also that $f'(c) = 0$. We can then conclude that

1) $f(x)$ has a relative maximum at $x = c$, provided that $f''(c) < 0$.
2) $f(x)$ has a relative minimum at $x = c$, provided that $f''(c) > 0$.

Proof.   Consider Case 1.

$$f''(c) = \lim_{\Delta x \to 0} \frac{f'(c + \Delta x) - f'(c)}{\Delta x}$$

by definition of the derivative

$$f'(c) = 0$$

and

$$f''(c) < 0 \qquad \text{by hypothesis}$$

$$\therefore \ \lim_{\Delta x \to 0} \frac{f'(c + \Delta x)}{\Delta x} < 0$$

This implies that $f'(c + \Delta x)$ and Δx have opposite signs; that is, when $\Delta x > 0$, $f'(c + \Delta x) < 0$, and when $\Delta x < 0$, $f'(c + \Delta x) > 0$. This, in turn, implies that $f(x)$ has a relative maximum at $x = c$ by Theorem 2.

The proof for Case 2 follows analogously.

Note that this theorem says nothing about the case where $f'(c) = 0$ and $f''(c) = 0$. In such an event, the second-derivative test cannot be used to ascertain the existence of maxima or minima. The first-derivative test must be utilized.

Illustration.   In an earlier illustration we inquired about maxima and minima for the function

$$y = x^3 - 6x^2 + 9x + 1$$

We located critical points at $x = 3$ and $x = 1$ and employed the first-derivative test to ascertain whether either of these were maximum or minimum points. Let us now employ the second-derivative test.

$$f(x) = x^3 - 6x^2 + 9x + 1$$

$$f'(x) = 3x^2 - 12x + 9$$

$$f''(x) = 6x - 12$$

$$f''(3) = 6 > 0$$

Therefore, $x = 3$ is a relative minimum point by Theorem 3.

$$f''(1) = -6 < 0$$

Therefore, $x = 1$ is a relative maximum point by Theorem 3.

We can now summarize the procedure to follow in locating maximum and minimum points of a function over a certain interval.

First, find the derivative of the function $f'(x)$; set it equal to zero and solve for values of x. These are critical points.

Second, test all critical points to ascertain whether they are relative maximum or minimum points or neither, by using the first-derivative test as given in Theorem 2 or the second-derivative test as given in Theorem 3. The second-derivative test will generally be easier and involve less computation. However, in the event that it is inconclusive, the first-derivative test must be used.

Third, find the points, if any, on the interval for which $f'(x)$ is not defined. These could possibly be maximum or minimum points. Determine what they are by using the first-derivative test; that is, if $f'(x)$ is positive for values immediately to the left of such a point and negative for values immediately to the right, then a relative maximum exists at that point, while if $f'(x)$ is negative for values immediately to the left and positive for values immediately to the right, then a relative minimum exists.

Fourth, consider any end points that exist for the interval and ascertain whether the value of the function at the end point is greater or smaller than for neighboring points within the interval. In the former case, a relative maximum exists; while in the latter case a relative minimum exists.

Fifth, consider all relative maximum points found in the previous steps and find the value of $f(x)$ for each of these points. The point that yields the greatest value for $f(x)$ is the absolute maximum point of the function on the particular interval. Similarly, consider all relative minimum points. The point that yields the smallest value for $f(x)$ is the absolute minimum point of the function on the particular interval. In the event that no end points are given, the function may continue to increase or decrease without bounds. In such a case, no absolute maximum or minimum would exist. See, for example, the illustration that follows Theorem 2.

Exercises

Find maximum and minimum points of each of the following functions.

1. $y = 2x^3 - 9x^2 - 60x + 7$

2. $y = 2x^3 - 27x^2 + 48x + 5$

3. $y = 3x^4 - 4x^3 - 72x^2 + 18$

4. $y = \dfrac{3x}{4 + x^2}$

5. $y = \dfrac{6}{9 + 2x}$

6. $y = 10(x - 4)^4$

7. $y = 400 + 4x^2 - x^3$

SECTION 9·2   SIGNIFICANCE OF SIGN OF SECOND DERIVATIVE FOR FUNCTIONS IN GENERAL, CONCAVITY, AND POINTS OF INFLECTION

In the previous section we saw that the sign of the second derivative indicates whether a maximum or minimum value is attained at a critical point. We now examine the significance of the sign of the second derivative for values of a function in general.

Consider a continuous function $y = f(x)$ with continuous derivatives. In Section 7.7 it was shown that a positive value for the derivative dy/dx at any point indicates that the function $y = f(x)$ is increasing at that point. Similarly, a negative value for the derivative indicates that the function is decreasing.

Now, the second derivative of any function $y = f(x)$ is simply the derivative of the first derivative. Therefore if $d^2y/dx^2 > 0$ at any point, this implies that (at that point) the first derivative is increasing, while if $d^2y/dx^2 < 0$, the first derivative is decreasing.

Illustration.

$$TR = -2q^3 + 35q^2 - 100q$$

At which levels of output is *marginal revenue* increasing, and at which levels is it decreasing?

Because marginal revenue is the first derivative of total revenue, we must find those points for which the second derivative is positive and those points for which it is negative. This is accomplished as follows:

$$\frac{d(TR)}{dq} = MR = -6q^2 + 70q - 100$$

$$\frac{d^2(TR)}{dq^2} = -12q + 70$$

We find those values for which the second derivative is positive by setting

$-12q + 70 > 0$

which yields

$12q < 70$

$q < \frac{35}{6}$

This implies that for any output level less than $\frac{35}{6}$, the first derivative, that is, marginal revenue, is increasing. Similarly, we could show that for any $q > \frac{35}{6}$, the first derivative is decreasing.

The sign of the second derivative also has a graphical interpretation. If, within a certain range, the second derivative is positive, then the graph of the function within that range of points opens upwards:

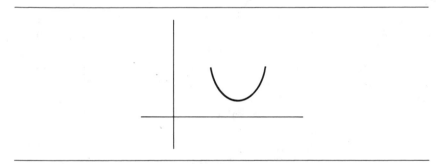

This curve is then said to be *concave upward*. On the other hand if, within a certain range, the second derivative is negative, then the graph of the function within that range of points opens downward:

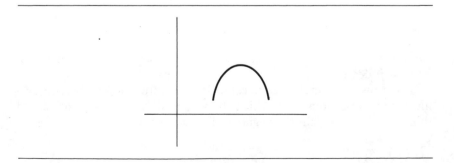

This curve is said to be *concave downward*.

In general, for any function, we shall find that its graphical representation will usually be a combination of portions where it is concave upward and portions where it is concave downward. The point at which a curve changes from concave upward to concave downward or vice versa is said to be an *inflection point*.

To locate points of inflection for any function $y = f(x)$ (assuming that the second derivative is continuous), it is only necessary to find at which points $d^2y/dx^2 = 0$. Such points are points of inflection, provided that the third derivative, $d^3y/dx^3 \neq 0$.

Illustration. We have already considered the function

$$y = x^3 - 6x^2 + 9x + 1$$

and found $x = 3$ to be a relative minimum point and $x = 1$ a relative maximum point. Let us now investigate direction of concavity and points of inflection. We have

$$f(x) = x^3 - 6x^2 + 9x + 1$$
$$f'(x) = 3x^2 - 12x + 9$$
$$f''(x) = 6x - 12$$

Now, to find where the function is concave upward, we locate the points for which $f''(x) > 0$:

$$6x - 12 > 0$$
$$6x > 12$$
$$x > 2 \quad \textit{concave upward}$$

The function is concave downward for those points where $f''(x) < 0$, which yields

$$6x - 12 < 0$$
$$6x < 12$$
$$x < 2 \quad \textit{concave downward}$$

To find possible inflection points, set $f''(x) = 0$, which yields

$$6x - 12 = 0$$
$$6x = 12$$
$$x = 2$$

Now $f'''(x) = 6$. Therefore, at $x = 2, f'''(x) \neq 0$. Thus $x = 2$ is a *point of inflection.*

Taking all this information together, it is quite easy to sketch the curve of this function, which would appear as follows:

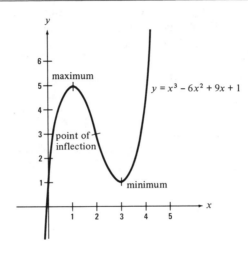

Exercises

Find direction of concavity and points of inflection for each of the following:

1. $y = 2x^3 - 9x^2 - 60x + 7$

2. $y = 2x^3 - 27x^2 + 48x + 5$

3. $y = \dfrac{6}{9 + 2x}$

4. $y = \dfrac{10}{(1 + x)^2}$

5. $y = 10(x - 4)^4$

6. $y = 400 + 4x^2 - x^3$

SECTION 9·3   ILLUSTRATIVE ECONOMIC FUNCTIONS

The concepts of the previous two sections can be readily applied to various economic functions. Let us consider the following illustrations, which taken together summarize the theorems, procedures, and different types of solutions that arise when maximizing and minimizing functions of one variable.

Illustration.   Find maximum and minimum points, direction of concavity, and points of inflection for the following revenue function:

$$TR = -2q^3 + 35q^2 - 100q \qquad \text{where } 4 \leqslant q \leqslant 13.9$$

Solution.   Our first step is to find any critical points, because these are possible maxima or minima. This we do by setting the first derivative equal to zero:

$$\frac{d(TR)}{dq} = MR = -6q^2 + 70q - 100 = 0$$

$$(-3q + 5)(2q - 20) = 0$$

$$q = \tfrac{5}{3} \qquad q = 10$$

We have two critical points. But $q = \tfrac{5}{3}$ is outside the interval for which our function is defined. Therefore the only remaining critical point for us to consider is $q = 10$. To decide whether $q = 10$ is a maximum, minimum, or neither, we use the second-derivative test:

$$TR'' = -12q + 70$$

Now, at $q = 10$, the second derivative

$$TR'' = -12(10) + 70 = -120 + 70 < 0$$

The second derivative is negative at this critical point, so we are assured that $q = 10$ is a relative maximum point.

The only other possible maximum or minimum points are end points of the interval over which the function is defined and any points for which the first derivative is undefined. Because the first derivative is defined for all points within the interval under consideration, we need consider only the end points.

At $q = 4$, $TR = 32$. As q increases beyond a value of 4, TR increases. Therefore $q = 4$ is a relative minimum. Note that we did not consider what occurs when q is less than 4, because the function is not defined for such points.

The other end point is $q = 13.9$. At this point $TR = 1.112$. For points to the immediate left of $q = 13.9$, TR is greater than 1.112. Therefore $q = 13.9$ is also a relative minimum. Here again, we did not examine the function for points greater than $q = 13.9$, because they are outside the domain for which the function is defined.

We therefore have one relative maximum point, $q = 10$, and two relative minima at the two end points, $q = 4$ and $q = 13.9$.

Because the point $q = 10$ is the only relative maximum point, it is also the absolute maximum point. At that point, $TR = 500$. The absolute minimum point occurs at one of the relative minimum points, $q = 4$ or $q = 13.9$. Because $TR = 32$ for $q = 4$ and $TR = 1.112$ for $q = 13.9$, we conclude that $q = 13.9$ is the absolute minimum point.

To find direction of concavity, we consider the second derivative of the TR function, which is

$$TR'' = -12q + 70$$

The function will be concave upward where

$$TR'' > 0$$

or where

$$-12q + 70 > 0$$

or

$$70 > 12q$$

$$\tfrac{70}{12} > q$$

$$\tfrac{35}{6} > q$$

The function will be concave downward where

$$TR'' < 0$$

or where

$$-12q + 70 < 0$$

$$70 < 12q$$

$$\tfrac{70}{12} < q$$

$$\tfrac{35}{6} < q$$

Thus the function is concave upward when $q < \tfrac{35}{6}$ and concave downward when $q > \tfrac{35}{6}$.

To find points of inflection, we set $TR'' = 0$, which yields

$$-12q + 70 = 0$$
$$12q = 70$$
$$q = \tfrac{35}{6}$$

We test this by evaluating TR'''. At $q = \tfrac{35}{6}$, $TR''' \neq 0$. Therefore $q = \tfrac{35}{6}$ is a point of inflection.

The information we have compiled enables us to sketch the graph of the TR function.

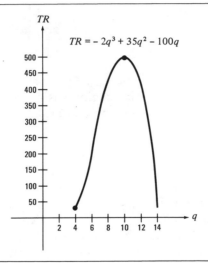

$$TR = -2q^3 + 35q^2 - 100q$$

Illustration. Find maximum and minimum points for the following function:

$$TR = \begin{cases} -2q^3 + 35q^2 - 100q & \text{for} \quad 4 \leqslant q \leqslant 11 \\ 35q^2 - 3762 & \text{for} \quad 11 < q \leqslant 14 \end{cases}$$

Solution. In order to find critical points, we must compute the first derivative of the function. There are two different functional representations for the two subintervals, so we shall find the first derivative for each one separately. This yields the following:

$$\frac{d(TR)}{dq} = MR = \begin{cases} -6q^2 + 70q - 100 & \text{for} \quad 4 \leqslant q < 11 \\ 70q & \text{for} \quad 11 < q \leqslant 14 \end{cases}$$

Note that we could not compute a derivative for the function at the point $q = 11$, because

$$\lim_{\Delta q \to 0} \frac{f(q + \Delta q) - f(q)}{\Delta q}$$

would vary depending on whether $q = 11$ is approached from the left side or the right side. Therefore $d(TR)/dq$ is undefined at $q = 11$.

Setting the first derivative equal to zero, we have

$-6q^2 + 70q - 100 = 0$ for $4 \leqslant q < 11$ $70q = 0$ for $11 < q < 14$

$(-3q + 5)(2q - 20) = 0$ $q = 0$ which is not

$q = \frac{5}{3}, q = 10$ within the
                                                                                        domain of

$q = \frac{5}{3}$ is not within the   definition
domain of definition

Therefore the only critical point remaining is $q = 10$. We now take the second derivative of the TR function and evaluate it at $q = 10$, which yields

$$TR'' = 12q + 70$$

At $q = 10$, we have $TR'' = -120 + 70 < 0$. Therefore $q = 10$ is a relative maximum point. This is the same result as we arrived at in the preceding illustration. But now we must consider any points for which $d(TR)/dq$ is undefined. Because $q = 11$ is such a point, we must test it for a possible maximum or minimum. We do this by ascertaining whether the value of $d(TR)/dq$ changes in sign as q varies from points to the left of $q = 11$ to points to the right of $q = 11$.

For points to the left of $q = 11$, the first derivative would be

$$\frac{d(TR)}{dq} = -6q^2 + 70q - 100 < 0$$

for points slightly less than 11, such as $q = 10.9$. For points to the right of $q = 11$, the first derivative would be

$$\frac{d(TR)}{dq} = 70q > 0$$

for points slightly more than 11, such as $q = 11.1$. Therefore $q = 11$ is a relative minimum point.

As in the previous illustration, we must also consider end points. At $q = 4$, $TR = 32$; and as q increases, TR increases. Therefore $q = 4$ is a relative minimum point. At $q = 14$, $TR = 3098$. For points to the immediate left of $q = 14$, TR is less than 3098. Therefore $q = 14$ is a relative maximum.

We thus have two relative maximum points, $q = 10$ and $q = 14$. Now, at $q = 10$, $TR = 500$; while at $q = 14$, $TR = 3098$. Therefore $q = 14$ is the absolute maximum point.

We also have two relative minimum points, $q = 4$ and $q = 11$. At $q = 4$, $TR = 32$; while at $q = 11$, $TR = 1804$. Therefore $q = 4$ is the absolute minimum point.

Illustration.   Find maximum and minimum points, direction of concavity, and points of inflection for the following revenue function:

$$TR = 30q^2 - q^3 \qquad \text{where} \quad q \geqslant 0$$

Solution.   We locate critical points by setting the first derivative equal to zero:

$$\frac{d(TR)}{dq} = 60q - 3q^2 = 0$$

$$3q(20 - q) = 0$$

$$q = 0 \qquad q = 20$$

We now test each of these critical points by evaluating the second derivative at these points. This yields

$$TR'' = 60 - 6q$$

At $q = 0$, the second derivative is equal to 60. This is positive, so $q = 0$ is a relative minimum point. At $q = 20$, the second derivative is equal to $60 - 6(20) < 0$. This is negative, so $q = 20$ is a relative maximum point.

The only other possible maximum or minimum points are at points where the first derivative does not exist or at the end points. However, the first derivative exists for all points. The only end point we have is $q = 0$, which was already found to be a relative minimum. Therefore $q = 0$ is the only relative minimum.

To find the absolute minimum point, we consider the value of the function at $q = 0$, which yields $TR = 0$. But we also notice that TR

would be negative for large values of q. These are real possibilities, because q has no upper end point. In fact, TR could become increasingly negative beyond any bound. Therefore we say that there is no absolute minimum for the function.

   To find the absolute maximum, we consider the value of the function at $q = 20$, which yields $TR = 30(20)^2 - (20)^3 = 4000$. There are no other relative maximum points to consider, and when q increases without bounds TR is certainly below the value of 4000. Therefore $q = 20$ is the absolute maximum.

   The function will be concave upward for those points where the second derivative is positive, which yields

$$TR'' = 60 - 6q > 0$$
$$60 > 6q$$
$$10 > q$$

The function will be concave downward for those points where the second derivative is negative, which yields

$$TR'' = 60 - 6q < 0$$
$$60 < 6q$$
$$10 < q$$

Thus the function is concave upward when $q < 10$ and concave downward when $q > 10$.

   Points of inflection occur where the second derivative equals zero, or

$$TR'' = 60 - 6q = 0$$
$$60 = 6q$$
$$q = 10$$

We must verify this by examining the third derivative, which is

$$TR''' = -6$$

Because the third derivative is $\neq 0$ at $q = 10$, we conclude that $q = 10$ is an inflection point.

   With the information we have derived, we can easily sketch the graph of this revenue function. It would appear as follows.

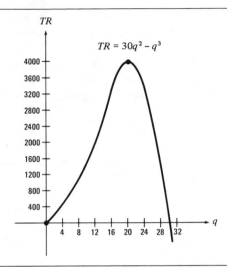

$$TR = 30q^2 - q^3$$

Illustration. Find maximum and minimum points, direction of concavity, and points of inflection for the following supply function:

$$q_s = 10(p - 4)^3 + 640 \qquad \text{when} \quad p \geqslant 0$$

Solution. We find critical points by setting the first derivative equal to zero:

$$\frac{dq_s}{dp} = 30(p - 4)^2 = 0$$

$$(p - 4) = 0$$

$$p = 4$$

We now test this critical value by evaluating the second derivative at $p = 4$.

$$q_s'' = 60(p - 4)$$

At $p = 4$, the second derivative is zero. Therefore the second-derivative test is inconclusive. We must use the first-derivative test. When p is slightly less than 4, such as $p = 3.9$, the first derivative is positive. When p is slightly more than 4, such as $p = 4.1$, the first derivative is still positive. The derivative does not change signs as it moves from the left of $p = 4$ to the right of that point, so we conclude that $p = 4$ is neither a maximum nor a minimum. This illustrates how a critical point may be neither a maximum or a minimum.

The only possible maximum or minimum points are therefore at points for which the first derivative is undefined or at the end points of the function. The first derivative exists at all points, so we are left to consider the end points, of which we have only one, namely, $p = 0$.

At $p = 0$, $q_s = 0$. As p increases, q_s increases. Therefore $p = 0$ is a relative minimum. It is the only relative minimum, and the function gets very large when p increases without bound, so we conclude that $p = 0$ is also the absolute minimum.

There are no relative maximum points for this function. The function becomes larger and larger beyond bounds as p gets larger and larger, so there are no absolute maximum points either.

The function will be concave upward whenever the second derivative is positive, or when

$$q_s'' = 60(p - 4) > 0$$

$$p - 4 > 0$$

$$p > 4$$

It will be concave downward whenever the second derivative is negative, or when

$$q_s'' = 60(p - 4) < 0$$

$$p - 4 < 0$$

$$p < 4$$

Points of inflection occur when the second derivative equals zero, or

$$q_s'' = 60(p - 4) = 0$$

$$p - 4 = 0$$

$$p = 4$$

To verify that this is a point of inflection, we must compute the third derivative. We find

$$q_s''' = 60 \neq 0$$

Therefore $p = 4$ is a point of inflection.

Exercises

Find maximum and minimum points, direction of concavity, and points of inflection for the following functions.

1. $TR = 18q^2 - 4q^3$, where $q \geqslant 0$

2. $TR = -q^3 + 48q^2 - 180q$, where $0 \leqslant q \leqslant 100$

3. $TR = \begin{cases} -q^3 + 48q^2 - 180q, & \text{where} \quad 0 \leqslant q \leqslant 50 \\ 50q^2 - 25{,}000, & \text{where} \quad 50 < q \leqslant 100 \end{cases}$

4. $TR = -q^4 + 20q^3 - 100q^2$, where $3 \leqslant q \leqslant 15.$

5. $TR = -2q^3 - 18q^2 - 48q$, where $q \geqslant 0$

6. $q_d = \dfrac{p}{1 + p^2}$, where $p \geqslant 0$

7. $q_s = 1000 - \dfrac{100}{p}$, where $p > 0$

8. $q_s = 100p^3 - 20p^2$, where $p \geqslant 1$

9. $q_d = 400 - 2p + 3.5p^2 - p^3$, where $0 \leqslant p \leqslant 8$

10. $q_s = 3(2p - 10)^3 + 3000$, where $p \geqslant 0$

CHAPTER

$$\boxed{10}$$

FUNCTIONS OF
SEVERAL VARIABLES

> Those skilled in mathematical analysis know that its object is not simply to calculate numbers, but that it is also employed to find relations between magnitudes which cannot be expressed in numbers and between functions whose law is not capable of algebraic expression.
>
> —Augustin Cournot

In past chapters we have applied the concepts of limits, continuity, and differentiation to functions of one independent variable. In the real economic world, however, we most frequently encounter cases where several independent variables affect economic phenomena. In this chapter we therefore extend earlier concepts and procedures to functions of several variables.

SECTION 10·1 FUNCTIONS, LIMITS, AND CONTINUITY

Suppose that we are given information that tells us that for each possible price of a product and income of consumers there is some unique quantity that will be demanded. This is the same as saying that quantity demanded is a *function* of price and income. Thus, a function of several variables is a relationship or association between several independent variables and one dependent variable. In our case, once price and income are set, quantity is determined by the nature of the functional relationship.

Functions can be defined for any number of independent variables. If, for example, quantity demanded depends not only on product price and consumer income but also upon the prices of a host of related products, we would represent this by

$$q_{d_A} = f(p_A, p_B, p_C, \ldots, y)$$

where q_{d_A} denotes the quantity demanded of product A; p_A is the price of product A; p_B the price of product B; and so on.

It can be seen that the definition of a function of several variables is completely analogous to that given in Chapter 4 for functions of one variable. We have also seen that we can view functions involving one independent and one dependent variable as sets of ordered pairs. Similarly, functions involving two independent variables and one dependent variable can be viewed as sets of ordered triplets. In general, for any number of variables, functions are sets of ordered tuples.

The *limit* of a function of several variables is also defined in a manner analogous to that for a function of one variable. Consider the following function of two variables:

$$q_d = f(p, y)$$

We say that

$$\lim_{\substack{p \to a \\ y \to b}} f(p, y) = L$$

if for $p \neq a$, $y \neq b$, $f(p, y)$ is as close as we desire to L when p is sufficiently close to a and y sufficiently close to b.

Such a statement tells us that when p is close to a and y to b, $f(p, y)$ is close to L. How close is close enough? The answer is that $f(p, y)$ can be made as close to L as we desire simply by taking p close enough to a and y close enough to b.

Limits of functions of three or more variables are defined in like manner.

Note: See the appendix at the end of this chapter for a more formal and rigorous expression of limits.

Illustration.   Consider the demand function given by

$$q_d = 100 - 3p^3 + 2\sqrt{y}$$

Find $\lim_{\substack{p \to 2 \\ y \to 100}} q_d$

Solution.   As p moves closer and closer to 2 and y moves closer and closer to 100, $3p^3$ approaches 24 and $2\sqrt{y}$ approaches 20. Therefore $f(p, y) = 100 - 3p^3 + 2\sqrt{y}$ will be as close as we desire to $100 - 24 + 20 = 96$ as long as p is sufficiently close to 2 and y to 100.

Therefore, $\lim_{\substack{p \to 2 \\ y \to 100}} q_d = 96$

We now turn to the definition of continuity of a function of several variables, which will also be seen to be analogous to that for a function of one variable.

Definition. The function $f(p, y)$ is continuous at $p = a$, $y = b$ if

1) $f(a, b)$ exists.
2) $f(p, y)$ approaches some limit as p approaches a and y approaches b.
3) $\lim\limits_{\substack{p \to a \\ y \to b}} f(p, y) = f(a, b)$.

Illustration. In the previous illustration we considered the function

$$q_d = 100 - 3p^3 + 2\sqrt{y}$$

and found that $\lim\limits_{\substack{p \to 2 \\ y \to 100}} q_d = 96$

Now $f(2, 100) = 96$. Therefore this function is continuous at $(2, 100)$.

Illustration. Consider the following demand function:

$$q_d = \frac{10y}{5p + y - 10}$$

This function is undefined at the point $p = 1$, $y = 5$. Therefore it is discontinuous at this point.

A function is said to be continuous in a region if it is continuous at all points in the region.

Continuity of functions of three or more variables are defined in like manner.

SECTION 10·2 PARTIAL DERIVATIVES

Consider the demand function

$$q_d = f(p, y)$$

and suppose that y is held fixed. q_d thus becomes a function of p only. If we can then find the derivative of this function with respect to p, the result is called the *partial derivative* of q_d with respect to p. It is denoted by one of the following symbols:

$$\frac{\partial q_d}{\partial p} \quad \text{or} \quad \frac{\partial f}{\partial p} \quad \text{or} \quad f_p(p, y)$$

Similarly, if p is held fixed and we then find the derivative of the function with respect to y, the result is the *partial derivative* of q_d with respect to y.

Using more concise terminology, partial derivatives can be defined by the following:

$$\frac{\partial q_d}{\partial p} = \lim_{\Delta p \to 0} \frac{f(p + \Delta p, y) - f(p, y)}{\Delta p}$$

and

$$\frac{\partial q_d}{\partial y} = \lim_{\Delta y \to 0} \frac{f(p, y + \Delta y) - f(p, y)}{\Delta y}$$

It can thus be seen that $\partial q_d/\partial p$ is the *instantaneous rate of change* of quantity demanded with respect to p as y is held constant.

In like manner, $\partial q_d/\partial y$ is the *instantaneous rate of change* of quantity demanded with respect to y as p is held constant.

The process of actually computing partial derivatives of specific functions is essentially the same as for derivatives of functions of one variable. We use the same rules of differentiation as developed in Chapter 8, remembering, all the while, that if we want $\partial q_d/\partial p$, we must consider y, wherever it appears, as a constant. Similarly, if we want $\partial q_d/\partial y$, we must consider p, wherever it appears, as a constant.

Illustration.

$$q_d = 100 - 3p^3 + 2\sqrt{y}$$

$$\frac{\partial q_d}{\partial p} = -9p^2$$

$$\frac{\partial q_d}{\partial y} = 2 \cdot \tfrac{1}{2} y^{-1/2} = y^{-1/2}$$

We can find the value of partial derivatives at particular points by merely substituting the respective values for the variables. Thus, at $p = 2$, $y = 100$, we would have

$$\frac{\partial q_d}{\partial p} = -36 \qquad \frac{\partial q_d}{\partial y} = \frac{1}{10}$$

Illustration.

$$q_d = \frac{10y}{5p + y - 10}$$

To find $\partial q_d/\partial p$, we treat y as if it were a constant and differentiate with respect to p. We then use the quotient rule, which yields

$$\frac{\partial q_d}{\partial p} = \frac{(5p + y - 10)(0) - 10y(5)}{(5p + y - 10)^2}$$

$$= \frac{-50y}{(5p + y - 10)^2}$$

To find $\partial q_d / \partial y$, we treat p as if it were a constant and differentiate with respect to y. Therefore,

$$\frac{\partial q_d}{\partial y} = \frac{(5p + y - 10)(10) - 10y(1)}{(5p + y - 10)^2} = \frac{50p + 10y - 100 - 10y}{(5p + y - 10)^2}$$

$$= \frac{50p - 100}{(5p + y - 10)^2}$$

At the point $p = 10$, $y = 160$, we have

$$\frac{\partial q_d}{\partial p} = \frac{-50(160)}{(50 + 160 - 10)^2} = \frac{-8000}{40,000} = \frac{-1}{5} = -0.2$$

$$\frac{\partial q_d}{\partial y} = \frac{500 - 100}{(50 + 160 - 10)^2} = \frac{400}{40,000} = \frac{1}{100} = 0.01$$

Illustration.

$$q_d = 100 - 2p^4 - \tfrac{1}{100}py + \tfrac{1}{100}y^2$$

To find $\partial q_d / \partial p$, we treat y as if it were a constant. We then have

$$\frac{\partial q_d}{\partial p} = -8p^3 - \tfrac{1}{100}y$$

Similarly, to find $\partial q_d / \partial y$, we treat p as a constant. This yields

$$\frac{\partial q_d}{\partial y} = -\tfrac{1}{100}p + \tfrac{1}{50}y$$

At the point $p = 2$, $y = 200$, we have

$$\frac{\partial q_d}{\partial p} = -8(8) - \tfrac{200}{100} = -64 - 2 = -66$$

$$\frac{\partial q_d}{\partial y} = -\tfrac{1}{100}(2) + \tfrac{1}{50}(200) = -\tfrac{1}{50} + 4 = \tfrac{199}{50} = 3.98$$

We have discussed partial derivatives of functions of two variables. But the concept can easily be extended to functions of any number of variables. For any such function, we would hold fixed all independent variables except one and then take the derivative of the resulting function of one variable. Suppose that we have

$$q_{d_A} = F(p_A, p_B, p_C, \ldots, p_N)$$

where q_{d_A} is the quantity demanded of product A, p_A is the price of product A, p_b is the price of product B, and so on. We can then find the N partial derivatives:

$$\frac{\partial F}{\partial p_A}, \frac{\partial F}{\partial p_B}, \frac{\partial F}{\partial p_C}, \ldots, \frac{\partial F}{\partial p_N}$$

Illustration. In Chapter 8 we discussed utility functions of the simplest kind; that is, utility of a product was given as a function of the quantity consumed of that product. Suppose that we are given a function that expresses the utility received from a combination of products in varying quantities, such as

$$u = 10q_1^{1/2} + 5q_2^{1/2} + 3q_3^{2/3} + \ln 2q_4$$

where u is the utility received from some bundle of the four products labeled product 1, product 2, product 3, and product 4, and q_1 is the quantity of product 1, q_2 the quantity of product 2, and so on. We would find the respective partial derivatives in the following manner:

$$\frac{\partial u}{\partial q_1} = 10 \cdot \tfrac{1}{2}q_1^{-1/2} = 5q_1^{-1/2}$$

$$\frac{\partial u}{\partial q_2} = 5 \cdot \tfrac{1}{2}q_2^{-1/2} = \tfrac{5}{2}q_2^{-1/2}$$

$$\frac{\partial u}{\partial q_3} = 3 \cdot \tfrac{2}{3}q_3^{-1/3} = 2q_3^{-1/3}$$

$$\frac{\partial u}{\partial q_4} = \frac{1}{2q_4} \cdot 2 = \frac{1}{q_4}$$

The reader will recall that, in Chapter 8, we showed that if we had a utility function of one variable, such as

$$u = f(q)$$

then du/dq represented the marginal utility of the product, that is, the additional utility that would ensue from the consumption of a small incremental amount of product x. In analogous fashion, if we have a utility function of several variables, then the partial derivatives represent the marginal utility of the respective products 1, 2, 3, and 4. Thus, $\partial u/\partial q_1$

indicates the additional utility from consuming an incremental amount of product 1; $\partial u / \partial q_2$ the additional utility of product 2; and so on. We shall have more to say about the whole concept of utility in Chapter 12.

Exercises

For each of the following, find the partial derivatives with respect to each of the independent variables at the indicated points or in general terms if no points are given.

1. $q_d = 200 - 4p^{3/2} + \frac{1}{10}y$ at $p = 9$, $y = 200$

2. $q_d = 500 - 3(2p - 4)^{4/3} + \ln y$

3. $q_d = 100 - \ln(4p - \frac{1}{20}y)$

4. $q_d = \dfrac{2y}{(15p + 1)^2}$ at $p = 1$, $y = 100$

5. $q_d = 400 - e^{2p} - \frac{1}{50}py + \sqrt{2y}$

6. $u = q_1^2 + \frac{1}{2}q_2 e^{q_1} + 2q_2^3$

7. $u = q_1^2 + q_2^2 - 3q_1 q_2$ at $q_1 = 3$, $q_2 = 5$

8. $u = 3q_1^2 + 4q_2^2 + \sqrt{10q_3}$

9. $q_{d_A} = 1000 - 6p_A^2 + \frac{1}{3}p_B^{2/3} - \frac{1}{2}p_C^{1/2}$

10. $z = \dfrac{x + y}{2x - 3y}$ at $x = 8$, $y = 4$

11. $z = 2x^2 y^3 + xy^2$ at $x = 6$, $y = 4$

12. $z = \dfrac{1}{\sqrt{2x^2 + y^2}}$

SECTION 10·3   ELASTICITIES FOR FUNCTIONS OF SEVERAL VARIABLES

In Chapter 7 we discussed, at some length, the concept of price elasticity of demand. But we considered only functions of one variable in the form of

$$q_d = f(p)$$

that is, quantity demanded of a particular product was a function of the price of that product. Under such circumstances, we defined

marginal demand $= \dfrac{dq_d}{dp}$

elasticity of demand $= E_d = \dfrac{dq_d}{dp} \dfrac{p}{q_d}$

We now recognize that the quantity demanded of product A is affected not only by the price of product A, but also by the prices of other products. These other products may be either substitutes or complements. The only way we can take account of all of these factors is to express quantity demanded as a function of several variables,

$$q_{d_A} = f(p_a, p_b, p_c, \ldots, p_n, y)$$

Here quantity demanded of product A is a function of the price of product A, the price of product B, and so on, and also consumer income.

If we find

$$\frac{\partial q_{d_A}}{\partial p_A}$$

we have the instantaneous rate of change of quantity demanded of product A with respect to changes in the price of A. This we call the marginal demand of A. In most instances it is preferable to have a relative measure of elasticity as explained in Chapter 7. This is defined as

price elasticity of demand for $A = E_{p_A} = \dfrac{\partial q_{d_A}}{\partial p_A} \dfrac{p_A}{q_{d_A}}$

Our definitions are analogous to those given in Chapter 7 except that for functions of several variables, we use partial derivatives in place of ordinary derivatives.

But this is not the only elasticity we can derive. Because the quantity demanded of A is also linked to the price of products B, C, and so on, and to consumer income, we can inquire into the effect that changes in those variables would have upon the quantity demanded for A.

If we find $\partial q_{d_A} / \partial p_B$, we have the instantaneous rate of change of quantity demanded of product A with respect to changes in the price of the related product B. To put this rate of change in relative terms, we make the following definition:

cross elasticity of demand $= E_{AB} = \dfrac{\partial q_{d_A}}{\partial p_B} \dfrac{p_B}{q_{d_A}}$

E_{AB} would therefore measure the responsiveness of the quantity demanded of product A to changes in the price of product B. Of course, cross elasticity of demand could be computed for changes in the prices of any other product included in the demand function. In general, for any product we would have

cross elasticity of demand $= E_{AI} = \dfrac{\partial q_{d_A}}{\partial p_I} \dfrac{p_I}{q_{d_A}}$ where $I \neq A$

The sign of the coefficient of cross elasticity, E_{AI}, conveys some interesting information. If E_{AI} is positive, then as the price of I increases, the quantity demanded of A increases. This indicates that product I is a substitute for product A. Therefore as the price of I increases, the substitute I becomes less attractive and more of A is used. On the other hand, if E_{AI} is negative, then as the price of I increases, the quantity demanded of A decreases. This indicates that I is a complementary product to A; that is, it is used in conjunction with A. Therefore as the price of I increases, less is used of both A and I.

It should now be evident that we can also derive an elasticity measure that will indicate the responsiveness of quantity demanded of product A to changes in consumer income. The expression $\partial q_d / \partial y$ would give us the instantaneous rate of change of quantity demanded of product A with respect to changes in consumer income. Again we usually put this in relative terms and introduce what is called

income elasticity of demand $= E_{y_A} = \dfrac{\partial q_{d_A}}{\partial y} \dfrac{y}{q_{d_A}}$

Illustration.   Find price elasticity of demand, cross elasticities of demand, and income elasticity of demand for the demand function

$$q_{d_A} = 200 - 5p_A^2 + \tfrac{1}{2}p_B^{2/3} - p_C^{1/2} + \tfrac{1}{10}y$$

when $p_A = 5$, $p_B = 8$, $p_C = 4$, and $y = 250$.
Solution.

price elasticity

$$= E_{p_A} = \frac{\partial q_{d_A}}{\partial p_A} \frac{p_A}{q_{d_A}} = -10p_A \frac{p_A}{q_{d_A}}$$

$$= \frac{-10p_A^2}{200 - 5p_A^2 + \tfrac{1}{2}p_B^{2/3} - p_C^{1/2} + \tfrac{1}{10}y}$$

At $p_A = 5$, $p_B = 8$, $p_C = 4$, and $y = 250$, we have

$$E_{p_A} = \frac{-250}{200 - 125 + 2 - 2 + 25} = \frac{-250}{100} = -2.5$$

This indicates that for every 1 percent price increase in product A, the quantity demanded of A decreases by 2.5 percent.

cross elasticity between A and B

$$= E_{AB} = \frac{\partial q_{d_A}}{\partial p_B} \frac{p_B}{q_{d_A}} = \frac{1}{2} \cdot \frac{2}{3} p_B^{-1/3} \frac{p_B}{q_{d_A}}$$

$$= \frac{\frac{1}{3} p_B^{2/3}}{200 - 5p_A^2 + \frac{1}{2} p_B^{2/3} - p_C^{1/2} + \frac{1}{10} y}$$

At the given point, we have

$$E_{AB} = \frac{\frac{4}{3}}{100} = \frac{4}{300} = 0.013$$

This indicates that for every 1 percent price increase in product B, the quantity demanded of product A increases by $\frac{13}{1000}$ percent. The sign of the coefficient is positive, so we know that B is a substitute for A (although not too strong a substitute, because the coefficient is only 0.013).

cross elasticity between A and C

$$= E_{AC} = \frac{\partial q_{d_A}}{\partial p_C} \frac{p_C}{q_{d_A}}$$

$$= -\frac{1}{2} p_C^{-1/2} \frac{p_C}{q_{d_A}} = \frac{-\frac{1}{2} p_C^{1/2}}{200 - 5p_A^2 + \frac{1}{2} p_B^{2/3} - p_C^{1/2} - p_C^{1/2} + \frac{1}{10} y}$$

At the given point, we have

$$E_{AC} = \frac{-\frac{1}{2} \cdot 2}{100} = -\frac{1}{100} = -0.01$$

This indicates that for every 1 percent price increase in product C, the quantity demanded of product A decreases by $\frac{1}{100}$ percent. In this case the sign of the coefficient is negative. Therefore product C is complementary to product A.

income elasticity

$$= E_{y_A} = \frac{\partial q_{d_A}}{\partial y} \frac{y}{q_{d_A}} = \frac{1}{10} \frac{y}{q_{d_A}}$$

$$= \frac{y}{10(200 - 5p_A^2 + \frac{1}{2}p_B^{2/3} - p_C^{1/2} + \frac{1}{10}y)}$$

At the given point, we have

$$E_{y_A} = \frac{250}{10(100)} = \frac{250}{1000} = \frac{1}{4} = 0.25$$

This indicates that for every 1 percent increase in consumer income, the quantity demanded of product A increases by $\frac{1}{4}$ percent.

Illustration.   Find price elasticity of demand, cross elasticity of demand, and income elasticity of demand for the following demand function:

$$q_{d_A} = p_A^{-1.58} p_B^{0.6} y^{0.2}$$

Solution.

price elasticity

$$= E_{p_A} = \frac{\partial q_{d_A}}{\partial p_A} \frac{p_A}{q_{d_A}} = -1.58 p_A^{-2.58} p_B^{0.6} y^{0.2} \left(\frac{p_A}{q_{d_A}}\right)$$

$$= \frac{-1.58 p_A^{-1.58} p_B^{0.6} y^{0.2}}{p_A^{-1.58} p_B^{0.6} y^{0.2}} = -1.58$$

Thus price elasticity is a constant regardless of the particular values of p_A, p_B, or y. The coefficient indicates that for every 1 percent price increase in product A, the quantity demanded of A decreases by 1.58 percent.

cross elasticity

$$= E_{AB} = \frac{\partial q_{d_A}}{\partial p_B} \frac{p_B}{q_{d_A}} = 0.6 p_A^{-1.58} p_B^{-0.4} y^{0.2} \frac{p_B}{q_{d_A}}$$

$$144 \quad = \frac{0.6 p_A^{-1.58} p_B^{0.6} y^{0.2}}{p_A^{-1.58} p_B^{0.6} y^{0.2}} = 0.6$$

Cross elasticity for this function is also a constant. The coefficient indicates that for every 1 percent price increase in product B, the quantity demanded of product A increases by $\frac{6}{10}$ percent. The sign of the coefficient is positive, so we know that B is a substitute for A.

income elasticity

$$= E_{y_A} = \frac{\partial q_d}{\partial y} \frac{y}{q_{d_A}} = 0.2 p_A^{-1.58} p_B^{0.6} y^{-0.8} \frac{y}{q_{d_A}}$$

$$= \frac{0.2 p_A^{-1.58} p_B^{0.6} y^{0.2}}{p_A^{-1.58} p_B^{0.6} y^{0.2}} = 0.2$$

Income elasticity for this function is also a constant. The coefficient indicates that for every 1 percent increase in consumer income, the quantity demanded of product A increases by $\frac{2}{10}$ percent.

We have discussed elasticity coefficients with regard to demand functions because they are most often encountered this way. However, the concept of elasticity can be applied to any function.

Consider any general function

$$u = f(x_1, x_2, x_3, \ldots)$$

We can define a coefficient of elasticity of u with respect to x_1 as

$$E_{u_{x_1}} = \frac{\partial u}{\partial x_1} \frac{x_1}{u}$$

Exercises

Find price elasticity, cross elasticity, and income elasticity (wherever relevant) for each of the following functions at the indicated points and determine whether products referred to are substitutes or complements. (Note that the first coordinate in each case refers to p_A, the second to $p_B, \ldots$, the last to y.)

1. $q_{d_A} = 1000 - 60 p_A^2 + \frac{1}{3} p_B^{2/3} - \frac{1}{2} p_C^{1/2} + y^{1/2}$ at $(3, 27, 16, 100)$

2. $q_{d_A} = 200 - 20 p_A^{3/2} + 3 p_B - p_C + \frac{1}{100} y$ at $(4, 10, 20, 1000)$

3. $q_{d_A} = \dfrac{2y + p_B}{15 p_A + 5}$ at $(3, 20, 90)$

4. $q_{d_A} = \dfrac{100}{p_A} + \dfrac{1}{20} p_B + \dfrac{20}{p_C} + \dfrac{1}{50} y$ at $(10, 40, 20, 350)$

5. $q_{d_A} = p_A^{-0.8} p_B^{0.2} y^{1.5}$

6. $q_{d_A} = p_A^{-2.5} p_B^{-0.2} p_C^{0.5} y$

7. $q_d = 500 - \ln(4p - \frac{1}{20} y)$

8. $q_{d_A} = 400 - e^{2 p_A} + \frac{1}{50} p_B + \sqrt{2y}$

SECTION 10·4 PARTIAL DERIVATIVES OF HIGHER ORDER

Consider the utility function

$$u = 10x^{1/2} + xy + 20 \ln y$$

where x and y represent the quantities consumed of product X and product Y, respectively, and u is the utility received from the various combinations of these products. We can easily find the partial derivatives of this function. We have

$$\frac{\partial u}{\partial x} = 5x^{-1/2} + y$$

This partial derivative represents the marginal utility of product X, that is, the additional utility to be obtained from incremental increases in that product.

Suppose that we are interested in determining how marginal utility, $\partial u/\partial x$, changes as x increases. We take the partial derivative (with respect to x) of $\partial u/\partial x$. This is written as

$$\frac{\partial}{\partial x}\left(\frac{\partial u}{\partial x}\right) = \frac{\partial^2 u}{\partial x^2} = -\tfrac{5}{2}x^{-3/2}$$

This *second partial* of u with respect to x is computed by viewing the first partial as a function in itself and merely partially differentiating it. In our case, we see that the second partial is always negative, because x is always positive. This indicates that the first partial, $\partial u/\partial x$, is decreasing as x increases. An equivalent way of expressing this is to say that the utility function is increasing (as x increases), but at a decreasing rate.

Similarly, we can find the other first partial of the utility function, which is

$$\frac{\partial u}{\partial y} = x + \frac{20}{y}$$

This represents the marginal utility of product Y.

If we are interested in determining how marginal utility of this product, $\partial u/\partial y$, changes, we take the partial derivative (with respect to y) of $\partial u/\partial y$. This gives us

$$\frac{\partial}{\partial y}\left(\frac{\partial u}{\partial y}\right) = \frac{\partial^2 u}{\partial y^2} = \frac{-20}{y^2}$$

This second partial is always negative, because y is always positive. This indicates that the first partial, $\partial u/\partial y$, is decreasing as y increases. Equivalently, we can say that the utility function is increasing (as y increases), but at a decreasing rate.

Suppose that we are interested in determining how the marginal utility of the first product, $\partial u/\partial x$, changes as the amount of the second product, y, changes. We then take the partial derivative (with respect to y) of $\partial u/\partial x$. This gives

$$\frac{\partial}{\partial y}\left(\frac{\partial u}{\partial x}\right) = 1$$

which indicates that $\partial u/\partial x$ increases by 1 unit for each unit increase in y.

Finally, we can determine how the marginal utility of the second product, $\partial u/\partial y$, changes as the amount of the first product, x, changes. We take the partial derivative (with respect to x) of $\partial u/\partial y$. This gives

$$\frac{\partial}{\partial x}\left(\frac{\partial u}{\partial y}\right) = 1$$

which indicates that $\partial u/\partial y$ increases by 1 unit for each unit increase in x.

We can now generalize the concept of higher-order partials. Given any function

$$u = f(x, y)$$

The partial derivatives

$$\frac{\partial u}{\partial x} \quad \text{and} \quad \frac{\partial u}{\partial y}$$

are themselves functions. As such, we can take their partial derivatives with respect to either x or y. When we do, we have the following *second partials*:

$$\frac{\partial}{\partial x}\left(\frac{\partial u}{\partial x}\right) = \frac{\partial^2 u}{\partial x^2} = f_{xx} \tag{1}$$

which indicates that we take the partial derivative with respect to x of $\partial u/\partial x$;

$$\frac{\partial}{\partial y}\left(\frac{\partial u}{\partial x}\right) = \frac{\partial^2 u}{\partial y\,\partial x} = f_{xy} \tag{2}$$

which indicates that we take the partial derivative with respect to y of $\partial u/\partial x$;

$$\frac{\partial}{\partial x}\left(\frac{\partial u}{\partial y}\right) = \frac{\partial^2 u}{\partial x\,\partial y} = f_{yx} \tag{3}$$

which indicates that we take the partial derivative with respect to x of $\partial u/\partial y$;

$$\frac{\partial}{\partial y}\left(\frac{\partial u}{\partial y}\right) = \frac{\partial^2 u}{\partial y^2} = f_{yy} \tag{4}$$

which indicates that we take the partial derivative with respect to y of $\partial u/\partial y$.

In a similar manner, we can compute third- and higher-partial derivatives. For example,

$$\frac{\partial}{\partial x}\left(\frac{\partial^2 u}{\partial x^2}\right) = \frac{\partial^3 u}{\partial x^3} = f_{xxx}$$

which indicates that we take the partial derivative with respect to x of $\partial^2 u/\partial x^2$, or

$$\frac{\partial}{\partial x}\left(\frac{\partial^2 u}{\partial x\, \partial y}\right) = \frac{\partial^3 u}{\partial x^2\, \partial y} = f_{yxx}$$

which indicates that we take the partial derivative with respect to x of $\partial^2 u/\partial x\, \partial y$, and similarly for other possible third- or higher-order partials.

Higher-order partials would be defined in completely analogous fashion for functions of three or more variables.

Illustration. Find the second partial derivatives of the following function:

$$u = x^2 y + xy + 2x - 3y + 7$$
Solution.

$$\frac{\partial u}{\partial x} = 2xy + y + 2 \quad \text{and} \quad \frac{\partial u}{\partial y} = x^2 + x - 3$$

$$\frac{\partial^2 u}{\partial x^2} = 2y \qquad\qquad \frac{\partial^2 u}{\partial y\, \partial x} = 2x + 1$$

$$\frac{\partial^2 u}{\partial y^2} = 0 \qquad\qquad \frac{\partial^2 u}{\partial x\, \partial y} = 2x + 1$$

Illustration. Find the second partial derivatives of the following function:

$$q_d = 100 - 2p^4 - \tfrac{1}{100}py + \tfrac{1}{100}y^2$$

Solution.

$$\frac{\partial q_d}{\partial p} = -8p^3 - \tfrac{1}{100}y \quad \text{and} \quad \frac{\partial q_d}{\partial y} = -\tfrac{1}{100}p + \tfrac{1}{50}y$$

$$\frac{\partial^2 q_d}{\partial p^2} = -24p^2 \qquad \frac{\partial^2 q_d}{\partial y \, \partial p} = -\tfrac{1}{100}$$

$$\frac{\partial^2 q_d}{\partial y^2} = \tfrac{1}{50} \qquad \frac{\partial^2 q_d}{\partial p \, \partial y} = -\tfrac{1}{100}$$

It is interesting to note that in each of our illustrations the mixed second partials,

$$\frac{\partial^2 u}{\partial x \, \partial y} \quad \text{and} \quad \frac{\partial^2 u}{\partial y \, \partial x}$$

turned out to be equal. This is no sheer accident, as is demonstrated by the next theorem.

Theorem. If $u = f(x, y)$ is defined in some region, the partial derivatives

$$\frac{\partial u}{\partial x} \qquad \frac{\partial u}{\partial y} \qquad \frac{\partial^2 u}{\partial x \, \partial y} \qquad \frac{\partial^2 u}{\partial y \, \partial x}$$

are also defined in that region, and suppose that

$$\frac{\partial^2 u}{\partial x \, \partial y} \quad \text{and} \quad \frac{\partial^2 u}{\partial y \, \partial x}$$

are continuous at some point within the region. Then

$$\frac{\partial^2 u}{\partial x \, \partial y} = \frac{\partial^2 u}{\partial y \, \partial x}$$

Exercises

Find the second partial derivatives of the following functions.

1. $q_d = 200 - 4p^{3/2} + \tfrac{1}{10}y$

2. $q_d = 500 - 3(2p - 4)^{4/3} + \ln y$

3. $q_d = 100 - \ln(4p - \tfrac{1}{20}y)$

4. $q_d = \dfrac{2y}{(15p + 1)^2}$

5. $q_d = 400 - e^{2p} - \frac{1}{50}py + \sqrt{2y}$

6. $u = q_1^2 + \frac{1}{2}q_2 e^{q_1} + 2q_2^3$

7. $u = q_1^2 + q_2^2 - 3q_1 q_2$

8. $u = 3q_1^2 + 4q_2^2 + \sqrt{10q_3}$

9. $q_{d_A} = 1000 - 6p_A^2 + \frac{1}{3}p_B^{2/3} - \frac{1}{2}p_C^{1/2}$

10. $z = \dfrac{x + y}{2x - 3y}$

11. $z = 2x^2 y^3 + xy^2$

12. $z = \dfrac{1}{\sqrt{2x^2 + y^2}}$

SECTION 10·5   THE TOTAL DIFFERENTIAL

In the preceding sections of this chapter we considered rates of change in functions of two or more variables such as $u = f(x, y)$ when either x alone changes or y alone changes. We next turn to the effects of simultaneous changes in both independent variables.

We state the following theorem on total increments.

Theorem.   If $u = f(x, y)$, $\partial u/\partial x$ and $\partial u/\partial y$ are continuous, and if x and y are given increments Δx and Δy, respectively, then the resulting total increment Δu of the function is given by

$$\Delta u = \frac{\partial u}{\partial x}\Delta x + \frac{\partial u}{\partial y}\Delta y + \varepsilon_1 \, \Delta x + \varepsilon_2 \, \Delta y$$

where ε_1 and ε_2 approach zero as Δx and Δy approach zero. This is known as the *total increment* formula.

In general, the last two terms of the total increment formula will be negligible compared to the first two terms. Therefore, if we drop the last two terms, the remaining terms will be a good approximation of the total increment. We therefore give a new name to the remaining terms, namely, the *total differential*, and denote this by *du*. The total increment (Δu) is thus the exact change in *u* due to changes in *x* and *y*. The total differential (*du*) is an approximation of this change. The smaller Δx and Δy are, the better will be the approximation.

For notational convenience, we make the following definitions:

Definition. The *differential* of the independent variable x shall be denoted by dx and defined as $dx = \Delta x$.

The *differential* of the independent variable y shall be denoted by dy and defined as $dy = \Delta y$.

As a result of these definitions, we can now state the following total differential formula:

$$du = \frac{\partial u}{\partial x} dx + \frac{\partial u}{\partial y} dy$$

Note again that dx is precisely equal to Δx and dy precisely equal to Δy. But du is only an approximation of Δu.

Illustration.   Find the total differential of

$$q_d = 100 - 3p^3 + 2\sqrt{y}$$

where $\sqrt{y}$ means the positive square root of y.
Solution.

$$dq_d = \frac{\partial q_d}{\partial p} dp + \frac{\partial q_d}{\partial y} dy$$

$$\frac{\partial q_d}{\partial p} = -9p^2 \qquad \frac{\partial q_d}{\partial y} = 2 \cdot \tfrac{1}{2} y^{-1/2} = y^{-1/2}$$

$$\therefore dq_d = -9p^2 \, dp + y^{-1/2} \, dy$$

We have thus found an expression for the change in q_d that results from any change in p and y. If we desire, we could evaluate the total differential at a specific point and for specific changes.

In particular, if at a price of \$2 and income of \$100, p increases by \$0.01 and y by \$10, what change will take place in quantity demanded? We merely evaluate the total differential at this point:

$$dq_d = -9(2)^2(0.01) + \frac{1}{\sqrt{100}} 10$$

$$= -0.36 + 1 = 0.64$$

Quantity demanded will thus increase by 0.64 unit.

Illustration.   Find the total differential of the following utility function:

$$u = 5q_1^{1/3} + \frac{1}{20} q_1 q_2 + \ln 10q_2$$

Solution.

$$du = \frac{\partial u}{\partial q_1} dq_1 + \frac{\partial u}{\partial q_2} dq_2$$

$$\frac{\partial u}{\partial q_1} = \frac{5}{3} q_1^{-2/3} + \frac{1}{20} q_2 \qquad \frac{\partial u}{\partial q_2} = \frac{1}{20} q_1 + \frac{10}{10 q_2} = \frac{1}{20} q_1 + \frac{1}{q_2}$$

$$\therefore du = \left(\frac{5}{3} q_1^{-2/3} + \frac{1}{20} q_2 \right) dq_1 + \left(\frac{1}{20} q_1 + \frac{1}{q_2} \right) dq_2$$

There are many occasions where values of independent variables are determined by some form of estimation and may therefore be in error. If this is the case, it is important to know the corresponding error in the dependent variable that would result from particular errors in the independent variables. The total differential formula is ideally suited for this purpose, because the possible errors in the independent variables can be viewed as increments in those variables, and the corresponding increment or error in the dependent variable can then be computed.

Illustration.

$$u = x^2 y + x y^2$$

x and y are estimated as 10 units and 20 units, respectively, but with a possible error of ± 0.05 unit in x and a possible error of ± 0.10 unit in y. What is the maximum possible error in u?

Solution.

$$du = \frac{\partial u}{\partial x} dx + \frac{\partial u}{\partial y} dy$$

$$\frac{\partial u}{\partial x} = 2xy + y^2 \qquad \frac{\partial u}{\partial y} = x^2 + 2xy$$

$$\therefore du = (2xy + y^2) dx + (x^2 + 2xy) dy$$

Now, for x, substitute its estimated value of 10; for y, its estimated value of 20; for dx, the maximum error of ± 0.05; and for dy, its maximum error of ± 0.10. We then have

$$du = (800)(\pm 0.05) + (500)(\pm 0.10)$$

The maximum error in u is therefore

$$du = \pm 40 \pm 50 = \pm 90$$

Thus u could be in error anywhere from -90 units to $+90$ units.

We have so far dealt with total differentials for functions of two variables. But our work can be generalized for functions of any number of variables.

If $u = f(x_1, x_2, \ldots, x_n)$, the total differential is defined as

$$du = \frac{\partial u}{\partial x_1} dx_1 + \frac{\partial u}{\partial x_2} dx_2 + \cdots + \frac{\partial u}{\partial x_n} dx_n$$

where $dx_1 = \Delta x_1$, $dx_2 = \Delta x_2$, $\ldots$, $dx_n = \Delta x_n$ are the increments in the independent variables.

In particular, note that a function of one variable,

$$y = f(x)$$

is a special case of the generalized function. We would therefore have

$$dy = \frac{dy}{dx} dx$$

where $dx = \Delta x$ is the increment in the independent variable x. In this case dy is referred to simply as the *differential* of the function rather than the total differential, because it is composed of only one term rather than a sum of terms. In addition, the ordinary derivative dy/dx is used rather than a partial derivative. This is due to the fact that there is only one independent variable, so that any derivative taken is an ordinary derivative.

Illustration. Find the differential of the following demand function:

$$q_d = 100 - 2p^2$$

Solution. The differential formula for a function of one variable is

$$dq_d = \frac{dq_d}{dp} dp$$

Now the derivative

$$\frac{dq_d}{dp} = -4p$$

$$\therefore dq_d = -4p \, dp$$

At a price of $5, if price changes by $0.10, quantity will change by approximately dq_d, or

$$dq_d = -4(5)(0.10)$$

$$= -2$$

Quantity demanded will thus decrease by approximately 2 units.

Illustration. Find the total differential of the following utility function:

$$u = 10q_1^{1/2} + 5q_2^{1/2} + 3q_3^{2/3} + \ln 2q_4$$

Solution. The total differential for this function of four variables would be given as

$$du = \frac{\partial u}{\partial q_1}\, dq_1 + \frac{\partial u}{\partial q_2}\, dq_2 + \frac{\partial u}{\partial q_3}\, dq_3 + \frac{\partial u}{\partial q_4}\, dq_4$$

Now

$$\frac{\partial u}{\partial q_1} = 5q_1^{-1/2} \qquad \frac{\partial u}{\partial q_2} = \frac{5}{2} q_2^{-1/2}$$

$$\frac{\partial u}{\partial q_3} = 2q_3^{-1/3} \qquad \frac{\partial u}{\partial q_4} = \frac{1}{q_4}$$

$$\therefore\; du = 5q_1^{-1/2}\, dq_1 + \frac{5}{2} q_2^{-1/2}\, dq_2 + 2q_3^{-1/3}\, dq_3 + \frac{1}{q_4}\, dq_4$$

Exercises

Find the total differential of each of the functions in Exercises 1–8, and evaluate for the stated points and increments.

1. $q_d = 200 - 4p^{3/2} + \frac{1}{10}y$; $p = 9$, $y = 200$, $\Delta p = 0.10$, $\Delta y = 2$

2. $q_d = 500 - 3(2p - 4)^{4/3} + \ln y$; $p = 6$, $y = 200$, $\Delta p = \frac{1}{4}$, $\Delta y = -5$

3. $q_d = \dfrac{2y}{(15p + 1)^2}$; $p = 1$, $y = 100$, $\Delta p = 0.04$, $\Delta y = -1$

4. $u = q_1^2 + \frac{1}{2}q_2 e^{q_1} + 2q_3^3$

5. $u = q_1^2 + q_2^2 - 3q_1 q_2$; $q_1 = 3$, $q_2 = 5$, $\Delta q_1 = \frac{1}{2}$, $\Delta q_2 = -\frac{1}{3}$

6. $q_d = 1000 - 6p_A^2 + \frac{1}{3}p_B^{2/3} - \frac{1}{2}p_C^{1/2}$

7. $z = \dfrac{x + y}{2x - 3y}$; $x = 8$, $y = 4$, $\Delta x = -\frac{1}{2}$, $\Delta y = 1$

8. $u = 100 \ln q_1 + 50 \ln q_2 + 40 \ln 3q_3 + 10 \ln \frac{1}{2}q_4$

9. What is the maximum possible error in z if $z = 2x^2 y^3 + xy^2$ and x and y are estimated as 4 units and 2 units, respectively, but with a possible error of 0.01 unit in x and a possible error of 0.05 in y?

10. Find the differential of $q_s = 50p^3 - 40$.

11. Find the differential of $q_d = 50 - \ln p$.

12. Find the differential of $q_s = \dfrac{p^2 + 4}{p - 1}$

SECTION 10·6 THE TOTAL DERIVATIVE

Consider a function of two variables,

$$u = f(x, y)$$

where both x and y are functions of some other variable such as

$$x = g(t)$$

$$y = h(t)$$

    In effect, u is a function of t, because for any particular value of t, corresponding values of x and y can be found that will, in turn, determine a particular value for u. We may therefore wish to find the instantaneous rate of change of u with respect to t. This is defined as

$$\frac{du}{dt} = \lim_{\Delta t \to 0} \frac{\Delta u}{\Delta t}$$

    In order to derive an expression for this rate of change, let us go back to the total increment formula introduced in the previous section. Assume that the conditions for the continuity of the requisite partial derivatives are satisfied. Then we have

$$\Delta u = \frac{\partial u}{\partial x} \Delta x + \frac{\partial u}{\partial y} \Delta y + \varepsilon_1 \, \Delta x + \varepsilon_2 \, \Delta y$$

Let Δt represent the incremental change in t. Divide both sides of the equation by the quantity Δt. This yields

$$\frac{\Delta u}{\Delta t} = \frac{\partial u}{\partial x} \frac{\Delta x}{\Delta t} + \frac{\partial u}{\partial y} \frac{\Delta y}{\Delta t} + \varepsilon_1 \frac{\Delta x}{\Delta t} + \varepsilon_2 \frac{\Delta y}{\Delta t}$$

Next consider the limit of each side of the equation as $\Delta t \to 0$. We have

$$\lim_{\Delta t \to 0} \frac{\Delta u}{\Delta t} = \lim_{\Delta t \to 0} \left(\frac{\partial u}{\partial x} \frac{\Delta x}{\Delta t} + \frac{\partial u}{\partial y} \frac{\Delta y}{\Delta t} + \varepsilon_1 \frac{\Delta x}{\Delta t} + \varepsilon_2 \frac{\Delta y}{\Delta t} \right)$$

Now as $\Delta t \to 0$, so will Δx and Δy. But $\varepsilon_1 \to 0$ as $\Delta x \to 0$ and $\varepsilon_2 \to 0$ as $\Delta y \to 0$. Therefore the limit as $\Delta t \to 0$ of the last two terms is zero.

Moreover,

$$\lim_{\Delta t \to 0} \frac{\Delta x}{\Delta t} = \frac{dx}{dt}$$

because x is a function of the one variable t. Similarly,

$$\lim_{\Delta t \to 0} \frac{\Delta y}{\Delta t} = \frac{dy}{dt}$$

Therefore,

$$\frac{du}{dt} = \frac{\partial u}{\partial x}\frac{dx}{dt} + \frac{\partial u}{\partial y}\frac{dy}{dt}$$

$\dfrac{du}{dt}$ is known as the *total derivative of u.*

The total derivative is an instantaneous rate of change and is thus analogous to derivatives of functions of one variable, which were considered in earlier chapters. It differs from the total differential of a function, which is an approximation of the actual change in u (rather than a rate of change) due to changes in its independent variables.

Illustration.   Find the total derivative of quantity demanded, where q_d is a function of price and income but each of the latter is, in turn, some function of time; that is, with the passage of time both price and income change in predictable ways:

$$q_d = 100 - 3p^3 + 2\sqrt{y}$$
$$p = 2 + \tfrac{1}{8}t$$
$$y = 36 + t^2$$

Solution.   The total derivative is given by

$$\frac{dq_d}{dt} = \frac{\partial q_d}{\partial p}\frac{dp}{dt} + \frac{\partial q_d}{\partial y}\frac{dy}{dt}$$

Now

$$\frac{\partial q_d}{\partial p} = -9p^2 \qquad \frac{\partial q_d}{\partial y} = y^{-1/2}$$

$$\frac{dp}{dt} = \tfrac{1}{8} \qquad \frac{dy}{dt} = 2t$$

$$\therefore \quad \frac{dq_d}{dt} = -9p^2(\tfrac{1}{8}) + y^{-1/2}(2t)$$

$$= -\tfrac{9}{8}p^2 + 2ty^{-1/2}$$

This is the total derivative of q_d for any t (note that once t is specified, p and y can easily be determined.) If we desire, we can evaluate the total derivative at any specific point.

In particular, at $t = 8$, we have

$$p = 2 + \tfrac{1}{8}(8) = 3$$

$$y = 36 + 64 = 100$$

and

$$\frac{dq_d}{dt} = -\tfrac{9}{8}(9) + \frac{16}{\sqrt{100}} = -\tfrac{81}{8} + \tfrac{16}{10} = -10.125 + 1.6$$

$$= -8.525$$

Thus, for each unit increase in t, quantity demanded decreases by 8.525 units.

The concept of total derivatives can be extended to functions of any number of variables. Thus, if we have a function of three variables such as

$$u = f(x_1, x_2, x_3)$$

$$x_1 = g(t)$$

$$x_2 = h(t)$$

$$x_3 = j(t)$$

then

$$\frac{du}{dt} = \frac{\partial u}{\partial x_1}\frac{dx_1}{dt} + \frac{\partial u}{\partial x_2}\frac{dx_2}{dt} + \frac{\partial u}{\partial x_3}\frac{dx_3}{dt}$$

Illustration. Find the total derivative of quantity demanded of product A, where q_{d_A} is a function of the prices of products A, B, and C but each of the latter is, in turn, some function of time:

$$q_{d_A} = 200 - 5p_A^2 + \tfrac{1}{2}p_B^{2/3} - p_C^{1/2}$$

$$p_A = 10 + \tfrac{1}{20}t$$

$$p_B = 26 + \tfrac{1}{10}t$$

$$p_C = 14 + \tfrac{1}{5}t$$

Solution. The total derivative is given by

$$\frac{dq_{d_A}}{dt} = \frac{\partial q_{d_A}}{\partial p_A}\frac{dp_A}{dt} + \frac{\partial q_{d_A}}{\partial p_B}\frac{dp_B}{dt} + \frac{\partial q_{d_A}}{\partial p_C}\frac{dp_C}{dt}$$

Now

$$\frac{\partial q_{d_A}}{\partial p_A} = -10p_A \qquad \frac{\partial q_{d_A}}{\partial p_B} = \tfrac{1}{2} \cdot \tfrac{2}{3} p_B^{-1/3} = \tfrac{1}{3} p_B^{-1/3}$$

$$\frac{\partial q_{d_A}}{\partial p_C} = -\tfrac{1}{2} p_C^{-1/2}$$

$$\frac{dp_A}{dt} = \tfrac{1}{20} \qquad \frac{dp_B}{dt} = \tfrac{1}{10} \qquad \frac{dp_C}{dt} = \tfrac{1}{5}$$

$$\therefore \quad \frac{dq_{d_A}}{dt} = -10p_A(\tfrac{1}{20}) + \tfrac{1}{3} p_B^{-1/3}(\tfrac{1}{10}) - \tfrac{1}{2} p_C^{-1/2}(\tfrac{1}{5})$$

$$= -\tfrac{1}{2} p_A + \tfrac{1}{30} p_B^{-1/3} - \tfrac{1}{10} p_C^{-1/2}$$

At the particular point where $t = 10$, we have

$$p_A = 10 + \tfrac{10}{20} = 10.5$$

$$p_B = 26 + \tfrac{10}{10} = 27$$

$$p_C = 14 + \tfrac{10}{5} = 16$$

and

$$\frac{dq_{d_A}}{dt} = -\tfrac{1}{2}(10.5) + \tfrac{1}{30}(\tfrac{1}{9}) - \tfrac{1}{10}(\tfrac{1}{4})$$

$$= -5.25 + 0.004 - 0.063 = -5.309$$

which indicates that for each unit increase in t, quantity demanded decreases by 5.309 units.

When dealing with a function of several variables such as $u = f(x, y)$, it may happen that x and y may not be independent of each other but related by some functional expression $y = g(x)$. In such cases, if we reconsider the formula for the total derivative given above,

$$\frac{du}{dt} = \frac{\partial u}{\partial x}\frac{dx}{dt} + \frac{\partial u}{\partial y}\frac{dy}{dt}$$

and we let $t = x$, we have

$$\frac{du}{dx} = \frac{\partial u}{\partial x} + \frac{\partial u}{\partial y}\frac{dy}{dx}$$

where du/dx is the total derivative of $u = f(x, y)$ for the special case where y itself is some function of x.

Illustration. Find the total derivative of the utility function

$$u = 10q_1^{2/3} + 6q_2^{1/2}$$

where q_1 and q_2 are products that are used jointly and where the relation between the amount of q_1 and the amount of q_2 is given by

$$q_2 = 4q_1$$

Solution. The total derivative for this case is given by

$$\frac{du}{dq_1} = \frac{\partial u}{\partial q_1} + \frac{\partial u}{\partial q_2}\frac{dq_2}{dq_1}$$

Now

$$\frac{\partial u}{\partial q_1} = 10 \cdot \tfrac{2}{3}q_1^{-1/3} = \tfrac{20}{3}q_1^{-1/3}$$

$$\frac{\partial u}{\partial q_2} = 6 \cdot \tfrac{1}{2}q_2^{-1/2} = 3q_2^{-1/2}$$

$$\frac{dq_2}{dq_1} = 4$$

$$\therefore \quad \frac{du}{dq_1} = \tfrac{20}{3}q_1^{-1/3} + 3q_2^{-1/2}(4)$$

$$= \tfrac{20}{3}q_1^{-1/3} + 12q_2^{-1/2}$$

An alternative approach to this problem involves substituting the value of q_2 into the original functional relationship, thus transforming the original function of two variables into a function of one variable:

$$u = 10q_1^{2/3} + 6q_2^{1/2}$$
$$q_2 = 4q_1$$
$$\therefore u = 10q_1^{2/3} + 6(4q_1)^{1/2}$$
$$= 10q_1^{2/3} + 12q_1^{1/2}$$

and

$$\frac{du}{dq_1} = \tfrac{20}{3}q_1^{-1/3} + 6q_1^{-1/2}$$

which is seen to be identical to the earlier result if we recall that $q_2 = 4q_1$.

While, in this case, the alternative approach is no more difficult to apply, this is not always so. On certain occasions, it is extremely cumbersome to substitute back into the original function.

As in earlier cases, similar formulas hold for functions of more than two variables.

Illustration. Find the total derivative of the utility function

$$u = q_1^{1/3} + 2q_2^{1/2} + \ln 2q_3$$

where

$$q_2 = 5q_1$$
$$q_3 = 3q_1 + 10$$

Solution. The total derivative for this case is given by

$$\frac{du}{dq_1} = \frac{\partial u}{\partial q_1} + \frac{\partial u}{\partial q_2}\frac{dq_2}{dq_1} + \frac{\partial u}{\partial q_3}\frac{dq_3}{dq_1}$$

Now

$$\frac{\partial u}{\partial q_1} = \tfrac{1}{3}q_1^{-2/3}$$

$$\frac{\partial u}{\partial q_2} = 2 \cdot \tfrac{1}{2}q_2^{-1/2} = q_2^{-1/2}$$

$$\frac{\partial u}{\partial q_3} = \frac{2}{2q_3} = \frac{1}{q_3}$$

$$\frac{dq_2}{dq_1} = 5 \qquad \frac{dq_3}{dq_1} = 3$$

$$\therefore \quad \frac{du}{dq_1} = \tfrac{1}{3}q_1^{-2/3} + q_2^{-1/2}(5) + \frac{1}{q_3}(3)$$

$$= \tfrac{1}{3}q_1^{-2/3} + 5q_2^{-1/2} + \frac{3}{q_3}$$

Let us consider again a function of two variables:

$$u = f(x, y)$$

But now x and y are functions, not of a single variable as previously, but of two other variables:

$$x = g(r, s)$$
$$y = h(r, s)$$

Because u is a function of x and y, which, in turn, are functions of r and s, u is also a function of r and s. We may therefore inquire into the rates of change of u with respect to r or with respect to s.

In order to derive an expression for this rate of change, consider again the total increment formula and assume that the conditions for the continuity of the requisite partial derivatives are satisfied. We have

$$\Delta u = \frac{\partial u}{\partial x} \Delta x + \frac{\partial u}{\partial y} \Delta y + \varepsilon_1 \, \Delta x + \varepsilon_2 \, \Delta y$$

If we wish to find the rate of change of u with respect to r, we hold s constant and assume that r undergoes an incremental change of Δr. This produces changes Δx and Δy in x and y, respectively, which, in turn, result in an increment Δu.

Dividing both sides of the total increment formula by Δr, we have

$$\frac{\Delta u}{\Delta r} = \frac{\partial u}{\partial x} \frac{\Delta x}{\Delta r} + \frac{\partial u}{\partial y} \frac{\Delta y}{\Delta r} + \varepsilon_1 \frac{\Delta x}{\Delta r} + \varepsilon_2 \frac{\Delta y}{\Delta r}$$

Next, taking the limit of each side of the equation as $\Delta r \to 0$,

$$\lim_{\Delta r \to 0} \frac{\Delta u}{\Delta r} = \lim_{\Delta r \to 0} \left(\frac{\partial u}{\partial x} \frac{\Delta x}{\Delta r} + \frac{\partial u}{\partial y} \frac{\Delta y}{\Delta r} + \varepsilon_1 \frac{\Delta x}{\Delta r} + \varepsilon_2 \frac{\Delta y}{\Delta r} \right)$$

Now, as $\Delta r \to 0$, so will Δx and Δy, which, in turn, implies that ε_1 and $\varepsilon_2 \to 0$. Therefore the limit as $\Delta r \to 0$ of the last two terms is zero. Moreover,

$$\lim_{\Delta r \to 0} \frac{\Delta x}{\Delta r} = \frac{\partial x}{\partial r}$$

because x is a function of r and s and s is being held constant.

Similarly,

$$\lim_{\Delta r \to 0} \frac{\Delta y}{\Delta r} = \frac{\partial y}{\partial r}$$

and

$$\lim_{\Delta r \to 0} \frac{\Delta u}{\Delta r} = \frac{\partial u}{\partial r}$$

Therefore,

$$\frac{\partial u}{\partial r} = \frac{\partial u}{\partial x} \frac{\partial x}{\partial r} + \frac{\partial u}{\partial y} \frac{\partial y}{\partial r}$$

In like manner, if we would hold r constant and vary s, we can derive the following:

$$\frac{\partial u}{\partial s} = \frac{\partial u}{\partial x}\frac{\partial x}{\partial s} + \frac{\partial u}{\partial y}\frac{\partial y}{\partial s}$$

All the differentiation formulas in this section are sometimes referred to as *chain-rule* differentiation or differentiation by the *composite function* rule.

Illustration. Find

$$\frac{\partial u}{\partial p_1} \quad \text{and} \quad \frac{\partial u}{\partial p_2}$$

for the following function, where utility is a function of the quantities consumed of two products (q_1 and q_2) but where the quantities consumed are themselves functions of the prices of the products (p_1 and p_2):

$$u = 10q_1^{1/2} + q_1 q_2 + 20 \ln q_2$$

$$q_1 = 200 - p_1^2 + \tfrac{1}{2}p_2$$

$$q_2 = 500 + 2p_1^{1/2} - 10p_2$$

Solution.

$$\frac{\partial u}{\partial p_1} = \frac{\partial u}{\partial q_1}\frac{\partial q_1}{\partial p_1} + \frac{\partial u}{\partial q_2}\frac{\partial q_2}{\partial p_1}$$

Now

$$\frac{\partial u}{\partial q_1} = 5q_1^{-1/2} + q_2 \qquad \frac{\partial u}{\partial q_2} = q_1 + \frac{20}{q_2}$$

$$\frac{\partial q_1}{\partial p_1} = -2p_1 \qquad\qquad \frac{\partial q_2}{\partial p_1} = p_1^{-1/2}$$

$$\therefore \frac{\partial u}{\partial p_1} = (5q_1^{-1/2} + q_2)(-2p_1) + \left(q_1 + \frac{20}{q_2}\right)(p_1^{-1/2})$$

$$= -10q_1^{-1/2}p_1 - 2q_2 p_1 + q_1 p_1^{-1/2} + \frac{20p_1^{-1/2}}{q_2}$$

Similarly,

$$\frac{\partial u}{\partial p_2} = \frac{\partial u}{\partial q_1}\frac{\partial q_1}{\partial p_2} + \frac{\partial u}{\partial q_2}\frac{\partial q_2}{\partial p_2}$$

and

$$\frac{\partial q_1}{\partial p_2} = \frac{1}{2} \qquad \frac{\partial q_2}{\partial p_2} = -10$$

$$\therefore \; \frac{\partial u}{\partial p_2} = (5q_1^{-1/2} + q_2)\left(\frac{1}{2}\right) + \left(q_1 + \frac{20}{q_2}\right)(-10)$$

$$= \frac{5}{2}q_1^{-1/2} + \frac{1}{2}q_2 - 10q_1 - \frac{200}{q_2}$$

These formulas can again be generalized to functions of any number of variables. If $u = f(x_1, x_2, \ldots, x_n)$ with continuous partial derivatives, and if $x_1, x_2, \ldots, x_n$ are themselves continuous functions of the variables $r, s, t, \ldots$, then

$$\frac{\partial u}{\partial r} = \frac{\partial u}{\partial x_1}\frac{\partial x_1}{\partial r} + \frac{\partial u}{\partial x_2}\frac{\partial x_2}{\partial r} + \cdots + \frac{\partial u}{\partial x_n}\frac{\partial x_n}{\partial r}$$

$$\frac{\partial u}{\partial s} = \frac{\partial u}{\partial x_1}\frac{\partial x_1}{\partial s} + \frac{\partial u}{\partial x_2}\frac{\partial x_2}{\partial s} + \cdots + \frac{\partial u}{\partial x_n}\frac{\partial x_n}{\partial s}$$

$$\frac{\partial u}{\partial t} = \frac{\partial u}{\partial x_1}\frac{\partial x_1}{\partial t} + \frac{\partial u}{\partial x_2}\frac{\partial x_2}{\partial t} + \cdots + \frac{\partial u}{\partial x_n}\frac{\partial x_n}{\partial t}$$

$$\vdots$$

In using these formulas, it is to be understood that if any of the variables $x_1, x_2, \ldots, x_n$ are functions of only a single variable, then instead of computing the relevant partial derivative, the ordinary derivative is to be found.

Exercises

For each of the following, find the total derivative dq_d/dt and evaluate at the indicated points, or express in general terms if no points are indicated.

1. $q_d = 200 - 4p^{3/2} + \frac{1}{10}y$, where $p = 4 + \frac{1}{5}t^2$, $y = 50 + 10t$; at $t = 5$

2. $q_d = 500 - 3(2p - 4)^{4/3} + \ln y$, where $p = 10 + \sqrt{t}$,

$$y = 100 + \tfrac{1}{10}t^2$$

3. $q_d = 100 - \ln(4p - \frac{1}{20}y)$, where $p = \frac{1}{10}t^2$, $y = 200 + 20t$

4. $q_d = \dfrac{2y}{(15p + 1)^2}$, where $p = 2 + 2t$, $y = 100t$; at $t = 1$

5. $q_d = 400 - e^{2p} - \frac{1}{50}py + \sqrt{2y}$, where $p = \frac{1}{2}t$, $y = 200t - 200$

For each of the following, find the total derivative dq_{d_A}/dt.

6. $q_{d_A} = 1000 - 6p_A^2 + \frac{1}{3}p_B^{2/3} - \frac{1}{2}p_C^{1/2}$,   where $p_A = 2t$, $p_B = 2 + t^2$,
    $p_C = 1 + 2\sqrt{t}$

7. $q_{d_A} = \dfrac{100}{p_A} + \dfrac{1}{20}p_B + \dfrac{20}{p_C}$, where

    $p_A = 2 + 3t$, $p_B = \dfrac{1}{2}t$, $p_C = 4t^{1/2}$

8. $q_{d_A} = p_A^{-2.5}p_B^{-0.2}p_C^{0.5}p_D^{0.1}$, where $p_A = 5 + t$, $p_B = 1 + 2t$, $p_C = \frac{1}{3}t$,
    $p_D = 2t^2$

For each of the following, find the total derivative du/dq_1.

9. $u = q_1^2 + \frac{1}{2}q_2 e^{q_1} + 2q_2^3$, where $q_2 = 2q_1$

10. $u = q_1^2 + q_2^2 - 3q_1 q_2$, where $q_2 = \sqrt{q_1} + 4$

11. $u = 3q_1^2 + 4q_2^2 + \sqrt{10q_3}$, where $q_2 = 2 + 2q_1$ and $q_3 = \frac{1}{2}q_1 + 1$

For each of the following, find the total derivative dz/dt.

12. $z = \dfrac{x + y}{2x - 3y}$, where $x = 1 - t^2$, $y = \dfrac{1}{t}$

13. $z = 2x^2 y^3 + xy^2$, where $x = e^t$, $y = t^{1/2}$

14. $z = \dfrac{1}{\sqrt{2x^2 + y^2}}$, where $x = \ln 5t$, $y = \dfrac{t^3}{1 - t}$

15. $z = \ln(x^2 + y^2 + w^2)$, where $x = \dfrac{1}{t}$, $y = t^2$, $w = 1 - t^2$

For each of the following, find $\partial u/\partial p_1$ and $\partial u/\partial p_2$.

16. $u = q_1^2 + q_2^2 - 3q_1 q_2$, where $q_1 = 100 - 2p_1 + \frac{1}{100}p_2^2$ and
     $q_2 = 150 + p_1^{3/2} - 5p_2^2$

17. $u = q_1^2 + \frac{1}{2}q_2 e^{q_1} + 2q_2^3$, where $q_1 = 200 - p_1 + \frac{1}{4}p_2$ and
     $q_2 = 400 + \frac{1}{2}p_1 - \frac{1}{10}p_2$

18. $u = 3q_1^2 + \sqrt{10q_2}$, where $q_1 = \dfrac{100}{p_1} - \dfrac{200}{p_2^2}$ and

$q_2 = \dfrac{500}{p_1} - \ln 2p_2$

19. $u = 100 \ln q_1 + 50 \ln q_2 + 10 \ln \frac{1}{2}q_3$, where

$q_1 = 600 - 2p_1 + p_2 - \frac{1}{2}p_3$,

$q_2 = 100 + p_1^2 - 2p_2^2 + p_3 , q_3 = 200 - p_1 + \frac{1}{2}p_2 - 20 \ln p_3$

For each of the following, find $\partial u/\partial r$ and $\partial u/\partial s$.

20. $u = 2xe^y + ye^{2x}$, where $x = 2rs, y = \dfrac{r}{2s}$

21. $u = e^{xy}$, where $x = r^2 - s^2, y = rs$

22. $u = \sqrt{x^2 + y^2}$, where $x = r^2 + s^2, y = e^s$

SECTION 10·7   DIFFERENTIATION OF IMPLICIT FUNCTIONS

In Section 8.11, we showed that if we had an implicit function $F(x, y) = 0$, we could find the derivative of y with respect to x by differentiating the function term by term. We are now in a position to derive an alternative method for implicit differentiation, which will turn out to be simpler and more useful.

Consider the implicit function $F(x, y) = 0$. Let

$u = F(x, y)$

and assume that this function and its first partial derivatives are continuous. We can now apply the total derivative formula to this function, because u is a function of x and y, and y is itself a function of x as given by $F(x, y) = 0$. The total derivative for this case, as stated in the previous section, is

$\dfrac{du}{dx} = \dfrac{\partial F}{\partial x} + \dfrac{\partial F}{\partial y}\dfrac{dy}{dx}$

It is easily seen, however, that $u = 0$ by the way we defined u at the outset. Therefore,

$\dfrac{du}{dx} = 0$

which implies

$$0 = \frac{\partial F}{\partial x} + \frac{\partial F}{\partial y}\frac{dy}{dx}$$

which is the same as

$$\frac{dy}{dx} = \frac{-\dfrac{\partial F}{\partial x}}{\dfrac{\partial F}{\partial y}} \qquad \text{provided that} \quad \frac{\partial F}{\partial y} \neq 0$$

This enables us to state the following theorem.

Theorem. If $F(x, y) = 0$ is an implicit function involving x and y and, moreover, $F(x, y)$ and its first partial derivatives are continuous, then

$$\frac{dy}{dx} = \frac{-\dfrac{\partial F}{\partial x}}{\dfrac{\partial F}{\partial y}} \qquad \text{provided that} \quad \frac{\partial F}{\partial y} \neq 0$$

Illustration. If $2x^2 - xy + y^2 + 6 = 0$, find dy/dx.

Solution. By the implicit function theorem, we have

$$\frac{dy}{dx} = \frac{-\dfrac{\partial F}{\partial x}}{\dfrac{\partial F}{\partial y}}$$

Now,

$$\frac{\partial F}{\partial x} = 4x - y \qquad \frac{\partial F}{\partial y} = -x + 2y$$

$$\therefore \frac{dy}{dx} = \frac{-(4x - y)}{-x + 2y} = \frac{4x - y}{x - 2y}$$

Note that this is precisely what we arrived at in Section 8.11 by using term-by-term differentiation.

Illustration. Find elasticity of demand at a price of $0.50 for the following demand function:

$$p + pq_d + q_d - 2 = 0$$

Solution.   Elasticity of demand is given by

$$E_d = \frac{p}{q_d} \frac{dq_d}{dp}$$

We must therefore find the derivative dq_d/dp. This is given by the implicit function theorem as

$$\frac{dq_d}{dp} = - \frac{\dfrac{\partial F}{\partial p}}{\dfrac{\partial F}{\partial q_d}}$$

Now,

$$\frac{\partial F}{\partial p} = 1 + q_d \qquad \frac{\partial F}{\partial q_d} = p + 1$$

$$\therefore \quad \frac{dq_d}{dp} = \frac{-(1 + q_d)}{p + 1} = \frac{-1 - q_d}{p + 1}$$

Therefore elasticity of demand is

$$E_d = \frac{p}{q_d} \left(\frac{-1 - q_d}{p + 1} \right)$$

From the original demand function, we find that when $p = 0.50$, $q_d = 1$. At a price of \$0.50, elasticity of demand is

$$E_d = \frac{0.50}{1.00} \left(\frac{-2}{1.50} \right) = -0.667$$

which is also precisely what we arrived at in Section 8.11 by using term-by-term differentiation.

The theorem on implicit differentiation can be extended to functions of any number of variables.

Theorem.   If $F(x_1, x_2, \ldots, x_n) = 0$ is an implicit function involving x_1, $x_2, \ldots, x_n$ and the function and its first partial derivatives are continuous, then

$$\frac{\partial x_i}{\partial x_j} = - \frac{\dfrac{\partial F}{\partial x_j}}{\dfrac{\partial F}{\partial x_i}} \qquad \text{where } i \neq j \text{ provided that} \quad \frac{\partial F}{\partial x_i} \neq 0$$

Illustration.   If $2x^2 - xy + y^2 + 2z^3 + 6 = 0$, find $\partial z/\partial x$ and $\partial z/\partial y$.

Solution.   By the generalized implicit function theorem, we have

$$\frac{\partial z}{\partial x} = -\frac{\dfrac{\partial F}{\partial x}}{\dfrac{\partial F}{\partial z}} \quad \text{and} \quad \frac{\partial z}{\partial y} = -\frac{\dfrac{\partial F}{\partial y}}{\dfrac{\partial F}{\partial z}}$$

Now,

$$\frac{\partial F}{\partial x} = 4x - y \qquad \frac{\partial F}{\partial y} = -x + 2y \qquad \frac{\partial F}{\partial z} = 6z^2$$

$$\therefore \frac{\partial z}{\partial x} = -\frac{(4x - y)}{6z^2} \qquad \frac{\partial z}{\partial y} = \frac{-x + 2y}{6z^2} = \frac{x - 2y}{6z^2}$$

$$= \frac{-4x + y}{6z^2}$$

Illustration.   Demand is given by the following implicit function:

$$q_{d_A}^2 p_A^3 p_B = 10$$

Find price elasticity of product A, cross elasticity of demand of product A with respect to changes in the price of product B, and determine whether A and B are substitutes or complements.

Solution.   Price elasticity of demand for product A is given by

$$E_{p_A} = \frac{\partial q_{d_A}}{\partial p_A} \frac{p_A}{q_{d_A}}$$

By the generalized theorem on implicit differentiation, we have

$$\frac{\partial q_{d_A}}{\partial p_A} = -\frac{\dfrac{\partial F}{\partial p_A}}{\dfrac{\partial F}{\partial q_{d_A}}}$$

Express the demand function as

$$F(q_{d_A}, p_A, p_B) = q_{d_A}^2 p_A^3 p_B - 10$$

Now,

$$\frac{\partial F}{\partial p_A} = 3q_{d_A}^2 p_A^2 p_B \quad \text{and} \quad \frac{\partial F}{\partial q_{d_A}} = 2q_{d_A} p_A^3 p_B$$

$$\therefore \frac{\partial q_{d_A}}{\partial p_A} = \frac{-3q_{d_A}^2 p_A^2 p_B}{2q_{d_A} p_A^3 p_B} = \frac{-3q_{d_A}}{2p_A}$$

and

price elasticity $E_{p_A} = \dfrac{-3q_{d_A}}{2p_A} \dfrac{p_A}{q_{d_A}} = -\dfrac{3}{2}$

Cross elasticity of demand for product A with respect to changes in the price of product B is given by

$$E_{AB} = \frac{\partial q_{d_A}}{\partial p_B} \frac{p_B}{q_{d_A}}$$

By the generalized theorem on implicit differentiation, we have

$$\frac{\partial q_{d_A}}{\partial p_B} = \frac{-\dfrac{\partial F}{\partial p_B}}{\dfrac{\partial F}{\partial q_{d_A}}}$$

Now,

$$\frac{\partial F}{\partial p_B} = q_{d_A}^2 p_A^3$$

$$\therefore \frac{\partial q_{d_A}}{\partial p_B} = \frac{-q_{d_A}^2 p_A^3}{2q_{d_A} p_A^3 p_B} = \frac{-q_{d_A}}{2p_B}$$

and

cross elasticity $E_{AB} = \dfrac{-q_{d_A}}{2p_B} \dfrac{p_B}{q_{d_A}} = -\dfrac{1}{2}$

The coefficient of cross elasticity is negative, so the products are complements.

Exercises

Use the theorem on differentiation of implicit functions to find the relevant derivatives for each of the following.

1. $p^2 - q_s^2 = 100$. Find dq_s/dp.

2. $q_d^2 + 4p^2 = 160$. Find elasticity of demand at a price of $6.

3. $10p^2 q_d = 7$. Find elasticity of demand at a price of $3.

4. $x^2 + y^2 - 4y = 0$. Find dy/dx.

5. $x^2 + 2xy - 5y^2 = 4$. Find dy/dx.

6. $10p_A q_{d_A} + 5q_{d_A} - p_B = 100$. Find price elasticity of demand for product A, cross elasticity of demand of product A with respect to changes in the price of product B, and determine whether A and B are substitutes or complements.

7. $p_A q_{d_A}^2 + 4q_{d_A} - 3p_B - 2y = 50$. Find price elasticity of demand for product A, cross elasticity of demand of product A with respect to changes in the price of product B, and income elasticity of demand of product A.

8. $15p_A q_{d_A} + 5q_{d_A} - 2y = 10$. Find price elasticity of demand for product A and income elasticity of demand of product A.

9. $q_{d_A}^{1.5} p_A^{0.8} p_B^{0.3} = 40$. Find price elasticity of product A, cross elasticity of demand of product A with respect to changes in the price of product B, and determine whether A and B are substitutes or complements.

10. $q_{d_A}^{2.5} p_A^{1.5} p_B^{-0.5} y^{-1.5} = 60$. Find price elasticity of product A, cross elasticity of demand of product A with respect to changes in the price of product B, and income elasticity of demand of product A.

11. $2x^2 y^2 + y^2 z^2 + 2z^2 x^2 = 4$. Find $\partial z/\partial x$ and $\partial z/\partial y$.

12. $xe^{yz} + ye^{zx} + ze^{xy} = 10$. Find $\partial z/\partial x$ and $\partial z/\partial y$.

SECTION 10·8   HOMOGENEOUS FUNCTIONS

Consider the following demand function, which relates quantity demanded to price and consumer income:

$$q_d = \frac{y^2}{100p}$$

Suppose that each of the independent variables, that is, y and p, is multiplied by any constant t. We then have

$$q_d = \frac{(ty)^2}{100tp} = \frac{t^2 y^2}{100tp} = \frac{ty^2}{100p} = t\,\frac{y^2}{100p}$$

The resulting demand function is the same as the original demand function multiplied by t. This implies that if income and price are both increased by, say, 10 percent, then quantity demanded also increases by 10 percent. Such a function is said to be a *homogeneous function*.

We shall now speak of homogeneous functions in general terms. Suppose that we are given any function

$$u = f(x, y)$$

such that whenever each of the independent variables is multiplied by any constant t, the resulting function is t^k multiplied by the original function. We then say that $u = f(x, y)$ is a *homogeneous function of degree K.*

In symbols, this is equivalent to saying that a function $f(x, y)$ is homogeneous of degree K if

$$f(tx, ty) = t^k f(x, y)$$

for all values of x, y, and t for which the function is defined. The degree K is a constant, which may be positive, negative, or zero. It need not necessarily be an integer. If $K = 1$, we sometimes say that the function is *linearly homogeneous.* This is not to imply that the function is linear, but only that the degree of homogeneity is 1.

Illustration 1.   Is the following function homogeneous and, if so, of what degree?

$$f(x, y) = 2x^2 + 3xy + y^2$$

Solution.   Multiply x and y by t, any constant. Then

$$
\begin{aligned}
f(tx, ty) &= 2(tx)^2 + 3(tx)(ty) + (ty)^2 \\
&= 2t^2x^2 + 3t^2xy + t^2y^2 \\
&= t^2(2x^2 + 3xy + y^2) \\
&= t^2 f(x, y)
\end{aligned}
$$

$f(x, y)$ is homogeneous of degree 2.

Illustration 2.   Is the following demand function homogeneous and, if so, of what degree?

$$q_d = \frac{y}{20p}$$

Solution.   Multiply y and p by t. We have

$$f(tp, ty) = \frac{ty}{20tp} = \frac{y}{20p} = t^0 f(p, y)$$

Therefore, $f(p, y)$ is homogeneous of degree zero. This implies that when p and y change by any proportion, q_d will remain unchanged.

Illustration 3.   Is the following utility function homogeneous and, if so, of what degree?

$$u = 10q_1^{1/2} + 5q_2^{1/2}$$
Solution.   Multiply q_1 and q_2 by t. We have

$$
\begin{aligned}
f(tq_1, tq_2) &= 10(tq_1)^{1/2} + 5(tq_2)^{1/2} \\
&= 10t^{1/2}q_1^{1/2} + 5t^{1/2}q_2^{1/2} \\
&= t^{1/2}(10q_1^{1/2} + 5q_2^{1/2}) \\
&= t^{1/2}f(q_1, q_2)
\end{aligned}
$$

Therefore, $f(q_1, q_2)$ is homogeneous of degree $\frac{1}{2}$.

Illustration 4.   Is the following utility function homogeneous and, if so, of what degree?

$$u = 10q_1 + 5q_2^{1/2}$$
Solution.   Multiply q_1 and q_2 by t. We have

$$
\begin{aligned}
f(tq_1, tq_2) &= 10tq_1 + 5(tq_2)^{1/2} \\
&= 10tq_1 + 5t^{1/2}q_2^{1/2}
\end{aligned}
$$

We cannot express this as t^k multiplied by the original function. Therefore this utility function is not homogeneous.

The definition of homogeneity can be extended in like manner to functions of any number of variables. A function of n variables $f(x_1, x_2, \ldots, x_n)$ is homogeneous of degree k if

$$f(tx_1, tx_2, \ldots, tx_n) = t^k f(x_1, x_2, \ldots, x_n)$$

for all values of $x_1, x_2, \ldots, x_n$ and t for which the function is defined.

Illustration 5.   Is the following demand function homogeneous and, if so, of what degree?

$$q_{d_A} = \frac{p_B}{p_A^2} + \frac{2y}{p_A^2}$$

Solution. Multiply p_A, p_B and y by t. We have

$$f(tp_A, tp_B, ty) = \frac{tp_B}{(tp_A)^2} + \frac{2ty}{(tp_A)^2}$$

$$= \frac{tp_B}{t^2 p_A^2} + \frac{2ty}{t^2 p_A^2}$$

$$= \frac{p_B}{tp_A^2} + \frac{2y}{tp_A^2}$$

$$= \frac{1}{t}\left(\frac{p_B}{p_A^2} + \frac{2y}{p_A^2}\right)$$

$$= t^{-1}f(p_A, p_B, y)$$

Therefore, the demand function is homogeneous of degree -1.

We next state an important theorem concerning homogeneous functions, which is known as *Euler's theorem*, named after the great Swiss mathematician.

Euler's Theorem.   If $z = f(x, y)$ is a homogeneous function of degree k, then

$$x\frac{\partial f}{\partial x} + y\frac{\partial f}{\partial y} = kf(x, y)$$

for all points where the function $f(x, y)$ is differentiable.

Proof.   Because $z = f(x, y)$ is homogeneous of degree k, it follows that

$$f(tx, ty) = t^k f(x, y) \qquad \text{for all possible } t$$

Now, let $u = tx$ and $v = ty$. We then have

$$f(u, v) = t^k f(x, y) \tag{1}$$

We differentiate both sides of the equation with respect to t. For the left side, using chain-rule differentiation, we get

$$\frac{\partial}{\partial t}f(u, v) = \frac{\partial f(u, v)}{\partial u}\frac{\partial u}{\partial t} + \frac{\partial f(u, v)}{\partial v}\frac{\partial v}{\partial t}$$

$$= x\frac{\partial f(u, v)}{\partial u} + y\frac{\partial f(u, v)}{\partial v}$$

Differentiating the right side, we have

$$\frac{\partial}{\partial t} t^k f(x, y) = t^k \frac{\partial f(x, y)}{\partial t} + kt^{k-1}f(x, y) \qquad \text{by the product rule}$$

$$= (t^k)(0) + kt^{k-1}f(x, y)$$

$$= kt^{k-1}f(x, y)$$

Because the left side of (1) is equal to the right side of (1), so will the results of differentiating both sides, so that

$$x\frac{\partial f(u, v)}{\partial u} + y\frac{\partial f(u, v)}{\partial v} = kt^{k-1}f(x, y)$$

This equality holds for all values of t. In particular, it must therefore hold when $t = 1$. If we set $t = 1$, we get $u = x$ and $v = y$, giving us

$$x\frac{\partial f(x, y)}{\partial x} + y\frac{\partial f(x, y)}{\partial y} = kf(x, y)$$

which proves the theorem.

Euler's theorem can easily be extended to functions of any number of variables. For the general case, we would have the following.

Euler's Theorem for the General Case. If $u = f(x_1, x_2, \ldots, x_n)$ is a homogeneous function of degree k, then

$$x_1\frac{\partial f}{\partial x_1} + x_2\frac{\partial f}{\partial x_2} + \cdots + x_n\frac{\partial f}{\partial x_n} = kf(x_1, x_2, \ldots, x_n)$$

Illustration 6. Apply Euler's theorem to the function given in Illustration 1.

Solution. In Illustration 1, we found that the function

$$f(x, y) = 2x^2 + 3xy + y^2$$

was homogeneous of degree 2. Applying Euler's Theorem, we have

$$x\frac{\partial f}{\partial x} + y\frac{\partial f}{\partial y} = 2(2x^2 + 3xy + y^2)$$

$$= 4x^2 + 6xy + 2y^2$$

We could check this by actually computing $\partial f/\partial x$ and $\partial f/\partial y$:

$$\frac{\partial f}{\partial x} = 4x + 3y \qquad \frac{\partial f}{\partial y} = 3x + 2y$$

and

$$x\frac{\partial f}{\partial x} + y\frac{\partial f}{\partial y} = x(4x + 3y) + y(3x + 2y)$$

$$= 4x^2 + 3xy + 3xy + 2y^2$$

$$= 4x^2 + 6xy + 2y^2$$

Illustration 7. Apply Euler's theorem to the function given in Illustration 2.

Solution. In Illustration 2 we found that the demand function

$$q_d = \frac{y}{20p}$$

was homogeneous of degree zero. Applying Euler's theorem, we have

$$p\frac{\partial q_d}{\partial p} + y\frac{\partial q_d}{\partial y} = 0\left(\frac{y}{20p}\right) = 0$$

We could check this by actually computing $\partial q_d/\partial p$ and $\partial q_d/\partial y$:

$$\frac{\partial q_d}{\partial p} = \frac{-20y}{(20p)^2} = \frac{-y}{20p^2} \qquad \frac{\partial q_d}{\partial y} = \frac{1}{20p}$$

and

$$p\frac{\partial q_d}{\partial p} + y\frac{\partial q_d}{\partial y} = p\left(\frac{-y}{20p^2}\right) + y\left(\frac{1}{20p}\right)$$

$$= \frac{-y}{20p} + \frac{y}{20p} = 0$$

Illustration 8. Apply Euler's theorem to the function given in Illustration 3.

Solution. In Illustration 3 we found that the utility function

$$u = 10q_1^{1/2} + 5q_2^{1/2}$$

was homogeneous of degree $\frac{1}{2}$.

Applying Euler's theorem, we have

$$q_1\frac{\partial u}{\partial q_1} + q_2\frac{\partial u}{\partial q_2} = \tfrac{1}{2}(10q_1^{1/2} + 5q_2^{1/2})$$

$$= 5q_1^{1/2} + \tfrac{5}{2}q_2^{1/2}$$

Illustration 9. Apply Euler's theorem to the function given in Illustration 5.

Solution. In Illustration 5 we found that the demand function

$$q_{d_A} = \frac{p_B}{p_A^2} + \frac{2y}{p_A^2}$$

was homogeneous of degree -1.

Applying Euler's theorem, we have

$$p_A \frac{\partial q_{d_A}}{\partial p_A} + p_B \frac{\partial q_{d_A}}{\partial p_B} + y \frac{\partial q_{d_A}}{\partial y} = -1\left(\frac{p_B}{p_A^2} + \frac{2y}{p_A^2}\right)$$

$$= -\frac{p_B}{p_A^2} - \frac{2y}{p_A^2}$$

Exercises

Decide whether each of the following functions is homogeneous and, if so, of what degree, and then apply Euler's theorem.

1. $q_d = \dfrac{2y^2}{15p^2}$

2. $u = q_1^2 + q_2^2 - 3q_1 q_2$

3. $u = 3q_1^2 + 4q_2^2 + \sqrt{10q_3^4}$

4. $q_d = \dfrac{y^2}{p + y}$

5. $u = q_1^{1/2} + q_2^{1/2} + q_1^{1/4}q_2^{1/4} \log \dfrac{q_1}{q_2}$

6. $q_d = y^{1/3} + yp^{-2/3}$

7. $z = \dfrac{x^2 - 2y^2}{2x^2 + y^2}$

8. $q_d = 200 - 4p^{3/2} + \frac{1}{10}y$

9. $q_{d_A} = \dfrac{p_B^{1/2}}{p_A^2} + 2yp_A^{-5/2}$

10. $u = q_1^{3/2} + q_1 q_2^{1/2} + q_2$

11. $z = \dfrac{x^2 + y^2}{2x - 3y}$

12. $z = 2x^2y + xy^2 + y^3$

13. $z = \dfrac{1}{\sqrt{2x^2 + y^2}}$

APPENDIX

The purpose of this appendix is to provide a more formal and rigorous definition of limits than is given in the text of the chapter. This more precise definition is completely analogous to that given for functions of one variable in the appendix to Chapter 6.

Definition. A function $f(x, y)$ is said to approach a limit L as x approaches a and y approaches b if, for any positive number ε, there is a positive number δ such that

$$|f(x, y) - L| < \varepsilon \qquad \text{when} \quad 0 < \sqrt{(x - a)^2 + (y - b)^2} < \delta$$

This is equivalent to saying that $f(x, y)$ approaches the limit L as x approaches a and y approaches b if we can bring the value of $f(x, y)$ within any ε distance from L by bringing x and y to within some neighborhood with radius δ of a and b.

11

MAXIMA AND MINIMA FOR FUNCTIONS OF SEVERAL VARIABLES: WITH AND WITHOUT CONSTRAINTS

Mathematics I regard as a supremely grand study but a very unsatisfactory life employment. It gives delight as a dessert but little nutriment as the main course. By exercise it generates penetration but by neglect it tends to fossilization. It broadens a man as a thinker but it narrows him as a factor in the world. Few realize what a terrible isolation a professionally devoted mathematician must suffer.

—Irving Fisher

In Chapter 9 we discussed the theory and procedure for finding maximum and minimum points for functions of one independent variable. We now extend our purview to functions of several independent variables. At the outset we deal with functions of two independent variables and subsequently extend the results to functions of any number of variables.

SECTION 11·1 RELATIVE AND ABSOLUTE EXTREMA FOR FUNCTIONS OF TWO OR MORE VARIABLES

Consider the function $z = f(x, y)$ defined for some region. Suppose that there is a point (a, b) in this region such that $f(a, b) > f(x, y)$ for all points within the region. We then say that the function $f(x, y)$ has an *absolute maximum* at the point (a, b). Similarly, suppose that there is some point (c, d) in the region such that $f(c, d) < f(x, y)$ for all points in the region. We then say that the function $f(x, y)$ has an *absolute minimum* at the point (c, d). An absolute maximum is often referred to as a *global maximum*, while an absolute minimum is analogously termed a *global minimum*.

A point (i, j) is said to be a *relative maximum* for the function given above if there is some neighborhood of (i, j) such that $f(i, j) > f(x, y)$ for all points in this neighborhood. Analogously, a point (k, l) is a *relative minimum* for the function if there is some neighborhood of (k, l) such that $f(k, l) < f(x, y)$ for all points in that neighborhood. Relative maxima and minima are frequently referred to as *local maxima* and *local minima*, respectively.

In cases where we wish to find absolute maximum or minimum points, it is usually wise to look first for relative extrema. If there are only a few of these, it is often easy to select which of the relative maxima or minima is an absolute maximum or absolute minimum.

The following theorem on relative extrema is therefore very useful for finding both relative and absolute extrema.

Theorem 1. Suppose that $f(x, y)$ is defined for a certain region and has a relative maximum or minimum at the point (a, b), where (a, b) is an interior point of the defined region (not on the boundary). Suppose also that the first partial derivatives at (a, b) exist. We can then conclude that at the point (a, b),

$$\frac{\partial f}{\partial x} = 0 \quad \text{and} \quad \frac{\partial f}{\partial y} = 0$$

In other words, if a function has a relative extremum at an interior point of a region and if its first partial derivatives are defined at that point, then these partials are equal to zero. However, relative extrema can occur at boundary points of the region without the first partial derivatives being equal to zero.

It should be noted that the vanishing of the first partial derivatives is a necessary, but not sufficient, condition for a relative extremum. It may happen that the first partials are equal to zero and yet there may be no relative extrema.

This implies that if we locate the points for which the first partial derivatives vanish, we know that such points are the only possible extreme points in the interior of the region (assuming that the first partials are defined for all points within the region). To verify whether such points are, indeed, extrema, it is necessary to satisfy the additional conditions given in the next theorem.

Theorem 2. Suppose that $f(x, y)$ and its first and second partial derivatives are defined and continuous throughout a region of which (a, b) is an interior point, and suppose that the first partial derivatives vanish at that point. Then we can conclude that:

1. $f(x, y)$ has a relative maximum at (a, b), provided that at that point one of the unmixed second partials of $f(x, y)$ is negative, that is, $f_{xx} < 0$ or $f_{yy} < 0$, and provided that $f_{xx}f_{yy} - (f_{xy})^2 > 0$.
2. $f(x, y)$ has a relative minimum at (a, b), provided that at that point one of the unmixed second partials of $f(x, y)$ is positive, that is, $f_{xx} > 0$ or $f_{yy} > 0$, and provided that $f_{xx}f_{yy} - (f_{xy})^2 > 0$.
3. $f(x, y)$ has neither a maximum nor a minimum at (a, b) if at that point $f_{xx}f_{yy} - (f_{xy})^2 < 0$. In this case, the function is said to have a *saddle point* at (a, b), which implies that a movement from that point parallel to one of the axes results in greater values for the function, but a movement parallel to another axis results in lower values for the function.
4. If, at (a, b), it turns out that $f_{xx}f_{yy} - (f_{xy})^2 = 0$, then we cannot immediately say whether any extrema occur. Any one of the possibilities outlined in 1–3 may occur.

The necessary conditions for extrema stated in Theorem 1 are sometimes referred to as *first-order conditions*, because they involve first partial derivatives; while the conditions stated in Theorem 2 are referred to as *second-order conditions*, because they involve second partial derivatives. The second-order conditions, when taken in combination with the first-order conditions, provide sufficient conditions for extrema.

Illustration 1. Find maximum and minimum points for the revenue function

$$TR = -5q_1^2 - 8q_2^2 - 2q_1q_2 + 14q_1 + 34q_2 \qquad \text{where } q_1 \text{ and } q_2 \geq 0$$

and where q_1 and q_2 are the respective quantities of two products sold by a firm.

Solution. We first locate possible relative maxima and minima by setting the first partials equal to zero.

$$\frac{\partial TR}{\partial q_1} = -10q_1 - 2q_2 + 14 = 0 \qquad \frac{\partial TR}{\partial q_2} = -16q_2 - 2q_1 + 34 = 0$$

We now have two first-order conditions for extreme points. Solve these simultaneously to find the points that satisfy both equations.

$$-10q_1 - 2q_2 + 14 = 0$$

$$-2q_1 - 16q_2 + 34 = 0$$

Multiply the second equation by -5 and leave the first unchanged. Then add the two resulting equations.

$$-10q_1 - 2q_2 + 14 = 0$$

$$10q_1 + 80q_2 - 170 = 0$$

$$78q_2 - 156 = 0$$

$$78q_2 = 156$$

$$q_2 = 2$$

$$q_1 = 1$$

By Theorem 1, we know that this point $(1, 2)$ is the only possible extreme point within the interior of the defined region for the revenue function. In order to verify whether the point is a maximum, minimum, or neither, we utilize Theorem 2. This necessitates finding the second partial derivatives, which are

$$f_{q_1 q_1} = -10 \qquad f_{q_2 q_2} = -16 \qquad f_{q_1 q_2} = -2$$

Therefore,

$$f_{q_1 q_1} < 0$$

and

$$f_{q_1 q_1} f_{q_2 q_2} - (f_{q_1 q_2})^2 = (-10)(-16) - (-2)^2 = 156 > 0$$

Therefore, we have satisfied the sufficient conditions for a relative maximum. The only extreme point on the interior of the function is $q_1 = 1$, $q_2 = 2$, at which $TR = 41$.

However, this does not guarantee that the point we found is also the absolute maximum for the function. Before deciding on the absolute maximum and minimum points, we must consider the behavior of the revenue function on its boundary of definition. The method of finding extrema provided by Theorems 1 and 2 does not apply to boundary points, so we must consider such points separately.

The revenue function is defined for all values for which $q_1 \geq 0$ and $q_2 \geq 0$. Therefore its boundaries are given by $q_1 = 0$ and $q_2 = 0$. Let us then consider these two possibilities.

If $q_1 = 0$, we have

$$TR = -8q_2^2 + 34q_2$$

Let us find the maximum or minimum points attained by the revenue function on this boundary. TR is now a function of one variable, so we can use the ordinary first derivative to locate critical points. We proceed as follows:

$$TR' = -16q_2 + 34 = 0$$

$$16q_2 = 34$$

$$q_2 = \tfrac{34}{16} = \tfrac{17}{8}$$

To verify whether $q_2 = \tfrac{17}{8}$ is a maximum, minimum, or neither, we take the second derivative, which is

$$TR'' = -16$$

The second derivative is negative, so the point $q_1 = 0$, $q_2 = \tfrac{17}{8}$ is a boundary maximum. At this point

$$TR = -8(\tfrac{17}{8})^2 + 34(\tfrac{17}{8}) = \tfrac{289}{8} = 36.125$$

The remaining boundary to consider is $q_2 = 0$. In that case, we have

$$TR = -5q_1^2 + 14q_1$$

To find the maximum or minimum on this boundary, we set the first derivative equal to zero.

$$TR' = 10q_1 + 14 = 0$$

$$10q_1 = 14$$

$$q_1 = \tfrac{7}{5}$$

To verify whether this point is a maximum, minimum, or neither, we find the second derivative, which is

$$TR'' = -10$$

The second derivative is negative, so the point $q_1 = \tfrac{7}{5}$, $q_2 = 0$ is a boundary maximum. At this point

$$TR = -5(\tfrac{7}{5})^2 + 14(\tfrac{7}{5}) = \tfrac{147}{5} = 29.4$$

We have thus located one interior maximum and two boundary maxima. To find the absolute maximum, we compare the values of TR for each of these points. We get the following:

At $q_1 = 1$, $q_2 = 2$, we have $TR = 41$

At $q_1 = 0$, $q_2 = \frac{17}{8}$, we have $TR = 36.125$

At $q_1 = \frac{7}{5}$, $q_2 = 0$, we have $TR = 29.4$

Therefore we conclude that the *absolute maximum* of the revenue function is at $q_1 = 1$, $q_2 = 2$.

We note that our process has not uncovered any minimum points. This is because TR decreases without end as q_1 and q_2 become large. Therefore there is no absolute minimum for this revenue function.

Illustration 2.   Find the maximum points for the following revenue function:

$$TR = -3q_1^2 - q_2^2 - 10q_1 q_2 + 24q_1 + 18q_2 \qquad \text{where } q_1 \text{ and } q_2 \geqslant 0$$

Solution.   We locate possible maxima by setting the first partials equal to zero.

$$\frac{\partial TR}{\partial q_1} = -6q_1 - 10q_2 + 24 = 0 \qquad \frac{\partial TR}{\partial q_2} = -2q_2 - 10q_1 + 18 = 0$$

We have two first-order conditions for extreme points. Solve these simultaneously to find the points that satisfy both equations.

$$-6q_1 - 10q_2 + 24 = 0$$

$$-10q_1 - 2q_2 + 18 = 0$$

Multiply the second equation by -5 and leave the first unchanged. Then add the resulting equations:

$$-6q_1 - 10q_2 + 24 = 0$$

$$50q_1 + 10q_2 - 90 = 0$$

$$44q_1 - 66 = 0$$

$$q_1 = \tfrac{3}{2}$$

$$q_2 = \tfrac{3}{2}$$

By Theorem 1, we know that this point $(\frac{3}{2}, \frac{3}{2})$ is the only possible maximum within the interior of the defined region for the revenue function. In order to verify whether the point is a maximum or not, we utilize Theorem 2. This necessitates finding the second partial derivatives, which are

$$f_{q_1 q_1} = -6 \qquad f_{q_2 q_2} = -2 \qquad f_{q_1 q_2} = -10$$

Now

$$f_{q_1 q_1} < 0$$

But

$$f_{q_1 q_1} f_{q_2 q_2} - (f_{q_1 q_2})^2 = (-6)(-2) - (-10)^2 = -88 < 0$$

The sufficient conditions for either a maximum or minimum are thus not satisfied. Therefore the point $q_1 = 1$, $q_2 = 2$ is only a saddle point.

We next search for maxima on the boundary of definition. There are two boundaries, $q_1 = 0$ and $q_2 = 0$. Consider each one separately.

If $q_1 = 0$, we have

$$TR = -q_2^2 + 18q_2$$

To find possible extreme points on this boundary, we set the first derivative equal to zero:

$$TR' = -2q_2 + 18 = 0$$

$$q_2 = 9$$

To verify whether this point is a boundary maximum, we take the second derivative, which is

$$TR'' = -2$$

The second derivative is negative, so the point $q_1 = 0$, $q_2 = 9$ is a boundary maximum. At this point

$$TR = -81 + 18(9) = 81$$

The remaining boundary is $q_2 = 0$. In that case we have

$$TR = -3q_1^2 + 24q_1$$

We set the first derivative equal to zero:

$$TR' = -6q_1 + 24 = 0$$

$$q_1 = 4$$

To verify whether this point is a boundary maximum, we take the second derivative, which is

$$TR'' = -6$$

The second derivative is negative, so the point $q_1 = 4$, $q_2 = 0$ is a boundary maximum. At this point

$$TR = -3(4)^2 + 24(4) = 48$$

We therefore have two boundary maxima. To find the absolute maximum, we compare the values of TR for each of these points. We notice that

At $q_1 = 0$, $q_2 = 9$ and $TR = 81$

At $q_1 = 4$, $q_2 = 0$ and $TR = 48$

We conclude that the *absolute maximum* of the revenue function is at $q_1 = 0$, $q_2 = 9$. Because this point is on the boundary of the region, it is sometimes called a *corner solution*.

Theorems 1 and 2 can be extended so as to provide necessary and sufficient conditions for maxima and minima of functions of any number of variables. We now state these theorems in general terms for any function $f(x_1, x_2, \ldots, x_n)$.

Theorem 3.   Suppose that $f(x_1, x_2, \ldots, x_n)$ is defined for a certain region and has a relative maximum or minimum at the point $(a, b, \ldots, n)$ where $(a, b, \ldots, n)$ is an interior point of the defined region (not on the boundary). Suppose also that the first partial derivatives at $(a, b, \ldots, n)$ exist. We can then conclude that at the point $(a, b, \ldots, n)$

$$\frac{\partial f}{\partial x_1} = 0, \ \frac{\partial f}{\partial x_2} = 0, \ldots, \ \frac{\partial f}{\partial x_n} = 0$$

Thus the vanishing of all the first partial derivatives is a necessary condition for the existence of relative extrema of functions of any number of variables. These conditions are also called first-order conditions.

To verify whether points that satisfy the condition of Theorem 3 are maxima, minima, or neither, we make use of Theorem 4.

Theorem 4.   Suppose that $f(x_1, x_2, \ldots, x_n)$ and its first and second partial derivatives are defined and continuous throughout a region of which $(a, b, \ldots, n)$ is an interior point, and suppose that the first partial derivatives vanish at that point. Then construct the determinants

$$f_{x_1 x_1}, \ \begin{vmatrix} f_{x_1 x_1} & f_{x_1 x_2} \\ f_{x_2 x_1} & f_{x_2 x_2} \end{vmatrix}, \ \begin{vmatrix} f_{x_1 x_1} & f_{x_1 x_2} & f_{x_1 x_3} \\ f_{x_2 x_1} & f_{x_2 x_2} & f_{x_2 x_3} \\ f_{x_3 x_1} & f_{x_3 x_2} & f_{x_3 x_3} \end{vmatrix}, \ldots,$$

$$\begin{vmatrix} f_{x_1 x_1} & f_{x_1 x_2} & \cdots & f_{x_1 x_n} \\ f_{x_2 x_1} & f_{x_2 x_2} & \cdots & f_{x_2 x_n} \\ \vdots & \vdots & & \vdots \\ f_{x_n x_1} & f_{x_n x_2} & \cdots & f_{x_n x_n} \end{vmatrix}$$

where each partial is to be evaluated at the point $(a, b, \ldots, n)$. We can conclude that a relative maximum exists at the point $(a, b, \ldots, n)$ if the determinants of odd order are negative and those of even order are positive. The point will be a relative minimum if all of the above determinants are positive. The conditions given by Theorem 4 are sometimes referred to as second-order conditions because they involve second derivatives.

It will be noted that the elements of each of the determinants given above are second partial derivatives. Such determinants are sometimes called *Hessians*. The nth-order Hessian is the last determinant given above. The Hessian of order $n - 1$ would be formed by deleting the final row and column of the nth-order determinant. It would thus be an $n - 1$ determinant. Similarly, the third-order Hessian would be a third-order determinant formed by taking all the possible second partials with respect to the three variables x_1, x_2, x_3. In like manner, the second-order Hessian is simply the second-order determinant formed by taking all the possible second partials with respect to the two variables x_1 and x_2. The first-order Hessian is the single term $f_{x_1 x_1}$, which can be viewed as equivalent to a determinant whose single term is the second partial with respect to the one variable x_1.

We are assuming that the second partials are all continuous, so we know by the theorem given in Section 10.4 that the mixed partials will be equal; that is, $f_{x_1 x_2} = f_{x_2 x_1}$ and $f_{x_1 x_3} = f_{x_3 x_1}, \ldots, f_{x_1 x_j} = f_{x_j x_i}$. This will prove helpful in particular problems because it will enable us to combine such terms.

Theorem 4, when taken together with Theorem 3, provides sufficient conditions for extrema of any function of n variables. In particular, when $n = 2$, we have the special case of a function of two independent variables. Using Theorem 4, we conclude that for such a function to have a maximum point, the first partials with respect to the two variables would have to vanish and, in addition,

$$f_{x_1 x_1} < 0 \quad \text{and} \quad \begin{vmatrix} f_{x_1 x_1} & f_{x_1 x_2} \\ f_{x_2 x_1} & f_{x_2 x_2} \end{vmatrix} > 0$$

when evaluated at the particular point. Expansion of the last determinant yields

$$f_{x_1 x_1} f_{x_2 x_2} - (f_{x_1 x_2})^2 > 0$$

where we utilized the fact that $f_{x_1 x_2} = f_{x_2 x_1}$. It is easily seen that these conditions are identical to those stated in Theorem 2, which dealt only with a function of two variables.

Similarly, the sufficient condition for a minimum at a particular point is that the first partials vanish and, in addition,

$$f_{x_1x_1} > 0 \quad \text{and} \quad \begin{vmatrix} f_{x_1x_1} & f_{x_1x_2} \\ f_{x_2x_1} & f_{x_2x_2} \end{vmatrix} > 0$$

Expansion of the last determinant again shows that this condition is identical to that stated in Theorem 2. Thus Theorems 1 and 2 are concerned with a special case of the more generalized Theorems 3 and 4.

Illustration 3. Find maxima and minima of the following function:

$$f(x, y, z) = x^2 - 3x + xy + xz + y^2 + z^2$$

Solution. We locate possible maximum and minimum points by setting the first partial derivatives equal to zero and solving simultaneously.

$$\frac{\partial f}{\partial x} = 2x - 3 + y + z = 0$$

$$\frac{\partial f}{\partial y} = x + 2y = 0 \quad \text{or} \quad y = -\frac{x}{2}$$

$$\frac{\partial f}{\partial z} = x + 2z = 0 \quad \text{or} \quad z = -\frac{x}{2}$$

Substituting

$$y = -\frac{x}{2} \quad \text{and} \quad z = -\frac{x}{2}$$

into the first equation, we have

$$2x - 3 - \frac{x}{2} - \frac{x}{2} = 0$$

$$2x - 3 - x = 0$$

$$x = 3$$

and

$$y = -\frac{x}{2} = -\frac{3}{2}$$

$$z = -\frac{x}{2} = -\frac{3}{2}$$

Thus the only possible extreme point is at $(3, -\frac{3}{2}, -\frac{3}{2})$. To verify whether this point is a maximum, minimum, or neither, we consider the second-

order conditions. We have three independent variables, so we must form
the following three determinants:

$$f_{xx} \qquad \begin{vmatrix} f_{xx} & f_{xy} \\ f_{yx} & f_{yy} \end{vmatrix} \qquad \begin{vmatrix} f_{xx} & f_{xy} & f_{xz} \\ f_{yx} & f_{yy} & f_{yz} \\ f_{zx} & f_{zy} & f_{zz} \end{vmatrix}$$

We shall have a relative minimum at the point $(3, -\frac{3}{2}, -\frac{3}{2})$ if all the
above determinants are positive. We shall have a relative maximum at
that point if the first determinant, that is, f_{xx}, is negative, the second
determinant is positive, and the third determinant is negative.

Let us therefore evaluate the various second partials.

$$f_{xx} = 2 \qquad f_{xy} = f_{yx} = 1 \qquad f_{xz} = f_{zx} = 1$$

$$f_{yy} = 2 \qquad f_{yz} = f_{zy} = 0 \qquad f_{zz} = 2$$

Now, $f_{xx} > 0$

$$\begin{vmatrix} f_{xx} & f_{xy} \\ f_{yx} & f_{yy} \end{vmatrix} = \begin{vmatrix} 2 & 1 \\ 1 & 2 \end{vmatrix} = 4 - 1 = 3 > 0$$

and

$$\begin{vmatrix} f_{xx} & f_{xy} & f_{xz} \\ f_{yx} & f_{yy} & f_{yz} \\ f_{zx} & f_{zy} & f_{zz} \end{vmatrix} = \begin{vmatrix} 2 & 1 & 1 \\ 1 & 2 & 0 \\ 1 & 0 & 2 \end{vmatrix}$$

$$= 2 \begin{vmatrix} 2 & 0 \\ 0 & 2 \end{vmatrix} - 1 \begin{vmatrix} 1 & 1 \\ 0 & 2 \end{vmatrix} + 1 \begin{vmatrix} 1 & 1 \\ 2 & 0 \end{vmatrix} = 8 - 2 - 2 = 4 > 0$$

Therefore all the required determinants are positive, and the point
$(3, -\frac{3}{2}, -\frac{3}{2})$ is a relative minimum.

Exercises

Find maxima and minima for each of the following functions.

1. $TR = -2q_1^2 - 3q_2^2 - q_1 q_2 + 20q_1 + 28q_2$, where q_1 and $q_2 \geqslant 0$
2. $TR = -10q_1^2 - 6q_2^2 + 5q_1 q_2 + 52q_1 + 30q_2$, where q_1 and $q_2 \geqslant 0$
3. $TR = -4q_1^2 - 3q_2^2 - 4q_1 q_2 + 18q_1 + 25q_2$, where q_1 and $q_2 \geqslant 0$
4. $TR = -q_1^2 - 4q_2^2 + 5q_1 q_2 - 10q_1 - 11q_2$, where q_1 and $q_2 \geqslant 0$
5. $TR = -3q_1^2 - 2q_2^2 - 6q_1 q_2 + 21q_1 + 31q_2$, where q_1 and $q_2 \geqslant 0$
6. $TR = -2q_1^3 - q_2^2 + 2q_1 q_2 - 20q_1 + 40q_2$, where q_1 and $q_2 > 0$
7. $z = x^3 + y^3 - 3xy$

8. $f(x, y, z) = 10z - z^2 - x^2 - y^2 - zy - zx$

9. $z = x^3 + y^3 - 3x - 3y + 1$

10. Does the function $f(x, y, z) = x^4 + y^4 + z^4 - 4xyz$ have a maximum or minimum at the point $(1, 1, 1)$?

SECTION 11·2 MAXIMA AND MINIMA OF FUNCTIONS WITH CONSTRAINTS

In this section we consider the problem of finding maxima and minima of a function subject to certain conditions or constraints. Such a problem arises, for example, when we wish to maximize a utility function subject to the condition that the consumer has only a fixed amount of money to spend on all products combined. A similar situation exists if we wish to maximize total revenue received from producing two products, where $TR = f(q_1, q_2)$ subject to the constraint that there is a fixed relation between the quantities of the two products, such as $q_1 = 2q_2$. The latter condition could represent a certain joint production process, where for each unit of product 2 created, two units of product 1 are simultaneously produced.

Suppose, then, that we wish to find extrema of any function $z = f(x, y)$ subject to the condition that $g(x, y) = 0$. One method that might be employed is to use the equation of constraint to express one variable in terms of the other. This expression is then substituted into the function that is to be maximized or minimized. The solution is then attained by the same methods as previously outlined for functions without constraints. This method is known as *direct elimination*. In effect, the constraint helps to eliminate one variable and reduces the number of independent variables.

Illustration 1. Find the point at which a consumer will maximize his utility when his utility function is given by

$$u = 2q_1 + q_2 + 2q_1 q_2$$

where q_1 and $q_2 \geqslant 0$; his budget is fixed at $100 and the prices of the two products are set at $2 and $1, respectively.

Solution. Because the consumer's budget is fixed at $100 and the product prices are $2 and $1, respectively, the following constraint must be satisfied,

$$100 = 2q_1 + q_2$$

that is, the price of the first product multiplied by its quantity plus the price of the second product multiplied by its quantity will exhaust the total budget. We now wish to maximize

$$u = 2q_1 + q_2 + 2q_1 q_2$$

subject to the condition $100 = 2q_1 + q_2$. The first step is to express one variable in terms of the other, or $q_2 = 100 - 2q_1$. We then substitute this value of q_2 into the utility function, which gives

$$u = 2q_1 + (100 - 2q_1) + 2q_1(100 - 2q_1)$$
$$= 2q_1 + 100 - 2q_1 + 200q_1 - 4q_1^2$$
$$= 100 + 200q_1 - 4q_1^2$$

To find critical points of this function, we set its first derivative equal to zero:

$$\frac{du}{dq_1} = 200 - 8q_1 = 0$$

$$8q_1 = 200$$

$$q_1 = 25$$

Note that after the substitution, u became a function of just one variable, q_1. We therefore took the ordinary derivative rather than some partial derivative.

To verify whether $q_1 = 25$ is a maximum, minimum, or neither, we find the second derivative, which is

$$\frac{d^2u}{dq^2} = -8 < 0$$

Therefore $q_1 = 25$ is, indeed, a maximum of the utility function subject to the given constraint. From the equation of constraint, we find that when $q_1 = 25$, $q_2 = 50$. At this point the utility level is given by

$$u = 2(25) + 50 + 2(25)(50)$$

$$= 2600$$

As in earlier problems, our procedure enables us only to find extreme points on the interior of the defined region. It is possible, however, that there may be extreme points on the boundary of the function.

The utility function under consideration is defined for q_1 and $q_2 \geqslant 0$. Therefore its boundaries are given by $q_1 = 0$ and $q_2 = 0$. Let us consider each case separately.

If $q_1 = 0$, we find from the equation of constraint that $q_2 = 100$. At $q_1 = 0$, $q_2 = 100$, we have $u = 100$.

If $q_2 = 0$, we find from the equation of constraint that $q_1 = 50$. At $q_1 = 50$, $q_2 = 0$, we have $u = 100$.

We then see that the boundary values for the utility function are smaller than that attained by the interior maximum. We therefore conclude that the point $q_1 = 25$, $q_2 = 50$ is an absolute or global maximum for the utility function with the given constraint.

In the illustration we just considered, we had no difficulty solving the constraint equation for one variable in terms of the other and then substituting into the original function. However, this procedure frequently becomes very difficult or even impossible when the equation is more complex. This is particularly so when we deal with functions of many variables. Moreover, the method of direct elimination suffers from a lack of symmetry, because one variable is arbitrarily eliminated from the function while others are retained. It is for these reasons that an alternative, more elegant, and more powerful method, known as *Lagrange multipliers*, is most often used in practice. We shall first outline this method for a function of two variables subject to one constraint and then generalize to functions of any number of variables and constraints.

Suppose that we wish to find extrema of any function $z = f(x, y)$ subject to the condition that $g(x, y) = 0$. Form a new function

$$F = f(x, y) + \lambda g(x, y)$$

where λ is some unknown constant, sometimes called Lagrange's multiplier. This new function is known as the Lagrangian function. It is constructed by taking the function that is to be maximized or minimized and adding to it the equation of constraint multiplied by an unknown constant. Note that the equation of constraint must first be set equal to zero.

A necessary condition for an extreme point on the interior of the original function $z = f(x, y)$ subject to the constraint $g(x, y) = 0$ is that any such point must satisfy the following equations involving the partial derivatives of the Lagrangian function.

$$\frac{\partial F}{\partial x} = 0 \qquad \frac{\partial F}{\partial y} = 0$$

To locate these points, we find the first partials of the Lagrangian function and set them equal to zero. The two equations

$$\frac{\partial F}{\partial x} = 0 \quad \text{and} \quad \frac{\partial F}{\partial y} = 0$$

are then solved simultaneously with the equation of constraint to yield values for the three unknowns x, y, and λ. It is interesting to observe that the constraint equation can be expressed as $\partial F / \partial \lambda$ so that the three equations could all be stated in terms of partial derivatives of the Lagrangian function.

Any points we find by the above procedure are, of course, only possible maxima or minima. To verify whether they are maxima, minima, or neither, we must consider the second-order or sufficient conditions that apply to Lagrangian functions. These conditions can be stated most compactly in the following form:

Consider the following determinant whose elements are either second partial derivatives of the Lagrangian function or first partials of the constraint equation $g(x, y) = 0$. If, at a point that satisfies the necessary conditions given above, the determinant

$$\begin{vmatrix} F_{xx} & F_{xy} & g_x \\ F_{yx} & F_{yy} & g_y \\ g_x & g_y & 0 \end{vmatrix} > 0$$

then a relative maximum exists at that point. On the other hand, if the above determinant is less than zero, a relative minimum exists at that point.

The determinant given above is sometimes called the *bordered Hessian*, because it is formed by taking the Hessian determinant as defined in Section 11.1 and bordering it by an additional column and row made up of the first partials of the constraint equation and a zero term in the corner.

Illustration 2. Use the Lagrangian method to maximize the utility function

$$u = 2q_1 + q_2 + 2q_1 q_2$$

where q_1 and $q_2 > 0$ subject to the budget constraint $100 = 2q_1 + q_2$.

Solution. We first form the Lagrangian function, which is

$$F(q_1, q_2) = 2q_1 + q_2 + 2q_1 q_2 + \lambda(2q_1 + q_2 - 100)$$

The necessary or first-order conditions for a maximum are derived by setting the first partials of the Lagrangian function equal to zero.

$$\frac{\partial F}{\partial q_1} = 2 + 2q_2 + 2\lambda = 0$$

$$\frac{\partial F}{\partial q_2} = 1 + 2q_1 + \lambda = 0$$

The constraint equation is the same as

$$\frac{\partial F}{\partial \lambda} = 2q_1 + q_2 - 100 = 0$$

We now solve these three equations simultaneously. From the second, we get

$$\lambda = -2q_1 - 1$$

Inserting this value of λ into the first equation, we get

$$2 + 2q_2 - 4q_1 - 2 = 0$$

or

$$-4q_1 + 2q_2 = 0$$

But we also have, from the third equation,

$$2q_1 + q_2 = 100$$

Solving these simultaneously by multiplying the last equation by -2, we have

$$-4q_1 + 2q_2 = 0$$
$$-4q_1 - 2q_2 = -200$$
$$\overline{\; -8q_1 = -200}$$
$$q_1 = 25$$
$$q_2 = 50$$

To verify whether this point is a maximum, minimum, or neither, we must evaluate the bordered Hessian. We compute the following:

$$F_{q_1 q_1} = 0 \qquad F_{q_1 q_2} = F_{q_2 q_1} = 2 \qquad F_{q_2 q_2} = 0$$

$$g_{q_1} = 2 \quad \text{and} \quad g_{q_2} = 1$$

and

$$\begin{vmatrix} F_{q_1 q_1} & F_{q_1 q_2} & g_{q_1} \\ F_{q_2 q_1} & F_{q_2 q_2} & g_{q_2} \\ g_{q_1} & g_{q_2} & 0 \end{vmatrix} = \begin{vmatrix} 0 & 2 & 2 \\ 2 & 0 & 1 \\ 2 & 1 & 0 \end{vmatrix}$$

$$= -2 \begin{vmatrix} 2 & 2 \\ 1 & 0 \end{vmatrix} + 2 \begin{vmatrix} 2 & 2 \\ 0 & 1 \end{vmatrix} = 4 + 4 = 8 > 0$$

The determinant is positive, so the second-order conditions for a maximum are satisfied and the point $q_1 = 25$, $q_2 = 50$ is a maximum. At this point $u = 2600$.

This point is the only possible maximum on the interior of the function subject to the given budget constraint. We must still consider the possibility of a boundary maximum.

The given utility function is defined for q_1 and $q_2 \geqslant 0$. Therefore its boundaries are given by $q_1 = 0$ and $q_2 = 0$. Let us consider each case separately.

If $q_1 = 0$, we have from the equation of constraint that $q_2 = 100$. At this point, we find $u = 100$.

If $q_2 = 0$, we have from the equation of constraint that $q_1 = 50$. At this point, we find $u = 100$.

Thus the boundary values of the utility function are smaller than that attained by the interior maximum. We therefore conclude that the point $q_1 = 25$, $q_2 = 50$ is an absolute or global maximum for the utility function with the given constraint.

Our solution is, of course, identical to the one we arrived at in Illustration 1, where we employed the method of direct elimination.

Illustration 3.   Maximize the revenue function

$$TR = -5q_1^2 - 8q_2^2 - 2q_1q_2 + 14q_1 + 34q_2$$

when q_1 and $q_2 \geqslant 0$ subject to the condition that $q_1 = 2q_2 - \frac{1}{11}$, where q_1 and q_2 are two products that are jointly produced.

Solution.   We form the Lagrangian function, which is

$$F(q_1, q_2) = -5q_1^2 - 8q_2^2 - 2q_1q_2 + 14q_1 + 34q_2 + \lambda(q_1 - 2q_2 + \tfrac{1}{11})$$

We set the first partial derivatives equal to zero in order to satisfy the first-order or necessary conditions for an extreme point.

$$\frac{\partial F}{\partial q_1} = -10q_1 - 2q_2 + 14 + \lambda = 0 \tag{1}$$

$$\frac{\partial F}{\partial q_2} = -16q_2 - 2q_1 + 34 - 2\lambda = 0 \tag{2}$$

$$\frac{\partial F}{\partial \lambda} = q_1 - 2q_2 + \tfrac{1}{11} = 0 \tag{3}$$

From the first equation, we solve for λ and get

$$\lambda = 10q_1 + 2q_2 - 14$$

Substituting this value into the second equation, we have

$$-16q_2 - 2q_1 + 34 - 2(10q_1 + 2q_2 - 14) = 0$$
$$-16q_2 - 2q_1 + 34 - 20q_1 - 4q_2 + 28 = 0$$
$$-22q_1 - 20q_2 + 62 = 0$$

Now, from equation (3), we find

$$q_1 = 2q_2 - \tfrac{1}{11}$$

Therefore, substituting for q_1, we get

$$-22(2q_2 - \tfrac{1}{11}) - 20q_2 + 62 = 0$$
$$-44q_2 + 2 - 20q_2 + 62 = 0$$
$$-64q_2 + 64 = 0$$
$$q_2 = 1$$
$$q_1 = \tfrac{21}{11}$$

To verify whether this point is a maximum, minimum, or neither, we must evaluate the bordered Hessian. We have

$$F_{q_1 q_1} = -10 \qquad F_{q_1 q_2} = F_{q_2 q_1} = -2 \qquad F_{q_2 q_2} = -16$$

$$g_{q_1} = 1 \qquad g_{q_2} = -2$$

and

$$\begin{vmatrix} F_{q_1 q_1} & F_{q_1 q_2} & g_{q_1} \\ F_{q_2 q_1} & F_{q_2 q_2} & g_{q_2} \\ g_{q_1} & g_{q_2} & 0 \end{vmatrix} = \begin{vmatrix} -10 & -2 & 1 \\ -2 & -16 & -2 \\ 1 & -2 & 0 \end{vmatrix}$$

$$= -10 \begin{vmatrix} -16 & -2 \\ -2 & 0 \end{vmatrix} + 2 \begin{vmatrix} -2 & 1 \\ -2 & 0 \end{vmatrix} + \begin{vmatrix} -2 & 1 \\ -16 & -2 \end{vmatrix}$$

$$= -10(-4) + 2(2) + (4 + 16) = 40 + 4 + 20 = 64 > 0$$

The determinant is positive, so the second-order conditions for a maximum are satisfied and the point $q_1 = 1$, $q_2 = \tfrac{21}{11}$ is a maximum. At this point, $TR = 40 + \tfrac{113}{121}$.

We must, however, still consider the possibility of a boundary maximum.

The given revenue function is defined for q_1 and $q_2 \geqslant 0$. Therefore its boundaries are given by $q_1 = 0$ and $q_2 = 0$. Let us consider each case separately.

If $q_1 = 0$, we find from the equation of constraint that $q_2 = \tfrac{1}{22}$. At this point, we find $TR = \tfrac{185}{121}$.

If $q_2 = 0$, we find from the equation of constraint that $q_1 = -\frac{1}{11}$. Because q_1 cannot be negative, we dismiss this possibility.

The value for TR attained at the interior maximum is greater than the boundary values. Therefore we conclude that the point $q_1 = 1$, $q_2 = \frac{21}{11}$ is an absolute or global maximum for the total revenue function with the given production constraint.

The method of Lagrange multipliers can be extended to functions of any number of variables.

Suppose that we wish to find extrema of any function $f(x_1, x_2, \ldots, x_n)$ subject to the condition that $g(x_1, x_2, \ldots, x_n) = 0$. Form a Lagrangian function

$$F = f(x_1, x_2, \ldots, x_n) + \lambda g(x_1, x_2, \ldots, x_n)$$

A necessary condition for an extreme point on the interior of the original function $f(x_1, x_2, \ldots, x_n)$ subject to the constraint $g(x_1, x_2, \ldots, x_n) = 0$ is that any such point must satisfy the equations

$$\frac{\partial F}{\partial x_1} = 0 \qquad \frac{\partial F}{\partial x_2} = 0 \quad \cdots \quad \frac{\partial F}{\partial x_n} = 0 \quad \text{and} \quad \frac{\partial F}{\partial \lambda} = 0$$

In other words, the first partial derivatives of the Lagrangian function with respect to each variable must vanish at the point in question.

To locate such points, we solve simultaneously the n equations involving the first partials together with the equation of constraint, that is,

$$\frac{\partial F}{\partial \lambda} = 0$$

This yields values for the $n + 1$ unknowns $x_1, x_2, \ldots, x_n$ and λ.

The resulting points are then possible maxima or minima. To verify whether any such point is a maximum, minimum, or neither, we must consider the sufficient or second-order conditions. These are stated in terms of the following bordered Hessians or determinants.

$$\begin{vmatrix} F_{x_1 x_1} & F_{x_1 x_2} & g_{x_1} \\ F_{x_2 x_1} & F_{x_2 x_2} & g_{x_2} \\ g_{x_1} & g_{x_2} & 0 \end{vmatrix} \qquad \begin{vmatrix} F_{x_1 x_1} & F_{x_1 x_2} & F_{x_1 x_3} & g_{x_1} \\ F_{x_2 x_1} & F_{x_2 x_2} & F_{x_2 x_3} & g_{x_2} \\ F_{x_3 x_1} & F_{x_3 x_2} & F_{x_3 x_3} & g_{x_3} \\ g_{x_1} & g_{x_2} & g_{x_3} & 0 \end{vmatrix}$$

$$\cdots \begin{vmatrix} F_{x_1 x_1} & F_{x_1 x_2} & \cdots & F_{x_1 x_n} & g_{x_1} \\ F_{x_2 x_1} & F_{x_2 x_2} & \cdots & F_{x_2 x_n} & g_{x_2} \\ \vdots & \vdots & & \vdots & \vdots \\ F_{x_n x_1} & F_{x_n x_2} & \cdots & F_{x_n x_n} & g_{x_n} \\ g_{x_1} & g_{x_2} & \cdots & g_{x_n} & 0 \end{vmatrix}$$

Note that these determinants comprise the bordered Hessians of all orders. If, at a point that satisfies the necessary conditions given above, all the determinants (or bordered Hessians) are less than zero, then a relative minimum is attained at that point. If, at such a point, the determinants alternate in sign beginning with a positive sign, then a relative maximum is attained.

The Lagrangian procedure can also be applied to the case of more than one constraint provided that the number of constraints is smaller than the number of variables.

Suppose that we wish to find extrema of any function $f(x_1, x_2, \ldots, x_n)$ subject to two constraints $g(x_1, x_2, \ldots, x_n) = 0$ and $h(x_1, x_2, \ldots, x_n) = 0$.

Form a Lagrangian function

$$F = f(x_1, x_2, \ldots, x_n) + \lambda_1 g(x_1, x_2, \ldots, x_n) + \lambda_2 h(x_1, x_2, \ldots, x_n)$$

where λ_1 and λ_2 are undetermined Lagrangian constants. A necessary condition for an interior maximum or minimum is that any such point must satisfy the following:

$$\frac{\partial F}{\partial x_1} = 0 \quad \frac{\partial F}{\partial x_2} = 0 \quad \cdots \quad \frac{\partial F}{\partial x_n} = 0 \quad \text{and} \quad \frac{\partial F}{\partial \lambda_1} = 0 \quad \frac{\partial F}{\partial \lambda_2} = 0$$

To verify whether any such point satisfying the necessary conditions is a maximum, minimum, or neither, we must consider the sufficient conditions. These are stated in terms of the following bordered Hessians.

$$\begin{vmatrix}
F_{x_1x_1} & F_{x_1x_2} & F_{x_1x_3} & g_{x_1} & h_{x_1} \\
F_{x_2x_1} & F_{x_2x_2} & F_{x_2x_3} & g_{x_2} & h_{x_2} \\
F_{x_3x_1} & F_{x_3x_2} & F_{x_3x_3} & g_{x_3} & h_{x_3} \\
g_{x_1} & g_{x_2} & g_{x_3} & 0 & 0 \\
h_{x_1} & h_{x_2} & h_{x_3} & 0 & 0
\end{vmatrix}$$

$$\begin{vmatrix}
F_{x_1x_1} & F_{x_1x_2} & F_{x_1x_3} & F_{x_1x_4} & g_{x_1} & h_{x_1} \\
F_{x_2x_1} & F_{x_2x_2} & F_{x_2x_3} & F_{x_2x_4} & g_{x_2} & h_{x_2} \\
F_{x_3x_1} & F_{x_3x_2} & F_{x_3x_3} & F_{x_3x_4} & g_{x_3} & h_{x_3} \\
F_{x_4x_1} & F_{x_4x_2} & F_{x_4x_3} & F_{x_4x_4} & g_{x_4} & h_{x_4} \\
g_{x_1} & g_{x_2} & g_{x_3} & g_{x_4} & 0 & 0 \\
h_{x_1} & h_{x_2} & h_{x_3} & h_{x_4} & 0 & 0
\end{vmatrix}$$

$$\cdots \begin{vmatrix}
F_{x_1x_1} & F_{x_1x_2} & \cdots & F_{x_1x_n} & g_{x_1} & h_{x_1} \\
F_{x_2x_1} & F_{x_2x_2} & \cdots & F_{x_2x_n} & g_{x_2} & h_{x_2} \\
\vdots & \vdots & & \vdots & \vdots & \vdots \\
F_{x_nx_1} & F_{x_nx_2} & \cdots & F_{x_nx_n} & g_{x_n} & h_{x_n} \\
g_{x_1} & g_{x_2} & \cdots & g_{x_n} & 0 & 0 \\
h_{x_1} & h_{x_2} & \cdots & h_{x_n} & 0 & 0
\end{vmatrix}$$

If, at a point that satisfies the necessary conditions given above, all the determinants are greater than zero, then a relative minimum is attained at that point. If, at such a point, the determinants alternate in sign beginning with a negative sign, then a relative maximum is attained.

Note that the second-order conditions for two constraints are somewhat different than those for one constraint. Further note that in forming the bordered Hessians for the two constraint case, we begin with the Hessian involving the first three variables, unlike the one-constraint case where we began with the Hessian involving the first two variables.

Suppose that we wished to find extrema of a function of n variables subject to m constraints, where $m < n$. The necessary conditions would again be the vanishing of all the first partials of the Lagrangian function, that is, with respect to all variables and all Lagrangian coefficients λ_1, $\lambda_2, \ldots, \lambda_n$. To verify maxima or minima, we would again consider the bordered Hessians. But we would begin with the Hessian involving the first $m + 1$ variables. The sufficient (or second-order) condition for a minimum would then be that all the determinants have the sign $(-1)^m$. The sufficient condition for a maximum would be that all the determinants alternate in sign beginning with the sign $(-1)^{m+1}$.

The significance of extrema problems with n variables or m constraints is not so much for specific functions as to enable us to prove economic theorems for the general case involving any number of commodities, factors of production, and so on. In subsequent chapters, we shall consider applications of these general concepts.

Exercises

Maximize the following functions subject to the given constraints.

1. $u = 5q_1 + 2q_2 + 20q_1 q_2$ subject to $200 = 5q_1 + 2q_2$, where q_1 and $q_2 \geqslant 0$

2. $u = 10q_1 + q_2 + q_1 q_2$ subject to $100 = 20q_1 + 2q_2$, where q_1 and $q_2 \geqslant 0$

3. $u = q_1^2 + 2q_2 + 2q_1 q_2$ subject to $50 = 2q_1 + 2q_2$, where q_1 and $q_2 \geqslant 0$

4. $u = 2q_1^2 + 2q_2^2 + 10q_1 q_2$ subject to $240 = 4q_1 + 8q_2$, where q_1 and $q_2 \geqslant 0$

Find extrema for the following functions subject to the given constraints.

5. $TR = -2q_1^2 - 3q_2^2 + 3q_1 q_2 + 10q_1 + 20q_2$ subject to $q_1 = 3q_2$, where q_1 and $q_2 \geqslant 0$

6. $TR = -2q_1^2 - 3q_2^2 - q_1 q_2 + 20q_1 + 28q_2$ subject to $q_1 = \frac{1}{2}q_2$, where q_1 and $q_2 \geqslant 0$

7. $z = xy$ subject to $x + 3y = 5$

8. $z = x^2 y$ subject to $x^2 + y^2 = 9$

12

THEORY OF CONSUMER CHOICE

There is every indication that, in the future, mathematics will receive a tremendous stimulus from the social sciences. There are clear indications of this development at present, and it is interesting to note that more and more mathematicians begin to look with interest at economic and social problems. More gifted young people turn to economics, attracted by its new life and outlook, most of it involving a far more significant use of mathematics than has ever been the case.

—Oskar Morgenstern

In Chapter 4 we discussed the determination of equilibrium price and quantity in a purely competitive market. We saw that such solutions depend on supply and demand conditions existing in the market. But such recognition is merely the beginning of our inquiry. An understanding of what underlies supply and demand is essential. We were not able to turn immediately to such considerations in Chapter 4, because we had not yet developed adequate mathematical tools. This was accomplished in Chapters 5–11. It is therefore time to return to the economic analysis of what is responsible for the determination of both demand and supply. What distinctive shapes, characteristics, or properties can we discern in regard to these forces?

In this chapter we focus our attention on the demand side. Subsequently, in Chapter 13, the supply side takes center stage. The consumer is the key to the demand side, because market demand is an aggregate of the demand of many different consumers. It therefore becomes imperative to understand consumer decision making when confronted with some degree of choice. The basic analysis of consumer choice will be seen to apply not only to purely competitive markets but to any type of market.

SECTION 12·1   THE PROBLEM FACING THE CONSUMER

By a consumer, we mean a purchasing or spending unit. A consumer may thus be a single individual or a family or spending unit (usually smaller than a family) sharing a common budget. In each case, the consumer must somehow decide how to allocate the available budget among competing commodities. Commodities are defined in their broadest sense to include both physical products and services that can be purchased.

Any consumer typically desires countless different commodities. The intensity of his desire, however, varies from item to item and even from unit to unit. He[1] thus has a scale of preferences among units of commodities. If he could satisfy all his desires without any limit or constraint, there would be no problem. He would simply choose units of all commodities for which he had any desire. But if the consumer is subject to some constraint, namely, that his budget is limited, he must then choose some combination of commodities from among all those that seem desirable. How to make this selection is the basic problem facing the consumer. The remainder of this chapter is concerned with various approaches to the problem and the consequences that follow therefrom.

SECTION 12·2   MARSHALLIAN CARDINAL UTILITY APPROACH

The earliest analysis of the stated problem was made by the leading neoclassical economists in the latter part of the nineteenth century— Gossen, Jevons, Walras, and Marshall. Because Marshall's formulation became most popular and exerted most influence over economic thought, we refer to this type of analysis as Marshallian. Its starting point is that the consumer wishes to maximize utility, by which is meant satisfaction. Any commodity the consumer desires has positive utility. This is not the same thing as saying that the item is intrinsically good, healthful, socially beneficial, or morally superior. Satisfaction is completely subjective and varies from individual to individual. It may arise from physical needs, psychological drives, social motivations, or, more frequently, from a combination of all of these. Each consumer evaluates the utility of a particular unit of any commodity and of combinations of commodities based upon the intensity of desire that he feels for that unit and commodity.

The assumption is made that the consumer has sufficient knowledge and is capable of actually measuring the utility he will derive from each

---

[1] The terms "he" and "his" as used in our discussions refer to either males, females, or spending units.

unit of any commodity or combination of commodities. Thus a typical consumer can actually assign particular numbers, such as 10 units of utility (sometimes called utils) to the ith unit of some commodity and 50 units of utility to the jth unit of another commodity. Such numbers are known as *cardinal numbers* (as opposed to the following manner of counting: first, second, third, etc., which only ranks alternatives but does not actually assign measurable quantities to them). This approach can therefore be referred to as *cardinal utility analysis*. An item associated with 50 units of utility is not only preferable to one with 10 units of utility, but is, in fact, 40 utils more preferable.

In essence, then, the cardinal utility theorists said that for each consumer, utility was a function of the quantities of commodities received. This can be expressed as

$$u = f(q_1, q_2, \ldots, q_n)$$

where $q_1, q_2, \ldots, q_n$ represent the quantities of the n commodities Q_1, $Q_2, \ldots, Q_n$ received. For each possible combination of $q_1, q_2, \ldots, q_n$, there exists a unique value of u that would measure the amount of utility derived from that combination. The aim of the consumer is to maximize the value of u within the constraint of a limited budget. His actions will reflect this aim.

Another crucial assumption made by this school of thought is known as the *law of diminishing marginal utility*. This states that the more of a commodity acquired, the less an additional unit of that commodity is worth to the consumer. An equivalent way of expressing this is that utility increases as quantity increases, but by diminishing amounts. The justification given by proponents of this assumption is that it seems to accord well with our experiences.

It should be readily apparent to readers of earlier chapters that the marginal utility of any commodity is simply the first partial derivative of the utility function with respect to the quantity of that particular commodity. Thus the marginal utility of commodity Q_1 is given by $\partial u / \partial q_1$ and the marginal utility of any commodity Q_i is given by $\partial u / \partial q_i$. These first partials are positive, because additional units of commodities yield some positive amount of utility. The law of diminishing marginal utility is nothing other than the statement that as the quantity of any commodity increases, the first partial derivative with respect to that commodity decreases. This is equivalent to asserting that

$$\frac{\partial^2 u}{\partial q_i^2} < 0$$

that is, all the second partials are negative.

Illustration. Consider the following utility function for a consumer who, for simplicity, has only two commodities available to him.

$$u = 100 \ln q_1 + 50 \ln q_2 \qquad \text{where} \quad q_1 \quad \text{and} \quad q_2 \geqslant 1$$

According to the cardinal utility approach, this implies that if the consumer acquires 3 units of the first commodity and 5 units of the second commodity, he will experience

$$u = 100 \ln(3.00) + 50 \ln(5.00)$$

or $u = 100(1.0986) + 50(1.6094) = 190$ utils of satisfaction. (See the table of natural logarithms at the end of the book.)

On the other hand, if the consumer acquires 6 units of the first commodity and 8 units of the second commodity, then $u = 100 \ln(6.00) + 50 \ln(8.00) = 283$ utils of satisfaction. The cardinal utility theorists would conclude that the second combination yields 93 more utils than the first combination. Similar comparisons could be made between any other possible combinations.

We find the marginal utility of each commodity by computing first partial derivatives. Thus,

$$\frac{\partial u}{\partial q_1} = \frac{100}{q_1}$$

is the marginal utility of the first commodity, and

$$\frac{\partial u}{\partial q_2} = \frac{50}{q_2}$$

is the marginal utility of the second commodity.

The marginal utilities are positive for all values of q_1 and q_2, indicating that additional units of each commodity increase total utility. But notice that as q_1 increases, the value of marginal utility decreases. Thus, if $q_1 = 5$, the marginal utility of an additional unit of that commodity is $\frac{100}{5} = 20$. If $q_1 = 10$, the marginal utility of an additional unit of that commodity is, however, $\frac{100}{10} = 10$. More generally, if we take the second partials, we find

$$\frac{\partial^2 u}{\partial q_1^2} = -\frac{100}{q_1^2} \quad \text{and} \quad \frac{\partial^2 u}{\partial q_2^2} = -\frac{50}{q_2^2}$$

It is evident that the second partials are always negative, which indicates that the marginal utilities (i.e., first partials) become smaller as the quantities increase. This illustrates diminishing marginal utility.

It should be pointed out that the utility function given in the illustration above implies that the utility of one commodity is independent of the other commodity; that is, the utility accruing from units of one commodity is not affected by the quantity consumed of the second commodity. This follows from the fact that the first partials with respect to each commodity involve only the quantity consumed of that commodity. Cardinal utility theorists did, in fact, talk as if this were generally true. However, it is easily seen that such is not necessarily the case. In general, the utility received from consuming some item is definitely affected by the quantities of related products the consumer is able to acquire simultaneously. The basic analysis of cardinal utility theory, however, remains intact even if we discard the notion of independent utilities. The utility function is merely given in some mathematical form that allows utilities to be interdependent. The utility function given in Illustration 2 of Section 12·4 falls in this category and can easily be given a cardinal interpretation.

SECTION 12·3   HICKSIAN ORDINAL UTILITY APPROACH

The assumption made in the previous section that a consumer can actually measure the utility of all possible combinations of commodities was historically rooted in the general philosophy of utilitarianism, which believed in the feasibility of an actual calculus of pleasure and pain as the basis for all action (not just market behavior). By the twentieth century there was hardly anyone who still subscribed to this general philosophy. It is therefore not surprising that attacks were mounted against the cardinal utility assumptions. The alternative approach is most often associated with the name of Hicks, although others shared in its development.

The basic objection raised to the earlier cardinal approach was based on the belief that a consumer is totally incapable of measuring the utility to be derived from specific amounts of any commodity or combination of commodities. Consequently, the *ordinal utility* theorists assumed only that a consumer could rank different commodities in order of preference. Confronted with *n* alternative bundles of commodities, a consumer can state which he most prefers, which is his second choice, third choice, and so on. Numerical quantities such as first, second, third, and so on are termed *ordinal numbers*, because they provide only an order of priorities without indicating the actual utility to be derived from each alternative. Thus, a typical consumer can state that he prefers combination *A* to combination *B*, but cannot state by how much *A* is preferred to *B*. Of course, the possibility exists that the consumer may rank two or more different combinations of commodities equally; that is, he may be indifferent to different alternatives. The essential point, however, is that the consumer is always able to state either that he prefers A to B, B to A, or is indifferent between them. His preferences are also assumed to be *transitive*, which implies that if he prefers A to B and B to C, then he also prefers A to C. Finally, it is assumed that any consumer prefers more of any commodity to less of that commodity. This is sometimes referred to as *nonsatiety*.

Preferences or rankings of a consumer can be expressed by a utility function, provided that it is properly interpreted. This would appear as

$$u = f(q_1, q_2, \ldots, q_n)$$

which looks identical to the functional formulation given in the preceding section using the cardinal utility approach. There is, however, a crucial difference. According to the ordinal approach, the values of u associated with particular combinations of $q_1, q_2, \ldots, q_n$ do not indicate the amount of utility to be derived from such combinations, but instead only portray the relative ranking of the particular combinations. Higher utility numbers indicate higher-rank preferences, while lower utility numbers are associated with lower-rank preferences. A combination that has a utility number of 50 associated with it is not necessarily 40 utils more preferable than one that has a utility number of 10. We know only that the former combination is preferable to the latter, because it has a higher rank score, but we do not know by how much it is preferred.

Because the consumer always prefers combinations associated with higher utility numbers than those with lower ones, he will seek to maximize his utility function, that is, choose the alternative that yields the highest utility number subject to his limited budget.

It should be noted that any such utility function is defined for some' particular time period. As the consumer experiences changes in tastes (broadly defined to include biological, psychological, and sociological factors), his utility function will change.

Because utility numbers indicate only the relative ordering of different combinations, an ordinal utility function is not unique. This means that there are many different functions that will portray the same relative ranking of different alternatives. To illustrate, suppose that there is a utility function

$$u = f(q_1, q_2, \ldots, q_n)$$

that ranks all possible alternatives for the consumer. Let us introduce a new utility function

$$u' = h(q_1, q_2, \ldots, q_n)$$

where $u' = 2u + 1$; that is, for each combination of commodities q_1, $q_2, \ldots, q_n$, the new function associates a utility number that is twice the original utility number plus 1. It is easily seen that all the relative rankings of alternatives are precisely preserved. If combination A is ranked ahead of combination B by the original function, it will still be in the same relative position according to the new function. The only difference will be that all the utility numbers will be doubled and then increased by 1. But under ordinal utility theory, the actual utility numbers have no significance in terms of their absolute magnitude anyway. They portray only a certain ordering of preferences, and this remains invariant.

In general, if u is a utility function, then $F(u)$ can serve the same purpose provided that $F(u_i) > F(u_j)$ whenever $u_i > u_j$. This is equivalent to the statement that any monotonic transformation of a utility function is itself an equivalent utility function in the ordinal sense.

The basic thrust of ordinal theory is to consider the utility of a commodity not in its own absolute terms, but in terms of its rank relative to other commodities. It is not surprising, therefore, that the assumption of diminishing marginal utility adopted by cardinal theorists was replaced by the assumption of a *diminishing marginal rate of substitution*, which involves relative preferences.

Suppose that a consumer possesses some combination of commodities $Q_1, Q_2, \ldots, Q_n$. Let us increase the amount of Q_1 and diminish the amount of Q_2 (holding all other quantities fixed) in such a way that the consumer remains neither better off nor worse off. This implies that the consumer is indifferent between the original and the new combinations. It seems likely that the more the consumer has of Q_2, the greater the number of units he will be willing to forego in order to receive an additional unit of Q_1. This is assumed to hold in general and is known as *diminishing marginal rate of substitution*. It occurs because a consumer with a great amount of some commodity tends to value marginal units of that commodity relatively lower relative to other commodities than when he has a smaller amount of the same commodity.

For the case where the consumer has two commodities available, the utility function appears as

$$u = f(q_1, q_2)$$

We are considering changes in q_1 and q_2 that will leave the utility number unchanged, so we may consider the utility number to be any constant. We then have

$$f(q_1, q_2) = c$$

The marginal rate of substitution can then be expressed as the instantaneous rate of change of q_2 with respect to q_1, which is the same as dq_2/dq_1.

The assumption of diminishing marginal rate of substitution states that the absolute value of this first derivative (i.e., the magnitude of dq_2/dq_1 without regard to sign) decreases as q_1 increases. Now, we know that dq_2/dq_1 will always have a negative sign attached to it, because if the consumer is to remain indifferent between alternatives, it must be that as one commodity is increased the other is decreased. This implies, however that as q_1 increases, dq_2/dq_1 becomes a smaller and smaller negative number which, in turn, is equivalent to the expression

$$\frac{d^2q_2}{dq_1^2} > 0$$

The reader may have expected that the term diminishing marginal rate of substitution would be associated with a negative second derivative. However, by definition, the marginal rate of substitution refers only to the absolute value of the first derivative, whereas when we take the actual signed value, the first derivative will become a smaller and smaller negative number, thus, in fact, getting larger. The second derivative will therefore be positive, because it is the rate of change of the first derivative.[2]

For the case of n commodities, it is assumed that there is present diminishing marginal rates of substitution between any pair of commodities.

Illustration. We now consider the same utility function as given in the illustration of Section 12·2, but it is now to be given an ordinal interpretation: $u = 100 \ln q_1 + 50 \ln q_2$, where q_1 and $q_2 \geqslant 1$.

If the consumer acquires 3 units of the first commodity and 5 units of the second commodity, the utility number is

$$u = 100 \ln(3.00) + 50 \ln(5.00) = 190$$

For 6 units of the first commodity and 8 units of the second commodity, we would have

$$u = 100 \ln(6.00) + 50 \ln(8.00) = 283$$

According to ordinal utility theory, this does not mean that the first combination yields 190 utils of satisfaction or that the second combination yields 283 utils of satisfaction. The only inference to be made from utility numbers is that a combination with a higher utility number is

---

[2] From a mathematical point of view, it would probably be less confusing to talk about increasing rates of substitution and refer to the actual signed value rather than its absolute value. We, nevertheless, follow current usage of the term, which dates back to Hicks' desire to use terminology that would be analogous to Marshall's diminishing marginal utility. See J. R. Hicks, *Value and Capital* (Oxford: Clarendon Press, 1946), p. 20n.

preferred to one with a lower utility number. We can therefore say only that the second combination is preferred to the first, but not by how much.

Notice, too, that we can compute the marginal utility of each product. Thus the marginal utility of the first product is

$$\frac{\partial u}{\partial q_1} = \frac{100}{q_1}$$

When using the ordinal approach, however, this does not indicate the actual amount of utility to be gained by an additional unit of the commodity, because that is immeasurable. The partial derivative has significance only in that its positive sign indicates that additional units of the commodity increase utility.

It has been pointed out that utility functions in the ordinal sense are not unique. As an example, the function $u' = 200 \ln q_1 + 100 \ln q_2 + 10$ could serve as an equivalent to the original utility function given above, because u' increases whenever u does. For a combination of 3 units of the first commodity and 5 units of the second commodity, this new function would assign the utility number

$$u' = 200 \ln(3.00) + 100 \ln(5.00) + 10 = 390$$

and for the combination of 6 units of the first and 8 units of the second commodity, the utility number

$$u' = 200 \ln(6.00) + 100 \ln(8.00) = 576$$

The utility numbers assigned by this function to the two combinations are different than those obtained using the original utility function. Yet this is of no consequence, because the magnitudes of these numbers are meaningless anyway, the only thing of significance being the relative ranking assigned to the various combinations. It is obvious that the two functions assign the same relative ranking to the alternative combinations.

Let us now find the marginal rate of substitution from our original utility function. We set u equal to any constant c, which yields

$$100 \ln q_1 + 50 \ln q_2 = c$$

or

$$100 \ln q_1 + 50 \ln q_2 - c = 0$$

To find the value of dq_2/dq_1, we recall the theorem in Section 10·7 concerning the differentiation of implicit functions, which tells us that

$$\frac{dq_2}{dq_1} = \frac{-f_{q_1}}{f_{q_2}} \quad \text{where } f_{q_1} = \frac{\partial f}{\partial q_1} \quad \text{and } f_{q_2} = \frac{\partial f}{\partial q_2}$$

Now

$$f_{q_1} = \frac{100}{q_1} \quad \text{and} \quad f_{q_2} = \frac{50}{q_2}$$

Therefore,

$$\frac{dq_2}{dq_1} = \frac{-100/q_1}{50/q_2} = \frac{-2q_2}{q_1}$$

Because q_1 and q_2 are always positive, the marginal rate of substitution is seen to be negative.

To verify whether diminishing marginal rate of substitution applies, it is necessary to take the second derivative, that is, d^2q_2/dq_1^2. We thus seek the derivative of the first derivative. But note that the expression for the first derivative involves the two variables q_2 and q_1. Consequently, we must use the total derivative formula as given in Section 10·6. As applied to our case, this is

$$\frac{d^2q_2}{dq_1^2} = \frac{\partial(-2q_2/q_1)}{\partial q_1} + \frac{\partial(-2q_2/q_1)}{\partial q_2} \frac{dq_2}{dq_1}$$

where d^2q_2/dq_1^2 is the total derivative of the function and where q_2 is itself a function of q_1. Evaluating the partials in the above expression, we have

$$\frac{d^2q_2}{dq_1^2} = \frac{2q_2}{q_1^2} + \left(\frac{-2}{q_1}\right)\left(\frac{-2q_2}{q_1}\right)$$

$$= \frac{2q_2}{q_1^2} + \frac{4q_2}{q_1^2}$$

$$= \frac{6q_2}{q_1^2} > 0 \quad \text{because } q_2 > 0$$

The utility function under consideration therefore satisfies the condition that

$$\frac{d^2q_2}{dq_1^2} > 0$$

which is equivalent to a diminishing marginal rate of substitution.

It should be noted that throughout the discussion of consumer choice, we have made no restrictions as to the type of market in which products are being purchased. Thus the analysis applies equally well for monopolistic or oligopolistic markets as for purely competitive cases.

Caution: Consumer Sovereignty Versus Contrived Demand

Economic theory frequently makes the explicit or, more often, implicit assumption that the market system exists to cater to consumer wants and that firms seek to satisfy such desires. This is known as *consumer sovereignty*. Galbraith has, however, poignantly stressed that, in our advanced industrial society, we find a preponderance of instances where firms actually mold or create consumer demand.[3] There is a good deal of controversy over the extent to which this is true. Views range all the way from negligible to enormous.[4] Without going into the question of degree, we take the position that the phenomenon described by Galbraith is, at least in part, realistic. This being the case, utility functions, whether of the cardinal or ordinal variety, will be influenced by this factor. Nevertheless, this does not affect the basic analysis of how a consumer makes decisions given a certain utility function. Regardless of whether the consumer's utility function is a product of his innate desires or of the advertising efforts of large firms, there will be some combination of products that will maximize such a function. It is, however, necessary to be wary about conclusions concerning the optimality of the solution chosen by the consumer. We do not attempt to make any such conclusions, so our analysis remains intact.

A possibly significant shortcoming in the usual theory of consumer choice can, however, arise if the ability of firms to create demand is very effective. In such cases, merely to assume that this factor is somehow incorporated into the consumer's utility function without understanding how it operates, how potent it is, and under what circumstances it is effective would leave a definite void in our comprehension of consumer choice and decision making. The same comment applies with regard to all the general psychological, sociological, and cultural forces that shape consumer thought.

---

[3] John K. Galbraith, *The Affluent Society* (Boston: Houghton Mifflin, 1958), pp. 134–154, and *The New Industrial State* (Boston: Houghton Mifflin, 1967), pp. 198–218.

[4] See, for example, George Katona, *The Mass Consumption Society* (New York: McGraw-Hill, 1964), pp. 50–68; John K. Galbraith, "Economics as a System of Belief," *American Economic Review*, LX (May 1970), pp. 470–478; Eli Goldstein, "Discussion," *American Economic Review*, LX (May 1970), pp. 478–481; Harold Demsetz, "Discussion," *American Economic Review*, LX (May 1970), pp. 481–484; Abba Lerner, "The Economics and Politics of Consumer Sovereignty," *American Economic Review*, LXII (May 1972), pp. 258–266; Herbert Gintis, "Consumer Behavior and the Concept of Sovereignty: Explanations of Social Decay," *American Economic Review*, LXII (May 1972), pp. 267–278.

Exercises

Verify whether diminishing marginal utility and/or diminishing marginal rate of substitution holds for each of the following utility functions, where q_1, q_2, and $u \geqslant 0$.

1. $u = q_1 q_2$
2. $u = q_1^2 q_2^3$
3. $u = \ln q_1 + 2 \ln q_2$
4. $u = 100 \ln(2q_1^2 + q_2^2)$
5. $u = 4q_1 + q_1 q_2 + 2q_2$
6. $u = q_1^{1/2} + q_2^{1/2}$, where only positive square roots are to be taken
7. $u = q_1^2 q_2$
8. $u = \ln(10q_1^{1/2} + q_2^{1/2})$, where only positive square roots are to be taken
9. $u = 100 \ln q_1 + 20 \ln q_2$
10. $u = 8q_1^2 + 4q_2^2$

SECTION 12·4   CONSUMER EQUILIBRIUM

A consumer has many options open to him. Within the constraint of his limited budget, there are numerous possible combinations of commodities. For a stated time period, he must select one of these possibilities. He will, of course, desire to choose the "best" alternative available to him. We are now concerned with how to arrive at this "best" alternative.

According to cardinal utility theory, the consumer will seek to maximize his utility, that is, choose that combination which yields the greatest number of utils, subject to his limited budget. We have seen that ordinal theorists believe that measurement of utility is not feasible. Nevertheless, the consumer could determine that combination which is ranked highest along his scale of preferences subject to the limited available budget. The consumer thus would seek to maximize his utility number, which indicates the relative ranking of combinations of products.

It turns out, therefore, that whether one uses the cardinal or the ordinal utility approaches, the problem of finding the point of consumer equilibrium involves the same mathematical process, namely, maximizing the utility function subject to a budget constraint. The approaches differ in their interpretation of the information conveyed by the utility function, but both the process and the final result are unaffected by this difference.

We shall therefore consider simultaneously the conditions for consumer equilibrium according to both approaches. For simplicity, we deal first with a consumer making choices between two commodities. Of course, each of these two commodities can be thought of as a bundle of several other products. Subsequently, we shall show how the results can be extended to any number of commodities.

The starting point of the analysis is the consumer's utility function, which according to either the cardinal or ordinal approaches can be stated in the following form:

$$u = f(q_1, q_2) \qquad \text{where } q_1 \text{ and } q_2 \geqslant 0$$

which is assumed to be a continuous function with continuous first and second partial derivatives. The values of u will be actual amounts of satisfaction according to the cardinal approach, but only relative rankings of satisfaction according to the ordinal approach. According to either approach, the consumer wishes to maximize the value of u. His income, however, is limited. His budget constraint can be written as

$$I = p_1 q_1 + p_2 q_2$$

where I is his income, and p_1 and p_2 are the market prices of the first and second commodities, respectively. The amount spent on any commodity is given by the price of that commodity multiplied by the quantity of that commodity. Therefore $p_1 q_1$ is the amount spent on the first commodity and $p_2 q_2$ is the amount spent on the second commodity. Because we are considering only two alternatives, the amounts spent on both commodities exhaust the available budget, namely, I.

We employ the method of Lagrange multipliers, which enables us to maximize a function subject to some constraint as explained in Section 11.2. We wish to maximize

$$u = f(q_1, q_2)$$

subject to $I = p_1 q_1 + p_2 q_2$, so we form the Lagrangian function

$$F = f(q_1 q_2) + \lambda(I - p_1 q_1 - p_2 q_2)$$

Setting the first partial derivatives of the Lagrangian function equal to zero yields

$$\frac{\partial F}{\partial q_1} = \frac{\partial f}{\partial q_1} - \lambda p_1 = 0 \tag{1}$$

$$\frac{\partial F}{\partial q_2} = \frac{\partial f}{\partial q_2} - \lambda p_2 = 0 \tag{2}$$

$$\frac{\partial F}{\partial \lambda} = I - p_1 q_1 - p_2 q_2 = 0 \tag{3}$$

from which we get

$$\frac{\partial f}{\partial q_1} = \lambda p_1 \qquad \frac{\partial f}{\partial q_2} = \lambda p_2 \tag{4}$$

which is equivalent to

$$\frac{\partial f/\partial q_1}{\partial f/\partial q_2} = \frac{\lambda p_1}{\lambda p_2} = \frac{p_1}{p_2} \tag{5}$$

Alternatively, this condition can be expressed as

$$\frac{\partial f/\partial q_1}{p_1} = \frac{\partial f/\partial q_2}{p_2} \tag{6}$$

Thus, in order for a consumer to maximize utility, it is necessary that the ratio of marginal utilities of the commodities be equal to the ratio of their respective prices. This is the same as saying that marginal utility divided by the price must be identical for all commodities.

Because the derivation presented above is independent of whether cardinal or ordinal assumptions are made, the required conditions for consumer equilibrium apply in either case. Only the interpretation varies. According to the cardinal approach, $\partial f/\partial q_1$ = marginal utility of Q_1 represents the actual amount of additional utility to be bestowed by an additional unit of Q_1; while according to the ordinal approach, the marginal utility of $Q_1 = \partial f/\partial q_1$ indicates only the change in the utility number or rank preference resulting from an additional unit of Q_1. The fact that ordinal utility theory is able to derive the same conditions for consumer equilibrium as cardinal utility without making the same stringent assumptions is itself a noteworthy achievement.

From equation (4), we also have

$$\frac{\partial f/\partial q_1}{p_1} = \lambda$$

Therefore condition (6) can also be extended to

$$\frac{\partial f/\partial q_1}{p_1} = \frac{\partial f/\partial q_2}{p_2} = \lambda$$

λ is seen to be the ratio of the marginal utility of any commodity divided by the price of that commodity, that is, marginal utility per dollar. This is referred to as the *marginal utility of money or income*. According to cardinal theory, it measures the additional utility that could be acquired by spending another unit of money (i.e., dollar). Ordinal theorists would, however, simply interpret the marginal utility of money as the change in the utility number forthcoming from an additional dollar.

The equation stated in (5) or (6) is only a necessary condition for utility maximization. If we are to be certain that equilibrium is, indeed, achieved when this condition is satisfied, we must find the second-order or sufficient conditions for maximization as explained in Section 11.2.

The second-order conditions for a maximum require that the following determinant be positive, where F is the Lagrangian function and g is the equation of constraint:

$$\begin{vmatrix} F_{q_1q_1} & F_{q_1q_2} & g_{q_1} \\ F_{q_2q_1} & F_{q_2q_2} & g_{q_2} \\ g_{q_1} & g_{q_2} & 0 \end{vmatrix} > 0$$

In our case this is equivalent to

$$\begin{vmatrix} f_{q_1q_1} & f_{q_1q_2} & -p_1 \\ f_{q_2q_1} & f_{q_2q_2} & -p_2 \\ -p_1 & -p_2 & 0 \end{vmatrix} > 0$$

By expanding the determinant, we get

$$f_{q_1q_1}(-p_2^2) - f_{q_2q_1}(-p_2p_1) - p_1(-f_{q_1q_2}p_2 + f_{q_2q_2}p_1) > 0$$

and

$$-f_{q_1q_1}p_2^2 + 2f_{q_1q_2}p_1p_2 - f_{q_2q_2}p_1^2 > 0 \qquad (7)$$

This latter second-order condition must be satisfied, along with the first-order condition given by equation (5), in order to ensure consumer equilibrium. Again, it will be seen that this latter condition applies both for the cardinal and ordinal approaches. Of course, the interpretation of the partial derivatives differs, as stated earlier.

We could rewrite the condition given in (7) by making use of the relationship given by equation (4), namely

$$\frac{\partial f}{\partial q_1} = \lambda p_1 \qquad \frac{\partial f}{\partial q_2} = \lambda p_2$$

which is equivalent to

$$p_1 = \frac{f_{q_1}}{\lambda} \quad \text{and} \quad p_2 = \frac{f_{q_2}}{\lambda}$$

where

$$f_{q_1} = \frac{\partial f}{\partial q_1} \quad \text{and} \quad f_{q_2} = \frac{\partial f}{\partial q_2}$$

Substituting for p_1 and p_2 into (7), we have

$$-f_{q_1 q_1} \frac{f^2_{q_2}}{\lambda^2} + 2f_{q_1 q_2} \frac{f_{q_1} f_{q_2}}{\lambda^2} - f_{q_2 q_2} \frac{f^2_{q_1}}{\lambda^2} > 0$$

Multiplying both sides of the inequality by λ^2 yields

$$-f_{q_1 q_1} f^2_{q_2} + 2f_{q_1 q_2} f_{q_1} f_{q_2} - f_{q_2 q_2} f^2_{q_1} > 0 \tag{8}$$

It will be seen that if one assumes (as the cardinal theorists did) diminishing marginal utility and that the utility of one commodity is independent of any other, then the second-order conditions will always be satisfied. Diminishing marginal utility implies that $f_{q_1 q_1}$ and $f_{q_2 q_2}$ are each negative, as shown in Section 12.2. The independence of utilities of different commodities ensures that $f_{q_1 q_2} = 0$, as indicated in the same section. The middle term therefore vanishes. The first term is positive, because it is the negative of a negative number. A similar situation applies to the third term. We then have the sum of two positive terms, which clearly satisfies the inequality.

It was pointed out earlier that one could drop the independence of utilities assumption and still adhere to the cardinal approach. In that case, the middle term would not necessarily vanish. If $f_{q_1 q_2}$ had a positive sign, the inequality would again be satisfied, because f_{q_1} and f_{q_2} are positive by the assumption of nonsatiety. Each of the three terms of the inequality would therefore be positive, thus satisfying the inequality. If, however, $f_{q_1 q_2}$ were negative, the middle term would be negative. In order to satisfy the inequality, it would be necessary for the first and third terms combined to outweigh the middle term if utility were to be maximized.

The key assumption, according to the cardinal theorists, was diminishing marginal utility. If that assumption were somehow not satisfied, then $f_{q_1 q_1}$ and $f_{q_2 q_2}$ could be positive, which, in turn, would imply that the first and third terms of the inequality were negative. This could very well lead to the inequality not being satisfied.

The ordinal utility theorists did not make the assumption of diminishing marginal utility. But it will be recalled that they did assume a diminishing marginal rate of substitution, which, as shown in Section 12.3, is equivalent to the statement

$$\frac{d^2 q_2}{dq_1^2} > 0$$

We know by the implicit function theorem of Section 10.7 that

$$\frac{dq_2}{dq_1} = \frac{-f_{q_1}}{f_{q_2}}$$

The expression just given involves the two variables q_1 and q_2. To find the second derivative, that is, the derivative of dq_2/dq_1, it is therefore necessary to use the total derivative formula given in Section 10.6. We have

$$\frac{d^2 q_2}{dq_1^2} = \frac{\partial(-f_{q_1}/f_{q_2})}{\partial q_1} + \frac{\partial(-f_{q_1}/f_{q_2})}{\partial q_2}\frac{dq_2}{dq_1}$$

$$= \frac{-f_{q_2}f_{q_1q_1} + f_{q_1}f_{q_2q_1}}{f_{q_2}^2} + \frac{-f_{q_2}f_{q_1q_2} + f_{q_1}f_{q_2q_2}}{f_{q_2}^2}\left(\frac{-f_{q_1}}{f_{q_2}}\right)$$

$$= \frac{-f_{q_2}^2 f_{q_1q_1} + f_{q_1}f_{q_2}f_{q_1q_2}}{f_{q_2}^3} + \frac{f_{q_1}f_{q_2}f_{q_1q_2} - f_{q_1}^2 f_{q_2q_2}}{f_{q_2}^3}$$

$$= \frac{-f_{q_1q_1}f_{q_2}^2 + 2f_{q_1q_2}f_{q_1}f_{q_2} - f_{q_2q_2}f_{q_1}^2}{f_{q_2}^3}$$

Because $d^2 q_2/dq_1^2$ is assumed positive by ordinal theorists and f_{q_2} is positive by the assumption of nonsatiety, it follows that

$$-f_{q_1q_1}f_{q_2}^2 + 2f_{q_1q_2}f_{q_1}f_{q_2} - f_{q_2q_2}f_{q_1}^2 > 0 \quad ,$$

thus satisfying the second-order conditions for the maximization of utility provided that diminishing marginal rate of substitution holds.

A diminishing marginal rate of substitution seems to be a reasonable assumption, as explained in Section 12.2. In the event, however, that it does not hold and

$$\frac{d^2 q_2}{dq_1^2} < 0$$

inequality (8) would be reversed so that a point satisfying the first-order conditions would actually minimize consumer utility. There would be no maximum point on the interior of the function. A movement away from the minimum point in either direction would increase utility until the boundary points or corner values of the function are attained (i.e., $q_1 = 0$ or $q_2 = 0$). The function would have to be examined to see which corner point attains the highest utility number. The corner point with the highest utility value would maximize consumer utility. This would imply that the consumer would choose not to buy one commodity at all, spending all his income on the other commodity (or commodities, if there are several).

A similar situation could be expected according to cardinal utility theory if the assumption of diminishing marginal utility does not pertain.

The possibility also exists that the first-order conditions given by (5) or (6) may not be satisfied at any point within the range of definition, that is, q_1 and $q_2 \geqslant 0$. This could occur if the ratio

$$\frac{\partial f/\partial q_1}{\partial f/\partial q_2}$$

is greater than p_1/p_2 or smaller than p_1/p_2 for all positive values of q_1 and q_2. In that event, no maximum would be attained within the interior of the function. One of the boundary or corner points would then be the absolute maximum utility position. The utility function would again have to be examined at each boundary point, that is, $q_1 = 0$ and $q_2 = 0$, to see which yields the greatest utility number.

Even if the first- and second-order conditions are satisfied at some point, this implies only that such a point is a maximum within the interior of the defined function. As explained in Section 11.2, nothing is implied regarding boundary points, that is, $q_1 = 0$ or $q_2 = 0$. Thus it would be necessary to evaluate the utility function at the interior point found to be a maximum and also at each boundary point. The point corresponding to the highest utility number would be an absolute maximum point of the utility function subject to the given constraint.

In spite of the fact that boundary or corner solutions are possible, the basic condition for utility maximization, that is, marginal utility divided by price being identical for all commodities, is still widely applicable. In the case of two commodities, a corner solution would imply that one product will not be purchased at all, the entire budget being spent on the remaining product—a very unusual occurrence. If there are n commodities, it will again be possible to have corner solutions, in which case at least one of the commodities will not be bought. This is quite conceivable, because at any time there is some commodity that a consumer does not purchase. However, suppose that there are K products that will not be bought. The maximization problem can then be expressed in terms of the remaining $n - k$ commodities that should be bought. The first-order conditions will then require the equality of marginal utility divided by price for all such commodities.

Thus, while corner solutions cannot be ruled out entirely, the basic result still holds, provided that it is applied only to those commodities that will be bought in some amount.

Illustration 1.   Find the equilibrium point for a consumer whose utility function is given by

$$u = 100 \ln q_1 + 50 \ln q_2 \qquad \text{where } q_1 \text{ and } q_2 \geqslant 1$$

and where the price of commodity Q_1 is \$3, the price of Q_2 is \$1, and the available budget is \$10.

Solution.   A consumer achieves equilibrium by maximizing utility subject to the budget limitation. Thus, whether the utility function is to be interpreted in a cardinal or an ordinal sense, the mathematical problem is the same. The budget constraint is given by

$$I = p_1 q_1 + p_2 q_2$$

which in this case becomes $10 = 3q_1 + q_2$. We must therefore maximize $u = 100 \ln q_1 + 50 \ln q_2$ subject to the constraint $10 = 3q_1 + q_2$.

We form the Lagrangian function, which is

$$F = 100 \ln q_1 + 50 \ln q_2 + \lambda(10 - 3q_1 - q_2)$$

Setting the first partials of the Lagrangian function equal to zero yields

$$\frac{\partial F}{\partial q_1} = \frac{100}{q_1} - 3\lambda = 0$$

$$\frac{\partial F}{\partial q_2} = \frac{50}{q_2} - \lambda = 0$$

$$\frac{\partial F}{\partial \lambda} = 10 - 3q_1 - q_2 = 0$$

From the second equation, we find

$$\lambda = \frac{50}{q_2}$$

which we substitute into the first equation:

$$\frac{100}{q_1} - 3\left(\frac{50}{q_2}\right) = 0$$

or

$$\frac{100}{q_1} = \frac{150}{q_2}$$

and

$$150q_1 = 100q_2$$

$$3q_1 = 2q_2$$

Finally, substituting the value of $3q_1$ into the third of our equations, we have

$$10 - 2q_2 - q_2 = 0$$

$$3q_2 = 10$$

$$q_2 = 3.33$$

from which we find

$$q_1 = 2.22$$

   Thus the point $q_1 = 2.22$, $q_2 = 3.33$ is the only point that satisfies the first-order conditions for the maximization of utility. We must, of course, investigate whether the second-order or sufficient conditions are also fulfilled at this point.

   The second-order condition for a maximization requires that the bordered determinant of partials of the Lagrangian function be positive. We have already shown that for any utility function $u = f(q_1, q_2)$ subject to any budget constraint this reduces to the condition

$$-f_{q_1q_1} p_2^2 + 2f_{q_1q_2} p_1 p_2 - f_{q_2q_2} p_1^2 > 0$$

In our case, we have $u = 100 \ln q_1 + 50 \ln q_2$, and

$$\frac{\partial f}{\partial q_1} = \frac{100}{q_1} \qquad \frac{\partial f}{\partial q_2} = \frac{50}{q_2}$$

$$f_{q_1q_1} = \frac{-100}{q_1^2} \qquad f_{q_2q_2} = \frac{-50}{q_2^2} \qquad f_{q_1q_2} = 0$$

After evaluating at $q_1 = 2.22$, $q_2 = 3.33$ and substituting into the inequality, we get as our second-order condition:

$$-\left[\frac{-100}{(2.22)^2}\right](1)^2 + 0 - \left[\frac{-50}{(3.33)^2}\right](3)^2$$

$$= \frac{100}{4.9284} + \frac{450}{11.0889} = 20.3 + 40.6 > 0$$

The sufficient condition is therefore satisfied and $q_1 = 2.22$, $q_2 = 3.33$ is a maximum utility position. At that point, we find $u = 139.45$.

   We must yet, however, consider boundary values of the utility function, because the Lagrangian process only locates maximum points on the interior of the function. The boundaries of our function are given by $q_1 = 1$ and $q_2 = 1$. Let us therefore evaluate the utility function at these boundary points.

When $q_1 = 1$, we find $q_2 = 7$ and

$$u = 100 \ln(1) + 50 \ln(7) = 0 + 50(1.9459) = 97.3$$

When $q_2 = 1$, we find $q_1 = 3$ and

$$u = 100 \ln(3) + 50 \ln(1) = 100(1.0986) = 109.86$$

We see that the utility numbers associated with either boundary point are smaller than that for the interior point located by the Lagrangian process. We conclude that $q_1 = 2.22$, $q_2 = 3.33$ is the point that maximizes utility for the consumer given his utility function and his budget constraint.

In the illustration given in Section 12·3, we pointed out that the function $u' = 200 \ln q_1 + 100 \ln q_2 + 10$ could serve as an equivalent to the original utility function according to ordinal utility theory. To test this, suppose that we use the Lagrangian process for u' subject to the same budget constraint. We have

$$F = 200 \ln q_1 + 100 \ln q_2 + 10 + \lambda(10 - 3q_1 - q_2)$$

and

$$\frac{\partial F}{\partial q_1} = \frac{200}{q_1} - 3\lambda = 0$$

$$\frac{\partial F}{\partial q_2} = \frac{100}{q_2} - \lambda = 0$$

$$\frac{\partial F}{\partial \lambda} = 10 - 3q_1 - q_2 = 0$$

from which we find

$$\lambda = \frac{100}{q_2}$$

and

$$\frac{200}{q_1} - \frac{3(100)}{q_2} = 0$$

$$\frac{200}{q_1} = \frac{300}{q_2}$$

$$300q_1 = 200q_2$$

$$3q_1 = 2q_2$$

which is exactly what we had for the original utility function.

It can also easily be shown that the second-order conditions for the new function are satisfied whenever the original second-order conditions are.

The utility function given in the previous Illustration implied that the utility of one commodity was independent of the utility of the other commodity. We have already pointed out that the basic analysis of consumer equilibrium would be essentially unchanged even if this were not the case. The following illustration introduces a utility function where the utility of one commodity depends not only on the amount of that commodity, but also on the amount of the alternative commodity.

Illustration 2.   Find the position of consumer equilibrium where

$$u = 100 \ln(4q_1^{1/2} + 2q_2^{1/2}) \qquad \text{where} \quad q_1, q_2, \quad \text{and} \quad u \geqslant 0$$

it being understood that only positive square roots are to be taken and where the price of Q_1 is \$4, the price of Q_2 is \$1, and the available budget is \$100.

Solution.   We wish to maximize the utility function

$$u = 100 \ln(4q_1^{1/2} + 2q_2^{1/2})$$

subject to the budget constraint $100 = 4q_1 + q_2$.
    Form the Lagrangian function

$$F = 100 \ln(4q_1^{1/2} + 2q_2^{1/2}) + \lambda(100 - 4q_1 - q_2)$$

Set the first partials of the Lagrangian function equal to zero:

$$\frac{\partial F}{\partial q_1} = 100 \frac{2q_1^{-1/2}}{4q_1^{1/2} + 2q_2^{1/2}} - 4\lambda = 0$$

$$\frac{\partial F}{\partial q_2} = 100 \frac{q_2^{-1/2}}{4q_1^{1/2} + 2q_2^{1/2}} - \lambda = 0$$

$$\frac{\partial F}{\partial \lambda} = 100 - 4q_1 - q_2 = 0$$

From the second equation, we have

$$\lambda = \frac{100q_2^{-1/2}}{4q_1^{1/2} + 2q_2^{1/2}}$$

which we substitute into the first equation:

$$\frac{200q_1^{-1/2}}{4q_1^{1/2} + 2q_2^{1/2}} - \frac{400q_2^{-1/2}}{4q_1^{1/2} + 2q_2^{1/2}} = 0$$

$$\frac{200q_1^{-1/2} - 400q_2^{-1/2}}{4q_1^{1/2} + 2q_2^{1/2}} = 0$$

which implies that

$$200q_1^{-1/2} - 400q_2^{-1/2} = 0$$

or

$$200q_1^{-1/2} = 400q_2^{-1/2}$$

$$q_1^{-1/2} = 2q_2^{-1/2}$$

$$\frac{1}{q_1^{1/2}} = \frac{2}{q_2^{1/2}}$$

$$2q_1^{1/2} = q_2^{1/2}$$

$$q_2 = 4q_1$$

Substituting this value of q_2 into the budget equation, we have

$$100 - q_2 - q_2 = 0$$

$$2q_2 = 100$$

$$q_2 = 50$$

and

$$q_1 = 12.5$$

The point $q_1 = 12.5$, $q_2 = 50$ is the only set of values that satisfies the first-order conditions for the maximization of utility. An investigation of the second-order conditions will confirm that this point is, indeed, the maximum utility position.

It is now time to show how utility analysis can be extended to any number of commodities. If there are n alternative commodities, the utility function will appear as

$$u = f(q_1, q_2, \ldots, q_n)$$

and the budget constraint will be given by

$$I = p_1 q_1 + p_2 q_2 + \cdots + p_n q_n$$

A shorthand way of writing the budget equation is to employ the summation sign $\sum$. The symbol $\sum_{i=1}^{n} p_i q_i$ indicates that the terms $p_i q_i$ should be summed together for all values of i, where i goes from 1 to n. It follows that

$$\sum_{i=1}^{n} p_i q_i = p_1 q_1 + p_2 q_2 + \cdots + p_n q_n$$

Our problem is therefore to maximize the function

$$u = f(q_1, q_2, \ldots, q_n)$$

subject to the constraint

$$I = \sum_{i=1}^{n} p_i q_i$$

We form the Lagrangian function

$$F = f(q_1, q_2, \ldots, q_n) + \lambda\left(I - \sum_{i=1}^{n} p_i q_i\right)$$

take the partial derivatives of F with respect to $q_1, q_2, \ldots, q_n$ and set them equal to zero. For any one of these q_i, we shall have

$$\frac{\partial F}{\partial q_i} = \frac{\partial f}{\partial q_i} - \lambda p_i = 0 \qquad \text{for all } i = 1, 2, \ldots, n$$

or, equivalently,

$$\frac{\partial f}{\partial q_i} = \lambda p_i \qquad \text{for all } i = 1, 2, \ldots, n$$

This implies that

$$\frac{\partial f / \partial q_i}{\partial f / \partial q_j} = \frac{\lambda p_i}{\lambda p_j} = \frac{p_i}{p_j} \qquad \text{for} \qquad \begin{array}{l} i = 1, \ldots, n \\ j = 1, \ldots, n \end{array}$$

which is equivalent to

$$\frac{\partial f / \partial q_1}{p_1} = \frac{\partial f / \partial q_2}{p_2} = \cdots = \frac{\partial f / \partial q_n}{p_n} = \lambda$$

Thus, in order for a consumer to maximize utility, it is necessary that the marginal utility divided by price be identical for all commodities. This result is seen to be a generalization of the result we arrived at for two commodities. Again it is seen that the result is independent of whether the cardinal or ordinal approach is followed.

The equality stated above is, of course, only the first-order or necessary conditions. To verify that a maximum is actually attained at such a point, it is necessary to check the second-order conditions.

The second-order conditions for a maximum require that the following determinants alternate in sign:

$$\begin{vmatrix} f_{q_1q_1} & f_{q_1q_2} & -p_1 \\ f_{q_2q_1} & f_{q_2q_2} & -p_2 \\ -p_1 & -p_2 & 0 \end{vmatrix} > 0 \qquad \begin{vmatrix} f_{q_1q_1} & f_{q_1q_2} & f_{q_1q_3} & -p_1 \\ f_{q_2q_1} & f_{q_2q_2} & f_{q_2q_3} & -p_2 \\ f_{q_3q_1} & f_{q_3q_2} & f_{q_3q_3} & -p_3 \\ -p_1 & -p_2 & -p_3 & 0 \end{vmatrix} < 0$$

$$\cdots \quad (-1)^n \begin{vmatrix} f_{q_1q_1} & f_{q_1q_2} & \cdots & f_{q_1q_n} & -p_1 \\ f_{q_2q_1} & f_{q_2q_2} & \cdots & f_{q_2q_n} & -p_2 \\ \vdots & \vdots & & \vdots & \vdots \\ f_{q_nq_1} & f_{q_nq_2} & \cdots & f_{q_nq_n} & -p_n \\ -p_1 & -p_2 & \cdots & -p_n & 0 \end{vmatrix} > 0$$

Notice that when $n = 2$, these sufficient conditions reduce to those given when we earlier considered two commodities. In the case of two commodities, we saw that the second-order condition would be satisfied provided that a diminishing marginal rate of substitution holds. In analogous fashion, for the general case of n commodities, a decreasing marginal rate of substitution between every pair of commodities is required in order to satisfy the second-order conditions.

Illustration 3. Find the equilibrium position for a consumer whose utility function is given by

$$u = 10q_1 q_2 q_3 \qquad \text{where} \quad q_1, q_2, \quad \text{and} \quad u \geqslant 0$$

and where the price of Q_1 is \$2, the price of Q_2 is \$1, the price of Q_3 is \$4, and the available budget is \$120.
Solution. We wish to maximize the utility function $u = 10q_1 q_2 q_3$ subject to the budget constraint $120 = 2q_1 + q_2 + 4q_3$. Form the Lagrangian function

$$F = 10q_1 q_2 q_3 + \lambda(120 - 2q_1 - q_2 - 4q_3)$$

Set the first partials of this function equal to zero:

$$\frac{\partial F}{\partial q_1} = 10q_2 q_3 - 2\lambda = 0$$

$$\frac{\partial F}{\partial q_2} = 10q_1 q_3 - \lambda = 0$$

$$\frac{\partial F}{\partial q_3} = 10q_1 q_2 - 4\lambda = 0$$

$$\frac{\partial F}{\partial \lambda} = 120 - 2q_1 - q_2 - 4q_3 = 0$$

From the second of these equations, we find

$$\lambda = 10q_1 q_3$$

Substituting this value into the first and third equations yields

$$10q_2 q_3 - 20q_1 q_3 = 0$$
$$10q_1 q_2 - 40q_1 q_3 = 0$$

Factoring each of these latter equations, we get

$$10q_3(q_2 - 2q_1) = 0$$
$$10q_1(q_2 - 4q_3) = 0$$

Now, if either q_1 or q_3 were equal to zero, the value of u would also be zero. This could not be a maximum utility position, because any positive set of values for $q_1, q_2,$ and q_3 would yield a positive u. Therefore the only possible maximum points occur when

$$q_2 - 2q_1 = 0$$

and

$$q_2 - 4q_3 = 0$$

from which it follows that

$$2q_1 = q_2$$

and

$$4q_3 = q_2$$

Substituting these values into the budget constraint gives

$$120 - q_2 - q_2 - q_2 = 0$$
$$120 - 3q_2 = 0$$
$$3q_2 = 120$$
$$q_2 = 40$$
$$q_1 = 20$$
$$q_3 = 10$$

This combination is the only possible maximum utility position. To verify whether it is, in fact, a maximum, we consider the second-order conditions.

The second-order conditions appear as follows:

$$\begin{vmatrix} f_{q_1q_1} & f_{q_1q_2} & -p_1 \\ f_{q_2q_1} & f_{q_2q_2} & -p_2 \\ -p_1 & -p_2 & 0 \end{vmatrix} > 0 \qquad \begin{vmatrix} f_{q_1q_1} & f_{q_1q_2} & f_{q_1q_3} & -p_1 \\ f_{q_2q_1} & f_{q_2q_2} & f_{q_2q_3} & -p_2 \\ f_{q_3q_1} & f_{q_3q_2} & f_{q_3q_3} & -p_3 \\ -p_1 & -p_2 & -p_3 & 0 \end{vmatrix} < 0$$

We therefore evaluate the relevant partials at the point $q_1 = 20$, $q_2 = 40$, $q_3 = 10$.

The utility function is $u = 10q_1 q_2 q_3$. Therefore,

$$\frac{\partial f}{\partial q_1} = 10q_2 q_3 \qquad \frac{\partial f}{\partial q_2} = 10q_1 q_3 \qquad \frac{\partial f}{\partial q_3} = 10q_1 q_2$$

$$f_{q_1q_1} = 0 \qquad f_{q_1q_2} = 10q_3 = 100 \qquad f_{q_1q_3} = 10q_2 = 400$$

$$f_{q_2q_1} = 10q_3 = 100 \qquad f_{q_2q_2} = 0 \qquad f_{q_2q_3} = 10q_1 = 200$$

$$f_{q_3q_1} = 10q_2 = 400 \qquad f_{q_3q_2} = 10q_1 = 200 \qquad f_{q_3q_3} = 0$$

Substituting the relevant values into the 3×3 determinant, we get

$$\begin{vmatrix} 0 & 100 & -2 \\ 100 & 0 & -1 \\ -2 & -1 & 0 \end{vmatrix} = -100 \begin{vmatrix} 100 & -2 \\ -1 & 0 \end{vmatrix} - 2 \begin{vmatrix} 100 & -2 \\ 0 & -1 \end{vmatrix}$$

$$= 200 + 200 > 0$$

Next, substituting the relevant values into the 4×4 determinant gives

$$\begin{vmatrix} 0 & 100 & 400 & -2 \\ 100 & 0 & 200 & -1 \\ 400 & 200 & 0 & -4 \\ -2 & -1 & -4 & 0 \end{vmatrix}$$

The easiest way to evaluate this determinant is to convert it to one containing a column with all zeros except for one element. This can be done by multiplying one of the rows by a suitable constant and adding the result to some other row, as explained in Section 5·3.

In our case, multiply the bottom row by 50 and add the result to the second row. We get

$$\begin{vmatrix} 0 & 100 & 400 & -2 \\ 0 & -50 & 0 & -1 \\ 400 & 200 & 0 & -4 \\ -2 & -1 & -4 & 0 \end{vmatrix}$$

Next, multiply the bottom row by 200 and add the result to the third row. We get

$$\begin{vmatrix} 0 & 100 & 400 & -2 \\ 0 & -50 & 0 & -1 \\ 0 & 0 & -800 & -4 \\ -2 & -1 & -4 & 0 \end{vmatrix} = 2 \begin{vmatrix} 100 & 400 & -2 \\ -50 & 0 & -1 \\ 0 & -800 & -4 \end{vmatrix}$$

We have thus reduced the 4×4 determinant to an equivalent expression involving only a 3×3 determinant. This 3×3 determinant can, in turn, be simplified by multiplying its second row by 2 and adding the result to the first row. This yields

$$2 \begin{vmatrix} 0 & 400 & -4 \\ -50 & 0 & -1 \\ 0 & -800 & -4 \end{vmatrix} = 2(50) \begin{vmatrix} 400 & -4 \\ -800 & -4 \end{vmatrix}$$

$$= 100(-1600 - 3200) = 100(-4800) = -48,000 < 0$$

The relevant 3×3 determinant is positive and the relevant 4×4 determinant is negative, so the sufficient conditions for a maximum are satisfied at $q_1 = 20$, $q_2 = 40$, $q_3 = 10$. For this combination, the utility number is computed to be $u = 80,000$.

The possibility of corner or boundary solutions must, of course, be considered. The boundaries of the utility function are given by $q_1 = 0$, $q_2 = 0$, and $q_3 = 0$. In any of these cases, the value of u would be zero. Thus the interior maximum, that is, $q_1 = 20, q_2 = 40, q_3 = 10$, is, indeed, the equilibrium position of the consumer.

Exercises

Find the equilibrium position of a consumer given the following utility functions and budget information. In each case q_1, q_2, and $u \geqslant 0$ unless otherwise stated.

1. $u = q_1 q_2$, $I = 200$, $p_1 = 1$, $p_2 = 5$. Show that the result will be unaffected if the utility function is transformed into $u' = 3u$.
2. $u = q_1^2 q_2^3$, $I = 100$, $p_1 = 1$, $p_2 = 4$. Show that the result will be unaffected if the utility function is transformed into $u' = u + 50$.
3. $u = \ln q_1 + 2 \ln q_2$, where q_1 and $q_2 \geqslant 1$, $I = 90$, $p_1 = 0.40$, $p_2 = 0.20$.
4. $u = 100 \ln(2q_1^2 + q_2^2)$, $I = 11$, $p_1 = 3$, $p_2 = 1$
5. $u = 4q_1 + q_1 q_2 + 2q_2$, $I = 402$, $p_1 = 5$, $p_2 = 2$

6. $u = q_1^{1/2} + q_2^{1/2}$, where only positive square roots are to be taken,
    $I = 300$, $p_1 = 2$, $p_2 = 4$
7. $u = q_1^2 q_2$, $I = 120$, $p_1 = 8$, $p_2 = 2$
8. $u = \ln(2q_1^{1/2} + q_2^{1/2})$, where only positive square roots are to be
    taken, $I = 320$, $p_1 = 1$, $p_2 = 1$.
9. $u = 100 \ln q_1 + 20 \ln q_2$, where q_1 and $q_2 \geqslant 1$, $I = 10$, $p_1 = 3$,
    $p_2 = 1$
10. $u = 8q_1^2 + 4q_2^2$, $I = 180$, $p_1 = 4$, $p_2 = 8$
11. $u = \ln q_1 + \ln q_2 + \ln q_3$, where $q_1, q_2,$ and $q_3 \geqslant 1$, $I = 60$, $p_1 = 2$,
    $p_2 = 5$, $p_3 = 1$
12. $u = q_1^2 q_2 q_3$, $I = 100$, $p_1 = 1$, $p_2 = 4$, $p_3 = 2$

SECTION 12·5   DEMAND FUNCTIONS

In earlier chapters we dealt with many different demand functions. In
general, we took them as given without investigating how they are
derived. We are now in a position to appreciate the elements that go into
the formation of a consumer demand function.

Consider a consumer possessing a utility function $u = f(q_1, q_2)$ and
a budget constraint $I = p_1 q_1 + p_2 q_2$. As shown in the previous section,
the equilibrium position of the consumer can be found by forming a
Lagrangian function and setting its partial derivatives equal to zero. The
three equations involving q_1, q_2, and λ that ensue can then be solved for
q_1 and q_2. The solutions will be in terms of p_1, p_2, and I. If, as is usually
the case, the second-order conditions for a maximization of utility are
satisfied and no boundary solutions exist, then the expressions for q_1 and
q_2 are, in fact, the *demand functions* for commodities Q_1 and Q_2.

In the event that the second-order conditions are not satisfied, then,
as shown in the previous section, the consumer will maximize utility by
attaining a corner or boundary position, that is, spending all his income
on one commodity. His demand function can then easily be derived from
his budget constraint by simply solving for q_1 or q_2, whichever he buys.

An analogous situation exists if n commodities are available. The
utility function is given by

$$u = f(q_1, q_2, \ldots, q_n)$$

with a budget constraint of $I = \sum_{i=1}^{n} p_i q_i$. It is then possible to solve for
$q_1, \ldots, q_n$ from the equations produced by setting the partial derivatives
of the Lagrangian function equal to zero. These expressions are the
demand functions for commodities $Q_1, \ldots, Q_n$, provided that the second-
order conditions are satisfied. If they are not satisfied, then one or more of
the n commodities is not bought at all and the equations can be restated

in terms of those that are bought. Demand functions can then be derived for those commodities that are purchased.

In any case, market demand functions are an aggregation of all consumer's demand functions.

Illustration 1. Derive the demand functions for the commodities Q_1 and Q_2 if

$$u = 100 \ln q_1 + 50 \ln q_2 \qquad \text{where} \quad q_1 \quad \text{and} \quad q_2 \geq 1$$

Solution. We are not given any particular values of p_1, p_2, and I because we are to find an expression for quantity demanded of each commodity for each possible value of price and income. The budget equation in general form is

$$I = p_1 q_1 + p_2 q_2$$

The Lagrangian function is therefore

$$F = 100 \ln q_1 + 50 \ln q_2 + \lambda(I - p_1 q_1 - p_2 q_2)$$

Setting its first partial derivatives equal to zero gives

$$\frac{\partial F}{\partial q_1} = \frac{100}{q_1} - p_1 \lambda = 0$$

$$\frac{\partial F}{\partial q_2} = \frac{50}{q_2} - p_2 \lambda = 0$$

$$\frac{\partial F}{\partial \lambda} = I - p_1 q_1 - p_2 q_2 = 0$$

From the first of these equations, we find

$$p_1 \lambda = \frac{100}{q_1}$$

$$\lambda = \frac{100}{p_1 q_1}$$

We then substitute the value of λ into the second equation, which gives

$$\frac{50}{q_2} - \frac{100 p_2}{p_1 q_1} = 0$$

and

$$\frac{50}{q_2} = \frac{100p_2}{p_1 q_1}$$

$$50p_1 q_1 = 100p_2 q_2$$

$$p_1 q_1 = 2p_2 q_2$$

The value of $p_1 q_1$ is then inserted into the third of the partial derivative equations:

$$I - 2p_2 q_2 - p_2 q_2 = 0$$

$$3p_2 q_2 = I$$

$$q_2 = \frac{I}{3p_2}$$

This latter expression is the demand function for Q_2. To find the demand function for Q_1, we insert the value of $p_2 q_2$ into the third of the partial derivative equations:

$$I - p_1 q_1 - \tfrac{1}{2}p_1 q_1 = 0$$

$$\tfrac{3}{2}p_1 q_1 = I$$

$$q_1 = \frac{2I}{3p_1}$$

The demand functions for q_1 and q_2 indicate how much of each commodity will be purchased by the consumer at the various prices and incomes. They are based on the consumer's utility function. In the particular case where $p_1 = 3$, $p_2 = 1$, and $I = 10$, we find that $q_1 = 2.22$, $q_2 = 3.33$. This is the result we arrived at in Illustration 1 of the previous section. These equations are, however, more general, because they show what demand is for all possible prices and incomes.

The expressions just derived for q_1 and q_2 are, we must remember, demand functions only for those values for which the second-order conditions are satisfied. It is easy, however, to show that these conditions are, indeed, satisfied for all values of q_1 and q_2.

As shown earlier, the second-order conditions reduce to

$$-f_{q_1 q_1} p_2^2 + 2f_{q_1 q_2} p_1 p_2 - f_{q_2 q_2} p_1^2 > 0$$

For the utility function in our illustration, we find

$$f_{q_1 q_1} = \frac{-100}{q_1^2} \qquad f_{q_2 q_2} = \frac{-50}{q_2^2} \qquad f_{q_1 q_2} = 0$$

Thus the second-order conditions are satisfied regardless of the particular values of q_1 and q_2. The possibility of a boundary solution, however, still exists. For any particular set of values of p_1, p_2, and I, such a possibility should be checked out.

Illustration 2. Derive demand functions for Q_1 and Q_2 if

$$u = 100 \ln(4q_1^{1/2} + 2q_2^{1/2}) \qquad \text{where } q_1, q_2, \text{ and } u \geqslant 0$$

it being understood that only positive square roots are to be taken.
Solution. The budget constraint in general form is

$$I = p_1 q_1 + p_2 q_2$$

Therefore the Lagrangian function will appear as

$$F = 100 \ln(4q_1^{1/2} + 2q_2^{1/2}) + \lambda(I - p_1 q_1 - p_2 q_2)$$

Setting the first partial derivatives equal to zero gives

$$\frac{\partial F}{\partial q_1} = \frac{200 q_1^{-1/2}}{4q_1^{1/2} + 2q_2^{1/2}} - p_1 \lambda = 0$$

$$\frac{\partial F}{\partial q_2} = \frac{100 q_2^{-1/2}}{4q_1^{1/2} + 2q_2^{1/2}} - p_2 \lambda = 0$$

$$\frac{\partial F}{\partial \lambda} = I - p_1 q_1 - p_2 q_2 = 0$$

From the first equation, we have

$$\lambda = \frac{200 q_1^{-1/2}}{p_1(4q_1^{1/2} + 2q_2^{1/2})}$$

which we substitute into the second equation:

$$\frac{100 q_2^{-1/2}}{4q_1^{1/2} + 2q_2^{1/2}} - \frac{200 p_2 q_1^{-1/2}}{p_1(4q_1^{1/2} + 2q_2^{1/2})} = 0$$

$$\frac{100 q_2^{-1/2}}{4q_1^{1/2} + 2q_2^{1/2}} = \frac{200 p_2 q_1^{-1/2}}{p_1(4q_1^{1/2} + 2q_2^{1/2})}$$

which reduces to

$$p_1 q_2^{-1/2} = 2p_2 q_1^{-1/2}$$

$$p_1 q_1^{1/2} = 2p_2 q_2^{1/2}$$

$$p_1^2 q_1 = 4p_2^2 q_2$$

$$q_1 = \frac{4p_2^2 q_2}{p_1^2}$$

Substituting this value of q_1 into the third partial derivative equation, that is, the budget equation, gives us

$$I - \frac{4p_2^2 q_2}{p_1} - p_2 q_2 = 0$$

$$I = \left(\frac{4p_2^2}{p_1} + p_2\right) q_2$$

$$= \left(\frac{4p_2^2 + p_1 p_2}{p_1}\right) q_2$$

$$q_2 = \frac{p_1 I}{4p_2^2 + p_1 p_2}$$

and consequently,

$$q_1 = \frac{4p_2^2}{p_1^2} \frac{p_1 I}{4p_2^2 + p_1 p_2}$$

$$= \frac{4p_2 I}{p_1(4p_2 + p_1)} = \frac{4p_2 I}{4p_1 p_2 + p_1^2}$$

The expressions for q_1 and q_2 are the demand functions for the two commodities, provided that the second-order conditions are satisfied and that no boundary solutions appear. The second-order conditions can be shown to be satisfied for all applicable values. The possibility of a boundary solution should be checked for any particular set of values of p_1, p_2, and I under consideration. In particular, when $p_1 = 4$, $p_2 = 1$, and $I = 100$, we find that $q_1 = 12.5$ and $q_2 = 50$, which is what we arrived at when we considered this case in Illustration 2 of the previous section.

The reader will notice that the demand for Q_1 in our illustration depends on p_1, p_2, and I. This is generally to be expected, because quantity demanded of any commodity depends not only on the price of that commodity, but also on the price of related products and on consumer income.

An interesting property of demand functions is stated in the following theorem.

Theorem. Demand functions are homogeneous of degree zero relative to prices and income; that is, if all prices and income change by the same proportion, quantity demanded is unaffected.[5]

---

[5] For a review of homogeneous functions, see Section 10.8.

Proof.   We shall prove this theorem for the case of two commodities. The proof can readily be generalized for any number of commodities. We begin with a consumer utility function of the form

$$u = f(q_1, q_2)$$

and a budget constraint of $I = p_1 q_1 + p_2 q_2$. We have already dealt with this case in the previous section and derived the equilibrium position by setting the partial derivatives of the Lagrangian function equal to zero.

Assume now that the price of each commodity and income changes by a multiple, K. The budget equation will, consequently, be altered to

$$KI = Kp_1 q_1 + Kp_2 q_2$$

The Lagrangian function then appears as

$$F = f(q_1, q_2) + \lambda(KI - Kp_1 q_1 - Kp_2 q_2)$$

Setting the first partial derivatives of this function equal to zero gives

$$\frac{\partial F}{\partial q_1} = \frac{\partial f}{\partial q_1} - \lambda K p_1 = 0$$

$$\frac{\partial F}{\partial q_2} = \frac{\partial f}{\partial q_2} - \lambda K p_2 = 0$$

$$\frac{\partial F}{\partial \lambda} = KI - Kp_1 q_1 - Kp_2 q_2 = 0$$

From the first and second of these equations, we get

$$\frac{\partial f}{\partial q_1} = \lambda K p_1 \qquad \frac{\partial f}{\partial q_2} = \lambda K p_2$$

which is equivalent to

$$\frac{\partial f/\partial q_1}{\partial f/\partial q_2} = \frac{\lambda K p_1}{\lambda K p_2} = \frac{p_1}{p_2} \tag{1}$$

This is exactly the same first-order condition that we arrived at in Section 12.4. Moreover, the budget equation can be written as

$$KI - Kp_1 q_1 - Kp_2 q_2 = K(I - p_1 q_1 - p_2 q_2) = 0$$

Because $K \neq 0$, this is equivalent to

$$I - p_1 q_1 - p_2 q_2 = 0 \tag{2}$$

which is the same as the original budget equation.

Demand functions are derived from (1) and (2). They are seen to be the same as for the original prices and income, provided, of course, that the second-order conditions hold. We must therefore show that the second-order conditions are the same as for the original prices and income.

The second-order conditions for the original prices and income were given by the determinant

$$\begin{vmatrix} f_{q_1q_1} & f_{q_1q_2} & -p_1 \\ f_{q_2q_1} & f_{q_2q_2} & -p_2 \\ -p_1 & -p_2 & 0 \end{vmatrix} > 0$$

which expands to

$$-f_{q_1q_1}p_2^2 + 2f_{q_1q_2}p_1p_2 - f_{q_2q_2}p_1^2 > 0$$

The proportionate changes in prices and income will affect only the p terms. Each p term will be prefixed by a K. The second-order condition will therefore become

$$-f_{q_1q_1}K^2p_2^2 + 2f_{q_1q_2}K^2p_1p_2 - f_{q_2q_2}K^2p_1^2 > 0$$

or

$$K^2(-f_{q_1q_1}p_2^2 + 2f_{q_1q_2}p_1p_2 - f_{q_2q_2}p_1^2) > 0$$

Now K^2 is certainly positive. Therefore the above condition is equivalent to

$$(-f_{q_1q_1}p_2^2 + 2f_{q_1q_2}p_1p_2 - f_{q_2q_2}p_1^2) > 0$$

which is precisely the second-order condition for the original prices and income.

Exercises

Derive demand functions for each of the commodities included in the following utility functions defined for q_1, q_2, and $u \geqslant 0$.

1. $u = q_1 q_2$
2. $u = q_1^2 q_2^3$
3. $u = \ln q_1 + 2 \ln q_2$, where q_1 and $q_2 \geqslant 1$
4. $u = 4q_1 + q_1 q_2 + 2q_2$
5. $u = q_1^{1/2} + q_2^{1/2}$, where only positive square roots are to be taken
6. $u = q_1^2 q_2$
7. $u = \ln(2q_1^{1/2} + q_2^{1/2})$, where only positive square roots are to be taken

8. $u = 8q_1^2 + 4q_2^2$
9. $u = 10q_1 q_2 q_3$, where q_1, q_2, and $u \geqslant 0$
10. $u = \ln q_1 + \ln q_2 + \ln q_3$, where q_1, q_2, and $q_3 \geqslant 1$

SECTION 12·6   SUBSTITUTION AND INCOME EFFECTS

In Section 12.4, we showed that in order to maximize a utility function $u = f(q_1, q_2)$ subject to the constraint $I = p_1 q_1 + p_2 q_2$, the following conditions must be satisfied.

$$\frac{\partial f}{\partial q_1} = \lambda p_1 \tag{1}$$

$$\frac{\partial f}{\partial q_2} = \lambda p_2 \tag{2}$$

$$-p_1 q_1 - p_2 q_2 = -I \tag{3}$$

These equations can, in general, be solved to yield values for q_1 and q_2 that represent the equilibrium position for the consumer (provided that the second-order conditions are also satisfied). It is evident that the values of q_1 and q_2 will depend upon the particular values of p_1, p_2, and I. As p_1, p_2, and I change, the equilibrium solution for q_1 and q_2 will also vary. We are now interested in ascertaining the precise effect that changes in price and income have upon equilibrium quantities.

Let us vary p_1, p_2, and I and see what happens to the equations given above. Using total differentiation[6] for both sides of each equation, we get

$$f_{q_1 q_1}\, dq_1 + f_{q_1 q_2}\, dq_2 = \lambda\, dp_1 + p_1\, d\lambda$$

$$f_{q_2 q_1}\, dq_1 + f_{q_2 q_2}\, dq_2 = \lambda\, dp_2 + p_2\, d\lambda$$

$$-p_1\, dq_1 - q_1\, dp_1 - p_2\, dq_2 - q_2\, dp_2 = -dI$$

Rearranging terms gives us

$$f_{q_1 q_2}\, dq_1 + f_{q_1 q_2}\, dq_2 - p_1\, d\lambda = \lambda\, dp_1 \tag{4}$$

$$f_{q_2 q_1}\, dq_1 + f_{q_2 q_2}\, dq_2 - p_2\, d\lambda = \lambda\, dp_2 \tag{5}$$

$$-p_1\, dq_1 - p_2\, dq_2 = -dI + q_1\, dp_1 + q_2\, dp_2 \tag{6}$$

---

[6] For a review of total differentiation, see Section 10.6.

These three linear equations are arranged so that each has a dq_1 term, a dq_2 term, and a $d\lambda$ term. We can solve these equations for dq_1 by use of Cramer's rule,[7] which yields

$$dq_1 = \frac{\begin{vmatrix} \lambda\, dp_1 & f_{q_1q_2} & -p_1 \\ \lambda\, dp_2 & f_{q_2q_2} & -p_2 \\ -dI + q_1\, dp_1 + q_2\, dp_2 & -p_2 & 0 \end{vmatrix}}{\begin{vmatrix} f_{q_1q_1} & f_{q_1q_2} & -p_1 \\ f_{q_2q_1} & f_{q_2q_2} & -p_2 \\ -p_1 & -p_2 & 0 \end{vmatrix}} \tag{7}$$

The denominator is the determinant whose elements are the coefficients of the dq_1, dq_2, and $d\lambda$ terms. It turns out that this determinant is identical to the bordered Hessian introduced in Section 12.4 in connection with second-order conditions. Let us denote this determinant by H.

The numerator of the above fraction is the same determinant as the denominator except that the coefficients of the dq_1 term are replaced by the terms on the right-hand side of equations (4), (5), and (6).

Let us now hold p_2 and I constant, that is, $dp_2 = dI = 0$, and also divide both sides of (7) by dp_1. It will be recalled from Section 5.3 that dividing a determinant by any number is equivalent to dividing each term in any one column or row by that number. Consequently, we have

$$\frac{\partial q_1}{\partial p_1} = \frac{\begin{vmatrix} \lambda & f_{q_1q_2} & -p_1 \\ 0 & f_{q_2q_2} & -p_2 \\ q_1 & -p_2 & 0 \end{vmatrix}}{H}$$

The term on the left side is expressed as a partial derivative because some variables, that is, p_2 and I, are being held constant.

Expanding the determinant in the numerator gives us

$$\frac{\partial q_1}{\partial p_1} = \frac{-\lambda p_2^2 + q_1(-f_{q_1q_2}p_2 + f_{q_2q_2}p_1)}{H} \tag{8a}$$

or

$$\frac{\partial q_1}{\partial p_1} = \frac{-\lambda p_2^2 - f_{q_1q_2}p_2 q_1 + f_{q_2q_2}p_1 q_1}{H} \tag{8b}$$

[7] See Section 5.3 for a discussion of Cramer's rule.

We have thus derived an expression for the instantaneous rate of change of quantity purchased of Q_1 with respect to its price when all other prices and income are held constant.

In a similar manner, we could derive an analogous expression for $\partial q_2 / \partial p_2$.

We next wish to find the rate of change of quantity purchased with respect to income. Return to equation (7) and now hold p_1 and p_2 constant, that is, $dp_1 = dp_2 = 0$, and divide by dI. This leads to

$$\frac{\partial q_1}{\partial I} = \frac{\begin{vmatrix} 0 & f_{q_1 q_2} & -p_1 \\ 0 & f_{q_2 q_2} & -p_2 \\ -1 & -p_2 & 0 \end{vmatrix}}{H}$$

which after expansion of the top determinant becomes

$$\frac{\partial q_1}{\partial I} = \frac{f_{q_1 q_2} p_2 - f_{q_2 q_2} p_1}{H} \tag{9}$$

We have thus examined separately the effect of a change in price and the effect of a change in income. Let us now consider the effect of a change in the price of Q_1 that is accompanied by a change in income just enough to compensate the consumer exactly for the price change, so that he remains neither better nor worse off. The net result of the two changes is that the consumer achieves the same amount of utility; that is, $du = 0$.

Now,

$$u = f(q_1, q_2)$$

and

$$du = \frac{\partial f}{\partial q_1} dq_1 + \frac{\partial f}{\partial q_2} dq_2$$

by the total differentiation formula. Because $du = 0$, we have

$$0 = \frac{\partial f}{\partial q_1} dq_1 + \frac{\partial f}{\partial q_2} dq_2$$

which is equivalent to

$$\frac{-dq_2}{dq_1} = \frac{\partial f / \partial q_1}{\partial f / \partial q_2}$$

But in Section 12.4 we have already derived that the following condition holds for a consumer in equilibrium:

$$\frac{\partial f/\partial q_1}{\partial f/\partial q_2} = \frac{p_1}{p_2}$$

It follows that

$$\frac{-dq_2}{dq_1} = \frac{p_1}{p_2}$$

or

$$p_1\, dq_1 + p_2\, dq_2 = 0$$

which, from equation (6), implies that

$$-dI + q_1\, dp_1 + q_2\, dp_2 = 0$$

Let us now return to equation (7) and allow p_1 to vary, but hold p_2 and u constant; that is, $dp_2 = du = 0$. Divide both sides of (7) by dp_1 and recall that $-dI + q_1\, dp_1 + q_2\, dp_2 = 0$. We get

$$\left(\frac{\partial q_1}{\partial p_1}\right)_{u=\text{constant}} = \frac{\begin{vmatrix} \lambda & f_{q_1 q_2} & -p_1 \\ 0 & f_{q_2 q_2} & -p_2 \\ 0 & -p_2 & 0 \end{vmatrix}}{H}$$

from which it follows that

$$\left(\frac{\partial q_1}{\partial p_1}\right)_{u=\text{constant}} = \frac{-\lambda p_2^2}{H} \tag{10}$$

We now notice that if we take the expression for

$$\left(\frac{\partial q_1}{\partial p_1}\right)_{u=\text{constant}}$$

and from it subtract q_1 multiplied by the expression for $\partial q_1/\partial I$, we get precisely the expression as we derived for $\partial q_1/\partial p_1$. Therefore we have established what is known as the *Slutsky equation*:

$$\frac{\partial q_1}{\partial p_1} = \left(\frac{\partial q_1}{\partial p_1}\right)_{u=\text{constant}} - q_1\left(\frac{\partial q_1}{\partial I}\right)$$

A change in the price of any single commodity accomplishes two things. Firstly, it affects the attractiveness of the commodity relative to other substitute commodities. Second, it alters the real income of the consumer, thus affecting the total utility he can attain. The term $\partial q_1/\partial p_1$ is the rate of change in quantity with respect to price. Its magnitude thus depends upon (1) the change in the product's attractiveness relative to substitutes and (2) the change in real income, both of which occur due to the price change. The former is known as the *substitution effect*, while the latter is the *income effect*.

The term

$$\left(\frac{\partial q_1}{\partial p_1}\right)_{u=\text{constant}}$$

is the rate of change of quantity with respect to price while total utility is held constant; that is, the consumer is compensated sufficiently so that he is able to attain the same utility level as before the price change. The resulting quantity change can therefore be attributed only to the change in the attractiveness of the commodity relative to its substitutes. It is thus a measure of the *substitution effect*.

When the term

$$-q_1\left(\frac{\partial q_1}{\partial I}\right)$$

is added to the substitution effect, the result is the rate of change in quantity due to both the substitution and income effects. The term

$$-q_1\left(\frac{\partial q_1}{\partial I}\right)$$

is therefore the *income effect*.

The Slutsky equation states that $\partial q_1/\partial p_1$ (i.e., marginal demand with respect to changes in p_1) is the summation of

$$\left(\frac{\partial q_1}{\partial p_1}\right)_{u=\text{constant}} = \frac{-\lambda p_2^2}{H} \quad \text{plus} \quad -q_1\left(\frac{\partial q_1}{\partial I}\right) = -q_1\frac{[f_{q_1q_2}p_2 - f_{q_2q_2}p_1]}{H}$$

Let us see if we can determine whether each of these components is positive or negative.

We have already shown in Section 12.4 that λ is equal to the marginal utility of income or money. This must be positive as long as there is some commodity that yields positive utility. We also know from Section 12.4 that $H > 0$ if the second-order conditions for a maximization of utility are to be satisfied. Moroeover, p_2^2 is certainly positive. Therefore the substitution effect,

$$\left(\frac{\partial q_1}{\partial p_1}\right)_{u=\text{constant}} = \frac{-\lambda p_2^2}{H}$$

must always be negative. The income effect,

$$-q_1 \left(\frac{\partial q_1}{\partial I} \right) = -q_1 \frac{(f_{q_1 q_2} p_2 - f_{q_2 q_2} p_1)}{H}$$

however, can be of either sign, because $f_{q_1 q_2} p_2 - f_{q_2 q_2} p_1$ can be either positive or negative. Nevertheless, we can say that in most cases $\partial q_1 / \partial I$ is positive, because consumers can be expected to buy more of a commodity when their income increases and to buy less when their income decreases. In the usual case, therefore,

$$\text{income effect} = -q_1 \left(\frac{\partial q_1}{\partial I} \right)$$

will be negative.

Consequently, the total effect of a price change upon quantity purchased, namely, $\partial q_1 / \partial p_1$, would certainly be negative in the usual case, because it would be the summation of two negative components.

If it happens that $\partial q_1 / \partial I$ is negative for some commodity, this implies that as the consumer receives more income, he purchases less of the commodity that is not wanted so much for its own sake but rather because it is cheap. A consumer would reduce expenditures on such an item ause it is cheap. A consumer would reduce expenditures on such an item as his income increased, because he would be better able to buy more expensive items. In the case of inferior goods, because $\partial q_1 / \partial I$ is negative,

$$\text{income effect} = -q_1 \left(\frac{\partial q_1}{\partial I} \right)$$

will be positive. Consequently, the total effect of a price change upon quantity purchased, that is, $\partial q_1 / \partial p_1$, could be either positive or negative. If the substitution effect is greater in absolute magnitude than the income effect, the total effect will still be negative. Only in the event that the income effect is both positive and greater than the substitution effect will the total effect $\partial q_1 / \partial p_1$ be positive. In such a case the commodity is referred to as a *Giffen good*. A Giffen good is thus an inferior good, but also one with an income effect large enough to outweigh the negative substitution effect. We expect this to occur only if the consumer is so poor that he must spend a substantial portion of his budget on the inferior good.

We have determined that in all cases other than Giffen goods, $\partial q_1 / \partial p_1$ will be negative. This is the justification for the general assumption of a negatively sloping demand curve, that is, the inverse relationship between price and quantity demanded. We did, however, note that $\partial q_1 / \partial p_1$ could conceivably be positive. This would occur only in very rare cases, because it would require (1) that the commodity be an inferior good and (2) that the income effect outweigh the substitution effect.

The approach used above to derive the Slutsky equation for $\partial q_1/\partial p_1$ can also be applied to the analysis of cross effects, that is, the effect of a change in the price of one commodity upon the quantity of a second commodity. Suppose that we wish to find $\partial q_1/\partial p_2$. We go back to equation (7), but now hold $dp_1 = dI = 0$ and divide by dp_2. We get

$$\frac{\partial q_1}{\partial p_2} = \frac{\begin{vmatrix} 0 & f_{q_1q_2} & -p_1 \\ \lambda & f_{q_2q_2} & -p_2 \\ q_2 & -p_2 & 0 \end{vmatrix}}{H}$$

which is equivalent to

$$\frac{\partial q_1}{\partial p_2} = \frac{\lambda p_1 p_2 + q_2(-f_{q_1q_2}p_2 + f_{q_2q_2}p_1)}{H}$$

$$\frac{\partial q_1}{\partial p_2} = \frac{\lambda p_1 p_2}{H} - \frac{q_2(f_{q_1q_2}p_2 - f_{q_2q_2}p_1)}{H}$$

It can be shown that the first term is the *cross substitution effect* and the second term the *cross income effect*. Unlike direct effects, the signs of cross substitution effects are not known. They may be positive or negative. If the cross substitution effect between two commodities is positive, they are substitute products. It its sign is negative, they are complementary products.

The Slutsky equation can also be generalized for any number of variables.

Illustration. Find the Slutsky equation for $\partial q_1/\partial p_1$ and $\partial q_1/\partial p_2$ where the utility function is $u = 100 \ln q_1 + 50 \ln q_2$, where q_1 and $q_2 \geqslant 1$.
Solution. The Slutsky equation for $\partial q_1/\partial p_1$ states that

$$\frac{\partial q_1}{\partial p_1} = \left(\frac{\partial q_1}{\partial p_1}\right)_{u=\text{constant}} - q_1\left(\frac{\partial q_1}{\partial I}\right)$$

We have shown that

$$\left(\frac{\partial q_1}{\partial p_1}\right)_{u=\text{constant}} = \frac{-\lambda p_2^2}{H} = \text{substitution effect}$$

and

$$-q_1\left(\frac{\partial q_1}{\partial I}\right) = \frac{-q_1(f_{q_1q_2}p_2 - f_{q_2q_2}p_1)}{H} = \text{income effect}$$

Because in our case $u = 100 \ln q_1 + 50 \ln q_2$, we have

$$\frac{\partial f}{\partial q_1} = \frac{100}{q_1} \qquad \frac{\partial f}{\partial q_2} = \frac{50}{q_2}$$

and

$$f_{q_1 q_1} = \frac{-100}{q_1^2} \qquad f_{q_1 q_2} = 0 \qquad f_{q_2 q_2} = \frac{-50}{q_2^2}$$

We also know from Section 12.4 that for a consumer in equilibrium,

$$\lambda = \frac{\partial f / \partial q_1}{p_1}$$

In our case this would become

$$\lambda = \frac{100}{p_1 q_1}$$

Furthermore, we also showed in Section 12.4 that

$$H = -f_{q_1 q_1} p_2^2 + 2 f_{q_1 q_2} p_1 p_2 - f_{q_2 q_2} p_1^2$$

which in our case is

$$H = \frac{100 p_2^2}{q_1^2} + \frac{50 p_1^2}{q_2^2}$$

Therefore,

$$\left(\frac{\partial q_1}{\partial p_1} \right)_{u=\text{constant}} = \frac{-\lambda p_2^2}{H}$$

$$= \frac{-100 p_2^2 / p_1 q_1}{(100 p_2^2 / q_1^2) + (50 p_1^2 / q_2^2)} = \text{substitution effect}$$

$$-q_1 \left(\frac{\partial q_1}{\partial I} \right) = \frac{-q_1 (f_{q_1 q_2} p_2 - f_{q_2 q_2} p_1)}{H}$$

$$= \frac{-50 p_1 q_1 / q_2^2}{(100 p_2^2 / q_1^2) + (50 p_1^2 / q_2^2)} = \text{income effect}$$

and the Slutsky equation is

$$\frac{\partial q_1}{\partial p_1} = \frac{-100 p_2^2 / p_1 q_1}{(100 p_2^2 / q_1^2) + (50 p_1^2 / q_2^2)} - \frac{50 p_1 q_1 / q_2^2}{(100 p_2^2 / q_1^2) + (50 p_1^2 / q_2^2)}$$

It is evident that regardless of the particular values for the prices and quantities, both the substitution and income effects are negative, which is the usual situation.

In particular, if $p_1 = 3$, $p_2 = 1$, and $I = 10$, we found in Illustration 1 of Section 12.4 that the equilibrium quantities would be $q_1 = 2.22$ and $q_2 = 3.33$. We would therefore have

$$\left(\frac{\partial q_1}{\partial p_1}\right)_{u=\text{constant}} = \frac{-100p_2^2/p_1 q_1}{(100p_2^2/q_1^2) + (50p_1^2/q_2^2)}$$

$$= \frac{-100/6.66}{[100/(2.22)^2] + [450/(3.33)^2]}$$

$$= \frac{-15}{60.9} = -0.25 = \text{substitution effect}$$

$$-q_1\left(\frac{\partial q_1}{\partial I}\right) = \frac{-50p_1 q_1/q_2^2}{(100p_2^2/q_1^2) + (50p_1^2/q_2^2)} = \frac{-50(6.66)/(3.33)^2}{60.9}$$

$$= -0.49 = \text{income effect}$$

and

$$\frac{\partial q_1}{\partial p_1} = -0.25 - 0.49 = -0.74$$

This implies that for each dollar increase in the price of Q_1, the quantity purchased of Q_1 decreases by 0.74 unit. The fact that with a price increase, Q_1 becomes more expensive relative to its substitutes is responsible for 0.25 unit reduction, while the fact that the consumer's real income is simultaneously cut accounts for the remaining reduction of 0.49 of a unit.

The Slutsky equation for $\partial q_1/\partial p_2$ is found in a similar manner. We have shown that

$$\frac{\partial q_1}{\partial p_2} = \frac{\lambda p_1 p_2}{H} + \frac{q_2(-f_{q_1 q_2} p_2 + f_{q_2 q_2} p_1)}{H}$$

where the first term on the right-hand side of the equation represents the cross substitution effect and the second term represents the cross income effect.

In our case we find

$$\frac{\lambda p_1 p_2}{H} = \frac{(100/p_1 q_1)p_1 p_2}{(100p_2^2/q_1^2) + (50p_1^2/q_2^2)} = \frac{100p_2/q_1}{(100p_2^2/q_1^2) + (50p_1^2/q_2^2)}$$

$$= \text{cross substitution effect}$$

and

$$\frac{-q_2(f_{q_1 q_2} p_2 - f_{q_2 q_2} p_1)}{H} = \frac{-50 p_1/q_2}{(100 p_2^2/q_1^2) + (50 p_1^2/q_2^2)}$$

$$= \text{cross income effect}$$

The Slutsky equation then becomes

$$\frac{\partial q_1}{\partial p_2} = \frac{100 p_2/q_1}{(100 p_2^2/q_1^2) + (50 p_1^2/q_2^2)} - \frac{50 p_1/q_2}{(100 p_2^2/q_1^2) + (50 p_1^2/q_2^2)}$$

The cross substitution effect is clearly positive regardless of the particular values for the prices and quantities. This indicates that an increase in the price of Q_2 will induce the consumer to buy more of Q_1. This, in turn, implies that Q_1 and Q_2 are substitute products. The cross income effect is negative, arising from the fact that an increase in the price of Q_2 will reduce the real income of the consumer, thus making him less able to buy all products.

In particular, if $p_1 = 3$, $p_2 = 1$, $q_1 = 2.22$, $q_2 = 3.33$, we find that

$$\text{cross substitution effect} = \frac{100 p_2/q_1}{(100 p_2^2/q_1^2) + (50 p_1^2/q_2^2)}$$

$$= \frac{100/2.22}{60.9} = \frac{45}{60.9} = 0.74$$

and

$$\text{cross income effect} = \frac{-50 p_1/q_2}{(100 p_2^2/q_1^2) + (50 p_1^2/q_2^2)}$$

$$= \frac{-150/3.33}{60.9} = \frac{-45}{60.9} = -0.74$$

and

$$\frac{\partial q_1}{\partial p_2} = 0.74 - 0.74 = 0$$

This indicates that variations in the price of Q_2 do not affect the quantity of Q_1 that is purchased. This is not really surprising in light of the fact that we had earlier found (Illustration 1 of Section 12.5) that the demand function for q_1 is independent of p_2. The Slutsky equation shows us that there is a positive cross substitution effect that, by itself, tends to increase the quantity of Q_1 as the price of Q_2 increases. But the equation also demonstrates that, at least at the particular values we chose, there is a negative cross income effect that exactly matches the positive cross substitution effect. The two effects thus cancel each other, and no net effect is realized. This result will also appear for other specified points.

We should emphasize that this result should not be generalized for other utility functions. In most cases, as a matter of fact, the cross substitution and cross income effects will not necessarily cancel each other. As an example, the reader may refer to the utility function given in Illustration 2 of Section 12.5.

The present illustration is also enlightening in showing us that the precise way of determining whether two products are substitutes is by examining the cross substitution effect and not simply by looking at the demand function as we did in earlier sections before we had developed the Slutsky equation.

Exercises

For each of the following utility functions, find the Slutsky equation for $\partial q_1/\partial p_1$ and $\partial q_1/\partial p_2$ in general terms and then for the specific values indicated below.

1. $u = q_1 q_2; I = 200, p_1 = 1, p_2 = 5$
2. $u = q_1^2 q_2^3; I = 100, p_1 = 1, p_2 = 4$
3. $u = \ln q_1 + 2 \ln q_2$, where q_1 and $q_2 \geqslant 1$; $I = 90$, $p_1 = 0.40$, $p_2 = 0.20$
4. $u = 4q_1 + q_1 q_2 + 2q_2; I = 402, p_1 = 5, p_2 = 2$
5. $u = q_1^{1/2} + q_2^{1/2}$, where only positive square roots are to be taken; $I = 300, p_1 = 2, p_2 = 4$
6. $u = q_1^2 q_2; I = 120, p_1 = 8, p_2 = 2$

SECTION 12·7   SHORTCOMINGS OF ORDINAL UTILITY THEORY

Caution: The reader will recall that ordinal utility theory was developed because of the desire to escape the restrictive assumptions of cardinal utility theory. Ordinal theorists rejected the notion that utility was measurable, and instead substituted the more plausible assumption that a consumer is merely capable of ordering all conceivable alternatives that he could possibly attain. It is, indeed, remarkable that all of the results derived by the cardinal theorists could be derived without employing the totally unrealistic cardinal assumption. Moreover, ordinal theorists were able to advance our understanding of the process of consumer decision making by uncovering such significant concepts as the substitution and income effects and by deriving the Slutsky equation.

Nevertheless, one may, in turn, question the reasonableness of the ordinal utility assumption. Is it not unrealistic to expect a consumer to be able to rank in order all conceivable combinations of commodities? If it can be shown that consumers can, by and large (even if not always) rank alternatives, then the theory could serve as an adequate approximation to reality. But if the consumer's inability to do what is implied by the ordinal assumption is pervasive, how useful are the results?

Moreover, if consumer preferences can frequently be molded, created, or destroyed by producers, how much faith can we have in the apparently unshakable assumptions of rationality and transitivity that are common to both the cardinal and ordinal theories?

The approaches to understanding consumer behavior introduced in the next few sections attempt to remedy some—but not all—of the deficiencies possessed by ordinal utility theory.

SECTION 12·8   REVEALED PREFERENCE THEORY

We now turn to an approach that was first pioneered by Paul Samuelson and further developed by others such as Arrow, Houthakker, and Little. Adherents to the "revealed preference" point of view do not assume that a consumer is capable of ordering all conceivable combination of commodities. In fact, the consumer may be unable to supply any information regarding his preferences. Yet we can derive meaningful conclusions regarding consumer choice by merely observing consumer market behavior. The essential point is that actual consumer actions, when observed in a variety of situations, reveal many features of his preferences without us having to rely on any introspective information.

Suppose that there are n commodities available, $Q_1, Q_2, \ldots, Q_n$, and a consumer chooses to buy a combination consisting of $q_1, q_2, \ldots, q_n$ units of these commodities at their stated prices of $p_1, p_2, \ldots, p_n$. Total expenditures would be

$$p_1 q_1 + p_2 q_2 + \cdots + p_n q_n$$

This can be written as $\sum_{i=1}^{n} p_i q_i$, where the sign $\sum$ indicates summation and the notation below and above the sign signifies that the process is to begin at $i = 1$ and end at $i = n$. Thus

$$\sum_{i=1}^{n} p_i q_i = p_1 q_1 + p_2 q_2 + \cdots + p_n q_n$$

At any time a consumer has many alternatives open to him; that is, instead of buying the collection $q_1, q_2, \ldots, q_n$, the consumer could have bought other combinations of these commodities. The fact that collection $q_1, q_2, \ldots, q_n$ was chosen does not necessarily indicate that it is preferred to any other possible collection. An alternative collection could well have been preferable and yet not chosen because of its high purchase price. But, suppose that there is some alternative collection $q_1', q_2', \ldots, q_n'$ that is no more expensive than the combination actually chosen. Under such circumstances, one can only conclude that the chosen combination is preferred to the alternative.

This leads us to the following definition. If a consumer chooses to buy a collection of commodities $q_1, q_2, \ldots, q_n$ at prices $p_1, p_2, \ldots, p_n$ and if the cost of some alternative collection $q_1', q_2', \ldots, q_n'$ is no more than his total expenditures for the chosen alternative, that is,

$$\sum_{i=1}^{n} p_i q_i' \leqslant \sum_{i=1}^{n} p_i q_i$$

then we say that combination $q_1, q_2, \ldots, q_n$ has been *revealed to be preferred* to combination $q_1', q_2', \ldots, q_n'$.

We now make what is sometimes referred to as the *consistency assumption*. If a combination $q_1, q_2, \ldots, q_n$ is revealed to be preferred to some other combination $q_1', q_2', \ldots, q_n'$, then it is not possible that the consumer would take any action that would indicate that the latter combination is revealed to be preferred to the former.

Suppose that prices change so that they are now given by $p_1', p_2', \ldots, p_n'$ and as a result the consumer now chooses combination $q_1', q_2', \ldots, q_n'$. It cannot be that expenditures on this latter combination are greater than those that would occur for the original combination $q_1, q_2, \ldots, q_n$, because that would imply that $q_1', q_2', \ldots, q_n'$ is revealed to be preferred to $q_1, q_2, \ldots, q_n$, which contradicts our earlier conclusion. In other words, if it were true that $\sum_{i=1}^{n} p_i' q_i \leqslant \sum_{i=1}^{n} p_i' q_i'$, then $q_1', q_2', \ldots, q_n'$ would be revealed preferred to $q_1, q_2, \ldots, q_n$, which would violate the consistency assumption.

Therefore if, as in the above case, we know that

$$\sum_{i=1}^{n} p_i q_i' \leqslant \sum_{i=1}^{n} p_i q_i$$

it follows that

$$\sum_{i=1}^{n} p_i' q_i > \sum_{i=1}^{n} p_i' q_i'$$

It can be shown that all the results derived from ordinal utility theory may be deduced by using the revealed preference approach even though no assumption is made that a consumer can introspectively rank-order alternative combinations. These include the Slutsky equation, the homogeneity (zero degree) of demand functions, and even construction of the consumer's indifference map on the basis of sufficient observations of market behavior. Furthermore, the general analysis of n-commodity choice is greatly simplified. To illustrate, we shall show how this approach can be utilized to prove that the substitution effect is always negative.

Assume that with a given set of prices $p_1, p_2, \ldots, p_n$, a consumer chooses to buy a collection $q_1, q_2, \ldots, q_n$. Now let prices change to $p'_1, p'_2, \ldots, p'_n$ and at the same time allow income to change so as to compensate exactly for the change in real income that has occurred; that is, the consumer is exactly as well off as before the price change. Under these circumstances, the consumer will purchase some collection $q'_1, q'_2, \ldots, q'_n$. The consumer must be indifferent between the collection $q_1, q_2, \ldots, q_n$ and $q'_1, q'_2, \ldots, q'_n$, because he is exactly as well off as before the price change.

From the fact that at the original prices $p_1, p_2, \ldots, p_n$, he purchases $q_1, q_2, \ldots, q_n$, we can deduce that this combination is no more expensive than $q'_1, q'_2, \ldots, q'_n$. Thus we know that

$$\sum_{i=1}^{n} p_i q_i \leqslant \sum_{i=1}^{n} p_i q'_i \tag{1}$$

But we also know that at prices $p'_1, p'_2, \ldots, p'_n$ (holding real income constant) the consumer buys $q'_1, q'_2, \ldots, q'_n$ even though he is just as well off with collection $q_1, q_2, \ldots, q_n$. This implies that at the new price $p'_1, p'_2, \ldots, p'_n$, the combination $q'_1, q'_2, \ldots, q'_n$ is no more expensive than $q_1, q_2, \ldots, q_n$. This is the same as

$$\sum_{i=1}^{n} p'_i q'_i \leqslant \sum_{i=1}^{n} p'_i q_i \tag{2}$$

Now, from (1), we have

$$\sum_{i=1}^{n} p_i q_i - \sum_{i=1}^{n} p_i q'_i \leqslant 0$$

which is equivalent to

$$\sum_{i=1}^{n} (p_i q_i - p_i q'_i) \leqslant 0$$

or

$$\sum_{i=1}^{n} p_i(q_i - q_i') \leqslant 0$$

or

$$\sum_{i=1}^{n} - p_i(q_i' - q_i) \leqslant 0 \tag{3}$$

From (2), we get

$$\sum_{i=1}^{n} p_i' q_i' - \sum_{i=1}^{n} p_i' q_i \leqslant 0$$

which is equivalent to

$$\sum_{i=1}^{n} (p_i' q_i' - p_i' q_i) \leqslant 0$$

or

$$\sum_{i=1}^{n} p_i'(q_i' - q_i) \leqslant 0 \tag{4}$$

Adding (3) and (4) together gives us

$$\sum_{i=1}^{n} - p_i(q_i' - q_i) + \sum_{i=1}^{n} p_i'(q_i' - q_i) \leqslant 0$$

which is equivalent to

$$\sum_{i=1}^{n} - p_i(q_i' - q_i) + p_i'(q_i' - q_i) \leqslant 0$$

or

$$\sum_{i=1}^{n} (p_i' - p_i)(q_i' - q_i) \leqslant 0 \tag{5}$$

$(p_i' - p_i)$ represents the change in price, while $(q_i' - q_i)$ is the change in quantity of any commodity. Neither of these can be zero, because we have assumed some definite price change, which, in turn, leads to some change in quantity. Therefore we drop the equality sign in (5) and remain with

$$\sum_{i=1}^{n} (p_i' - p_i)(q_i' - q_i) < 0 \tag{6}$$

This indicates that if price increases, quantity will decrease and vice versa, so that the two factors within the summation will have unlike signs. Because we have held real income constant while varying prices, our result represents the substitution effect. This is seen to be negative, bec·ause quantity decreases in response to price increases.

Caution : Shortcomings of Revealed Preference Theory

It should be recognized that while revealed preference theory rectifies some of the weaknesses of earlier approaches, it, too, has short-comings. First, it does not allow for uncertainty on the part of consumers. According to revealed preference theory, if a consumer chooses a certain collection of commodities that is not cheaper than an alternative collec-tion, this reveals his preference for the former. But suppose that there is uncertainty of some kind associated with one or more of the collections under consideration. This could perhaps arise from uncertainty about the quality of a particular unit of the commodity, or there could be a variety of other uncertain economic circumstances. The consumer's choice of a particular collection may then reflect, not preference, but rather the degree of risk associated with the various alternatives.

Revealed preference theory also does not adequately explain con-sumer decision making with regard to durable products. Such products by their very nature have a considerable useful life. A consumer who chooses a new automobile rather than a new refrigerator does not neces-sarily reveal that he prefers the former to the latter if he has a three-year-old refrigerator at home that he may plan on replacing in a year or two. Only if the alternative commodities are instantly perishable is it true that preferences are revealed in the sense implied by the theory.

Moreover, the theory does not in any way show the relative effects of the diverse forces that influence consumer decision making. In particu-lar, the role of the producer in creating or inducing consumer demand is not given any attention at all.

Even with regard to its basic consistency assumption, revealed preference theory can be criticized. It sometimes happens that product A is preferred to product B as long as it is more expensive than B. When prices change so that B becomes more expensive than A, the consumer may change his preferences so that he then may actually prefer B. Its attractiveness could sometimes increase as a result of becoming more expensive. This clearly violates the consistency assumption, because A is first revealed to be preferred to B but then B is revealed to be preferred to A.

SECTION 12·9   UNCERTAINTY AND CONSUMER CHOICE

In previous sections we have seen that one of the weaknesses of utility theory stems from the difficulty in deriving utility numbers (whether of a cardinal or ordinal nature). A second weakness arises from the assumption that the consumer is faced with alternatives whose outcomes are certain and involve no risk. An approach developed in recent years by Von Neumann and Morgernstern attempts to remedy these difficulties.

Suppose that someone is offered a lottery ticket that offers a 30-day, all-expenses-paid vacation in Europe as the winning prize, and a pair of sunglasses as a consolation prize to all nonwinners. The utility of this ticket can be expressed as

probability of winning the vacation multiplied by the utility derived from the vacation plus the probability of not winning multiplied by the utility of a pair of sunglasses

If 1000 tickets are issued, each with an equal chance of selection, the utility of the lottery ticket is

$$U(\text{lottery ticket}) = 0.001 U(\text{vacation}) + 0.999 U(\text{sunglasses}),$$

where U denotes utility.

It now remains for us somehow to evaluate the utility of the vacation, $U(\text{vacation})$, and the utility of the pair of sunglasses, $U(\text{sunglasses})$. In order to establish a system of units that can be used to express the utility of any object, we choose two items as our utility base. One of these items should be something that bestows enormous utility and the other something that yields only negligible utility. We choose as our first base item (denoted by A) a luxurious 15-room home on a 5-acre plot in a prestigious location. Our other base item (denoted by B) is a dilapidated, unheated, two-room shack in a depressed neighborhood. Assign any arbitrary utility numbers to A and B. For our illustration, let $U(A) = 1000$ utils and $U(B) = 1$ util.

We are now in a position to derive utility numbers for any commodity. As an example, suppose that we wished to compute the utility of the vacation described earlier (denoted by V). We would ask the individual to weigh in his mind the following two alternatives: (1) a paid vacation without any uncertainty or (2) a chance of receiving either A or B as defined above. A moment's reflection will establish that, in general, the choice between (1) and (2) will depend upon the probabilities associated with possibilities A and B. For very high probabilities of A, the individual will undoubtedly select alternative (2), while for very low probabilities of A, the individual will select alternative (1). There will, in the usual case, be some probability for which the individual will weigh the two alternatives equally. Assume that we are told by the individual that, for example, he would take the sure vacation if possibility A had a probability less than 0.3, but that he would take the risky alternative (2) if the probability of A were more than 0.3. We then know that when $p(A) = 0.3$, the individual is indifferent between alternatives (1) and (2). This implies that with $p(A) = 0.3$, the expected utility derived from alternatives (1) and (2) are equal. We then have

$$U(V) = 0.3U(A) + 0.7U(B)$$

$$= 0.3(1000) + 0.7(1)$$

$$= 300 + 0.7 = 300.7 \text{ utils}$$

We have thus succeeded in deriving a utility number for the all-expenses-paid vacation. The same procedure could be followed with regard to any commodity or combination of commodities for all possible quantities. In this way a complete utility index or function could be built up for any individual. The procedure could also be applied to find the utility of money or income in any amount.

Because we now have a method to evaluate the utility of any commodity, it is only one step more to derive the utility of an uncertain event or payoff. We showed how the utility of an all-expenses-paid vacation could be calculated. But now suppose, as in our earlier illustration, that we are given a lottery ticket, so that the vacation is only a possible payoff. What is the utility of this ticket? It is certainly not the 300.7 utils we computed earlier, because that is the utility of actually getting the vacation, not simply having a possibility of getting such a vacation. To find the utility of the lottery ticket, we must first know the utilities of the two possible outcomes, namely, receiving the vacation or the sunglasses. We have already evaluated the former as 300.7. The latter is similarly found by asking the individual to weigh the following two alternatives: (1) a pair of sunglasses or (2) a chance of receiving either A or B as described above. Suppose that the individual would take the sunglasses only if possibility A had a probability less than 0.01. We then know that when $P(A) = 0.01$, the individual is indifferent between alternatives (1) and (2). This implies that

$$U(\text{sunglasses}) = 0.01U(A) + 0.99U(B)$$

$$= 0.01(1000) + 0.99(1)$$

$$= 10 + 0.99 = 10.99 \text{ utils}$$

We are now in a position to find the utility of a lottery ticket that offers a $\frac{1}{1000}$ chance of winning a vacation in Europe and a $\frac{999}{1000}$ chance of winning a pair of sunglasses. The utility of the lottery ticket (denoted by L) is given by

$$U(L) = 0.001U(\text{vacation}) + 0.999U(\text{sunglasses})$$

$$= 0.001(300.7) + 0.999(10.99)$$

$$= 0.3007 + 10.979 = 11.28 \text{ utils}$$

If the individual had to make a choice between the lottery ticket described above and some other lottery ticket that offered different prizes with different probabilities, he would have to compute the utility of the latter ticket and compare it with the former. He should then select the ticket that offers the greater utility.

This approach can be applied not only to lottery tickets offering prizes, but also to any uncertain outcome facing a consumer, as the following illustration shows.

Illustration.   Suppose that an individual is contemplating the purchase of a six-room home on a 40×100 ft plot of land in a certain middle-class neighborhood. He is, however, concerned about reports that middle-class families are gradually leaving the neighborhood. The possibility exists that in the near future the neighborhood may become a lower-class area, with the resulting reduction in status or deterioration of property values. The utility derived from a home in a middle-class neighborhood is greater for the individual than that realized from the same home in a depressed area.

We thus have an example of a consumer who is faced with an uncertain outcome. He must somehow calculate his expected utility considering the different possibilities. It is then necessary first to compute the utility of a home in a middle-class neighborhood (denoted by H-M) and subsequently the utility of the same home in a low-class neighborhood (denoted by H-L). This is done by asking the consumer to compare: (1) a home, as described above, in a middle-class neighborhood to (2) a chance of receiving either A or B, which are our base commodities. Suppose that we are informed that he would select (1) if the probability of A was less than 0.2 but that he would choose (2)if the probability of A was more than 0.2. This would imply that at a probability of 0.2, the alternatives (1) and (2) are equal in utility. We would then find the utility of the home in the middle-class neighborhood as

$$U(H\text{-}M) = 0.2U(A) + 0.8U(B)$$

$$= 0.2(1000) + 0.8(1)$$

$$= 200 + 0.8 = 200.8 \text{ utils}$$

The consumer must next compare (1)a home in a low-class neigh-borhood to (2)a chance of receiving either A or B. Suppose that he would select (1) only if the probability of A was less than 0.05. When $p(A) = 0.05$, he would be indifferent between alternatives (1) and (2). We would compute the utility of a home in a low-class neighborhood as

$$U(H\text{-}L) = 0.05U(A) + 0.95U(B)$$

$$= 0.05(1000) + 0.95(1)$$

$$= 50 + 0.95 = 50.95 \text{ utils}$$

We are now in a position to compute the expected utility of the above-described home when it is uncertain whether its neighborhood will be middle class or low class in the immediate future. Suppose that there is a 60 percent chance of the neighborhood remaining middle class. The utility of the home, taking into account its uncertainty is

$$U(\text{home with uncertain neighborhood}) = 0.6U(H\text{-}M) + 0.4U(H\text{-}L)$$

$$= 0.6(200.8) + 0.4(50.95)$$

$$= 120.48 + 20.38$$

$$= 140.86 \text{ utils}$$

We have already pointed out that the utility of any amount of money or income can be computed in a manner similar to that for any commodity. A consumer will purchase a commodity if its expected utility is greater than that yielded by the money that must be paid to acquire the commodity. Thus, if the home in the previous illustration costs $40,000, the consumer should purchase it only if the utility of $40,000 is less than 140.86 utils to him. Similarly, the lottery ticket considered above should be bought only if the money it costs is valued at less than 11.28 utils to the individual. These examples involve uncertainty. The same principle would also apply to commodities that do not involve any uncertainty. Such a commodity should be bought if the utility it yields is greater than the utility of the money that must be paid for the item.

The Neumann-Morgenstern method of deriving utility numbers is sometimes referred to as a cardinal utility measure because it deals with measurable quantities of utils. However, it is important to realize that this sort of measure is very different from the concept of utility introduced by the early cardinal utility theorists. The distinction lies in that utility meas-urements according to Neumann-Morgenstern do not, in fact, purport to gauge the absolute amount of satisfaction or pleasure to be derived from a commodity. Instead, they merely indicate the relative standing in the mind of the consumer of a commodity compared to other possible commodities with varying degrees of risk associated with them. Calculations in terms of base commodities are made only to enable us to establish a common denominator so that it becomes possible to compare diverse alternatives.[8]

Caution : Shortcomings of the Neumann-Morgenstern Approach

Although the Neumann-Morgenstern utility approach rectifies some of the glaring weaknesses inherent in the older theories, it is not without its own shortcomings. There are many who doubt whether a consumer can simultaneously make all the necessary calculations for the approach to have applicability. It is also doubtful that individuals approach every risky situation in cool, rational, and consistent terms, as implied by the theory. Certainly, there are people for whom gambling or risk taking provides its own set of thrills aside from the expected payoffs. Such behavior is, however, precluded under the Neumann-Morgenstern theory.

Finally, this theory, in common with the others previously studied, does not show the relative effects of the various forces that influence consumer decision making. In particular, the role of the producer in creating or inducing consumer demand is given no attention at all.

In this chapter, we have carefully developed the various economic theories of consumer choice. In the process, we have not hesitated to elaborate on various shortcomings inherent in all the theories. This is not, however, to imply that they do not reveal interesting facets of consumer choice. Just how much of the total picture they uncover is difficult to say. One thing that appears certain is that there is a great deal more to learn about consumer choice.

Exercises

1. Choose any two items as your utility base and assign utility numbers to them. Use this base for the remaining exercises.
2. Find the utility you would derive from (a) a new Datsun automobile, (b) a color TV, (c) a pack of cigarettes, (d) this textbook, (e) a hot dog, (f) a cup of coffee.
3. Find the expected utility of a two-year-old automobile that has a

[8] The reader who wishes to pursue this point further should see William J. Baumol, *Economic Theory and Operations Analysis* (Englewood Cliffs, N.J.: Prentice-Hall, 1972), pp. 547–548.

40 percent probability of being in excellent condition, and a 60 percent probability of being in poor condition.

4. For the automobile mentioned in the preceding exercise, suppose that
there was a 30 percent probability of it being in excellent condition, a
50 percent probability of it being in fair condition, and a 20 percent
probability of it being in poor condition. Find your expected utility.

5. What is your expected utility from a lottery ticket that offers a grand
prize of a Cadillac to the winner and a small transistor radio to
everyone else? Assume that 10,000 tickets are sold.

6. Find the expected utility of a college education to you if there is a
70 percent probability that you will earn $80,000 more lifetime by
going to college and a 30 percent probability that you will not earn
any more and, in fact, lose the $20,000 you could have made by
working full time instead of going to college.

7. What is the utility of a four-room apartment close to the school you
attend rented to you for one year if there is a 10 percent probability
that you will be surrounded by noisy neighbors?

8. What is the utility to you of (1) $1, (2) $100, (3) $1000?

9. Using the results of Exercise 8, suppose that you could buy a color
TV for $100. How would you decide whether or not to make the
purchase?

13

THE THEORY OF THE FIRM AND ITS DECISIONS

But mathematical economists form no school in any meaningful sense of the term, any more than do those economists who read Italian; all the differences of opinion that can be conceived to exist between economists at all—a certain class of errors alone excepted—may and do exist between the mathematically trained ones.

—Joseph Schumpeter

The previous chapter was concerned with consumer decision making. We now turn to the other side of the market, namely, the enterprises that produce and sell goods and services.

SECTION 13·1   THE FIRM: PRODUCTION AND COSTS

A "firm" in economic theory is an enterprise that produces some output for the purpose of selling and reaping a profit. As such, a firm may represent a one-man business establishment producing a single product as well as a large corporation producing multiple products. It may produce a physical product such as wheat or steel, but it may be in the business of providing some nontangible product such as the services of a doctor, musician, or entertainer.

One of the most crucial decisions that any firm must make is the quantity of output it will produce during any specified period of time. To this end, it is vital for firms to know what returns will accrue from different levels of production. These must be compared to the corresponding costs that will thereby be incurred. It is easily seen that any theory of the firm must deal with production, costs, returns, and aims of business enterprises. We begin with the case of a firm that produces a single product in a single plant and then adapt our analysis to more complex cases such as firms producing in multiple plants or selling multiple products.

The production of any commodity involves the utilization of inputs. These inputs may be classified in broad categories such as units of labor, capital, and raw materials; in more detailed terms such as units of skilled labor, semiskilled labor, unskilled labor, and so on; or even more precisely by specifying the exact type of labor such as bricklayer, the various machines to be used, and the particular materials to be employed.

For any period of time, the quantity of output that a firm is able to produce can be expressed as some function of the various inputs it utilizes. Thus

$$q = f(x_1, x_2, \ldots, x_n)$$

where $x_1, x_2, \ldots, x_n$ are the quantities of the variable inputs $X_1, X_2, \ldots, X_n$ that are to be employed in combination with any fixed or unvarying inputs available to the firm. q is the quantity of output that ensues from such use of inputs, and the function is known as a *production function*.

If all inputs are held constant except for one, x_i, which is allowed to vary, we can inquire into the resulting effect upon output. The instantaneous rate of change of output is then given by the partial derivative

$$\frac{\partial q}{\partial x_i}$$

which is also referred to as the *marginal productivity* (or *MP*) of X_i. The *average productivity* of X_i when all other inputs are at some fixed level is the total output divided by its quantity x_i, or

$$AP_i = \frac{q}{x_i}$$

One important feature common to almost all production processes is known as the *law of diminishing returns*, sometimes more accurately called the *law of variable proportions*. This states that when all inputs are held fixed except for one, additional units of the variable input will increase total output by successively smaller amounts. This is equivalent to the statement

$$\frac{\partial^2 q}{\partial x_i^2} < 0$$

that is, the first partial derivatives of the production function (or marginal productivities) decrease as the amount of any input increases with the others held constant. Note that in the typical case marginal productivity (which is the first partial $\partial q/\partial x_i$), even though decreasing, is still positive, indicating that total output is increased somewhat by an increase in any input. It is, however, possible to reach a stage where marginal productivity can decline so much as actually to become negative, indicating that output falls as more of that input is added. This might occur due to severe crowding, for example, as when more and more workers are added to a fixed plant with fixed machinery, and so on. It should also be pointed out that the law of diminishing returns does not necessarily apply to those initial stages of production where very little of an input is used. Under such circumstances, as the input is increased, such as by adding a few workers to cultivate a vast acreage of land, marginal productivity may actually increase because of the possibilities of specialization. Generally, however, as any input is increased while other inputs remain fixed, diminishing returns will eventually set in.

Why is diminishing returns so ever-present? The key lies in the proportionate relationship among inputs. As one input, such as labor, is increased without corresponding increases in other inputs, such as capital, each unit of the variable input has less and less of the fixed input to work with. Thus, if initially there are 100 machines and 100 workers, each worker has full use of a machine. But if this changes to 200 workers operating the same 100 machines, then each machine must be shared by two workers. Marginal productivity can only fall as a consequence. We can now see that the term, "the law of variable proportions," is actually a more apt description for the condition we are describing than the more popular term, "diminishing returns." It is the variation in the relative proportion of inputs that results in declining marginal product. It is thus evident that this law does not apply at all to the case where all inputs are increased simultaneously.

Illustration.   For simplicity, consider the following production function where there are only two variable inputs:

$$q = 100 \ln x_1 + 50 \ln x_2 \qquad \text{where } x_1 \text{ and } x_2 \geqslant 1$$

For any specified amounts of the two inputs, the production function expresses the amount of output that would ensue. Thus, if 6 units of x_1 are utilized along with 8 units of x_2, then

$$q = 100 \ln(6.00) + 50 \ln(8.00) = 283 \text{ units of output}$$

The marginal productivity of each input can be found simply by computing the first partial derivatives. Thus

$$\frac{\partial q}{\partial x_1} = \frac{100}{x_1} = MP_1$$

and

$$\frac{\partial q}{\partial x_2} = \frac{50}{x_2} = MP_2$$

It is seen that the marginal productivities are positive for all values of x_1 and x_2, indicating that additional units of each input increase total output.

Let us now find the second partials of the production function. We get

$$\frac{\partial^2 q}{\partial x_1^2} = \frac{-100}{x_1^2} \quad \text{and} \quad \frac{\partial^2 q}{\partial x_2^2} = \frac{-50}{x_2^2}$$

It is evident that the second partials are negative, which indicates that the first partials (or marginal productivities) are decreasing. This, in turn, implies diminishing returns.

The production function given in the preceding illustration implies that the productivity of one input is independent of the quantity of the other unit that is utilized. This follows from the fact that the marginal productivities (or first partials) of each input involve only the quantity of that particular input. This is, of course, not necessarily true, and we do not assume that such is the general case. The basic interpretation and analysis of production functions is not, however, appreciably affected in any event. For an example of a production function where input productivities are interdependent, see Illustration 2 in Section 13.2.

Every utilization of inputs involves costs. If we assume pure competition in the factor market (i.e., the markets where inputs are purchased or hired) the *cost equation* can be expressed as

$$C = r_1 x_1 + r_2 x_2 + \cdots + r_n x_n + b$$

where $r_1, r_2, \ldots, r_n$ are the prices of the respective variable inputs and b is the cost of the fixed or unvarying inputs. $r_1 x_1$ is the price of the first input multiplied by the quantity of that input, which therefore represents the total amount spent on that input, and similarly for $r_2 x_2, \ldots, r_n x_n$. When the amounts spent on all variable inputs are added to the fixed costs, b, we have total costs of production, C.

It may, by now, be apparent that the theory of the firm is, in many respects, analogous to the theory of the consumer. Just as the consumer has a utility function and a linear budget equation, so the firm has a production function and a linear cost equation. The analogy is, however, not perfect. While it may be impossible to state in cardinal terms how much utility is realized from particular combinations of products, it is only a question of sufficient engineering expertise to be able to compute the amount of output accruing from the use of particular combinations of inputs. The crucial difference is that utility functions are subjective and not even measurable by the consumer, while production functions are objective and, at least theoretically, relatively easy to measure. A second difference is that the consumer, at any point in time, always has a fixed budget, while the firm can usually vary its total expenditures.

Exercises

Verify whether diminishing returns holds for each of the following production functions defined for x_1, x_2, and $q \geqslant 0$

1. $q = x_1 x_2$
2. $q = x_1^2 x_2$
3. $q = \ln x_1 + 2 \ln x_2$
4. $q = 4x_1 + x_1 x_2 + 2x_2$
5. $q = x_1 + 2x_1 x_2 + x_2$
6. $q = x_1^{1/2} + x_2^{1/2}$
7. $q = 100x_1 x_2 - 5x_1^2 - 10x_2^2$

8. $q = 10 - \dfrac{1}{x_1} - \dfrac{1}{x_2}$

9. $q = 100 \ln x_1 + 100 \ln x_2$
10. $q = 8x_1 + 4x_2^2$

SECTION 13·2   MINIMIZING COSTS
FOR ANY LEVEL OF PRODUCTION

Suppose that a firm has decided to produce a specific amount of its product. There will typically be several ways that this can be achieved. It might, for example, be possible to use a great deal of labor together with small amounts of capital or, alternatively, to produce the same output by using a combination that is more capital intensive. The production function of the firm will give this type of information. In general form, it appears as

$$q = f(x_1, x_2, \ldots, x_n)$$

If the firm wishes to produce the specific output q_0, then any combination of values for $x_1, x_2, \ldots, x_n$ that satisfies

$$q_0 = f(x_1, x_2, \ldots, x_n)$$

is a possible method of production.

A firm faced with several alternative ways of producing the same output can reasonably be expected to choose the one with least cost. The problem before us is therefore one of minimizing costs subject to the constraint of achieving a given level of production. The method of Lagrangian multipliers is suited for this purpose.

For simplicity, we deal with the case where there are only two variable inputs. The results can easily be extended to any number of inputs, just as we extended the analysis of consumer equilibrium from two to n commodities.

We wish to minimize the cost equation

$$C = r_1 x_1 + r_2 x_2 + b \qquad \text{where } x_1 \text{ and } x_2 \geqslant 0$$

subject to the constraint

$$q_0 = f(x_1, x_2)$$

where q_0 is some specific level of output. We assume that $f(x_1, x_2)$ is a continuous function with continuous first and second partial derivatives.

The relevant Lagrangian function is therefore

$$F = r_1 x_1 + r_2 x_2 + b + \lambda[q_0 - f(x_1, x_2)]$$

Setting the first partial derivatives of the Lagrangian function equal to zero yields

$$\frac{\partial F}{\partial x_1} = r_1 - \lambda \frac{\partial f}{\partial x_1} = 0 \tag{1}$$

$$\frac{\partial F}{\partial x_2} = r_2 - \lambda \frac{\partial f}{\partial x_2} = 0 \tag{2}$$

$$\frac{\partial F}{\partial \lambda} = q_0 - f(x_1, x_2) = 0 \tag{3}$$

from which we get

$$r_1 = \lambda \frac{\partial f}{\partial x_1} \qquad r_2 = \lambda \frac{\partial f}{\partial x_2} \tag{4}$$

which is equivalent to

$$\frac{r_1}{r_2} = \frac{\lambda(\partial f/\partial x_1)}{\lambda(\partial f/\partial x_2)} = \frac{\partial f/\partial x_1}{\partial f/\partial x_2} \tag{5}$$

Alternatively, this condition can be expressed as

$$\frac{\partial f/\partial x_1}{r_1} = \frac{\partial f/\partial x_2}{r_2} \tag{6}$$

The first-order conditions thus require that the ratio of marginal productivities of the inputs be equal to the ratio of their respective prices. This is the same as saying that the marginal productivity divided by the price be equal for all inputs. This is sometimes referred to as the *least-cost rule*.

The second-order conditions for the minimization of costs at a specific output require that the following determinant be negative, where F is the Lagrangian function and g is the equation of constraint.

$$\begin{vmatrix} F_{x_1x_1} & F_{x_1x_2} & g_{x_1} \\ F_{x_2x_1} & F_{x_2x_2} & g_{x_2} \\ g_{x_1} & g_{x_2} & 0 \end{vmatrix} < 0$$

In our case, this is equivalent to

$$\begin{vmatrix} -\lambda f_{x_1x_1} & -\lambda f_{x_1x_2} & -f_{x_1} \\ -\lambda f_{x_2x_1} & -\lambda f_{x_2x_2} & -f_{x_2} \\ -f_{x_1} & -f_{x_2} & 0 \end{vmatrix} < 0$$

By expanding the determinant, we get

$$-\lambda f_{x_1x_1}(-f_{x_2}^2) + \lambda f_{x_2x_1}(-f_{x_1}f_{x_2}) - f_{x_1}(\lambda f_{x_1x_2}f_{x_2} - \lambda f_{x_2x_2}f_{x_1}) < 0$$

which is equivalent to

$$\lambda f_{x_1x_1} f_{x_2}^2 - 2\lambda f_{x_1x_2} f_{x_1} f_{x_2} + \lambda f_{x_2x_2} f_{x_1}^2 < 0 \tag{7}$$

Now, from equation (4), we know that

$$\lambda = \frac{\partial f/\partial x_1}{r_1}$$

and because both $\partial f/\partial x_1$ and r_1 are positive, it follows that λ is also positive. Therefore we can divide each term of (7) by λ without changing the sense of the inequality. This yields

$$f_{x_1x_1} f_{x_2}^2 - 2f_{x_1x_2} f_{x_1} f_{x_2} + f_{x_2x_2} f_{x_1}^2 < 0 \tag{8}$$

This second-order condition must be satisfied, along with the first-order condition given by equation (5), in order to ensure the minimization of costs when producing a specific output.

In Section 13.1, we showed that the law of diminishing returns implies that $f_{x_1x_1}$ and $f_{x_2x_2}$ are each negative. The first and third terms of inequality (8) will therefore be negative. If, in addition, $f_{x_1x_2}$ is positive, inequality (8) will be satisfied because f_{x_1} and f_{x_2} are positive as long as the inputs yield any productivity at all. If $f_{x_1x_2}$ is, on the other hand, negative, the inequality can still be satisfied provided that the first and third terms outweigh the middle term. Only if $f_{x_1x_2}$ is negative and the middle term outweighs the first and third terms combined will the second-order conditions fail to be satisfied.

In the event that the second-order condition is not satisfied, no minimum-cost point will be attained on the interior of the function. The boundary or corner values (i.e., $x_1 = 0$ or $x_2 = 0$) must then be examined to see which one yields the lowest cost subject to the constraint. The implication of such a result is that the given level of output could be most economically produced by utilizing only one of the inputs and not using the other at all.

The possibility also exists that the first-order conditions given by (5) or (6) may not be satisfied at any point within the region of definition, that is, x_1 and $x_2 \geqslant 0$. This could happen if the ratio r_1/r_2 is greater than $(\partial f/\partial x_1)/(\partial f/\partial x_2)$ or smaller than $(\partial f/\partial x_1)/(\partial f/\partial x_2)$ for all positive values of x_1 and x_2. In that case, no minimum would be attained within the interior of the function. One of the boundary points will then be the absolute minimum-cost position. The cost function will again have to be examined at each boundary point, that is, $x_1 = 0$ and $x_2 = 0$, to see which yields the least cost.

Even if the first- and second-order conditions are satisfied at some point, this implies only that such a point is a minimum-cost position within the interior of the defined function. Nothing is implied regarding boundary points, that is, $x_1 = 0$ or $x_2 = 0$. Thus it would be necessary to compute the cost of production at the interior minimum point and also at each boundary point in order to find the least-cost position.

In spite of the fact that boundary or corner solutions are possible, the basic condition for cost minimization, that is, marginal productivity divided by price being identical for all inputs, is still widely applicable. In the case of two inputs, a corner solution implies that one input will not be utilized at all and the product will be produced by using only one input, not a very usual occurrence. If there are n variable inputs, it will again be possible to have corner solutions, in which case some of the variable inputs, say, K, will not be utilized. The least-cost conditions can then be expressed in terms of the remaining $n - k$ inputs. The first-order conditions will then require the equality of marginal productivity divided by price for all such inputs.

Thus, while corner solutions cannot be ruled out entirely, the basic result still holds provided it is applied only to those inputs that will actually be utilized.

When a least-cost solution is found according to the above procedure, it applies only for a specified level of output. We can, however, find such a cost minimization for every level of output. We would then have a series of input combinations (x_1, x_2), where each combination represents a minimization of costs for some particular output level. These points can be expressed as some function $g(x_1 x_2) = 0$, which is then known as the *expansion path* of the firm. A firm wishing to expand must do so by moving along the curve or path traced out by $g(x_1, x_2) = 0$.

Illustration 1.   Find the least-cost way of producing any fixed level of output q_0 and, in particular, an output of 100 units if the firm's production function is given by

$$q = 100 \ln x_1 + 50 \ln x_2 \qquad \text{where } x_1 \text{ and } x_2 \geqslant 1$$

and the price of input X_1 is \$3 per unit, the price of input X_2 is \$1 per unit, and the fixed costs are \$2.

Solution.   The cost equation is given by

$$C = r_1 x_1 + r_2 x_2 + b$$

which, in this case, becomes

$$C = 3x_1 + x_2 + 2$$

We wish to minimize the costs of producing a fixed level of output q_0, which means that we wish to minimize

$$C = 3x_1 + x_2 + 2$$

subject to the constraint

$$q_0 = 100 \ln x_1 + 50 \ln x_2$$

We form the Lagrangian function

$$F = 3x_1 + x_2 + 2 + \lambda[q_0 - 100 \ln x_1 - 50 \ln x_2]$$

Setting the first partials of the Lagrangian function equal to zero yields

$$\frac{\partial F}{\partial x_1} = 3 - \frac{100\lambda}{x_1} = 0 \tag{1}$$

$$\frac{\partial F}{\partial x_2} = 1 - \frac{50\lambda}{x_2} = 0 \tag{2}$$

$$\frac{\partial F}{\partial \lambda} = q_0 - 100 \ln x_1 - 50 \ln x_2 = 0 \tag{3}$$

From the second equation, we find

$$1 = \frac{50\lambda}{x_2}$$

$$\frac{x_2}{50} = \lambda$$

which we substitute into the first equation:

$$3 - \frac{100(x_2/50)}{x_1} = 0$$

or

$$3 = \frac{2x_2}{x_1}$$

or

$$x_1 = \tfrac{2}{3}x_2 \tag{4}$$

Substituting the value of x_1 into equation (3) gives

$$q_0 - 100 \ln \tfrac{2}{3}x_2 - 50 \ln x_2 = 0$$

and

$$q_0 = 100 \ln \tfrac{2}{3}x_2 + 50 \ln x_2$$

$$= 50(2 \ln \tfrac{2}{3}x_2 + \ln x_2)$$

$$\frac{q_0}{50} = 2 \ln \tfrac{2}{3}x_2 + \ln x_2$$

which by the rules for operations with logarithms given in Chapter 4 becomes

$$\frac{q_0}{50} = \ln(\tfrac{2}{3}x_2)^2 + \ln x_2$$

$$= \ln[(\tfrac{2}{3}x_2)^2 x_2]$$

$$= \ln[\tfrac{4}{9}x_2^3]$$

$$= \ln \tfrac{4}{9} + 3 \ln x_2$$

$$= \ln 4 - \ln 9 + 3 \ln x_2$$

$$= 1.3863 - 2.1972 + 3 \ln x_2$$

$$= -0.8109 + 3 \ln x_2$$

$$\frac{q_0}{50} + 0.8109 = 3 \ln x_2$$

$$\ln x_2 = \frac{q_0}{150} + 0.2703 \tag{5}$$

For any fixed level of production q_0, we can easily evaluate x_2 by consulting a table of natural logarithms. Once we know the value of x_2, we can find x_1 from equation (4). This will give us the least-cost way of producing any fixed output, provided that the second-order conditions are satisfied for the particular values.

In particular, if we wish to produce an output of 100 units, then $q_0 = 100$, and from (5) we have

$$\ln x_2 = \tfrac{100}{150} + 0.2703$$

$$= 0.9370$$

$$x_2 = 2.55$$

and from (4),

$$x_1 = \tfrac{2}{3}(2.55) = 1.70$$

which means that the least-cost way of producing 100 units is to utilize 1.7 units of the first variable input and 2.55 of the second variable input, provided that the second-order conditions are satisfied.

The second-order condition for a minimization requires that the bordered determinant of partials of the Lagrangian function be negative. We have already shown that for a cost equation subject to the production constraint $q_0 = f(x_1, x_2)$, this reduces to

$$f_{x_1 x_1} f_{x_2}^2 - 2 f_{x_1 x_2} f_{x_1} f_{x_2} + f_{x_2 x_2} f_{x_1}^2 < 0$$

In our case, we have

$$q_0 = 100 \ln x_1 + 50 \ln x_2$$

and

$$f_{x_1} = \frac{\partial f}{\partial x_1} = \frac{100}{x_1} \qquad f_{x_2} = \frac{\partial f}{\partial x_2} = \frac{50}{x_2}$$

$$f_{x_1 x_1} = \frac{-100}{x_1^2} \qquad f_{x_1 x_2} = 0 \qquad f_{x_2 x_2} = \frac{-50}{x_2^2}$$

When evaluated at $x_1 = 1.70$, $x_2 = 2.55$ and substituted into the inequality, we get as our second-order condition

$$\frac{-100}{(1.7)^2} \left(\frac{50}{2.55} \right)^2 + 0 - \frac{50}{(2.55)^2} \left(\frac{100}{1.7} \right)^2 < 0$$

The sufficient condition is therefore satisfied, and $x_1 = 1.70$, $x_2 = 2.55$ is the least-cost utilization of inputs in order to produce 100 units of output. At that level of production, costs will be $C = 3(1.70) + 2.55 + 2 = 9.65$.

We have yet to consider the boundary values of our function. These are given by $x_1 = 1$ and $x_2 = 1$. From our production function, we find that with $q_0 = 100$ and $x_1 = 1$, we have $x_2 = 7.39$ and costs are

$$C = 3(1) + 7.39 + 2 = 12.39$$

When $q_0 = 100$ and $x_2 = 1$, we find that $x_1 = 2.72$ and costs are

$$C = 3(2.72) + 1 + 2 = 11.16$$

We thus see that the costs associated with either boundary point are greater than that for the interior point located by the Lagrangian process. We conclude that the best way of producing 100 units output is, indeed, by utilizing 1.70 units of input X_1 and 2.55 units of input X_2.

The general expansion path of the firm is given by equation (4),

$$x_1 = \tfrac{2}{3} x_2$$

that is, when expanding output, the firm should utilize $\tfrac{2}{3}$ unit of input X_1 for each additional unit of input X_2. Each of the combinations of inputs given by equation (4) is the least-cost way of producing a certain level of output.

The production function given in the previous illustration implied that the productivity of one input was independent of the other input. We have already pointed out that the basic analysis of the firm would be essentially unchanged even if this were not the case. The following illustration employs a production function where the productivity of one input depends not only on the amount of that input, but also on the amount of the other input.

Illustration 2.   Find the least-cost way of producing any fixed level of output q_0 and, in particular, an output of 350 units of the firm's production function, which is given by

$$q = 8x_1 x_2 - x_1^2 - 2x_2^2 \qquad \text{where } x_1 \text{ and } x_2 \geqslant 0$$

and the price of input X_1 is \$4 per unit, the price of input X_2 is \$2 per unit, and the fixed costs are \$5.
Solution.   We wish to minimize $C = 4x_1 + 2x_2 + 5$, subject to the constraint $q_0 = 8x_1 x_2 - x_1^2 - 2x_2^2$.
   Form the Lagrangian function

$$F = 4x_1 + 2x_2 + 5 + \lambda[q_0 - 8x_1 x_2 + x_1^2 + 2x_2^2]$$

Setting the first partials of the Lagrangian function equal to zero yields

$$\frac{\partial F}{\partial x_1} = 4 - 8\lambda x_2 + 2\lambda x_1 = 0 \tag{1}$$

$$\frac{\partial F}{\partial x_2} = 2 - 8\lambda x_1 + 4\lambda x_2 = 0 \tag{2}$$

$$\frac{\partial F}{\partial \lambda} = q_0 - 8x_1 x_2 + x_1^2 + 2x_2^2 = 0 \tag{3}$$

From the first equation, we find

$$8\lambda x_2 - 2\lambda x_1 = 4$$

$$2\lambda(4x_2 - x_1) = 4$$

$$\lambda = \frac{2}{4x_2 - x_1}$$

which we then substitute into the second equation:

$$2 - \frac{16x_1}{4x_2 - x_1} + \frac{8x_2}{4x_2 - x_1} = 0$$

$$\frac{8x_2 - 2x_1 - 16x_1 + 8x_2}{4x_2 - x_1} = 0$$

$$16x_2 - 18x_1 = 0$$

$$x_1 = \tfrac{8}{9}X_2 \tag{4}$$

Substituting the value of x_1 into equation (3) gives

$$q_0 - \tfrac{64}{9}x_2^2 + \tfrac{64}{81}x_2^2 + 2x_2^2 = 0$$

$$q_0 = \tfrac{64}{9}x_2^2 - \tfrac{64}{81}x_2^2 - 2x_2^2 = 0$$

$$q_0 = \frac{576x_2^2 - 64x_2^2 - 162x_2^2}{81}$$

$$q_0 = \frac{350x_2^2}{81}$$

$$x_2^2 = \tfrac{81}{350}q_0$$

$$x_2 = \sqrt{\tfrac{81}{350}q_0} \qquad\qquad (5)$$

For any fixed level of production, we can easily evaluate x_2 and then find x_1 from equation (4).

In particular, if we wish to produce an output of 350 units, then $q_0 = 350$ and from (5) we have

$$x_2 = \sqrt{81} = 9$$

and from (4),

$$x_1 = \tfrac{8}{9}(9) = 8$$

The point $x_1 = 8$, $x_2 = 9$ is the only one that satisfies the first-order conditions for the minimization of costs. An investigation of the second-order conditions will confirm that this point also satisfies the sufficient conditions. The possibility of boundary solutions, that is, $x_1 = 0$ or $x_2 = 0$, can also be eliminated, because an examination of the production function will show that at such points, no positive output will ensue.

We can therefore conclude that the least-cost way of producing 350 units of output would be to utilize 8 units of the first input in combination with 9 units of the second input. The general expansion path of the firm is given by (4)

$$x_1 = \tfrac{8}{9}x_2$$

that is, when expanding output, the firm should utilize $\tfrac{8}{9}$ unit of input X_1 for each additional unit of input X_2.

We now wish to show how least-cost analysis can be extended to any number of inputs. If there are n variable inputs, the production function will appear as

$$q = f(x_1, x_2, \ldots, x_n)$$

and the cost equation as

$$C = \sum_{i=1}^{n} r_i x_i + b = r_1 x_1 + r_2 x_2 + \cdots + r_n x_n + b$$

Our problem is therefore to minimize the cost equation

$$C = \sum_{i=1}^{n} r_i x_i + b$$

subject to the constraint

$$q_0 = f(x_1, x_2, \ldots, x_n)$$

We form the Lagrangian function

$$F = \sum_{i=1}^{n} r_i x_i + b + \lambda[q_0 - f(x_1, x_2, \ldots, x_n)]$$

take the partial derivatives of F with respect to $x_1, x_2, \ldots, x_n$, and set them equal to zero. For any one of these, x_i, we shall have

$$\frac{\partial F}{\partial x_i} = r_i - \lambda \frac{\partial f}{\partial x_i} = 0 \qquad \text{for all } i = 1, 2, \ldots, n$$

or

$$r_i = \lambda \frac{\partial f}{\partial x_i} \qquad \text{for all } i = 1, 2, \ldots, n$$

This implies that

$$\frac{r_i}{r_j} = \frac{\lambda(\partial f/\partial x_i)}{\lambda(\partial f/\partial x_j)} = \frac{\partial f/\partial x_i}{\partial f/\partial x_j} \qquad \text{for } i = 1, \ldots, n, j = 1, \ldots, n$$

which is equivalent to

$$\left(\frac{\partial f/\partial x_1}{r_1}\right)\left(\frac{\partial f/\partial x_2}{r_2}\right) = \cdots = \frac{\partial f/\partial x_n}{r_n} = \frac{1}{\lambda}$$

Thus a necessary condition for achieving production at least cost is that the marginal productivity divided by price be identical for all inputs. This result is seen to be a generalization of what we found for two commodities.

The second-order conditions for the minimization of costs at a specific output require that the following determinants all be negative:

$$
\begin{vmatrix}
-\lambda f_{x_1x_1} & -\lambda f_{x_1x_2} & -f_{x_1} \\
-\lambda f_{x_2x_1} & -\lambda f_{x_2x_2} & -f_{x_2} \\
-f_{x_1} & -f_{x_2} & 0
\end{vmatrix} < 0
$$

$$
\begin{vmatrix}
-\lambda f_{x_1x_1} & -\lambda f_{x_1x_2} & -\lambda f_{x_1x_3} & -f_{x_1} \\
-\lambda f_{x_2x_1} & -\lambda f_{x_2x_2} & -\lambda f_{x_2x_3} & -f_{x_2} \\
-\lambda f_{x_3x_1} & -\lambda f_{x_3x_2} & -\lambda f_{x_3x_3} & -f_{x_3} \\
-f_{x_1} & -f_{x_2} & -f_{x_3} & 0
\end{vmatrix} < 0
$$

$$
\vdots
$$

$$
\begin{vmatrix}
-\lambda f_{x_1x_1} & -\lambda f_{x_1x_2} & \cdots & -\lambda f_{x_1x_n} & -f_{x_1} \\
-\lambda f_{x_2x_1} & -\lambda f_{x_2x_2} & \cdots & -\lambda f_{x_2x_n} & -f_{x_2} \\
\vdots & \vdots & & \vdots & \vdots \\
-\lambda f_{x_nx_1} & -\lambda f_{x_nx_2} & \cdots & -\lambda f_{x_nx_n} & -f_{x_n} \\
-f_{x_1} & -f_{x_2} & \cdots & -f_{x_n} & 0
\end{vmatrix} < 0
$$

Notice that when $n = 2$, these sufficient conditions reduce to those given when we earlier considered the case of two inputs.

Exercises

Find the least-cost way of producing an output of q_0, given the following production functions and cost information. Also find the expansion path of the firm. In each case, unless otherwise stated, x_1, x_2, and $q > 0$.

1. $q = x_1 x_2$; $C = x_1 + 5x_2 + 10$; for $q_0 =$ any fixed output and for $q_0 = 125$

2. $q = x_1^2 x_2$; $C = 2x_1 + x_2 + 20$; for $q_0 =$ any fixed output and for $q_0 = 64$

3. $q = \ln x_1 + 2 \ln x_2$, where x_1 and $x_2 \geqslant 1$; $C = 3x_1 + 2x_2 + 5$; for $q_0 =$ any fixed output and for $q_0 = 9$

4. $q = 4x_1 + x_1 x_2 + 2x_2$; $C = 10x_1 + 4x_2 + 25$; for $q_0 = 32$

5. $q = x_1 + 2x_1 x_2 + x_2$; $C = x_1 + 2x_2 + 25$; for $q_0 = \frac{7}{2}$

6. $q = x_1^{1/2} + x_2^{1/2}$, where only positive square roots are to be taken; $C = 4x_1 + x_2 + 100$; for $q_0 =$ any fixed output and for $q_0 = 25$

7. $q = 100x_1 x_2 - 5x_1^2 - 10x_2$; $C = 20x_1 + 10x_2 + 200$; for

$$q_0 = 490$$

8. $q = 10 - \dfrac{1}{x_1} - \dfrac{1}{x_2}$; $C = x_1 + 4x_2 + 20$, where x_1 and $x_2 > 0$;

   for $q_0 =$ any fixed output and for $q_0 = 5$

9. $q = 100 \ln x_1 + 100 \ln x_2$; $C = 5x_1 + 2x_2 + 50$, where x_1 and $x_2 \geqslant 1$; for $q_0 = 400$

10. $q = 8x_1^2 + 4x_2^2$; $C = 4x_1 + 8x_2 + 150$; for $q_0 =$ any fixed output and for $q_0 = 72$

11. $q = 10x_1 x_2 x_3$; $C = 2x_1 + x_2 + 4x_3 + 120$; for $q_0 = 270$

12. $q = \ln x_1 + \ln x_2 + \ln x_3$; $C = 2x_1 + 5x_2 + x_3 + 250$, where x_1, x_2, and $x_3 \geqslant 1$; for $q_0 = 6$

SECTION 13·3   PROFIT MAXIMIZATION:
PRODUCTION FUNCTION APPROACH

In the previous section we showed that for any level of output, we can determine which combination of inputs will minimize costs. The next question we must tackle is which level of output will actually be chosen by the firm. To proceed, it is necessary to consider the ultimate objective of a firm. The assumption most often made in economic theory is that the central aim of a firm is to maximize profits. To achieve this objective, a firm will make calculations and comparisons and follow the path that promises the greatest attainable level of profits. We shall begin by making this assumption and see its logical consequences. Subsequently, in Section 13.8, we shall discuss the limitations of such an assumption.

If we denote profit by π, total revenue by TR, and costs by C, then we can make the following definition:

$$\pi = TR - C$$

that is, the amount of profit realized by a firm is merely the difference between the amount it receives by selling its product and the total cost of producing that product.

Now, we know that

$$TR = pq$$

that is, revenue is simply the price per unit multiplied by the number of units sold.

We therefore have

$$\pi = pq - C$$

The production function expresses q in terms of the firm's variable inputs, $q = f(x_1, x_2)$, where there are two variable inputs. The cost equation appears as

$$C = r_1 x_1 + r_2 x_2 + b$$

Therefore,

$$\pi = pf(x_1, x_2) - r_1 x_1 - r_2 x_2 - b$$

where there are only two variable inputs.

We assume pure competition in both the product and the input market, so that the firm has no control over either the product price or the input price. Consequently, the values of p, r_1, and r_2 can be treated as constants given by the market. In the following chapter we discuss other market structures.

To maximize profits, we have to find extreme points for this function of two variables. As shown in Section 11.1, the first-order conditions require that the first partials be set equal to zero:

$$\frac{\partial \pi}{\partial x_1} = p \frac{\partial f}{\partial x_1} - r_1 = 0 \qquad \frac{\partial \pi}{\partial x_2} = p \frac{\partial f}{\partial x_2} - r_2 = 0$$

$$p \frac{\partial f}{\partial x_1} = r_1 \qquad\qquad p \frac{\partial f}{\partial x_2} = r_2$$

Now, $\partial f / \partial x_i$ is the marginal productivity of the ith input or factor of production, and $p(\partial f / \partial x_i)$ is the additional revenue that would accrue as a result of selling the marginal product (sometimes called the marginal revenue product).

The necessary conditions for profit maximization therefore requires that the marginal revenue product of each input or factor of production be equal to the input price. In addition, the second-order or sufficient conditions must also be examined. These are

$$\pi_{x_1 x_1} < 0 \tag{1}$$

and

$$\pi_{x_1 x_1} \pi_{x_2 x_2} - (\pi_{x_1 x_2})^2 > 0 \tag{2}$$

We then find

$$\pi_{x_1 x_1} = p f_{x_1 x_1}$$

$$\pi_{x_1 x_2} = p f_{x_1 x_2}$$

$$\pi_{x_2 x_2} = p f_{x_2 x_2}$$

The sufficient conditions are then equivalent to

$$pf_{x_1x_1} < 0 \qquad\qquad (1)$$

and

$$pf_{x_1x_1} pf_{x_2x_2} - p^2(f_{x_1x_2})^2 > 0 \qquad\qquad (2)$$

which becomes

$$p^2[f_{x_1x_1} f_{x_2x_2} - (f_{x_1x_2})^2] > 0$$

But $p > 0$. Therefore, the sufficient conditions become

$$f_{x_1x_1} < 0 \qquad\qquad (1)$$

$$f_{x_1x_1} f_{x_2x_2} - (f_{x_1x_2})^2 > 0 \qquad\qquad (2)$$

Now $(f_{x_1x_2})^2$ is certainly greater than zero. Also, $f_{x_1x_1} < 0$ if the first condition (1) is to hold. Therefore, the only way (2) can be satisfied is if $f_{x_2x_2} < 0$.

Thus a maximization of profits will occur only where the marginal product of each input is decreasing, that is, when diminishing returns has already set in. This is not surprising because, with a constant product price, if either marginal product were increasing, it would pay to increase production by using more of that input.

Illustration 1. Find the profit maximization output for a firm whose production function is $q = 100 \ln x_1 + 50 \ln x_2$, where x_1 and $x_2 \geqslant 1$ and whose costs are given by $C = 3x_1 + x_2 + 2$. The market price for the product is set at \$4.
Solution. We form the profit function, which is

$$\pi = TR - C$$

$$= pq - C$$

$$= 4(100 \ln x_1 + 50 \ln x_2) - (3x_1 + x_2 + 2)$$

$$= 400 \ln x_1 + 200 \ln x_2 - 3x_1 - x_2 - 2$$

Setting the first partials equal to zero gives

$$\frac{\partial \pi}{\partial x_1} = \frac{400}{x_1} - 3 = 0 \qquad\qquad \frac{\partial \pi}{\partial x_2} = \frac{200}{x_2} - 1 = 0$$

$$\frac{400}{x_1} = 3 \qquad\qquad \frac{200}{x_2} = 1$$

$$x_1 = 133.33 \qquad\qquad x_2 = 200$$

Thus a necessary condition for the maximization of profit is that 133.33 units of the first input be used together with 200 units of the second input. This combination of inputs will produce

$$q = 100 \ln(133.33) + 50 \ln(200) = 100(4.8904) + 50(5.2983)$$

$$= 753.96 \text{ units of output}$$

For this level of output, we find

$$TR = pq = 4(753.96) = 43{,}015.84$$

$$C = 3(133.33) + 2\overset{\cdot}{0}0 + 2 = \$602$$

$$\pi = TR - C = 3{,}015.84 - 602 = \$2{,}413.84 \text{ profit}$$

To be assured that this output level yields the maximum feasible profit, we must check the second-order conditions, which are

$$\pi_{x_1 x_1} < 0 \quad \text{and} \quad \pi_{x_1 x_1} \pi_{x_2 x_2} - (\pi_{x_1 x_2})^2 > 0$$

Now,

$$\pi_{x_1} = \frac{\partial \pi}{\partial x_1} = \frac{400}{x_1} - 3 \qquad \pi_{x_2} = \frac{\partial \pi}{\partial x_2} = \frac{200}{x_2} - 1$$

$$\pi_{x_1 x_1} = \frac{-400}{x_1^2} \qquad \pi_{x_2 x_2} = \frac{-200}{x_2^2} \qquad \pi_{x_1 x_2} = 0$$

At $x_1 = 133.33$, $x_2 = 200$,

$$\pi_{x_1 x_1} < 0$$

and

$$\pi_{x_1 x_1} \pi_{x_2 x_2} - (\pi_{x_1 x_2})^2 > 0$$

The second-order or sufficient conditions are therefore satisfied. The possibility of a boundary solution must still be considered. The boundaries of our function are given by $x_1 = 1$ and $x_2 = 1$. If $x_1 = 1$, we have

$$q = 50 \ln x_2 \qquad C = 3 + x_2 + 2 = x_2 + 5$$

and

$$\pi = pq - C$$

$$= 4(50 \ln x_2) - (x_2 + 5) = 200 \ln x_2 - x_2 - 5$$

Maximizing this function with respect to x_2 gives

$$\frac{d\pi}{dx_2} = \frac{200}{x_2} - 1 = 0$$

$$\frac{200}{x_2} = 1$$

$$x_2 = 200$$

At $x_1 = 1$, $x_2 = 200$, we find

$$q = 50 \ln 200 = 50(5.2983) = 264.92$$

and

$$\pi = pq - C = 4(264.92) - 205 = \$854.68$$

Thus the level of profit at this boundary point is lower than for the interior maximum point.

In a similar manner, considering the remaining boundary point, $x_2 = 1$, we have

$$q = 100 \ln x_1 \qquad C = 3x_1 + 1 + 2 = 3x_1 + 3$$

and

$$\pi = pq - C = 4(100 \ln x_1) - (3x_1 + 3) = 400 \ln x_1 - 3x_1 - 3$$

Maximizing this function with respect to x_1 gives

$$\frac{d\pi}{dx_1} = \frac{400}{x_1} - 3 = 0$$

$$\frac{400}{x_1} = 3$$

$$x_1 = \tfrac{400}{3} = 133.33$$

At $x_1 = 133.33$, $x_2 = 1$, we find

$$q = 100 \ln(133.33) = 100(4.8904) = 489.04$$

and

$$\pi = pq - C = 4(489.04) - 403 = \$1553.16$$

This level of profit is again lower than for the interior maximum point.

We therefore conclude that profit is maximized by utilizing 133.33 units of the first input and 200 units of the second input to produce an output of 753.96 units.

Illustration 2.   Find the profit maximization output for a firm whose production function is $q = 8x_1 x_2 - x_1^2 - 2x_2^2$, where $0 \leqslant x_1 \leqslant 10$ and $x_2 \geqslant 0$ and whose costs are given by $C = 4x_1 + 2x_2 + 5$. The market price for the product is set at \$0.50.

Solution.   We form the profit function

$$\pi = TR - C = pq - C$$

$$= \tfrac{1}{2}(8x_1 x_2 - x_1^2 - 2x_2^2) - (4x_1 + 2x_2 + 5)$$

$$= 4x_1 x_2 - \tfrac{1}{2}x_1^2 - x_2^2 - 4x_1 - 2x_2 - 5$$

Setting the first partials equal to zero yields

$$\frac{\partial \pi}{\partial x_1} = 4x_2 - x_1 - 4 = 0 \qquad \frac{\partial \pi}{\partial x_2} = 4x_1 - 2x_2 - 2 = 0$$

$$x_1 = 4x_2 - 4$$

Substituting the value of x_1 into the second equation gives

$$4(4x_2 - 4) - 2x_2 - 2 = 0$$

$$16x_2 - 16 - 2x_2 - 2 = 0$$

$$14x_2 = 18$$

$$x_2 = \tfrac{9}{7}$$

$$x_1 = 4(\tfrac{9}{7}) - 4 = \tfrac{8}{7}$$

Thus a necessary condition for the maximization of profit is that $\tfrac{8}{7}$ units of the first input be used together with $\tfrac{9}{7}$ units of the second input. This combination of inputs will produce

$$q = 8(\tfrac{8}{7})(\tfrac{9}{7}) - \tfrac{64}{49} - \tfrac{162}{49} = \tfrac{350}{49} = \tfrac{50}{7} \text{ units of output}$$

For this level of output, we find

$$TR = pq = \tfrac{1}{2}(\tfrac{50}{7}) = \tfrac{25}{7}$$

$$C = 4(\tfrac{8}{7}) + 2(\tfrac{9}{7}) + 5 = \tfrac{85}{7}$$

$$\pi = TR - C = \tfrac{25}{7} - \tfrac{85}{7} = -\tfrac{60}{7} = -\$8.57$$

A negative value for π indicates that losses will, in fact, be realized. It is still possible for this to be a maximum point on the interior of the profit function, provided that the second-order conditions are satisfied. Such an event would imply simply that for every other utilization of inputs (aside from the boundary points), the level of profit would be even lower; that is, greater losses would ensue. Subsequently, boundary points would have to be checked to see if the profit position is any better at such values.

Let us therefore check the second-order conditions. We find

$$\pi_{x_1} = \frac{\partial \pi}{\partial x_1} = 4x_2 - x_1 - 4 \qquad \pi_{x_2} = 4_{x_1} - 2x_2 - 2$$

$$\pi_{x_1 x_1} = -1 \qquad \pi_{x_1 x_2} = 4 \qquad \pi_{x_2 x_2} = -2$$

At $x_1 = \frac{8}{7}$, $x_2 = \frac{9}{7}$, we have

$$\pi_{x_1 x_1} < 0$$

but

$$\pi_{x_1 x_1} \pi_{x_2 x_2} - (\pi_{x_1 x_2})^2 < 0$$

The latter inequality fails to satisfy the second-order conditions. Therefore the point $x_1 = \frac{8}{7}$, $x_2 = \frac{9}{7}$ is not, in fact, a maximum point on the interior of the function. Because there are no interior maximum points, we conclude that the profit function becomes progressively larger and larger or smaller and smaller. In either case, one of the boundary values will give us the maximum profit position.

The boundaries of our function are given by $x_1 = 0$, $x_2 = 0$, and $x_1 = 10$. The first two boundaries exclude, for obvious reasons, negative values for input use. The last boundary, $x_1 = 10$ indicates that this particular firm is subject to an upper limit on the utilization of one of its inputs.

It is clear from a quick examination of the profit function that if either $x_1 = 0$ or $x_2 = 0$, profit will be negative.

Let us consider the remaining boundary, $x_1 = 10$. If $x_1 = 10$, we find

$$\pi = 40x_2 - 50 - x_2^2 - 40 - 2x_2 - 5$$

$$= 38x_2 - x_2^2 - 95$$

Maximizing this function with respect to x_2 yields

$$\frac{d\pi}{dx_2} = 38 - 2x_2 = 0$$

$$2x_2 = 38$$

$$x_2 = 19$$

and

$$\frac{d^2\pi}{dx_2} = -2 < 0$$

so that $x_2 = 19$ does maximize the profit function, assuming that $x_1 = 10$. At the point $x_1 = 10$, $x_2 = 19$, we find

$$\pi = 38(19) - (19)^2 - 95 = 266$$

We conclude that profits are maximized by utilizing 10 units of the first input and 19 units of the second input to produce an output of

$$q = 8(10)(19) - (10)^2 - 2(19)^2 = 698 \text{ units}$$

Exercises

Find the profit maximization output for a firm whose production function, cost information, and product price are given below. In each case, unless otherwise stated, x_1, x_2, and $q > 0$.

1. $q = \ln x_1 + 2 \ln x_2$; $C = 3x_1 + 2x_2 + 5$; where x_1 and $x_2 \geqslant 1$ and $p = 6$

2. $q = x_1^{1/2} + x_2^{1/2}$, where only positive square roots are to be taken; $C = 4x_1 + x_2 + 100$ and $p = 32$

3. $q = 10 - \dfrac{1}{x_1} - \dfrac{1}{x_2}$; $C = x_1 + 4x_2 + 20$;

    where x_1 and $x_2 > 0$ and $p = 9$

4. $q = 100x_1 x_2 - 5x_1^2 - 10x_2^2$; $C = 20x_1 + 10x_2 + 200$; where

    $x_1 \geqslant 0, 0 \leqslant x_2 < 5$, and $p = \$1$

5. $q = 100 \ln x_1 + 100 \ln x_2$; $C = 5x_1 + 2x_2 + 50$; where x_1 and $x_2 \geqslant 1$ and $p = \$0.25$

6. $q = 100 \ln x_1 + 100 \ln x_2$; $C = 5x_1 + 2x_2 + 100$; where x_1 and $x_2 \geqslant 1$ and $p = \$0.25$

7. $q = 8x_1^2 + 4x_2^2$; $C = 4x_1 + 8x_2 + 150$; where $p = \$2$

8. $q = \ln x_1 + \ln x_2 + \ln x_3$; $C = 2x_1 + 5x_2 + x_3 + 2$; where $x_1, x_2,$ and $x_3 \geqslant 1$ and $p = \$10$

SECTION 13·4   PROFIT MAXIMIZATION:
COST FUNCTION APPROACH

An alternative, but equivalent, approach to finding the profit maximization output involves the derivation of cost functions. In Section 13·2 we have shown that, given a production function and cost equation, we can derive an expansion path function. Taking all of these together, we have

$$q = f(x_1, x_2) \qquad \text{production function} \tag{1}$$

$$C = r_1 x_1 + r_2 x_2 + b \qquad \text{cost equation} \tag{2}$$

$$g(x_1, x_2) = 0 \qquad \text{expansion path} \tag{3}$$

Solving equation (3) for x_1 in terms of x_2 and substituting its value into equation (1) enables us to express q in terms of x_2 alone, as $q = j(x_2)$. This, in turn, allows us to express x_2 as a function of q. The process can then be repeated for x_1 so that x_1 can also be expressed as a function of q. The values of both x_1 and x_2 (in terms of q) can then be substituted into equation (2), which will then give costs in terms of the single variable q:

$$C = h(q) + b$$

We refer to this last formulation as a *cost function*; that is, costs are expressed as a function of the level of output. This should not be confused with the *cost equation* (2), which expresses costs in terms of the amounts of inputs used.

If we have any cost function

$$C = h(q) + b$$

we can easily find *average costs* (AC):

$$AC = \frac{h(q) + b}{q}$$

that is, average cost per unit is total cost divided by the number of units produced. We also see that a cost function has two components, namely $h(q)$, which we call *variable costs*, and b, which we call *fixed costs*. Variable costs depend upon the number of units, q_1, produced, as illustrated by the increased number of workers or materials that would have to be utilized in order to increase output. But there are also certain fixed costs that are incurred regardless of how many units are produced, as illustrated by the rent that must be paid on a plant irrespective of output levels. Fixed costs therefore appear as a constant, b.

Average variable costs per unit (AVC) can be computed by dividing total variable costs by the number of units produced, which gives

$$AVC = \frac{h(q)}{q}$$

Similarly, *average fixed costs per unit* (AFC) is simply the total fixed costs divided by the number of units, or

$$AFC = \frac{b}{q}$$

It is immediately evident that

$$AC = AVC + AFC$$

We next inquire into the instantaneous rate of change of total costs with respect to changes in output. In other words, what affect will very small changes in output have upon total costs? We recognize that what we seek is the derivative of the cost function with respect to q, which we call *marginal costs* (MC). We have

$$MC = \frac{dC}{dq} = h'(q)$$

Profit can now be expressed as

$$\pi = TR - C$$
$$= pq - h(q) - b$$

What we have achieved is that profit (π) has now been expressed in terms of the single variable q, because the market price p is taken as a constant.

To maximize profits, we set the first derivative of the profit function equal to zero:

$$\frac{d\pi}{dq} = p - h'(q) = 0$$

and we have

$$p = h'(q)$$

which is equivalent to the statement that in order to maximize profits in a competitive market, it is necessary that price be equal to marginal cost.

To ensure that maximum profit is, in fact, attained at a point satisfying the above condition, it is necessary to check the second-order condition. This is

$$\frac{d^2\pi}{dq^2} = -h''(q) < 0$$

which is equivalent to $h''(q) > 0$; that is, marginal cost must be increasing.

Thus, a firm will maximize profits by producing that level of output for which its marginal cost equals market price, provided that at such an output level marginal costs are increasing. If, instead, marginal costs are decreasing, we have, in fact, a minimization of profits.

This clears up a point of possible confusion that arises when graphical analysis is used without the methods of calculus. It is often found that the price line intersects the marginal cost curve in two points:

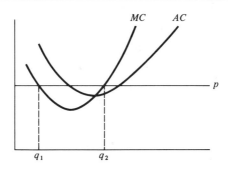

The question then arises as to which point (q_1 or q_2) is the profit-maximizing output. We have just shown that $p = MC$ is only a necessary and not a sufficient condition for profit maximization. Sufficient conditions require both that $p = MC$ and that MC be increasing, which is satisfied only by the point q_2.

Illustration 1.   Derive the cost function and then find the profit maximization output for a firm whose production function is $q = 100 \ln x_1 + 50 \ln x_2$, where x_1 and $x_2 \geqslant 1$ and whose costs are given by $C = 3x_1 + x_2 + 2$. The market price for the product is set at \$4.

Solution.   The information given us is identical to that in Illustration 1 of Section 13·2 and Illustration 1 of Section 13·3. Here, however, we employ the cost-function approach. In Illustration 1 of Section 13·2, we found the expansion path of the firm to be

$$x_1 = \tfrac{2}{3}x_2$$

Substituting the value of x_1 into the given production function gives

$$q = 100 \ln \tfrac{2}{3}x_2 + 50 \ln x_2$$

and

$$q = 50(2 \ln \tfrac{2}{3}x_2 + \ln x_2)$$

$$\frac{q}{50} = 2 \ln \tfrac{2}{3}x_2 + \ln x_2$$

which by the rules for operations with logarithms becomes

$$\frac{q}{50} = \ln(\tfrac{2}{3}x_2)^2 + \ln x_2$$

$$= \ln(\tfrac{2}{3}x_2)^2 x_2$$

$$= \ln \tfrac{4}{9}x_2^3$$

$$= \ln \tfrac{4}{9} + 3 \ln x_2$$

$$= \ln 4 - \ln 9 + 3 \ln x_2$$

$$= 1.3863 - 2.1972 + 3 \ln x_2$$

$$\frac{q}{50} + 0.8109 = 3 \ln x_2$$

$$\ln x_2 = \frac{q}{150} + 0.2703$$

and

$$x_2 = e^{(q/150) + 0.2703} = e^{q/150} e^{0.2703} = 1.31 e^{q/150}$$

Thus x_2 has been expressed in terms of the single variable q. Because $x_1 = \tfrac{2}{3}x_2$, it follows that

$$x_1 = 0.873 e^{q/150}$$

We therefore have values for both x_1 and x_2 in terms of q. These are now substituted into the given cost equation to give

$$C = 2.619 e^{q/150} + 1.31 e^{q/150} + 2$$

and

$$C = 3.929 e^{q/150} + 2$$

This is the cost function of the firm. For any level of output, we can compute the corresponding cost of production.

To find the profit maximization position, we form the profit function, which is

$$\pi = pq - c$$

$$= 4q - 3.929 e^{q/150} - 2$$

We then set the first derivative equal to zero:

$$\frac{d\pi}{dq} = 4 - \frac{3.929}{150} e^{q/150} = 0$$

and

$$e^{q/150} = \frac{600}{3.929} = 152.71$$

$$\frac{q}{150} = \ln 152.71$$

$$= 5.03$$

$$q = 754.50$$

which, except for a small round-off error, is the same output as we found in Illustration 1 of Section 13·3. At this output level, profit = $24? /.

We must, of course, remember that we have, so far, only found the output level that satisfies the first-order conditions. To verify an actual maximum, we check the second-order condition by computing the second derivative:

$$\frac{d^2\pi}{dq^2} = \frac{-3.929}{(150)^2} e^{q/150} < 0$$

The second derivative is clearly negative for our value of q, so we are assured that $q = 754.5$ is a maximum profit position on the interior of the function.

The possibility of a boundary solution still remains. The boundaries of the original production function are given by $x_1 = 1$ and $x_2 = 1$. If $x_1 = 1$, then

$$q = 50 \ln x_2$$

and

$$e^{q/50} = x_2$$

Substituting the values of x_1 and x_2 into the cost equation gives

$$C = 3 + e^{q/50} + 2$$

$$= e^{q/50} + 5$$

Forming the profit function, we have

$$\pi = pq - c = 4q - e^{q/50} - 5$$

Setting the first derivative equal to zero to maximize this function, we get

$$\frac{d\pi}{dq} = 4 - \frac{1}{50} e^{q/150} = 0$$

and

$$e^{q/150} = 200$$

$$\frac{q}{50} = \ln 200 = 5.2983$$

$$q = 264.92$$

at which output we find that $\pi = 854.68$, which is considerably below the profit that would be realized at the interior maximum point. A similar consideration for the other boundary point $(x_2 = 1)$ would show that it, too, would produce a lower profit than for the interior maximum.

We conclude that profit is maximized by producing 754.5 units of output.

Illustration 2.   A firm has derived its cost function to be

$$C = 10q^3 - 35q^2 + 24q + 3 \qquad \text{where } q \geqslant 0$$

The market price for its product is \$4. Find the firm's average cost, average variable cost, marginal cost, and profit-maximizing output.
Solution.

$$AC = \frac{10q^3 - 35q^2 + 24q + 3}{q}$$

$$AVC = \frac{10q^3 - 35q^2 + 24q}{q} = 10q^2 - 35q + 24$$

$$MC = \frac{dC}{dq} = 30q^2 - 70q + 24$$

To find the profit maximization output, we form the profit function, which is

$$\pi = pq - C$$

$$= 4q - 10q^3 + 35q^2 - 24q - 3$$

$$= -10q^3 + 35q^2 - 20q - 3$$

and setting the first derivative equal to zero,

$$\frac{d\pi}{dq} = -30q^2 + 70q - 20 = 0$$

$$30q^2 - 70q + 20 = 0$$

$$10(3q^2 - 7q + 2) = 0$$

$$10(3q - 1)(q - 2) = 0$$

which yields

$q = \frac{1}{3}, q = 2$

We thus have two points that satisfy the first-order conditions for an extremum. To verify whether either point is, in fact, a maximum, we must consider the second-order conditions:

$$\frac{d^2\pi}{dq^2} = -60q + 70$$

At $q = \frac{1}{3}$,

$$\frac{d^2\pi}{dq^2} = 50 > 0$$

Therefore this point is, in reality, a minimum profit position.

At $q = 2$,

$$\frac{d^2\pi}{dq^2} = -50 < 0$$

Therefore this point does maximize the profit function. With an output of 2 units, profit is

$\pi = -10(8) + 35(4) - 20(2) - 3 = \$17$

The possibility of a boundary solution can be quickly dismissed, because at the point $q = 0$, profits would actually be negative.

We therefore conclude that the firm should produce 2 units if it desires to maximize profits.

Exercises

Derive the cost function and then find the profit maximization output for a firm whose production function, cost information, and product price are given in Exercises 1–5. In each case, unless otherwise stated, x_1, x_2, and $q \geqslant 0$.

1. $q = \ln x_1 + 2 \ln x_2$; $C = 3x_1 + 2x_2 + 5$; where x_1 and $x_2 \geqslant 1$ and $p = 6$.

2. $q = x_1^{1/2} + x_2^{1/2}$, where only positive square roots are to be taken; $C = 4x_1 + x_2 + 100$; and $p = 32$.

3. $q = 10 - \dfrac{1}{x_1} - \dfrac{1}{x_2}$; $C = x_1 + 4x_2 + 20$;

    where x_1 and $x_2 > 0$ and $p = 9$.

4. $q = 100 \ln x_1 + 100 \ln x_2$; $C = 5x_1 + 2x_2 + 50$; where x_1 and $x_2 \geqslant 1$ and $p = \frac{1}{4}$.

5. $q = \ln x_1 + \ln x_2 + \ln x_3$; $C = 2x_1 + 5x_2 + x_3 + 2$; where x_1, x_2, and $x_3 \geqslant 1$ and $p = 10$.

For each of the cost functions and product prices given in Exercises 6–8, find the firm's average cost, average variable cost, marginal cost, profit-maximizing output, and profit earned. In each case $q \geqslant 0$.

6. $C = 24q - 9q^2 + q^3 + 5$; $p = 9$
7. $C = 50q - 8q^2 + q^4 + 10$, $p = 50$
8. $C = 80q - 18q^2 + q^3 + 100$, $p = 20$
9. Prove that marginal cost is equal to average cost at the minimum average cost point. (*Hint:* Consider the general form of the average cost function, i.e.,

$$AC = \frac{h(q) + b}{q}$$

Minimize this function by setting its derivative equal to zero and then rearrange terms to show the equality of AC and MC.
10. For the cost function in Exercise 6, show that at the minimum point of AC, $MC = AC$.
11. For the cost function in Exercise 7, show that at the minimum point of AC, $MC = AC$.
12. For the cost function in Exercise 8, show that at the minimum point of AC, $MC = AC$.

SECTION 13·5   COST FUNCTIONS AND PROFIT MAXIMIZATION IN THE LONG RUN

The cost functions we have considered until this point have all applied to the *short run,* that is, a period of time where some inputs are fixed and some variable. It is for this reason that these functions have appeared in the form

$$C = h(q) + b$$

The constant b represents the fixed costs that are incurred regardless of the level of output. This is illustrated by a firm that has a plant of fixed size, but within that plant can vary the other inputs it uses. The $h(q)$ then represents the cost of all the varying inputs, while b is the fixed cost of the plant.

The *long run* is a period of time where all inputs are variable. Thus, pursuing the illustration of the previous paragraph, the firm's contractual commitment to a certain plant will eventually expire. When this happens, the firm is free to consider anew all the different possible plant sizes. Assume that K represents the plant size; that is, the greater the value of K, the greater the plant size. K is known as a *parameter*, by which is meant an unspecified constant. The moment K is given a specified value, plant size is fixed and the firm is operating in the short run. But as long as K can vary—and we assume it can take on all continuous values—the firm is making long-run decisions. Under these circumstances, costs will depend not only upon the quantity produced (q), but also upon the plant size (K) selected to produce the particular output.

To illustrate, consider a firm whose costs are given by

$$C = 10q^2 + 2q - Kq + 5K^2 \qquad \text{where } q, K \geqslant 0$$

Note that if we assign any positive value to K, we have the exact form of the short-run cost functions we considered in the previous section. But because K may take on any positive value, the above expression is really a *family* of cost functions, that is, many cost functions (one for each value of K), but all of the same form. While it is true that any particular output level can be produced in different plant sizes, there will, in fact, be an optimal plant size for each output level. This optimal plant size will be the one that yields the output at least cost. Thus, for every particular level of production in the long run, the firm should choose a specific plant size that will put it on a particular short-run cost function. But as it contemplates changes in this long-run output, the optimum plant size and hence the relevant short-run cost function will change.

The upshot of all of this is that the firm's long-run cost function will be made up of many points, each of which coincides with a different short-run cost function. We say that the long-run cost is the *envelope* of all the short-run cost functions. In general, a function or curve C is the envelope of a family of functions or curves if it coincides or is tangent at each of its points to a different member of the family.

If a family of functions is known, then any envelope function that may exist can be found by expressing the family in implicit form and then setting its partial derivative with respect to the parameter equal to zero. Thus, in our illustration above, we had a family of short-run cost functions that, expressed in implicit form, becomes

$$C - 10q^2 - 2q + Kq - 5K^2 = 0$$

Differentiating partially with respect to the parameter K gives us

$$q - 10K = 0$$

$$K = \frac{q}{10}$$

This gives us a relationship between output (q) and optimum plant size, K. Substituting this value of K into the family of cost functions gives

$$C = 10q^2 + 2q - \frac{q^2}{10} + \frac{5q^2}{100}$$

and

$$C = \tfrac{199}{20}q^2 + 2q$$

which is then the *long-run cost function* of the firm, assuming that any output will be produced in the optimum way.

Suppose now that the market price for the firm's product is $22, which can be expected to remain fixed over a long period of time. The firm can determine how much to produce and what plant size to use by maximizing its long-run profit function. For the illustration above, we have

$$\pi = TR - TC$$

$$= pq - C$$

$$= 22q - \tfrac{199}{20}q^2 - 2q$$

$$= 20q - \tfrac{199}{20}q^2$$

Setting the first derivative equal to zero gives

$$\frac{d\pi}{dq} = 20 - 19.9q = 0$$

$$19.9q = 20$$

$$q = \tfrac{20}{19.9} = 1.01$$

We then check the second-order conditions to ensure that this is a maximum profit point. We get

$$\frac{d^2\pi}{dq^2} = -19.9 < 0$$

The second derivative is negative, so the point $q = 1.01$ is, indeed, a maximum point. At this point the level of profit is

$$\pi = 20(1.01) - \tfrac{199}{20}(1.01)^2 = \$10.05$$

The optimum plant size is

$$K = \frac{1.01}{10} = 0.101$$

Any possibility of a boundary solution can be dismissed, because at $q = 0$, profit is zero.

Exercises

For each of the families of cost functions and product prices given below, find the long-run cost function, the long-run average cost function, the long-run marginal cost function, and the long-run profit-maximizing output and size of plant. In each case, q and $K \geqslant 0$.

1. $C = q^3 - 9q^2 + 20q - Kq + 2K^2$; $p = 20$
2. $C = \frac{1}{2}q^4 - 8q^2 + 50q - Kq + \frac{1}{4}K^2$; $p = 50$
3. $C = 6q^2 + 8q - Kq + \frac{1}{8}K^2$; $p = 32$

SECTION 13·6 THE MULTIPLE-PLANT FIRM

We have until this point assumed that the firm produces its product in a single plant. We now turn to the possibility that the firm may have two or more plants with different costs of production in each. Under these circumstances, the firm must decide how much of its output to produce in each plant.

Let q_1 denote the quantity of the product produced in plant 1 and q_2 the quantity produced in plant 2. Total output is then $q = q_1 + q_2$. Costs of production vary from plant to plant, so there will be two separate cost functions, which may be denoted by $C_1(q_1)$ and $C_2(q_2)$. Total cost is the sum of the costs in each plant, or $C = C_1(q_1) + C_2(q_2)$. Total revenue is simply the price of the product multiplied by total output, or

$$TR = pq = p(q_1 + q_2) = pq_1 + pq_2$$

The profit function can then be expressed as

$$\pi = TR - C$$
$$= pq_1 + pq_2 - C_1(q_1) - C_2(q_2)$$

A firm desiring to maximize profits would set the first partial derivatives of the profit function equal to zero:

$$\frac{\partial \pi}{\partial q_1} = p - C'_1(q_1) = 0 \quad \text{and} \quad \frac{\partial \pi}{\partial q_2} = p - C'_2(q_2) = 0$$

$$p = C'_1(q_1) \qquad\qquad\qquad p = C'_2(q_2)$$

or

$$p = C'_1(q_1) = C'_2(q_2)$$

This is equivalent to the statement that in order to maximize profits in a competitive market, a two-plant firm must equate price to the marginal cost in each separate plant.

To ensure that maximum profit is, in fact, attained at a point satisfying the above condition, it is necessary to check the second-order conditions. These are

$$\pi_{q_1 q_1} < 0 \tag{1}$$

$$\pi_{q_1 q_1} \pi_{q_2 q_2} - (\pi_{q_1 q_2})^2 > 0 \tag{2}$$

We find that

$$\pi_{q_1 q_1} = -C''_1(q_1)$$

$$\pi_{q_1 q_2} = 0$$

$$\pi_{q_2 q_2} = -C''_2(q_2)$$

The sufficient conditions are therefore equivalent to

$$-C''_1(q_1) < 0 \tag{1}$$

or $C''_1(q_1) > 0$, that is, marginal cost in plant 1 must be increasing, and

$$C''_1(q_1)C''_2(q_2) > 0 \tag{2}$$

Because $C''_1(q_1) > 0$ by condition (1), $C''_2(q_2)$ must also be > 0, thus implying that the marginal cost in both plants must be increasing.

This analysis can, in like manner, be extended to a firm with any number of plants. In this regard, see Exercise 7 at the end of this section.

Illustration.   A firm has the following cost functions for its two plants:

$$C_1 = 20q_1^3 - 24q_1 + 5 \qquad C_2 = 27q_2^2 + 10$$

where q_1 and $q_2 \geqslant 0$. The market price for its product is \$216. Find the firm's profit-maximizing output and the amount it will produce in each plant.

Solution.   The profit function can be expressed as

$$\pi = TR - C$$
$$= pq_1 + pq_2 - C_1(q_1) - C_2(q_2)$$

which in our case becomes

$$\pi = 216q_1 + 216q_2 - 20q_1^3 + 24q_1 - 5 - 27q_2^2 - 10$$
$$= 240q_1 + 216q_2 - 20q_1^3 - 27q_2^2 - 15$$

Setting the first partials equal to zero gives

$$\frac{\partial \pi}{\partial q_1} = 240 - 60q_1^2 = 0 \qquad\qquad \frac{\partial \pi}{\partial q_2} = 216 - 54q_2 = 0$$

$$60q_1^2 = 240 \qquad\qquad 54q_2 = 216$$

$$q_1^2 = 4 \qquad\qquad q_2 = 4$$

$$q_1 = 2$$

When $q_1 = 2$ and $q_2 = 4$, we find that $\pi = 737$.
   To check second-order conditions, we find

$$\pi_{q_1 q_1} = -120q_1 \qquad \pi_{q_1 q_2} = 0 \qquad \pi_{q_2 q_2} = -54$$

At $q_1 = 2$, $q_2 = 4$, we have

$$\pi_{q_1 q_1} < 0$$

and

$$\pi_{q_1 q_1}\pi_{q_2 q_2} - (\pi_{q_1 q_2})^2 > 0$$

Therefore the sufficient conditions for a relative maximum are satisfied at $q_1 = 2$, $q_2 = 4$.
   To investigate the possibility of boundary solutions, we consider first the boundary $q_1 = 0$, that is, all production should take place in the second plant. We get

$$\pi = 216q_2 - 27q_2^2 - 15$$

Maximizing this function by setting its derivative equal to zero gives

$$\frac{d\pi}{dq_2} = 216 - 54q_2 = 0$$

$$54q_2 = 216$$

$$q_2 = 4$$

for which $\pi = 417$, which is a lower profit than for $q_1 = 2$, $q_2 = 4$.

The other boundary is $q_2 = 0$, for which we get

$$\pi = 240q_1 - 20q_1^3 - 15$$

Maximizing this function gives

$$\frac{d\pi}{dq_1} = 240 - 60q_1^2 = 0$$

$$60q_1^2 = 240$$

$$q_1^2 = 4$$

$$q_1 = 2$$

for which $\pi = 305$, which is again a lower profit than for $q_1 = 2, q_2 = 4$.

We therefore conclude that the profit-maximizing output is $q = q_1 + q_2 = 2 + 4 = 6$ units. Two of these units will be produced in the first plant and 4 units in the second plant, and \$737 will be earned in profits.

Exercises

In each of the following cases, find the firm's profit-maximizing output and the amount that will be produced in each plant.

1. The firm's cost functions for its two plants are

    $C_1 = 2q_1^3 - 8q_1 + 20 \qquad C_2 = 12q_2^3 - 12q_2 + 25$
    where q_1 and $q_2 \geqslant 0$

    The market price for the product is \$88.

2. The firm's cost functions for its two plants are

    $C_1 = 18q_1^2 - 20q_1 + 40 \qquad C_2 = 2q_2^3 - 10q_2 + 10$
    where q_1 and $q_2 > 0$

    The market price for the product is \$44.

3. The firm's cost functions for its two plants are

    $C_1 = 6q_1^2 - 8q_1 + 50 \qquad C_2 = 4q_2^2 - 4q_2 + 15$
    where q_1 and $q_2 \geqslant 0$

    The market price for the product is \$52.

4. The firm's cost functions for its two plants are

    $C_1 = q_1^3 - 2q_1 + 18 \qquad C_2 = 10q_2^2 - 5q_2 + 36$
    where q_1 and $q_2 \geqslant 0$

    The market price for the product is \$145.

5. The firm's cost functions for its two plants are

$C_1 = \frac{1}{2}q_1^4 - 3q_1 + 16 \qquad C_2 = 5q_2^2 - 7q_2 + 9$
where q_1 and $q_2 \geqslant 0$

The market price for the product is $13.

6. The firm's cost functions for its three plants are

$C_1 = 10q_1^2 - 2q_1 + 25 \qquad C_2 = 3q_2^2 - 4q_2 + 8, \qquad C_3 = 5q_3^2 + 40$
where q_1, q_2, and $q_3 \geqslant 0$

The market price for the product is $98.

7. Prove that a firm with n plants in a competitive market must equate price to the marginal cost in each separate plant if it is to maximize profits.

SECTION 13·7 THE MULTIPLE-PRODUCT FIRM

In all previous sections we have dealt with firms that produce only one product. We now consider the case of a firm that produces two or more products. Such instances are fairly common even in purely competitive markets. Consider, for example, a farmer who grows several crops on a fixed acreage of land. In this and similar situations, decisions must be made as to how much of each product to produce.

For simplicity, we shall deal with the case of a firm that produces two products, A and B. The results can, without difficulty, be extended to any number of products. Let q_A denote the quantity of product A, q_B the quantity of product B, p_A the market price of product A, and p_B the market price of product B. Total revenue is then $TR = p_A q_A + p_B q_B$. Costs of production are some function of the amounts of A and B produced, or $C = C(q_A, q_B)$.

The profit function can then be expressed as

$\pi = TR - C$

$= p_A q_A + p_B q_B - C(q_A, q_B)$

To find the profit-maximizing outputs, we set the first partial derivatives of the profit function equal to zero:

$$\frac{\partial \pi}{\partial q_A} = p_A - \frac{\partial C}{\partial q_A} = 0 \qquad \frac{\partial \pi}{\partial q_B} = p_B - \frac{\partial C}{\partial q_B} = 0$$

$$p_A = \frac{\partial C}{\partial q_A} \qquad\qquad p_B = \frac{\partial C}{\partial q_B}$$

which is equivalent to the statement that in order to maximize profits in a competitive market, a two-product firm must equate the market price of each product to the marginal cost of that product.

To ensure that maximum profit is, in fact, attained at a point satisfying the above conditions, it is necessary to check the second-order conditions. These are

$$\pi_{q_A q_A} < 0 \tag{1}$$

and

$$\pi_{q_A q_A} \pi_{q_B q_B} - \left(\pi_{q_A q_B}\right)^2 > 0 \tag{2}$$

We find that

$$\pi_{q_A q_A} = -\frac{\partial^2 C}{\partial q_A^2}$$

$$\pi_{q_A q_B} = -\frac{\partial^2 C}{\partial q_A \, \partial q_B}$$

$$\pi_{q_B q_B} = -\frac{\partial^2 C}{\partial q_B^2}$$

The sufficient conditions are therefore equivalent to

$$-\frac{\partial^2 C}{\partial q_A^2} < 0 \tag{1}$$

or

$$\frac{\partial^2 C}{\partial q_A^2} > 0$$

that is, the marginal cost of product A must be increasing, and

$$\frac{\partial^2 C}{\partial q_A^2} \frac{\partial^2 C}{\partial q_B^2} - \left(\frac{\partial^2 C}{\partial q_A \, \partial q_B}\right)^2 > 0 \tag{2}$$

Because

$$\frac{\partial^2 C}{\partial q_A^2} > 0$$

by condition (1),

$$\frac{\partial^2 C}{\partial q_B^2} > 0$$

if the expression is to be positive. This implies that the marginal cost of both products must be increasing. In addition,

$$\frac{\partial^2 C}{\partial q_A^2} \frac{\partial^2 C}{\partial q_B^2}$$

must be greater than

$$\left(\frac{\partial^2 C}{\partial q_A \, \partial q_B} \right)^2$$

in order to satisfy the sufficient conditions for maximum profit.

In some cases it may happen that

$$\frac{\partial^2 C}{\partial q_A \, \partial q_B} = 0$$

This indicates that the two products, A and B, are technically unrelated in production, that is, the level of output of A does not affect the marginal costs of producing B and vice versa. However, in many cases the products are, in fact, technically related in production, so that the mixed partial derivative of the cost function does not vanish.

This analysis can, in like manner, be extended to a firm producing any number of products. In this regard see Exercise 7 at the end of this section.

Illustration.   A two-product firm has the following cost function:

$$C = \tfrac{1}{2} q_A^2 - q_A + q_A q_B + q_B^2 - 4q_B \qquad \text{where } q_A \text{ and } q_B \geqslant 0$$

The market prices for A and B are \$30 and \$50, respectively. Find the firm's profit-maximizing output of each product.

Solution.   The firm's revenue function is

$$TR = p_A q_A + p_B q_B = 30q_A + 50q_B$$

The cost function is given as

$$C = \tfrac{1}{2} q_A^2 - q_A + q_A q_B + q_B^2 - 4q_B$$

The two products are seen to be technically related in production, because

$$\frac{\partial C}{\partial q_A} = q_A - 1 + q_B$$

which indicates that the level of output of B affects the marginal cost of A.

The profit function can be expressed as

$$\pi = TR - C$$

$$= 30q_A + 50q_B - \tfrac{1}{2}q_A^2 + q_A - q_Aq_B - q_B^2 + 4q_B$$

$$= -\tfrac{1}{2}q_A^2 + 31q_A - q_Aq_B - q_B^2 + 54q_B$$

Setting the first partials equal to zero yields

$$\frac{\partial \pi}{\partial q_A} = -q_A + 31 - q_B = 0 \qquad \frac{\partial \pi}{\partial q_B} = -q_A - 2q_B + 54 = 0$$

Solving these two equations simultaneously, we have

$$q_A + q_B = 31$$

$$q_A + 2q_B = 54$$

and by subtracting the first equation from the second,

$$q_B = 23$$

$$q_A = 8$$

for which we find $\pi = 745$.

To check second-order conditions, we find

$$\pi_{q_Aq_A} = -1 \qquad \pi_{q_Aq_B} = -1 \qquad \pi_{q_Bq_B} = -2$$

Therefore,

$$\pi_{q_Aq_A} < 0$$

and

$$\pi_{q_Aq_A}\pi_{q_Bq_B} - (\pi_{q_Aq_B})^2 > 0$$

The sufficient conditions for a relative maximum are thus satisfied at $q_A = 8$, $q_B = 23$.

To investigate the possibility of boundary solutions, we consider first the boundary $q_A = 0$; that is, only product B should be produced. We get

$$\pi = -q_B^2 + 54q_B$$

Maximizing this function by setting its derivative equal to zero gives

$$\frac{d\pi}{dq_B} = -2q_B + 54 = 0$$

$$2q_B = 54$$

$$q_B = 27$$

for which $\pi = 729$, which is a lower profit than for $q_A = 8$, $q_B = 23$.

The other boundary is $q_B = 0$; that is, only A should be produced. We get

$$\pi = -\tfrac{1}{2}q_A^2 + 31q_A$$

Maximizing this function gives

$$\frac{d\pi}{dq_A} = -q_A + 31 = 0$$

$$q_A = 31$$

for which $\pi = 480.5$, which is again a lower profit than for $q_A = 8$, $q_B = 23$.

We therefore conclude that the profit-maximizing outputs are $q_A = 8$, $q_B = 23$.

Exercises

In each of the following cases, find the firm's profit-maximizing output of each product. Also indicate whether the products are technically related in production.

1. The firm's cost function for its two products is

    $$C = q_A^2 + 2q_A q_B + 5q_B^2 + 5 \qquad \text{where } q_A \text{ and } q_B > 0$$

    The market prices for A and B are \$12 and \$36, respectively.

2. The firm's cost function for its two products is

    $$C = 3q_A^2 - 4q_A + 3q_A q_B + 6q_B^2 + 10 \qquad \text{where } q_A \text{ and } q_B \geqslant 0$$

    The market prices for A and B are \$12 and \$50, respectively.

3. The firm's cost function for its two products is

    $$C = 12q_A^2 - 3q_A + 4q_A q_B + 2q_B^2 - q_B \qquad \text{where } q_A \text{ and } q_B \geqslant 0$$

    The market prices for A and B are \$200 and \$102, respectively.

4. The firm's cost function for its two products is

    $$C = 4q_A^2 - 5q_A + 8q_B^2 - 3q_B + 17 \qquad \text{where } q_A \text{ and } q_B \geqslant 0$$

    The market prices for A and B are \$43 and \$45, respectively.

5. The firm's cost function for its two products is

    $$C = 2q_A^3 - 6q_A + 3q_B^3 - 4q_B \qquad \text{where } q_A \text{ and } q_B \geqslant 0$$

    The market prices for A and B are \$48 and \$32, respectively.

6.   The firm's cost function for its three products is

$$C = 5q_A^2 - q_A + q_B^2 - 2q_B + 2q_D^2 \qquad \text{where } q_A, q_B, \text{ and } q_D \geqslant 0$$

The market prices for A, B, and D are \$19, \$12, and \$36, respectively.

7.   Prove that a firm with n products in competitive markets must equate the market price of each product to the marginal cost of that product if it is to maximize profits.

SECTION 13·8   THE PROFIT MAXIMIZATION HYPOTHESIS

Caution: The analysis presented in the preceding sections of this chapter is predicated upon the assumption that the central objective of any firm is to maximize profits. This assumption has, however, come in for its share of criticism over the years. There are those who point to the myriad of other motives that often govern business behavior, such as the desire to be large and wield power, the desire to be socially responsive, the desire for security, the often-encountered feelings of complacency on the part of some and aggressive hostility by others. To the extent that these other motives and drives operate, decisions may be made that could, in fact, be inimical to attaining maximum profits. Thus a firm may expand beyond the optimum profit-maximizing level, or it may shy away from certain policies because of its social consciousness, or it may not take full advantage of its economic opportunities because of timidity or out of fear of becoming involved in an economic war with other enterprises. Moreover, those managing firms may, upon occasion, be negligent, thoughtless, blindly repetitive, or even irrational. Even if firms are intent on maximizing profits, it is doubtful that they are able to obtain the mass of intricate and detailed information necessary to achieve that objective.

Those who employ the assumption of profit maximization are not oblivious to the other possible motives mentioned in the preceding paragraph. They insist, however, that the motive of profit maximization, while not perfectly or universally realistic, is a sufficiently good approximation of business behavior so that meaningful and relevant conclusions may be derived therefrom. It is true that any one particular firm may deviate considerably from the rational profit-maximizing model. Nevertheless, it is claimed that profit maximization is still the overriding factor governing the actions of the vast majority of firms.

It should then be understood that the basic justification for employing the profit maximization hypothesis rests on there being present a large number of firms, so that even if some firms deviate from the assumption, the overall market effects will be left intact. This implies that a more realistic theory — even if more complex — may be required where there are only a few large firms in the industry and where there is not much competitive rivalry between these firms. Unfortunately, the attempts that have been made to develop alternative models of economic behavior have not been highly successful. In dealing with monopolistic and oligopolistic markets in the next chapter, we introduce the traditional profit maximization model, which should be viewed only as a starting point for the analysis of such markets. In some cases, the results achieved will be tolerably close to reality. But in applying these results, great care should be exercised to see whether the model is really relevant.

Exercises

1. Assume that you are in the process of opening a business of your choice. By introspection, try to determine what your primary objective would be at the outset and ten years later. Then make a guess as to what you think will be the major objectives of your classmates and whether you expect them to answer realistically. Finally, compare answers.
2. Would your answers to the preceding exercise vary according to the type or nature of business being considered?

SECTION 13·9   PRODUCTION FUNCTIONS FOR AN ENTIRE INDUSTRY OR ECONOMY

We have dealt extensively with production functions in previous sections of this chapter. In each case we were referring to a particular firm and its production possibilities. This concept can easily be extended so that we can talk about the production function of an industry or even of the economy as a whole. The former indicates the production capabilities of an entire industry; that is, industry-wide output will be some function of the various inputs utilized by all firms. The latter portrays the production capabilities of the entire economy; that is, total aggregate output will be a function of the various inputs utilized throughout the economy.

One of the most often used production functions for these purposes is known as the *Cobb-Douglas* production function, named for Senator Paul Douglas and C. W. Cobb, who first suggested its use. In its original formulation, it was applied to all manufacturing output in the United States and was given by

$$Q = AL^{\alpha}C^{1-\alpha}$$

where Q is total manufacturing output, L is the amount of labor used, C is the amount of capital used, A is some positive constant, and $0 < \alpha < 1$.

It is easy to verify that this is a homogeneous function. In Section 10.8 we showed that in order to determine whether or not a function is homogeneous, we multiply each of the independent variables by a constant t and observe the effect upon the function. Applying this procedure for the Cobb-Douglas function, we get

$$f(tL, tC) = A(tL)^{\alpha}(tC)^{1-\alpha} = At^{\alpha}L^{\alpha}t^{1-\alpha}C^{1-\alpha}$$

$$= tAL^{\alpha}C^{1-\alpha} = tf(L, C)$$

Thus the resulting function is t times the original function. As explained in Section 10.8, this means that the Cobb-Douglas function is homogeneous of degree 1, which implies that if both labor and capital are doubled, for example, then total product will also double.

We can also compute the marginal product of labor from the Cobb-Douglas function,

$$MP_L = \frac{\partial Q}{\partial L} = A\alpha L^{\alpha-1}C^{1-\alpha}$$

Let us now multiply each of the independent variables by a constant t and see the resulting effect upon marginal product. We have

$$f_L(tL, tC) = A\alpha(tL)^{\alpha-1}(tC)^{1-\alpha} = A\alpha t^0 L^{\alpha-1}C^{1-\alpha}$$

$$= t^0 f_L(L, C)$$

The marginal product of labor function is thus homogeneous of degree 0. This implies that if labor and capital are doubled, the marginal product of labor will remain unchanged.

A similar situation applies to the marginal product of capital, which we compute to be

$$MP_C = \frac{\partial Q}{\partial C} = A(1 - \alpha)L^{\alpha}C^{-\alpha}$$

Multiplying each independent variable by t gives us

$$f_C(tL, tC) = A(1 - \alpha)(tL)^{\alpha}(tC)^{-\alpha} = A(1 - \alpha)t^0 L^{\alpha}C^{-\alpha}$$

$$= t^0 f_C(L, C)$$

The marginal product of capital function is also homogeneous of degree 0, which implies that doubling labor and capital will leave the marginal product of capital unchanged.

In general, we can state that a production function that is linearly homogeneous, that is, homogeneous of degree 1, implies constant returns to scale. When all inputs are increased by the same percentage, total output is increased by the very same percentage. The Cobb-Douglas function thus implies constant returns to scale. On the other hand, a production function that is homogeneous of degree greater than 1 implies increasing returns to scale. When all inputs are increased by some percentage, total output is increased by a greater percentage. Finally, a production function that is homogeneous of degree less than 1 exhibits decreasing returns to scale. When all inputs are increased by some percentage, total output is increased, but only by a smaller percentage.

It should be noted that returns to scale have nothing to do with diminishing returns, which was discussed in Section 13.1. The latter applies only to a situation where some inputs are varied while others are held fixed. The former, on the other hand, refers to a situation where all inputs are varied by some percentage. Thus it is entirely consistent to encounter diminishing returns in the short run and constant or even increasing returns to scale in the long run when all inputs can be varied.

This can be illustrated by the Cobb-Douglas function, which we have already shown exhibits constant returns to scale. Yet we can show that diminishing returns is also present. We have already computed the marginal product of labor to be

$$MP_L = \frac{\partial Q}{\partial L} = A\alpha L^{\alpha-1}C^{1-\alpha}$$

Let us now find the second partial derivative of the production function with respect to L. We have

$$\frac{\partial^2 Q}{\partial L^2} = A\alpha(\alpha - 1)L^{\alpha-2}C^{1-\alpha}$$

Now $\alpha - 1$ is negative, because $0 < \alpha < 1$, while all other terms are positive. Therefore

$$\frac{\partial^2 Q}{\partial L^2} < 0$$

As shown in Section 13.1, this implies diminishing returns.

We shall now apply Euler's theorem, as discussed in Section 10.8, to the Cobb-Douglas production function, $Q = f(L, C)$. The theorem asserts that

$$L\frac{\partial Q}{\partial L} + C\frac{\partial Q}{\partial C} = Kf(L, C)$$

where K is the degree of homogeneity. Because we have already established that the Cobb-Douglas function is homogeneous of degree 1, this translates into

$$L \frac{\partial Q}{\partial L} + C \frac{\partial Q}{\partial C} = f(L, C)$$

Now L is the amount of labor utilized, and $\partial Q/\partial L$ is the marginal product of a unit of labor. Similarly, C is the amount of capital utilized, and $\partial Q/\partial C$ is the marginal product of a unit of capital. Euler's theorem, as applied to the Cobb-Douglas function, therefore implies that if each unit of labor and capital is paid its marginal product, the total product $f(L, C)$ is exhausted. This means that nothing is left over in the form of a surplus or, equivalently, that long-term profits are zero. This should not be taken to mean that those owning and/or managing the firm will not be rewarded. Their return arises as a return to their labor and/or capital contributed to the firm.

In Section 13.3, we showed that a necessary condition for profit maximization is that

$$r_i = p \frac{\partial f}{\partial x_i}$$

or that any input is paid the equivalent of its marginal productivity in money terms, that is, $p(\partial f/\partial x_i)$ is the money value of the input's marginal product. Thus, if the Cobb-Douglas function is the relevant production function, then payments to the inputs would, indeed, be just enough to exhaust the total product. This result is sometimes referred to as the *adding-up theorem*.

Caution: Production Functions and Reality

In dealing with production functions, one must be wary of oversimplification and the temptation to generalize results that apply only in special circumstances. The adding-up theorem, which follows as a logical consequence from the Cobb-Douglas production function, has frequently been accepted as generally true. However, if the production function is altered somewhat so that, for example, it is not linearly homogeneous or in some other manner, the results could be vastly different.

Illustration.   Given the following aggregate production function:

$$Q = 2L^{0.60}C^{0.20}$$

Is this function homogeneous and, if so, of what degree? What type of returns to scale are present? What percentage of total product will be available as a surplus after labor and capital are paid their shares?

Solution.

$$f(tL, tC) = 2(tL)^{0.60}(tC)^{0.20} = 2t^{0.80}L^{0.60}C^{0.20}$$

$$= t^{0.80}f(L, C)$$

The function is therefore homogeneous of degree 0.80. The degree of homogeneity is less than 1, so we can conclude that decreasing returns to scale are present; that is, if labor and capital are each increased by 10 percent, total product increases by only 8 percent.

Euler's theorem, as applied to this function, states that

$$L\frac{\partial Q}{\partial L} + C\frac{\partial Q}{\partial C} = 0.8Q$$

If labor and capital are each paid their respective marginal products, then only 80 percent of the total product is exhausted, leaving a surplus of 20 percent of the product as a profit return.

In the event that the production function is homogeneous of degree greater than one, it will be found that if each input is paid its marginal product, the aggregate payments will more than exhaust total product. As an example, see Exercise 1 at the end of this section. Such a situation cannot, of course, be maintained. The result is that inputs will not be paid their marginal products. There will, in effect, be a tug of war between owners of the various inputs, with those inputs possessing the greater market power gaining at the expense of the others. Such market power can, for example, arise from union organization, which may strengthen the labor input, or from the emergence of some monopsonistic (one-buyer) control over workers, thus weakening the labor share. In either case, the competitive nature of the input market may be destroyed.

Exercises

For each of the following aggregate production functions, determine degree of homogeneity (if homogeneous), what type of returns to scale, what percentage of total product will be available as a surplus if labor and capital are paid their marginal products, and whether the adding-up theorem applies.

1. $Q = 5L^{0.80}C^{0.30}$
2. $Q = 10L^{0.70}C^{0.25}$
3. $Q = 2L^{0.75}C^{0.25}$
4. $Q = 8L^{0.65}C^{0.35} + L$
5. $Q = L^{0.6}C^{0.4} + L^2$

SECTION 13·10 NONPHYSICAL PRODUCTION

Caution: The theory of production, cost, and profit, as we have developed it, lends itself most readily to physical output, that is, production of tangible items. Theoretically, these concepts can be extended to the production of intangible services. But what do we mean by the productivity of a doctor? Is it measured by the number of patients he sees per hour, by the kinds of treatment afforded to patients, by the resulting improvement in their health? If by the latter, how is such measurement achieved? We are in a similar dilemma when we consider the productivity of a teacher, a hospital administrator, or an office manager. If a precise definition of productivity escapes us in these cases, then it makes little sense to talk about marginal productivity, returns to scale, or the least-cost method of producing some level of output.

This situation would be but a slight annoyance if production of such services accounted for only a negligible proportion of all productive activity. It becomes a very significant conceptual problem, however, the moment we recognize that nonphysical activities are responsible for approximately half of the gross national product in the United States. Moreover, as time passes, the proportion of economic activity engaged in nonphysical production is increasing.

This is not to say that insights gained from considering the production of physical output are useless when considering nonphysical production. Doubtless, such results can be very suggestive. But a great deal remains to be done in this area if the present theory of the firm is to become a truly general explanation of economic action on the micro level.

Exercises

1. List five productive activities for which it would be difficult to define productivity and related concepts.
2. For each of the items listed in response to Exercise 1, make an attempt to define productivity and its related concepts as best you can.

SECTION 13·11   MARKET EQUILIBRIUM
UNDER PURE COMPETITION

In Chapter 4, we showed that market equilibrium under pure competition occurs at the intersection of market demand and market supply. Such intersection points could be found, for the most part, by simple algebraic methods. The crucial questions of what determines or lies behind market demand and supply were left unanswered. Chapter 12 utilized concepts and methods of the calculus to show how an individual's demand function is derived. Market or overall demand is then merely the algebraic sum of the demand functions of all consumers. Similarly, by using calculus techniques, this chapter has shown how an individual firm determines what output to produce and offer for sale on the market. Essentially, we saw that the firm will continue production until its marginal cost has increased to the point where it is equal to the product price given by the market. In general, for each possible market price there will be a different output level forthcoming from the firm. All of these possible combinations of product prices and the associated output levels comprise the supply function of the firm. Market or overall supply can then be viewed as the algebraic sum of the supply functions of all firms. Setting market demand equal to market supply, then, allows us to find the market price that will prevail in the competitive market.

Illustration.   In Illustration 1 of Section 13.4, we derived the following cost function for a firm: $C = 3.929e^{q/150} + 2$. We now wish to find the supply function of the firm. We know that for any market price, the firm will equate marginal cost and price. Therefore we find the marginal cost function and then set it equal to price:

$$MC = \frac{dC}{dq} = \frac{3.929}{150} e^{q/150}$$

But $MC = p$. Therefore,

$$p = \frac{3.929}{150} e^{q/150}$$

$$e^{q/150} = 38.2p$$

$$\frac{q}{150} = \ln(38.2p)$$

$$= \ln 38.2 + \ln p$$

$$= 3.6429 + \ln p$$

$$q_s = 546.44 + 150 \ln p$$

We insert the subscript s under the q symbol because the quantity refers to the number of units that will be supplied by the firm. For any possible price, we have an associated quantity that the firm will offer for sale. It will be noted that, in Illustration 1 of Section 13.4, we considered the profit maximization output for this firm when the product price was set at \$4. We found this to be $q = 754.50$. If we substitute $p = 4$ into our supply function, we get

$$q_s = 546.44 + 150 \ln 4$$

$$= 546.44 + 150(1.3863)$$

$$= 754.39$$

which, except for a round-off error, is the same as we found earlier.

To find the market supply, we would add together the supply functions of all firms. Assume that we have 1000 identical firms in the industry. We then have

$$q_S = 1000(546.44 + 150 \ln p)$$

$$= 546440 + 150{,}000 \ln p$$

where q_S denotes market supply.

Suppose that the demand function of a consumer is given by

$$q_d = 100 - 5 \ln p$$

and there are 10,000 identical consumers. Then

$$q_D = 1{,}000{,}000 - 50{,}000 \ln p$$

where q_D is the market demand.

To find competitive equilibrium, we set

$$q_D = q_S$$

which gives

$$1{,}000{,}000 - 50{,}000 \ln p = 546{,}440 + 150{,}000 \ln p$$

$$200{,}000 \ln p = 453{,}564$$

$$\ln p = 2.2678$$

$$p = 9.66$$

Thus $p = 9.66$ is the equilibrium market price. At that price 886,610 units will be offered for sale on the market and an equivalent amount will be bought by consumers.

We have until this point assumed that costs of production for a firm are a function of its own level of output. On many occasions, however, costs for a firm depend not only upon its own output, but also upon the industry output level. Thus it may be that as an industry expands, costs of training may decline for each individual firm because the government, noting the increasing number of jobs of a certain sort becoming available, may subsidize such training or schools may gear some of their instruction to such opportunities. Alternatively, transportation or finance costs may decline as government or banks become more willing to aid expanding industries. In such cases, we say that *external economies* exist; that is, the firm will benefit from the expansion of the industry. Such economies are external to the firm because they are beyond the control of any one firm. Conversely, it may happen that, as the whole industry expands, costs of production increase for each firm. This could occur if certain specialized inputs are in great demand by the industry, thus raising input prices as the industry expands. Such costs are referred to as *external diseconomies*. Again, any single firm has no control over such increased costs.

In the event that no external effects exist, costs of production for the ith firm can be expressed as a function of its own output level:

$$C_i = f(q_i)$$

The cost functions with which we have dealt have all been of this variety.

However, if external economies or diseconomies exist, costs of production for the ith firm must be expressed as a function of its own output and also of the industry output as well. The function is then of the form

$$C_i = f(q_i, q)$$

where q_i is the output of the ith firm and $q = \sum_{i=1}^{n} q_i$ is the sum of the output of all n firms in the industry. Each firm must make some estimation of expected industry output. Once having made such an estimate, q can be treated as a constant and the firm can proceed to maximize its own profit function. If the estimate of industry output is grossly out of line, the firm may realize unanticipated gains or losses, in which case it must recalculate its profit function and adjust its output level.

Caution: Limitations of Static Analysis

Our analysis has, so far, been of a *static nature*; that is, we have not considered the time it takes for adjustments to be made by either the consumer or the firm, nor have we considered what occurs during the adjustment process. When consideration is given to the time element and how changes occur over time, we are then dealing with *dynamic analysis*.

The analysis is certainly more realistic, because it would be rare for adjustments to be instantaneous. We shall consider dynamic analysis in Chapter 17. Suffice it is to say that even then our statements will be subject to definite limitations.

Exercises

For each of the following, derive the firm's supply function, the market supply function, and the equilibrium market price.

1. The cost function of the firm is $C = 0.99e^{q/3} + 5$; there are 500 identical firms in the industry; the demand function for a consumer is $q_d = 5 - 3 \ln p$; there are 1000 identical consumers.
2. The cost function of the firm is $C = \frac{4}{5}q^2 + 100$; there are 8000 identical firms in the industry; the demand function for a consumer is $q_d = 1000 - 2p$; there are 10,000 identical consumers.
3. The cost function of the firm is $C = 100e^q + 20$; there are 1000 identical firms in the industry; the demand function for a consumer is $q_d = 50 - 19 \ln p$; there are 1000 identical consumers.
4. The cost function of the firm is $C = 10q^2 + 100q + 250$; there are 2000 identical firms in the industry; the demand function for a consumer is $q_d = 20 - \frac{1}{5}p$; there are 5000 identical consumers.

14

MONOPOLY AND OLIGOPOLY EQUILIBRIUM

> There is no reason why theoretical economics should be a monopoly of the reactionaries.
>
> —H. J. Davenport

Our discussions of profit maximization until this point have all assumed purely competitive markets. We wish now to extend our analysis to other market structures. It will become evident that a good deal of our previous work will help us enormously. In many respects all that will be needed is to make adjustments in some of our expressions. This is not, however, to say that the consideration of other market structures is without difficulties.

SECTION 14·1 MONOPOLY AND PROFIT MAXIMIZATION

A *monopolistic* market structure exists whenever there is one seller of a product with no close substitutes. The monopolistic firm is thus the whole industry. This market structure is the opposite extreme of pure competition, where any single firm is too small to influence the market price or even to determine its own price. A monopolist can certainly influence and, in fact, set price. However, consumer demand places sharp restrictions upon what even the monopolist can do.

Suppose that the demand function of all consumers for the product of the monopolist is

$$q_d = f(p)$$

that is, quantity demanded is a function of the price of the product. In virtually all cases, we expect that

$$\frac{dq_d}{dp} < 0$$

that is, as price increases, quantity demanded decreases and vice versa. Assuming that the demand function has an inverse, we can solve for p in terms of q_d, which will give something in the form of

$$p = h(q_d)$$

with

$$\frac{dp}{dq_d} < 0$$

Total revenue is given by $TR = pq$, where q is the quantity sold at a price p (q and q_d are interchangeable in this context). In Section 8·16, we differentiated this expression for TR and found

$$MR = \frac{d(TR)}{dq} = p + q\frac{dp}{dq}$$

Because $dp/dq_d < 0$, $MR < p$. This will generally hold true for all firms other than pure competitors. A monopolist or some other imperfectly competitive firm must reduce market price for all products he wishes to sell in greater amount. The revenue he gains by selling an additional unit is less than the price, because his gain is offset by the lower price he receives for all units. On the other hand, a pure competitor can increase sales indefinitely without reducing the price, because he is too small to influence the market price. As a result, $dp/dq = 0$ and $MR = p$ for a pure competitor.

Total revenue, for a monopolist, can also be expressed as a function of the single variable q. This is achieved by substituting for p its value in terms of q, as indicated by the following:

$$TR = pq$$

$$p = h(q_d)$$

which is, the demand function in inverse form and

$$TR = h(q)q$$

recalling that q_d and q are interchangeable for purposes of this discussion. In concise form, we write this as

$$TR = R(q)$$

that is, total revenue is some function of quantity sold.

The monopolist's cost function can also be expressed as a function of quantity, $C = C(q)$, just as was done for the pure competitor in earlier sections. The derivation of such cost functions is based on production functions and input prices, as we showed earlier.

Profit for a monopolist, as for everyone, is the difference between total revenue and costs:

$$\pi = TR - C$$
$$= R(q) - C(q)$$

This differs from the case of a pure competitor only in that revenue for a pure competitor could be expressed as $TR = pq$ and p regarded as a constant, because such a firm has no effect upon market price. The output level of a monopolist, on the other hand, certainly does influence the market price in the way indicated by the demand function for his product. Therefore p must be first converted into terms of q in order that the profit function be stated in terms of the single variable q. Because

$$\pi = R(q) - C(q)$$

we can find the point of maximum profit by differentiating with respect to q and setting the result equal to zero:

$$\frac{d\pi}{dq} = R'(q) - C'(q) = 0$$

$$R'(q) = C'(q)$$

Thus a necessary condition for profit maximization is that marginal revenue equal marginal cost.

To ensure that a maximum profit position is actually attained, it is necessary to check second-order conditions, which are

$$\frac{d^2\pi}{dq^2} = R''(q) - C''(q) < 0$$

or

$$R''(q) < C''(q)$$

that is, the rate of change in marginal revenue must be less than that in marginal cost. If, as is commonly thought, marginal revenue is decreasing and marginal cost is increasing, the second-order condition is clearly satisfied. In the case where both are decreasing, MR must decrease more rapidly than MC in order for the conditions to be satisfied.

In Section 13·4, we saw that a condition for the maximization of profits under pure competition is that price equal marginal cost. We have also established that $MR < p$ for a monopolist. When a monopolist equates MR to MC, he is restricting output, because he ceases production at a point where $p > MC$, while under pure competition, production would still go on. This result ensues only if the cost function of the monopolist is identical to what would have been the aggregate cost function were the industry purely competitive. It may, however, be possible for the monopolist to reduce the overall cost of production because of economies of scale, in which case there would not necessarily be adverse effects upon the quantity offered on the market.

Illustration. The demand function for a monopolist is given by $p = 15 - 6q_d$, where $q_d \geqslant 0$, and where p is expressed as a function of q_d. Its cost function is

$$C = 2q^3 - 3q^2 + 3q + 2 \qquad \text{where } q \geqslant 0$$

Find the firm's profit-maximizing output, the price it will charge, and the amount of profit it will make.

Solution.   Total revenue is given by

$$TR = pq = (15 - 6q)q = 15q - 6q^2$$

The profit function is

$$\begin{aligned} \pi = TR - C &= 15q - 6q^2 - 2q^3 + 3q^2 - 3q - 2 \\ &= 12q - 3q^2 - 2q^3 - 2 \end{aligned}$$

To maximize the profit function, we set its first derivative equal to zero.

$$\frac{d\pi}{dq} = 12 - 6q - 6q^2 = 0$$

$$-6(q + 2)(q - 1) = 0$$

$$q = -2 \quad \text{or} \quad q = 1$$

Because $q = -2$ is outside the range of definition of the function, we are left with one possible maximum point.

To confirm whether this point is, in fact, a maximum profit position, we check the second-order condition:

$$\frac{d^2\pi}{dq^2} = -6 - 12q$$

At $q = 1$,

$$\frac{d^2\pi}{dq^2} < 0$$

Therefore the second-order condition is satisfied and $q = 1$ is the maximum profit point on the interior of the function. At $q = 1$, we find the profit level to be $\pi = 5$.

We must, of course, consider the possibility of a boundary solution. The boundary is given by $q = 0$. When $q = 0$, we find $\pi = -2$. This is less than the profit level we found earlier, so we reject the possibility of a boundary solution.

We conclude that the monopolist will maximize profits by producing 1 unit. The price he will charge is determined from his demand function $p = 15 - 6q_d$. When $q_d = 1$, $p = q$ and his profit level is $\pi = 5$.

Exercises

In each of the following cases, find the monopolist's profit-maximizing output, the price it will charge, and the amount of profit it will make.

1. The demand function for the monopolist is given by $p = 60 - 2q_d$, where $q_d \geqslant 0$. Its cost function is $C = 39q - 11q^2 + q^3 + 5$, where $q \geqslant 0$.
2. The demand function for the monopolist is given by $p = 100 + 17q_d - 3q_d^2$, where $q_d \geqslant 0$. Its cost function is $C = 50q - 8q^2 + q^3 + 10$, where $q \geqslant 0$.
3. The demand function for the monopolist is given by $p = 200 - 4q_d^2$, where $q_d \geqslant 0$. Its cost function is $C = 80q - 15q^2 + q^3 + 100$, where $q \geqslant 0$.
4. The demand function for the monopolist is given by $p = 80 - 12q_d - 2q_d^2$, where $q_d \geqslant 0$. Its cost function is $C = 32q - 12q^2 + 2q^3 + 25$, where $q \geqslant 0$.
5. The demand function for the monopolist is given by $p = 45 - q_d$, where $q_d \geqslant 0$. Its cost function is $C = 5q$, where $q \geqslant 0$.
6. The demand function for the monopolist is given by $p = 12 - 2q_d$, where $q_d \geqslant 0$. Its cost function is $C = 4q + 4$, where $q \geqslant 0$.
7. The demand function for the monopolist is given by $p = 120 - 3q_d$, where $q_d \geqslant 0$. Its cost function is $C = q^2 + 100$, where $q \geqslant 0$.

SECTION 14·2 MONOPOLY PROFIT MAXIMIZATION USING PRODUCTION FUNCTIONS[1]

In considering profit maximization for a monopolist in the previous section, we used the cost function approach, which is the usual form such analysis takes. We know from earlier sections (see Section 13·4) that cost functions are derived from information given by the firm's production

[1] This section can be omitted without disturbing the continuity of presentation.

function (which expresses production possibilities in terms of amounts of input use) and the cost equation (which expresses cost in terms of input use). A monopolist derives his cost function in the same manner as a pure competitor. There is no need to consider such derivations anew, because the procedure already outlined is perfectly general.

We also showed earlier (Section 13·3) that the profit-maximizing output can be derived through direct use of the production function. In the process, however, we assumed the existence of pure competition. Let us therefore show how the basic approach can easily be extended to the monopoly case.

The production function for a firm with two variable inputs, x_1 and x_2, is given by

$$q = f(x_1, x_2)$$

The cost equation is $C = r_1 x_1 + r_2 x_2 + b$, where r_1 and r_2 are the input prices. The demand function for the monopolist's product is given by $p = h(q_d)$. Total revenue is given by $TR = pq$, which can then be expressed as $TR = R(q)$. The monopolist's profit function is then

$$\pi = TR - C$$

$$= R(q) - r_1 x_1 - r_2 x_2$$

where we understand that $R(q)$ can be expressed as a function of x_1 and x_2 by substituting the value of q given by the production function.

To find the maximum profit position, it is necessary to set the first partial derivatives equal to zero:

$$\frac{\partial \pi}{\partial x_1} = \frac{\partial R}{\partial x_1} - r_1 = 0 \qquad \frac{\partial \pi}{\partial x_2} = \frac{\partial R}{\partial x_2} - r_2 = 0$$

Now R is a function of q, which, in turn, is a function of two other variables, x_1 and x_2. Therefore, applying the generalized formula for the total derivative given in Section 10·6 gives us

$$\frac{\partial R}{\partial x_1} = \frac{dR}{dq} \frac{\partial q}{\partial x_1} \quad \text{and} \quad \frac{\partial R}{\partial x_2} = \frac{dR}{dq} \frac{\partial q}{\partial x_2}$$

We then get

$$\frac{\partial \pi}{\partial x_1} = \frac{dR}{dq} \frac{\partial q}{\partial x} - r_1 = 0 \quad \text{and} \quad \frac{\partial \pi}{\partial x_2} = \frac{dR}{dq} \frac{\partial q}{\partial x} - r_2 = 0$$

and

$$\frac{dR}{dq} \frac{\partial q}{\partial x_1} = r_1 \qquad \frac{dR}{dq} \frac{\partial q}{\partial x_2} = r_2$$

Now $\partial q/\partial x_1$ is the marginal productivity of the ith input and dR/dq is the marginal revenue of an additional unit produced. Therefore

$$\frac{dR}{dq}\frac{\partial q}{\partial x_1}$$

is the marginal revenue that would accrue to the monopolist as a result of selling the marginal product, sometimes called the *marginal revenue product*.

The necessary conditions for monopoly profit maximization therefore require that the marginal revenue product of each input be equal to the input price. This is analogous to the condition for profit maximization under pure competition derived in Section 13·3. In each case the marginal revenue product must be equal to the input price. An essential difference, however, is that under pure competition, marginal revenue product is equal to product price multiplied by the marginal product, while under monopoly, marginal revenue product is equal to marginal revenue multiplied by the marginal product. This difference arises because, as explained earlier, marginal revenue is product price for a pure competitor, while for a monopolist, marginal revenue is less than product price.[2]

To ensure a point of maximum profit, second-order conditions must be examined and the possibility of boundary solutions considered.

Illustration.   Find the profit-maximizing output and product price for a monopolist whose production function is $q = 100 \ln x_1 + 50 \ln x_2$, where x_1 and $x_2 \geqslant 1$, and whose costs are given by $4x_1 + x_2 + 2$. The demand function for the monopolist's product is

$$p = 50 + \frac{100}{q_d}$$

Solution.   We form the profit function, which is

$$\pi = TR - C$$

$$= pq - C$$

$$= \left(50 + \frac{100}{q}\right)q - 4x_1 - x_2 - 2$$

$$= 50q + 100 - 4x_1 - x_2 - 2$$

$$= 50(100 \ln x_1 + 50 \ln x_2) + 100 - 4x_1 - x_2 - 2$$

$$= 5000 \ln x_1 + 2500 \ln x_2 - 4x_1 - x_2 + 98$$

---

[2] Indeed, because of this difference, marginal revenue product for a pure competitor is often called the *value of the marginal product*, which differentiates it from the marginal revenue product of a monopolist.

Setting the first partials equal to zero gives

$$\frac{\partial \pi}{\partial x_1} = \frac{5000}{x_1} - 4 = 0 \qquad\qquad \frac{\partial \pi}{\partial x_2} = \frac{2500}{x_2} - 1 = 0$$

$$\frac{5000}{x_1} = 4 \qquad\qquad\qquad \frac{2500}{x_2} = 1$$

$$x_1 = 1250 \qquad\qquad\qquad x_2 = 2500$$

Thus a necessary condition for the maximization of profit is that 1250 units of the first input be used together with 2500 units of the second input. This combination of inputs will produce

$$q = 100 \ln(1250) + 50 \ln(2500) = 100(7.1309) + 50(7.8633)$$

$$= 1106.26 \text{ units of output}$$

For this level of output, we find

$$\pi = 5000 \ln(1250) + 2500 \ln(2500) - 4(1250) - 2500 + 98$$

$$= \$44,370.75 \text{ profit}$$

To be assured that this output level yields the maximum possible profit, we must check the second-order conditions, which are

$$\pi_{x_1 x_1} < 0 \quad \text{and} \quad \pi_{x_1 x_1} \pi_{x_2 x_2} - (\pi_{x_1 x_2})^2 > 0$$

Now

$$\pi_{x_1} = \frac{\partial \pi}{\partial x_1} = \frac{5000}{x_1} - 4 \qquad \pi_{x_2} = \frac{\partial \pi}{\partial x_2} = \frac{2500}{x_2} - 1$$

$$\pi_{x_1 x_1} = \frac{-5000}{x_1^2} \qquad \pi_{x_1 x_2} = 0 \qquad \pi_{x_2 x_2} = \frac{-2500}{x_2^2}$$

At $x_1 = 1250$, $x_2 = 2500$,

$$\pi_{x_1 x_1} < 0$$

and

$$\pi_{x_1 x_1} \pi_{x_2 x_2} - (\pi_{x_1 x_2})^2 > 0$$

The second-order or sufficient conditions are therefore satisfied.

The possibility of a boundary solution must still be considered. The boundaries of our function are given by $x_1 = 1$ and $x_2 = 1$. If $x_1 = 1$, we have

$$\pi = 2500 \ln x_2 - x_2 + 98$$

Maximizing this function with respect to x_2 gives

$$\frac{d\pi}{dx_2} = \frac{2500}{x_2} - 1 = 0$$

$$\frac{2500}{x_2} = 1$$

$$x_2 = 2500$$

At $x_1 = 1$, $x_2 = 2500$, we find

$$\pi = 2500 \ln(2500) - 2500 + 98 = \$13{,}716.25$$

Thus the level of profit at this boundary point is lower than for the interior maximum point.

In a similar manner, considering the other boundary point, $x_2 = 1$, we have

$$\pi = 5000 \ln x_1 - 4x_1 + 98$$

Maximizing this function with respect to x_1 gives

$$\frac{d\pi}{dx_1} = \frac{5000}{x_1} - 4 = 0$$

$$\frac{5000}{x_1} = 4$$

$$x_1 = 1250$$

At $x_1 = 1250$, $x_2 = 1$, we find

$$\pi = \$30{,}752.50$$

This level of profit is again lower than for the interior maximum point.

We therefore conclude that profit is maximized by utilizing 1250 units of the first input and 2500 of the second input to produce an output of 1106.26 units. The price to be charged is determined from the demand function for the product; that is,

$$p = 50 + \frac{100}{q_d} \quad \text{or} \quad p = 50 + \frac{100}{1106.26} = \$50.09$$

Exercises

In each of the following cases, find the monopolist's profit-maximizing output and the price it will charge.

1. The monopolist's production function is

$$q = \ln x_1 + 2 \ln x_2$$

where x_1 and $x_2 \geqslant 1$; its costs are given by

$$C = 3x_1 + 2x_2 + 5$$

its demand function is

$$p = 100 + \frac{500}{q_d}$$

2. The monopolist's production function is

$$q = x_1^{1/2} + x_2^{1/2}$$

where only positive square roots are to be taken; its costs are given by

$$C = 4x_1 + x_2 + 100$$

its demand function is

$$p = 200 + \frac{300}{q_d}$$

3. The monopolist's production function is

$$q = 10 - \frac{1}{x_1} - \frac{1}{x_2}$$

where x_1 and $x_2 > 0$; its costs are given by

$$C = x_1 + 4x_2 + 20$$

its demand function is

$$p = 64 + \frac{50}{q_d}$$

4. The monopolist's production function is

$$q = 100 \ln x_1 + 100 \ln x_2$$

where x_1 and $x_2 \geqslant 1$; its costs are given by

$$C = 5x_1 + 2x_2 + 50$$

its demand function is

$$p = 10 + \frac{800}{q_d}$$

SECTION 14·3   MONOPOLY AND PRICE DISCRIMINATION

In previous sections we have assumed that the firm sells all its output at a single market price—whatever that may be. This is certainly always true for a pure competitor, who has no control over the market price. Once market forces of supply and demand determine the equilibrium market price, the firm has no choice but to sell however much it desires at this market price. However, in other market structures where firms have some degree of control over the product price, it may sometimes be profitable to break the total product market into two or more submarkets and vary the price from submarket to submarket.

The practice of setting different prices in different markets for the same product is known as *price discrimination*. It occurs where consumers in one market are unable to purchase in the other markets because of barriers that exist naturally or are created by the seller. Thus utility companies, such as gas, electricity, and telephone companies, can arbitrarily separate industrial users from consumers who use the product for personal use. The firm can then charge different rates to these different classes of buyers. Doctors, lawyers, and others selling personal services may vary their rate depending on their estimation of clients' prosperity. Markets may sometimes be separated geographically so that buyers in the higher-priced market are unable (in a practical sense) to buy in the lower-priced market because of high transportation costs. Domestic markets may be separated from foreign markets, with a lower price being set in the latter market. Domestic buyers can be disuaded from purchasing in the foreign market through use of import tariffs. Railroad rates for specific mileages may differ according to location. Students may be given lower rates on international flights.

As the illustrations of the preceding paragraph indicate, price discrimination will be profitable only where consumer demand differs from market to market. Thus, industrial users of power invariably have more elastic demand functions than personal users. Demand is also more elastic in foreign than in domestic markets because of more intense competition from foreign products.

To demonstrate profit maximization and price setting under price discrimination, we consider the case of a monopolist who has ascertained that there are separate and distinct demand conditions in the two segments of its market. Assume that the demand functions for the product in the two markets are $p_1 = f_1(q_1)$ and $p_2 = f_2(q_2)$, where p_1 and p_2 are the prices and q_1 and q_2 the quantities consumers purchase in the two markets. Because demand varies from market to market, so will revenue. The monopolist will therefore have two revenue functions, $R_1(q_1)$ in the first market and $R_2(q_2)$ in the second market. Costs will, however, be given by the single function $C = C(q_1 + q_2)$, because the production process is unaffected by whether or not the total market is broken into subdivisions.

Profits can therefore be expressed as the difference between total revenue from both markets and total cost of production. The profit function is therefore

$$\pi = R_1(q_1) + R_2(q_2) - C(q_1 + q_2)$$

To maximize profits, the first partials must be set equal to zero:

$$\frac{\partial \pi}{\partial q_1} = \frac{dR_1}{dq_1} - \frac{\partial C}{\partial q_1} = 0 \qquad \frac{\partial \pi}{\partial q_2} = \frac{dR_2}{dq_2} - \frac{\partial C}{\partial q_2} = 0$$

or

$$\frac{dR_1}{dq_1} = \frac{\partial C}{\partial q_1} \qquad \frac{dR_2}{dq_2} = \frac{\partial C}{\partial q_2}$$

This implies that, in each market, the marginal revenue must be equal to the marginal cost of producing another unit. It is easy to see that the marginal cost of producing a unit of output is the same whether that unit is to be sold in market 1 or market 2. Therefore

$$\frac{\partial C}{\partial q_1} = \frac{\partial C}{\partial q_2}$$

so that the necessary conditions are equivalent to

$$\frac{dR_1}{dq_1} = \frac{dR_2}{dq_2} = \frac{\partial C}{\partial q_1} = \frac{\partial C}{\partial q_2}$$

that is, marginal revenue in each market must be equal to each other and each equal to the marginal cost of producing a unit of output.

In Section 8·16 we derived the following relationship between marginal revenue and price:

$$MR = p\left(1 + \frac{1}{E}\right)$$

where E is the elasticity of demand. Now, marginal revenue in the two markets must be equal, so

$$p_1\left(1 + \frac{1}{E_1}\right) = p_2\left(1 + \frac{1}{E_2}\right)$$

where p_1 and p_2 are the market prices and E_1 and E_2 are the elasticities of demand in the two markets. It is immediately evident, therefore, that if elasticity of demand varies from market to market, so will the market prices set by the monopolist. In the event that elasticity of demand is the same in each market, the market price will be identical in each market, implying that price discrimination is unrewarding unless there are variations in elasticities of demand.

Second-order conditions must, of course, be checked to ensure that a maximum profit position is actually attained when the first-order conditions are satisfied. The possibility of boundary solutions must also be considered.

This result can be extended to cases where a monopolist breaks down his total market into any number of submarkets. In this regard see Exercise 7 at the end of this section.

Illustration. The cost function for a monopolist is given by $C = 2q^2 - 5q + 3$, where q is total output and $q \geqslant 0$. The demand for its product in its two markets is $p_1 = 8 - 5q_1$, where $q_1 \geqslant 0$, and $p_2 = 7 - 2q_2$, where $q_2 \geqslant 0$. Find the firm's profit-maximizing output in each market, the price it will charge in each market, and the amount of overall profit it will make.

Solution. Total revenue in the first market is given by

$$TR_1 = p_1 q_1 = 8q_1 - 5q_1^2$$

Total revenue in the second market is

$$TR_2 = p_2 q_2 = 7q_2 - 2q_2^2$$

The cost function is given as

$$C = 2q^2 - 5q + 3.$$

Because $q = q_1 + q_2$, this is equivalent to

$$C = 2(q_1 + q_2)^2 - 5(q_1 + q_2) + 3$$
$$= 2q_1^2 + 4q_1 q_2 + 2q_2^2 - 5q_1 - 5q_2 + 3$$

The profit function is

$$\pi = TR_1 + TR_2 - C$$
$$= 8q_1 - 5q_1^2 + 7q_2 - 2q_2^2 - 2q_1^2 - 4q_1 q_2 - 2q_2^2 + 5q_1 + 5q_2 - 3$$
$$= 13q_1 - 7q_1^2 + 12q_2 - 4q_2^2 - 4q_1 q_2 - 3$$

To maximize profits, we set the first partials equal to zero:

$$\frac{\partial \pi}{\partial q_1} = 13 - 14q_1 - 4q_2 = 0 \qquad \frac{\partial \pi}{\partial q_2} = 12 - 8q_2 - 4q_1 = 0$$

We then solve these two equations simultaneously:

$$14q_1 + 4q_2 = 13$$
$$4q_1 + 8q_2 = 12$$

Multiplying the first equation by 2 gives

$$28q_1 + 8q_2 = 26$$
$$4q_1 + 8q_2 = 12$$

Subtracting the second equation from the first gives

$$24q_1 = 14$$
$$q_1 = \tfrac{7}{12}$$
$$q_2 = \tfrac{29}{24}$$

To confirm whether this point is, in fact, a maximum profit position, we check the second-order conditions. These are

$$\pi_{q_1 q_1} < 0 \quad \text{and} \quad \pi_{q_1 q_1}\pi_{q_2 q_2} - (\pi_{q_1 q_2})^2 > 0$$

Now,

$$\pi_{q_1 q_1} = -14 \qquad \pi_{q_1 q_2} = -4 \qquad \pi_{q_2 q_2} = -8$$

Therefore,

$$\pi_{q_1 q_1} < 0 \quad \text{and} \quad \pi_{q_1 q_1}\pi_{q_2 q_2} - (\pi_{q_1 q_2})^2 > 0$$

and the second-order conditions are satisfied. $q_1 = \tfrac{7}{12}$, $q_2 = \tfrac{29}{24}$ is the maximum profit position on the interior of the function. At this point, we find the profit level to be

$$\pi = \frac{\$1079}{72} = \$14.99$$

We should, of course, consider the possibility of a boundary solution. The boundary is given by $q_1 = 0$, $q_2 = 0$. When $q_1 = 0$, we have

$$\pi = 12q_2 - 4q_2^2 - 3$$

To maximize this function of q_2, we set its first derivative equal to zero:

$$\frac{d\pi}{dq_2} = 12 - 8q_2 = 0$$

$$8q_2 = 12$$

$$q_2 = \tfrac{3}{2}$$

At $q_1 = 0$, $q_2 = \tfrac{3}{2}$, we find $\pi = \$6$. Thus the level of profit at this boundary point is lower than for the interior maximum point.

In a similar manner, considering the other boundary point, $q_2 = 0$, we have

$$\pi = 13q_1 - 7q_1^2 - 3$$

Maximizing the function with respect to q_1 gives

$$\frac{d\pi}{dq_1} = 13 - 14q_1 = 0$$

$$14q_1 = 13$$

$$q_1 = \tfrac{13}{14}$$

At $q_1 = \tfrac{13}{14}$, $q_2 = 0$, we find $\pi = \$3.04$. This level of profits is again lower than for the interior maximum point.

We therefore conclude that profit is maximized by placing $\tfrac{7}{12}$ unit on the first market and $\tfrac{29}{24}$ units on the second market. The prices in each market are then determined from the respective demand functions.

$$p_1 = 8 - 5q_1 = 8 - 5(\tfrac{7}{12}) = 8 - \tfrac{35}{12} = \tfrac{61}{12} = \$5.08$$

$$p_2 = 7 - 2q_2 = 7 - 2(\tfrac{29}{24}) = 7 - 2.42 = \$4.58$$

Exercises

In each of the following cases, find the monopolist's profit-maximizing output in each market, the price it will charge in each market, and the amount of overall profit it will make.

1. The monopolist's cost function is $C = q^2 - 14q + 39$, where $q \geqslant 0$. The demand for its product in its two markets is $p_1 = 40 - 2q_1$, where $q_1 \geqslant 0$; and $p_2 = 30 - q_2$, where $q_2 \geqslant 0$.
2. The monopolist's cost function is $C = q^2 + 100$, where $q \geqslant 0$. The demand for its product in its two markets is $p_1 = 100 - 2q_1$, where $q_1 \geqslant 0$; and $p_2 = 80 - q_2$, where $q_2 \geqslant 0$.

3. The monopolist's cost function is $C = q^2 - 15q + 80$, where $q \geqslant 0$. The demand for its product in its two markets is $p_1 = 105 - 2q_1$, where $q_1 \geqslant 0$; and $p_2 = 45 - q_2$, where $q_2 \geqslant 0$.
4. The monopolist's cost function is $C = 5q$, where $q \geqslant 0$. The demand for its product in its two markets is $p_1 = 85 - 2q_1$, where $q_1 \geqslant 0$; and $p_2 = 20 - q_2$, where $q_2 \geqslant 0$.
5. The monopolist's cost function is $C = 4q + 4$, where $q \geqslant 0$. The demand for its product in its two markets is $p_1 = 40 - q_1$, where $q_1 \geqslant 0$; and $p_2 = 10 - \frac{1}{2}q_2$, where $q_2 \geqslant 0$.
6. The monopolist's cost function is $C = 4q$, where $q \geqslant 0$. The demand for its product in its three markets is $p_1 = 100 - 2q_1^2$, where $q_1 \geqslant 0$; $p_2 = 50 - q_2$, where $q_2 \geqslant 0$; $p_3 = 40 - q_3$, where $q_3 \geqslant 0$.
7. Prove that a monopolist who has n submarkets must equate marginal revenue to marginal cost in each separate market if profit maximization is to ensue.

SECTION 14·4   THE MULTIPLE-PLANT MONOPOLIST

In Section 13·6 we showed how a competitive firm with two or more plants would maximize profits. In this section, we consider a monopolist who has more than one plant with different costs of production and who must decide how much output to produce in each plant.

Let q_1 denote the quantity of the product produced in the first plant and q_2 the quantity produced in the second plant. Total output is then $q = q_1 + q_2$. Costs of production vary from plant to plant, so there will be two distinct cost functions, which may be denoted by $C_1(q_1)$ and $C_2(q_2)$. Total cost is the sum of the costs in each plant, or $C = C_1(q_1) + C_2(q_2)$. Suppose that the demand for the monopolist's product is given by $p = h(q_d)$. Total revenue is the price of the product multiplied by the quantity sold, or $TR = pq = h(q_1, q_2) = R(q) = R(q_1 + q_2)$.

The profit function can then be expressed as

$$\pi = TR - C$$

$$= R(q_1 + q_2) - C_1(q_1) - C_2(q_2)$$

To find the profit-maximizing output, we set the first partial derivatives of this function equal to zero.

$$\frac{\partial \pi}{\partial q_1} = \frac{\partial R}{\partial q_1} - \frac{dC_1}{dq_1} = 0 \qquad \frac{\partial \pi}{\partial q_2} = \frac{\partial R}{\partial q_2} - \frac{dC_2}{dq_2} = 0$$

or

$$\frac{\partial R}{\partial q_1} = \frac{dC_1}{dq_1} \qquad \frac{\partial R}{\partial q_2} = \frac{dC_2}{dq_2}$$

which implies that marginal revenue must be equal to the marginal cost of a unit for each plant. It is easy to see that the marginal revenue of a unit is the same regardless of which plant the unit is produced in. Therefore

$$\frac{\partial R}{\partial q_1} = \frac{\partial R}{\partial q_2}$$

so that the necessary conditions are equivalent to

$$\frac{\partial R}{\partial q_1} = \frac{\partial R}{\partial q_2} = \frac{dC_1}{dq_1} = \frac{dC_2}{dq_2}$$

that is, marginal cost in each plant must be equal to each other and each equal to the marginal revenue of a unit of the product.

Second-order conditions must, of course, be checked to ensure that a maximum profit position is actually attained. The possibility of boundary solutions must also be considered.

The analysis can, in like manner, be extended to a firm with any number of plants. In this regard see Exercises 6 and 7 at the end of the section.

Illustration.   A monopolistic firm has the following cost functions for its two plants:

$$C_1 = 4q_1^2 + 5 \qquad C_2 = 2q_2^2 + 10 \qquad \text{where } q_1 \text{ and } q_2 \geqslant 0$$

The demand for its product is given by $p = 100 - 2q_d$. Find the firm's profit-maximizing output, the amount it will produce in each plant, and the price it will charge for its product.

Solution.   Total revenue for the monopolist is

$$TR = pq = 100q - 2q^2 = 100(q_1 + q_2) - 2(q_1 + q_2)^2$$
$$= 100q_1 + 100q_2 - 2q_1^2 - 4q_1 q_2 - 2q_2^2$$

The profit function can be expressed as

$$\pi = R(q_1 + q_2) - C_1(q_1) - C_2(q_2)$$

which, in our case, becomes

$$\pi = 100q_1 + 100q_2 - 2q_1^2 - 4q_1 q_2 - 2q_2^2 - 4q_1^2 - 5 - 2q_2^2 - 10$$
$$= 100q_1 + 100q_2 - 6q_1^2 - 4q_1 q_2 - 4q_2^2 - 15$$

Setting the first partials equal to zero gives

$$\frac{\partial \pi}{\partial q_1} = 100 - 12q_1 - 4q_2 = 0 \qquad \frac{\partial \pi}{\partial q_2} = 100 - 4q_1 - 8q_2 = 0$$

Solving simultaneously, we get

$$12q_1 + 4q_2 = 100$$
$$4q_1 + 8q_2 = 100$$

Multiplying the second equation by 3 gives

$$12q_1 + 4q_2 = 100$$
$$12q_1 + 24q_2 = 300$$

Subtracting the first equation from the second gives

$$20q_2 = 200$$
$$q_2 = 10$$
$$q_1 = 5$$

When $q_1 = 5$ and $q_2 = 10$, we find that $\pi = \$735$.

To check second-order conditions, we find

$$\pi_{q_1 q_1} = -12 \qquad \pi_{q_1 q_2} = -4 \qquad \pi_{q_2 q_2} = -8$$

from which we see that

$$\pi_{q_1 q_1} < 0 \quad \text{and} \quad \pi_{q_1 q_1} \pi_{q_2 q_2} - (\pi_{q_1 q_2})^2 > 0$$

Therefore the sufficient conditions for a relative maximum are satisfied at $q_1 = 5$, $q_2 = 10$.

To consider the possibility of boundary solutions, we first examine the boundary $q_1 = 0$, that is, all production should take place in the second plant. We get

$$\pi = 100q_2 - 4q_2^2 - 15$$

Maximizing this function of q_2 by setting its derivative equal to zero gives

$$\frac{d\pi}{dq_2} = 100 - 8q_2 = 0$$
$$8q_2 = 100$$
$$q_2 = 12.5$$

for which $\pi = 610$, which is a lower profit than for $q_1 = 5$, $q_2 = 10$.

The other boundary is $q_2 = 0$, for which we get

$$\pi = 100q_1 - 6q_1^2 - 15$$

Maximizing this function of q_1 by setting its derivative equal to zero gives

$$\frac{d\pi}{dq_1} = 100 - 12q_1 = 0$$

$$12q_1 = 100$$

$$q_1 = \tfrac{25}{3}$$

for which

$$\pi = \frac{1205}{3} = 401.7$$

which is again a lower profit than for $q_1 = 5$, $q_2 = 10$.

We therefore conclude that the profit-maximizing output is $q = q_1 + q_2 = 5 + 10 = 15$ units. Five of these units should be produced in the first plant and 10 units in the second plant. The product price is derived from the demand function, which is $p = 100 - 2q_d$. Total output is 15 units, so market price will be $p = 100 - 2(15) = \$70$.

Exercises

In each of the following cases, find the monopolist's profit-maximizing output, the amount that will be produced in each plant, and the price it will charge for its product.

1. The monopolist's cost functions for its two plants are

$$C_1 = 2q_1^2 - 8q_1 + 20 \qquad C_2 = 12q_2^2 + 25$$

where q_1 and $q_2 \geqslant 0$
The demand for the product is

$$p = 60 - 2q_d$$

2. The monopolist's cost functions for its two plants are

$$C_1 = 15q_1^2 - 20q_1 + 40 \qquad C_2 = 2q_2^3 - 50q_2 + 10$$

where q_1 and $q_2 \geqslant 0$. The demand for the product is

$$p = 100 + \frac{500}{q_d}$$

3. The monopolist's cost functions for its two plants are

$$C_1 = 6q_1^2 - 8q_1 + 50 \qquad C_2 = 4q_2^2 - 16q_2 + 15$$

where q_1 and $q_2 \geqslant 0$. The demand for the product is

$$p = 45 - q_d$$

4. The monopolist's cost functions for its two plants are

$$C_1 = q_1^3 - 12q_1 + 18 \qquad C_2 = 10q_2^2 - 20q_2 + 36$$

where q_1 and $q_2 \geqslant 0$. The demand for the product is

$$p = 180 + \frac{300}{q_d}$$

5. The monopolist's cost functions for its two plants are

$$C_1 = \tfrac{1}{2}q_1^2 + 16 \qquad C_2 = 5q_2^2 + 19$$

where q_1 and $q_2 \geqslant 0$. The demand for the product is

$$p = 64 + \frac{50}{q_d}$$

6. The monopolist's cost functions for its three plants are

$$C_1 = 10q_1^2 - 10q_1 + 25 \qquad C_2 = 3q_2^2 - 2q_2 + 8$$
$$C_3 = 5q_3^2 + 40$$

where q_1, q_2, and $q_3 \geqslant 0$. The demand for the product is

$$p = 10 + \frac{800}{q_d}$$

7. Prove that a monopolist with n plants must equate marginal revenue to the marginal cost in each separate plant if it is to maximize profits.

SECTION 14·5 THE MULTIPLE-PRODUCT MONOPOLIST

In Section 13·7 we showed how a competitive firm with two or more products would maximize profits. In this section we consider a monopolist of two or more products. It is, in fact, very common to find large producers selling several products. In such cases, decisions must be made as to how much of each product to produce.

Let q_A denote the quantity of product A and q_B the quantity of product B. The demand for these two products (assuming they are related to each other either as substitutes or complements) is given by $p_A = h(q_A, q_B)$ and $p_B = j(q_A, q_B)$. Total revenue derived from product A is given by

$$TR_A = p_A q_A = h(q_A, q_B)q_A = R_A(q_A, q_B)$$

that is, total revenue of A can be expressed as a function of the quantities of A and B. Total revenue derived from product B is, similarly,

$$TR_B = p_B q_B = j(q_A, q_B)q_B = R_B(q_A, q_B)$$

that is, total revenue of B can be expressed as a function of the quantities of A and B. Costs of production are some function of the amounts of A and B produced, or $C = C(q_A, q_B)$.

The profit function can then be expressed as

$$\pi = TR - C$$

But total revenue overall is equal to total revenue derived from product A plus total revenue derived from product B; that is,

$$TR = TR_A + TR_B$$

Therefore,

$$\pi = TR_A + TR_B - C$$
$$= R_A(q_A, q_B) + R_B(q_A, q_B) - C(q_A, q_B)$$

To find the profit-maximizing output, we set the first partial derivatives of the profit function equal to zero:

$$\frac{\partial \pi}{\partial q_A} = \frac{dR_A}{dq_A} - \frac{\partial C}{\partial q_A} = 0 \qquad \frac{\partial \pi}{\partial q_B} = \frac{dR_B}{dq_B} - \frac{\partial C}{\partial q_B} = 0$$

$$\boxed{\frac{dR_A}{dq_A} = \frac{\partial C}{\partial q_A}} \qquad\qquad \boxed{\frac{dR_B}{dq_B} = \frac{\partial C}{\partial q_B}}$$

This is equivalent to the statement that in order to maximize profits, a two-product monopolist must equate the marginal revenue of each product to the marginal cost of that product.

Second-order conditions must, of course, be checked to ensure that a maximum profit position is actually attained. The possibility of boundary solutions must also be considered.

The analysis can, in like manner, be extended to a firm with any number of products.

Illustration.   A two-product monopolistic firm has the cost function $C = q_A^2 - q_A + q_A q_B + q_B^2 - 4q_B$ where q_A and $q_B \geqslant 0$. The demand function for its two products are $p_A = 8 - 5q_A - q_B$ and $p_B = 7 - q_A - 2q_B$, where q_A and $q_B \geqslant 0$. Find the firm's profit-maximizing output of each product, the price it will charge for each product, and the amount of overall profit it will make.

Solution.   From the demand functions for A and B, we see that they are related products; that is, the price and quantity of one influences the price and quantity of the other. Total revenue for product A is given by

$$TR_A = p_A q_A = 8q_A - 5q_A^2 - q_A q_B$$

Total revenue for product B is given by

$$TR_B = p_B q_B = 7q_B - q_A q_B - 2q_B^2$$

The profit function can be expressed as

$$
\begin{aligned}
\pi &= TR_A + TR_B - C \\
&= 8q_A - 5q_A^2 - q_A q_B + 7q_B - q_A q_B - 2q_B^2 \\
&\quad - q_A^2 + q_A - q_A q_B - q_B^2 + 4q_B \\
&= 9q_A - 6q_A^2 - 3q_A q_B + 11q_B - 3q_B^2
\end{aligned}
$$

Setting the first partials equal to zero yields

$$\frac{\partial \pi}{\partial q_A} = 9 - 12q_A - 3q_B = 0 \qquad \frac{\partial \pi}{\partial q_B} = -3q_A + 11 - 6q_B$$

Solving these two equations simultaneously, we have

$$12q_A + 3q_B = 9$$
$$3q_A + 6q_B = 11$$

Multiplying the first equation by 2 gives

$$24q_A + 6q_B = 18$$
$$3q_A + 6q_B = 11$$

Subtract the second equation from the first and we get

$$21q_A = 7$$
$$q_A = \tfrac{1}{3}$$
$$q_B = \tfrac{5}{3}$$

for which we find $\pi = \tfrac{32}{3} = \$10.67$.

To check second-order conditions, we find

$$\pi_{q_A q_A} = -12 \qquad \pi_{q_A q_B} = -3 \qquad \pi_{q_B q_B} = -6$$

Therefore,

$$\pi_{q_A q_A} < 0$$

and

$$\pi_{q_A q_A} \pi_{q_B q_B} - (\pi_{q_A q_B})^2 > 0$$

The sufficient conditions for a relative maximum are thus satisfied at $q_A = \frac{1}{3}$, $q_B = \frac{5}{3}$.

To investigate the possibility of boundary solutions, we consider first the boundary $q_A = 0$, that is, only B should be produced. We get $\pi = 11q_B - 3q_B^2$. Maximizing this function by setting its derivative equal to zero gives

$$\frac{d\pi}{dq_B} = 11 - 6q_B = 0$$

$$6q_B = 11$$

$$q_B = \tfrac{11}{6}$$

for which $\pi = \frac{121}{12} = \$10.08$, which is a lower profit than for $q_A = \frac{1}{3}$, $q_B = \frac{5}{3}$.

The other boundary is $q_B = 0$, that is, only A should be produced. We get

$$\pi = 9q_A - 6q_A^2$$

Maximizing this function gives

$$\frac{d\pi}{dq_A} = 9 - 12q_A = 0$$

$$12q_A = 9$$

$$q_A = \tfrac{3}{4}$$

for which $\pi = \frac{27}{8} = \$3.38$, which is again a lower profit than for $q_A = \frac{1}{3}$, $q_B = \frac{5}{3}$.

We therefore conclude that the profit-maximizing outputs are $q_A = \frac{1}{3}$, $q_B = \frac{5}{3}$. The prices of each product are derived from the demand functions for each product.

$$p_A = 8 - 5q_A - q_B = 8 - 5(\tfrac{1}{3}) - \tfrac{5}{3} = \tfrac{14}{3} = \$4.67$$

$$p_B = 7 - q_A - 2q_B = 7 - \tfrac{1}{3} - 2(\tfrac{5}{3}) = \tfrac{10}{3} = \$3.33$$

Exercises

In each of the following cases, find the monopolist's profit-maximizing output of each product, the price it will charge for each product, and the amount of overall profit it will make.

1. The monopolist's cost function for its two products is $C = q_A^2 + 2q_A q_B + 4q_B^2 + 5$, where q_A and $q_B \geqslant 0$. The demand functions for its two products are $p_A = 40 - 2q_A - 2q_B$ and $p_B = 31 - q_A - q_B$, where q_A and $q_B \geqslant 0$.
2. The monopolist's cost function for its two products is $C = 3q_A^2 - 4q_A + 3q_A q_B + 6q_B^2 + 10$, where q_A and $q_B \geqslant 0$. The demand function for its two products are $p_A = 100 - 2q_A - q_B$ and $p_B = 75 - q_A - q_B$, where q_A and $q_B \geqslant 0$.
3. The monopolist's cost function for its two products is $C = 12q_A^2 - 3q_A + 4q_A q_B + 2q_B^2 - q_B$, where q_A and $q_B \geqslant 0$. The demand functions for its two products are $p_A = 105 - 4q_A - 2q_B$ and $p_B = 47 - 2q_A - 6q_B$, where q_A and $q_B \geqslant 0$.
4. The monopolist's cost function for its two products is $C = 4q_A^2 - 5q_A + 8q_B^2 - 3q_B + 17$, where q_A and $q_B \geqslant 0$. The demand functions for its two products are $p_A = 90 - 5q_A + q_B$ and $p_B = 34 + q_A - 4q_B$, where q_A and $q_B \geqslant 0$.
5. The monopolist's cost function for its three products is $C = 5q_A^2 - 12q_A + q_B^2 - 2q_B + q_B^2$, where q_A, q_B, and $q_D \geqslant 0$. The demand functions for its three products are $p_A = 100 - 2q_A$, $p_B = 50 - q_B$, $p_C = 40 - q_D$, where q_A, q_B, $q_C \geqslant 0$.
6. Prove that a monopolist with n products must equate the marginal revenue of each product to the marginal cost of that product.

SECTION 14·6   TAXING THE MONOPOLIST

In this section, we consider the effect of government-imposed taxation upon the monopolist. Taxation may take several different forms, each of which may have distinctive effects upon a monopolistic market.

Assume, first, that a lump-sum tax of T dollars is imposed upon the monopolist. This means that the monopolist must pay such an amount to the government regardless of how many units it sells or how much profit it makes. As a result, the profit function of the monopolist must be modified to read

$$\pi = R(q) - C(q) - T$$

where $R(q)$ and $C(q)$ are the revenue and cost functions as stated previously and T is the amount of tax.

The point of maximum profit is derived by setting the first derivative of the profit function equal to zero, which gives

$$\frac{d\pi}{dq} = R'(q) - C'(q) = 0$$

or

$$R'(q) = C'(q)$$

The necessary condition for a maximum is thus seen to be exactly the same as derived in Section 14·1 for a monopolist without any tax imposed. Second-order conditions will also be identical, because $d\pi/dq$ and hence the second derivatives of the profit function are the same in either case.

Thus, a lump-sum tax will have no effect whatever on the quantity produced by the monopolist. The price charged by the monopolist is derived from its demand function. Because both the demand function and the quantity offered for sale remain the same whether or not this tax is imposed, the market price for the product will also be unchanged. The sole effect of the lump-sum tax will be to reduce the level of profits by the amount of the tax. If the amount of profit was excessive to begin with, this reduction would seem to have only beneficial effects. However, if the amount of profit enjoyed by the monopolist was minimal or no higher than could be attained through alternative investments, a lump-sum tax, by reducing profits, could impede investment of new capital into the industry. This, in turn, could eventually lead to adverse effects upon consumers.

The reader may recall that in Sections 4·10 and 4·11, when we considered the effects of various alternative taxes upon a purely competitive firm, we did not deal with the possibility of a lump-sum tax. The reason for this was that we expect that under pure competition any long-run excessive profits that are earned will be gradually dissipated by market forces, because free entry is present. Excessive profits will attract more firms to enter the industry, thus increasing market supply and reducing price and profits until the profit level is at a reasonable level. This situation, of course, does not pertain to a monopolistic industry, where entry is certainly not free. Excessive profits beyond reasonable returns can persist, thus inviting the possibility of a government-imposed lump-sum tax.

Illustration 1.   In Section 14·1, we considered the illustration of a monopolist with a demand function given by $p = 15 - 6q_d$, where $q_d \geqslant 0$, and a cost function of $C = 2q^3 - 3q^2 + 3q + 2$, where $q \geqslant 0$. Suppose that a lump-sum tax of \$2 is imposed. What effect will this have upon the firm's output, the product price, and the amount of profit received?

Solution.   In the illustration of Section 14·1, we found that the profit-maximizing output in this case is 1 unit, the market price \$9, and the profit level \$5. A lump-sum tax of \$2 is now imposed.

The total revenue function remains as previously:

$$TR = pq = (15 - 6q)q = 15q - 6q^2$$

The profit function becomes

$$\pi = TR - C - T$$

where T is the lump-sum tax and

$$\pi = 15q - 6q^2 - 2q^3 + 3q^2 - 3q - 2 - 2$$
$$= 12q - 3q^2 - 2q^3 - 4$$

To maximize the profit function, we set its first derivative equal to zero.

$$\frac{d\pi}{dq} = 12 - 6q - 6q^2 = 0$$

$$-6(q + 2)(q - 1) = 0$$

$$q = -2 \quad \text{or} \quad q = 1$$

Because $q = -2$ is outside the range of definition of the function, we are left with one possible maximum point, namely, $q = 1$. This is the same point arrived at in the earlier illustration where no tax was imposed upon the monopolist. Second-order conditions will be satisfied at this point as in the earlier illustration. The product price at this level of output will be $p = 9$ as found previously. The profit received will, however, be $\pi = 3$ as compared to $\pi = 5$ in the earlier illustration. The possibility of a boundary solution can again be dismissed, because such a solution will yield a still lower profit figure.

Thus the sole effect of the lump-sum tax is to reduce monopoly profits by the amount of the tax. Product price and quantity remain the same.

Suppose now that the government wishes to tax a certain proportion of the monopolist's profits. This is known as a profits tax and differs from a lump-sum tax in that the latter takes the same dollar amount regardless of how much profit is made, while the former tax levy varies according to the amount of profits received.

A profits tax is equivalent to a tax on the difference between total revenue and total costs. Consider a tax at the fixed rate of t, where $0 < t < 1$, that is, some positive proportion less than 1. The profit function can then be written as

$$\pi = R(q) - C(q) - t[R(q) - C(q)]$$

which means that profit is equal to total revenue minus total cost minus the amount of the tax, which happens to be a certain proportion of pretax profits. This can further be written as

$$\pi = (1 - t)[R(q) - C(q)]$$

To maximize profits, we set the first derivative equal to zero.

$$\frac{d\pi}{dq} = (1 - t)[R'(q) - C'(q)] = 0$$

Now $(1 - t) \neq 0$. Therefore

$$R'(q) - C'(q) = 0$$

or

$$R'(q) = C'(q)$$

which is again the same first-order condition for a maximization of profits as we derived in Section 14.1 for a monopolist without any tax imposed. Second-order conditions require that

$$\frac{d^2\pi}{dq^2} = (1 - t)[R''(q) - C''(q)] < 0$$

Because $0 < t < 1$, it follows that $1 - t$ is positive. Therefore the second-order condition is equivalent to

$$R''(q) - C''(q) < 0$$

or

$$R''(q) < C''(q)$$

which is the same second-order condition as we derived in Section 14.1 for a monopolist without any tax imposed.

Thus a profits tax of less than 100 percent will also have no effect on the quantity produced by the monopolist and hence upon the product price. It will, however, reduce the level of profits.

In the event that a 100 percent profits tax is imposed upon the monopolist, then $t = 1.00$, meaning that 100 percent of profits would be taxed away. Thus the monopolist's after profit level can be no greater than zero. If $R(q) > C(q)$, there will be a pretax profit, but this will be taxed away. Thus it is entirely immaterial to the monopolist by how much $R(q)$ exceeds $C(q)$, because there will be nothing left for the firm in any event. The monopolist, however, must still guard against the possibility of $R(q) < C(q)$, in which case there will be losses accruing. Under these circumstances, the monopolist will produce an output for which there is no negative profit, but there will usually be many alternative output levels among which the monopolist will be indifferent. The solution is, in fact, indeterminate. The actual output may be the output the monopolist had produced in a former year or some other output level, but maximizing behavior will not be able to determine it.

The question may arise as to why a monopolist will remain in business at all when not earning any profit. The answer may be that in the short run, if operations are terminated, losses may actually be incurred due to existing fixed costs. Moreover, even with a zero profit level, the firm is presumably earning a reasonable return on its labor and capital invested in the business, that is, a return equal to what can be made in other investment opportunities with comparable risk. To be sure, it is not receiving any payment above the usual economy-wide return and thus not particularly benefitting from its monopolistic status. Nevertheless, there may be sufficient incentive to stay put, at least until some more attractive channel for its capital opens up.

Illustration 2.   Consider again the example of a monopolist with a demand function given by $p = 15 - 6q_d$, where $q_d \geqslant 0$, and a cost function of $C = 2q^3 - 3q^2 + 3q + 2$, where $q \geqslant 0$. Suppose that a 25 percent profits tax is imposed. What effect will this have upon the firm's output, the product price, and the amount of profit received? What effect will a 100 percent profits tax have upon output, price, and profit?
Solution.   Total revenue remains as previously:

$$TR = pq = (15 - 6q)q = 15q - 6q^2$$

The profit function, assuming a 25 percent profits tax, becomes

$$\pi = TR - C - 0.25(TR - C) = 0.75(TR - C)$$
$$= 0.75(15q - 6q^2 - 2q^3 + 3q^2 - 3q - 2)$$
$$= 0.75(12q - 3q^2 - 2q^3 - 2)$$

To maximize the profit function, we set its first derivative equal to zero.

$$\frac{d\pi}{dq} = 0.75(12 - 6q - 6q^2) = 0$$

$$-4.5(-2 + q + q^2) = 0$$

$$-4.5(q + 2)(q - 1) = 0$$

$$q = -2 \quad \text{or} \quad q = 1$$

Because $q = -2$ is outside the range of definition of the function, we are left with one possible maximum point, namely, $q = 1$. This is the same point arrived at in the earlier illustration where no tax was imposed. Second-order conditions will again be satisfied at this point as in the earlier illustration. The product price, at this level of output, will be $p = 9$, as found previously. The profit received will, however, be $\pi = 0.75(5) = 3.75$ as compared to $\pi = 5$ in the earlier illustration. The possibility of a boundary solution can again be dismissed, because such a solution will yield a still lower profit figure.

Thus the sole effect of the 25 percent profits tax is to reduce monopoly profits by 25 percent. Product price and quantity remain the same.

In the case of a 100 percent profits tax, after-tax profit can be no more than zero. Thus, as long as $R(q) \geqslant C(q)$, it is immaterial what level of output is chosen, because the resulting profit will be taxed away anyway. The monopolist will, however, have to ensure that $R(q) \geqslant C(q)$. This is equivalent to

$$15q - 6q^2 \geqslant 2q^3 - 3q^2 + 3q + 2$$

or

$$12q - 3q^2 - 2q^3 - 2 \geqslant 0$$

It is evident that there are many values of q for which this inequality holds, such as $q = \frac{1}{4}$, $q = \frac{1}{2}$, $q = 1$, $q = \frac{3}{2}$, and so on. Any such value will produce a positive pretax profit. There should be no reason to prefer one such output level to another, because the profit will be taxed away in any event. Thus the solution in this case is indeterminate.

We next turn to the case where the government imposes a specific tax of S dollars per unit of output. The profit function of the monopolist is then

$$\pi = R(q) - C(q) - Sq$$

that is, profit is revenue minus costs of production minus the tax levy (Sq), which is the tax per unit multiplied by the number of units.

The point of maximum profit is derived by setting the first derivative of the profit function equal to zero.

$$\frac{d\pi}{dq} = R'(q) - C'(q) - S = 0$$

$$R'(q) = C'(q) + S$$

that is, the monopolist must equate marginal revenue to marginal cost plus the tax per unit. This yields a different result than the first-order condition derived for a monopolist without any tax imposed. The second-order condition for a maximization of profits is

$$\frac{d^2\pi}{dq^2} = R''(q) - C''(q) < 0$$

We now wish to determine how monopolistic output changes as the amount of the tax changes, that is, an expression for dq/dS. We notice that the first-order conditions can be written as

$$S = R'(q) - C'(q)$$

From this expression, we can easily find

$$\frac{dS}{dq} = R''(q) - C''(q)$$

By the inverse function theorem given in Section 8.10, we know that

$$\frac{dq}{dS} = \frac{1}{dS/dq}$$

Therefore,

$$\frac{dq}{dS} = \frac{1}{R''(q) - C''(q)}$$

But $R''(q) - C''(q) < 0$ by the second-order conditions. Therefore

$$\frac{dq}{dS} < 0$$

This means that as the specific tax increases, the profit-maximizing output decreases. As a result of this decrease in output, product price will increase, as indicated by the usual negatively sloped demand function.

The effect of a specific tax is, then, to reduce the quantity and increase the price of the product. The profit level will also decrease somewhat, because the new quantity and price levels cannot yield as much profit as would have been received without any tax, as indicated by the fact that the firm did not choose such levels originally.

Illustration 3. Return to the monopolist of prior illustrations, who has a demand function given by $p = 15 - 6q_d$, where $q_d \geqslant 0$, and a cost function of $C = 2q^3 - 3q^2 + 3q + 2$, where $q \geqslant 0$. Suppose that a specific tax of $2 per unit is imposed upon the monopolist. What effect will this have upon the firm's output, the product price, and on profits?
Solution. Total revenue remains $TR = pq = (15 - 6q)q = 15q - 6q^2$. The profit function, assuming a $2 per unit specific tax, becomes

$$\pi = TR - C - 2q$$

$$= 15q - 6q^2 - 2q^3 + 3q^2 - 3q - 2 - 2q$$

$$= 10q - 3q^2 - 2q^3 - 2$$

To maximize the profit function, we set its first derivative equal to zero.

$$\frac{d\pi}{dq} = 10 - 6q - 6q^2 = 0$$

$$-2(3q^2 + 3q - 5) = 0$$

This expression cannot be factored, so the quadratic formula as given in Chapter 4 must be used. We have

$$q = \frac{-3 \pm \sqrt{9 + 60}}{6} = \frac{-3 \pm \sqrt{69}}{6} = \frac{-3 \pm 8.3}{6}$$

$$q = -1.88 \quad \text{or} \quad q = 0.88$$

Because $q = -1.88$ is outside the range of definition of the function, we are left with one possible maximum point, namely, $q = 0.88$.
The second-order condition for a maximum is

$$\frac{d^2\pi}{dq^2} = -6 - 12q < 0$$

When $q = 0.88$,

$$\frac{d^2\pi}{dq^2} < 0$$

Therefore a maximum is attained at $q = 0.88$. From the demand function, we find that when $q = 0.88$, $p = 15 - 6(0.88) = \$9.72$. The profit level will be $\pi = 3.12$. The possibility of a boundary solution, that is, $q = 0$, can be dismissed because the profit level would then be negative.

Thus the result of the specific tax of $2 per unit is to reduce quantity from 1.00 to 0.88, raise price from $9.00 to $9.72, and reduce profits from $5.00 to $3.12. As a consequence of the $2 per unit tax, product price increases by $0.72. The consumer pays $0.72 of the $2.00 tax levy. The monopolist receives $9.72 per unit, but must pay $2 per unit to the government. He remains with $7.72 per unit and, in effect, pays $1.28 of the $2.00 tax levy. The specific tax is thus partly shifted to the consumer.

Finally, let us consider the case where the government imposes a sales tax of rate h, where $0 < h < 1$. This implies a payment of a certain proportion of the dollar value of sales or total revenue. The profit function of the monopolist is then

$$\pi = R(q) - C(q) - hR(q)$$

that is, profit is revenue minus costs of production minus the tax levy, where the tax levy is given by $hR(q)$, which is the tax rate multiplied by sales or revenue. This can further be written as

$$\pi = (1 - h)R(q) - C(q)$$

The point of maximum profit is derived by setting the first derivative of the profit function equal to zero.

$$\frac{d\pi}{dq} = (1 - h)R'(q) - C'(q) = 0$$

$$(1 - h)R'(q) = C'(q)$$

that is, the monopolist must equate $1 - h$ of marginal revenue to marginal cost. This yields a different result than the first-order condition derived for a monopolist without any tax imposed. The second-order condition for a maximization of profits is

$$\frac{d^2\pi}{dq^2} = (1 - h)R''(q) - C''(q) < 0$$

To determine how monopolistic output changes as the sales tax rate changes, we wish to find an expression for dq/dh. The first-order condition can be written as

$$R'(q) - hR'(q) - C'(q) = 0$$

Remembering that both q and h are now to be considered variable, we differentiate implicitly with respect to q. This yields

$$R''(q) - hR''(q) - R'(q)\frac{dh}{dq} - C''(q) = 0$$

$$R'(q)\frac{dh}{dq} = R''(q) - hR''(q) - C''(q)$$

$$\frac{dh}{dq} = \frac{(1 - h)R''(q) - C''(q)}{R'(q)}$$

By the inverse function theorem, we know that

$$\frac{dq}{dh} = \frac{1}{dh/dq}$$

Therefore,

$$\frac{dq}{dh} = \frac{R'(q)}{(1 - h)R''(q) - C''(q)}$$

Now, the first-order condition for profit maximization requires $R'(q)$ to be positive, because $C'(q)$ is positive for any economic good. The second-order condition requires that $(1 - h)R''(q) - C''(q)$ be negative. Therefore, we may conclude that

$$\frac{dq}{dh} < 0$$

if profits are being maximized. This implies that an increase in the sales tax rate will reduce output. As a result of the decrease in output, product price will increase, as indicated by the usual negatively sloped demand function.

A sales tax thus has similar effects to a specific tax in that it reduces the quantity and increases the price of the product. The profit level will also decrease somewhat for the same reason as explained in the case of a specific tax.

Illustration 4.   Once more consider the monopolist who has a demand function given by $p = 15 - 6q_d$, where $q_d \geqslant 0$, and a cost function of $C = 2q^3 - 3q^2 + 3q + 2$, where $q \geqslant 0$. Suppose that a sales tax of 10 percent is imposed upon the monopolist. What effect will this have upon the firm's output, the product price, and profits?

Solution. The profit function becomes

$$\pi = TR - TC - 0.10(TR)$$
$$= 15q - 6q^2 - 2q^3 + 3q^2 - 3q - 2 - 0.10(15q - 6q^2)$$
$$= 10.5q - 2.4q^2 - 2q^3 - 2$$

To maximize the profit function, we set its first derivative equal to zero.

$$\frac{d\pi}{dq} = 10.5 - 4.8q - 6q^2 = 0$$

$$-(6q^2 + 4.8q - 10.5) = 0$$

This expression cannot be factored, so the quadratic formula must be used. We find

$$q = \frac{-4.8 \pm \sqrt{23.04 + 252}}{12} = \frac{-4.8 \pm \sqrt{275.04}}{12} = \frac{-4.8 \pm 16.6}{12}$$

$$q = -1.78 \quad \text{or} \quad q = 0.98$$

Because $q = -1.78$ is outside the range of definition of the function, we are left with one possible maximum point, namely, $q = 0.98$.
    The second-order condition for a maximum is

$$\frac{d^2\pi}{dq^2} = -4.8 - 12q < 0$$

When $q = 0.98$,

$$\frac{d^2\pi}{dq^2} < 0$$

Therefore a maximum is attained at $q = 0.98$. From the demand function, we find that when $q = 0.98$, $p = 15 - 6(0.98) = \$9.12$. The profit level will be $\pi = 4.11$. The possibility of a boundary solution, that is, $q = 0$, can be dismissed because the profit level would then be negative.
    Thus, the result of the 10 percent sales tax is to reduce quantity from 1.00 to 0.98, raise price from \$9.00 to \$9.12, and reduce profits from \$5.00 to \$4.11. As for the case of a specific tax considered earlier, the sales tax is partly shifted to the consumer but also borne, in part, by the monopolist.

Exercises

In each of the following cases, find the effect upon output, price, and profit of (a) a lump-sum tax of $10, (b) a 20 percent profits tax, (c) a specific tax of $5 per unit, (d) a 5 percent sales tax imposed upon the monopolist.

1. The demand function for the monopolist is given by $p = 60 - 2q_d$, where $q_d \geqslant 0$. Its cost function is $C = 39q - 11q^2 + q^3 + 5$, where $q \geqslant 0$.
2. The demand function for the monopolist is given by $p = 100 + 17q - 3q_d^2$, where $q_d \geqslant 0$. Its cost function is $C = 50q - 8q^2 + q^3 + 10$, where $q \geqslant 0$.
3. The demand function for the monopolist is given by $p = 200 - 4q_d^2$, where $q_d \geqslant 0$. Its cost function is $C = 80q - 15q^2 + q^3 + 100$, where $q \geqslant 0$.
4. The demand function for the monopolist is given by $p = 80 - 12q_d - 2q_d^2$, where $q_d \geqslant 0$. Its cost function is $C = 32q - 12q^2 + 2q^3 + 25$, where $q \geqslant 0$.
5. The demand function for the monopolist is given by $p = 45 - q_d$, where $q_d \geqslant 0$. Its cost function is $C = 5q$, where $q \geqslant 0$.
6. The demand function for the monopolist is given by $p = 12 - 2q_d$, where $q_d \geqslant 0$. Its cost function is $C = 4q + 4$, where $q \geqslant 0$.
7. The demand function for the monopolist is given by $p = 120 - 3q_d$, where $q_d \geqslant 0$. Its cost function is $C = q^2 + 100$, where $q \geqslant 0$.

SECTION 14·7   MONOPOLY AND REVENUE MAXIMIZATION

In Section 13.8 it was pointed out that while profit maximization is most often assumed to be the objective of business firms, it is possible that other objectives may sometimes be more important. One such alternative goal has been emphasized by William Baumol.[3] It is Baumol's contention that many large firms are more concerned with the level of sales than with the level of profits. The ability to raise funds in the money market for future expansion is often tied more closely to size than to profitability. Moreover, with the separation of ownership and control that is prevalent in most large enterprises, management has more to gain from the expansion of sales than from increased profits. Increased sales promote the

[3] See William Baumol, *Business Behavior, Value and Growth*, (New York: Harcourt Brace Jovanovich, 1967).

growth of firms and the number of workers and other inputs that must be managed. This, in turn, increases the power of management. Moreover, the larger the firm, the more likely it is for the salaries, bonuses, and other management perquisites to increase.

Of course, management is to some degree accountable, in the final analysis, to the stockholders. But it is felt by Baumol that as long as the firm is able to earn a minimally acceptable profit return, this will satisfy its stockholders. Thus, according to this hypothesis, management will strive to maximize sales or revenue subject to the proviso that it must earn the minimally acceptable profit level.

We now consider how the management of a monopolistic firm would determine its output and product price with the goal of revenue maximization in mind. This approach can be extended to the case of an industry with a few large firms. It is also possible to hypothesize other goals on the part of firms and to see the resulting effects.

Suppose that the profit-maximizing output for a monopolist occurs at q_0 at which a profit of π_0 could be realized. Assume, however, that the monopolist wishes to maximize revenue $R(q)$ subject to the condition that profit must be at least as great as π_1. If $\pi_0 \leqslant \pi_1$, there will be no difference in the level of output between the profit maximizer and the revenue maximizer. The latter will not expand sales, because the minimum profit will not have been surpassed.

On the other hand, if $\pi_0 > \pi_1$, the revenue maximizer will realize that it could expand sales and still preserve the minimum acceptable profit level of π_1. Such a firm will therefore continue to increase output until it reaches either the maximum possible revenue point or the point where $\pi = \pi_1$.

This suggests to us that we can find the equilibrium level of output for the revenue maximizer subject to a minimum profit by first finding the maximum revenue output. If at such a point $\pi \geqslant \pi_1$, then this will be the output level. If at such a point $\pi < \pi_1$, then the minimum profit is not realized and output must be curtailed by a sufficient amount so that $\pi = \pi_1$. The firm's equilibrium then occurs at the point where $\pi = \pi_1$. If there is more than one value of q for which $\pi = \pi_1$, then the one that yields the greater revenue will be selected.

Illustration. The cost function for a monopolist is given by $C = 3q^2 + 10$, where $q \geqslant 0$. The demand for its product is $p = 60 - 3q_d$, where $q_d \geqslant 0$. The firm wishes to maximize revenue subject to the constraint that profit is at least \$44. Find the firm's output, the price it will charge, and the amount of profit it will make, and compare these to what would pertain for a profit-maximizing monopolist.

Solution. Total revenue is given by $TR = pq = 60q - 3q^2$. The profit function is $\pi = TR - C = 60q - 3q^2 - 3q^2 - 10 = 60q - 6q^2 - 10$. If the firm wished to maximize profits, it would set the first derivative of the profit function equal to zero:

$$\frac{d\pi}{dq} = 60 - 12q = 0$$

$$12q = 60$$

$$q = 5$$

At $q = 5$, we find the product price to be $p = 60 - 3q = 45$ and profit to be $\pi = 140$. The second-order condition for a maximum is satisfied, because

$$\frac{d^2\pi}{dq^2} = -12 < 0$$

The possibility of a boundary solution can quickly be dismissed, because at $q = 0$ there will be negative profits.

A firm that wishes to maximize revenue subject to the constraint that profits are at least \$44 should attempt to maximize its revenue function:

$$TR = 60q - 3q^2$$

$$\frac{d(TR)}{dq} = 60 - 6q = 0$$

$$q = 10$$

The second-order condition for a maximization of the revenue function is satisfied, because

$$\frac{d^2(TR)}{dq^2} = -6 < 0$$

At $q = 10$, we find the market price to be $p = 60 - 3q = 30$ and profit to be $\pi = -10$.

This indicates that at the point where revenue is maximized, a negative profit is realized. Such a profit level is certainly below the minimum acceptable profit, so the firm will seek some other output level such that the minimum profit is achieved. This can be found by setting the profit function equal to \$44, which is the minimum acceptable profit. We then have

$$60q - 6q^2 - 10 = 44$$

$$6q^2 - 60q + 54 = 0$$

$$6(q^2 - 10q + 9) = 0$$

$$6(q - 9)(q - 1) = 0$$

$$q = 9 \quad \text{or} \quad q = 1$$

At either $q = 9$ or $q = 1$, profit will be $\pi = 44$, just satisfying the minimum profit constraint. We then find that at $q = 9$, revenue is $TR = 60q - 3q^2 = 297$, while at $q = 1$, revenue is $TR = 60q - 3q^2 = 57$.

We conclude that the firm will produce an output of 9 units, charge a price of $p = 60 - 3q = 60 - 27 = \$33$, make a profit of \$44, and receive revenue of \$297. This compares to an output of 5 units, a price of \$45, a profit of \$140, and a revenue of \$225 for the profit-maximizing firm.

Exercises

In each of the following cases, find the firm's output, the price it will charge, and the amount of profit it will make assuming that the firm wishes to maximize revenue subject to the given profit constraint. Compare the results to those that would pertain for a profit-maximizing firm.

1. The demand function for the monopolist is given by $p = 100 - 2q_d$, where $q_d \geqslant 0$. Its cost function is $C = 2q^2 + 50$, where $q \geqslant 0$. Profit must be at least \$350.
2. The demand function for the monopolist is given by $p = 120 - 3q_d$, where $q_d \geqslant 0$. Its cost function is $C = q^2 + 100$, where $q \geqslant 0$. Profit must be at least \$500.
3. The demand function for the monopolist is given by $p = 120 - 4q_d$, where $q_d \geqslant 0$. Its cost function is $C = 2q^2 + 120$, where $q \geqslant 0$. Profit must be at least \$456.
4. The demand function for the monopolist is given by $p = 12 - 2q_d$, where $q_d \geqslant 0$. Its cost function is $C = 4q + 4$, where $q \geqslant 0$. Profit must be at least \$3.

5. The demand function for the monopolist is given by $p = 45 - q_d$, where $q_d \geqslant 0$. Its cost function is $C = 5q$, where $q \geqslant 0$. Profit must be at least \$399.

SECTION 14·8   OLIGOPOLY

In previous sections we dealt with market structures that were extreme situations, namely, pure competition and monopoly. The former applied only where there were so many firms that no single one had any influence over the price of the product. The latter presupposes only one seller of a product. Either of these cases is not very likely to be encountered in practice. We spent so much time with them only because the consideration of the two extreme poles enables us to develop a basic approach that can then be applied, with the necessary adjustments, to more realistic cases.

We now turn to oligopoly, which is probably the most prevalent market structure in the U.S. economy. Oligopoly is characterized by few sellers. The product sold by the different sellers may be either homogeneous or differentiated. The most important aspect of this market structure is the interdependence of firms. Actions taken by one firm affect the other firms and invariably lead to reactions by such other firms. Thus, in deciding whether a particular industry is oligopolistic or not, there is no specific number that serves as a criterion for satisfying the "fewness" requirement. Rather, what is crucial is whether price, quantity, or other decisions made by one firm influence the decisions of the remaining firms. If an industry contains only two firms, it is said to be a duopoly, which is a special case of the more general term oligopoly.

Because any firm in an oligopolistic market is dependent not only on what it does but also upon the actions and reactions of other firms, it is difficult or perhaps impossible to conceive of a general solution to the oligopoly problem. There are many different patterns of behavior that characterize oligopolistic rivals. Results will vary depending upon the type of responses that can be expected. Thus, in some industries, rival firms typically act cooperatively; that is, they practice collusion. In others, firms frequently act to thwart the aims and intentions of their rivals. In still other cases, one or two firms emerge as leaders, with the remaining firms acting as followers.

In the succeeding sections we shall therefore consider how equilibrium will be attained given specific patterns of behavior on the part of firms in the oligopolistic industry. Theoretically the number of such models is infinite, but we shall deal with some of the more common types of behavior. Hopefully, such analysis should be suggestive as to how one would treat other varieties of oligopolistic behavior.

SECTION 14·9 PROFIT MAXIMIZATION UNDER OLIGOPOLY, ASSUMING COLLUSION

Oligopolistic firms may agree to act as one common entity with the aim of maximizing joint profits and thereby increasing expected profits for each firm. Such firms will set a common price (assuming a homogeneous product), decide how much output each will produce, and divide profits by some predetermined formula. If this happens, they are said to have formed a cartel.

The formation of cartels and the practice of collusion are generally illegal in the United States because they violate antitrust laws. In some other countries, this is not the case. Moreover, even in the United States, the law allows for certain exceptions, which, for example, enables producers' associations—cartels—to fix the price of milk in many parts of the country.

For simplicity, we deal with a two-firm industry and with a homogeneous product. The results can easily be generalized for any number of firms and extended to the case of differentiated products.

Let q_1 denote the output level of the first firm and q_2 the output level of the second firm. Total industry output is then $q = q_1 + q_2$. Costs of production vary from firm to firm, so there will be two distinct cost functions, which may be denoted by $C_1(q_1)$ and $C_2(q_2)$. Total industry cost is the sum of the costs of each firm, or $C = C_1(q_1) + C_2(q_2)$. Suppose that the demand for the product is given by $p = h(q_d)$. Total revenue for the industry is the product price multiplied by the industry quantity sold, or

$$TR = pq = h(q)q = R(q) = R(q_1 + q_2)$$

The industry profit function can then be expressed as

$$\pi = TR - C$$
$$= R(q_1 + q_2) - C_1(q_1) - C_2(q_2)$$

To find the profit-maximizing output, we set the first partial derivatives
equal to zero.

$$\frac{\partial \pi}{\partial q_1} = \frac{\partial R}{\partial q_1} - \frac{dC_1}{dq_1} = 0 \qquad \frac{\partial \pi}{\partial q_2} = \frac{\partial R}{\partial q_2} - \frac{dC_2}{dq_2} = 0$$

or

$$\frac{\partial R}{\partial q_1} = \frac{dC_1}{dq_1} \qquad \frac{\partial R}{\partial q_2} = \frac{dC_2}{dq_2}$$

which implies that marginal revenue must be equal to marginal cost for
each firm. It is easy to see that industry marginal revenue of a unit of
output is the same regardless of which firm produces that unit. Therefore,

$$\frac{\partial R}{\partial q_1} = \frac{\partial R}{\partial q_2}$$

so that the necessary conditions are equivalent to

$$\frac{\partial R}{\partial q_1} = \frac{\partial R}{\partial q_2} = \frac{dC_1}{dq_1} = \frac{dC_2}{dq_2}$$

that is, marginal cost of each firm must be equal to each other and each
equal to the marginal revenue of a unit of the product.

Second-order conditions must, of course, be checked to ensure that
a maximum profit position is actually attained. The possibility of boundary solutions must also be considered.

Illustration 1. An oligopolistic industry is composed of two firms that
sell a homogeneous product and practice collusion. The cost functions of
these two firms are given by

$$C_1 = 4q_1^2 \qquad C_2 = q_2^2 \qquad \text{where } q_1 \text{ and } q_2 \geqslant 0$$

The demand for the product is given by $p = 140 - 2q_d$. Find the output
to be produced by each firm and the price charged for the product.
Solution. The two firms that practice collusion will attempt to maximize
joint profits. They will therefore look at total revenue for the industry,
which is

$$TR = pq = 140q - 2q^2 = 140(q_1 + q_2) - 2(q_1 + q_2)^2$$
$$= 140q_1 + 140q_2 - 2q_1^2 - 4q_1q_2 - 2q_2^2$$

The industry profit function can be expressed as

$$\pi = R(q_1 + q_2) - C_1(q_1) - C_2(q_2)$$

which, in our case, becomes

$$\pi = 140q_1 + 140q_2 - 2q_1^2 - 4q_1q_2 - 2q_2^2 - 4q_1^2 - q_2^2$$
$$= 140q_1 + 140q_2 - 6q_1^2 - 4q_1q_2 - 3q_2^2$$

To maximize joint profits, we set the first partials equal to zero, which gives

$$\frac{\partial \pi}{\partial q_1} = 140 - 12q_1 - 4q_2 = 0 \qquad \frac{\partial \pi}{\partial q_2} = 140 - 4q_1 - 6q_2 = 0$$

Solving simultaneously, we get

$$12q_1 + 4q_2 = 140$$

$$4q_1 + 6q_2 = 140$$

Multiplying the second equation by 3 gives

$$12q_1 + 4q_2 = 140$$

$$12q_1 + 18q_2 = 420$$

Subtracting the first equation from the second gives

$$14q_2 = 280$$

$$q_2 = 20$$

$$q_1 = 5$$

When $q_1 = 5$ and $q_2 = 20$, we find that joint profits are $\pi = \$1750$. The two firms will divide these profits according to some predetermined formula, which could simply be to share profits equally, or firm 2 may get a larger proportion of the profits because it is the low-cost firm and does, in fact, produce 80 percent of the industry output.

To check second-order conditions, we find

$$\pi_{q_1q_1} = -12 \qquad \pi_{q_1q_2} = -4 \qquad \pi_{q_2q_2} = -6$$

from which we see that

$$\pi_{q_1q_1} < 0 \quad \text{and} \quad \pi_{q_1q_1}\pi_{q_2q_2} - (\pi_{q_1q_2})^2 > 0$$

Therefore the sufficient conditions for a relative maximum are satisfied at $q_1 = 5$, $q_2 = 20$.

To consider the possibility of boundary solutions, we consider first the boundary $q_1 = 0$, that is, the second firm should produce all output. We get

$$\pi = 140q_2 - 3q_2^2$$

Maximizing this function of q_2 by setting its derivative equal to zero gives

$$\frac{d\pi}{dq_2} = 140 - 6q_2 = 0$$

$$6q_2 = 140$$

$$q_2 = 23.3$$

for which $\pi = 1633.33$, which is a lower joint profit than for $q_1 = 5$, $q_2 = 20$.

The other boundary is $q_2 = 0$, for which we get

$$\pi = 140q_1 - 6q_1^2$$

Maximizing this function of q_1 by setting its derivative equal to zero gives

$$\frac{d\pi}{dq_1} = 140 - 12q_1 = 0$$

$$12q_1 = 140$$

$$q_1 = 11.7$$

for which $\pi = 816.66$, which is again a lower joint profit than for $q_1 = 5$, $q_2 = 20$.

We therefore conclude that the profit-maximizing industry output is $q = q_1 + q_2 = 5 + 20 = 25$ units. Five of these units should be produced by the first firm and 20 units by the second firm. The product price is derived from the demand function for the product, which is $p = 140 - 2q_d$. Total output is 25 units, so market price will be $p = 140 - 2(25) = \$90$.

The following illustration shows how collusion can be used to determine prices and quantities even where firms produce differentiated or nonhomogeneous products.

Illustration 2. An oligopolistic industry is composed of two firms that sell a differentiated product but that practice collusion. The cost functions for these two firms are given by $C_1 = 1.5q_1^2$, $C_2 = 2q_2^2$, where q_1 and $q_2 \geqslant 0$. The demands for the products produced by the two firms are given by $p_1 = 8 - 5q_1 - q_2$, $p_2 = 7 - q_1 - 2q_2$. Find the output to be produced by each firm and the prices charged by each firm.
Solution. The objective of the two firms is to maximize joint profits, so they must consider total revenue for the industry. This is given by

$$TR = TR_1 + TR_2$$

that is, joint total revenue is the sum of total revenue for each firm. This leads to

$$TR = p_1 q_1 + p_2 q_2$$
$$= 8q_1 - 5q_1^2 - q_1 q_2 + 7q_2 - q_1 q_2 - 2q_2^2$$
$$= 8q_1 - 5q_1^2 - 2q_1 q_2 + 7q_2 - 2q_2^2$$

The industry profit function can be expressed as

$$\pi = TR - C_1 - C_2$$
$$= 8q_1 - 5q_1^2 - 2q_1 q_2 + 7q_2 - 2q_2^2 - 1.5q_1^2 - 2q_2^2$$
$$= 8q_1 - 6.5q_1^2 - 2q_1 q_2 + 7q_2 - 4q_2^2$$

To maximize joint profits, we set the first partials equal to zero, which gives

$$\frac{\partial \pi}{\partial q_1} = 8 - 13q_1 - 2q_2 = 0 \qquad \frac{\partial \pi}{\partial q_2} = -2q_1 + 7 - 8q_2 = 0$$

Solving simultaneously, we get

$$13q_1 + 2q_2 = 8$$
$$\underline{2q_1 + 8q_2 = 7}$$

Multiplying the first equation by 4 gives

$$52q_1 + 8q_2 = 32$$
$$\underline{2q_1 + 8q_2 = 7}$$

Subtracting the second equation from the first gives

$$50q_1 = 25$$
$$q_1 = \tfrac{1}{2}$$
$$q_2 = \tfrac{3}{4}$$

We then find the prices charged by each firm from the respective demand functions:

$$p_1 = 8 - 5(\tfrac{1}{2}) - \tfrac{3}{4} = \tfrac{19}{4} = \$4.75$$
$$p_2 = 7 - \tfrac{1}{2} - 2(\tfrac{3}{4}) = \$5.00$$

When $q_1 = \tfrac{1}{2}$ and $q_2 = \tfrac{3}{4}$, we find that joint profits are $= \$4.625$.

The reader can verify that the second-order conditions for a maximization of profits are satisfied and that no boundary solutions exist.

We conclude that the first firm will produce $\frac{1}{2}$ unit of its product and charge a price of \$4.75, while the second firm will produce $\frac{3}{4}$ unit of its product and charge \$5.00. Joint profits will then be divided according to some predetermined arrangement.

Exercises

In each of the following cases, an oligopolistic industry is composed of firms selling a homogeneous product and practicing collusion. Find the output to be produced by each firm and the price charged for the product.

1. The cost functions for the two firms are $C_1 = 2q_1^2 - 8q_1 + 20$, $C_2 = 12q_2^2 + 25$, where q_1 and $q_2 \geq 0$. The demand for the product is $p = 60 - 2q_d$.
2. The cost functions for the two firms are $C_1 = 6q_1^2 - 8q_1 + 50$, $C_2 = 4q_2^2 - 16q_2 + 15$, where q_1 and $q_2 \geq 0$. The demand for the product is $p = 45 - q_d$.
3. The cost functions for the two firms are $C_1 = q_1^3 - 2q_1 + 18$, $C_2 = 10q_2^2 - 20q_2 + 36$, where q_1 and $q_2 \geq 0$. The demand for the product is

$$p = 180 + \frac{300}{q_d}$$

4. The cost functions for the three firms are $C_1 = 10q_1^2 - 10q_1 + 25$, $C_2 = 3q_2^2 - 2q_2 + 8$, $C_3 = 5q_3^3 + 40$, where q_1, q_2, and $q_3 \geq 0$. The demand for the product is

$$p = 10 + \frac{800}{q_d}$$

In each of the following cases, an oligopolistic industry is composed of firms selling a differentiated product and practicing collusion. Find the output to be produced by each firm and the prices charged by each firm.

5. The cost functions for the two firms are $C_1 = q_1^2 + 5$, $C_2 = 3q_2^2 + 8$, where q_1 and $q_2 \geq 0$. The demands for the products produced by the firms are $p_1 = 40 - 2q_1 - 2q_2$, $p_2 = 37 - q_1 - 2q_2$.
6. The cost functions for the two firms are $C_1 = 2q_1^2 + 4$, $C_2 = 6.5q_2^2 + 10$, where q_1 and $q_2 \geq 0$. The demands for the products produced by the firms are $p_1 = 100 - 2q_1 - q_2$, $p_2 = 75 - q_1 - q_2$.

SECTION 14·10   PROFIT MAXIMIZATION UNDER OLIGOPOLY, ASSUMING DOMINANT FIRM LEADERSHIP

Price leadership is a phenomenon frequently observed in oligopolistic industries. The firm that is the recognized price leader sets its price after considering the potential profitability of various alternatives. The remaining firms in the industry then generally follow suit. If the product is a homogeneous one, the industry price may well be uniform. In the case of a differentiated product, the expectation is that prices will vary somewhat from firm to firm. The essential feature of price leadership is that a price increase by the leader will be approximately matched by other firms. A similar result will occur when the leader reduces price.

The reasons that are responsible for one firm being the price leader rather than others are many and varied. One firm may be recognized as very astute in forseeing market conditions, thus attracting others to follow out of respect for its judgment. More frequently, it may happen that one firm can exert its leadership because of its dominant position in the market, that is, being the largest firm, the low-cost firm, or the most aggressive. This is known as *dominant-firm price leadership* and is the kind of price leadership with which we are concerned with in this section.

Consider an oligopolistic industry with k firms selling a homogeneous product. Assume that one firm is the dominant price leader. Let q_1 denote the output level of this leader and q_i the output of the ith firm, where $i = 2, 3, \ldots, k$. Total industry output is then $q = q_1 + q_2 + \cdots + q_k = \sum_{i=1}^{k} q_i$. Suppose that the overall demand for the product is given by $q_d = f(p)$.

In such an industry the price leader will set some price which the remaining firms will accept. These firms will then adjust their output levels in order to maximize profits given the price set by the leader. Thus all firms except the leader will, in effect, act in a way similar to pure competitors, who accept the market price and adjust output to maximize their profits.

For each firm other than the leader, we have $\pi_i = TR_i - C_i$; that is, the profit of the ith firm is its total revenue minus its cost of production. This is equivalent to $\pi_i = pq_i - C_i(q_i)$. To maximize profits, we must differentiate the profit function and set it equal to zero while considering p as a constant, because it is set by the leader. This gives

$$\frac{d\pi}{dq_i} = p - \frac{dC_i}{dq_i} = 0$$

$$p = \frac{dC_i}{dq_i}$$

This is a necessary condition for the maximization of profits for any firm other than the leader. Such firms will therefore equate the price set by the leader to their marginal costs and thereby determine how much to produce, provided, of course, that second-order conditions are satisfied and that no boundary solution exists. As the price set by the leader varies, so will the profit-maximizing output of the remaining firms. Thus

$$q_i = g_i(p)$$

that is, the output of the ith firm will be some function of the price set by the leader.

The dominant firm will compute the output that will be produced by all other firms at each possible price. It will then substitute these values of q_i into the market demand function in order to arrive at the demand function for its own product.

Now, market demand is given by

$$q_d = f(p)$$

where q_d is a composite of the quantities of all firms. This is equivalent to

$$q_1 + q_2 + \cdots + q_k = f(p)$$

or

$$q_1 = f(p) - \sum_{i=2}^{k} q_i$$

that is, the demand for the leader's product is the market demand minus the sum of the outputs of all other firms. But $q_i = g_i(p)$. Therefore,

$$q_1 = f(p) - \sum_{i=2}^{k} g_i(p) \tag{1}$$

The dominant firm will then find its total revenue function by solving expression (1) for p in terms of q_1 and then multiplying by q_1. It will also have a cost function expressing costs as a function of its output q_1. Its profit function will then appear as $TR_1 - C_1$. A necessary condition for the maximization of its profits is then the equality of its marginal revenue with its marginal costs. Thus the dominant firm, unlike the remaining firms, will maximize profits by equating marginal revenue to marginal costs and not price to marginal costs.

Illustration. An oligopolistic industry is composed of 17 firms that sell a homogeneous product. One of these firms is the dominant price leader. The cost function of the leader is given by $c_1 = 2q_1^2$ and the cost functions of the others are given by $c_i = 4q_i^2$, where q_1 and $q_i \geqslant 0$. The overall demand for the product is given by $q_d = 1000 - 2p$. Find the output to be produced by each firm, the price charged for the product, and the profit received by each firm.

Solution. The price leader will set the price, with the other 16 firms following. Therefore these 16 firms will consider the price as fixed and attempt to adjust their output so as to maximize profits. The profit function will appear as

$$\pi_i = pq_i - C_i$$

$$= pq_i - 4q_i^2$$

Set the first derivative equal to zero:

$$\frac{d\pi_i}{dq_i} = p - 8q_i = 0$$

$$8q_i = p$$

$$q_i = \frac{p}{8}$$

Thus a necessary condition for the maximization of profits, on the part of all firms other than the leader, is that output be equal to the product price divided by 8.

To check second-order conditions, we find

$$\frac{d^2\pi_i}{dq_i^2} = -8 < 0$$

The second derivative is negative, so the sufficient conditions for a maximization of profits are satisfied.

The possibility of a boundary solution, that is, $q_i = 0$, can be dismissed as long as some positive profit results from setting

$$q_i = \frac{p}{8}$$

because at $q_i = 0$, profit will be nil.

Each of the firms other than the price leader will produce $p/8$ units, so we can now find the demand function facing the leader. Demand for the leader will be overall market demand minus the output of the 16 nonleader firms. This will be

$$q_1 = 1000 - 2p - 16\left(\frac{p}{8}\right)$$

$$= 1000 - 2p - 2p$$

$$= 1000 - 4p$$

which is equivalent to

$$4p = 1000 - q_1$$

$$p = 250 - \tfrac{1}{4}q_1$$

We can now find the revenue of the price leader, which is

$$TR_1 = pq_1 = 250q_1 - \tfrac{1}{4}q_1^2$$

The profit function of the price leader is

$$\pi_1 = TR_1 - C_1$$

$$= 250q_1 - \tfrac{1}{4}q_1^2 - 2q_1^2$$

$$= 250q_1 - \tfrac{9}{4}q_1^2$$

To maximize profits, the price leader will set the first derivative of the profit function equal to zero:

$$\frac{d\pi_1}{dq_1} = 250 - \tfrac{9}{2}q_1 = 0$$

$$\tfrac{9}{2}q_1 = 250$$

$$q_1 = \tfrac{500}{9}$$

The price that corresponds to this quantity is found from the demand function facing the price leader, which we know to be

$$p = 250 - \tfrac{1}{4}q_1$$

Therefore, at $q_1 = \tfrac{500}{9}$,

$$p = \frac{2125}{9} \quad \text{and} \quad \pi_1 = \frac{250{,}000}{36}$$

Second-order conditions for the maximization of profits are satisfied, because

$$\frac{d^2\pi_1}{dq_1^2} = -\tfrac{9}{2} < 0$$

We can dismiss the possibility of a boundary solution, that is, $q_1 = 0$, because such a solution would yield zero profit.

Thus the price leader will set a price of \$2125/9, produce 500/9 units, and make a profit of \$250,000/36. The other 16 firms will each charge the same price, produce

$$q_i = \frac{p}{8} = \frac{2125}{72}$$

and make a profit of

$$\pi_i = pq_1 - 4q_i^2 = \frac{2125}{9} \cdot \frac{2125}{72} - 4\left(\frac{2125}{72}\right)^2 = \frac{\$2125}{1296}$$

Exercises

In each of the following cases, an oligopolistic industry is composed of one dominant price leader and several other firms, all selling a homogeneous product. Find the output to be produced by each firm, the price charged for the product, and the profit received by each firm.

1. The cost function of the dominant firm is given by $C_1 = 3q_1^2$, while the cost functions of the other ten firms are given by $C_i = 10q_i^2$, where q_1 and $q_i \geqslant 0$. The overall demand for the product is $q_d = 600 - 3p$.
2. The cost function of the dominant firm is given by $C_1 = 5q_1^2 + q_1 + 10$, while the cost functions of the other 16 firms are given by $C_i = 8q_i^2 + 15$, where q_1 and $q_i \geqslant 0$. The overall demand for the product is $q_d = 2000 - 5p$.
3. The cost function of the dominant firm is given by $C_1 = \frac{1}{3}q_1^2 + 2q_1 + 5$, while the cost functions of the other six firms are given by $C_i = \frac{1}{2}q_i^2 + 20$, where q_1 and $q_i \geqslant 0$. The overall demand for the product is $q_d = 800 - 4p$.
4. The cost function of the dominant firm is given by $C_1 = \frac{1}{5}q_1^2$; the cost functions of seven other firms in the industry are given by $C_i = \frac{1}{4}q_i^2$; and the cost functions of the eight remaining firms in the industry are given by $C_j = q_j^2$, where q_1, q_i, and $q_j \geqslant 0$. The overall demand for the product is $q_d = 500 - 2p$.
5. The cost function of the dominant firm is given by $C_1 = \frac{1}{4}q_1^2 + q_1 + 2$; the cost function of a second firm is given by $C_2 = \frac{1}{2}q_2^2 + 2q_2 + 3$; the cost function of a third firm is given by $C_3 = q_3^2 + q_3 + 6$; and the cost function of the remaining firm in the industry is given by $C_4 = 2q_4^2 + 10$, where q_1, q_2, q_3, and $q_4 \geqslant 0$. The overall demand for the product is $q_d = 437.5 - p$.

SECTION 14·11 PROFIT MAXIMIZATION UNDER OLIGOPOLY, ASSUMING FIXED MARKET SHARES

It sometimes happens in oligopolistic markets that all sellers are content to allow one firm to be the price leader provided that they are able to retain fixed shares of the market. Thus, if the leader changes its price, the other firms will react by changing their prices so as to preserve their share of the market. We shall deal with a two-firm industry for simplicity, but the results can be extended to any number of firms.

Let q_1 denote the output level of the first firm and q_2 the output level of the second firm. Total industry output is $q = q_1 + q_2$. Assume that the second firm allows the first firm to be the price leader, provided that fixed market shares are maintained. Suppose that the fixed market share of the second firm is a certain proportion, K. Then we can write

$$K = \frac{q_2}{q_1 + q_2}$$

Solving for q_2, we get

$$q_2 = K(q_1 + q_2)$$
$$= Kq_1 + Kq_2$$

and

$$(1 - K)q_2 = Kq_1$$

$$q_2 = \frac{Kq_1}{1 - K} \tag{1}$$

Consider the case where the two firms sell homogeneous products. Overall market demand for the product is given by

$$p = f(q)$$

or, equivalently, $p = f(q_1 + q_2)$. The profit function of the first firm is then

$$\pi_1 = TR_1 - C_1$$
$$= pq_1 - C_1(q_1)$$
$$= q_1 f(q_1 + q_2) - C_1(q_1)$$

Substituting the value of q_2 found in (1), we have

$$\pi_1 = q_1 f\left(q_1 + \frac{Kq_1}{1 - K}\right) - C_1(q_1)$$

Thus profit for the first firm can be expressed as a function of q_1 alone. It can therefore be maximized by differentiating with respect to q_1 and setting the result equal to zero. This will yield a value of q_1, and q_2 can then be found from (1).

In the event that the two firms sell a differentiated product, demand for the products of the two firms is given by

$$p_1 = h_1(q_1, q_2)$$
$$p_2 = h_2(q_1, q_2)$$

The profit function of the first firm is then

$$\pi_1 = TR_1 - C_1$$
$$= p_1 q_1 - C_1(q_1)$$
$$= q_1 h_1(q_1, q_2) - C_1(q_1)$$

Substituting the value of q_2 found in (1), we have

$$\pi = q_1 h_1\left(q_1, \frac{Kq_1}{1 - K}\right) - C_1(q_1)$$

Thus profit for the first firm is again a function of the single variable q_1. It can be maximized by differentiating with respect to q_1 and setting the result equal to zero. This procedure will yield a value for q_1, and q_2 can then be found from (1).

Illustration 1.   An oligopolistic industry is composed of two firms that sell a homogeneous product. One firm is the price leader, with the second firm content to follow provided that it maintains its one-third share of the total market. The cost functions of the two firms are given by $C_1 = 3q_1^2$, $C_2 = 4q_2^2$, where q_1 and $q_2 \geqslant 0$. The demand for the product is given by $p = 200 - 3q_d$. Find the output to be produced by each firm, the price charged for the product, and the profit received by each firm.
Solution.   The second firm is interested in maintaining its one-third market share. It has been shown that

$$q_2 = \frac{Kq_1}{1 - K}$$

so we have

$$q_2 = \frac{\frac{1}{3}q_1}{1 - \frac{1}{3}} = \frac{1}{2}q_1$$

The overall market demand for the product is

$$p = 200 - 3q_d = 200 - 3(q_1 + q_2) = 200 - 3q_1 - 3q_2$$

The profit function for the first firm is

$$\pi_1 = TR_1 - C_1$$
$$= pq_1 - C_1(q_1)$$
$$= (200 - 3q_1 - 3q_2)q_1 - 3q_1^2$$
$$= 200q_1 - 6q_1^2 - 3q_1q_2$$
$$= 200q_1 - 6q_1^2 - 3q_1(\tfrac{1}{2}q_1)$$
$$= 200q_1 - \tfrac{15}{2}q_1^2$$

To maximize this function, we set its first derivative equal to zero:

$$\frac{d\pi_1}{dq_1} = 200 - 15q_1 = 0$$
$$15q_1 = 200$$
$$q_1 = \tfrac{40}{3}$$

To check second-order conditions, we find the second derivative, which is

$$\frac{d^2\pi}{dq_1^2} = -15$$

This is negative, so we are assured of a maximum point at $q_1 = \tfrac{40}{3}$. The possibility of a boundary solution, that is, $q_1 = 0$ or $q_2 = 0$, can be dismissed.

We therefore conclude that the profit-maximizing output of the first firm is $q_1 = \tfrac{40}{3}$. Because $q_2 = \tfrac{1}{2}q_1$, we find that $q_2 = \tfrac{40}{6}$.

The product price is derived from the demand function for the product, which is $p = 200 - 3q_d = 200 - 3q_1 - 3q_2$. Because $q_1 = \tfrac{40}{3}$ and $q_2 = \tfrac{40}{6}$, the product price will be

$$p = 200 - 3(\tfrac{40}{3}) - 3(\tfrac{40}{6}) = \$140$$

The profit of the first firm is given by

$$\pi_1 = pq_1 - C_1(q_1)$$
$$= (200 - 3q_1 - 3q_2)q_1 - 3q_1^2$$

Therefore when $q_1 = \tfrac{40}{3}$ and $q_2 = \tfrac{40}{6}$, we find

$$\pi_1 = \frac{\$4000}{3} = \$1,333.33$$

The profit of the second firm is given by

$$\pi_2 = pq_2 - C_2(q_2)$$
$$= (200 - 3q_1 - 3q_2)q_2 - 4q_2^2$$

Therefore when $q_1 = \frac{40}{3}$ and $q_2 = \frac{40}{6}$, we find

$$\pi_2 = \frac{13,600}{18} = \$755.55$$

Illustration 2. An oligopolistic industry is composed of two firms selling differentiated products. One firm is the price leader, with the second firm content to follow provided that it maintains its one-fourth share of the total market. The cost functions of the two firms are given by $C_1 = 2q_1^2$, $C_2 = 3q_2^2$, where q_1 and $q_2 \geq 0$. The demand for the product of the first firm is $p_1 = 50 - 5q_1 - 2q_2$, while the demand for the product of the second firm is $p_2 = 60 - 3q_1 - 4q_2$. Find the output to be produced by each firm and the price charged by each firm.

Solution. The second firm is intent on maintaining its one-fourth market share. Because

$$q_2 = \frac{Kq_1}{1 - K}$$

we find

$$q_2 = \frac{\frac{1}{4}q_1}{1 - \frac{1}{4}} = \frac{1}{3}q_1$$

The profit function for the first firm is

$$\pi_1 = TR_1 - C_1$$
$$= p_1 q_1 - C_1(q_1)$$
$$= (50 - 5q_1 - 2q_2)q_1 - 2q_1^2$$
$$= 50q_1 - 7q_1^2 - 2q_1 q_2$$
$$= 50q_1 - 7q_1^2 - 2q_1(\tfrac{1}{3}q_1)$$
$$= 50q_1 - \tfrac{23}{3}q_1^2$$

To maximize this function, we set its first derivative equal to zero:

$$\frac{d\pi_1}{dq_1} = 50 - \tfrac{46}{3}q_1 = 0$$
$$\tfrac{46}{3}q_1 = 50$$
$$q_1 = \tfrac{150}{46}$$

The reader can verify that the second-order conditions are satisfied and
that no boundary solutions exist. Because $q_2 = \frac{1}{3}q_1$, we find that

$q_2 = \frac{150}{138}$

The price of the first firm's product can easily be computed from

$p_1 = 50 - 5q_1 - 2q_2$

Similarly, the price of the second firm's product is derived from

$p_2 = 60 - 3q_1 - 4q_2$

Exercises

In each of the following cases, an oligopolistic industry is composed
of a price leader and one or more other firms content to follow, provided
that the given market shares are maintained. Find the output to be
produced by each firm, the price charged, and the profit received by each
firm.

1. The cost functions for the two firms selling a homogeneous product
    are $C_1 = 2q_1^2 - 8q_1 + 20$, $C_2 = 12q_2^2 + 25$, where q_1 and $q_2 \geq 0$.
    The market share of the second firm is one-half. The demand for the
    product is $p = 60 - 2q_d$.
2. The cost functions for the two firms selling a homogeneous product
    are $C_1 = 6q_1^2 - 8q_1 + 50$, $C_2 = 4q_2^2 - 16q_2 + 15$, where q_1 and
    $q_2 \geq 0$. The market share of the second firm is three-eighths. The
    demand for the product is $p = 45 - q_d$.
3. The cost functions for the two firms selling a differentiated product
    are $C_1 = q_1^2 + 5$, $C_2 = 3q_2^2 + 8$, where q_1 and $q_2 \geq 0$. The market
    share of the second firm is one-sixth. The demands for the products
    produced by the firms are $p_1 = 40 - 2q_1 - 2q_2$, $p_2 = 17 - q_1 - 2q_2$.
4. The cost functions for the two firms selling a differentiated product
    are $C_1 = 2q_1^2 + 4$, $C_2 = 6.5q_2^2 + 10$, where q_1 and $q_2 \geq 0$. The
    market share of the second firm is two-fifths. The demand for the
    products produced by the firms are $p_1 = 100 - 2q_1 - q_2$,
    $p_2 = 75 - q_1 - q_2$.
5. The cost functions for the two firms selling a homogeneous product
    are $C_1 = q_1^3 - 12q_1 + 18$, $C_2 = 10q_2^2 - 20q_2 + 36$, where q_1 and
    $q_2 \geq 0$. The market share of the second firm is five-eighths. The
    demand for the product is

    $$p = 180 + \frac{300}{q_d}$$

6. The cost functions for the three firms selling a homogeneous product are $C_1 = 10q_1^2 - 10q_1 + 25$, $C_2 = 3q_2^2 - 2q_2 + 8$, $C_3 = 5q_3^2 + 40$, where q_1, q_2, and $q_3 \geqslant 0$. The market share of the second firm is one-third, and the market share of the third firm is one-fourth. The demand for the product is

$$p = 10 + \frac{800}{q_d}$$

SECTION 14·12 THE GIANT CORPORATION

Caution: The growth of giant corporations during this century has caused many to question whether the traditional theory of the firm, as outlined in previous sections, is relevant to major segments of the economy. Large, diversified corporations have significant impact, not only in product markets but also in input and money markets. They are not simple extensions of smaller firms. They are qualitatively different, because they are sub-economies in themselves, affecting the destinies of multitudes of workers and influencing or perhaps contriving consumer demand.

Moreover, these giant corporations often exert not only economic power but also political power. Indeed, their intricate structures, with the accompanying layers of management and bureaucracy, may make such organizations more similar to governments than to the traditional firm of economic theory.

Under such conditions, the true goals of these corporations may be difficult to ascertain. Indeed, there may not be one overriding goal pursued by management, but rather a complex combination of sometimes competing goals may be more typical. Maximizing profits may suit the stockholders, but they invariably have little or no control over these large institutions. The models of economic theory therefore fall far short of serving as a good approximation of market behavior in noncompetitive market structures. On the other hand, we should not preclude the possibility that our simplified models may adequately describe many real market situations. It is thus important to be aware of the limitations in such models, to search for new and better models and, above all, to evaluate the adequacy of the particular model used to predict or describe a specific market situation.

15

INCOME AND EMPLOYMENT THEORY

> With all its acknowledged deficiencies, the Keynesian analysis still stands as the most useful point of departure in macroeconomic theory. Itself incomplete and imperfect, it remains the foundation of the great majority of the significant theoretical works in macroeconomics of the past two decades. It has long provided the basic framework for most governmental analyses of economic conditions and forecasts, and, increasingly, of the analysis and forecasts made by private groups and firms.
>
> —Gardner Ackley

In this chapter we consider macroeconomic theory, which deals with aggregates such as national income and product, employment, and the general price level. This is contrasted to the microeconomic theory of previous chapters, which dealt with the determination of prices, quantities, and costs of individual products. The name most prominently associated with modern macroeconomic theory is John Maynard Keynes, although many others have also made significant contributions.

SECTION 15·1 NATIONAL INCOME AND PRODUCT

The market value of all goods and services produced in a country over a specified period of time (usually a year) is known as *gross national product* (GNP). No product is to be counted more than once. This means, for example, that the steel produced within a certain year that becomes part of a newly built automobile during the same year should be counted only in its final state, as part of the automobile, and not in its intermediate stage, as a raw material.

Gross national product, assuming no foreign trade, can be represented as

$$GNP = C + I + G$$

where C is the amount of expenditures on consumption products; I is the amount spent on investment products, that is, additions to the stock of capital including plant and equipment, housing, and additions to the level of inventories; G is the value of governmental goods and services, and does not include transfer payments which simply transfer money without producing anything.

In any period of time there is always a certain portion of the capital stock that becomes depleted or used up. This can be referred to as depreciation of capital. If we then subtract from GNP an allowance for capital depreciation, we have *net national product* (NNP). The difference between GNP and NNP is thus that the latter includes net investment instead of gross investment. We can therefore represent net national product as

$$NNP = C + \text{net } I + G$$

Whenever I is used to represent investment, it must be ascertained whether net or gross investment is being referred to. In subsequent discussions, unless otherwise stated, the symbol I will refer to net investment. Net national product is a more meaningful figure than GNP, because it makes allowance for depreciation of capital; but for this very reason, it is much more difficult to estimate accurately.

Net national product can be viewed not only from a production perspective, but also from an income perspective. This follows from the fact that all money spent on production becomes income to some person or entity, albeit in different forms (wages, interest, rent, profits, whether distributed or not, and government income such as sales taxes). Thus NNP is a measure not only of national product, but also of national income.

We wish now to develop some relationships between simple macro constructs. At the outset, we assume that there is neither government nor foreign trade. We shall subsequently relax these restrictive assumptions.

If we look at NNP from the income side, we can say that all such income is either consumed or saved (personal savings or corporate savings). Thus we have

$$Y = C + S \qquad \text{where } Y \text{ is NNP}$$

If we look at NNP from the production side, we can say that all production is in the form either of consumption products or investment products. Thus we get

$$Y = C + I \qquad \text{where } I \text{ is net investment}$$

We have already shown that the two approaches toward NNP are identical, so it follows that

$$C + S = C + I$$

and

$$S = I$$

We have thus derived a basic identity; that is, it must always be true that over any specified period of time, actual savings that take place in the economy are equal to the actual investment that occurs. The reader will recall that investment expenditures include additions to inventory stocks. Such additions are not always voluntary; that is, they occur when a smaller than anticipated amount of any product is sold. Thus the statement that actual savings equal actual investment does not imply that desired savings also equal desired investment.

Our next step is to introduce government into our model. We then find that viewing NNP from the income side gives us

$$Y = C + S + T$$

Where T = government taxes minus government transfer payments. In effect, transfer payments are negative taxes. The equation thus states that all income is used for consumption, savings, or paying taxes. On the other hand, if we look at the production side of NNP, we can say that all production is either in the form of consumption, investment, or governmental products. This gives us

$$Y = C + I + G$$

The two approaches are identical, so we conclude that

$$C + S + T = C + I + G$$

and

$$S + T = I + G$$

Thus, with the introduction of government, our basic identity states that actual savings plus taxes during any period must be equal to actual investment and government expenditures.

We are now in a position to extend our results to include foreign trade. From the income side, NNP can still be viewed as

$$Y = C + S + T$$

All income is used for either consumption, savings, or paying taxes. From the production side, NNP can be expressed as

$$Y = C + I + G + E_x - I_m$$

where E_x denotes exports and I_m denotes imports. Exports are added to $C + I + G$ because a portion of domestic production is shipped out of the country. Imports are subtracted from the other elements in the equation because, with a foreign sector, some of the expenditures on C, I, and G are used to buy foreign products. The two approaches are identical, so we conclude finally that

$$C + S + T = C + I + G + E_x - I_m$$

and

$$S + T = I + G + E_x - I_m$$

Thus we have generalized our very simple identity $S = I$, which applied with no governmental or foreign sectors, to the more realistic case where those sectors are included.

SECTION 15·2   THE CONSUMPTION FUNCTION

One of the cornerstones of modern macroeconomic theory is the assertion that the level of aggregate consumption expenditures is associated with the level of national income; that is, changes in Y result in changes in C. This can be expressed by writing

$$C = C(Y)$$

that is, consumption is some function of national income. Such a function, which could be statistically derived from sufficient data, is known as a *consumption function*. Note that this statement is not an identity, but rather a behavioral assertion that can be verified.

If we take the first derivative of the consumption function, we get an expression indicating the instantaneous rate of change of consumption with respect to changes in national income. This rate of change is known as the *marginal propensity to consume* (*MPC*). Thus we have

$$MPC = \frac{dC}{dY} = C'(Y)$$

The value of the *MPC* indicates how much of an additional dollar of income will be spent on consumption. Instead of talking about the additional consumption that results from increases in consumption, we could talk about the average amount of consumption per dollar of overall income. This is known as the *average propensity to consume (APC)* and can be expressed as

$$APC = \frac{C}{Y}$$

Now, consumption is a function of national income and savings is a residual of income after expenditures are made for consumption, so it follows that savings should also be a function of income. For simplicity, let us, at first, assume no government or foreign sector. We have already established that

$$Y = C + S$$

We also know that we can write $C = C(Y)$. Therefore

$$Y = C(Y) + S$$

$$S = Y - C(Y)$$

and

$$S = S(Y)$$

that is, savings in some function of national income. Moreover, the savings function can be derived from the consumption function, because

$$S(Y) = Y - C(Y)$$

If we take the first derivative of the savings function, we get an expression indicating the instantaneous rate of change of savings with respect to changes in national income. This rate of change is known as the *marginal propensity to save (MPS)*. Thus we have

$$MPS = \frac{dS}{dY} = S'(Y) = 1 - C'(Y) = 1 - MPC$$

The value of the *MPS* indicates how much of an additional dollar of income will be saved. We can also talk about the average amount of savings per dollar of income. This is known as the *average propensity to save (APS)* and can be expressed as

$$APS = \frac{S}{Y} = \frac{Y - C}{Y} = 1 - \frac{C}{Y} = 1 - APC$$

A general assumption that is invariably made in macroeconomic theory is that

$$0 < \frac{dC}{dY} < 1$$

that is, the marginal propensity to consume is a positive fraction smaller than 1. This implies that as income increases, so does consumption, but by a smaller amount than the increase in income. All available data certainly support this assumption.

Illustration 1. Suppose that the consumption function is given by $C = 40 + 0.9Y$. Find the MPC, APC, the savings function, MPS, and APS.

Solution.

$$C = 40 + 0.9Y$$

$$MPC = \frac{dC}{dY} = 0.9$$

In this case MPC is a constant; that is, the MPC is the same regardless of the level of income. For every additional dollar in national income, there will be $0.90 more consumption. Similarly, a reduction in income of any amount will lead to a reduction in consumption of $\frac{9}{10}$ that amount.

We also find

$$APC = \frac{C}{Y} = \frac{40 + 0.9Y}{Y}$$

Thus the APC is not a constant, because its value depends upon the particular value of Y. To see how the APC changes as Y changes, let us find the derivative of APC. We get

$$\frac{d(APC)}{dY} = \frac{-40}{y^2} < 0$$

Thus, as income increases, the APC decreases. To illustrate, if $Y = 1000$, the APC is $\frac{940}{1000} = 0.94$, while if $Y = 2000$, the APC is $\frac{1840}{2000} = 0.92$.

The savings function can be derived from

$$S = Y - C$$

$$S = Y - 40 - 0.9Y = (1 - 0.9)Y - 40 = 0.1Y - 40$$

and

$$MPS = \frac{dS}{dY} = 0.1$$

$$APS = \frac{S}{Y} = \frac{0.1Y - 40}{Y} = 0.1 - \frac{40}{Y}$$

Again to illustrate, if $Y = 1000$, the $APS = \frac{60}{1000} = 0.06$, while if $Y = 2000$, the $APS = \frac{160}{2000} = 0.08$.

Illustration 2. Suppose that the consumption function is given by $C = a + bY + cY^2$. Find the MPC, APC, savings function, MPS, and APS.

Solution.

$$C = a + bY + cY^2$$

$$MPC = \frac{dC}{dY} = b + 2cY$$

$$APC = \frac{C}{Y} = \frac{a + bY + cY^2}{Y} = \frac{a}{Y} + b + cY$$

$$S = Y - C = Y - a - bY - cY^2 = (1 - b)Y - a - cY^2$$

$$MPS = \frac{dS}{dY} = 1 - b - 2cY$$

$$APS = \frac{S}{Y} = \frac{(1 - b)Y - a - cY^2}{Y} = 1 - b - \frac{a}{Y} - cY$$

If we introduce government into the picture, then it seems logical that consumption will depend not only on the level of NNP (which is pretax income), but also upon the amount of income paid out in taxes. In that event, the consumption function can be expressed as

$$C = C(Y - T)$$

where, as in Section 15·1, T is government taxes minus transfer payments. This means that consumption, C, is linked to aftertax income, $Y - T$, rather than pretax income, Y. In a similar manner, it can be seen that if there is present a significant amount of undistributed corporate profits (i.e., retained earnings), consumption should be linked to the income at the disposal of the consumer and not to total NNP. Recognizing this, we express consumption as a function of disposable income (Y_d), so that

$$C = C(Y_d) = C(Y - T - U)$$

where U represents the amount of undistributed corporate profits and where $Y_d = Y - T - U$.

The level of national income, Y, is the most important variable in determining consumption. This is the justification for writing $C = C(Y)$ or $C = C(Y_d)$. However, other variables may also affect consumption. For some purposes, it may therefore be desirable to express consumption as a function of several variables. One of these other variables is the rate of interest. As the interest rate increases, people may save more and consume less; or it is possible that the interest rate may operate in different ways—for example, a higher interest rate, which returns a greater yield to savings, may actually increase consumption.

Other factors that could possibly exert a significant influence upon consumption include the level of financial assets and the amount of durables owned by consumers. Consumption could then be expressed as a function of several variables in the form

$$C = C(Y, i, A_F, A_D)$$

Where i is the interest rate, A_F is the amount of financial assets, and A_D is the amount of durable goods. Moreover, still other income variables (aside from Y, which is present income) could be used, such as expected future income, past income, peak income, and so on. For many purposes, however, it is sufficient to consider only the most important independent variable, so we shall continue to write

$$C = C(Y)$$

Caution: Consumption of Durables Versus Nondurables

In dealing with the consumption function, we lumped together all the various types of consumption. In fact, the consumption of durables is unlike that of nondurables in many respects. The effects of current income, past income, wealth, and so on upon the former could be very different than their effects upon the latter. If such is the case, then it would be necessary to derive separate consumption functions for durables and nondurables.

Exercises

In each of the following cases, find the MPC, APC, savings function, MPS, and APS. Also evaluate each of these assuming that NNP $= 1000$.

1. $C = 0.9Y$
2. $C = 100 + 0.8Y$
3. $C = bY$, where $b > 0$
4. $C = a + bY$, where $b > 0$
5. $C = 200 - 0.1Y + 0.0004Y^2$
6. $C = 50 + Y - 0.0001Y^2$
7. $C = 900 \ln Y - 950$
8. $C = 0.86Y$
9. $C = 80 + 0.85Y$
10. $C = 500 + 0.00045Y^2$

SECTION 15·3 INVESTMENT

In Section 15·1 we divided nongovernmental production into the two components of consumption and investment. The former refers to products that provide utility or satisfaction to consumers and that are exhausted either completely or substantially within the income period under consideration (usually a year). The latter refers to products that do not yield direct consumer utility within the usual income period of a year, but instead are produced because they facilitate and increase the capability of producing consumer goods. Investment products are also called capital goods, because investment is the process of adding to the existing stock of capital. The largest item within this category is business expenditures on plant and equipment. Residential construction and additions to inventory stocks are also considered investment. While it is true that housing provides direct utility to consumers, any residential structure has a life that extends over a considerable period of time. A house is not built to be consumed within the usual income period of a year, but rather for a long span of years. In this sense it is considered an investment in the future. Additions to the inventory stock do not increase consumer utility during the stated income period, because they do not reach the consumer within that time. In fact, they are a preliminary step toward achieving utility at some future time. Consequently, they are considered investment goods. When we refer to investment, we shall be talking about net investment; that is, expenditures made to replace worn-out or depleted capital will not be considered.

While it is individuals who consume, it is firms, by and large, that invest in capital goods. Consumers purchase consumption products in order to achieve utility or satisfaction, but why do firms spend money on investment projects? It seems likely that the expectation of profits is the overriding motive. Firms must therefore compute the returns over and beyond costs that will be derived from investment projects. Such returns (expressed as a percentage) were referred to by Keynes as the *marginal efficiency of capital* (*MEC*) or, as later writers have suggested, the *marginal efficiency of investment*. An investment project will be undertaken only if the *MEC* is greater than the interest rate, because if the interest rate is greater than the *MEC*, it would be more profitable to lend out internal funds or not borrow external funds.

In a short-run period, we may assume that the *MEC* is relatively fixed in comparison to the interest rate, which may vary greatly. Investment can therefore be viewed as a function of the interest rate assuming a constant *MEC*. This is expressed as

$$I = I(i)$$

where I is the level of investment expenditures and i is the standard market rate of interest. Now we easily see that (with a constant MEC), as the interest rate declines, the level of investment will increase, because projects previously unprofitable become profitable. Similarly, as the interest rate increases, investment decreases. This is expressed as

$$\frac{dI}{di} < 0$$

There is an inverse relation between investment and the interest rate. Of course, if the MEC changes, the whole function will shift.

Illustration 1. Suppose that the investment function is given by $I = 200 - 2000i$. Show that

$$\frac{dI}{di} < 0$$

and find the values of I and dI/di at an interest rate of 5 percent.

Solution.

$$I = 200 - 2000i$$

$$\frac{dI}{di} = -2000 < 0$$

When $i = 0.05$,

$$I = 200 - 2000(0.05) = 100$$

$$\frac{dI}{di} = -2000$$

which means that an increase in the interest rate will be accompanied by a 2000-fold decrease in investment. For example, an increase in the interest rate of 1 percent will result in declining investment by $(2000)(0.01) = 20$.

Illustration 2. The investment function is given by

$$I = \frac{a}{bi} \qquad \text{where } a \text{ and } b > 0$$

Show that

$$\frac{dI}{di} < 0$$

and find the values of I and dI/di at an interest rate of 5 percent.

Solution.

$$I = \frac{a}{bi} \qquad a \text{ and } b > 0$$

$$\frac{dI}{di} = \frac{-a}{bi^2} < 0$$

When $i = 0.05$,

$$I = \frac{a}{0.05b} = \frac{20a}{b}$$

$$\frac{dI}{di} = \frac{-a}{0.0025b} = -\frac{400a}{b}$$

A bit of reflection will show us that investment depends not only upon the interest rate, but also on variations in the level of national income. This follows from the fact that increased national income will result in increased consumption and sales, thus enhancing prospective profits, which, in turn, will induce increased business investment. It is thus more realistic to write

$$I = I(i, Y) \qquad \text{where } Y \text{ is NNP}$$

We expect that

$$\frac{\partial I}{\partial i} < 0 \quad \text{and} \quad \frac{\partial I}{\partial Y} > 0$$

Illustration 3. The investment function is given by $I = 200 - 2000i + 0.02Y$. Show that

$$\frac{\partial I}{\partial i} < 0 \quad \text{and} \quad \frac{\partial I}{\partial Y} > 0.$$

Find the values of I, $\partial I/\partial i$, and $\partial I/\partial Y$ when the interest rate is 4 percent and NNP is 1000.
Solution.

$$I = 200 - 2000i + 0.02Y$$

$$\frac{\partial I}{\partial i} = -2000 < 0$$

$$\frac{\partial I}{\partial Y} = 0.02 > 0$$

When $i = 0.04$ and $Y = 1000$,

$$I = 200 - 2000(0.04) + 0.02(1000) = 140$$

$$\frac{\partial I}{\partial i} = -2000$$

$$\frac{\partial I}{\partial Y} = 0.02$$

Illustration 4. The investment function is given by

$$I = \frac{aY}{bi} \qquad \text{where } a \text{ and } b > 0.$$

Show that

$$\frac{\partial I}{\partial i} < 0 \quad \text{and} \quad \frac{\partial I}{\partial Y} > 0.$$

Find the values of I, $\partial I/\partial i$, and $\partial I/\partial Y$ when the interest rate is 4 percent and NNP is 1000.
Solution.

$$I = \frac{aY}{bi} \qquad a \text{ and } b > 0$$

$$\frac{\partial I}{\partial i} = \frac{-aY}{bi^2} < 0$$

$$\frac{\partial I}{\partial Y} = \frac{a}{bi} > 0$$

When $i = 0.04$ and $Y = 1000$,

$$I = \frac{1000a}{0.04b} = \frac{25,000a}{b}$$

$$\frac{\partial I}{\partial i} = -\frac{1000a}{0.0016b} = -\frac{625,000a}{b}$$

$$\frac{\partial I}{\partial Y} = \frac{a}{0.04b} = \frac{25a}{b}$$

Caution: Investment in Plant and Equipment
Versus Residential Construction

Our analysis of investment has assumed that profitability is the motivation for such expenditures. While this is probably true in the case of the expenditures on plant and equipment, it can hardly be extended to residential construction, which is also included in aggregate investment. Thus, it should be clear that different forces affect these different components of investment. As such, it would be desirable and possibly necessary to disaggregate investment into at least two categories. It can even further be argued that the third subcategory of investment, namely, changes in inventories, is important and distinctive enough as to merit a separate investment function as well.

Exercises

In each of the following cases, show that

$$\frac{dI}{di} < 0$$

and find the values of I and dI/di at an interest rate of 8 percent.

1. $I = 300 - 1500i$

2. $I = 550 - 4000i$

3. $I = a - bi$, where $b > 0$

4. $I = \dfrac{5}{i}$

5. $I = \dfrac{450}{99i}$

6. $I = 400 - 3000i + 2000i^2$

7. $I = 500 - 100e^{100i}$

In each of the following cases, show that

$$\frac{\partial I}{\partial i} < 0 \quad \text{and} \quad \frac{\partial I}{\partial Y} > 0.$$

Find the values of I, $\partial I/\partial i$, and $\partial I/\partial Y$ when the interest rate is 8 percent and NNP is 900.

8. $I = 300 - 1500i + 0.03Y$

9. $I = 550 - 4000i + 0.01Y$

10. $I = a - bi + cY$, where b and $c > 0$

11. $I = \dfrac{3Y}{100i}$

12. $I = \dfrac{2Y}{99i}$

13. $I = 400 - 3000i + 0.001Y^2$

14. $I = 500 - 100e^{100i} + 0.1Y$

SECTION 15·4 INCOME DETERMINATION ASSUMING A FIXED INTEREST RATE

We have shown that both consumption and savings are functions of national income. Investment is, at least in part, a function of income. The question that now arises is what will determine the actual level of national income at any specified time. Assume at the outset that there is no government sector in the economy. We know from Section 15·1 that $Y = C + I$ or, alternatively, that $S = I$. These are identities and thus must always be true. This does not mean that people desire to save precisely as much as they wish to invest. In fact, savings and investment are not necessarily done by the same people. But even if desired savings and investment are not equal, it will turn out that actual savings equal actual investment.

Equilibrium is attained when no forces are acting to change things. In this connection, we saw (when dealing with microeconomics) in Chapter 4 that market equilibrium for any product is attained at a market price such that the quantity supplied is equal to the quantity demanded. If the two were not equal, there would be forces in operation causing the price to change. In an analogous manner for the macro market, the equilibrium level of national income will ensure that consumers, savers, and investors are achieving what they desire given the prevailing market conditions. If this is not the case, forces will be in operation that will cause continued changes in national income. Thus a nonequilibrium level of national income cannot be maintained, even if existing market conditions remain the same. An equilibrium level of national income will, on the other hand, endure as long as market conditions do not change.

For equilibrium to exist, it must be that

desired savings = actual savings

desired investment = actual investment

because if people are not achieving what they intend, there will be forces
tending to change things. The operation of such forces and their effects
will be described shortly. We also know that it is *always true* (i.e., whether
or not equilibrium is attained) that

actual savings = actual investment

It therefore follows that, *to attain equilibrium*, it is necessary that

desired savings = desired investment

It should be stressed that this last equation is not an identity, because it is
true only when the economy is in equilibrium—unlike the statement,
actual savings = actual investment, which is always true.

To see how forces work in the absence of equilibrium, let us assume
that the above condition are not satisfied. Suppose that at a certain level
of national income (Y_1), desired $S >$ desired I. This means that the
amount that people wish to withdraw from the income stream is not
matched by the amount firms wish to invest. The income level (Y_1) cannot
be maintained under such conditions. Inventories will involuntarily pile
up, thus raising I above desired I and ensuring that actual $S =$ actual I.
An inevitable consequence will be cuts in production, which will, in turn,
lower national income and savings.

On the other hand, if, at a certain level of national income (Y_2),
desired $S <$ desired I, this would mean that the amount firms wish to
invest more than matches the amount that people wish to withdraw from
the income stream in the form of savings. The income level (Y_2) will
therefore increase, because inventories will be involuntarily depleted—
thus reducing I below desired I and ensuring that actual $S =$ actual I.
The inevitable consequence will be increased production, which, in turn,
will raise national income and savings.

Only at a level of national income (Y_0) where desired $S =$ desired I
will the amount people wish to withdraw from the income stream be
exactly matched by the amount that firms wish to invest. The income
level Y_0 can thus be maintained and it is, in fact, the only possible equilibrium national income.

An alternative, but equivalent, way of expressing the equilibrium condition is to say that national income must be the same as the amount that consumers and investors, in combination, desire to spend on consumption and investment. If desired $C + I$ is smaller than the sum of all incomes being received, inventories will pile up, thus involuntarily increasing investment but, consequently, reducing production and national income. If, on the other hand, $C + I$ is greater than the sum of all incomes being received, inventories will be depleted, thus involuntarily reducing investment but, consequently, increasing production and national income. Only at a level of income where desired $C + I$ is equal to the sum of all incomes being received will equilibrium be attained.

We can therefore find the equilibrium level of national income by setting the savings function equal to the investment function and solving for Y. Assume a fixed interest rate in the economy. At a later point we shall show how any such rate is actually determined. We have

$$S(Y) = I(Y, i_0)$$

Because i_0 is some constant, there is only one variable, namely, Y in the expression. The solution is easily found. Alternatively, we can use the second formulation of the equilibrium condition, which is

$$Y = C(Y) + I(Y, i_0)$$

Again, there is only one variable, Y, and this can easily be found.

Illustration 1.   The consumption and investment functions are given by $C = 800 + 0.88Y$ and $I = 200 - 2000i + 0.02Y$. Assume that the market rate of interest is 5 percent. Find the equilibrium level of national income.

Solution.   The condition for equilibrium is that

$$S(Y) = I(Y, i_0)$$

We are given $I = 200 - 2000i + 0.02Y$ and $i_0 = 0.05$. Therefore we have

$$I = 200 - 2000(0.05) + 0.02Y = 100 + 0.02Y$$

We can derive the savings function from the given consumption function in the following manner:

$$
\begin{aligned}
S &= Y - C \qquad \text{by definition} \\
&= Y - 800 - 0.88Y \\
&= 0.12Y - 800
\end{aligned}
$$

We now set the savings function equal to the investment function, which gives us

$$0.12Y - 800 = 100 + 0.02Y$$
$$0.1Y = 900$$
$$Y = 9000$$

Alternative Method. An equivalent way of expressing the equilibrium condition is

$$Y = C(Y) + I(Y, i_0)$$

which gives us

$$Y = 800 + 0.88Y + 100 + 0.02Y$$

or

$$0.1Y = 900$$
$$Y = 9000$$

Illustration 2. The consumption and investment functions are given by $C = aY^2$ and $I = b - di + eY$. The market rate of interest is i_0. Find the equilibrium level of national income.
Solution. The equilibrium condition is

$$S(Y) = I(Y, i_0)$$

We are given $I = b - di_0 + eY$. The savings function is derived as follows:

$$S = Y - C$$
$$= Y - aY^2$$

Setting $S = I$, we get

$$Y - aY^2 = b - di_0 + eY$$

and

$$aY^2 + eY - Y + b - di_0 = 0$$

or

$$aY^2 + (e - 1)Y + b - di_0 = 0$$

This is a quadratic equation, which can be solved for Y by use of the quadratic formula:

$$Y = \frac{1 - e \pm \sqrt{(e - 1)^2 - 4a(b - di_0)}}{2a}$$

$$= \frac{1 - e \pm \sqrt{e^2 - 2e + 1 - 4ab + 4adi_0}}{2a}$$

Alternative Method.

$$Y = C(Y) + I(Y, i_0)$$

$$= aY^2 + b - di_0 + eY$$

$$aY^2 + eY - Y + b - di_0 = 0$$

$$aY^2 + (e - 1)Y + b - di_0 = 0$$

which is the same as we arrived at using the first method. The solution will obviously be identical.

It is easily seen that nothing in the derivation of the equilibrium level of national income assures us that this equilibrium level will correspond to full employment. It may be possible to generate the indicated national income or product with 90 percent, 95 percent, or 100 percent of the labor force employed.

It is now time to introduce a government sector into the economy. We know from Section 15·1 that our basic identities change to

$$S + T = I + G$$

and

$$Y = C + I + G$$

where G represents governmental expenditures on goods and services and T represents taxes minus transfer payments.

The equilibrium conditions change correspondingly to:

desired savings + taxes = desired investment
+ government expenditures

national income = desired consumption + desired investment
+ government expenditures

To find the equilibrium level of national income, we therefore solve the following equation:

$$S(Y - T) + T = I(Y, i_0) + G$$

Note that with a government sector, savings is written as a function of aftertax income $(Y - T)$ instead of the simple NNP (Y) that applies when there is no government sector (see Section 15·2). The interest rate is again taken as fixed at i_0 as in the previous case. Assuming that T and G are determined by government policy makers, the equilibrium equation involves only one variable, Y, and the solution is easily found.

Alternatively, we can use the second formulation of the equilibrium condition, which is

$$Y = C(Y - T) + I(Y, i_0) + G$$

Consumption is a function of posttax income $(Y - T)$ and G, T, and i_0 are fixed. Again, we have only one variable, Y, and the solution is easily found.

Illustration 3.   The consumption and investment functions are given by $C = 800 + 0.88(Y - T)$ and $I = 200 - 2,000i + 0.02Y$. The market rate of interest is fixed at 5 percent, while government expenditures are 110 and $T = 100$. Find the equilibrium level of national income.
Solution.   The equilibrium condition is

$$S(Y - T) + T = I(Y, i_0) + G$$

We are given

$$I = 200 - 2000i + 0.02Y \quad \text{and} \quad i_0 = 0.05.$$

Therefore we have

$$I = 200 - 2000(0.05) + 0.02Y = 100 + 0.02Y$$

The savings function can be derived from the consumption function in the following manner:

$$
\begin{aligned}
S &= Y - C - T \\
  &= Y - 800 - 0.88(Y - T) - T \\
  &= Y - 800 - 0.88Y + 0.88T - T \\
  &= 0.12Y - 0.12T - 800
\end{aligned}
$$

Because $T = 100$, we find

$$
\begin{aligned}
S &= 0.12Y - 0.12(100) - 800 \\
  &= 0.12Y - 812
\end{aligned}
$$

We now set savings plus taxes equal to investment plus government expenditures, which gives us

$$0.12Y - 812 + 100 = 100 + 0.02Y + 110$$
$$0.1Y = 922$$
$$Y = 9220$$

Alternative Method. An equivalent way of expressing the equilibrium condition is

$$Y = C(Y - T) + I(Y, i_0) + G$$
$$= 800 + 0.88(Y - T) + 100 + 0.02Y + G$$

or, because $G = 110$ and $T = 100$,

$$Y = 800 + 0.88(Y - 100) + 100 + 0.02Y + 110$$
$$= 922 + 0.9Y$$

and

$$0.1Y = 922$$
$$Y = 9220$$

In the event that taxes are not a simply stated dollar amount but depend on the level of income (e.g., income taxes), we would have

$$T = T(Y) \quad \text{instead of} \quad T = T_0$$

However, the equilibrium condition would still involve only the single variable Y and the solution should not pose any problem.

Caution: Interactions Between Governmental and Nongovernmental Expenditures

The government component of the national income model is generally assumed to be exogenous or independent of the workings of the model; that is, it is determined by policy makers and can be assumed to be fixed or constant for the purpose of finding the solution for the other variables. In reality, however, the public sector is also dependent on the other variables that affect the model and therefore is not rigidly fixed. Government expenditures on education, health care, mass transit, housing, and other social projects depend, to some degree, upon the levels of

population and income. Moreover, government investment is both affected by and affects private investment. Consumer spending on such
things as automobiles and recreation are connected to the government-
built highways, parks, and so on. It is therefore a gross simplification to
consider all government actions as exogeneous.

Exercises

Find the equilibrium level of national income in each of the following cases.

1. $C = 0.87Y, I = 300 - 1500i + 0.03Y, i_0 = 0.02$

2. $C = 100 + 0.79Y, I = 550 - 4000i + 0.01Y, i_0 = 0.08$

3. $C = 80 + 0.85Y, I = \dfrac{Y}{200i}, i = 0.05$

4. $C = a + bY, I = d - ei + fY, i = i_0$

5. $C = 200 - 0.1Y + 0.0004Y^2, I = \dfrac{3Y}{100i}, i = 0.06$

6. $C = 50 + Y - 0.0002Y^2, I = 500 - 3000i + 0.0001Y^2, i = 0.05$

7. $C = 500 + 0.00025Y^2, I = 140 - 1000i + 0.00015Y^2, i = 0.04$

8. $C = 900 \log Y + Y - 3100, I = 200 - 1000i + 100 \log Y,$

   $i = 0.10$

9. $C = 0.87(Y - T), I = 300 - 1500i + 0.03Y, i_0 = 0.02, T = 200,$

   $G = 250$

10. $C = 100 + 0.79(Y - T), I = 550 - 4000i + 0.01Y, i_0 = 0.08,$

   $T = 30, G = 20$

11. $C = 80 + 0.85(Y - T), I = \dfrac{Y}{200i}, i = 0.05, T = 160, G = 180$

12. $C = a + b(Y - T), I = d - ei + fY, i = i_0, T = T_0, G = G_0$

13. $C = 100 - 0.1(Y - T) + 0.0004(Y - T)^2, I = \dfrac{3Y}{100i}, i = 0.06,$

   $T = 100, G = 86$

SECTION 15·5 THE MULTIPLIER

In the previous section we showed how the equilibrium level of national income is determined assuming a fixed interest rate. We now consider the effect that *changes* in investment, consumption, or government expenditures will have upon the level of national income.

We know that the equilibrium condition can be written as

$$Y = C + I + G$$

Assume that consumption is a function of aftertax income $(Y - T)$, investment is fixed at some level I_0, government expenditures are G_0, and taxes minus transfers are fixed at T_0. We then have as our equilibrium condition

$$Y = C(Y - T_0) + I_0 + G_0$$

A change now occurs in investment. To find the resulting effect upon national income, we must find $\partial Y / \partial I$.

If we write the equilibrium condition as

$$Y - C(Y - T_0) - I_0 - G_0 = 0$$

we can use the theorem on the differentiation of implicit functions presented in Section 10·7. This gives us

$$\frac{\partial Y}{\partial I} = \frac{-F_I}{F_Y} = -\frac{-1}{1 - \partial C/\partial Y} = \frac{1}{1 - \partial C/\partial Y} = \frac{1}{1 - MPC} = \frac{1}{MPS}$$

Thus the instantaneous rate of change of Y with respect to changes in I is the reciprocal of the marginal propensity to save. This means that if investment increases by ΔI, national income will increase by $(1/MPS)(\Delta I)$.

The expression

$$\frac{\partial Y}{\partial I} = \frac{1}{1 - MPC} = \frac{1}{MPS}$$

is called the *investment multiplier* (more frequently simply referred to as the *multiplier*), because it indicates the multiple by which national income will increase in response to an increase in investment. Now, the marginal propensity to save is a positive fraction less than 1. Therefore,

$$\frac{1}{MPS} > 1$$

so the multiplier is greater than 1. An increase of ΔI in investment will lead to a greater-than-ΔI increase in national income.

The reason for this result is that an increased investment of ΔI generates many rounds of respending. Thus national income and product will initially increase by ΔI, but this increased income is, in turn, at least partially respent by income recipients, thus generating more national product and income, which, in turn, is also partially respent, and so on. The magnitude of the respending will depend on the marginal propensity to consume. The total respending stream, including the initial investment, can be expressed as

$$\Delta I + \Delta I \frac{\partial C}{\partial Y} + \Delta I \left(\frac{\partial C}{\partial Y}\right)^2 + \Delta I \left(\frac{\partial C}{\partial Y}\right)^3 + \cdots = \frac{\Delta I}{1-r} = \frac{\Delta I}{1 - \partial C/\partial Y}$$

$$= \frac{\Delta I}{MPS}$$

The first term, ΔI, is the initial new investment. The second term, $\Delta I (\partial C/\partial Y)$, which is the new investment multiplied by the marginal propensity to consume, is the first round of respending that would occur. The second round of respending is the amount of new income generated in the previous round multiplied by the MPC. This amounts to $\Delta I(\partial C/\partial Y)^2$, and similarly for subsequent rounds of respending. The sum is computed by the well-known formula for the sum of an infinite geometric series. In this case it is given by $(\Delta I/1 - r)$, where r is the geometric rate of progression, which turns out to be $\partial C/\partial Y$.

Our result is the same as we computed earlier by use of implicit differentiation; that is, equilibrium national income will increase by $\Delta I/MPS$. But it now becomes evident that the achievement of this new equilibrium level of national income will take time and the operation of several income rounds in order to come to fruition. If we happen to be interested in the multiplier effect over some short period of time, it may be more appropriate to consider the resulting increase in national income after the workings of only two or three rounds.

Illustration 1. The consumption function is given by $C = 800 + 0.8(Y - T)$. Investment is some fixed constant, as are government expenditures and taxes. Find the value of the investment multiplier in general. In particular, by how much will income change if investment increases by 20?
Solution. The multiplier is given by

$$\frac{\partial Y}{\partial I} = \frac{1}{1 - MPC} = \frac{1}{1 - (\partial C/\partial Y)} = \frac{1}{1 - 0.8} = \frac{1}{0.2} = 5$$

This means that for each dollar increase in investment, national income will increase by $5. In particular, an increase in investment of 20 will result in national income expanding by $(5)(20) = 100$.

Note that even though we did not know the values of I, G, or T and thus could not compute the precise level of national income, we could nevertheless find the *change* in the equilibrium level of national income.

Suppose now that instead of a change in investment, there is a parallel shift or change in the consumption function. This means that the slope or derivative of the consumption function, that is, $\partial C/\partial Y$ remains the same but the constant term increases or decreases by amount a. The consumption function is then given by

$$C' = C(Y - T) + a$$

To find the resulting effect upon national income, we seek to determine $\partial Y/\partial a$, that is, the rate of change of income with respect to changes in the constant term a. Assume again that $I = I_0$, $G = G_0$, and $T = T_0$.

The equilibrium condition is

$$Y = C' + I_0 + G_0$$

or

$$Y = C(Y - T_0) + a + I_0 + G_0$$

which can be written as

$$Y - C(Y - T_0) - a - I_0 - G_0 = 0$$

The formula for implicit differentiation then gives us

$$\frac{\partial Y}{\partial a} = \frac{-F_a}{F_Y} = -\frac{-1}{1 - (\partial C/\partial Y)} = \frac{1}{1 - (\partial C/\partial Y)} = \frac{1}{1 - MPC} = \frac{1}{MPS}$$

Thus we have shown that the *consumption multiplier* is the same as the *investment multiplier*. An increase in either consumption or investment by some constant amount will have the same multiplier effect upon national income.

Illustration 2. The consumption function is given by $C = 800 + 0.8(Y - T)$. Investment, government expenditures, and taxes are fixed constants. Find the value of the consumption multiplier in general. In particular, by how much will income change if consumption increases by 20?

Solution.   The multiplier is given by

$$\frac{\partial Y}{\partial a} = \frac{1}{1 - MPC} = \frac{1}{1 - (\partial C/\partial Y)} = \frac{1}{1 - 0.8} = \frac{1}{0.2} = 5$$

This means that for each dollar increase in consumption, national income will increase by \$5. In particular, an increase in consumption of 20 will result in national income expanding by $(5)(20) = 100$. The consumption multiplier is seen to be identical to the investment multiplier of Illustration 1.

We now consider the case where I is not a fixed constant but depends upon the level of income. The investment function is then written $I = I(Y, i_0)$, where i_0 is a constant. Suppose that a parallel shift occurs in the investment function. This means that the slope or derivative of the investment function, that is, $\partial I/\partial Y$, remains the same but the constant term increases or decreases by some constant b. The investment function is then given by

$$I' = I(Y, i_0) + b$$

To find the resulting effect upon national income, we compute $\partial Y/\partial b$, that is, the rate of change of income with respect to changes in the constant term b. Assume again that consumption is a function of aftertax income $(Y - T)$, government expenditures are G_0, and $T = T_0$.

The equilibrium condition is then

$$Y = C + I' + G_0$$

or

$$Y = C(Y - T_0) + I(Y, i_0) + b + G_0$$

which can be written as

$$Y - C(Y - T_0) - I(Y, i_0) - b - G_0 = 0$$

The formula for implicit differentiation gives us

$$\frac{\partial Y}{\partial b} = \frac{-F_b}{F_Y} = -\frac{-1}{1 - (\partial C/\partial Y) - (\partial I/\partial Y)} = \frac{1}{1 - (\partial C/\partial Y) - (\partial I/\partial Y)}$$

$$= \frac{1}{1 - MPC - MPI} = \frac{1}{MPS - MPI}$$

where MPI is the marginal propensity to invest, that is, the proportion of an additional dollar of national income that will be invested.

The expression $\partial Y/\partial b$ is the *investment multiplier when investments is a function of income.* It differs from the earlier investment multiplier, which assumed that investment is a constant.

Illustration 3. The consumption function is given by $C = 800 + 0.88(Y - T)$, while the investment function is $I = 200 - 2000i + 0.02Y$. The interest rate, government expenditures, and taxes are fixed constants. Find the value of the investment multiplier in general. In particular, by how much will income change if investment increases by 20?
Solution.   The multiplier is given by

$$\frac{\partial Y}{\partial b} = \frac{1}{1 - MPC - MPI} = \frac{1}{1 - (\partial C/\partial Y) - (\partial I/\partial Y)} = \frac{1}{1 - 0.88 - 0.02}$$

$$= \frac{1}{0.1} = 10$$

For each dollar increase in investment, national income will increase by $10. In particular, an increase in investment of 20 will result in national income expanding by $(10)(20) = 200$.

It is easily seen that the multiplier effect works both ways; that is, if investment increases by ΔI, national income will increase by a multiplied amount but, conversely, if investment decreases by ΔI, national income will decrease by a multiplied amount.

Illustration 4.   Return to Illustration 3. By how much will income change if investment decreases by 15?
Solution.   The multiplier is the same as in the previous illustration, because the functions remain unchanged. It is given by

$$\frac{\partial Y}{\partial b} = \frac{1}{1 - (\partial C/\partial Y) - (\partial I/\partial Y)} = 10$$

If investment declines by 15, national income will decline by 10 times that amount, or $(10)(15) = 150$.

We now wish to explore the effects of a change in government expenditures upon national income. Assume that consumption is a function of aftertax income $(Y - T)$, investment is fixed at I_0, and $T = T_0$. To find the effect of a change in G upon national income, we must determine $\partial Y/\partial G$.
The equilibrium condition is

$$Y = C(Y - T_0) + I_0 + G$$

which can be written as

$$Y - C(Y - T_0) - I_0 - G = 0$$

The formula for implicit differentiation gives

$$\frac{\partial Y}{\partial G} = \frac{-F_G}{F_Y} = -\frac{-1}{1 - (\partial C/\partial Y)} = \frac{1}{1 - MPC} = \frac{1}{MPS}$$

This is the *government expenditures multiplier*. It is easily seen that this is the same as the investment and consumption multipliers computed earlier.

The government expenditures multiplier has important policy implications. If government policy makers are dissatisfied with the equilibrium level of national income (e.g., because of too much unemployment), they can increase government expenditures by ΔG and national income will rise by a multiplied amount $[(1/MPS)\,\Delta G]$. This, of course, assumes that increased government expenditures will have no adverse effects upon private investment.

Illustration 5. The consumption function is given by $C = 800 + 0.8(Y - T)$. Investment, government expenditures, and taxes are at some constant levels. Find the value of the government expenditures multiplier in general. In particular, by how much will income change if government expenditures increase by 20?

Solution.   The multiplier is given by

$$\frac{\partial Y}{\partial G} = \frac{1}{1 - MPC} = \frac{1}{1 - (\partial C/\partial Y)} = \frac{1}{1 - 0.8} = \frac{1}{0.2} = 5$$

This means that for each dollar increase in government expenditures, national income will increase by \$5. In particular, an increase in G of 20 will result in national income expanding by $(5)(20) = 100$. The government expenditure multiplier is seen to be identical to the investment and consumption multipliers of Illustrations 1 and 2.

In computing the government expenditures multiplier, we assumed that I was a fixed constant. In the event that I depends upon the level of national income, the government expenditures multiplier is computed in a similar manner. The result is analogous to the earlier case where we computed the investment multiplier under the assumption that I was a function of income. The multiplier expression in such cases will involve not only the MPC but also the MPI.

Suppose that we next wish to consider the effect of a change in taxes upon national income. Assume that consumption is a function of aftertax income, $Y - T$, investment is fixed at I_0, and $G = G_0$. To find the effect of a change in T upon national income, we must determine $\partial Y/\partial T$.

The equilibrium condition is

$$Y = C(Y - T) + I_0 + G_0$$

which can be written as

$$Y - C(Y - T) - I_0 - G_0 = 0$$

By the formula for implicit differentiation, we get

$$\frac{\partial Y}{\partial T} = \frac{-F_T}{F_Y} = \frac{\partial C/\partial T}{1 - (\partial C/\partial Y)} \tag{1}$$

We shall now show that $\partial C/\partial T$ and $\partial C/\partial Y$ are related. Because $C = f(Y - T)$, we can write $C = f(u)$, where $u = Y - T$. We then use the rule for differentiation of a composite function given in Chapter 10, which gives us

$$\frac{\partial C}{\partial Y} = \frac{\partial C}{\partial u}\frac{\partial u}{\partial Y} = \left(\frac{\partial C}{\partial u}\right)(1) = \frac{\partial C}{\partial u}$$

and

$$\frac{\partial C}{\partial T} = \frac{\partial C}{\partial u}\frac{\partial u}{\partial T} = \left(\frac{\partial C}{\partial u}\right)(-1) = -\frac{\partial C}{\partial u}$$

we therefore conclude that

$$\frac{\partial C}{\partial T} = -\frac{\partial C}{\partial Y}$$

which enables us to go back to (1) and write

$$\frac{\partial Y}{\partial T} = \frac{\partial C/\partial T}{1 - \partial C/\partial Y} = \frac{-\partial C/\partial Y}{1 - (\partial C/\partial Y)} = \frac{-MPC}{1 - MPC}$$

This is the *tax multiplier*. It indicates that a tax increase of ΔT will lead to a reduction in national income by

$$\left(\frac{\partial C/\partial Y}{1 - (\partial C/\partial Y)}\right)\Delta T$$

Conversely, a tax reduction of ΔT will increase national income by

$$\left(\frac{\partial C/\partial Y}{1 - (\partial C/\partial Y)}\right)\Delta T$$

Government transfer payments are, of course, negative taxes, and as such an increase in transfer payments will have the same effect as a decrease in taxes and vice versa for a decrease in transfer payments.

Let us now add the number 1 to the tax multiplier. We get

$$\frac{\partial C/\partial Y}{1 - (\partial C/\partial Y)} + 1 = \frac{(\partial C/\partial Y) + 1 - (\partial C/\partial Y)}{1 - (\partial C/\partial Y)} = \frac{1}{1 - (\partial C/\partial Y)}$$

which turns out to be the government expenditures multiplier.

We have thus shown that the tax multiplier is always one less than the government expenditures multiplier. The explanation for this is that government expenditures create national product immediately. When a portion is respent, additional income is created, a portion of which is again respent, and similarly for further rounds. This creates a full multiplier effect. In the case of a reduction in taxes, however, no new national product is created until a portion of the tax saving is respent. The resulting multiplier chain then falls short of that generated by government expenditures.

Illustration 6.   The consumption function is given by $C = 800 + 0.8(Y - T)$. Investment, government expenditures, and taxes are at some constant levels. Find the value of the tax multiplier in general. In particular, how much will income change if taxes decrease by 20?
Solution.   The multiplier is given by

$$\frac{\partial Y}{\partial T} = \frac{-MPC}{1 - MPC} = \frac{-(\partial C/\partial Y)}{1 - (\partial C/\partial Y)} = \frac{-0.8}{1 - 0.8} = -4$$

This means that for each dollar increase in taxes, national income decreases by $4, and conversely for tax reductions. In particular, a tax reduction of 20 will result in a change in national income of $(-4)(-20) = 80$. The tax multiplier is seen to be one less than the government expenditures multiplier.

Suppose that there occurs an equal increase in both taxes and government expenditures. The positive government expenditures multiplier would be one multiple greater than the negative tax multiplier. It follows that the net combined multiplier will be one. Consequently, national income will increase by the amount of the increased government expenditures. This is known as the *balanced budget theorem*. The impact of a balanced budget (i.e., equivalent amounts of expenditures and taxes on the part of government) exerts an expansionary effect upon national income.

Illustration 7. The consumption function is given by $C = 800 + 0.8(Y - T)$. Investment, government expenditures, and taxes are at some constant levels. What effect will an increase of 20 in both government expenditures and taxes have?

Solution. The government expenditures multiplier is given by

$$\frac{\partial Y}{\partial G} = \frac{1}{1 - (\partial C/\partial Y)} = \frac{1}{1 - 0.8} = 5$$

The tax multiplier is given by

$$\frac{\partial Y}{\partial T} = \frac{-(\partial C/\partial Y)}{1 - (\partial C/\partial Y)} = \frac{-0.8}{1 - 0.8} = -4$$

Therefore the increase of 20 in government expenditures will raise national income by $(5)(20) = 100$. The increase in taxes of 20 will reduce national income by $(-4)(20) = -80$. The net effect of both the expenditure and tax increase will be $100 - 80 = 20$, which is the same as the new expenditures.

Caution: Limitation of Multiplier Analysis

In each of the above illustrations, consumption was given as a linear function of income. This ensured that the marginal propensity to consume, that is, $\partial C/\partial Y$, would be a constant. Under such circumstances the multiplier is not difficult to compute, provided that the consumption function is relatively stable over a period of time. However, in the event that the consumption function is nonlinear, the marginal propensity to consume, $\partial C/\partial Y$, will not be a constant but rather some expression containing Y (i.e., national income). It will then be impossible to find the value of the multiplier that would pertain for some increase in, say, G, unless we know the new level of national income (i.e., Y). But if we already know the new equilibrium, Y, we hardly need the multiplier formulation to tell us by how much national income has increased.

Illustration 8. The consumption function is given by $C = 50 + Y - 0.0002Y^2$. Investment, government expenditures, and taxes are at some constant levels. By how much will income change if government expenditures increase by 20?

Solution. The multiplier is given by

$$\frac{\partial Y}{\partial G} = \frac{1}{1 - MPC} = \frac{1}{1 - (\partial C/\partial Y)} = \frac{1}{1 - (1 - 0.0004Y)} = \frac{1}{0.0004Y}$$

We cannot find this precise value unless we know the equilibrium level of income associated with the new level of government expenditures. But if we somehow know this level of income, there is no need to find the value of the multiplier, because the purpose of the latter is to enable us to determine the level of income that would ensue given a change in government expenditures.

In the final analysis, the adequacy of the multiplier analysis given in this section will depend upon how well the consumption function can be approximated by a linear function.

Exercises

1. $C = 0.85(Y - T)$, $I = I_0$, $G = G_0$, $T = T_0$. Find the investment, consumption, government expenditures, and tax multipliers. By how much will national income change if investment increases by 10? If consumption declines by 5? If government expenditures increase by 20? If taxes increase by 10? If government expenditures and taxes each increase by 15?

2. $C = 150 + 0.9(Y - T)$, $I = I_0$, $G = G_0$, $T = T_0$. Find the investment, consumption, government expenditures, and tax multipliers. By how much will national income change if investment decreases by 5? If consumption increases by 8? If government expenditures increase by 12? If taxes increase by 4? If government expenditures and taxes each increase by 14?

3. $C = 200 + 0.75(Y - T)$, $I = I_0$, $G = G_0$, $T = T_0$. Find the investment consumption, government expenditures, and tax multipliers. By how much will national income change if investment increases by 15? If consumption increases by $\frac{1}{2}$? If government expenditures increase by 6? If taxes decrease by 2? If government expenditures increase by 8 and taxes increase by 10?

4. $C = a + b(Y - T)$, $I = I_0$, $G = G_0$, $T = T_0$. Find the investment, consumption, government expenditures, and tax multipliers.

5. $C = 0.87(Y - T)$, $I = 300 - 1500i + 0.03Y$, $i = i_0$, $G = G_0$, $T = T_0$. Find the investment multiplier. By how much will national income change if investment declines by 15?

6. $C = 100 + 0.79(Y - T)$, $I = 550 - 4000i + 0.01Y$, $i = i_0$, $G = G_0$, $T = T_0$. Find the investment multiplier. By how much will national income change if investment increases by 11?

7. $C = a + b(Y - T)$, $I = d - ei + fY$, $i = i_0$, $G = G_0$, $T = T_0$. Find the investment and government expenditures multiplier.

SECTION 15·6   MONEY AND LIQUIDITY

Anything that is universally accepted as payment for debts or for purchases is *money*. Coins and paper currency are common forms of money, but the most important type of money arises from checking account balances. Payments by check account for the bulk of all monetary transactions.

Why do people hold money rather than spend it or lend it out? For one thing, people need a certain amount of money to cover their expected transactions for the period between paychecks and also to serve as a precaution for any unexpected contingencies that may arise. This combined need may be broadly referred to as the *transactions motive* for holding money. In addition, people will also seek to hold money for speculative reasons; that is, they may feel that there is a substantial probability that the interest rate may soon increase, making it wise to keep their money liquid so as to be able to lend it out at increased interest rates in the near future. This is known as the *speculative motive* for holding money.

The aggregate transactions demand clearly depends upon the level of national income. The greater the aggregate demand, the larger the number of transactions that take place and hence the greater the need for money on hand to be available for such spending. This can be written as

$$M_t = KPY$$

where M_t is the transactions demand for money, Y is net national product in real terms, P is a price index that measures changes in the overall price level, and K is some constant generally less than 1. The expression indicates that the transactions demand for money is some constant multiplied by net national product in current prices (as prices increase, transaction demand increases even if physical national product remains the same, because people need more money to buy the same amount of goods). The constant K is generally less than 1, because a given amount of money is turned over several times during a year. We also have

$$\frac{dM_t}{dY} > 0$$

that is, as national income increases, the demand for transactions balances also increases, and vice versa for decreases in national income.

The speculative demand for money, on the other hand, depends primarily upon the interest rate. The lower the interest rate, the more people will wish to hold in idle cash because of the likelihood that the interest rate will rise. Furthermore, when interest rates are low, not much is lost by holding idle balances. Conversely, as interest rates rise, people wish to hold less in idle balances because of the reduced likelihood that the rate will go up even further. Moreover, when interest rates are high, there is more to lose by holding idle balances and thus foregoing the income that could be earned by lending money.

The speculative demand (M_s) can therefore be written as

$$M_s = L(i)$$

where i is the market rate of interest (e.g., the prime rate). We shall also generally have

$$\frac{dM_s}{di} < 0$$

This means that increases in the interest rate will reduce the speculative demand to hold money in the form of idle cash balances, and vice versa for decreases in the interest rate.

The total demand for money, which is known as the *liquidity preference*, is the sum of the transactions plus speculative demands, that is, $M_t + M_s$. The actual supply of money (M_0) is, however, fixed by government authorities. If the demand for money turns out to be greater than the supply of money, this means that people on the aggregate desire to hold onto more money than is available. The result is an increase in the interest rate which is the price paid to induce people to give up their liquidity or cash balances. The increased interest rate will reduce speculative demand as explained above. On the other hand, if the demand for money is smaller than the supply of money, it means that people on the aggregate do not desire to hold onto as much money as is available. The result is a decrease in the interest rate, which will increase speculative demand.

Only at an interest rate level where the demand for money is equal to the supply of money will a state of equilibrium exist. At such a level there will be no forces exerting pressure to change things.

Thus the condition for equilibrium in the money market can be written as

$$M_0 = M_t + M_s$$

which is equivalent to

$$M_0 = KPY + L(i)$$

Assume a fixed price level P_0. It is evident that for any level of income Y_0, we can determine the equilibrium interest rate that will equate the two sides of the equation

$$M_0 = KP_0Y_0 + L(i) \tag{1}$$

But what will be the actual level of income? We found in Section 15·4 that by equating

$$S(Y) = I(Y, i_0) \tag{2}$$

or equivalently,

$$Y = C(Y) + I(Y, i_0)$$

we could find the equilibrium level of national income. That, however, assumed a fixed interest rate. Keynes thought that by stating the two equilibrium conditions (1) and (2), he was providing a solution to the national income model. The level of national income can be determined from equation (2), while the interest rate can be found from equation (1). It was, however, pointed out by both Hicks and Hansen that equation (2) could determine the level of national income only if the interest rate was known. But the interest rate could only be determined from (1) provided that the level of national income was known. There seemed to be some circular reasoning involved.

Hicks and Hansen then showed that while neither (1) nor (2) alone could provide a solution, the simultaneous consideration of both (1) and (2) was capable of producing a determinate solution for the equilibrium rate of interest and level of national income. If we take together the two equations, assuming that neither Y nor i is fixed, we have

$$S(Y) = I(Y, i)$$
$$M_0 = KP_0 Y + L(i)$$

This is a system of two equations in two unknowns, Y and i, which can generally be easily solved. Keynes thus provided the two key building blocks for a solution, but did not connect them. It remained for Hicks and Hansen to finish Keynes' work in this regard by showing that a determinate solution could indeed be derived.

Illustration 1. The transactions demand for money is given by

$$M_t = \tfrac{1}{4}PY$$

and the speculative demand for money by

$$M_s = \frac{10}{i}$$

Suppose that the level of national income is $Y_0 = 9000$, the price index is $P_0 = 1.00$, and the money supply is $M_0 = 3000$. Find the equilibrium interest rate.

Solution. The equilibrium interest rate is one that will equate the supply of money and the demand for money. The former is given as $M_0 = 3000$. The latter is the sum of the transactions and speculative demands for money, that is, $M_t + M_s$. We thus get

$$M_0 = M_t + M_s$$

$$3000 = \frac{1}{4}PY + \frac{10}{i}$$

The level of national income is given as $Y_0 = 9000$ and $P_0 = 1.00$, so we have

$$3000 = \frac{1}{4}(9000) + \frac{10}{i}$$

$$750 = \frac{10}{i}$$

$$750i = 10$$

$$i = \frac{1}{75} = 0.013$$

The equilibrium interest rate is then 1.3 percent.

Illustration 2.   The savings function is given by

$$S = 0.12Y - 800$$

the investment function by $I = 200 - 2000i + 0.02Y$; the transaction demand for money by $M_t = \frac{1}{4}PY$; the speculative demand for money by $M_s = 10/i$; the price index by $P_0 = 1.00$; and the money supply by $M_0 = 3000$. Find the equilibrium rate of interest and level of national income.

Solution.   Unlike the previous illustration, the level of national income is not given. Therefore it is necessary to solve the following equations simultaneously.

$$S = I$$

$$M_0 = M_t + M_s$$

By inserting the information given to us, we get

$$0.12Y - 800 = 200 - 2000i + 0.02Y \tag{1a}$$

$$3000 = \frac{1}{4}Y + \frac{10}{i} \tag{2a}$$

Now, equation (2a) can be solved for Y:

$$\frac{1}{4} Y = 3000 - \frac{10}{i}$$

and

$$Y = 12,000 - \frac{40}{i}$$

Equation (1a) can be rearranged to read

$$0.10Y = 1000 - 2000i$$

The value of Y can then be substituted into this equation to give

$$0.10\left(12,000 - \frac{40}{i}\right) = 1000 - 2000i$$

$$1200 - \frac{4}{i} = 1000 - 2000i$$

and

$$2000i - \frac{4}{i} + 200 = 0$$

Multiplying each side of the equation by i, we get

$$2000i^2 - 4 + 200i = 0$$

and $500i^2 + 50i - 1 = 0$, which is a quadratic equation in i and can be solved by use of the quadratic formula:

$$i = \frac{-50 \pm \sqrt{2500 + 2000}}{1000} = \frac{-50 \pm \sqrt{4500}}{1000} = \frac{-50 \pm 67}{1000} = 0.017$$

Because we had earlier determined that

$$Y = 12,000 - \frac{40}{i}$$

we now get

$$Y = 12,000 - \frac{40}{0.017} = 12,000 - 2353 = 9647$$

We have thus found the equilibrium interest rate to be 1.7 percent and the equilibrium national income to be 9647.

If we introduce a government sector, the equilibrium condition that requires the equality of savings and investment must be modified, as indicated in Section 15·4, to

$$S(Y - T) + T = I(Y, i) + G$$

Savings, which is a function of aftertax income plus taxes, must now equal investment plus government expenditures.

The two equilibrium conditions therefore become

$$S(Y - T) + T = I(Y, i) + G \tag{3}$$

$$M_0 = KP_0 Y + L(i) \tag{4}$$

As previously, there are two equations in two unknowns, Y and i, which can generally be solved.

Illustration 3.   The consumption and investment functions are given by $C = 800 + 0.88(Y - T)$ and $I = 200 - 2000i + 0.02Y$. Government expenditures are $G = 110$ and $T = 100$. The transactions demand for money is given by $M_t = \frac{1}{4}PY$; the speculative demand for money by $M_s = 10/i$; the price level by $P_0 = 1.00$; and the money supply by $M_0 = 3000$. Find the equilibrium rate of interest and level of national income.

Solution.   The savings function can be derived from the consumption function in the following manner.

$$S = Y - C - T$$
$$= Y - 800 - 0.88(Y - T) - T$$
$$= Y - 800 - 0.88Y + 0.88T - T$$
$$= 0.12Y - 0.12T - 800$$

Because $T = 100$, we find

$$S = 0.12Y - 0.12(100) - 800$$
$$= 0.12Y - 812$$

The two equilibrium conditions become in this case

$$0.12Y - 812 + 100 = 200 - 2000i + 0.02Y + 110 \tag{3a}$$

$$3000 = \frac{1}{4}Y + \frac{10}{i} \tag{4a}$$

From equation (4a) we find

$$\frac{1}{4} Y = 3000 - \frac{10}{i}$$

and

$$Y = 12,000 - \frac{40}{i}$$

Equation (3a) can be rearranged to read

$$0.10Y + 2000i - 1022 = 0$$

Substituting the value of Y into this equation gives

$$0.10\left(12,000 - \frac{40}{i}\right) + 2000i - 1022 = 0$$

$$1200 - \frac{4}{i} + 2000i - 1022 = 0$$

$$2000i + 178 - \frac{4}{i} = 0$$

Multiplying both sides of the equation by i gives us

$$2000i^2 + 178i - 4 = 0$$
$$1000i^2 + 89i - 2 = 0$$

which we solve by the quadratic formula:

$$i = \frac{-89 \pm \sqrt{7921 + 8000}}{2000} = \frac{-89 \pm 126}{2000} = \frac{37}{2000} = 0.0185$$

We earlier found that

$$Y = 12,000 - \frac{40}{i}$$

so we have

$$Y - 12,000 = \frac{40}{0.0185} = 12,000 - 2162 = 9838$$

Thus the equilibrium interest rate is 1.85 percent and the equilibrium national income 9838.

Suppose now that in the previous illustration government expenditures were increased by 18 so that there was a change in G from 110 to 128. The two equilibrium conditions would then become

$$0.12Y - 812 + 100 = 200 - 2000 + 0.02Y + 128 \qquad \text{(3b)}$$

$$3000 = \frac{1}{4}Y + \frac{10}{i} \qquad \text{(4b)}$$

We would have, as before,

$$Y = 12,000 - \frac{40}{i}$$

Equation (3b) could now be rearranged to

$$0.10Y + 2000i - 1040 = 0$$

Substituting the value of Y into this equation gives

$$0.10\left(12,000 - \frac{40}{i}\right) + 2000i - 1040 = 0$$

$$1200 - \frac{4}{i} + 2000i - 1040 = 0$$

$$2000i + 160 - \frac{4}{i} = 0$$

and

$$2000i^2 + 160i - 4 = 0$$

or

$$500i^2 + 40i - 1 = 0$$

which we solve for i by use of the quadratic formula:

$$i = \frac{-40 \pm \sqrt{1600 + 2000}}{1000} = \frac{-40 \pm \sqrt{3600}}{1000} = \frac{20}{1000} = 0.02$$

Because

$$Y = 12,000 - \frac{40}{i}$$

we have

$$Y = 12,000 - \frac{40}{0.02} = 12,000 - 2000 = 10,000$$

Thus, as a result of the increase of 18 in government expenditures, the interest rate will increase from 1.85 percent to 2.0 percent, and national income will increase from 9838 to 10,000.

It will, however, be seen that this increase in national income is not as great as would have been expected if we had computed the government expenditures multiplier (see Section 15·5). The government expenditures multiplier is given by

$$\frac{\partial Y}{\partial G} = \frac{1}{1 - MPC - MPI} = \frac{1}{1 - (\partial C/\partial Y) - (\partial I/\partial Y)}$$

For the function given in Illustration 3, we have

$$\frac{\partial C}{\partial Y} = 0.88 \quad \text{and} \quad \frac{\partial I}{\partial Y} = 0.02$$

Thus

$$\frac{\partial Y}{\partial G} = \frac{1}{1 - 0.88 - 0.02} = \frac{1}{0.10} = 10$$

Because the government expenditures multiplier is 10, we would expect national income to increase by 180 if government expenditures increase by 18. In our illustration, however, we found that national income actually increased by only 162.

The reason for this discrepancy is that previously we assumed a constant or fixed interest rate whereas, at the present, we are considering simultaneous changes in both national income and the interest rate. Only with a fixed interest rate is the full multiplier effect realized. In the more realistic case where the interest rate is allowed to fluctuate, some of the expansionary effect of an increase in government expenditures will be lost. This occurs because, as the multiplier effect works itself out, the interest rate increases due to the need for more transactions balances. The interest rate therefore exerts a dampening effect upon the increase in national income. The result is then something less than a full multiplier effect. This is seen in our illustration where, as a result of the increased government expenditures, the interest rate increased from 1.85 to 2.0 percent, thus preventing national income from expanding by the full multiplier amount of 180.

These results hold generally; that is, an increase in government expenditures will raise both the interest rate and national income. The increase in national income will be somewhat less than the full multiplier effect. A reduction in taxes will also increase both the interest rate and national income, although not by as great an amount as a similar increase in government expenditures. Conversely, a reduction in government expenditures or an increase in taxes will lower both the interest rate and national income. The reduction in national income will again be not quite as large as the full multiplier effects predicted by either the government expenditures multiplier or the tax multiplier.

We have seen that changes in government expenditures and taxes exert an impact upon national income. When such measures are used as part of an economic stabilization plan, they are grouped under the heading *fiscal policy*.

Because the money supply M_0 is under the control of government authorities, it, too, can be changed. Suppose that in Illustration 3, the money supply increases by 145, so that M_0 changes from 3000 to 3145. The two equilibrium conditions would then be

$$0.12Y - 812 + 100 = 200 - 2000i + 0.02Y + 110 \tag{3c}$$

$$3145 = \frac{1}{4}Y + \frac{10}{i} \tag{4c}$$

From equation (4c) we would have

$$Y = 12{,}580 - \frac{40}{i}$$

Equation (3c) can be rearranged to read

$$0.10Y + 2000i - 1022 = 0$$

Substituting the value of Y into this equation gives

$$0.10\left(12{,}580 - \frac{40}{i}\right) + 2000i - 1022 = 0$$

$$1258 - \frac{4}{i} + 2000i - 1022 = 0$$

$$2000i + 236 - \frac{4}{i} = 0$$

$$2000i^2 + 236i - 4 = 0$$

$$500i^2 + 59i - 1 = 0$$

which can be solved for i:

$$i = \frac{-59 \pm \sqrt{3481 + 2000}}{1000} = \frac{-59 \pm 74}{1000} = \frac{15}{1000} = 0.015$$

and because

$$Y = 12{,}580 - \frac{40}{i}$$

we get

$$Y = 12{,}580 - \frac{40}{0.015} = 12{,}580 - 2667 = 9913$$

Thus, as a result of an increase in the money supply of 145, the interest rate will decrease from 1.85 percent to 1.5 percent, and national income will increase from 9838 to 9913. This result will hold generally; that is, an increase in the money supply will reduce the interest rate while raising national income. Conversely, a reduction in the money supply will increase the interest rate and reduce national income.

We have already seen that government can affect the level of national income through expenditures and taxes. We now see that government can exert a similar effect by manipulating the money supply. When such a measure is used as part of an economic stabilization plan, it is known as *monetary policy*.

We have considered separately changes in government expenditures and in the money supply. The government can, of course, simultaneously vary both expenditures and the money supply. An increase in both government expenditures and the money supply will result in a higher level of national income, but the effect on the interest rate is uncertain. Increased expenditures cause higher interest rates, but a greater money supply reduces the interest rate. The net effect will depend on the particular combination.

Earlier, we saw that the full multiplier effect is not realized from an increase in government expenditures, because the accompanying higher interest rate dampens the multiplier. However, if, along with an increase in government expenditures, there is also an increase in the money supply of sufficient magnitude to compensate for the increased demand for transactions balances (i.e., the interest rate remains constant), then the full multiplier effect can be achieved. Thus the judicious use of fiscal and monetary policy in concert can be very beneficial.

Caution: Limitations of Liquidity Preference Analysis

The theory of liquidity preference, as presented by Keynes and his followers, takes explicit account of only the choice between holding money or lending it out. In fact the choice is a many-sided one, including the options of investing in short-term government bills, long-term bonds, cash, savings accounts, shares of stock, and goods and services. All of these possibilities should be considered. There may also be significant differences arising from changes in the class of holders of money, such as private households, banks, other financial institutions, nonfinancial companies, central bank, and government treasury.

The theory also assumes a fixed money supply completely determined by governmental authorities and not subject to the operation of the national income model. Writers such as Tobin, Brunner, and Meltzer have shown the importance of developing a more realistic theory of money supply. Public authorities, it cannot be denied, exert enormous influence over the money supply, but they cannot always determine its magnitude precisely. Decisions by private banks can affect the money supply. Moreover, conflicts often arise between central banking authorities and treasury policy makers. The resolution or persistence of such conflicts can have a significant influence upon the money supply.

Exercises

1. The transactions demand for money is given by $M_t = \frac{1}{5}PY$; the speculative demand for money by $M_s = 100 - 800i$; national income by $Y_0 = 7500$; the price index by $P_0 = 1.10$; the money supply by $M_0 = 1670$. Find the equilibrium interest rate.

2. The transactions demand for money is given by $M_t = \frac{1}{4}PY$; the speculative demand for money by $M_s = 200 - 10{,}000i^2$; national income by $Y_0 = 8000$; the price index by $P_0 = 1.00$; the money supply by $M_0 = 1700$. Find the equilibrium interest rate.

3. The transactions demand for money is given by $M_t = .3PY$; the speculative demand for money by $M_s = 20/i$; national income by $Y_0 = 6000$; the price index by $P_0 = 1.50$; the money supply by $M_0 = 2950$. Find the equilibrium interest rate.

4. The transactions demand for money is given by $M_t = \frac{1}{3}PY$; the speculative demand for money by $M_s = 150 - 1000i$; national income by $Y_0 = 8500$; the price index by $P_0 = 1.20$; the money supply by $M_0 = 3480$. Find the equilibrium interest rate.

5. The transactions demand for money is given by $M_t = \frac{1}{6}PY$; the speculative demand for money by $M_s = 5/i$; national income by $Y_0 = 5000$; the price index by $P_0 = 1.20$; the money supply by $M_0 = 1100$. Find the equilibrium interest rate.

6. The savings function is given by $S = 0.13Y$; the investment function by $I = 300 - 1500i + 0.03Y$; the transactions demand for money

by $M_t = \frac{1}{5}PY$; the speculative demand for money by $M_s = 100 - 800i$; the price index by $P_0 = 1.00$; and the money supply by $M_0 = 600$. Find the equilibrium rate of interest and level of national income.

7. The savings function is given by $S = 0.21Y - 100$; the investment function by $I = 552 - 4000i + 0.01Y$; the transactions demand for money by $M_t = 0.4PY$; the speculative demand for money by $M_s = 20/i$; the price index by $P_0 = 1.25$; and the money supply by $M_0 = 2950$. Find the equilibrium rate of interest and level of national income.

8. The savings function is given by $S = 0.15Y - 80$; the investment function by $I = 800 - 2000i + 0.05Y$; the transactions demand for money by $M_t = \frac{1}{6}PY$; the speculative demand for money by $M_s = 5/i$; the price index by $P_0 = 1.20$; and the money supply by $M_0 = 1100$. Find the equilibrium rate of interest and level of national income.

9. The consumption function is given by $C = 200 + 0.89Y$; the investment function by $I = 700 - 3000i + 0.01Y$; the transactions demand for money by $M_t = \frac{1}{3}PY$; the speculative demand for money by $M_s = 160 - 1000i$; the price index by $P_0 = 1.20$; and the money supply by $M_0 = 3480$. Find the equilibrium rate of interest and level of national income.

10. The consumption function is given by $C = 0.87(Y - T)$; the investment function by $I = 300 - 1500i + 0.03Y$; Government expenditures by $G = 250$; taxes by $T = 200$; the transactions demand for money by $M_t = \frac{1}{5}PY$; the speculative demand for money by $M_s = 100 - 800i$; the price index by $P_0 = 1.00$; and the money supply by $M_0 = 600$. Find the equilibrium rate of interest and level of national income.

11. The consumption function is given by $C = 100 + 0.79(Y - T)$; the investment function by $I = 552 - 4000i + 0.01Y$; Government expenditures by $G = 63$; taxes by $T = 100$; the transactions demand for money by $M_t = 0.4PY$; the speculative demand for money by $M_s = 20/i$; the price index by $P_0 = 1.25$; and the money supply by $M_0 = 2950$. Find the equilibrium rate of interest and level of national income.

12. The consumption function is given by $C = 80 + 0.85(Y - T)$; the investment function by $I = 800 - 2000i + 0.05Y$; government expenditures by $G = 180$; taxes by $T = 160$; the transactions demand for money by $M_t = \frac{1}{6}PY$; the speculative demand for money by $M_s = 8/i$; the price index by $P_0 = 1.20$; and the money supply by $M_0 = 2000$. Find the equilibrium rate of interest and level of national income.

13.   The consumption function is given by $C = 200 + 0.89(Y - T)$; the
      investment function by $I = 700 - 3000i + 0.01Y$; government ex-
      penditures by $G = 280$; taxes by $T = 200$; the transactions demand
      for money by $M_t = \frac{1}{3}PY$; the speculative demand for money by
      $M_s = 160 - 1000i$; the price index by $P_0 = 1.20$; and the money
      supply by $M_0 = 3480$. Find the equilibrium rate of interest and level
      of national income.

14–17. For each of Exercises 10–13, find the effect of
      a)   an increase in G of 30
      b)   an increase in T of 20
      c)   an increase in G of 20 and an increase in T of 20
      d)   an increase in M_0 of 100
      e)   an increase in M_0 of 100 and an increase in G of 30
      Then compare the answers given in (a), (b), and (c) to what you
      would have arrived at by using the multiplier and explain the
      discrepancy.

SECTION 15·7   PRICE AND WAGE LEVELS, INCOME, AND EMPLOYMENT: THE COMPLETE MODEL

The analysis of previous sections is adequate as long as prices are fixed at
a certain level P_0. However, if price levels are allowed to vary, we then
have an additional variable. The system of two equations given in the
previous section, namely,

$$S(Y) = I(Y, i) \tag{1}$$

$$M_0 = KPY + L(i) \tag{2}$$

does not have a determinate solution, because it contains the three variables Y, i, and P.

It is therefore necessary to introduce a relationship involving the
price level. Prices of products are, in turn, closely connected to wage rates,
profits, and production functions. These will therefore all have to be
considered.

Let us introduce a very simple aggregate production function:

$$Y = Y(N) \tag{3}$$

where Y is net national product and N is the number of employed persons or hours of labor. It will be noticed that capital is omitted as a
variable from the production function, thus implying that it is held at
some fixed level. This is in accord with the Keynesian presentation, which
assumed the capital stock to be constant in the short run. It is conceded

that any investment changes that may occur could amount to a significant percentage of previous investment levels. Nevertheless, it is argued, such investment changes would alter the total capital stock by only a minute percentage. It is also assumed that

$$\frac{dY}{dN} > 0,$$

that is, as employment increases, so does production.

We next turn to a consideration of economy-wide profits. Assume, for simplicity, a purely competitive economy. (The procedure can, with some modifications, be generalized to other market structures.) We found in Section 13·3 that a necessary condition for profit maximization for any firm is

$$p\frac{\partial f}{\partial x_i} = r_i$$

where $\partial f/\partial x_i$ is the marginal product of any input, r_i is the input price, and p is the product price. This is the same as

$$\frac{\partial f}{\partial x_i} = \frac{r_i}{p}$$

If we generalize this result to the economy as a whole, $\partial f/\partial x_i$ becomes dY/dN (the marginal product of labor), r_i becomes W (i.e., the average wage rate), and p becomes P the overall price index. We therefore have

$$\frac{dY}{dN} = \frac{W}{P} \tag{4}$$

Keynes assumed that wage rates are autonomous, that is, determined by bargaining, inertia, and custom, and not by the income-employment situation. Therefore we can write

$$W = W_0 \tag{5}$$

If we take together the equations we have generated, we have the following:

$$S(Y) = I(Y, i) \tag{1}$$

$$M_0 = KPY + L(i) \tag{2}$$

$$Y = Y(N) \tag{3}$$

$$\frac{dY}{dn} = \frac{W}{P} \tag{4}$$

$$W = W_0 \tag{5}$$

This is a system of five equations in five unknowns (Y, i, P, N, W), which can generally be solved (as long as each equation is an independent statement and not something that can be derived from the others). It is also significant to note that the equilibrium value for N may be a level of employment that diverges substantially from full employment.

In the event that wages are not rigidly set, then instead of a constant wage $W = W_0$, we would have a supply function of labor that would relate the real wage W/P to the number of workers N. Equation (5) would then appear in the form

$$N = N\left(\frac{W}{P}\right)$$

Although the expression is somewhat more complicated, no new variables are introduced. We would then still have five equations in the five unknowns, Y, i, P, N, W. It is also possible that the supply of labor may be more directly linked to the money wage rather than the real wage; that is, a money illusion might exist, making a greater money wage seem more attractive even if price levels rise by similar amounts. In that case the labor supply function would appear as $N = N(W)$, and again there would be no change in the number of variables overall.

The introduction of a government sector affects equation (1), as indicated in earlier sections. Instead of the simple equality between the savings and investment functions, we have

$$S(Y - T) + T = I(Y, i) + G$$

The resulting system of equations will still involve five equations and five unknowns, as illustrated by the following example.

Illustration. As in Illustration 3 of Section 15·6, the consumption function is given by $C = 800 + 0.88(Y - T)$; the investment function by $I = 200 - 2000i + 0.02Y$; government expenditures are $G = 110$, and $T = 100$; the transactions demand for money is given by $M_t = \frac{1}{4}PY$; the speculative demand for money is given by $M_s = 10/i$; the money supply by $M_0 = 3000$. Unlike Illustration 3 above, however, the price index is not given; the production function is given as $Y = 2N$, where N is the number of labor hours and the average wage rate is $W_0 = 4$. Find the equilibrium rate of interest, the level of national income, the price index, and the number of labor hours.

Solution. The savings function derived from the consumption function as in Illustration 3 of Section 15·6 is $S = 0.12Y - 812$. The equilibrium conditions (1) through (5) therefore become

$$0.12Y - 812 + 100 = 200 - 2000i + 0.02Y + 110 \tag{1d}$$

$$3000 = \frac{1}{4}PY + \frac{10}{i} \tag{2d}$$

$$Y = 2N \tag{3d}$$

$$2 = \frac{W}{P} \tag{4d}$$

$$W = 4 \tag{5d}$$

Note that we have utilized the modified form of equation (1) that applies with a government sector.

Substituting the value of W given by equation (5d) into equation (4d), we get

$$2 = \frac{4}{P}$$

and

$$2P = 4$$

$$P = 2$$

From equation (2d) we then get

$$3000 = \frac{1}{2}Y + \frac{10}{i}$$

$$Y = 6000 - \frac{20}{i}$$

Equation (1d) can be rearranged to read

$$0.10Y = 1022 - 2000i$$

Substituting the value of Y into this equation, we get

$$0.10\left(6000 - \frac{20}{i}\right) = 1022 - 2000i$$

$$600 - \frac{2}{i} = 1022 - 2000i$$

$$2000i - 422 - \frac{2}{i} = 0$$

$$2000i^2 - 422i - 2 = 0$$

$$1000i^2 - 211i - 1 = 0$$

which, solving by the quadratic formula, gives

$$i = \frac{211 \pm \sqrt{44{,}521 + 4000}}{2000} = \frac{211 \pm \sqrt{48{,}521}}{2000} = \frac{211 \pm 220}{2000}$$

$$= \frac{431}{2000} = 0.2155$$

We earlier found

$$Y = 6000 - \frac{20}{i}$$

so that we have

$$Y = 6000 - \frac{20}{0.2155} = 5907$$

From equation (3d), we have $Y = 2N$, which we can now solve for N:

$5907 = 2N$

$N = 2953.5$ hours of labor

We have now solved the complete system. Our solutions are

$i = 0.2155$

$Y = 5907$

$N = 2953.5$

$W = 4.00$

$P = 2.00$

Caution: Some Shortcomings of the Complete Macro Model

In developing the national income model, we have assumed a production function with only one variable, that is, labor. The omission of capital as a variable can sometimes lead to serious distortions. The claim that any short-run changes in investment will not affect the total capital stock by very much is often untrue. Even in a period of one or two years, changes in capital formation can be significant.

The national income model also pictures the entire economy as equivalent to one giant firm. The implicit assumption is present that the treatment of this macro firm is analogous to the micro theory of the single firm. It might, however, be more enlightening to break the economy into at least several sectors, because there may be significant differences between sectors.

The Keynesian model is a *static* model; that is, it considers economic relationships at a certain time and attempts to show what equilibrium position will ensue given these conditions. The model also enables us to compare one equilibrium position based on a certain set of conditions to another equilibrium position based upon another set of conditions. This is known as *comparative statics*. However, static analysis is not concerned with the time it takes to attain an equilibrium position, nor with the process or path that is followed in order to achieve the equilibrium. If we are interested in these questions, and sometimes they are quite important, we need a *dynamic* model, which will trace the path of change taken by variables over time. Moreover, some present variables depend upon previous aggregates; for example, present consumption may depend not only upon present income but also on previous year's income. Only a dynamic model can take proper account of such things. Finally, it is possible for a system never to attain an equilibrium position, in which case only a dynamic treatment can describe what does occur.

There have been many attempts to provide dynamic macromodels, but there is some question as to how realistic they are.[1]

Exercises

For each of the following, find the equilibrium rate of interest, the level of national income, the price index, and the number of labor hours.

1. The consumption function is given by $C = 0.87(Y - T)$; the investment function by $I = 300 - 1500i + 0.03Y$; government expenditures are $G = 250$, and $T = 200$; the transactions demand for money is given by $M_t = \frac{1}{5}PY$; the speculative demand for money by $M_s = 100 - 800i$; the money supply by $M_0 = 400$; the production function by $Y = 4N$, where N is the number of labor hours; the average wage rate by $W_0 = 5.00$.

2. The consumption function is given by $C = 100 + 0.79(Y - T)$; the investment function by $I = 552 - 4000i + 0.01Y$; government expenditures are $G = 63$, and $T = 100$; the transactions demand for money is given by $M_t = 0.4PY$; the speculative demand for money by $M_s = 20/i$; the money supply by $M_0 = 2950$; the production function by $Y = 5N$, where N is the number of labor hours; the average wage rate by $W_0 = 6.25$.

[1] For a more detailed discussion of economic dynamics in general, see Chapter 17.

3. The consumption function is given by $C = 80 + 0.85(Y - T)$; the investment function by $I = 800 - 2000i + 0.05Y$; government expenditures are $G = 180$, and $T = 160$; the transactions demand for money is given by $M_t = \frac{1}{6}PY$; the speculative demand for money by $M_s = 8/i$; the money supply by $M_0 = 2000$; the production function by $Y = 3N$; the average wage rate by $W_0 = 6.00$.

4. The consumption function is given by $C = 200 + 0.89(Y - T)$; the investment function by $I = 700 - 3000i + 0.01Y$; government expenditures are $G = 280$, and $T = 200$; the transactions demand for money is given by $M_t = \frac{1}{3}PY$; the speculative demand for money by $M_s = 160 - 1000i$; the money supply by $M_0 = 3480$; the production function by $Y = 1.5N$; the average wage rate by $W_0 = 4.50$.

16

INTEGRATION

Our speculations can scarce ever be too
fine provided they be just.
—David Hume

In previous chapters we dealt extensively with functions and their derivatives. Once a function was stated either in general or particular form, we
could find some expression for its derivative. In this chapter we consider
the inverse problem of deriving original functions from given derivatives.

SECTION 16·1   THE INDEFINITE INTEGRAL

In Chapters 13 and 14 we encountered many instances where a cost
function was given to us or we had sufficient information to derive one.
Once we knew the cost function, it was relatively easy to find the marginal
cost function by the process of differentiation. But suppose that a producer knows his marginal cost function from observing operations over a
long period of time. How can he derive his cost function?

For illustration, if a firm possesses the marginal cost function

$$MC = 30q^2 - 70q + 24$$

then we are seeking a function that when differentiated will give $30q^2 -
70q + 24$. We can readily see that the function we are searching for is

$$C = 10q^3 - 35q^2 + 24q + c$$

(where c is any constant whatever), because if we differentiate C, that is,
find dC/dq, we get the given MC function. The process we have used is the
reverse of differentiation and is called *integration*.

Note that in the above illustration, c can be any constant. But if we
also know that fixed costs are, for example, equal to 3, then we have $c = 3$
and

$$C = 10q^3 - 35q^2 + 24q + 3$$

More generally, if we wish to integrate any function $f(x)$, we denote this by

$$F(x) = \int f(x)\, dx$$

$F(x)$ is the function whose derivative is $f(x)$ or whose differential is $f(x)\, dx$. The symbol $\int$ denotes the operation of *integration* and is called the *integral sign*, while $f(x)$ is said to be the *integrand*. The term

$$\int f(x)\, dx$$

is read: "the integral of $f(x)$ with respect to x" or "the integral of $f(x)\, dx$." The expression

$$\int f(x)\, dx$$

is also said to be the *indefinite integral of* $f(x)$ or the *antiderivative of* $f(x)$.

The reader will quickly perceive that the concept of integration is applicable when we seek to derive revenue from marginal revenue, demand from marginal demand, supply from marginal supply, consumption from marginal propensity to consume, savings from marginal propensity to save, and a host of similar problems.

We now state the following rules of integration, which help make the concept of integration operational.

Rule 1.   If u and v are functions of x, then

$$\int (u + v)\, dx = \int u\, dx + \int v\, dx$$

that is, the integral of the sum of two functions is the sum of the integrals of the functions. This rule can be generalized to any number of functions, so that

$$\int (u + v + w)\, dx = \int u\, dx + \int v\, dx + \int w\, dx$$

where u, v, w are functions of x, and similarly for the integral of four or more functions.

Rule 2.   If u is any function of x and k is any constant, then

$$\int ku\, dx = k \int u\, dx$$

that is, the integral of a constant multiplied by a function is the constant multiplied by the integral of the function.

Rule 3.   If u is any function of x and n is any constant exponent except -1, then

$$\int u^n \, du = \frac{u^{n+1}}{n+1} + c$$

where $n \neq -1$ and c is any constant, that is, the integral of a function to a power is the function to that power increased by 1, all divided by the new power and then added to a constant.

In the event that $n = -1$, the expression u^n becomes

$$u^{-1} = \frac{1}{u}$$

and the following rule is applicable.

Rule 4.   If u is any function of x, then

$$\int \frac{1}{u} \, du = \ln u + c \qquad \text{if } u > 0$$

and

$$\int \frac{1}{u} \, du = \ln(-u) + c \qquad \text{if } u < 0$$

Note that we must consider separately the cases where u is positive and where u is negative, because the logarithm of a negative number is undefined. Therefore, if u is negative, we take $\ln(-u)$.

Illustration 1.

a) $\displaystyle \int x^4 \, dx = \frac{x^5}{5} + c \qquad$ using Rule 3

b) $\displaystyle \int x^{1/2} \, dx = \frac{x^{3/2}}{\frac{3}{2}} = \tfrac{2}{3}x^{3/2} + c \qquad$ using Rule 3

c) $\displaystyle \int x^{-4} \, dx = \frac{x^{-3}}{-3} + c \qquad$ using Rule 3

d) $\displaystyle \int 6p^5 \, dp = 6 \int p^5 \, dp = \frac{6p^6}{6} + c = p^6 + c \qquad$ using Rules 2 and 3

e) $\displaystyle \int dp = \int p^0 \, dp = \frac{p^1}{1} + c = p + c \qquad$ using Rule 3

f) $\int \frac{2}{3}p^{-1/3}\,dp = \frac{2}{3}\int p^{-1/3} = \frac{2}{3}\frac{p^{2/3}}{\frac{2}{3}} + c = \frac{3}{2}\cdot\frac{2}{3}p^{2/3} + c = p^{2/3} + c$

using Rules 2 and 3

g) $\int \frac{-400}{p^5}\,dp = -400\int p^{-5}\,dp = -400\frac{p^{-4}}{-4} + c = 100p^{-4}$

using Rules 2 and 3

h) $\int \frac{4}{p}\,dp = 4\int \frac{dp}{p} = 4\ln p + c$ using Rules 2 and 4

Illustration 2.

a) $\int \left(5x^6 + \frac{1}{2}x^3\right) dx = \frac{5x^7}{7} + \frac{x^4}{8} + c$ using Rules 1, 2, and 3

b) $\int (-4 - 4p)\,dp = -4p - 2p^2 + c$ using Rules 1, 2, and 3

c) $\int (6p + 6)\,dp = 3p^2 + 6p + c$ using Rules 1, 2, and 3

d) $\int (50 - q)\,dq = 5q - \frac{q^2}{2} + c$ using Rules 1 and 3

Illustration 3.   The marginal cost function of a firm is given by
$MC = 30q^2 - 70q + 24$
Find the cost function.
Solution.   Marginal cost is the derivative of total costs, dC/dq, so we find the cost function by integrating the MC function:

$$\int (30q^2 - 70q + 24)\,dq = \frac{30q^3}{3} - \frac{70q^2}{2} + 24q + c$$

$$= 10q^3 - 35q^2 + 24q + c$$

We have determined the cost function to within a constant.

Illustration 4.   The marginal propensity to consume is given as 0.9. Find the consumption function.
Solution.   The marginal propensity to consume is the derivative of the consumption function dC/dY, so we find the consumption function by integrating the MPC function:

$$\int 0.9\,dY = 0.9Y + c$$ where Y is national income

We have determined the consumption function to within a constant.

Illustration 5.   The marginal demand for a certain product is given by

$$MD = p - 6p^2 - \tfrac{2}{5}p^3$$

Find the demand function.

Solution.   Marginal demand is the derivative of the demand function, dq_d/dp, so we find the demand function by integrating the marginal demand function:

$$\int \left(p - 6p^2 - \frac{2p^3}{5} \right) dp = \frac{p^2}{2} - \frac{6p^3}{3} - \frac{2}{5}\frac{p^4}{4} + c$$

$$= \frac{p^2}{2} - 2p^3 - \frac{1}{10}p^4 + c$$

We have determined the demand function to within a constant.

Illustration 6.   The marginal supply for a certain product is given by

$$MS = 4p^3 + 12p^2 - 1$$

Find the supply function.

Solution.   Marginal supply is the derivative of the supply function, (dq_s/dp), so we find the supply function by integrating the marginal supply function:

$$\int (4p^3 + 12p^2 - 1)\, dp = \frac{4p^4}{4} + \frac{12p^3}{3} - p + c = p^4 + 4p^3 - p + c$$

We have determined the supply function to within a constant.

Indefinite integrals always involve a *constant of integration*, as in the examples given above. The constant can take on any value. Thus we are not provided with a unique solution to the problem of finding the original function (the cost function, demand function, etc.). However, if we are also given a set of coordinates linking the independent variable to the value of the function at some point, we can determine the value of the constant of integration.

Illustration 7.

$$\int x^4\, dx = \frac{x^5}{5} + c$$

Thus we can write the original function as

$$Y = \frac{x^5}{5} + c$$

If $Y = \frac{2}{5}$ when $x = 2$, we have

$\frac{2}{5} = \frac{32}{5} + c$

$c = \frac{30}{5} = 6$

and

$$Y = \frac{x^5}{5} + 6$$

is the original function.

Frequently, when given an integral, we know the initial conditions, that is, the value of the function when the independent variable is zero.

Illustration 8. In Illustration 3 we found that if

$MC = 30q^2 - 70q + 24$

then the cost function is

$C = 10q^3 - 35q^2 + 24q + c$

If, in addition, we are given that fixed costs are 20, we can determine a unique cost function. Because fixed costs are 20, this means that when $q = 0$, $c = 20$. We therefore have

$20 = c$

The cost function is then

$C = 10q^3 - 35q^2 + 24q + 20$

Illustration 9. In Illustration 5 we found that if

$MD = p - 6p^2 - \frac{2}{5}p^3$

then the demand function is

$q_d = \frac{p^2}{2} - 2p^3 - \frac{1}{10}p^4 + c$

If, in addition, we are given that people would desire 10,000 units of the product if it were a free good, we can determine a unique demand function. At $p = 0$, we have $q_d = 10,000$. Thus

$10,000 = c$

The demand function is then

$$q_d = \frac{p^2}{2} - 2p^3 - \tfrac{1}{10}p^4 + 10,000$$

In each of the illustrations we have considered, it was relatively simple to apply the rules of integration because u could always be taken as some single variable term, such as x, p, q, Y, and du was simply dx, dp, dq, or dY. It happens, however, in many cases that the only way to integrate some function is to take u as a more complicated expression. In such cases the value of du must be calculated to see that the integral is in the precise form of one of the rules for integration.

Illustration 10.   Find the value of

$$\int 2x(x^2 + 3)^3 \, dx$$

Solution.   To integrate this function, we seek to use Rule 3, which gives the integral of a power. The rule is in the form

$$\int u^n \, du = \frac{u^{n+1}}{n+1} + c \qquad \text{where } n \neq -1$$

Therefore we define u as $u = x^2 + 3$, which implies that $du = 2x\,dx$. Our integral is then in the form of

$$\int u^3 \, du$$

and can now easily be integrated. By the use of Rule 3, we have

$$\int u^3 \, du = \frac{u^4}{4} + c$$

But remembering that $u = x^2 + 3$, we conclude that

$$\int 2x(x^2 + 3)^3 \, dx = \frac{(x^2 + 3)^4}{4} + c$$

Illustration 11.   Evaluate

$$\int \frac{dx}{\sqrt{1 - x}}$$

Solution.   Set $u = 1 - x$. We then have $du = -dx$. In order to put this in a form suitable for integration, we must multiply the integrand by -1

and then compensate by placing a factor of -1 in front of the integral. We have

$$\int \frac{dx}{\sqrt{1-x}} = -\int (1-x)^{-1/2} - dx$$

This is in the form

$$-\int u^{-1/2} \, du = \frac{-u^{1/2}}{\frac{1}{2}} + c = -2u^{1/2} + c$$

Because $u = 1 - x$, we have

$$\int \frac{dx}{\sqrt{1-x}} = -2(1-x)^{1/2} + c$$

Illustration 12.   The marginal supply for a certain product is given by

$$MS = p\sqrt{p^2 - 4}$$

Find the supply function.
Solution.   Marginal supply is the derivative of the supply function, dq_s/dp, so we find the supply function by integrating the marginal supply function:

$$\int p\sqrt{p^2 - 4} \, dp$$

Set $u = p^2 - 4$, from which we derive $du = 2p \, dp$. The integrand contains only a $p \, dp$ term, so we multiply by 2 within the integral and by $\frac{1}{2}$ outside the integral to compensate. We then get

$$\int p\sqrt{p^2 - 4} \, dp = \tfrac{1}{2} \int (p^2 - 4)^{1/2} 2p \, dp$$

This is in the form

$$\frac{1}{2} \int u^{1/2} \, du = \frac{1}{2} \frac{u^{3/2}}{\frac{3}{2}} + c = \frac{1}{3} u^{3/2} + c$$

Because $u = p^2 - 4$, we have

$$\int p\sqrt{p^2 - 4} \, dp = \tfrac{1}{3}(p^2 - 4)^{3/2} + c$$

as the supply function.

Illustration 13.   The marginal supply for a certain product is given by

$$MS = \frac{p}{p^2 - 1}$$

Find the supply function.

Solution.   We find the supply function by evaluating

$$\int \frac{p}{p^2 - 1}\, dp$$

Set $u = p^2 - 1$, from which we derive $du = 2p\, dp$. The integrand contains only a $p\, dp$ term, so we multiply by 2 within the integral and by $\frac{1}{2}$ outside the integral in order to compensate. We get

$$\int \frac{p}{p^2 - 1}\, dp = \frac{1}{2} \int \frac{2p\, dp}{p^2 - 1}$$

This is in the form

$$\frac{1}{2} \int \frac{du}{u} = \frac{1}{2} \ln u + c \qquad \text{by Rule 4}$$

Because $u = p^2 - 1$, we have

$$\int \frac{p}{p^2 - 1}\, dp = \tfrac{1}{2} \ln(p^2 - 1) + c$$

as the supply function.

We now state two more rules of integration in order to enable us to integrate exponential functions.

Rule 5.   If u is any function of x, then

$$\int e^u\, du = e^u + c$$

Rule 6.   If u is any function of x, then

$$\int a^u\, du = \frac{a^u}{\ln a} + c, \qquad \text{when } a > 0,\, a \neq 1$$

These rules can be easily verified by differentiating the right-hand side of each expression and showing that the result is identical to the integrand of the left-hand side.

Illustration 14.   Evaluate

$$\int e^{3x-1}\, dx$$

Solution.   Set $u = 3x - 1$, from which we derive $du = 3\,dx$. Then multiply the integrand by 3 and compensate by placing $\frac{1}{3}$ outside the integral. We have

$$\int e^{3x-1}\,dx = \tfrac{1}{3}\int e^{3x-1}3\,dx$$

This is now in the form

$$\tfrac{1}{3}\int e^u\,du = \tfrac{1}{3}e^u + c \qquad \text{by Rule 5}$$

Because $u = 3x - 1$, we have

$$\int e^{3x-1}\,dx = \tfrac{1}{3}e^{3x-1} + c$$

Illustration 15.   Evaluate

$$\int (a^{2x} + a^{-x})\,dx$$

Solution.

$$\int (a^{2x} + a^{-x})\,dx = \int a^{2x}\,dx + \int a^{-x}\,dx$$

$$= \frac{1}{2}\int a^{2x}2\,dx - \int a^{-x}(-dx)$$

$$= \frac{1}{2}\cdot\frac{a^{2x}}{\ln a} - \frac{a^{-x}}{\ln a} + c$$

Illustration 16.   The marginal cost function of a firm is given by

$$MC = \tfrac{1}{50}e^{q/150}$$

Find the cost function.
Solution.   We find the cost function by integrating the MC function:

$$\int \tfrac{1}{50}e^{q/150}\,dq = 3\int e^{q/150}\tfrac{1}{150}\,dq = 3e^{q/150} + c$$

which is the cost function.

Illustration 17.   The marginal demand for a certain product is

$$MD = -4pe^{-p^2}$$

Find the demand function.

Solution. We find the demand function by integrating the marginal demand function:

$$\int -4pe^{-p^2} \, dp = 2 \int e^{-p^2}(-2p \, dp) = 2e^{-p^2} + c$$

which is the demand function.

Exercises

Evaluate each of the following.

1. $\int x^3 \, dx$

2. $\int \dfrac{2}{x^2} \, dx$

3. $\int \frac{1}{3}x^{4/3} \, dx$

4. $\int 6x^{-4} \, dx$

5. $\int x^{1/4} \, dx$

6. $\int \dfrac{dx}{x + 2}$

7. $\int (2p - 4) \, dp$

8. $\int (3p^2 - 3) \, dp$

9. $\int (-3p^{-2} + p^{-3}) \, dp$

10. $\int p^{-1/3} \, dp$

11. $\int (4q + 5) \, dq$

12. $\int (-9p^2 + 4) \, dp$

13. $\int \dfrac{dp}{3p + 2}$

14. $\int \dfrac{1 + p}{p^2}\, dp$

15. $\int \sqrt{p - 4}\, dp$

16. $\int p\sqrt{p^2 - 9}\, dp$

17. $\int \dfrac{p\, dp}{\sqrt{p^2 + 1}}$

18. $\int \dfrac{x + 2}{\sqrt{x^2 + 4x}}\, dx$

19. $\int (1 - p)^{3/2}\, dp$

20. $\int \dfrac{1 + 2p}{p^2 + p}\, dp$

21. $\int \dfrac{dp}{1 - p}$

22. $\int \dfrac{x^2\, dx}{x^3 + 3}$

23. $\int (e^p + e^{-p})\, dp$

24. $\int a^{2p - 1}\, dp$

25. $\int e^{p/2 - 3}\, dp$

26. $\int 2e^{-3x}\, dx$

27. $\int 3^x\, dx$

For each of the following marginal demand functions, find the original demand functions in general and then on the assumption that demand would be 2000 if the product were free.

28. $MD = 3 - 4p$

29. $MD = -9p^2 + 4$

30. $MD = \dfrac{1}{400p}$

31. $MD = -4e^{-2p}$

For each of the following marginal supply functions, find the original supply functions.

32. $MS = 3p^2 - \frac{1}{2}p - 2$

33. $MS = 2e^{p/2}$

34. $MS = \dfrac{p}{p^2 + 1}$

35. $MS = \dfrac{1}{\sqrt{2p + 1}}$

For each of the following marginal cost functions, find the original cost function in general and then on the assumption that fixed costs are 100.

36. $MC = 24 - 18q + 3q^2$

37. $MC = 50 - 16q + 4q^3$

38. $MC = 80 - 36q + 3q^2$

39. $MC = 39 - 22q + 3q^2$

40. $MC = \frac{1}{100}e^{q/200}$

For each of the following marginal propensities to consume, find the original consumption function.

41. $MPC = 0.85$

42. $MPC = -0.1 + 0.0008Y$

43. $MPC = 1 - 0.0002Y$

44. $MPC = \dfrac{900}{Y}$

45. $MPC = 0.0009Y$

SECTION 16·2   THE DEFINITE INTEGRAL

Consider the following demand function of a consumer,

$$p = 1600 - q_d^2$$

which appears graphically as

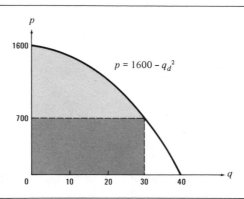

If the market price is $700, the consumer will purchase 30 units for a total expenditure of ($700)(30) = $21,000. The consumer pays a uniform price of $700 for each unit but, in fact, all units except the 30th are worth more to him—as evidenced by his demand function, which shows that he would have paid almost $1600 for some units and more than $700 for any unit preceding the final unit.

To find the total dollar value of the 30 units to the consumer, it is necessary to be able to compute the area under the demand curve from $q = 0$ to $q = 30$ (i.e., the total shaded area). Now, we know how to find the area of any rectangle, namely, by multiplying length by width. The area of the shaded rectangle is therefore $p \times q = ($700)(30) = $21,000$, which is what the consumer pays for the 30 units of the product. But the rectangle is only a portion of the total shaded area. We thus need some way of calculating areas of figures that are not rectilinear.

For any function $p = f(q)$ that is positive or zero throughout an interval (a, b), we can approximate the area bounded by the curve of the function, the horizontal axis, and the lines $x = a$ and $x = b$ by dividing the total area into many small rectangles. We then sum the areas of each rectangle, which could be expressed as

$$\sum_{i=1}^{n} f(q_i) \, \Delta q_i$$

where $f(q_i)$ is the vertical distance of the ith rectangle and Δq_i is the horizontal distance of the ith rectangle, as in the accompanying diagram.

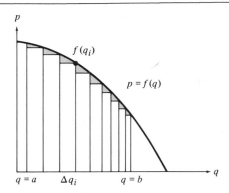

This summation, however, does not give the exact area—only an approximation because of the little pieces of area that are left out of the summation (shaded portions). But if we increase the number of rectangles so that the Δq_i, for all i, approach zero, we can form the limit

$$\lim_{n \to \infty} \sum_{i=1}^{n} f(q_i) \Delta q_i$$

where n is the number of subdivisions. Note that as $n \to \infty$, $\Delta q_i \to 0$. We can then define the area under the curve as this limit, because the error in the approximation $\to 0$ as $n \to \infty$.

We denote this summation in the following manner:

area under curve $f(q)$ over interval (a, b), where

$$a < b = \lim_{n \to \infty} \sum_{i=1}^{n} f(q_i) \Delta q_i = \int_{a}^{b} f(q)\, dq$$

The latter expression is known as the *definite integral* of $f(x)$ from a to b. a and b are also referred to as the *limits of integration*.

It can be proved that if $f(q)$ is continuous over the interval (a, b), then

$$\int_{a}^{b} f(q)\, dq = F(b) - F(a)$$

where $F(q)$ is the indefinite integral of $f(q)$. This is known as the *fundamental theorem of integral calculus*. It establishes the link between definite and indefinite integrals and enables us to evaluate definite integrals by finding the indefinite integral and evaluating it at the limits of integration. Note that we can omit constants of integration, because they will cancel when we take $F(b) - F(a)$. It is important to realize that while the value of an indefinite integral is a function, the value of a definite integral with constant limits is a number.

For convenience, we often write $F(b) - F(a)$ as $F(x)|_a^b$, which means that $F(x)$ is to be evaluated at b, then at a, and that the latter is to be subtracted from the former.

Illustration 1. Let us return to the problem presented at the outset of this section. We wish to find the area under the demand curve $p = 1600 - q_d^2$ from $q = 0$ to $q = 30$ (see Figure 1).
Solution. The area is given by

$$\int_a^b f(q)\, dq = \int_0^{30} (1600 - q^2)\, dq$$

Now, the fundamental theorem of integral calculus tells us that to evaluate this definite integral, we first find its indefinite integral and evaluate this at the limits of integration. We therefore have

$$\int_0^{30} (1600 - q^2)\, dq = 1600q - \frac{q^3}{3}\Big|_0^{30}$$

Now,

$$F(30) = 1600(30) - \frac{27,000}{3} = 48,000 - 9,000 = 39,000$$

and

$$F(0) = 0$$

so that

$$F(30) - F(0) = 39,000 - 0 = 39,000$$

Therefore

$$\int_0^{30} (1600 - q^2)\, dq = 39,000$$

and the total dollar value to the consumer of what he bought is $39,000. We have already determined that he pays only ($700)(30) = $21,000 for this bundle of the product. This leaves him with a *consumer surplus*[1] of $39,000 − $21,000 = $18,000.

Illustration 2. Consider the following demand function of a consumer:

$$p = (400 - q_d)^{1/2}$$

If the market price is $10, what is the consumer's surplus?
Solution. The demand curve is pictured below.

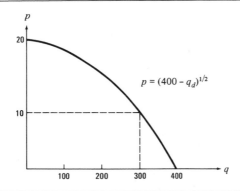

At $10, the consumer will purchase 300 units. The dollar value of the 300 units to the consumer is

$$\int_a^b f(q) \, dq = \int_0^{300} (400 - q)^{1/2} \, dq$$

$$= -\int_0^{300} (400 - q)^{1/2}(-dq) = -\tfrac{2}{3}(400 - q)^{3/2} \, \big|_0^{300}$$

$$= \$4,666.67$$

The consumer pays $10 per unit. His total expenditures are

($10)(300) = $3000

Consumer surplus is the difference between the dollar value of the units and the amount paid by the consumer. Thus

consumer surplus = $4666.67 − 3000 = $1666.67

[1] The concept of consumer surplus was elaborated upon by Alfred Marshall, but has gone through several reformulations. It is not our purpose to go into all of the subtleties involved. We are concerned only with illustrating the concept of finding areas under curves and the general evaluation of definite integrals.

In dealing with consumer surplus, we have computed areas under demand curves. The process is, however, a general one, and can in the same way be applied to finding areas under any curves.

Illustration 3.   Find the area bounded by the curve $y = x^3$, the x axis, and the lines $x = 2$, $x = 4$.
Solution.   The graph of the function within the stated interval appears as

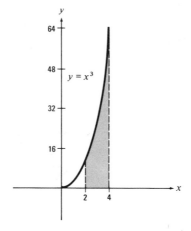

The area we seek is the shaded portion of the diagram and is given by

$$\text{area} = \int_2^4 x^3 \, dx = \frac{x^4}{4} \Big|_2^4 = \frac{256}{4} - \frac{16}{4} = 60 \text{ units of area}$$

In the event that a function $f(x)$ is negative throughout some interval, we could follow a similar procedure in order to find the area between the curve and the x axis. In that case the curve lies entirely below the x axis and the value of the definite integral will be negative, because all the $f(x_i) \leq 0$. We could then say that the resulting area is negative (in the sense that it appears below the x axis), or we can refer to the absolute value of the area and disregard the sign.

Illustration 4.   Find the area bounded by the curve $y = x^3$, the x axis, and the lines $x = -3$, $x = -4$.
Solution.   The graph of the function within the stated interval appears as

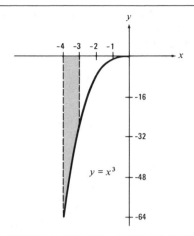

The area we seek is the shaded portion of the diagram and is given by

$$\text{area} = \int_{-4}^{-3} x^3 \, dx = \left.\frac{x^4}{4}\right|_{-4}^{-3} = \frac{(-3)^4}{4} - \frac{(-4)^4}{4} = \frac{81}{4} - \frac{256}{4} = -\frac{175}{4}$$

The absolute value of this area is thus $\frac{175}{4}$. Note that in computing this area we chose -4 as the lower limit of integration and -3 as the upper limit of integration. This is because $-4 < -3$.

On occasion, we may wish to consider the area under a curve that takes on both positive and negative values on some interval; that is, the curve is above the x axis for some portion and below the x axis for another portion. In such cases, we cannot compute the area by taking the definite integral over the entire interval, because the negative and positive areas will, at least partially, cancel each other. We are interested in the sum of the absolute value of the areas, so we wish to count both the negative and positive areas. In order to do this we make use of the following theorem.

Theorem. If c is any point within the interval (a, b), then

$$\int_a^b f(x) \, dx = \int_a^c f(x) \, dx + \int_c^b f(x) \, dx$$

Thus, to evaluate a definite integral over an interval, we can break down the interval into two subintervals and then sum the values of the integrals over these subintervals. This procedure can be generalized for any number of subintervals.

To find the area under a curve that takes on positive values for some portion of the interval and negative values for another portion of the interval, we find the relevant area for each subinterval separately and sum their absolute values.

Illustration 5.   Find the area bounded by the curve $y = x^3$, the x axis, and the lines $x = -4$, $x = 4$.
Solution.   The graph of the function within the stated interval appears as

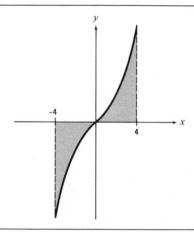

The area we seek is the total shaded portion of the diagram. The function is negative for $-4 < x < 0$ and positive for $0 < x < 4$, so we break the total interval into these two subintervals and compute the absolute value of each area separately.

$$\text{area} = \int_{-4}^{0} x^3 \, dx + \int_{0}^{4} x^3 \, dx = \frac{x^4}{4} \Big|_{-4}^{0} + \frac{x^4}{4} \Big|_{0}^{4}$$

$$= \left| -\tfrac{256}{4} \right| + \tfrac{256}{4} = 64 + 64 = 128$$

Notice that if we had not taken absolute values, the negative and positive areas would have canceled.

Some other interesting properties of definite integrals are given by the following theorems.

Theorem.   If k is any constant, then

$$\int_{a}^{b} kf(x) \, dx = k \int_{a}^{b} f(x) \, dx$$

Illustration 6.

$$\int_2^4 7x^3 \, dx = 7 \int_2^4 x^3 \, dx = 7(60) = 420$$

because we found in Illustration 3 that $\int_2^4 x^3 \, dx = 60$.

Theorem. If u and v are each continuous functions of x, then

$$\int_a^b (u + v) \, dx = \int_a^b u \, dx + \int_a^b v \, dx$$

A similar result holds for the sum of any number of functions.

Illustration 7.

$$\int_2^4 (7x^3 + x) \, dx = \int_2^4 7x^3 \, dx + \int_2^4 x \, dx$$

$$= 420 + \frac{x^2}{2} \Big|_2^4$$

$$= 420 + \tfrac{16}{2} - \tfrac{4}{2}$$

$$= 426$$

where we made use of the finding in Illustration 6 that $\int_2^4 7x^3 \, dx = 420$.

The reader should note that although the definite integral has been introduced as applying to area, it can be applied in general to any analogous process of finding

$$\lim_{n \to \infty} \sum_{i=1}^n f(x_i) \, \Delta x_i$$

Illustration 8. The marginal cost function of a firm is given by

$$MC = \tfrac{1}{50} e^{q/150}$$

Find the sum of the marginal costs of producing all units between 75 and 100.

Solution. We simply evaluate the following integral:

$$\int_{75}^{100} \tfrac{1}{50} e^{q/150} \, dq = 3 \int_{75}^{100} e^{q/150} \left(\tfrac{1}{150}\right) dq$$

$$= 3 e^{q/150} \Big|_{75}^{100} = 3(e^{2/3} - e^{1/2})$$

$$= 3(1.9739 - 1.6487)$$

$$= 3(0.3252) = 0.9756$$

Exercises

Evaluate each of the following.

1. $\displaystyle\int_{-1}^{3} \frac{2}{x^2} dx$

2. $\displaystyle\int_{1}^{8} \frac{1}{3}x^{4/3} dx$

3. $\displaystyle\int_{2}^{5} \frac{dx}{x + 2}$

4. $\displaystyle\int_{5}^{10} (2p - 4) dp$

5. $\displaystyle\int_{2}^{4} (3p^2 - 3) dp$

6. $\displaystyle\int_{1}^{6} (-3p^{-2} + p^{-3}) dp$

7. $\displaystyle\int_{1}^{3} \frac{1 + p}{p^2} dp$

8. $\displaystyle\int_{0}^{4} p\sqrt{p^2 + 9}\, dp$

9. $\displaystyle\int_{-1}^{8} \frac{p\, dp}{\sqrt{p^2 + 15}}$

10. $\displaystyle\int_{3/2}^{2} \frac{x^2\, dx}{x^3 - 2}$

11. $\displaystyle\int_{1}^{5} (e^p + e^{-p}) dp$

12. $\displaystyle\int_{10}^{20} e^{(p/2) - 3}\, dp$

For each of the following consumer demand functions, find the consumer's surplus at the given price (indicated by p_0).

13. $p = 1800 - 2q_d^2$; $p_0 = 1000$

14. $p = 200 - \frac{1}{2}q_d^2$; $p_0 = 150$

15. $p = 650 - q_d^2$; $p_0 = 25$

16. $p = (1000 - 2q_d)^{1/2}$; $p_0 = 30$

17. $p = (100 - 3q_d)^{1/2}$; $p_0 = 8$

18. $p = \dfrac{100}{q_d^{1/2}}$; $p_0 = 5$

19. $p = \dfrac{200}{q_d}$; $p_0 = 20$

20. $p = \dfrac{400}{q_d^2}$; $p_0 = 4$

21. $p = 3000 - e^{q_d}$; $p_0 = 19$

22. Find the area bounded by the curve $y = \frac{1}{2}x^2$, the x axis, and the lines $x = 4$, $x = 12$.

23. Find the area bounded by the curve $y = x^2 + 4$, the x axis, and the lines $x = -3$, $x = 5$.

24. Find the area bounded by the curve $y = 6 - x - x^2$, the x axis, and the lines $x = \frac{1}{2}$, $x = \frac{3}{2}$.

25. Find the area bounded by the curve $y = 2x + 10$, the x axis, and the lines $x = 5$, $x = 10$.

26. Find the area bounded by the curve $y = 2x + 10$, the x axis, and the lines $x = -1$, $x = -3$.

27. Find the area bounded by the curve $y = 2x + 10$, the x axis, and the lines $x = -3$, $x = 10$.

28. Find the area bounded by the curve $y = x^2 - 10$, the x axis, and the lines $x = -2$, $x = 2$.

29. Find the area bounded by the curve $y = \sqrt{3x + 16}$, the x axis, and the lines $x = 0$, $x = 3$.

30. Find the area bounded by the curve $y = x^2 - 6x + 8$, the x axis, and the lines $x = 0$, $x = 3$.

31. The marginal cost function of a firm is given by $MC = 24 - 18q + 3q^2$
     Find the sum of the marginal costs of producing all units between 5 and 8.

32. The marginal cost function of a firm is given by $MC = 10q + 2$
     Find the sum of the marginal costs of producing all units between 10 and 20.

33. The marginal cost function of a firm is given by

     $MC = \frac{1}{100}e^{q/200}$.

     Find the sum of the marginal costs of producing all units between 100 and 300.

SECTION 16·3 TABLES OF INTEGRALS

The reader will recall that when dealing with derivatives, it was possible to differentiate virtually any algebraic expression by using one or more of a small number of rules that we had developed. This, however, does not hold true for integration. As an illustration of relatively simple algebraic expressions that cannot be easily integrated, consider the following:

$$\int 4x\sqrt{x-2}\,dx \tag{1}$$

$$\int \frac{x^2}{3x-1}\,dx \tag{2}$$

Neither of these integrals can be put in the form $\int u^n\,du$, so the power rule (whether for $n \neq -1$ or for $n = -1$) does not apply.

There are many specialized methods that apply to integrals appearing in distinctive forms. Instead of considering any more of these, we wish to make the reader aware of the existence of tables of integrals and how they can be used. An abridged table of integrals is given at the end of the book. More extensive ones exist and can be consulted if the need arises. Each result in the table has been derived and stated in general form so that it can be used for any integral that can be expressed in such form.

Thus, to evaluate integral (1) given above, we look under the heading: "Forms Involving $\sqrt{a + bu}$." We find an entry that is applicable to the given integral, namely

$$\int u\sqrt{a+bu}\,du = \frac{2(3bu-2a)}{15b^2}(a+bu)^{3/2} + c$$

The integral we wish to evaluate can be written as

$$4\int x\sqrt{-2+x}\,dx$$

If we set $u = x$, $a = -2$, and $b = 1$, the given integral is in the same form as the entry in the table of integrals. Applying the result, we get

$$4\int x\sqrt{-2+x}\,dx = 4\left[\frac{2(3x+4)}{15}\right](-2+x)^{3/2} + c$$

$$= \frac{8(3x+4)}{15}(-2+x)^{3/2} + c$$

To evaluate integral (2) given above, we look under the heading: "Forms Involving $a + bu$." We find an entry that is applicable to the given integral, namely,

$$\int \frac{u^2}{a+bu}\,du = \frac{1}{b^3}\left[\frac{1}{2}(a+bu)^2 - 2a(a+bu) + a^2\ln(a+bu)\right] + c$$

The integral we wish to evaluate is

$$\int \frac{x^2 \, dx}{3x - 1}$$

If we set $u = x$, $a = 3$, and $b = -1$, the given integral is in the same form as the entry in the table of integrals. Applying the result, we get

$$\int \frac{x^2}{3x - 1} \, dx = \frac{1}{27} \left[\frac{1}{2} (3x - 1)^2 + 2(3x - 1) + \frac{1}{27} \ln(3x - 1) \right] + c$$

$$= \frac{1}{54} (3x - 1)^2 + \frac{2}{27} (3x - 1) + \frac{1}{27} \ln(3x - 1) + c$$

Exercises

Use the table of integrals at the end of the book to evaluate the following.

1. $\displaystyle \int \frac{x \, dx}{7x - 3}$

2. $\displaystyle \int x^2 \sqrt{4 - 3x} \, dx$

3. $\displaystyle \int x \sqrt{3 + 2x} \, dx$

4. $\displaystyle \int_0^2 \frac{x^3}{4 + x^2} \, dx$

5. $\displaystyle \int \frac{\sqrt{4 - x^2}}{2x} \, dx$

6. $\displaystyle \int \frac{\sqrt{9 + 4x^2}}{2x} \, dx$

7. $\displaystyle \int x e^x \, dx$

8. $\displaystyle \int x^2 e^x \, dx$

9. $\displaystyle \int_4^5 x^2 \sqrt{x^2 - 16} \, dx$

10. $\displaystyle \int x \ln x^2 \, dx$

11. $\int x^5 e^x \, dx$

12. $\int \ln 2x \, dx$

13. $\int x^2 e^{2x} \, dx$

14. $\int \dfrac{dx}{x\sqrt{x - x^2}}$

15. $\int_5^9 \dfrac{2 \, dx}{x^2 \sqrt{x^2 - 9}}$

16. $\int_9^{12} \dfrac{dx}{x^4 - 25}$

17. $\int \dfrac{dx}{x\sqrt{1 + 2x}}$

18. $\int \dfrac{x \, dx}{(1 + x^4)^{3/2}}$

19. $\int_2^6 \dfrac{dx}{2x(6 + 2x)^2}$

SECTION 16·4   INTEGRATION BY APPROXIMATION

There exist several methods of approximating the value of a definite integral. Such methods are invaluable when one is presented with integrals that are difficult to integrate or in cases where the function to be integrated is not known except for its values at specific points. In economics we frequently have little knowledge about the precise form of cost functions, revenue functions, demand functions, and so on, but yet may have a set of empirical values for marginal cost, marginal revenue, marginal demand, and so on. Under such circumstances, approximate integration should be investigated.

One very popular method of approximate integration is known as the *trapezoidal rule*, because it approximates the area under a curve by a series of trapezoids. Because the area of a trapezoid is known from geometry to be half the sum of the parallel sides multiplied by the altitude, a formula for total area can be easily derived. This is stated by the following.

Trapezoidal Rule.   If we wish to approximate the integral $\int_a^b f(x)\,dx$, where $y = f(x)$, then

$$\int_a^b f(x)\,dx \approx \frac{h}{2}\left(y_0 + 2y_1 + 2y_2 + 2y_3 + \cdots + 2y_{n-1} + y_n\right)$$

where the interval (a, b) is divided into n equal portions each of length h and where $y_0, y_1, y_2, \ldots, y_n$ are the values of $y = f(x)$ for $x = a, a + h$, $a + 2h, \ldots, b$. The symbol $\approx$ denotes "approximation." In general, the greater the value of n (i.e., the smaller the value of h), the better will be the approximation. It should also be noted that there exist formulas that estimate the errors arising from such approximations.

Illustration 1.   Evaluate

$$\int_0^1 \frac{x^2}{3x - 1}\,dx$$

by the trapezoidal rule, taking $n = 4$.
Solution.   Because $n = 4$, $h = \frac{1}{4}(b - a) = \frac{1}{4}(1 - 0) = \frac{1}{4}$. We then have $x_0 = 0$, $x_1 = \frac{1}{4}$, $x_2 = \frac{1}{2}$, $x_3 = \frac{3}{4}$, $x_4 = 1$. We know that

$$y = \frac{x^2}{3x - 1}$$

Therefore

$$y_0 = 0$$

$$y_1 = \frac{\frac{1}{16}}{\frac{3}{4} - 1} = -\frac{1}{4} = -0.25$$

$$y_2 = \frac{\frac{1}{4}}{\frac{3}{2} - 1} = \frac{1}{2} = 0.5$$

$$y_3 = \frac{\frac{9}{16}}{\frac{9}{4} - 1} = \frac{\frac{9}{16}}{\frac{5}{4}} = \frac{9}{20} = 0.45$$

$$y_4 = \frac{1}{2} = 0.5$$

Applying the trapezoidal rule, we get

$$\int_0^1 \frac{x^2}{3x - 1}\,dx \approx \frac{1}{2}\cdot\frac{1}{4}[0 + 2(-0.25) + 2(0.5) + 2(0.45) + 0.5] \approx 0.238$$

Illustration 2.   The following table gives marginal costs at several output levels

q	10.0	10.5	11.0	11.5	12.0
MC	1.80	2.00	2.05	2.15	2.30

Find the total cost of increasing output from 10 to 12 units.

Solution.   Total costs are derived by integrating the marginal cost function. We wish to find the cost of increasing output from 10 to 12 units, so we must evaluate the definite integral

$$\int_{10}^{12} MC \, dq$$

The problem, however, is that we do not know the MC function. We do, however, have information about marginal costs at several points between 10 and 12, so we can use approximate integration.

We have four equal subintervals, each of $\frac{1}{2}$ unit width, between 10 and 12. Therefore $n = 4$ and $h = \frac{1}{2}$. Our points are $q_0 = 10$, $q_1 = 10.5$, $q_2 = 11.0$, $q_3 = 11.5$, $q_4 = 12.0$. Corresponding to these we have $MC_0 = 1.80$, $MC_1 = 2.00$, $MC_2 = 2.05$, $MC_3 = 2.15$, and $MC_4 = 2.30$. Applying the trapezoidal rule, we get

$$\int_{10}^{12} MC \, dq \approx \tfrac{1}{2} \cdot \tfrac{1}{2}[1.80 + 2(2.00) + 2(2.05) + 2(2.15) + 2.30] \approx 4.125$$

Thus the cost of increasing output from 10 to 12 units is approximately $4.13. We were able to make this computation even though we did not know either the cost function or the marginal cost function between $q = 10$ and $q = 12$. All we really knew were particular numerical values for MC at specific points. It is for this reason that such methods of approximate integration are often referred to as *numerical integration.*

A second very popular and somewhat superior method of approximating integrals is given by *Simpson's rule.* It approximates the area under a curve by a series of parabolic arcs and is given by the following.

Simpson's Rule.   If we wish to approximate the integral $\int_a^b f(x) \, dx$, where $y = f(x)$, then

$$\int_a^b f(x) \, dx \approx \frac{h}{3}(y_0 + 4y_1 + 2y_2 + 4y_3 + 2y_4 + \cdots + 2y_{2n-2} + 4y_{2n-1} + y_{2n})$$

where the interval (a, b) is divided into an even number $(2n)$ of equal portions each of length h and where $y_0, y_1, y_2, \ldots, y_{2n}$ are the values of $y = f(x)$ for $x = a, a + h, a + 2h, \ldots, b$. As with the trapezoidal rule, the greater the value of n (i.e., the smaller the value of h), the better will be the approximation. Again, there exist formulas that estimate the errors arising from such approximations.

Illustration 3.   Evaluate

$$\int_0^1 \frac{x^2}{3x - 1}\, dx$$

by Simpson's rule, taking $2n = 4$.

Solution.   The number of subintervals is given by an even number, $2n = 4$. Therefore $h = \frac{1}{4}(b - a) = \frac{1}{4}(1 - 0) = \frac{1}{4}$. We then have $x_0 = 0$, $x_1 = \frac{1}{4}$, $x_2 = \frac{1}{2}$, $x_3 = \frac{3}{4}$, $x_4 = 1$. We know that

$$y = \frac{x}{3x - 1}$$

Therefore

$y_0 = 0$

$y_1 = -0.25$

$y_2 = 0.5$

$y_3 = 0.45$

$y_4 = 0.5$

Applying Simpson's rule, we get

$$\int_0^1 \frac{x^2}{3x - 1}\, dx \approx \frac{1}{3} \cdot \frac{1}{4}[0 + 4(-0.25) + 2(0.5) + 4(0.45) + 0.5] \approx 189$$

The value we now get is 0.049 less than what we arrived at by using the trapezoidal Rule. It can be shown that our present value is a better approximation than the former result.

Illustration 4.   As in Illustration 2, the following table gives marginal costs at several output levels:

q	10.0	10.5	11.0	11.5	12.0
MC	1.80	2.00	2.05	2.15	2.30

Find the total cost of increasing output from 10 to 12 units by using Simpson's rule.

Solution. Total costs are again derived by integrating the marginal cost function. We wish to evaluate the definite integral

$$\int_{10}^{12} MC \, dq$$

where we know the value of MC only at selected points.

The number of subintervals is given by an even number, $2n = 4$, each of $\frac{1}{2}$ unit width (i.e., $h = \frac{1}{2}$). Our points are $q_0 = 10.0$, $q_1 = 10.5$, $q_2 = 11.0$, $q_3 = 11.5$, $q_4 = 12.0$. Corresponding to these we have $MC_0 = 1.80$, $MC_1 = 2.00$, $MC_2 = 2.05$, $MC_3 = 2.15$, and $MC_4 = 2.30$.

Applying Simpson's rule, we get

$$\int_{10}^{12} MC \, dq \approx \frac{1}{3} \cdot \frac{1}{2}[1.80 + 4(2.00) + 2(2.05) + 4(2.15) + 2.30] \approx 4.133$$

The cost of increasing output from 10 to 12 units is approximately \$4.13, which, to the nearest penny, is the same as our earlier result.

Exercises

Evaluate each of the following definite integrals by first using the trapezoidal rule and then Simpson's rule. In each case use the indicated number of subintervals.

1. $\int_{1}^{3} \frac{x \, dx}{7x - 3}$, with eight subintervals

2. $\int_{0}^{2} \frac{x^3}{4 + x^2} \, dx$, with four subintervals

3. $\int_{2}^{5} xe^x \, dx$, with six subintervals

4. $\int_{1}^{4} \ln 2x \, dx$, with six subintervals

5. $\int_{0}^{3} \frac{dx}{1 + x^2}$ with six subintervals

6. $\int_{2}^{10} \frac{x \, dx}{4 - x}$, with eight subintervals

7. The following table gives marginal costs at several output levels

q	25.0	25.5	26.0	26.5	27.0	27.5	28.0
MC	10.0	10.5	11.1	12.0	13.0	14.0	15.5

Find the total cost of increasing output from 25 to 28 units.

8. The following table gives marginal revenue at several output levels

q	10	11	12	13	14	15	16	17	18
MR	40	39	37	33	30	25	24	20	15

Find the total revenue resulting from increasing output from 10 to 18 units.

9. The following table gives marginal costs at several output levels.

q	50.0	50.5	51.0	51.5	52.0	52.5	53.0
MC	2	6	8	10	10	10	12

Find the total cost of increasing output from 50 to 53 units.

DIFFERENCE AND DIFFERENTIAL EQUATIONS

> But times do change and move continually.
>
> —Edmund Spenser

As we have already pointed out, the economic analysis presented in earlier chapters is basically *static*. It deals with equilibrium positions and their characteristics without considering the role of time. To be sure, we have frequently considered changes in equilibrium positions due to changes in functional parameters. This is known as *comparative statics*, because different equilibrium situations are compared. But we did not investigate the transitional process involved in such changes, nor the time that might elapse while such changes occur. If we are interested in tracing the path leading to equilibrium, in ascertaining whether equilibrium will ever be achieved, or in variables that depend upon events that occurred in prior periods, we must provide a *dynamic analysis*. For this purpose, it is necessary to be conversant with the mathematics of difference and differential equations. In this chapter we provide an introductory treatment of these topics. The reader, however, should be aware that to cover this subject in an exhaustive manner would be beyond the scope of this book.

SECTION 17·1 DIFFERENCE EQUATIONS

There is evidence to suggest that a lag exists between the time that new income is received and the time it exerts its effect upon consumption patterns. If this is the case, then the consumption function should possibly be written in the form

$$C_t = C(Y_{t-1})$$

where t refers to any time period and $t - 1$ to the previous period. Consumption in any time period is thus a function of income in the previous period. This is known as a *difference equation*, because the variable in any time period, t, depends on what occurred in some previous time period. Analysis based on such equations is sometimes called *period analysis*.

As an illustration, consider the lagged consumption function

$$C_t = 40 + 0.9Y_{t-1}$$

Assume that investment is some fixed positive constant $I_t = I_0$ and there is no government sector. The general condition for the equilibrium level of national income as given in Section 15.4 can be written as $Y = C + I$. In our case this would be expressed as

$$Y_t = C_t + I_t$$

or

$$Y_t = 40 + 0.9Y_{t-1} + I_0$$
$$= 0.9Y_{t-1} + 40 + I_0$$

This equation is said to be a *first-order linear difference equation* with constant coefficients. It is first order because the variable (in this case income) depends on what occurred one period previous to the present and on no earlier periods. We could just as well encounter the case where income depends not only on what occurred in the previous period but also upon the situation that existed two periods prior to the present. Such a difference equation would be said to be of *second order*. Similarly, we can have difference equations of any order. The relationship

$$Y_t = 0.9Y_{t-1} + 40 + I_0$$

is linear because all terms involving the variable are raised to the first power. Finally, it has constant coefficients, such as 0.9, 40, and so on, and not coefficients that vary with time, such as $0.9t$, $40t^5$, and so on.

If we wish to find the equilibrium level of national income during any period, Y_t, we must be able to solve difference equations. Let us therefore consider general methods of finding solutions for difference equations and subsequently return to the specific problem given above.

The general form of an nth-order linear difference equation with constant coefficients is

$$Y_t = a_1 Y_{t-1} + a_2 Y_{t-2} + \cdots + a_n Y_{t-n} + b$$

where $a_1, a_2, \ldots, a_n$ and b are constants and where a_n is not zero. If a_n is zero and a_{n-1} is not zero, then the difference equation is of order $n - 1$. In the event that the value of b is zero, the difference equation is said to be *homogeneous*, while if it is any other constant the difference equation is *nonhomogeneous.* Thus the difference equation given earlier,

$$Y_t = 0.9Y_{t-1} + 40 + I_0$$

is nonhomogeneous, while the equation

$$Y_t = 0.9Y_{t-1}$$

is homogeneous.

In order to evaluate Y_t for all periods, where Y_t is given by a first-order difference equation, it is necessary to be given one initial condition. This means we must know the value of Y_t for some specified time, such as at the outset, Y_0. In the illustration given earlier, that is,

$$Y_t = 0.9Y_{t-1} + 40 + I_0$$

assume that we are given the initial condition $Y_0 = 1000$. We could easily compute Y_1 in the following way:

$$Y_1 = 0.9Y_0 + 40 + I_0$$
$$= 0.9(1000) + 40 + I_0$$
$$= 940 + I_0$$

Once knowing Y_1, we can find Y_2 by substitution:

$$Y_2 = 0.9Y_1 + 40 + I_0$$
$$= 0.9(940 + I_0) + 40 + I_0$$

Similarly, we can find all subsequent values of Y_t.

In the general case where we have an nth-order difference equation, it would be necessary to be given n initial conditions; that is, we must know the value of Y_t for n consecutive time periods. If, for example, we were given the values of Y_t for Y_0, Y_1, Y_2, ..., Y_{n-1}, we could then evaluate Y_n from the following:

$$Y_n = a_1 Y_{n-1} + a_2 Y_{n-2} + \cdots + a_n Y_0 + b$$

Once having found Y_n, we could proceed to find Y_{n+1} and then Y_{n+2}, and so on.

It will be seen that finding solutions using the procedure just outlined quickly becomes very time consuming. Suppose that we wish to find Y_{100}, where

$$Y_t = 0.9Y_{t-1} + 40 + I_0$$

and where the initial condition is $Y_0 = 1000$. In order to find Y_{100}, we would first have to find Y_1, Y_2, Y_3, ..., Y_{99}. To avoid such lengthy calculations, we are interested in deriving a general formula for solutions of difference equations. Such general formulas must have the properties of (1) satisfying the difference equation for all values of t and (2) satisfying the initial conditions.

In subsequent sections we shall show how to derive general solutions for some common forms of difference equations.

Exercises

For each of the following difference equations, determine the order, provide the necessary initial conditions, and then find Y_4 where appropriate.

1. $Y_t = 4Y_{t-1} - 3Y_{t-2} + 100$
2. $Y_t = 0.95Y_{t-1} + 120$
3. $Y_t = 0.90Y_{t-2} + 90$
4. $Y_t = 3Y_{t-1} - 2.5Y_{t-2} + 0.4Y_{t-3}$
5. $Y_t = 2Y_{t-1} - 1.2Y_{t-3}$
6. $Y_t = 1.5Y_{t-2} - 0.8Y_{t-3}$
7. $Y_t = 0.85Y_{t-1}$
8. $Y_t = 0.99Y_{t-1} - 0.1Y_{t-10}$
9. $Y_t = 1.5Y_{t-1} - 0.5Y_{t-3} - 0.2Y_{t-6}$
10. $Y_t = 0.8Y_{t-1} + 0.1Y_{t-2} + 200$

SECTION 17·2 SOLUTIONS OF FIRST-ORDER LINEAR HOMOGENEOUS DIFFERENCE EQUATIONS

Consider the general form of a first-order linear homogeneous difference equation,

$$Y_t = aY_{t-1}$$

Suppose that the initial condition is $Y_0 = K_0$. By substitution, we see that

$$Y_1 = aY_0 = aK_0$$

$$Y_2 = aY_1 = a(aK_0) = a^2K_0$$

$$Y_3 = aY_2 = a(a^2K_0) = a^3K_0$$

This leads us to expect that in general we would have

$$Y_t = a^tK_0$$

To verify that this is the general solution, we first check to see whether it satisfies the difference equation. If the proposed solution is correct, then we have

$$Y_t = a^t K_0$$

$$Y_{t-1} = a^{t-1} K_0$$

and

$$aY_{t-1} = a(a^{t-1}K_0) = a^t K_0$$

Because $Y_t = aY_{t-1}$, the difference equation is satisfied. We next check to see whether the initial conditions are satisfied. The proposed solution implies that

$$Y_0 = a^0 K_0 = K_0$$

which is the same as the initial condition. Therefore both the difference equation and the initial condition are satisfied.

We conclude that a general solution to the first-order linear homogeneous difference equation $Y_t = aY_{t-1}$ with initial condition $Y_0 = K_0$ is the formula

$$Y_t = a^t K_0$$

The value of Y for any time period can be found by merely inserting the appropriate value of t into the formula. As an example, if $t = 100$, we have

$$Y_{100} = a^{100} K_0$$

Expressing solutions of the difference equation in the general form $Y_t = a^t K_0$ also enables us to trace out the *time path* of the variable Y_t, which is, of course, one of the purposes of dynamic analysis. We can distinguish between different possibilities depending upon the values of a and K_0.

Assume first that $a > 1$ and K_0 is positive. In this case, a^t gets larger and larger as t increases. As time passes, Y_t will continually increase without any limit whatever. We sometimes say that such a function *explodes*, which indicates that it has no bounds.

Suppose that $0 < a < 1$, that is, a is a positive number less than 1, and K_0 is positive. As t increases, a^t gets smaller and smaller. As time passes, Y_t will continually decrease but will always be greater than zero. Such a function is sometimes said to be moving along a *damped path*.

If $a = 1$ and K_0 is positive, a^t will always be equal to 1 regardless of the value of t. Thus, as time passes, Y_t will be constant or *stationary*.

Assume next that $a < -1$ and K_0 is positive. In this case, a^t will get larger and larger in absolute value as t increases, but its sign will oscillate between negative and positive. Thus, as time passes, the magnitude of Y_t will continually increase but its sign will alternate from one period to the next. This function is said to *explode with oscillation*.

Suppose that $-1 < a < 0$, that is, a is a negative number smaller than 1 in magnitude and K_0 is positive. As t increases, a^t gets smaller and smaller in absolute value, but its sign will oscillate between negative and positive. Thus, as time passes, the magnitude of Y_t will continually decrease but its sign will alternate from one period to the next. Such a function is said to be moving along a *damped but oscillating path*.

If $a = -1$ and K_0 is positive, a^t will alternate between -1 and $+1$. Thus, as time passes, Y_t will be constant or stationary in absolute value but its sign will oscillate from one period to the next.

In the event that K_0 is negative, then for each of the various cases considered above, the signs will be reversed; that is, wherever we had a positive result, it will now be negative and vice versa.

Illustration.   Consumption is given by the following difference equation:

$$C_t = 0.99 Y_{t-1}$$

There is no net investment taking place; that is, $I_t = 0$, and there is no government sector. National income initially is $Y_0 = 1000$. Find the general solution for the equilibrium level of national income in any time period and, in particular, find national income in year 4. Also trace the time path of income.

Solution.   The condition for achieving equilibrium national income is

$$Y_t = C_t + I_t$$

which in our case becomes

$$Y_t = 0.99 Y_{t-1}$$

This is a first-order linear homogeneous difference equation. The general solution is therefore of the form

$$Y_t = a^t K_0$$

Applying this to our illustration gives

$$Y_t = (0.99)^t (1000)$$

$$= 1000(0.99)^t$$

In particular, when $t = 4$, we get

$Y_4 = 1000(0.99)^4$

$\qquad = 960.6$

It is evident that as time goes on, the equilibrium level of income continually decreases. This comes about because the marginal propensity to consume is less than 1 and there is no net investment or government spending taking place. In this case we have $0 < a < 1$ and K_0 is positive. Therefore, as indicated above, income will move along a damped nono-scillating path. As $t \to \infty$, $Y_t \to 0$.

Exercises

In each of the following cases, find the general solution for the equilibrium level of national income in any time period and, in particular, for $t = 5$. Also trace the time path of income. Assume that there is no government sector.

1. $C_t = 0.95 Y_{t-1}$, $I_t = 0$, $Y_0 = 500$
2. $C_t = 0.9 Y_{t-1}$, $I_t = 0$, $Y_0 = 600$
3. $C_t = Y_{t-1}$, $I_t = 0$, $Y_0 = 500$
4. $C_t = 1.1 Y_{t-1}$, $I_t = 0$, $Y_0 = 400$
5. $C_t = 0.95 Y_{t-1}$, $I_t = 0.05 Y_{t-1}$, $Y_0 = 500$
6. $C_t = 0.95 Y_{t-1}$, $I_t = 0.03 Y_{t-1}$, $Y_0 = 600$
7. $C_t = 0.95 Y_{t-1}$, $I_t = 0.1 Y_{t-1}$, $Y_0 = 400$
8. $C_t = 0.9 Y_{t-1}$, $I_t = 0.2 Y_{t-1}$, $Y_0 = 800$
9. $C_t = 0.5 Y_t + 0.4 Y_{t-1}$, $I_t = 0.1 Y_{t-1}$, $Y_0 = 1000$
10. $C_t = 0.5 Y_t + 0.4 Y_{t-1}$, $I_t = 0.2 Y_{t-1}$, $Y_0 = 1000$
11. $C_t = 0.6 Y_t + 0.4 Y_{t-1}$, $I_t = 0.08 Y_{t-1}$, $Y_0 = 1000$

SECTION 17·3   THE HARROD GROWTH MODEL

The Harrod growth model (introduced by Sir Roy Harrod) is an attempt to explain the dynamics of growth in the economy.[1]

---

[1] The purpose of this section is to demonstrate how simple difference equations can be applied to economic problems. Accordingly, we have made no attempt to go into all of the ramifications of the model. The interested reader is referred to R. F. Harrod, *Towards a Dynamic Economics* (London: Macmillan, 1948); William J. Baumol, *Economic Dynamics* (New York: Macmillan, 1959), pp. 37–55, 157–158, 165–166; and R. F. Harrod, "Domar and Dynamic Economics," *The Economic Journal*, LXIX (September 1959), pp. 451–464.

Assume that aggregate savings in an economy during any period t is a constant proportion α of the income of that period; that is, the marginal propensity to save is constant.[2] We have

$$S_t = \alpha Y_t$$

where S_t is aggregate savings in any time period, α is the marginal propensity to save (some positive constant less than 1) and Y_t is income in the same period.

Harrod also employs what is known as the *acceleration principle* as his theory of investment. This is equivalent to the statement that investment in any period is proportional to the rate of change in national product or income over time. The justification given for this is that increases in national product or income require increased capital equipment, and vice versa for decreases in national income. The aggregate investment function can therefore be stated as

$$I_t = b(Y_t - Y_{t-1})$$

where I_t is aggregate investment in any time period, b is some positive constant, Y_t is income in the same time period, and Y_{t-1} is income in the previous time period.

The condition for achieving equilibrium national income can be stated as

$$I_t = S_t$$

or

$$b(Y_t - Y_{t-1}) = \alpha Y_t$$
$$b Y_t - b Y_{t-1} = \alpha Y_t$$
$$(b - \alpha) Y_t = b Y_{t-1}$$

$$Y_t = \left(\frac{b}{b - \alpha}\right) Y_{t-1}$$

We recognize this as a first-order linear homogeneous difference equation.

This equation shows us how income grows over time in order to maintain equilibrium. Income during any period must be a constant $[b/(b - \alpha)]$ multiplied by the previous period national income.

Assume that we are given the initial condition

$$Y_0 = K_0 > 0$$

---

[2] It is possible to relax this assumption and to show that the basic implications of the model remain intact.

Following the procedure of the last section, we can write the general solution of the equation as

$$Y_t = \left(\frac{b}{b - \alpha}\right)^t K_0$$

We have already defined b and α to be positive. Moreover, we generally expect b to be greater than α, because α is invariably less than 1 and b is substantially more than 1, as all available empirical information indicates. Consequently, $b - \alpha$ is positive and $[b/(b - \alpha)]$ is not only positive but also greater than 1. Therefore, as $t \to \infty$, $Y_t \to \infty$. The time path of income is seen to be explosive and nonoscillating; that is, income will increase indefinitely so that in any period it is $[b/(b - \alpha)]$ times the income of the previous period. This implies a growth rate of

$$\frac{b}{b - \alpha} - 1 = \frac{\alpha}{b - \alpha}$$

This is known as the *warranted rate of growth*, which is the path upon which equilibrium is achieved. This explosive expansion could, however, be impeded by limitations in productive capabilities caused by such things as the full employment ceiling and bottlenecks in production due to shortages in specific types of capital or immobility of labor.

As an illustration, suppose that $\alpha = 0.15$ and $b = 3.15$. The general solution of the difference equation is

$$Y_t = \left(\frac{3.15}{3.15 - 0.15}\right)^t K_0$$

or

$$Y_t = (1.05)^t K_0$$

The time path of income is certainly explosive and nonoscillating. Income in any period will be 1.05 what it was in the previous period. The warranted growth rate is thus 0.05 or 5 percent.

In the unlikely event that $\alpha > b$, it would follow that $[b/(b - \alpha)]$ would be negative and greater than 1 in magnitude. The time path of income would then be explosive with oscillation; that is, the absolute value of income would get larger and larger but would alternate from negative to positive. Such a circumstance, of course, makes no sense from an economic point of view, but is what would be implied by the model if $\alpha > b$.

Exercises

For each of the following models: (a) Find the general solution of the equilibrium difference equation. (b) What are the implications for rates of growth? (c) What will the time path of income look like in general? (d) What would your answers be if $\alpha = 0.1$ and $b = 2$.

1. $S_t = \alpha Y_{t-1}; I_t = b(Y_t - Y_{t-1})$
2. $S_t = \alpha Y_{t-1}; I_t = b Y_t$
3. $S_t = \alpha Y_t; I_t = b Y_{t-1}$
4. $S_t = \alpha Y_t; I_t = b(Y_t - Y_{t-1})$
5. $S_t = \alpha Y_{t-1}; I_t = b Y_{t-1}$
6. $S_t = \alpha Y_t + \beta Y_{t-1}; I_t = b(Y_t - Y_{t-1})$

SECTION 17·4   SOLUTIONS OF FIRST-ORDER LINEAR NONHOMOGENEOUS DIFFERENCE EQUATIONS

We now turn to first-order linear difference equations that are not homogeneous. They appear in the form

$$Y_t = a Y_{t-1} + b$$

with initial condition $Y_0 = K_0$.

The procedure for solving such equations is as follows:

1. Find the solution to the reduced equation obtained by dropping b. The reduced equation is homogeneous and its solution is given by $Y_t = a^t M$, where M is some undetermined constant. Notice that we did not write $a^t K_0$ because K_0, in our case, is the initial condition satisfying the nonhomogeneous equation and not necessarily satisfying the reduced equation.
2. Find any solution to the complete nonhomogeneous equation without being concerned with satisfying the initial condition. To this end, try the simplest possible solution, $Y_t = c$, where c is some constant.
3. Substitute the solution $Y_t = c$ back into the original nonhomogeneous equation. This gives $c = ac + b$, because if $Y_t = c$ for all t, then $Y_{t-1} = c$ also. The equation $c = ac + b$ can be solved for c. Suppose that we get $c = c_0$. We say that $Y_t = c_0$ is a *particular solution*, because it is only one of the many possible solutions when we disregard initial conditions.
4. It can be shown that if x_t is an expression that satisfies the homogeneous equation without considering initial conditions and z_t is an expression that satisfies the nonhomogeneous equation without

considering initial conditions, then $x_t + z_t$ also satisfies the nonhomogeneous equation without considering initial conditions. We therefore know that a solution can be stated as $Y_t = a^t M + c_0$.

5. Determine the value of M that will satisfy the initial condition $Y_0 = K_0$. We get

$$K_0 = a^0 M + c_0$$

or

$$K_0 = M + c_0$$

This can be solved for M, say, $M = M_0$. The solution to the nonhomogeneous equation that satisfies the initial condition is then $Y_t = a^t M_0 + c_0$.

It is worth noting that such solutions can also be found by rote. From step 3, we see that

$$c = ac + b$$

or

$$(1 - a)c = b$$

$$c = \frac{b}{1 - a}$$

From step 5, above, we see that $K_0 = M + c_0$. Therefore

$$M = K_0 - c_0$$

which is equivalent to

$$M = K_0 - \frac{b}{1 - a}.$$

The complete solution can therefore be written as

$$Y_t = a^t \left(K_0 - \frac{b}{1 - a} \right) + \frac{b}{1 - a}$$

where a and b are given coefficients of the original equation and K_0 is the given initial condition.

Illustration 1. Consumption is given by the following difference equation:

$$C_t = 0.9 Y_{t-1} + 40$$

Net investment is constant at $I_t = 100$, and there is no government sector. National income is initially $Y_0 = 1000$. Find the equilibrium level of national income for any time period and, in particular, in year 4. Also trace the time path of income.

Solution.   The condition for achieving equilibrium national income is

$$Y_t = C_t + I_t$$

which in our case becomes

$$Y_t = 0.9Y_{t-1} + 40 + 100$$
$$= 0.9Y_{t-1} + 140$$

This is a first-order linear nonhomogeneous difference equation. To solve, we first consider the reduced equation, which is

$$Y_t = 0.9Y_{t-1}$$

The solution of the reduced equation can be written as

$$Y_t = (0.9)^t M$$

where M is some undetermined constant.

Our next step is to find a particular solution to the nonhomogeneous equation

$$Y_t = 0.9Y_{t-1} + 140$$

The simplest possibility is

$$Y_t = c \qquad \text{for all values of } t$$

Substituting $Y_t = Y_{t-1} = c$ into the nonhomogeneous equation, we get

$$c = .9c + 140$$
$$0.1c = 140$$
$$c = 1400$$

We now have a solution to the reduced equation, that is, $Y_t = (0.9)^t M$, and a particular solution to the nonhomogeneous equation, that is, $Y_t = c = 1400$. We know that the sum of these two is also a solution to the nonhomogeneous equation. Thus we can write this solution as

$$Y_t = (0.9)^t M + 1400$$

The complete solution must, however, also satisfy the initial condition, namely, $Y_0 = 100$. Substituting into the solution just arrived at, we
get

$$Y_0 = (0.9)^0 M + 1400$$

Because $Y_0 = 1000$, we have

$$1000 = M + 1400$$

$$M = -400$$

Therefore a complete solution to our problem is

$$Y_t = -400(0.9)^t + 1400$$

This solution can, in fact, be checked by substitution into the original equation

$$Y_t = 0.9 Y_{t-1} + 140$$

According to our solution,

$$Y_t = -400(0.9)^t + 1400$$

$$Y_{t-1} = -400(0.9)^{t-1} + 1400$$

$$0.9 Y_{t-1} + 140 = 0.9(-400)(0.9)^{t-1} + 0.9(1400) + 140$$

$$= (-400)(0.9)^t + 1400$$

$$Y_t = 0.9 Y_{t-1} + 140$$

The initial condition is also satisfied, because

$$Y_0 = -400(0.9)^0 + 1400$$

$$= 1000$$

Thus the solution is verified, because it satisfies the original equation and
the initial condition.

From our complete solution,

$$Y_t = -400(0.9)^t + 1400$$

we can find the equilibrium national income during any time period. In
particular, when $t = 4$, we have

$$Y_4 = -400(0.9)^4 + 1400$$

$$= -400(0.6561) + 1400$$

$$= 1137.56$$

The number raised to the t power in our solution is less than 1 and positive, so we have a damped, nonoscillating time path. In fact, we can see that as $t \to \infty$, $Y_t \to 1400$.

Illustration 2. Consumption is given by the following difference equation:

$$C_t = 0.8 Y_{t-1} + 100$$

Net investment is given by

$$I_t = 2(Y_t - Y_{t-1})$$

and there is no government sector. National income is initially $Y_0 = 2000$. Find the equilibrium level of national income for any time period and, in particular, in year 3. Also trace the time path of income.
Solution.   The condition for achieving equilibrium national income is

$$Y_t = C_t + I_t$$

which in our case becomes

$$Y_t = 0.8 Y_{t-1} + 100 + 2Y_t - 2Y_{t-1}$$

or

$$Y_t = 2Y_t - 1.2 Y_{t-1} + 100$$

and

$$-Y_t = -1.2 Y_{t-1} + 100$$
$$Y_t = 1.2 Y_{t-1} - 100$$

This is a first-order linear nonhomogeneous difference equation. To solve, we first consider the reduced equation, which is

$$Y_t = 1.2 Y_{t-1}$$

The solution of this reduced equation is

$$Y_t = (1.2)^t M$$

Where M is some undetermined constant.
We next find a particular solution to the nonhomogeneous equation

$$Y_t = 1.2 Y_{t-1} - 100$$

The simplest possibility is

$$Y_t = c \qquad \text{for all values of } t$$

Substituting $Y_t = Y_{t-1} = c$ into the nonhomogeneous equation, we get

$$c = 1.2c - 100$$

$$0.2c = 100$$

$$c = 500$$

The sum of the solution to the homogeneous equation and the solution to the nonhomogeneous equation will itself be a solution to the nonhomogeneous equation. This can be written as

$$Y_t = (1.2)^t M + 500$$

The complete solution must satisfy the initial condition, namely, $Y_0 = 2000$. Substituting into the solution just given, we get

$$Y_0 = (1.2)^0 M + 500$$

$$2000 = M + 500$$

$$M = 1500$$

Therefore a complete solution can be stated as

$$Y_t = 1500(1.2)^t + 500$$

In particular, when $t = 3$, we have

$$Y_3 = 1500(1.2)^3 + 500$$

$$= 1500(1.728) + 500$$

$$= 2592 + 500$$

$$= 3092$$

The number raised to the t power in our solution is more than 1 and positive, so we have an explosive nonoscillating time path. In fact, we can see that as $t \rightarrow \infty$, $Y_t \rightarrow \infty$.

In the illustrations we have considered, we encountered no difficulty in finding a simple solution to the nonhomogeneous equation of the form $Y_t = c$. In the event that the simplest possible solution, $Y_t = c$, is not a particular solution to the nonhomogeneous difference equation (which could happen under special circumstances), then the next simplest solution, $Y_t = ct$, should be tried. This should be substituted back into the original equation, thus yielding a value for c. The remaining procedure then follows analogously.

Exercises

In each of the following cases, find the equilibrium level of national income for any time period and, in particular, in year 4. Also trace the time path of income. Assume that there is no government sector.

1. $C_t = 0.95Y_{t-1} + 200$; $I_t = 300$; $Y_0 = 500$
2. $C_t = 0.99Y_{t-1} + 150$; $I_t = 250$; $Y_0 = 600$
3. $C_t = 1.1Y_{t-1} - 200$; $I_t = 300$; $Y_0 = 100$
4. $C_t = 0.95Y_{t-1} + 200$; $I_t = 3(Y_t - Y_{t-1})$; $Y_0 = 4500$
5. $C_t = 0.9Y_{t-1} + 150$; $I_t = 4(Y_t - Y_{t-1})$; $Y_0 = 2000$
6. $C_t = 0.96Y_{t-1} + 200$; $I_t = 0.2Y_t + 120$; $Y_0 = 200$
7. $C_t = 0.9Y_{t-1}$; $I_t = 0.3Y_{t-1} + 200$; $Y_0 = 1400$
8. $C_t = 0.5Y_t + 0.4Y_{t-1}$; $I_t = 0.15Y_{t-1} + 1000$; $Y_0 = 10{,}000$

SECTION 17·5   THE COBWEB THEOREM

The dynamic models that have been considered up to this point involved macroeconomic variables. We can also apply dynamic analysis to microeconomic problems. Suppose that we are given the following market demand and supply functions for a certain product:

$$q_{d_t} = ap_t + b$$

$$q_{s_t} = cp_{t-1} + d$$

where a, b, c, and d are any constants (i.e., either positive, negative, or zero). Note that we are not necessarily assuming a downward-sloping demand function or an upward-sloping supply function.

The given demand function is not much different than those considered in earlier chapters, because quantity demanded at a certain time depends on the price at that time. However, quantity supplied at any time depends on the price the product was able to fetch during the preceding time period. This is a realistic situation in many instances, where production decisions must be made before it is known what market price will prevail. The producer then uses previous-period price as a guide. One illustration of this occurs with regard to the supply of agricultural products, where farmers must decide how much to plant a good many months before the crop comes to the market.

Market equilibrium, assuming pure competition, is attained when quantity demanded is equal to quantity supplied. If quantity demanded were greater than quantity supplied, the current market price would be bid up, and vice versa if quantity demanded were smaller than quantity supplied. We thus have

$$q_{d_t} = q_{s_t}$$

which is equivalent to

$$ap_t + b = cp_{t-1} + d$$

and

$$ap_t = cp_{t-1} + d - b$$

$$p_t = \frac{c}{a}p_{t-1} + \frac{d-b}{a}$$

This is a first-order linear nonhomogeneous difference equation. If we are given the initial condition that price is p_0 when $t = 0$, we can solve the equation in the following way. First, consider the reduced equation, which is

$$p_t = \frac{c}{a}p_{t-1}$$

The solution of this reduced equation can be written as

$$p_t = \left(\frac{c}{a}\right)^t K$$

where K is some undetermined constant.

The next step is to find a particular solution to the nonhomogeneous equation

$$p_t = \frac{c}{a}p_{t-1} + \frac{d-b}{a}$$

The simplest possibility is

$$p_t = h \text{ (some constant)}$$

Substituting $p_t = p_{t-1} = h$ into the nonhomogeneous equation, we get

$$h = \left(\frac{c}{a}\right)h + \frac{d-b}{a}$$

and

$$\left(1 - \frac{c}{a}\right)h = \frac{d-b}{a}$$

$$h = \frac{(d-b)/a}{(a-c)/a} = \frac{d-b}{a-c}$$

Taking together the solution to the reduced equation with the particular solution of the nonhomogeneous equation, we get

$$p_t = \left(\frac{c}{a}\right)^t K + \frac{d-b}{a-c}$$

This solution must also satisfy the initial condition, namely, price, is p_0 when $t = 0$. Substituting into the solution just stated, we have

$$p_0 = \left(\frac{c}{a}\right)^0 K + \frac{d-b}{a-c}$$

$$= K + \frac{d-b}{a-c}$$

$$K = p_0 - \frac{d-b}{a-c}$$

Therefore a complete solution to our problem is

$$p_t = \left(p_0 - \frac{d-b}{a-c}\right)\left(\frac{c}{a}\right)^t + \frac{d-b}{a-c}$$

From this expression, we can find the equilibrium price at any time merely by substituting the appropriate value of t. Answers will, of course, be in terms of a, b, c, d, and p_0. If these constants are specified, we shall be able to arrive at a numerical answer.

The time path of price can also be derived from this expression. Whether price will move along an explosive or damped time path and whether it will oscillate or not will depend upon the values of the constants involved.

In the solution given above, p_t is the equilibrium price at any particular time, that is, the price that equates demand and supply during that time period. Each p_t is therefore a static equilibrium point, because it holds only for a certain time. We can also talk about a dynamic equilibrium price. By this we mean a price that, once achieved, prevails from period to period as long as the demand and supply functions remain unchanged.

To find such a dynamic equilibrium price, we equate demand and supply and set $p_t = p_{t-1}$. This gives us

$$ap_t + b = cp_{t-1} + d$$

and because $p_t = p_{t-1}$, we have

$$ap_t + b = cp_t + d$$

$$ap_t - cp_t = d - b$$

$$p_t = \frac{d - b}{a - c}$$

Thus the dynamic equilibrium price is a constant price from period to period:

$$p_e = \frac{d - b}{a - c}$$

To verify, if we go back to the complete solution written above, we see that if

$$p_0 = \frac{d - b}{a - c},$$

so will $p_1, p_2, \ldots$, and so on. Thus, if the dynamic equilibrium price,

$$\frac{d - b}{a - c}$$

is achieved, it will persist from period to period.

We can now consider the question of *stability* of equilibrium. An equilibrium point is said to be *stable* in a dynamic sense if, as time passes, there is convergence toward equilibrium. If, as time passes, there is divergence or movement away from equilibrium, it is said to be unstable. In our case, stability would require that $p_t \to p_e$ as $t \to \infty$.

Turning to the solution we found for any p_t,

$$p_t = \left(p_0 - \frac{d - b}{a - c}\right)\left(\frac{c}{a}\right)^t + \frac{d - b}{a - c}$$

we see that if

$$\frac{c}{a} < 1$$

in absolute value, the time path will be damped and price will converge to the equilibrium price

$$\frac{d - b}{a - c}$$

as $t \to \infty$. This is equivalent to the condition that the marginal demand, that is,

$$\frac{dq_d}{dp}$$

be greater in absolute value than marginal supply, that is,

$$\frac{dq_s}{dp}.$$

If this is true, then the equilibrium price is stable. In the usual case, of course, c and a will be of opposite sign (c positive and a negative), thus causing the time path to oscillate around the equilibrium (one period it will be below and the next period above the equilibrium). Even so, the price will be getting closer and closer to the dynamic equilibrium price. In the unlikely event that c and a are of like sign, the time path will not oscillate but will still be damped, ever approaching the equilibrium point.

On the other hand, if

$$\frac{c}{a} > 1$$

in absolute value (i.e., marginal demand less than marginal supply in absolute value), the time path of price will be explosive. As $t \to \infty$, price will move further and further away from the equilibrium price. In such a case, equilibrium will be unstable. In the usual event that c and a are of opposite sign, the time path will oscillate, but in any case it will be moving further away from equilibrium. In the unlikely event that c and a are of like sign, the time path will not oscillate but will still be exploding in one direction away from equilibrium.

The final possibility is that

$$c = a$$

in absolute value. In this case the time path of income will be constant in absolute terms. Price will always be the same distance from equilibrium. As $t \to \infty$, price will always be

$$p_0 - \frac{d - b}{a - c}$$

away from equilibrium. Thus, if price is at any nonequilibrium level, there is no movement toward equilibrium with the passage of time. Equilibrium is therefore unstable. In the usual case where a and c have different signs, there will be equal oscillations from period to period (price will be above equilibrium during one period and below equilibrium by the same amount during the next period). In the unusual case where a and c have the same sign, the time path will not oscillate but will always be a constant distance from equilibrium.

We conclude that the condition for stability is that

$$\left| \frac{c}{a} \right| < 1$$

In the event that

$$\left| \frac{c}{a} \right| \geqslant 1$$

the system is unstable.

These results are known as the *Cobweb theorem*, because in the usual case where c and a are of unlike sign, the oscillations that result resemble the tracing of a cobweb.

Illustration.   The demand and supply functions for a certain purely competitive market are given by

$$q_{d_t} = -2p_t + 100 \qquad q_{s_t} = p_{t-1} - 20$$

The initial price is $p_0 = 30$. Find the market price for any time period and, in particular, for period 4. Find the dynamic equilibrium price and determine if equilibrium is stable.

Solution.   To find market equilibrium, we set quantity demanded equal to quantity supplied:

$$-2p_t + 100 = p_{t-1} - 20$$
$$-2p_t = p_{t-1} - 120$$
$$p_t = -\tfrac{1}{2}p_{t-1} + 60$$

This is a first-order linear nonhomogeneous difference equation. The solution to the reduced equation is

$$p_t = (-\tfrac{1}{2})^t K$$

where K is some undetermined constant.

We find a particular solution by setting

$$p_t = c$$

Substituting $p_t = p_{t-1} = c$ into the nonhomogeneous equation gives

$$c = -\tfrac{1}{2}c + 60$$

$$\tfrac{3}{2}c = 60$$

$$c = 40$$

Taking together the solution to the reduced equation with the particular solution of the nonhomogeneous equation, we get

$$p_t = (-\tfrac{1}{2})^t K + 40$$

This solution must, however, satisfy the initial condition $p_0 = 30$. Substituting this value into the solution just stated gives us

$$p_0 = (-\tfrac{1}{2})^0 K + 40$$

$$30 = K + 40$$

$$K = -10$$

Therefore a complete solution to the problem is

$$p_t = -10(-\tfrac{1}{2})^t + 40$$

This is the market price for any t. In particular, for period 4, we have

$$p_4 = -10(-\tfrac{1}{2})^4 + 40$$

$$= -\tfrac{5}{8} + 40 = \tfrac{315}{8}$$

To find the dynamic equilibrium price, we equate demand and supply and set $p_t = p_{t-1}$. This gives us

$$-2p_t + 100 = p_t - 20$$

$$3p_t = 120$$

$$p_t = 40$$

The dynamic equilibrium price is $40.

To determine whether equilibrium is stable, we examine the complete solution and notice that the coefficient to be raised to the t power is $-\tfrac{1}{2}$. This number is negative but less than 1 in absolute value, so we have damped oscillations, and a stable equilibrium.

Exercises

In each of the following cases, (a) find the market price for any time period and, in particular, for period 4; (b) find the dynamic equilibrium price; and (c) determine if equilibrium is stable.

1. $q_{d_t} = -5p_t + 200; q_{s_t} = 2p_{t-1} - 45; p_0 = 50$
2. $q_{d_t} = -2p_t + 150; q_{s_t} = 2p_{t-1} - 50; p_0 = 20$
3. $q_{d_t} = -p_t + 50; q_{s_t} = \frac{1}{2}p_{t-1} - 40; p_0 = 10$
4. $q_{d_t} = -2p_t + 100; q_{s_t} = 3p_{t-1} - 80; p_0 = 200$
5. $q_{d_t} = -2p_t + 100; q_{s_t} = 3p_{t-1} - 80; p_0 = 40$
6. $q_{d_t} = -4p_t + 120; q_{s_t} = p_{t-1} - 40; p_0 = 5$
7. $q_{d_t} = 4p_t + 200; q_{s_t} = p_{t-1} - 40; p_0 = 16$
8. $q_{d_t} = -p_t + 50; q_{s_t} = 4p_{t-1} - 100; p_0 = 31$

SECTION 17·6   SOLUTIONS OF SECOND-ORDER LINEAR HOMOGENEOUS DIFFERENCE EQUATIONS

We shall now consider linear difference equations that are of second order. Methods similar to those developed in this section can be applied to difference equations of any order. In general form, a second-order linear homogeneous difference equation can be written as

$$Y_t = a_1 Y_{t-1} + a_2 Y_{t-2}$$

with the two initial conditions $Y_0 = K_0$ and $Y_1 = K_1$.

The procedure for solving such equations is given by the following:

1. Find a particular solution to the equation without being concerned about satisfying initial conditions. To this end, try the solution

    $$Y_t = x^t$$

    which the reader will notice is of the same form as solutions of first-order homogeneous equations.
2. Substitute this solution back into the original equation. This will give

    $$x^t = a_1 x^{t-1} + a_2 x^{t-2}$$

    Dividing both sides of the equation by x^{t-2} yields

    $$x^2 = a_1 x + a_2$$

    or

    $$x^2 - a_1 x - a_2 = 0$$

    This is a quadratic equation and can be solved for x. Two values will usually ensue, say, x_1 and x_2. We then have two particular solutions to the original difference equation:

    $$Y_t = x_1^t \quad \text{and} \quad Y_t = x_2^t$$

3. It can be shown that if x_1^t and x_2^t are solutions to the original difference equation, then so is $A(x_1)^t + B(x_2)^t$, where A and B are undetermined constants.[3] Thus a solution can be written as

$$Y_t = A(x_1)^t + B(x_2)^t$$

4. Determine the values of A and B that satisfy both initial conditions, that is, $Y_0 = K_0$ and $Y_1 = K_1$. We get

$$K_0 = A + B$$

$$K_1 = Ax_1 + Bx_2$$

which can be solved for A and B, say, $A = A_0$ and $B = B_0$.

5. The solution to the homogeneous equation that satisfies the initial condition is then

$$Y_t = A_0(x_1)^t + B_0(x_2)^t$$

Illustration. Consumption is given by the following difference equation:

$$C_t = 0.7Y_{t-1} + 0.3Y_{t-2}$$

Investment is given by

$$I_t = 2.3(Y_{t-1} - Y_{t-2})$$

National income is initially $Y_0 = 500$ and $Y_1 = 550$. Find the equilibrium level of national income for any time period and, in particular, in year 5. Also, trace the time path of income.

Solution. The condition for achieving equilibrium national income is

$$Y_t = C_t + I_t$$

which in our case becomes

$$Y_t = 0.7Y_{t-1} + 0.3Y_{t-2} + 2.3Y_{t-1} - 2.3Y_{t-2}$$

or

$$Y_t = 3Y_{t-1} - 2Y_{t-2}$$

This is a second-order linear homogeneous difference equation. To solve, we first find a particular solution to the equation without being concerned about satisfying initial conditions. To this end try the solution

$$Y_t = x^t$$

---

[3] This technique would have to be somewhat adjusted if the two roots of the quadratic equation were identical or imaginary. In any event, the basic approach would be unchanged. See Baumol, *op. cit.*, pp. 182–205 for these modifications.

Substitute this solution back into the original equation, which gives

$x^t = 3x^{t-1} - 2x^{t-2}$

Dividing both sides of the equation by x^{t-2}, we get

$x^2 = 3x - 2$

or

$x^2 - 3x + 2 = 0$

Solving this equation either by factoring or by the quadratic formula gives $x = 2$, $x = 1$.

We thus have two particular solutions to the original difference equation, namely,

$Y_t = 2^t$ and $Y_t = 1^t$

Because 2^t and 1^t are each solutions, so is

$A(2)^t + B(1)^t$

where A and B are undetermined constants. Thus a solution can be written as

$Y_t = A(2)^t + B(1)^t$

Our final solution must also satisfy the initial conditions, namely, $Y_0 = 500$, $Y_1 = 550$. Substituting these values into the solutions just stated, we get

$Y_0 = A(2)^0 + B(1)^0$

$Y_1 = A(2)^1 + B(1)^1$

or

$500 = A + B$

$550 = 2A + B$

Multiply the first equation by 2. We have

$1000 = 2A + 2B$

$550 = 2A + B$

Subtract the second equation from the first. This gives

$B = 450$

from which it follows that $A = 50$.

Therefore our final solution to the problem is

$$Y_t = 50(2)^t + 450(1)^t$$

From this expression, we can find the equilibrium national income during any time period. In particular, when $t = 5$, we have

$$Y_5 = 50(2)^5 + 450(1)^5$$

$$= 1600 + 450$$

$$= 2050$$

The numbers raised to the t power are both positive and at least one of them is greater than 1, so the time path is explosive and nonoscillating. In fact, we see that as $t \to \infty$, $Y_t \to \infty$.

Exercises

In each of the following cases, find the equilibrium level of national income for any time period and, in particular, in year 4. Also, trace the time path of income.

1. $C_t = 0.9Y_{t-1} + 0.1Y_{t-2}$; $I_t = 3.1(Y_{t-1} - Y_{t-2})$; $Y_0 = 600$, $Y_1 = 660$
2. $C_t = 0.8Y_{t-1} + 0.2Y_{t-2}$; $I_t = 4.2(Y_{t-1} - Y_{t-2})$; $Y_0 = 1000$,

$$Y_1 = 1100$$

3. $C_t = 0.6Y_{t-1} + 0.4Y_{t-2}$; $I_t = 3.4(Y_{t-1} - Y_{t-2})$; $Y_0 = 800$, $Y_1 = 840$
4. $C_t = 0.5Y_{t-1} + 0.5Y_{t-2}$; $I_t = 2.5(Y_{t-1} - Y_{t-2})$; $Y_0 = 400$, $Y_1 = 432$
5. $C_t = 0.9Y_{t-1}$; $I_t = 2.1Y_{t-1} - 2Y_{t-2}$; $Y_0 = 500$, $Y_1 = 520$
6. $C_t = 0.8Y_{t-1}$; $I_t = 3.2Y_{t-1} - 3Y_{t-2}$; $Y_0 = 440$, $Y_1 = 480$

SECTION 17·7   SOLUTIONS OF SECOND-ORDER LINEAR NONHOMOGENEOUS DIFFERENCE EQUATIONS

The process of solving second-order linear nonhomogeneous difference equations is analogous to the first-order case. We wish to find a solution to the general equation

$$Y_t = a_1 Y_{t-1} + a_2 Y_{t-2} + b$$

with the two initial conditions $Y_0 = K_0$, $Y_1 = K_1$. The procedure is as follows.

1. Find the solution to the reduced equation obtained by dropping b.
    The reduced equation is homogeneous, and its solution can be found
    by the procedure outlined in the previous section. In general, it is
    given by

    $$Y_t = A(x_1)^t + B(x_2)^t$$

    where x_1 and x_2 are the two values arrived at by substituting $Y_t = x^t$
    into the reduced equation and where A and B are undetermined
    constants.
2. Find any solution to the complete nonhomogeneous equation with-
    out being concerned about satisfying the initial conditions. To this
    end, try the simplest possible solution, $Y_t = c$, some constant.
3. Substitute the solution

    $$Y_t = c = Y_{t-1} = Y_{t-2}$$

    back into the original nonhomogeneous equation, which gives

    $$c = a_1 c + a_2 c + b$$

    This can be solved for c, say, $c = c_0$. $Y_t = c_0$ is then a particular
    solution, because it is only one of the many possible solutions when
    initial conditions are disregarded.
4. Add together the solution to the reduced equation with the particular
    solution to the nonhomogeneous equation. This yields another solu-
    tion to the original nonhomogeneous equation and appears as

    $$Y_t = A(x_1)^t + B(x_2)^t + c_0$$

5. Determine the values of A and B that satisfy both initial conditions,
    that is, $Y_0 = K_0$, $Y_1 = K_1$. We get

    $$K_0 = A + B + c_0$$

    $$K_1 = Ax_1 + Bx_2 + c_0$$

    which can be solved for A and B, say, $A = A_0$, $B = B_0$.
6. The complete solution to the nonhomogeneous equation that also
    satisfies the initial conditions is then

    $$Y_t = A_0(x_1)^t + B_0(x_2)^t + c_0$$

Illustration. Consumption is given by the difference equation

$$C_t = 0.5 Y_{t-1} + 0.75 Y_{t-2} + 50$$

and investment by

$$I_t = 1.5(Y_{t-1} - Y_{t-2})$$

National income is initially $Y_0 = 1000$, $Y_1 = 1100$. Find the equilibrium level of national income for any time period and, in particular, for year 3. Also, trace the time path of income.

Solution. The condition for equilibrium national income is

$$Y_t = C_t + I_t$$

which in our case becomes

$$Y_t = 0.5Y_{t-1} + 0.75Y_{t-2} + 50 + 1.5Y_{t-1} - 1.5Y_{t-2}$$

or

$$Y_t = 2Y_{t-1} - 0.75Y_{t-2} + 50$$

This is a second-order linear nonhomogeneous difference equation. To solve, we first find a solution to the reduced equation, which is

$$Y_t = 2Y_{t-1} - 0.75Y_{t-2}$$

We try the solution $Y_t = x^t$. Substituting back into the reduced equation gives

$$x^t = 2x^{t-1} - 0.75x^{t-2}$$

Dividing both sides of the equation by x^{t-2} gives us

$$x^2 = 2x - 0.75$$

or

$$x^2 - 2x + 0.75 = 0$$

Solving this quadratic gives $x = \frac{3}{2}$, $x = \frac{1}{2}$. A solution to the reduced equation can therefore be written as

$$A(\tfrac{3}{2})^t + B(\tfrac{1}{2})^t$$

where A and B are undetermined constants.

We now seek to find any particular solution of the nonhomogeneous equation. The simplest possibility is

$$Y_t = c \qquad \text{for all values of } t$$

Substituting into the nonhomogeneous equation, we get

$$c = 2c - 0.75c + 50$$

$$-0.25c = 50$$

$$c = -200$$

Taking together the solution to the reduced equation with the particular solution to the nonhomogeneous equation, we get

$$Y_t = A(\tfrac{3}{2})^t + B(\tfrac{1}{2})^t - 200$$

The final complete solution must satisfy the initial conditions, that is, $Y_0 = 1000$, $Y_1 = 1100$. Substituting these values gives

$$Y_0 = A(\tfrac{3}{2})^0 + B(\tfrac{1}{2})^0 - 200$$

$$Y_1 = A(\tfrac{3}{2})^1 + B(\tfrac{1}{2})^1 - 200$$

Because $Y_0 = 1000$ and $Y_1 = 1100$, we have

$$1000 = A + B - 200$$

$$1100 = \tfrac{3}{2}A + \tfrac{1}{2}B - 200$$

This is the same as

$$A + B = 1200$$

$$\tfrac{3}{2}A + \tfrac{1}{2}B = 1300$$

Multiplying the second equation by 2 and subtracting it from the first gives

$$-2A = -1400$$

$$A = 700$$

$$B = 500$$

The complete solution to the nonhomogeneous equation, that also satisfies the initial conditions is, then,

$$Y_t = 700(\tfrac{3}{2})^t + 500(\tfrac{1}{2})^t - 200$$

From this expression, we can find the equilibrium national income during any time period. In particular, when $t = 3$, we have

$$Y_3 = 700(\tfrac{3}{2})^3 + 500(\tfrac{1}{2})^3 - 200$$

$$= 700(\tfrac{27}{8}) + \tfrac{500}{8} - 200$$

$$= 2225$$

The numbers raised to the t power are both positive and at least one of them is greater than 1, so the time path of income will be explosive and nonoscillating. In fact, we see that as $t \to \infty$, $Y_t \to \infty$.

Exercises

In each of the following cases, find the equilibrium level of national income for any time period and, in particular, for year 3. Also, trace the time path of income.

1. $C_t = 0.6Y_{t-1} + 0.65Y_{t-2} + 100;$ $I_t = 1.4(Y_{t-1} - Y_{t-2});$ $Y_0 = 600,$
     $Y_1 = 660$
2. $C_t = 0.7Y_{t-1} + 0.55Y_{t-2} + 150;$ $I_t = 1.3(Y_{t-1} - Y_{t-2});$ $Y_0 = 900,$
     $Y_1 = 980$
3. $C_t = 0.8Y_{t-1} + 0.45Y_{t-2} + 200;$ $I_t = 1.2(Y_{t-1} - Y_{t-2});$ $Y_0 = 800,$
     $Y_1 = 840$
4. $C_t = 0.9Y_{t-1} + 300; I_t = 2.1Y_{t-1} - 1.25Y_{t-2}; Y_0 = 500, Y_1 = 520$
5. $C_t = 0.8Y_{t-1} + 400; I_t = 3.2Y_{t-1} - 1.75Y_{t-2}; Y_0 = 1200, Y_1 = 1280$
6. $C_t = 0.8Y_{t-1} + 525; I_t = 4.2Y_{t-1} - 2.25Y_{t-2}; Y_0 = 880, Y_1 = 1020$

SECTION 17·8   DIFFERENTIAL EQUATIONS

Consider the expression

$$\frac{dq_s}{dp} = \frac{1}{5}pq_s \tag{1}$$

where q_s is the quantity supplied of a certain product and p is the market price. This is an example of an equation that involves a derivative. In general, we say that any equation involving derivatives or differentials is a *differential equation*. If an equation contains derivatives with respect to only one independent variable, it is known as an *ordinary differential equation*. On the other hand, if it contains partial derivatives of a function of more than one independent variable, it is known as a *partial differential equation*.

Differential equations may involve first derivatives, second derivatives, or higher-order derivatives. The *order* of a differential equation is the order of the highest derivative contained in the equation. Differential equations may involve derivatives raised to any power. The *degree* of a differential equation is the power to which the derivative of highest order is raised.

Thus the differential equation given above is an ordinary differential equation of first order (because only the first derivative appears) and of first degree (because the derivative is raised to the first power). Other examples of differential equations are

$$\frac{d^2y}{dx^2} + 2\frac{dy}{dx} + 5y = 0 \tag{2}$$

$$\left(\frac{dy}{dx}\right)^2 + y = 16 \tag{3}$$

$$\frac{d^2y}{dx^2} + y = 4 \tag{4}$$

$$x\,dy + y\,dx = 12 \tag{5}$$

$$\frac{\partial u}{\partial x} + \frac{\partial u}{\partial y} = 9 \tag{6}$$

Equations (2)–(5) are ordinary differential equations, while equation (6) is a partial differential equation. Equation (2) is of second order and first degree. Equation (3) is of first order but second degree. Equation (4) is of second order and first degree. Equation (5) is of first order and first degree. Equation (6) is a first-order, first-degree partial differential equation.

By a *solution* to a differential equation involving x, y, and derivatives of y, we mean any function

$$y = f(x)$$

that satisfies the differential equation. Thus it can be seen that

$$y = \frac{x^2}{2} + 5x + 5$$

is a solution to the differential equation

$$\frac{dy}{dx} = x + 5$$

because if

$$y = \frac{x^2}{2} + 5x + 5$$

then

$$\frac{dy}{dx} = x + 5$$

A *general solution* of a differential equation of order n is a solution possessing n distinct arbitrary constants. Thus

$$y = \frac{x^2}{2} + 5x + c$$

(where c can be any constant) is a general solution to the differential equation

$$\frac{dy}{dx} = x + 5$$

as the reader can verify.

If we assign specific values to the arbitrary constants appearing in a general solution, we then have a *particular solution*. Thus $y = x^2/2 + 5x + 5$ is a particular solution of the differential equation

$$\frac{dy}{dx} = x + 5$$

Particular solutions are usually found by first determining the general solution and then using given information called *initial conditions* to evaluate the constants. Note that a constant of integration can be written in any convenient form, such as c, $3c$, c^2, $\ln c$, and so on. Judicious choice of the particular form of expressing the constant sometimes simplifies the expression.

Exercises

Find the order and degree of each of the following differential equations.

1. $\dfrac{d^2y}{dx^2} - 5\dfrac{dy}{dx} + 2y = x$

2. $\dfrac{dq_s}{dp} = \sqrt{pq_s}$

3. $\dfrac{dy}{dx} = 2x^5 - y$

4. $y\,dx + (2x - y)\,dy = 0$

5. $\dfrac{d^2y}{dt^2} = -\dfrac{1}{2}y$

6. $\dfrac{d^2y}{dx^2} - 2y = 2e^x$

Show that the following functions are solutions of the corresponding differential equations.

7. $y = 2e^x + 3e^{-x}$; $\dfrac{d^2y}{dx^2} - y = 0$

8. $y = \dfrac{x^4}{4} - \dfrac{2}{x}$; $x\dfrac{dy}{dx} - 4y = \dfrac{10}{x}$

9. $y = x^2 + xe^x$; $\dfrac{d^2y}{dx^2} - \dfrac{dy}{dx} = 2 - 2x$

10. $y = 7x^3 - 2x^{-4} - 2x^2$; $x^2\dfrac{d^2y}{dx^2} + 2x\dfrac{dy}{dx} - 12y = 12x^2$

SECTION 17·9 DIFFERENTIAL EQUATIONS OF THE FIRST ORDER AND FIRST DEGREE: VARIABLES SEPARABLE

A differential equation of first order and first degree can be written in the following form:

$$\frac{dy}{dx} = f(x, y)$$

An equivalent way of expressing this equation is to convert it into differential form:

$$u\,dx + v\,dy = 0$$

where u and v are each functions of x and y.

Equations of the first order and first degree are among the least difficult to solve. Nevertheless, not all such equations can be solved. This illustrates the essential point that not all differential equations can be solved. In this section we show how to solve equations of the first order and first degree when the *variables are separable*.

Consider a differential equation that can be put in the form

$$u(x)\,dx + v(y)\,dy = 0$$

that is, u is now a function of x only and v a function of y only. The variables are said to be separable because the dx term involves only functions of x and the dy term only functions of y. In this case, the solution to the differential equation is arrived at by simply integrating the dx and dy terms individually.

Illustration 1.   Find the general solution of the differential equation

$$\frac{dy}{dx} = 2xy^2$$

Also, find the particular solution if $y = 1$ when $x = 2$.
Solution.   This equation can be written in differential form as

$$dy = 2xy^2 \, dx$$

Dividing both sides of the equation by y^2 in order to separate the variables gives

$$\frac{dy}{y^2} = 2x \, dx$$

or

$$y^{-2} \, dy = 2x \, dx$$

Integrating each side of the equation gives

$$\frac{y^{-1}}{-1} = x^2 + c$$

where c is some arbitrary constant, and

$$\frac{-1}{y} = x^2 + c$$

so that

$$y = \frac{-1}{x^2 + c}$$

This is the general solution of the differential equation. We are also given the initial condition, $x = 2$, $y = 1$. Substituting these values into the general solution gives

$$1 = \frac{-1}{4 + c}$$

$$4 + c = -1$$

$$c = -5$$

Therefore the particular solution is

$$y = \frac{-1}{x^2 - 5}$$

Illustration 2. Find the general solution of the differential equation given at the beginning of Section 17·8,

$$\frac{dq_s}{dp} = \frac{1}{5} pq_s$$

where q_s is the quantity supplied of a certain product and p is the market price. Also, find the particular solution if $q_s = 2e^{10}$ when $p = 10$.
Solution. The equation can be written in differential form as

$$dq_s = \frac{1}{5} pq_s \, dp$$

Dividing both sides of the equation by q_s in order to separate the variables gives

$$\frac{dq_s}{q_s} = \frac{1}{5} p \, dp$$

Integrating each side of the equation gives

$$\ln q_s = \frac{p^2}{10} + \ln c$$

and

$$\ln q_s - \ln c = \frac{p^2}{10}$$

$$\ln\left(\frac{q_s}{c}\right) = \frac{p^2}{10}$$

$$\frac{q_s}{c} = e^{p^2/10}$$

$$q_s = ce^{p^2/10}$$

This is the supply function that is the general solution of the differential equation. Note that, as pointed out at the end of Section 17·8, the constant of integration may be expressed in any convenient form. In this case we wrote this constant as $\ln c$ so that the solution would lend itself to further simplification.

We are also given the initial condition $q_s = 2e^{10}$ when $p = 10$. Substituting these values into the general solution gives

$$2e^{10} = ce^{10}$$

$$c = 2$$

Therefore the particular solution is

$$q_s = 2e^{p^2/10}$$

For any market price, we can find the quantity that would be supplied.

Exercises

For each of the following differential equations, find the general solution and also the particular solution in those cases where initial conditions are given.

1. $\dfrac{dq_d}{dp} = \dfrac{-q_d}{p}$

2. $p\,dq_s - q_s\,dp = 0;$ $q_s = 10$ when $p = 2$

3. $\dfrac{dq_s}{dp} = \dfrac{p}{q_s};$ $q_s = 3$ when $p = 1$

4. $p\,dq_d + 2q_d\,dp = 0;$ $q_d = 1$ when $p = 2$

5. $\dfrac{dy}{dx} = 2x^5 - x$

6. $y\dfrac{dy}{dx} - 4x = \dfrac{10}{x}$

7. $\dfrac{dy}{dx} = \dfrac{2e^{-x}}{y^3}$

8. $\dfrac{dy}{dx} = -3xy^2$

9. $xy\,dx = (x^2 + 4)\,dy$

SECTION 17·10   LINEAR DIFFERENTIAL EQUATIONS OF THE FIRST ORDER

Consider the differential equation of form

$$\frac{dy}{dx} + Py = Q \qquad\qquad (1)$$

where P and Q are functions of x only. Such an equation is known as a *linear differential equation* of the first order. Note that like the differential equations of the previous section, this equation is of first order and first degree. But what distinguishes it from the others is that the dependent variable, y, appears only to the first power—hence the term linear.

Suppose that we multiply both sides of the equation by $e^{\int P\,dx}$. We get

$$e^{\int P\,dx}\frac{dy}{dx} + e^{\int P\,dx}Py = Qe^{\int P\,dx} \tag{2}$$

By using the product rule for differentiation, it can be shown that

$$\frac{d}{dx}\left(ye^{\int P\,dx}\right) = e^{\int P\,dx}\frac{dy}{dx} + e^{\int P\,dx}Py \tag{3}$$

We have thus shown that the integral of the left side of equation (2) is $ye^{\int P\,dx}$. Therefore if we integrate each side of equation (2) with respect to x, we get

$$ye^{\int P\,dx} = \int Qe^{\int P\,dx}\,dx + c \tag{4}$$

The term $e^{\int P\,dx}$ is known as an integrating factor of equation (1) because multiplication of both sides of the equation by this term enables us to find the integral of the equation. Equation (4) is the general solution of the linear differential equation. Frequently, the expression $e^{\int P\,dx}$ can be put into a convenient form so that the final answer, in many cases, appears in a simple form.

Illustration 1.   Find the general solution of the differential equation

$$\frac{dy}{dx} - 4y = 3e^x$$

Solution.   This is a linear differential equation because it is in the form

$$\frac{dy}{dx} + Py = Q$$

Where $P = -4$ and $Q = 3e^x$.

The general solution of such an equation is given by equation (4):

$$ye^{\int P\,dx} = \int Qe^{\int P\,dx}\,dx + c$$

We therefore evaluate

$$\int P\,dx = \int -4\,dx = -4x$$

and

$$e^{\int P\,dx} = e^{-4x}$$

Formula (4), as a result, becomes

$$ye^{-4x} = \int 3e^x e^{-4x}\, dx + c$$

$$= \int 3e^{-3x}\, dx + c$$

$$= -e^{-3x} + c$$

and

$$y = -e^x + ce^{4x}$$

This is the general solution of the linear differential equation given at the outset. Note that in evaluating $\int P\, dx$, we did not add a constant c_0 to the answer, because to do so would only multiply both sides of equation (4) by the constant e^{c_0} and have no effect upon the result.

Illustration 2.   Find the general solution of the differential equation

$$\frac{dq_s}{dp} + \frac{q_s}{p} = 3p^2$$

where q_s is the quantity supplied of a certain product and p is the market price. Also, find the particular solution if $q_s = 51$ when $p = 4$.

Solution.   This is a linear differential equation with p the independent variable. q_s, the dependent variable, appears only to the first power. For this equation, we have

$$P = \frac{1}{p} \quad \text{and} \quad Q = 3p^2$$

Note that p is the independent variable, while P is the coefficient of the dependent variable, which in this case happens to be $1/p$. We then evaluate

$$\int P\, dp = \int \frac{1}{p}\, dp = \ln p$$

and

$$e^{\int P\, dp} = e^{\ln p}$$

By a basic identity of logarithms, we know that

$$e^{\ln p} = p$$

Therefore,

$$e^{\int P \, dp} = p$$

Therefore the general solution (4) becomes

$$q_s p = \int 3p^2 p \, dp + c$$

$$q_s p = \int 3p^3 \, dp + c$$

$$q_s p = \frac{3p^4}{4} + c$$

$$q_s = \frac{3p^3}{4} + \frac{c}{p}$$

This is the supply function that is the general solution of the differential equation. We are also given the initial conditions $q_s = 51$ when $p = 4$. Substituting these values into the general solution gives

$$51 = 48 + \frac{c}{4}$$

and

$$\frac{c}{4} = 3$$

$$c = 12$$

Therefore the particular solution is

$$q_s = \frac{3p^3}{4} + \frac{12}{p}$$

For any market price, we can find the quantity that will be supplied.

In this section we have shown how to solve a linear differential equation of the first order. Of course, linear differential equations of higher order may also appear. Moreover, there are many nonlinear forms of differential equations. To consider all of the different types of differential equations that are soluble is beyond the scope of this book. We have, however, attempted to give the student an appreciation of the concept of such equations and the techniques of solving the simplest of these equations. The following section considers an interesting economic application of these techniques.

Exercises

For each of the following differential equations, find the general solution and also the particular solution in those cases where initial conditions are given.

1. $\dfrac{dy}{dx} - \dfrac{y}{x} = 3x^2$

2. $\dfrac{dy}{dx} = 2x + y$

3. $\dfrac{dy}{dx} + 4y = e^x$

4. $\dfrac{dq_s}{dp} + \dfrac{2q_s}{p} = 4;$ $q_s = 10$ when $p = 6$

5. $\dfrac{dq_s}{dp} = 3q_s + pe^{3p};$ $q_s = 403.43$ when $p = 2$

6. $\dfrac{p\, dq_d}{dp} + 2q_d = -p^2;$ $q_d = 50$ when $p = 20$

7. $p\, dq_s = (p^3 + q_s)\, dp;$ $q_s = 96$ when $p = 4$

8. $\dfrac{p^2\, dq_d}{dp} - 2pq_d = 2;$ $q_d = 10$ when $p = 5$

SECTION 17·11   THE DOMAR GROWTH MODEL

In Section 17·3 we utilized difference equations to analyze the Harrod growth model. Another growth model employing differential equations has been presented by Evsey Domar. In this section we introduce a modified version of the Domar growth model.[4] The Domar model was independently developed at about the same time and has a great deal of similarity to the Harrod model. Indeed, the points of similarity are so marked that in many textbooks (especially nonmathematical texts) they are discussed together under one heading, namely, the Harrod-Domar

---

[4] The modified version, as presented by Baumol, *op. cit.*, p. 281, is equivalent to the original formulation and differs only in the way the assumptions are expressed. We have chosen to follow Baumol's restatement because it shows most vividly the similarities and differences between the difference equation approach and the differential equation approach.

growth model. We shall, however, see that there are certain differences between the two formulations.

Assume that aggregate savings in the economy at any time t is a constant proportion α of the income at that time, that is, the marginal propensity to save is constant. We have

$$S(t) = \alpha Y(t)$$

where $S(t)$ is the savings function showing savings at any time, α is some positive marginal propensity to save and $Y(t)$ is the income function showing income at any time. Note that in the Domar formulation, savings and income are functions of the continuous variable t while in the Harrod version, savings and income are stated for discrete time periods, that is, $t = 1, 2, 3$, and so on.

The acceleration principle also appears in the Domar model, but instead of investment in any period being proportionate to the rate of change of income between the preceding and present periods, it is taken as proportionate to the instantaneous rate of change of income with respect to time. We therefore write

$$I(t) = b\frac{dY}{dt}$$

where I_t is aggregate investment at any time, b is some positive constant and dY/dt is the derivative of income with respect to time.

The condition for achieving equilibrium national income can be stated as

$$I(t) = S(t)$$

or

$$b\frac{dY}{dt} = \alpha Y(t)$$

$$\frac{dY}{dt} = \frac{\alpha}{b}Y(t)$$

which is equivalent to

$$\frac{dY/dt}{Y(t)} = \frac{\alpha}{b}$$

Thus, to maintain equilibrium, income must continually grow at a constant percentage α/b. This is sometimes referred to as the *razor's edge*; that is, the economy must proceed along a narrow, well-defined path. Any deviation will cause instability.

Let us now write our equation in the following form:

$$\frac{dY}{dt} - \frac{\alpha}{b} Y(t) = 0$$

This is a linear differential equation of the first order. Its general solution, as indicated in the previous section, is

$$Ye^{\int P\,dt} = \int Qe^{\int P\,dt}\,dt + c$$

In our case, $P = -\alpha/b$, and $Q = 0$. We therefore have

$$\int P\,dt = \int \frac{-\alpha}{b}\,dt = -\frac{\alpha}{b}t$$

so that

$$e^{\int P\,dt} = e^{-(\alpha/b)t}$$

and the general solution is

$$Ye^{-(\alpha/b)t} = c$$

$$Y = ce^{(\alpha/b)t}$$

Assume the initial condition $Y_0 = K_0 > 0$. We can then evaluate c by substituting the values $t = 0$, $Y = K_0$ into the last equation. This gives

$$K_0 = ce^{(\alpha/b)(0)}$$

$$= c$$

The particular solution thus becomes

$$Y = K_0 e^{(\alpha/b)t}$$

It is easily seen that as $t \to \infty$, $Yt \to \infty$, because K_0, α, and b are all positive. Thus the time path of income will be explosive; that is, income will increase indefinitely.

The same general conclusions result from using Domar's differential equation as from using Harrod's difference equation. The behavior assumptions, however, are not quite identical. While Harrod assumes that businessmen alter their investment policies from period to period, Domar assumes that such changes are made continuously.

Exercises

For each of the following set of values for α, b and K_0; (a) Find the solution of the Domar differential equation. (b) What are the implications for growth? (c) What will be the time path of income? (d) What will income be when $t = 4$?

1. $\alpha = 0.2, b = 2, K_0 = 1000$
2. $\alpha = 0.1, b = 3, K_0 = 800$
3. $\alpha = 0.15, b = 2.5, K_0 = 880$
4. $\alpha = 0.05, b = 4, K_0 = 600$
5. $\alpha = 0.01, b = 3.5, K_0 = 500$

REFERENCES FOR FURTHER STUDY

The following list of selected references is provided for those students who wish to pursue particular topics in mathematical economics more intensively or from different perspectives.

Allen, R. G. D., *Macro-Economic Theory*, Macmillan, London, 1968.
   (A mathematical treatment of much of macroeconomics.)
Allen, R. G. D., *Mathematical Economics*, 2nd ed., Macmillan, London, 1964.
   (Dynamic theories, complex variables, differential and difference equations, general equilibrium, matrix algebra, theory of games, linear programing.)
Almon, Clopper, *Matrix Methods in Economics*, Addison-Wesley, Reading, Mass., 1967.
   (Advanced treatment of matrix algebra and linear programing.)
Baumol, William, *Economic Theory and Operations Analysis*, 3rd ed., Prentice-Hall, Englewood Cliffs, N.J., 1972.
   (Introduction to microeconomic theory, mathematical programing, and game theory.)
Baumol, William, *Economic Dynamics*, 2nd ed., Macmillan, New York, 1959.
   (Difference and differential equation with economic applications.)
Bell, John F., *A History of Economic Thought*, Ronald, New York, 1967, pp. 680–708.
   (Contains interesting section on mathematical economics.)
Benavie, Arthur, *Mathematical Techniques for Economic Analysis*, Prentice-Hall, Englewood Cliffs, N.J., 1972.
   (Advanced mathematical methods.)
Boulding, Kenneth, *Economics as a Science*, McGraw-Hill, New York, 1970, Chapter V.
   (Discussion of uses and misuses of the mathematical method.)

Bowers, David A., and Robert N. Baird, *Elementary Mathematical Macroeconomics*, Prentice-Hall, Englewood Cliffs, N.J., 1971.
(A mathematical formulation of intermediate macroeconomic theory.)

Charlesworth, James C. (ed.), *Mathematics and the Social Sciences*, American Academy of Political and Social Science, Philadelphia, 1963.
(Concerned with uses and misuses of mathematics in the social sciences.)

Cohèn, Kalman J., and Richard M. Cyert, *Theory of the Firm*, Prentice-Hall, Englewood Cliffs, N.J., 1965.
(A mathematical treatment of the theory of the firm.)

Daniel, Coldwell, *Mathematical Models in Microeconomics*, Allyn & Bacon, Boston, 1970.
(A mathematical formulation of much of microeconomic theory.)

Dorfman, Robert, Paul A. Samuelson, and Robert M. Solow, *Linear Programming and Economic Analysis*, McGraw-Hill, New York, 1958.
(Linear programing, game theory, input/output analysis.)

Goldberg, Samuel, *Introduction to Difference Equations*, Wiley, New York, 1958.
(The mathematical theory and application of difference equations.)

Henderson, James M., and Richard Quandt, *Microeconomic Theory*, 2nd ed., McGraw-Hill, New York, 1971.
(A mathematical formulation of much of microeconomic theory.)

Kemeny, J. G., A. Schleifer, J. L. Snell, and G. L. Thompson, *Finite Mathematics*, Prentice-Hall, Englewood Cliffs, N.J., 1962.
(Set theory, logic of propositions, matrices, linear programing, and theory of games.)

Klein, Lawrence R., *The Keynesian Revolution*, 2nd ed., Macmillan, New York, 1966.
(Appendix contains a mathematical formulation of the Keynesian and classical macroeconomic models.)

Lancaster, Kelvin, *Mathematical Economics*, Macmillan, New York, 1968.
(Advanced mathematical treatment of mathematical programing, input/output analysis, general equilibrium, and growth theory.)

Newman, Peter (ed.), *Readings in Mathematical Economics*, Johns Hopkins Press, Baltimore, 1968.
(A collection of classic mathematical writings in value, capital, and growth theories.)

Pfouts, Ralph R., *Elementary Economics: A Mathematical Approach*, Wiley, New York, 1972.
(Principles of economics from a mathematical perspective.)

Puckett, Richard H., *Introduction to Mathematical Economics*, Heath, Lexington, Mass., 1971.
(Introduction to matrix algebra and linear programing.)
Roberts, Blaine, and David L. Schulze, *Modern Mathematics and Economic Analysis*, Norton, New York, 1973.
(An advanced treatment of mathematical techniques.)
Samuelson, Paul A., *Foundations of Economic Analysis*, Atheneum, New York, 1965.
(A rigorous mathematical treatment of much of microeconomic theory.)
Schumpeter, Joseph, *History of Economic Analysis*, Oxford University Press, New York, 1954, pp. 954–963.
(Contains interesting discussion of mathematical economics.)
Schwartz, Abraham, *Analytic Geometry and Calculus*, Holt, Rinehart & Winston, New York, 1960.
(Basic mathematical text.)
Spivey, W. Allen, *Linear Programming: An Introduction*, Macmillan, New York, 1963.
(An introduction to linear programing.)
Thomas, George B., *Calculus and Analytic Geometry*, 4th ed., Addison-Wesley, Reading, Mass., 1968.
(Basic mathematical text.)
Tintner, Gerhard, *Methodology of Mathematical Economics and Econometrics*, University of Chicago Press, Chicago, 1968.
(Discussion of uses of mathematical economics.)
Walsh, Vivian C., *Introduction to Contemporary Microeconomics*, McGraw-Hill, New York, 1970.
(Uses a set theoretic, axiomatic approach to develop choice and production theory.)
Yaari, Menahem E., *Linear Algebra for Social Sciences*, Prentice-Hall, Englewood Cliffs, N.J., 1971.
(Rigorous treatment of set theory and linear algebra.)

TABLE 1   **Squares, Square Roots, and Reciprocals**

n	n^2	$\sqrt{n}$	$\sqrt{10n}$	$1/n$	n	n^2	$\sqrt{n}$	$\sqrt{10n}$	$1/n$
1	1	1.000	3.162	1.00000	51	2601	7.141	22.583	.01961
2	4	1.414	4.472	.50000	52	2704	7.211	22.804	.01923
3	9	1.732	5.477	.33333	53	2809	7.280	23.022	.01887
4	16	2.000	6.325	.25000	54	2916	7.348	23.238	.01852
5	25	2.236	7.071	.20000	55	3025	7.416	23.452	.01818
6	36	2.449	7.746	.16667	56	3136	7.483	23.664	.01786
7	49	2.646	8.367	.14286	57	3249	7.550	23.875	.01754
8	64	2.828	8.944	.12500	58	3364	7.616	24.083	.01724
9	81	3.000	9.487	.11111	59	3481	7.681	24.290	.01695
10	100	3.162	10.000	.10000	60	3600	7.746	24.495	.01667
11	121	3.317	10.488	.09091	61	3721	7.810	24.698	.01639
12	144	3.464	10.954	.08333	62	3844	7.874	24.900	.01613
13	169	3.606	11.402	.07692	63	3969	7.937	25.100	.01587
14	196	3.742	11.832	.07143	64	4096	8.000	25.298	.01562
15	225	3.873	12.247	.06667	65	4225	8.062	25.495	.01538
16	256	4.000	12.649	.06250	66	4356	8.124	25.690	.01515
17	289	4.123	13.038	.05882	67	4489	8.185	25.884	.01493
18	324	4.243	13.416	.05556	68	4624	8.246	26.077	.01471
19	361	4.359	13.784	.05263	69	4761	8.307	26.268	.01449
20	400	4.472	14.142	.05000	70	4900	8.367	26.458	.01429
21	441	4.583	14.491	.04762	71	5041	8.426	26.646	.01408
22	484	4.690	14.832	.04545	72	5184	8.485	26.833	.01389
23	529	4.796	15.166	.04348	73	5329	8.544	27.019	.01370
24	576	4.899	15.492	.04167	74	5476	8.602	27.203	.01351
25	625	5.000	15.811	.04000	75	5625	8.660	27.386	.01333
26	676	5.099	16.125	.03846	76	5776	8.718	27.568	.01316
27	729	5.196	16.432	.03704	77	5929	8.775	27.749	.01299
28	784	5.292	16.733	.03571	78	6084	8.832	27.928	.01282
29	841	5.385	17.029	.03448	79	6241	8.888	28.107	.01266
30	900	5.477	17.321	.03333	80	6400	8.944	28.284	.01250
31	961	5.568	17.607	.03226	81	6561	9.000	28.460	.01235
32	1024	5.657	17.889	.03125	82	6724	9.055	28.636	.01220
33	1089	5.745	18.166	.03030	83	6889	9.110	28.810	.01205
34	1156	5.831	18.439	.02941	84	7056	9.165	28.983	.01190
35	1225	5.916	18.708	.02857	85	7225	9.220	29.155	.01176
36	1296	6.000	18.974	.02778	86	7396	9.274	29.326	.01163
37	1369	6.083	19.235	.02703	87	7569	9.327	29.496	.01149
38	1444	6.164	19.494	.02632	88	7744	9.381	29.665	.01136
39	1521	6.245	19.748	.02564	89	7921	9.434	29.833	.01124
40	1600	6.325	20.000	.02500	90	8100	9.487	30.000	.01111
41	1681	6.403	20.248	.02439	91	8281	9.539	30.166	.01099
42	1764	6.481	20.494	.02381	92	8464	9.592	30.332	.01087
43	1849	6.557	20.736	.02326	93	8649	9.644	30.496	.01075
44	1936	6.633	20.976	.02273	94	8836	9.695	30.659	.01064
45	2025	6.708	21.213	.02222	95	9025	9.747	30.822	.01053
46	2116	6.782	21.448	.02174	96	9216	9.798	30.984	.01042
47	2209	6.856	21.679	.02128	97	9409	9.849	31.145	.01031
48	2304	6.928	21.909	.02083	98	9604	9.899	31.305	.01020
49	2401	7.000	22.136	.02041	99	9801	9.950	31.464	.01010
50	2500	7.071	22.361	.02000	100	10000	10.000	31.623	.01000

TABLE 2   **Common Logarithms**

N	0	1	2	3	4	5	6	7	8	9
10	0000	0043	0086	0128	0170	0212	0253	0294	0334	0374
11	0414	0453	0492	0531	0569	0607	0645	0682	0719	0755
12	0792	0828	0864	0899	0934	0969	1004	1038	1072	1106
13	1139	1173	1206	1239	1271	1303	1335	1367	1399	1430
14	1461	1492	1523	1553	1584	1614	1644	1673	1703	1732
15	1761	1790	1818	1847	1875	1903	1931	1959	1987	2014
16	2041	2068	2095	2122	2148	2175	2201	2227	2253	2279
17	2304	2330	2355	2380	2405	2430	2455	2480	2504	2529
18	2553	2577	2601	2625	2648	2672	2695	2718	2742	2765
19	2788	2810	2833	2856	2878	2900	2923	2945	2967	2989
20	3010	3032	3054	3075	3096	3118	3139	3160	3181	3201
21	3222	3243	3263	3284	3304	3324	3345	3365	3385	3404
22	3424	3444	3464	3483	3502	3522	3541	3560	3579	3598
23	3617	3636	3655	3674	3692	3711	3729	3747	3766	3784
24	3802	3820	3838	3856	3874	3892	3909	3927	3945	3962
25	3979	3997	4014	4031	4048	4065	4082	4099	4116	4133
26	4150	4166	4183	4200	4216	4232	4249	4265	4281	4298
27	4314	4330	4346	4362	4378	4393	4409	4425	4440	4456
28	4472	4487	4502	4518	4533	4548	4564	4579	4594	4609
29	4624	4639	4654	4669	4683	4698	4713	4728	4742	4757
30	4771	4786	4800	4814	4829	4843	4857	4871	4886	4900
31	4914	4928	4942	4955	4969	4983	4997	5011	5024	5038
32	5051	5065	5079	5092	5105	5119	5132	5145	5159	5172
33	5185	5198	5211	5224	5237	5250	5263	5276	5289	5302
34	5315	5328	5340	5353	5366	5378	5391	5403	5416	5428
35	5441	5453	5465	5478	5490	5502	5514	5527	5539	5551
36	5563	5575	5587	5599	5611	5623	5635	5647	5658	5670
37	5682	5694	5705	5717	5729	5740	5752	5763	5775	5786
38	5798	5809	5821	5832	5843	5855	5866	5877	5888	5899
39	5911	5922	5933	5944	5955	5966	5977	5988	5999	6010
40	6021	6031	6042	6053	6064	6075	6085	6096	6107	6117
41	6128	6138	6149	6160	6170	6180	6191	6201	6212	6222
42	6232	6243	6253	6263	6274	6284	6294	6304	6314	6325
43	6335	6345	6355	6365	6375	6385	6395	6405	6415	6425
44	6435	6444	6454	6464	6474	6484	6493	6503	6513	6522
45	6532	6542	6551	6561	6571	6580	6590	6599	6609	6618
46	6628	6637	6646	6656	6665	6675	6684	6693	6702	6712
47	6721	6730	6739	6749	6758	6767	6776	6785	6794	6803
48	6812	6821	6830	6839	6848	6857	6866	6875	6884	6893
49	6902	6911	6920	6928	6937	6946	6955	6964	6972	6981
50	6990	6998	7007	7016	7024	7033	7042	7050	7059	7067
51	7076	7084	7093	7101	7110	7118	7126	7135	7143	7152
52	7160	7168	7177	7185	7193	7202	7210	7218	7226	7235
53	7243	7251	7259	7267	7275	7284	7292	7300	7308	7316
54	7324	7332	7340	7348	7356	7364	7372	7380	7388	7396

TABLE 2   **(Continued)**

N	0	1	2	3	4	5	6	7	8	9
55	7404	7412	7419	7427	7435	7443	7451	7459	7466	7474
56	7482	7490	7497	7505	7513	7520	7528	7536	7543	7551
57	7559	7566	7574	7582	7589	7597	7604	7612	7619	7627
58	7634	7642	7649	7657	7664	7672	7679	7686	7694	7701
59	7709	7716	7723	7731	7738	7745	7752	7760	7767	7774
60	7782	7789	7796	7803	7810	7818	7825	7832	7839	7846
61	7853	7860	7868	7875	7882	7889	7896	7903	7910	7917
62	7924	7931	7938	7945	7952	7959	7966	7973	7980	7987
63	7993	8000	8007	8014	8021	8028	8035	8041	8048	8055
64	8062	8069	8075	8082	8089	8096	8102	8109	8116	8122
65	8129	8136	8142	8149	8156	8162	8169	8176	8182	8189
66	8195	8202	8209	8215	8222	8228	8235	8241	8248	8254
67	8261	8267	8274	8280	8287	8293	8299	8306	8312	8319
68	8325	8331	8338	8344	8351	8357	8363	8370	8376	8382
69	8388	8395	8401	8407	8414	8420	8426	8432	8439	8445
70	8451	8457	8463	8470	8476	8482	8488	8494	8500	8506
71	8513	8519	8525	8531	8537	8543	8549	8555	8561	8567
72	8573	8579	8585	8591	8597	8603	8609	8615	8621	8627
73	8633	8639	8645	8651	8657	8663	8669	8675	8681	8686
74	8692	8698	8704	8710	8716	8722	8727	8733	8739	8745
75	8751	8756	8762	8768	8774	8779	8785	8791	8797	8802
76	8808	8814	8820	8825	8831	8837	8842	8848	8854	8859
77	8865	8871	8876	8882	8887	8893	8899	8904	8910	8915
78	8921	8927	8932	8938	8943	8949	8954	8960	8965	8971
79	8976	8982	8987	8993	8998	9004	9009	9015	9020	9025
80	9031	9036	9042	9047	9053	9058	9063	9069	9074	9079
81	9085	9090	9096	9101	9106	9112	9117	9122	9128	9133
82	9138	9143	9149	9154	9159	9165	9170	9175	9180	9186
83	9191	9196	9201	9206	9212	9217	9222	9227	9232	9238
84	9243	9248	9253	9258	9263	9269	9274	9279	9284	9289
85	9294	9299	9304	9309	9315	9320	9325	9330	9335	9340
86	9345	9350	9355	9360	9365	9370	9375	9380	9385	9390
87	9395	9400	9405	9410	9415	9420	9425	9430	9435	9440
88	9445	9450	9455	9460	9465	9469	9474	9479	9484	9489
89	9494	9499	9504	9509	9513	9518	9523	9528	9533	9538
90	9542	9547	9552	9557	9562	9566	9571	9576	9581	9586
91	9590	9595	9600	9605	9609	9614	9619	9624	9628	9633
92	9638	9643	9647	9652	9657	9661	9666	9671	9675	9680
93	9685	9689	9694	9699	9703	9708	9713	9717	9722	9727
94	9731	9736	9741	9745	9750	9754	9759	9763	9768	9773
95	9777	9782	9786	9791	9795	9800	9805	9809	9814	9818
96	9823	9827	9832	9836	9841	9845	9850	9854	9859	9863
97	9868	9872	9877	9881	9886	9890	9894	9899	9903	9908
98	9912	9917	9921	9926	9930	9934	9939	9943	9948	9952
99	9956	9961	9965	9969	9974	9978	9983	9987	9991	9996

TABLE 3   **Natural Logarithms**

N	0	1	2	3	4	5	6	7	8	9
1.0	0000	0100	0198	0296	0392	0488	0583	0677	0770	0862
1.1	0953	1044	1133	1222	1310	1398	1484	1570	1655	1740
1.2	1823	1906	1989	2070	2151	2231	2311	2390	2469	2546
1.3	2624	2700	2776	2852	2927	3001	3075	3148	3221	3293
1.4	3365	3436	3507	3577	3646	3716	3784	3853	3920	3988
1.5	4055	4121	4187	4253	4318	4383	4447	4511	4574	4637
1.6	4700	4762	4824	4886	4947	5008	5068	5128	5188	5247
1.7	5306	5365	5423	5481	5539	5596	5653	5710	5766	5822
1.8	5878	5933	5988	6043	6098	6152	6206	6259	6313	6366
1.9	6419	6471	6523	6575	6627	6678	6729	6780	6831	6881
2.0	6931	6981	7031	7080	7129	7178	7227	7275	7324	7372
2.1	7419	7467	7514	7561	7608	7655	7701	7747	7793	7839
2.2	7885	7930	7975	8020	8065	8109	8154	8198	8242	8286
2.3	8329	8372	8416	8459	8502	8544	8587	8629	8671	8713
2.4	8755	8796	8838	8879	8920	8961	9002	9042	9083	9123
2.5	9163	9203	9243	9282	9322	9361	9400	9439	9478	9517
2.6	9555	9594	9632	9670	9708	9746	9783	9821	9858	9895
2.7	9933	9969	1.0006	1.0043	1.0080	1.0116	1.0152	1.0188	1.0225	1.0260
2.8	1.0296	0332	0367	0403	0438	0473	0508	0543	0578	0613
2.9	0647	0682	0716	0750	0784	0818	0852	0886	0919	0953
3.0	1.0986	1019	1053	1086	1119	1151	1184	1217	1249	1282
3.1	1314	1346	1378	1410	1442	1474	1506	1537	1569	1600
3.2	1632	1663	1694	1725	1756	1787	1817	1848	1878	1909
3.3	1939	1969	2000	2030	2060	2090	2119	2149	2179	2208
3.4	2238	2267	2296	2326	2355	2384	2413	2442	2470	2499
3.5	1.2528	2556	2585	2613	2641	2669	2698	2726	2754	2782
3.6	2809	2837	2865	2892	2920	2947	2975	3002	3029	3056
3.7	3083	3110	3137	3164	3191	3218	3244	3271	3297	3324
3.8	3350	3376	3403	3429	3455	3481	3507	3533	3558	3584
3.9	3610	3635	3661	3686	3712	3737	3762	3788	3813	3838
4.0	1.3863	3888	3913	3938	3962	3987	4012	4036	4061	4085
4.1	4110	4134	4159	4183	4207	4231	4255	4279	4303	4327
4.2	4351	4375	4398	4422	4446	4469	4493	4516	4540	4563
4.3	4586	4609	4633	4656	4679	4702	4725	4748	4770	4793
4.4	4816	4839	4861	4884	4907	4929	4951	4974	4996	5019
4.5	1.5041	5063	5085	5107	5129	5151	5173	5195	5217	5239
4.6	5261	5282	5304	5326	5347	5369	5390	5412	5433	5454
4.7	5476	5497	5518	5539	5560	5581	5602	5623	5644	5665
4.8	5686	5707	5728	5748	5769	5790	5810	5831	5851	5872
4.9	5892	5913	5933	5953	5974	5994	6014	6034	6054	6074

TABLE 3 (Continued)

N	0	1	2	3	4	5	6	7	8	9
5.0	1.6094	6114	6134	6154	6174	6194	6214	6233	6253	6273
5.1	6292	6312	6332	6351	6371	6390	6409	6429	6448	6467
5.2	6487	6506	6525	6544	6563	6582	6601	6620	6639	6658
5.3	6677	6696	6715	6734	6752	6771	6790	6808	6827	6845
5.4	6864	6882	6901	6919	6938	6956	6974	6993	7011	7029
5.5	1.7047	7066	7084	7102	7120	7138	7156	7174	7192	7210
5.6	7228	7246	7263	7281	7299	7317	7334	7352	7370	7387
5.7	7405	7422	7440	7457	7475	7492	7509	7527	7544	7561
5.8	7579	7596	7613	7630	7647	7664	7681	7699	7716	7733
5.9	7750	7766	7783	7800	7817	7834	7851	7867	7884	7901
6.0	1.7918	7934	7951	7967	7984	8001	8017	8034	8050	8066
6.1	8083	8099	8116	8132	8148	8165	8181	8197	8213	8229
6.2	8245	8262	8278	8294	8310	8326	8342	8358	8374	8390
6.3	8405	8421	8437	8453	8469	8485	8500	8516	8532	8547
6.4	8563	8579	8594	8610	8625	8641	8656	8672	8687	8703
6.5	1.8718	8733	8749	8764	8779	8795	8810	8825	8840	8856
6.6	8871	8886	8901	8916	8931	8946	8961	8976	8991	9006
6.7	9021	9036	9051	9066	9081	9095	9110	9125	9140	9155
6.8	9169	9184	9199	9213	9228	9242	9257	9272	9286	9301
6.9	9315	9330	9344	9359	9373	9387	9402	9416	9430	9445
7.0	1.9459	9473	9488	9502	9516	9530	9544	9559	9573	9587
7.1	9601	9615	9629	9643	9657	9671	9685	9699	9713	9727
7.2	9741	9755	9769	9782	9796	9810	9824	9838	9851	9865
7.3	9879	9892	9906	9920	9933	9947	9961	9974	9988	2.0001
7.4	2.0015	0028	0042	0055	0069	0082	0096	0109	0122	0136
7.5	2.0149	0162	0176	0189	0202	0215	0229	0242	0255	0286
7.6	0281	0295	0308	0321	0334	0347	0360	0373	0386	0399
7.7	0412	0425	0438	0451	0464	0477	0490	0503	0516	0528
7.8	0541	0554	0567	0580	0592	0605	0618	0630	0643	0656
7.9	0669	0681	0694	0707	0719	0732	0744	0757	0769	0782
8.0	2.0794	0807	0819	0832	0844	0857	0869	0882	0894	0906
8.1	0919	0931	0943	0956	0968	0980	0992	1005	1017	1029
8.2	1041	1054	1066	1078	1090	1102	1114	1126	1138	1150
8.3	1163	1175	1187	1199	1211	1223	1235	1247	1258	1270
8.4	1282	1294	1306	1318	1330	1342	1353	1365	1377	1389
8.5	2.1401	1412	1424	1436	1448	1459	1471	1483	1494	1506
8.6	1518	1529	1541	1552	1564	1576	1587	1599	1610	1622
8.7	1633	1645	1656	1668	1679	1691	1702	1713	1725	1736
8.8	1748	1759	1770	1782	1793	1804	1815	1827	1838	1849
8.9	1861	1872	1883	1894	1905	1917	1928	1939	1950	1961

TABLE 3   (Continued)

N	0	1	2	3	4	5	6	7	8	9
9.0	2.1972	1983	1994	2006	2017	2028	2039	2050	2061	2072
9.1	2083	2094	2105	2116	2127	2138	2148	2159	2170	2181
9.2	2192	2203	2214	2225	2235	2246	2257	2268	2279	2289
9.3	2300	2311	2322	2332	2343	2354	2364	2375	2386	2396
9.4	2407	2418	2428	2439	2450	2460	2471	2481	2492	2502
9.5	2.2513	2523	2534	2544	2555	2565	2576	2586	2597	2607
9.6	2618	2628	2638	2649	2659	2670	2680	2690	2701	2711
9.7	2721	2732	2742	2752	2762	2773	2783	2793	2803	2814
9.8	2824	2834	2844	2854	2865	2875	2885	2895	2905	2915
9.9	2925	2935	2946	2956	2966	2976	2986	2996	3006	3016

NOTE: To find the logarithm of a number $N > 10$, use scientific notation to write $N = A \times 10^n$, where $0 < A \leq 1$, and compute $\ln N$ from the formula

$$\ln N = \ln A + n \times \ln 10$$

A table of values for $n \times \ln 10$ is included for your convenience.

n	$n \times \ln 10$	n	$n \times \ln 10$
1	2.30259	6	13.81551
2	4.60517	7	16.11810
3	6.90776	8	18.42068
4	9.21034	9	20.72327
5	11.51293	10	23.02585

TABLE 4   **The Exponential Function**

x	e^x	e^{-x}	x	e^x	e^{-x}
0.0	1.0000	1.0000	1.0	2.7183	0.36788
0.1	1.1052	0.90484	1.1	3.0042	0.33287
0.2	1.2214	0.81873	1.2	3.3201	0.30119
0.3	1.3499	0.74082	1.3	3.6693	0.27253
0.4	1.4918	0.67032	1.4	4.0552	0.24660
0.5	1.6487	0.60653	1.5	4.4817	0.22313
0.6	1.8221	0.54881	1.6	4.9530	0.20190
0.7	2.0138	0.49659	1.7	5.4739	0.18268
0.8	2.2255	0.44933	1.8	6.0496	0.16530
0.9	2.4596	0.40657	1.9	6.6859	0.14957

TABLE 4 **(Continued)**

x	e^x	e^{-x}	x	e^x	e^{-x}
2.0	7.3891	0.13534	6.0	403.43	0.00248
2.1	8.1662	0.12246	6.1	445.86	0.00224
2.2	9.0250	0.11080	6.2	492.75	0.00203
2.3	9.9742	0.10026	6.3	544.57	0.00184
2.4	11.023	0.09072	6.4	601.85	0.00166
2.5	12.182	0.08208	6.5	665.14	0.00150
2.6	13.464	0.07427	6.6	735.10	0.00136
2.7	14.880	0.06721	6.7	812.41	0.00123
2.8	16.445	0.06081	6.8	897.85	0.00111
2.9	18.174	0.05502	6.9	992.27	0.00101
3.0	20.086	0.04979	7.0	1096.6	0.00091
3.1	22.198	0.04505	7.1	1212.0	0.00083
3.2	24.533	0.04076	7.2	1339.4	0.00075
3.3	27.113	0.03688	7.3	1480.3	0.00068
3.4	29.964	0.03337	7.4	1636.0	0.00061
3.5	33.115	0.03020	7.5	1808.0	0.00055
3.6	36.598	0.02732	7.6	1998.2	0.00050
3.7	40.447	0.02472	7.7	2208.3	0.00045
3.8	44.701	0.02237	7.8	2440.6	0.00041
3.9	49.402	0.02024	7.9	2697.3	0.00037
4.0	54.598	0.01832	8.0	2981.0	0.00034
4.1	60.340	0.01657	8.1	3294.5	0.00030
4.2	66.686	0.01500	8.2	3641.0	0.00027
4.3	73.700	0.01357	8.3	4023.9	0.00025
4.4	81.451	0.01228	8.4	4447.1	0.00022
4.5	90.017	0.01111	8.5	4914.8	0.00020
4.6	99.484	0.01005	8.6	5431.7	0.00018
4.7	109.95	0.00910	8.7	6002.9	0.00017
4.8	121.51	0.00823	8.8	6634.2	0.00015
4.9	134.29	0.00745	8.9	7332.0	0.00014
5.0	148.51	0.00674	9.0	8103.1	0.00012
5.1	164.02	0.00610	9.1	8955.3	0.00011
5.2	181.27	0.00552	9.2	9897.1	0.00010
5.3	200.34	0.00499	9.3	10938	0.00009
5.4	221.41	0.00452	9.4	12088	0.00008
5.5	244.69	0.00409	9.5	13360	0.00007
5.6	270.43	0.00370	9.6	14765	0.00007
5.7	298.87	0.00335	9.7	16318	0.00006
5.8	330.30	0.00303	9.8	18034	0.00006
5.9	365.04	0.00274	9.9	19930	0.00005
			10.0	22026	0.00005

TABLE 5   An Abridged Table of Integrals

ELEMENTARY FORMS

1. $\int du = u + c$

2. $\int af(u)\,du = a \int f(u)\,du$

3. $\int (f + g + \cdots)\,du = \int f\,du + \int g\,du + \cdots$

4. $\int u^n\,du = \dfrac{u^{n+1}}{n+1} + c$ for $n \neq -1$

5. $\int \dfrac{du}{u} = \ln u + c$

6. $\int u\,dv = uv - \int v\,du$

FORMS INVOLVING $(a + bu)$

7. $\int \dfrac{du}{a + bu} = \dfrac{1}{b}\ln(a + bu) + c$

8. $\int \dfrac{u\,du}{a + bu} = \dfrac{1}{b^2}\left[a + bu - a\ln(a + bu)\right] + c$

9. $\int \dfrac{u^2\,du}{a + bu} = \dfrac{1}{b^3}\left[\tfrac{1}{2}(a + bu)^2 - 2a(a + bu) + a^2\ln(a + bu)\right] + c$

10. $\int \dfrac{du}{(a + bu)^2} = -\dfrac{1}{b(a + bu)} + c$

11. $\int \dfrac{u\,du}{(a + bu)^2} = \dfrac{1}{b^2}\left[\dfrac{a}{a + bu} + \ln(a + bu)\right] + c$

12. $\int \dfrac{u^2\,du}{(a + bu)^2} = \dfrac{1}{b^3}\left[a + bu - \dfrac{a^2}{a + bu} - 2a\ln(a + bu)\right] + c$

13. $\int \dfrac{du}{(a + bu)^3} = -\dfrac{1}{2b(a + bu)^2} + c$

14. $\int \dfrac{u\,du}{(a + bu)^3} = \dfrac{1}{b^2}\left[-\dfrac{1}{a + bu} + \dfrac{a}{2(a + bu)^2}\right]$

15. $\int \dfrac{u^2\,du}{(a + bu)^3} = \dfrac{1}{b^3}\left[\dfrac{2a}{a + bu} - \dfrac{a^2}{2(a + bu)^2} + \ln(a + bu)\right]$

16. $\int \dfrac{du}{u(a + bu)} = -\dfrac{1}{a}\ln\dfrac{a + bu}{u} + c$

17. $\int \dfrac{du}{u^2(a + bu)} = -\dfrac{1}{au} + \dfrac{b}{a^2}\ln\dfrac{a + bu}{u} + c$

TABLE 5   (Continued)

18. $\displaystyle \int \frac{du}{u(a + bu)^2} = \frac{1}{a(a + bu)} - \frac{1}{a^2} \ln \frac{a + bu}{u} + c$

19. $\displaystyle \int \frac{du}{u^2(a + bu)^2} = -\frac{a + 2bu}{a^2 u(a + bu)} + \frac{2b}{a^3} \ln \frac{a + bu}{u}$

FORMS INVOLVING $\sqrt{a + bu}$

---

20. $\displaystyle \int u\sqrt{a + bu}\, du = \frac{2(3bu - 2a)(a + bu)^{3/2}}{15b^2} + c$

21. $\displaystyle \int u^2\sqrt{a + bu}\, du = \frac{2(15b^2 u^2 - 12abu + 8a^2)(a + bu)^{3/2}}{105b^3} + c$

22. $\displaystyle \int \frac{u\, du}{\sqrt{a + bu}} = \frac{2(bu - 2a)\sqrt{a + bu}}{3b^2} + c$

23. $\displaystyle \int \frac{u^2\, du}{\sqrt{a + bu}} = \frac{2(3b^2 u^2 - 4abu + 8a^2)\sqrt{a + bu}}{15b^3} + c$

24. $\displaystyle \int \frac{du}{u\sqrt{a + bu}} = \frac{1}{\sqrt{a}} \ln \frac{\sqrt{a + bu} - \sqrt{a}}{\sqrt{a + bu} + \sqrt{a}} + c$ where $a > 0$

FORMS INVOLVING $a^2 - u^2$ AND $u^2 - a^2$

---

25. $\displaystyle \int \frac{du}{a^2 - u^2} = \frac{1}{2a} \ln \frac{a + u}{a - u} + c$ where $u^2 < a^2$

26. $\displaystyle \int \frac{du}{u^2 - a^2} = \frac{1}{2a} \ln \frac{u - a}{u + a} + c$ where $u^2 > a^2$

FORMS INVOLVING $\sqrt{a^2 - u^2}$

---

27. $\displaystyle \int \frac{\sqrt{a^2 - u^2}}{u}\, du = \sqrt{a^2 - u^2} - a \ln\left(\frac{a + \sqrt{a^2 - u^2}}{u}\right) + c$

28. $\displaystyle \int \frac{du}{u\sqrt{a^2 - u^2}} = -\frac{1}{a} \ln\left(\frac{a + \sqrt{a^2 - u^2}}{u}\right) + c$

29. $\displaystyle \int \frac{du}{u^2\sqrt{a^2 - u^2}} = -\frac{\sqrt{a^2 - u^2}}{a^2 u} + c$

FORMS INVOLVING $\sqrt{a^2 + u^2}$

---

30. $\displaystyle \int \frac{du}{\sqrt{a^2 + u^2}} = \ln(u + \sqrt{a^2 + u^2}) + c$

TABLE 5   (Continued)

31. $\int \sqrt{a^2 + u^2}\, du = \dfrac{u}{2}\sqrt{a^2 + u^2} + \dfrac{a^2}{2}\ln(u + \sqrt{a^2 + u^2}) + c$

32. $\int u^2\sqrt{a^2 + u^2}\, du = \dfrac{u}{8}(2u^2 + a^2)\sqrt{a^2 + u^2} - \dfrac{a^4}{8}\ln(u + \sqrt{a^2 + u^2}) + c$

33. $\int \dfrac{\sqrt{a^2 + u^2}}{u}\, du = \sqrt{a^2 + u^2} - a\ln\left(\dfrac{a + \sqrt{a^2 + u^2}}{u}\right) + c$

34. $\int \dfrac{\sqrt{a^2 + u^2}}{u^2}\, du = -\dfrac{\sqrt{a^2 + u^2}}{u} + \ln(u + \sqrt{a^2 + u^2}) + c$

35. $\int \dfrac{u^2\, du}{\sqrt{a^2 + u^2}} = \dfrac{u}{2}\sqrt{a^2 + u^2} - \dfrac{a^2}{2}\ln(u + \sqrt{a^2 + u^2}) + c$

36. $\int \dfrac{du}{u\sqrt{a^2 + u^2}} = -\dfrac{1}{a}\ln\left(\dfrac{\sqrt{a^2 + u^2} + a}{u}\right) + c$

37. $\int \dfrac{du}{u^2\sqrt{a^2 + u^2}} = -\dfrac{\sqrt{a^2 + u^2}}{a^2 u} + c$

38. $\int (a^2 + u^2)^{3/2}\, du = \dfrac{u}{8}(2u^2 + 5a^2)\sqrt{a^2 + u^2} + \dfrac{3a^4}{8}\ln(u + \sqrt{a^2 + u^2}) + c$

39. $\int \dfrac{du}{(a^2 + u^2)^{3/2}} = \dfrac{u}{a^2\sqrt{a^2 + u^2}} + c$

FORMS INVOLVING $\sqrt{u^2 - a^2}$

---

40. $\int \dfrac{du}{\sqrt{u^2 - a^2}} = \ln(u + \sqrt{u^2 - a^2}) + c$

41. $\int \sqrt{u^2 - a^2}\, du = \dfrac{u}{2}\sqrt{u^2 - a^2} - \dfrac{a^2}{2}\ln(u + \sqrt{u^2 - a^2}) + c$

42. $\int u^2\sqrt{u^2 - a^2}\, du = \dfrac{u}{8}(2u^2 - a^2)\sqrt{u^2 - a^2} - \dfrac{a^4}{8}\ln(u + \sqrt{u^2 - a^2}) + c$

43. $\int \dfrac{\sqrt{u^2 - a^2}}{u^2}\, du = -\dfrac{\sqrt{u^2 - a^2}}{u} + \ln(u + \sqrt{u^2 - a^2}) + c$

44. $\int \dfrac{u^2\, du}{\sqrt{u^2 - a^2}} = \dfrac{u}{2}\sqrt{u^2 - a^2} + \dfrac{a^2}{2}\ln(u + \sqrt{u^2 - a^2}) + c$

45. $\int \dfrac{du}{u^2\sqrt{u^2 - a^2}} = \dfrac{\sqrt{u^2 - a^2}}{a^2 u} + c$

46. $\int (u^2 - a^2)^{3/2}\, du = \dfrac{u}{8}(2u^2 - 5a^2)\sqrt{u^2 - a^2} + \dfrac{3a^4}{8}\ln(u + \sqrt{u^2 - a^2}) + c$

47. $\int \dfrac{du}{(u^2 - a^2)^{3/2}} = -\dfrac{u}{a^2\sqrt{u^2 - a^2}} + c$

TABLE 5 **(Continued)**

FORMS INVOLVING $\sqrt{2au - u^2}$

48. $\displaystyle\int \frac{du}{u\sqrt{2au - u^2}} = -\frac{\sqrt{2au - u^2}}{au} + c$

49. $\displaystyle\int \frac{du}{(2au - u^2)^{3/2}} = \frac{u - a}{a^2\sqrt{2au - u^2}} + c$

EXPONENTIAL AND LOGARITHMIC FORMS

50. $\displaystyle\int e^u \, du = e^u + c$

51. $\displaystyle\int a^u \, du = \frac{a^u}{\ln a} + c$

52. $\displaystyle\int ue^u \, du = e^u(u - 1) + c$

53. $\displaystyle\int u^n e^u \, du = u^n e^u - n\int u^{n-1} e^u \, du$

54. $\displaystyle\int \ln u \, du = u \ln u - u + c$

55. $\displaystyle\int u^n \ln u \, du = u^{n+1}\left[\frac{\ln u}{n + 1} - \frac{1}{(n + 1)^2}\right] + c$

ANSWERS TO SELECTED EXERCISES

(In most cases answers are given to odd numbered problems. In those instances where it was thought to be particularly instructive, answers are provided for even numbered exercises.)

Section 2·3

1. a) the set of all those who are either male or professional workers
c) the set of all male professional workers who are employed and over 50
e) the set of all those who are either male professional workers or who are employed professional workers over 50
2. a) no   **b)** yes   **c)** no

Section 2·5

1. invalid   **3.** valid   **5.** valid
7. a) invalid   **b)** invalid   **c)** invalid   **d)** valid
e) invalid
9. Anyone saying he knows all the alternative wages he can command, does in fact know them.

Section 2·6

3. a) F T T T   **b)** F T F F   **c)** T T T T
d) T F F T   **e)** F F F F   **f)** T T T T
4. a) tautology   **b)** neither   **c)** self contradiction

Section 3·8

7. a) $7 + 5i$ **c)** $-3 + 2i$ **e)** $21 + i$ **g)** $14 - 8i$
i) $-i$ **k)** $-i$ **m)** $(-1 + 8i)/5$

Section 3·11

1. a) $113_{(4)}$ **b)** $202_{(4)}$ **c)** $21_{(4)}$

Section 4·1

1. a) yes **b)** no **3. a)** no **b)** no
5. a) yes **b)** no

Section 4·5

1. $Y = 3X - 7$ **a)** 3 **b)** 11
3. a) $Y = 3X + 13$ **b)** $Y = -2X - 2$ **c)** $Y = 4$
5. -3

Section 4·6

1. a) $20 **b)** 92.5 **c)** decrease by 10 units
3. a) 64 **b)** 80 **c)** increase by 4 units
5. a) $b - 12$ **b)** b **c)** decrease by 12 units
7. a) 110 **b)** increase by 45 units
9. a) $49 - d$ **b)** increase by 4 units

Section 4·7

1. a) $p = $31, q = 45$ **b)** shortage of 99 units
c) surplus of 36 units

3. a) $p = \dfrac{\$140}{(c + a)}, q = \dfrac{(120c - 20a)}{c + a}$ **b)** $c + a = 7$

Section 4·8

1. a) $p = $54, \quad q = 137$ **b)** $p = $34, \quad q = 30$ **c)** $p = $57,$
$q = 122$

3. $p = \dfrac{(3b + 2d)}{7}, q = \dfrac{(12b - 6d)}{7}$

Section 4·10

1. **a)** price is increased by $4; quantity reduced by 20 units; consumer
    pays 44.4 percent of the tax
    b) $225

3. price is increased by $\dfrac{\$c}{(c + a)}$

5. 9

Section 4·11

Note that answers are rounded off
1. **a)** $p = \$31.85, q = 40.75$ **b)** $77.83

3. $p = \dfrac{140}{(c + 1.05a)}$

5. .346
7. **a)** price increases from $24 to $26.11; quantity decreases from 178
    to 170.80
    b) In former case price would be $26.18 and quantity 171.46. In
    latter case price would be $23.93 and quantity 177.44.

Section 4·12

1. $X = 6, -1$ 3. $X = 2 \pm \sqrt{3}$ 5. $p = -1 + \sqrt{115}$

7. $p = -1 + \sqrt{21}$ 9. $p = 3 + \sqrt{29}$ 11. $p = \dfrac{(-1 + \sqrt{461})}{2}$

Section 4·13

1. **a)** 2.4969   **b)** 1.3692   **c)** 0.7168   **d)** $8.7931 - 10$
    e) $7.7340 - 10$
3. 3.6246
5. **a)** 42.6145; 4.542   **b)** 1000; 35
7. **a)** 109.7696; 3.94   **b)** 1270; 95.17

Section 5·1

1. $p_A = 11, q_A = 30; p_B = 20, q_B = 40$
3. $p_A = 25, q_A = 15; p_B = 8, q_B = 80; p_C = 15, q_C = 30$
5. $p_A = 18, q_A = 16; p_B = 6, q_B = 6; p_C = 5, q_C = 50;$
    $p_C = 1, q_C = 100$

Section 5·2

1. $AP = B$

where $A = \begin{pmatrix} 9 & 10 \\ 3 & 18 \end{pmatrix}$ $P = \begin{pmatrix} p_A \\ p_B \end{pmatrix}$ $B = \begin{pmatrix} 299 \\ 393 \end{pmatrix}$

3. $AP = B$

where $A = \begin{pmatrix} 6 & -9 & 1 \\ 2 & -5 & 4 \\ 6 & -1 & 5 \end{pmatrix}$ $P = \begin{pmatrix} p_A \\ p_B \\ p_c \end{pmatrix}$ $B = \begin{pmatrix} 93 \\ 70 \\ 217 \end{pmatrix}$

7. a) $\begin{pmatrix} 7 & a & b \\ a & -2 & c \\ b & c & 1 \end{pmatrix}$ **b)** $\begin{pmatrix} 7 & 0 & 0 \\ 0 & -2 & 0 \\ 0 & 0 & 1 \end{pmatrix}$

9. a) $\begin{pmatrix} 1 & 0 \\ 0 & 1 \end{pmatrix}$ **b)** $\begin{pmatrix} 0 & 0 \\ 0 & 0 \end{pmatrix}$

11.

$$A + B = \begin{pmatrix} 4 & 7 \\ 2 & 0 \\ 11 & -5 \\ 8 & -1 \end{pmatrix}$$

13. not conformable for addition

15.

$$A - B = \begin{pmatrix} 4 & 1 & 3 \\ 0 & 0 & 1 \\ 2 & 1 & 2 \end{pmatrix}$$

17.

$$B - A = \begin{pmatrix} -8 & -1 \\ 0 & 0 \\ 7 & -11 \\ 6 & 5 \end{pmatrix}$$

19.

$$4A + 2B = \begin{pmatrix} 28 & 22 & 36 \\ 6 & 0 & 10 \\ 26 & 28 & 30 \end{pmatrix}$$

21.

$$AB = \begin{pmatrix} 79 & 74 & 63 \\ 20 & 19 & 14 \\ 52 & 46 & 36 \end{pmatrix} \qquad BA = \begin{pmatrix} 23 & 20 & 40 \\ 8 & 7 & 12 \\ 72 & 51 & 104 \end{pmatrix}$$

23. AB and BA are not conformable for multiplication

25.

$$AB = \begin{pmatrix} 15 & 12 & 23 & 67 \\ 1 & 0 & 1 & 5 \\ 12 & 9 & 18 & 54 \\ 5 & 3 & 7 & 23 \end{pmatrix} \qquad BA = \begin{pmatrix} 28 & 12 \\ 65 & 28 \end{pmatrix}$$

27.

$$IA = AI = A = \begin{pmatrix} 6 & 4 & 7 \\ 1 & 0 & 2 \\ 2 & 3 & 5 \end{pmatrix}$$

35.

$$(A')' = \begin{pmatrix} 6 & 4 & 7 \\ -1 & 0 & -2 \\ 2 & 3 & 5 \end{pmatrix}$$

37.

$$(2A)' = 2A' = \begin{pmatrix} 12 & -2 & 4 \\ 8 & 0 & 6 \\ 14 & -4 & 10 \end{pmatrix}$$

Section 5·3

1–5. same answers as Section 5.1, Exercises 1–5
7. 2, 0   **9.** 0   **11.** 86

Section 5·4

1. a) singular   **b)** nonsingular   **c)** singular
   d) singular   **e)** nonsingular   **f)** nonsingular
   g) singular
3. a) two   **b)** three   **c)** three   **d)** one
   e) two   **f)** one

4. a)
$$\begin{pmatrix} \frac{1}{2} & -\frac{1}{2} & -1 & \frac{1}{2} \\ -\frac{9}{2} & \frac{7}{2} & 11 & -\frac{7}{2} \\ -1 & 1 & 3 & -1 \\ -\frac{23}{2} & \frac{17}{2} & 29 & -\frac{19}{2} \end{pmatrix}$$

b)
$$\begin{pmatrix} \frac{1}{3} & \frac{1}{3} \\ -\frac{1}{3} & \frac{2}{3} \end{pmatrix}$$

c)
$$\begin{pmatrix} 1 & -2 & \frac{5}{4} \\ 0 & 0 & \frac{1}{4} \\ -1 & 3 & -\frac{7}{4} \end{pmatrix}$$

d) no inverse

e)
$$\begin{pmatrix} \frac{2}{5} & \frac{1}{25} \\ \frac{1}{10} & \frac{3}{50} \end{pmatrix}$$

f) no inverse

g)
$$\begin{pmatrix} -\frac{1}{17} & \frac{7}{17} & \frac{2}{17} \\ -\frac{5}{17} & \frac{1}{17} & -\frac{7}{17} \\ \frac{2}{17} & \frac{3}{17} & -\frac{4}{17} \end{pmatrix}$$

7. $p_A = 10$, $q_A = 12$; $p_B = 6$, $q_B = 20$

8–12. same answers as Section 5.1, Exercises 1–5.

Section 5·5

1. $X_1 = 4$, $X_2 = 8$ **3.** $X_1 = 20 - 5X_2$

5. $X_1 = 3$, $X_2 = 8$, $X_3 = 11$

7. $X_2 = 4X_4$, $X_1 = 0$, $X_3 = 10$

9. $X_1 = 5$, $X_2 = 2$, $X_3 = 4$, $X_4 = 10$ **11.** no solutions

13. $X_1 = 8 - 7X_3$, $X_2 = 11X_3$

15. no solutions   **17.** no solutions

19. $X_1 = \frac{22}{3}$, $X_2 = \frac{97}{6} - \frac{3}{2}X_4 + X_5$, $X_3 = -\frac{77}{18} + \frac{1}{2}X_4 - \frac{2}{3}X_5$

21. no solutions   **23.** no solutions   **25.** $X_1 = 5 - \frac{5}{2}X_2$

27. no solutions   **29.** $X_1 = 2X_3$, $X_2 = 10$

31. $X_1 = 0$, $X_2 = 0$, $X_3 = 0$

33. $X_1 = 0$, $X_3 = 0$, $X_2 = 4X_4$ **35.** $X_1 = -7X_3$, $X_2 = 11X_3$

37. $X_1 = -5X_2$

Section 6·3

1. 6   **3.** $\frac{3}{2}$ **5.** 0   **7.** 4   **9.** $\frac{1}{2}$ **11.** ∞

Section 6·4

1. 32   **3.** -1 **5.** $\frac{77}{3}$ **7.** 7   **9.** 0

Section 6·5

1. $p = 2$ **3.** none   **5.** $p = 100$ **7.** none   **9.** none

Section 7·3

1. $4p - 1;\ \dfrac{(4p^2 - p)}{(2p^2 - p + 4)}$

3. $2p - 4;\ 6$

5. $3p^2 - 3;\ \frac{36}{11}$

7. $-\dfrac{4p}{(p^2 + 4)^2}\ ;\ -\dfrac{2p^2}{(p^2 + 4)}$

Section 7·4

1. $2x$ **3.** $4x$ **5.** $\dfrac{1}{(x + 1)^2}$ **7.** 1

Section 7·6

1. a) $80q - 2q^2$ **b)** $80 - 4q$

3. $4q + 5$

Section 7·7

1. positive for $q < 20$ **3.** positive for $q > -\frac{5}{4}$

Appendix to Chapter 7

1. continuous, not differentiable
2. not continuous or differentiable
3. continuous, not differentiable

Section 8·5

1. $27x^8$ **3.** $-2x^{-3}$ **5.** $-3p^{-2} + p^{-3}$

7. $-\frac{2}{3}p^{-1/3}$ **9.** $-9p^2 + 4$

11. $15q - \frac{1}{2}q^2;\ 15 - q$

Section 8·7

1. $3x^3 + 4x - 3$ **3.** $6p^5 - 4p$ **5.** $3p^2 - 7$

7. $\dfrac{(-p^2 + 2p + 9)}{(p^2 + 9)^2}$ **9.** $-\dfrac{2 + 1}{(p + 1)^2}$

Section 8·8

1. $36x + 9$ **3.** $-18p - \dfrac{1}{(3p^2)}$

5. $162p^5 - 135p^4 - 36p^3 + 33p^2 + 14p - 3$

Section 8·9

1. $20(5x + 2)^3$ **3.** $\frac{3}{2}p^{1/2} + 4p^{-3}$ **5.** $10 + 6p^{-4}$

7. $-24000p(p^2 + 1)^{-4}$ **9.** $\frac{3}{2}p^4(p^3 + 1)^{-1/2} + 2p(p^3 + 1)^{1/2}$

11. $\dfrac{p^3(1 + p^2)^{-1/2} - 2p(1 + p^2)^{1/2}}{1 + p^2}$

Section 8·10

1. $\frac{1}{20}$ **3.** $\dfrac{1}{(3p^2 - 2)}$

Section 8·11

1. $\frac{5}{3}$ **3.** $\dfrac{p}{q_s}$ **5.** $-\dfrac{2q_d}{p}$ **7.** $\dfrac{3y}{(2y - 3x)}$

Section 8·12

1. $\dfrac{t}{6}$ **3.** $\dfrac{(-t^2 + 1)(2 + t)^2}{-100(t^2 + 1)^2}$ **5.** -1700

Section 8·13

1. $\dfrac{3}{p}$ 3. $-p - 2p \ln p$ 5. $-\dfrac{1}{(p \ln p)}$

7. $-\dfrac{2p}{(2p^2 - 4)}$ 9. $-\dfrac{p}{(4 - p)} + \ln(4 - p)$

Section 8·14

1. $\dfrac{(10p + 1)^2}{(p^2 - 4)^3}\left[\dfrac{20}{10p + 1} - \dfrac{6p}{p^2 + 4}\right]$

3. $\dfrac{4p^4 - 2}{p\sqrt{p^2 - 2}}\left[\dfrac{16p^3}{4p^4 - 2} - \dfrac{1}{p} - \dfrac{p}{p^2 - 2}\right]$

5. $\dfrac{(p^2 + 3)\sqrt{2p - 1}}{\sqrt[3]{p + 2}}\left[\dfrac{2p}{p^2 + 3} + \dfrac{1}{2p - 1} - \dfrac{1}{3p + 6}\right]$

Section 8·15

1. $(-8.047)5^{-p}$ 3. $-2e^{-2p}$

5. $10e^p - \tfrac{1}{2}e^{-p}$ 7. $\left(-\dfrac{p}{10}\right)e^{p/10} - e^{p/10}$

9. $\dfrac{(2pe^{2p} - e^{2p})}{p^2}$

Section 8·16

1. -40 3. -280 5. 0 7. -1700

Section 8·19

1. $216x^7$ 3. 4 5. $30p^4 - 4$ 7. $-1/x^2$

Section 9·1

1. $x = -2$ is a relative maximum; $x = 5$ is a relative minimum; no absolute maximum or minimum

3. $x = 0$ is a relative maximum; $x = 4$ is a relative minimum; $x = -3$ is a relative minimum; $x = 4$ is the absolute minimum point; no absolute maximum

5. no relative maximum or minimum; no absolute maximum or minimum

7. $x = \frac{8}{3}$ is a relative maximum; $x = 0$ is a relative minimum; no absolute maximum or minimum

Section 9·2

1. concave upward for $x > \frac{3}{2}$; concave downward for $x < \frac{3}{2}$ point of inflection for $x = \frac{3}{2}$

3. concave upward for $x < -\frac{9}{2}$; concave downward for $x > -\frac{9}{2}$; no points of inflection

5. concave upward for all values of x; no points of inflection

6. concave upward for $x < \frac{4}{3}$; concave downward for $x > \frac{4}{3}$; point of inflection for $x - \frac{4}{3}$

Section 9·3

1. $q = 3$ is a relative maximum; $q = 0$ is a relative minimum; $q = 3$ is the absolute maximum; no absolute minimum; concave upward for $q < \frac{3}{2}$; concave downward for $q > \frac{3}{2}$; point of inflection for $q = \frac{3}{2}$

3. $q = 0, 30, 100$ are relative maxima; $q = 2, 50$ are relative minima; $q = 100$ is the absolute maximum; $q = 50$ is the absolute minimum; concave upward for $0 \leq q < 16$ and $50 < q < 100$; concave downward for $16 < q < 50$; point of inflection for $q = 16$

5. $q = 0$ is a relative maximum; $q = 0$ is the absolute maximum; no absolute minimum; concave upward for $q \geq 0$

7. no relative or absolute maxima or minima; concave downward for $p > 0$

9. $p = 0, 2$ are relative maxima; $p = \frac{1}{3}, 8$ are relative minima; $p = 2$ is the absolute maximum; $p = 8$ is the absolute minimum; concave upward for $p < \frac{7}{6}$; concave downward for $p > \frac{7}{6}$; point of inflection for $p = \frac{7}{6}$

Section 10·2

1. $\dfrac{\partial q_d}{\partial p} = -18$ $\qquad$ $\dfrac{\partial q_d}{\partial y} = \dfrac{1}{10}$

3. $\dfrac{\partial q_d}{\partial p} = \dfrac{-1}{p - (\frac{1}{80})y}$ $\qquad$ $\dfrac{\partial q_d}{\partial y} = \dfrac{1}{80p - y}$

5. $\dfrac{\partial q_d}{\partial p} = -2e^{2p} - (\frac{1}{50})y$ $\qquad$ $\dfrac{\partial q_d}{\partial y} = -(\frac{1}{50})p + (2y)^{-1/2}$

7. $\dfrac{\partial u}{\partial q_1} = -9$ $\qquad$ $\dfrac{\partial u}{\partial q_2} = 1$

9. $\dfrac{\partial q_{dA}}{\partial p_A} = -12p_A$ $\qquad$ $\dfrac{\partial q_{dA}}{\partial p_B} = (\frac{2}{9})p_B^{-1/3}$

$\dfrac{\partial q_{dA}}{\partial p_C} = (-\frac{1}{4})p_C^{-1/2}$

11. $\dfrac{\partial z}{\partial x} = 1552$ $\qquad$ $\dfrac{\partial z}{\partial y} = 3504$

Section 10·3

1. $E_{pA} = \dfrac{-1080}{471}$

$E_{AB} = \frac{2}{471}, E_{AC} = -\frac{1}{471}, E_{yA} = \frac{5}{471}$
A and B are substitutes, A and C are complements

3. $E_{pA} = -0.9, E_{AB} = 0.1, E_{yA} = 0.9$
A and B are substitutes

5. $E_{pA} = -0.8, E_{AB} = 0.2, E_{yA} = 1.5$
A and B are substitutes

7. $E_{pA} = \dfrac{-4}{4p - \left(\dfrac{y}{20}\right)} \cdot \dfrac{p}{500 - \ln\left(4p - \dfrac{y}{20}\right)}$

$E_{yA} = \dfrac{1}{80p - y} \cdot \dfrac{y}{500 - \ln\left(4p - \dfrac{y}{20}\right)}$

Section 10·4

1. $\dfrac{\partial^2 q_d}{\partial p^2} = -3p^{-1/2}, \qquad \dfrac{\partial^2 q_d}{\partial y^2} = 0,$

$$\dfrac{\partial^2 q_d}{\partial p \, \partial y} = \dfrac{\partial^2 q_d}{\partial y \, \partial p} = 0$$

3. $\dfrac{\partial^2 q_d}{\partial p^2} = \dfrac{16}{\left(4p - \dfrac{y}{20}\right)^2} \qquad \dfrac{\partial^2 q_d}{\partial y^2} = \dfrac{1}{(80p - y)^2}$

$$\dfrac{\partial^2 q_d}{\partial p \, \partial y} = \dfrac{\partial^2 q_d}{\partial y \, \partial p} = \dfrac{-80}{(80p - y)^2}$$

5. $\dfrac{\partial^2 q_d}{\partial p^2} = -4e^{2p} \qquad \dfrac{\partial^2 q_d}{\partial y^2} = -(2y)^{-3/2}$

$$\dfrac{\partial^2 q_d}{\partial p \, \partial y} = \dfrac{\partial^2 q_d}{\partial y \, \partial p} = -\tfrac{1}{50}$$

7. $\dfrac{\partial^2 u}{\partial q_1^2} = 2 \qquad \dfrac{\partial^2 u}{\partial q_2^2} = 2 \qquad \dfrac{\partial^2 u}{\partial q_1 \, \partial q_2} = \dfrac{\partial^2 u}{\partial q_2 \, \partial q_1} = -3$

9. $\dfrac{\partial^2 q_{dA}}{\partial p_A^2} = -12, \qquad \dfrac{\partial^2 q_{dA}}{\partial p_B^2} = (-\tfrac{2}{27})p_B^{-4/3},$

$$\dfrac{\partial^2 q_{dA}}{\partial p_C^2} = (\tfrac{1}{8})p_C^{-3/2}$$

$$\dfrac{\partial^2 q_{dA}}{\partial p_A \, \partial p_B} = \dfrac{\partial^2 q_{dA}}{\partial p_A \, \partial p_C} = \dfrac{\partial^2 q_{dA}}{\partial p_B \, \partial p_C} = 0$$

11. $\dfrac{\partial^2 z}{\partial x^2} = 4y^3 \qquad \dfrac{\partial^2 z}{\partial y^2} = 12x^2 y + 2x$

$$\dfrac{\partial^2 z}{\partial x \, \partial y} = \dfrac{\partial^2 z}{\partial y \, \partial x} = 12xy^2 + 2y$$

Section 10·5

1. $dq_d = -1.6$
3. $dq_d = -\frac{17}{256}$
5. $du = -\frac{29}{6}$

7. $dz = \frac{25}{8}$

9. 21.32   **11.** $dq_d = \left(-\frac{1}{p}\right)dp$

Section 10·6

1. $\dfrac{dq_d}{dt} = -35$

3. $\dfrac{dq_d}{dt} = -\dfrac{t}{5p - (\frac{1}{16})y} + \dfrac{20}{80p - y}$

5. $\dfrac{dq_d}{dt} = -e^{2p} - (\frac{1}{100})y - 4p + 200(2y)^{-1/2}$

7. $\dfrac{dq_{dA}}{dt} = -\dfrac{300}{p_A^2} + \dfrac{1}{40} - \dfrac{40t^{-1/2}}{p_C^2}$

9. $\dfrac{du}{dq_1} = 2q_1 + (\frac{1}{2}q_2 + 1)e^{q_1} + 12q_2^2$

11. $\dfrac{du}{dq_1} = 6q_1 + 16q_2 + (\frac{5}{2})(10q_3)^{-1/2}$

13. $\dfrac{dz}{dt} = (4xy^3 + y^2)e^t + (3x^2y^2 + xy)t^{-1/2}$

17. $\dfrac{\partial u}{\partial p_1} = -2q_1 - (\frac{1}{2})q_2 e^{q_1} + (\frac{1}{4})e^{q_1} + 3q_2^2$

$\dfrac{\partial u}{\partial p_2} = (\frac{1}{2})q_1 + (\frac{1}{8})q_2 e^{q_1} - (\frac{1}{20})e^{q_1} - (\frac{3}{5})q_2^2$

19. $\dfrac{\partial u}{\partial p_1} = \dfrac{-200}{q_1} + \dfrac{100p_1}{q_2} - \dfrac{10}{q_3}$

21. $\dfrac{\partial u}{\partial r} = 2rye^{xy} + sxe^{xy}$

$\dfrac{\partial u}{\partial s} = -2sye^{xy} + rxe^{xy}$

Section 10·7

1. $\dfrac{p}{q_s}$ **3.** -2

5. $\dfrac{2x + 2y}{10y - 2x}$

7. $E_{pA} = \dfrac{-p_A q_{dA}}{2p_A q_{dA} + 4}$, $E_{AB} = \dfrac{3p_B}{(2p_A q_{dA} + 4)q_{dA}}$

$E_{yA} = \dfrac{2y}{(2p_A q_{dA} + 4)q_{dA}}$

9. $E_{pA} = \dfrac{-0.8}{1.5}$, $E_{AB} = -0.2$

   A and B are complements

11. $\dfrac{\partial z}{\partial x} = \dfrac{-4xy^2 + 4z^2 x}{2y^2 z + 4zx^2}$ $\dfrac{\partial z}{\partial y} = \dfrac{-4x^2 y + 2yz^2}{2y^2 z + 4zx^2}$

Section 10·8

1. homogeneous of degree zero
3. homogeneous of degree 2
5. homogeneous of degree $\frac{1}{2}$
7. homogeneous of degree zero
9. homogeneous of degree $-\frac{3}{2}$
11. homogeneous of degree 1
13. homogeneous of degree -1

Section 11·1

1. relative and absolute maximum at $q_1 = 4$, $q_2 = 4$
   boundary maxima at $q_1 = 0$,
   $q_2 = \frac{14}{3}$ and $q_1 = 5$, $q_2 = 0$
3. relative and absolute maximum at $q_1 = \frac{1}{4}$, $q_2 = 4$
   boundary maxima at $q_1 = 0$, $q_2 = \frac{25}{6}$ and $q_1 = \frac{9}{4}$, $q_2 = 0$
5. boundary maxima at $q_1 = 0$, $q_2 = \frac{31}{4}$ and $q_1 = \frac{7}{2}$, $q_2 = 0$
   absolute maximum at $q_1 = \frac{7}{2}$, $q_2 = 0$
7. relative minimum at $x = 1$, $y = 1$
9. relative maximum at $x = -1$, $y = -1$
   relative minimum at $x = 1$, $y = 1$

Section 11·2

1. $q_1 = 20$, $q_2 = 50$
3. $q_1 = 24$, $q_2 = 1$
5. absolute and relative maximum at $q_1 = \frac{25}{4}$, $q_2 = \frac{25}{12}$
7. absolute and relative maximum at $x = \frac{5}{2}$, $y = \frac{5}{6}$

Section 12·3

1. only diminishing marginal rate of substitution holds
3. both hold
5. only diminishing marginal rate of substitution holds
7. only diminishing marginal rate of substitution holds
9. both hold

Section 12·4

1. $q_1 = 100$, $q_2 = 20$
3. $q_1 = 75$, $q_2 = 300$
5. $q_1 = 40$, $q_2 = 101$
7. $q_1 = 10$, $q_2 = 20$
9. $q_1 = 2.80$, $q_2 = 1.67$
10. corner solution: $q_1 = 45$, $q_2 = 0$
11. $q_1 = 10$, $q_2 = 4$, $q_3 = 20$

Section 12·5

1. $q_1 = \dfrac{I}{2p_1}$, $\qquad q_2 = \dfrac{I}{2p_2}$

3. $q_1 = \dfrac{I}{3p_1}$, $\qquad q_2 = \dfrac{2I}{3p_2}$

5. $q_1 = \dfrac{Ip_2}{p_1^2 + p_1 p_2}$, $\qquad q_2 = \dfrac{Ip_1}{p_2^2 + p_1 p_2}$

7. $q_1 = \dfrac{4p_2 I}{4p_1 p_2 + p_1^2}$, $\qquad q_2 = \dfrac{p_1 I}{4p_2^2 + p_1 p_2}$

9. $q_1 = \dfrac{I}{3p_1}$, $\qquad q_2 = \dfrac{I}{3p_2}$, $\qquad q_3 = \dfrac{I}{3p_3}$

Section 12·6

1. $\dfrac{\partial q_1}{\partial p_1} = \dfrac{-p_2 q_2}{2p_1^2} - \dfrac{q_1}{2p_1} = -50 - 50 = -100$

$\dfrac{\partial q_1}{\partial p_2} = \dfrac{q_2}{2p_1} - \dfrac{q_2}{2p_1} = 0$

3. $\dfrac{\partial q_1}{\partial p_1} = \dfrac{\dfrac{-p_2^2}{p_1 q_1}}{\dfrac{p_2^2}{q_1^2} + \dfrac{2p_1^2}{q_2^2}} - \dfrac{\dfrac{2}{q_2^2}}{\dfrac{p_2^2}{q_1^2} + \dfrac{2p_1^2}{q_2^2}} = -20.83 - 10.42 = -31.25$

$\dfrac{\partial q_1}{\partial p_2} = \dfrac{\dfrac{p_2}{q_1}}{\dfrac{p_2^2}{q_1^2} + \dfrac{2p_1^2}{q_2^2}} - \dfrac{\dfrac{2p_1}{q_2}}{\dfrac{p_2^2}{q_1^2} + \dfrac{2p_1^2}{q_2^2}} = 41.67 - 41.67 = 0$

5. $\dfrac{\partial q_1}{\partial p_1} = \dfrac{\dfrac{-p_2^2}{2p_1 q_1^{1/2}}}{\dfrac{p_2^2}{4q_1^{3/2}} + \dfrac{p_1^2}{4q_2^{3/2}}} - \dfrac{\dfrac{p_1 q_1}{4q_2^{3/2}}}{\dfrac{p_2^2}{4q_1^{3/2}} + \dfrac{p_1^2}{4q_2^{3/2}}}$

$= -33.33 - 33.33 = -66.66$

$\dfrac{\partial q_1}{\partial p_2} = \dfrac{\dfrac{p_2}{2q_1^{1/2}}}{\dfrac{p_2^2}{4q_1^{3/2}} + \dfrac{p_1^2}{4q_2^{3/2}}} - \dfrac{\dfrac{p_1}{4q_2^{1/2}}}{\dfrac{p_2^2}{4q_1^{3/2}} + \dfrac{p_1^2}{4q_2^{3/2}}} = 16.67 - 8.33 = 8.34$

Section 13·1

1. No   3. Yes   5. No   7. Yes   9. Yes

Section 13·2

1. $x_1 = 25,\ x_2 = 5;\ x_1 = 5x_2$
3. $x_1 = 9.66,\ x_2 = 28.98;\ x_2 = 3x_1$
5. $x_1 = \frac{3}{2},\ x_2 = \frac{1}{2};\ x_1 = 2x_2 + \frac{1}{2}$
7. $x_1 = 2,\ x_2 = 3;\ x_1 = (\frac{2}{3})x_2$
9. $x_1 = 4.27,\ x_2 = 12.81;\ x_2 = 3x_1$
10. corner solution at $x_1 = 3,\ x_2 = 0$
11. $x_1 = 3,\ x_2 = 6,\ x_3 = \frac{3}{2};\ x_2 = 2x_1,\ x_3 = (\frac{1}{2})x_1$

Section 13·3

1. $q = 4.2767; x_1 = 2, x_2 = 6$
3. $q = 9; x_1 = 3, x_2 = \frac{3}{2}$
5. $q = 412.71; x_1 = 5, x_2 = 12.5$
7. Second order conditions not satisfied at any point. Firm will seek to increase output without limit as long as it can procure inputs.

Section 13·4

1. $C = e^{q/3} + 5; q = 8.67$
2. $C = (\frac{4}{5})q^2 + 100; q = 20$

3. $C = \dfrac{9}{10 - q} + 20; q = 9$

7. $q = 2, \pi = 6$

Section 13·5

1. $C = q^3 - (\frac{73}{8})q^2 + 20q, q = 6.08, K = 1.52$
3. $C = 4q^2 + 8q, q = 3, K = 12$

Section 13·6

1. $q = \frac{17}{3}, q_1 = 4, q_2 = \frac{5}{3}$
3. $q = 12, q_1 = 5, q_2 = 7$
5. $q = 4, q_1 = 2, q_2 = 2$

Section 13·7

1. $q_A = 3, q_B = 3$; technically related
3. $q_A = 5, q_B = \frac{83}{4}$; technically related
5. $q_A = 3, q_B = 2$; not technically related

Section 13·9

1. homogeneous of degree 1.1; increasing returns to scale; no available surplus; adding up Theorem doesn't apply
3. homogeneous of degree 1; constant returns to scale; no available surplus; adding up Theorem applies
5. not homogeneous; no available surplus; adding up Theorem doesn't apply

Section 13·11

1. $q_s = 3.3258 + \ln p$; $q_S = 1662.9 + 500 \ln p$; $p = 2.59$
3. $q_s = \ln p - 4.6052$; $q_S = 1000 \ln p - 4605.2$; $p = 9.68$

Section 14·1

1. $q = 7$, $p = 46$, $\pi = 240$
3. $q = 4$, $p = 136$, $\pi = 300$
5. $q = 20$, $p = 25$, $\pi = 400$
7. $q = 15$, $p = 75$, $\pi = 800$

Section 14·2

1. $x_1 = 33.3$, $x_2 = 100$, $q = 12.716$, $p = 139.32$
3. $x_1 = 8$, $x_2 = 4$, $q = 9.625$, $p = 64.19$

Section 14·3

1. $q_1 = 6.4$, $q_2 = 7.8$, $p_1 = 27.20$, $p_2 = 22.20$,
$\pi = 305.40$
3. $q_1 = 18$, $q_2 = 6$, $p_1 = 69$, $p_2 = 39$, $\pi = 1180$
5. $q_1 = 18$, $q_2 = 6$, $p_1 = 22$, $p_2 = 7$, $\pi = 338$

Section 14·4

1. $q_1 = 8$, $q_2 = 1$, $q = 9$, $p = 42$
3. $q_1 = 3$, $q_2 = 5.5$, $q = 8.5$, $p = 36.50$
5. $q_1 = 64$, $q_2 = 6.4$, $q = 70.4$, $p = 64.71$

Section 14·5

1. $q_A = 5$, $q_B = 2$, $p_A = 26$, $p_B = 24$, $\pi = 112$
3. $q_A = 3$, $q_B = 1.5$, $p_A = 90$, $p_B = 32$, $\pi = 198$
5. $q_A = 8$, $q_B = 13$, $q_C = 10$, $p_A = 84$, $p_B = 37$, $p_C = 30$,
$\pi = 986$

Section 14·7

1. $q = 20$, $p = 60$, $\pi = 350$
3. $q = 12$, $p = 72$, $\pi = 456$
5. $q = 21$, $p = 24$, $\pi = 399$

Section 14·9

1. $q_1 = 8, q_2 = 1, p = 42$

3. $q_1 = 8, q_2 = 10, p = 196.67$

5. $q_1 = \frac{17}{3}, q_2 = 2, p_1 = 24.67, p_2 = 27.33$

Section 14·10

1. $p = \frac{26400}{161}, q_1 = \frac{600}{23}, \pi_1 = \frac{360000}{161}$,

$q_i = \frac{1320}{161}, \pi_i = \dfrac{(13200)(1320)}{(161)^2}$

3. $p = 71, q_1 = 90, \pi_1 = 3510, q_i = 71, \pi_i = \frac{5001}{2}$

Section 14·11

1. $q_1 = \frac{17}{3}, q_2 = \frac{17}{3}, p = \frac{112}{3}$

3. $q_1 = \frac{100}{17}, q_2 = \frac{20}{17}, p_1 = \frac{440}{17}, p_2 = \frac{149}{17}$

Section 15·1

1. $MPC = 0.9, APC = 0.9, S = 0.1Y, MPS = 0.1, APS = 0.1$

3. $MPC = b, APC = b, S = (1 - b)Y, MPS = 1 - b, APS = 1 - b$

5. $MPC = .0008Y - 0.1, APC = \dfrac{(200 - 0.1Y + .0004Y^2)}{Y}$,

$S = 1.1Y - 200 - .0004Y^2, MPS = 1.1 - .0008Y$,

$APS = \dfrac{(1.1Y - 200 - .0004Y^2)}{Y}, MPC = \dfrac{900}{Y}$,

$APC = \dfrac{(900 \ln Y - 950)}{Y}, S = Y - 900 \ln Y + 950$,

$MPS = 1 - \dfrac{900}{Y}, APS = \dfrac{(Y - 900 \ln Y + 950)}{Y}$

Section 15·4

1. $Y = 2700,$ **3.** $Y = 1600$ **5.** $Y = 1000$ or 500

8. $Y = 1000,$ **9.** $Y = 4060,$ **11.** $Y = 2480$

Section 15·5

1. $6\frac{2}{3}$; $-5\frac{2}{3}$ **3.** 4; -3

5. 10   **7.** $\dfrac{1}{(1 - b - f)}$

Section 15·6

1. $i = .10$ **3.** $i = .08$
5. $i = .05$ **7.** $i = .014$, $Y = 3043$
9. $i = .022$, $Y = 8355$ **11.** $i = .013$, $Y = 2823$
13. $i = .053$, $Y = 8433$

Section 15·7

1. $i = .017$, $Y = 1254.5$, $N = 313.6$, $W = 5$, $P = 1.25$
3. $i = .169$, $Y = 5860$, $N = 1953$, $W = 6$, $P = 2$

Section 16·1

1. $\dfrac{x^4}{4} + c$ **3.** $(\frac{1}{7})x^{7/3} + c$

5. $(\frac{4}{5})x^{5/4} + c$ **7.** $p^2 - 4p + c$
9. $3p^{-1} - (\frac{1}{2})p^{-2} + c$ **11.** $2q^2 + 5q + c$
13. $(\frac{1}{3}) \ln (3p + 2) + c$ **15.** $(\frac{2}{3})(p - 4)^{3/2} + c$
19. $(-\frac{2}{5})(1 - p)^{5/2} + c$ **21.** $-\ln (1 - p) + c$
23. $e^p - e^{-p} + c$ **25.** $2e^{(p/2)-3} + c$

27. $\dfrac{3^x}{\ln 3} + c$ **29.** $q_d = -3p^3 + 4p + 2000$

31. $q_d = 2e^{-2p} + 1{,}998$ **33.** $q_s = 4e^{p/2} + c$
35. $q_s = (2p + 1)^{1/2}$ **37.** $C = 50q - 8q^2 + q^4 + 100$
39. $C = 39q - 11q^2 + q^3 + 100$
41. $C = .85Y + c$ **43.** $C = Y - .0001Y^2 + c$
45. $C = .00045Y^2 + c$

Section 16·2

1. $-\frac{8}{3}$ **3.** 0.5596   **5.** 50
7. 1.7653   **9.** 4.9   **11.** 146.055

13. 10,666.67   **15.** 10,416.67
17. 12.44   **19.** undefined   **21.** 20,868
23. 82.67   **25.** 125   **27.** 221
29. $\frac{122}{9}$ **31.** 108   **33.** 5.666

Section 17·2

1. $Y_t = 500(0.95)^t$, damped nonoscillating path
3. $Y_t = 500$, stationary path
5. $Y_t = 500$, stationary path
7. $Y_t = 400(1.05)^t$, explosive nonoscillating path
9. $Y_t = 1000$, stationary path
11. $Y_t = 1000(1.2)^t$, explosive nonoscillating path

Section 17·3

1. a) $Y_t = K_0\left(\dfrac{\alpha + b}{b}\right)^t$ **b)** growth rate of $\dfrac{\alpha}{b}$

   c) explosive nonoscillating

2. a) $Y_t = K_0\left(\dfrac{\alpha}{b}\right)^t$ **b)** growth rate of $\dfrac{(\alpha - b)}{b}$

   c) If $\alpha < b$, damped nonoscillating path
   If $\alpha > b$, explosive nonoscillating path
   If $\alpha = b$, stationary path

3. a) $Y_t = K_0\left(\dfrac{b}{\alpha}\right)^t$ **b)** growth rate of $\dfrac{(b - \alpha)}{\alpha}$

   c) If $\alpha < b$, explosive nonoscillating path
   If $\alpha > b$, damped nonoscillating path
   If $\alpha = b$, stationary path

Section 17·4

1. $Y_t = -9,500(.95)^t + 10,000$
3. $Y_t = 1100(1.1)^t - 1000$
5. $Y_t = 333.33(1.03)^t + 1666.67$
7. $Y_t = 2400(1.2)^t - 1000$

Section 17·5

1. **a)** $p_t = 15(-0.4)^t + 35$
   b) $p_t = 35$
   c) stable
3. **a)** $p_t = -50(-0.5)^t + 60$
   b) $p_t = 60$
   c) stable
5. **a)** $p_t = 4(-1.5)^t + 36$
   b) $p_t = 36$
   c) unstable
7. **a)** $p_t = -32(-0.25)^t + 48$
   b) $p_t = 48$
   c) stable

Section 17·6

1. $Y_t = 30(3)^t + 570(1)^t$
3. $Y_t = 20(3)^t + 780(1)^t$
5. $Y_t = 20(2)^t + 480(1)^t$

Section 17·7

1. $Y_t = 560(1.5)^t + 440(0.5)^t - 400$
3. $Y_t = 840(1.5)^t + 760(0.5)^t - 800$
5. $Y_t = 280(3.5)^t + 1240(0.5)^t - 320$

Section 17·8

1. second order, first degree
3. first order, first degree
5. second order, first degree

Section 17·9

1. $q_d = \dfrac{1}{cp}$ 3. $q_s^2 = p^2 + 8$

5. $y = \dfrac{x^6}{3} - \dfrac{x^2}{2} + c$ 7. $y^4 = -8e^{-x} + c$

9. $y = c(x^2 + 4)^{1/2}$

Section 17·10

1. $y = \dfrac{3x^3}{2} + cx$ **3.** $y = (\tfrac{1}{5})e^x + ce^{-4x}$

5. $q_s = \left(\dfrac{p^2}{2}\right)e^{3p} + ce^{3p}$ **7.** $q_s = p^{3/2} + cp$

Section 17·11

1. **a)** $Y = 1000e^{t/10}$ **b)** income must continually grow by 10 percent
   c) explosive   **d)** $Y = 1000e^{0.4}$
3. **a)** $Y = 880e^{.06t}$ **b)** income must continually grow by 6 percent
   c) explosive   **d)** $Y = 880e^{.24}$
5. **a)** $Y = 500e^{.0027t}$ **b)** income must continually grow by 0.27 percent

INDEX